NetWare Server Troubleshooting & Maintenance Handbook

The Communications Book Series

The Computing That Works Book Series

For more information about other McGraw-Hill materials, call 1-800-2-MCGRAW in the United States. In other countries, call your McGraw-Hill office.

NetWare Server Troubleshooting & Maintenance Handbook

Edward Liebing
Ken Neff

McGraw-Hill, Inc.
1221 Avenue of the Americas
New York, NY 10020

All products, names, and services are trademarks or registered trademarks of their respective companies.

Adaptec is a trademark of Adaptec, Ind.; ADIC is a registered trademark of Advanced Digital Information Corp.; Apple, AppleShare, AppleTalk, EtherTalk, LocalTalk, and Macintosh are registered trademarks of Apple Computer, Inc.; ARCnet is a registered trademark of Datapoint Corp.; Compaq is a trademark of Compaq Corp.; CompuServe is a registered trademark of H&R Block; dBASE and dBASE III Plus are registered trademarks of Ashton-Tate; DESQview is a trademark of Quarterdeck Office Systems Corp.; Hewlett-Packard is a trademark of Hewlett-Packard Company; IBM, IBM PC, IBM AT, IBM ProPrinter, Micro Channel, NetBIOS, PC-DOS, PS/2, and Token-Ring are registered trademarks of International Business Machines Corp.; Intel is a trademark of Intel Corp.; Lotus 1-2-3 is a registered trademark of Lotus Development Corp.; MS-DOS, OS/2, Windows, and Word are trademarks of Microsoft Corp.; Microline is a registered trademark of Oki America, Inc.; Novell and NetWare are registered trademarks and Hot Fix, LANSWER, Internetwork Packet Exchange (IPX), Sequenced Packet Exchange, SFT, RX-Net, and Transaction Tracking System (TTS) are trademarks of Novell, Inc.; Okidata is a registered trademark of Oki America, Inc.; Panasonic is a registered trademark of Matsushita Electric Industrial Co. Ltd.; Pinwriter and Spinwriter are registered trademarks of NEC Corp.; Star and Gemini are registered trademarks of Star Micronics America, Inc.; The Coordinator is a trademark of Action Technologies; Toshiba is a trademark of Toshiba America, Inc.; Wangtek is a trademark of Wangtek, Inc.; Western Digital is a trademark of Western Digital Corp.; WordPerfect is a trademark of WordPerfect Corp.; Xerox and Diablo are registered trademarks of Xerox Corp.; 286A and 286B are trademarks of Novell, Inc.; 3Com, EtherLink, EtherLink Plus, and 3Station are trademarks of 3Com Corp.

1234567890

Cover design by Kate Hennessy Johnson. The editor for this book was Vince Sondej and the production supervisor was David B. Doering. It was composed in PageMaker 3.01 by Doering & Associates.

Library of Congress Cataloging-in-Publication Data

Liebing, Edward.
    NetWare server troubleshooting and maintenance handbook/
Edward A. Liebing and Ken Neff.
        p.   cm.
    Includes index.
    ISBN 0-07-607028-X : $34.95
    1. NetWare (Computer operating system)   I. Neff, Ken, 1957
  II. Title
QA76.76.063L526   1990
005.7' 1369--dc20

                                                    90-42847
                                                      CIP

ACKNOWLEDGEMENTS

Thanks to:

Mark Hinckley, Ladd Timpson, Larry Tomkinson, Warren Harding, and Jason Lamb of Novell for technical reviews, product information, and other immense help.

Barbara Hume for her tireless editing efforts, and Dave Doering for his many days and nights spent pounding away at the Mac.

Vince Sondej for coordinating the whole project, however reluctantly, Gamal Herbon for his eager help and support, and Steve Heide for his assistance with Macintosh conversions.

Everyone else at McGraw-Hill for their help with the design, layout, paste-up, marketing, and other administrative details of producing this book.

Contributors to the LAN TIMES for providing much of the material from which this book was prepared.

Our families, who never want to hear the phrase "It's almost done" again, for their patience and support.

CONTENTS AT A GLANCE

Table of Contents

SECTION 1: INTRODUCTION

THE FILE SERVER AND NETWARE

SECTION 2: MAINTENANCE

MANAGING THE NETWORK ENVIRONMENT

CONTROLLING NETWORK PRINTING

MAINTAINING THE FILE SERVER

IMPROVING FILE SERVER PERFORMANCE

BACKING UP THE FILE SERVER

SECTION 3: TROUBLESHOOTING

TROUBLESHOOTING THE LAN

USING NETWARE'S DIAGNOSTICS AND REPAIR UTILITIES

HANDLING FILE SERVER ERROR MESSAGES

APPENDICES

INDEX

FOREWORD

According to a recent study by Infonetics, a market research firm based in Santa Clara, Calif., the average local area network is down six percent of the time. In a 2,080-hour working year, this average network downtime represents 15.6 days of disrupted employee productivity and millions of dollars in lost revenue.

Statistics like these provide little comfort to those charged with the responsibility of maintaining and troubleshooting Novell NetWare networks, especially when reference sources for NetWare management are so hard to come by. For example, Novell's documentation for NetWare 286 is a valuable resource for initially installing and setting up the network, but it seriously deficient in practical maintenance and troubleshooting information. Other books on NetWare try to cover every possible aspect of the network, from justifying the initial costs to analyzing bits in Ethernet 802.3 packets.

The *NetWare Server Troubleshooting and Maintenance Handbook* provides a focused, comprehensive reference source for managing NetWare 286-based file servers. System administrators, network supervisors, support technicians, and LAN consultants alike will benefit from the information presented in this book. To give the subject of file server maintenance and troubleshooting the depth of coverage it needs, we have limited the breadth of the information in two ways:

• First, this *Handbook* concentrates on managing the file server and its directly attached peripherals (hard disks, printers, and uninterruptible power supplies). A companion volume, the *NetWare Workstation Troubleshooting and Maintenance Handbook*, details the intricacies of diagnosing and troubleshooting problems with the three workstation platforms supported by NetWare: DOS, OS/2, and Macintosh.

• Second, we assume your file server has already been installed with either ELS, Advanced, or SFT NetWare 286 v2.1*x*, and that you have no network management tools at your disposal other than the utilities included with the NetWare operating system itself. While much of the information applies to pre-2.1*x* versions of NetWare 286 and to NetWare 386 as well, this book will prove most helpful to managers of the hundreds of thousands of servers currently running NetWare 286 v2.1*x*.

This book is divided into three main sections: an introduction, a maintenance section, and a troubleshooting section. The introductory section presents basic network concepts and gives the reader a broad overview of what a file server is and how the NetWare operating system works. The maintenance section contains suggestions to help you keep the file server running smoothly, fine-tune its performance, and make changes to the server when necessary. The troubleshooting section details methods for isolating, diagnosing, and fixing problems you may encounter with a NetWare 286 file server.

In addition, three appendices provide an overview of the differences between NetWare 286 versions, a routine file server checkup procedure, and a list of useful third-party NetWare management tools.

Throughout this book, we assume that you are familiar with the basics of operating a DOS-based personal computer; that you know, for instance, that you must press Enter after typing a command at the DOS prompt, and that you select an option in a menu by highlighting the option with the arrow keys and pressing Enter. The batch file examples assume that you are running DOS v3.3 or above; you may have to adjust the commands slightly for other versions of DOS.

We have tried to keep the command formats shown in this book as straightforward as possible. Commands that you are to type from the command line are shown in **boldface** type. For variables shown in *italics*, you must substitute the appropriate information; for example, in place of the variable *ServerName* in a command, you would type the name of your file server. Variable information in error messages is shown in *italics* as well. Names of keys on the keyboard are spelled out with an initial capital, as in Escape, Insert, and F1; names of programs and files are given in all capital letters, as in NETGEN and CONFIG.SYS.

We hope you find this book helpful as you face the challenges of maintaining your NetWare file server environment. By following the techniques described in this book, you should be more prepared to respond confidently the next time you hear the anguished cry, "The server's down again," from your network users.

Edward A. Liebing
Ken Neff
June 1990

Section 1

Introduction

THE FILE SERVER AND NETWARE

The file server is the heart of a NetWare 286 local area network. The NetWare operating system runs on the file server to control the operation of the entire network. The *NetWare Server Troubleshooting and Maintenance Handbook* focuses on maintaining and solving problems with these two key elements of a NetWare LAN. This first section serves as an introduction to the basic concepts, hardware, and software associated with the file server. A solid understanding of what goes on inside the file server provides the foundation which we'll build upon in the rest of the book.

     • Chapter 1 presents an overview of elementary local area network concepts and how they apply in NetWare networks. This chapter is mainly for those who are new to Novell's NetWare operating system and LANs in general. It discusses what LANs are, how LANs are used, and introduces the basic components of a NetWare network. This chapter also includes an introduction to network cabling, topologies, and protocols.

     • Chapter 2 looks at the various hardware components that make up a file server. The discussion centers around how each component contributes to the overall performance of the file server. It also discusses the peripherals commonly attached to the file server, such as external disk and tape drives, uninterruptible power supplies, and printers.

     • Chapter 3 dives headlong into the NetWare operating system and discusses the numerous processes and routines that all work together to keep the network running. Many discussions later in the book assume that you have read this chapter and understand at least the basic workings of NetWare.

1 Basic Network Concepts

This chapter presents fundamental concepts that anyone working with local area networks should understand. It will emphasize those aspects that are critical to maintaining and troubleshooting a NetWare file server and its associated hardware.

If you are already familiar with most of the basics of NetWare, you can use the information in this chapter strictly as a reference when you run across a term that is still fuzzy to you. For newcomers to the brave new world of networks in general and NetWare in particular, this chapter is must reading.

WHAT IS A LOCAL AREA NETWORK?

In its simplest (and somewhat outdated) definition, a local area network, or LAN, is an assortment of personal computers connected together in order to access common data, share peripherals, and communicate with each other.

The "local area" qualifier harks back to the early days when the networked computers had to be located physically close to each other. Over the years, advances in network cabling and communication hardware have extended the reach of the local area network. Even so, most LANs today are contained within a single department, building, office complex, or campus and do not physically extend beyond a mile or two. Figure 1-1 shows a typical LAN.

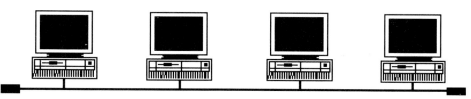

Figure 1-1: A typical local area network (LAN) consists of personal computers connected together.

Networks linked together to extend over a larger area are called wide area networks, or WANs. WANs typically involve electronic communication or data transmission between locations further than one or two miles apart. Often, a WAN is a collection of LANs connected through a slower, remote communications device such as a modem or T-1 link.

Uses of a LAN

Local area networks have a variety of uses. We'll mention only some of the main ones.

File Sharing. The most common use of LANs is to allow PC users to access files located on centralized hard disks. To accommodate a large amount of data, these shared disks typically have much more storage capacity than those normally installed in standalone PCs. Each network user can access common application programs and data files on the network. In this way, more than one person can be working with the same data (within the security bounds set by the network administrator).

Peripheral Sharing. In addition to consolidating hard disk storage, LANs also enable network users to share expensive peripherals such as printers, plotters, optical disk drives, and high-speed modems.

Electronic Communication. LANs also facilitate electronic communication between personal computer users. Inter-user communication on a network is accomplished through simple means (such as sending brief messages from one station to another) or through more sophisticated electronic-mail programs.

WHAT IS NETWARE 286?

Novell's NetWare 286 v2.1x is a high-performance local area network operating system designed specifically to provide network services in a multiuser, distributed processing environment. It uses a server-based processing model, in which clients (users) send requests for services to the server's operating system. The operating system processes the requests and responds accordingly.

The NetWare operating system is responsible for administering and controlling the users' connections to the network, their communications across the network, and their access to the network's resources (such as hard disks and printers). It also provides services that can, if used, protect network data from common hard disk and power failures.

Components of a NetWare LAN

To better understand NetWare, let's examine the components of a typical NetWare LAN and look briefly at how the NetWare operating system interacts with each component.

The File Server. In a general sense, a *server* is a computer that is set up to perform some kind of service for other computers. Hence, a *file server* is a computer that supplies file services to other computers. The file server is the central storage place for the network's directories and files. The file server runs the NetWare operating system, which coordinates all access to network data and provides other services necessary for the network to function. Figure 1-2 shows a typical NetWare 286 file server.

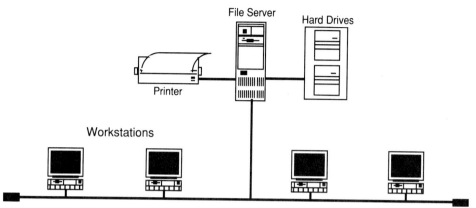

Figure 1-2: The file server is a personal computer that runs the NetWare operating system to control the activity of the network.

Workstations. Workstations are the personal computers from which network users run their applications. Each workstation has its own central processing unit (CPU) and runs its own operating system (such as DOS, OS/2, or the Macintosh OS). Being on the network, the workstation can read data from and write data to the file server, just as if it were reading or writing on a local hard disk.

In the case of a DOS workstation, memory-resident software called the *shell* sits on top of DOS. The shell intercepts all DOS requests. Those that DOS needs to handle locally are diverted back to DOS, and those that are for NetWare are sent to the file server. These requests are transmitted via some underlying delivery system to the NetWare operating system at the file server. Figure 1-3 illustrates the NetWare workstation shell.

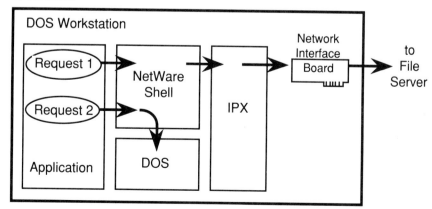

Figure 1-3: The NetWare shell sits on top of DOS in the workstation and intercepts application requests, redirecting all network-related requests (such as Request #1) to the file server. The shell passes local DOS requests (such as Request #2) back to DOS for handling.

OS/2 and Macintosh workstations use different schemes to send requests to the file server, but the principles of workstation-to-server communication are the same.

Network Interface Boards. In order to function on the LAN, the workstations and the file server must each contain a *network interface board*. The network boards are physically connected by means of a cabling system, using any of a number of different wiring schemes currently available. Network interface boards are also called adapters, network interface cards (NICs), or LAN interface boards. Figure 1-4 shows a typical network interface board with its corresponding cable and connec-

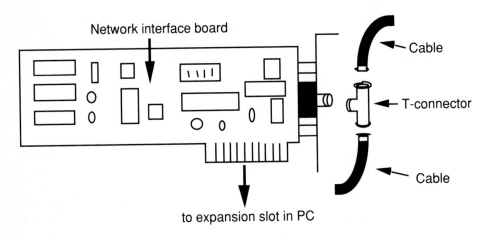

Network interface board

Cable

T-connector

Cable

to expansion slot in PC

tors.
Figure 1-4: A network interface board fits in the expansion slot of a personal computer and connects the computer to the network cabling.

NetWare communicates with a network interface board (and thereby with the network itself) through a specialized piece of software called a *communication driver* or *LAN driver*. Each type of network board that can be installed in a NetWare file server comes with a custom-written driver that enables the card to talk to NetWare. The LAN driver is linked in with the NetWare operating system as part of NetWare's installation procedure.

Each file server in a NetWare network can contain up to four network interface boards. This is called *internal bridging* in traditional Novell terminology. Figure 1-5 shows an example of internal bridging in a NetWare file server.

Somehow the NetWare operating system must keep track of which requests came in from which network board so it can route the response back to the appropriate place. Recently, Novell officially changed its terminology from *bridge* to *router* to more accurately reflect the process involved. (Routing will be explained more thoroughly in Chapter 3.)

Network Hard Disks. Because the file server is the central storage place for all network data, it typically has a large amount of hard disk storage attached to it. With

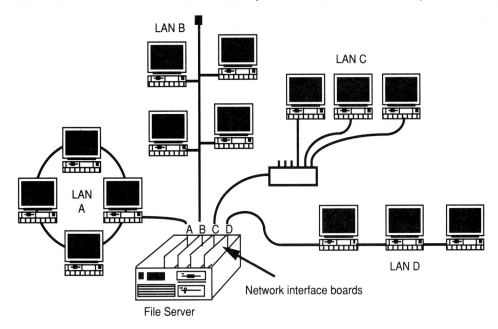

Figure 1-5: A file server can contain from one to four network interface boards, thus acting as an internal "bridge" between several networks.

SFT and Advanced NetWare, the disks can be either inside the file server itself or in some external housing connected to the file server (or both). The external housing is called a *disk subsystem*. ELS NetWare allows only internal hard disks.

NetWare 286 is primarily a file server operating system. For this reason, it was specifically designed to optimize disk read and write operations. One design goal was that the network data retrieval time had to rival the response time of a standalone system. NetWare achieves fast disk access times through the use of sophisticated caching and hashing techniques, elevator seeking, and multithreaded disk processing. (These terms will be explained in Chapter 3.)

Hard disks are connected to the file server via controller interface boards installed in the file server. As with network interface boards, a custom-written *disk driver* must be linked in with the NetWare operating system to enable communication with each particular disk/controller combination. Figure 1-6 shows a typical disk subsystem.

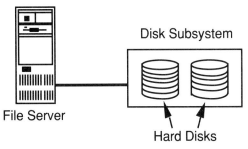

Figure 1-6: Hard disks can be attached to the file server in an external disk subsystem.

Network Backup Devices. Many personal computers designed for use as file servers have built-in tape drives for performing system backups. Another means of doing backups is to have an external backup device connected via a controller board inside the file server.

If you use Novell's backup and restore programs, the NetWare operating system will oversee the process of backing up and restoring data on the file server.

Network Printers. Typically, a file server has one or more printers connected to it. Through its built-in printing and queue services, NetWare makes these printers available to all network users and manages the print jobs that are sent to them. In this arrangement, the NetWare file server is acting as a print server as well. Alternatively, you could set up another computer on the network to act as the print server and offload this responsibility from the file server.

Uninterruptible Power Supply. Every NetWare file server should have a backup power supply to protect it against fluctuations in AC line voltage or power outages. If the AC power to a server is interrupted, an uninterruptible power supply (UPS) can supply battery power to the server long enough for it to be shut down properly. Figure 1-7 shows how a typical UPS is connected to a file server.

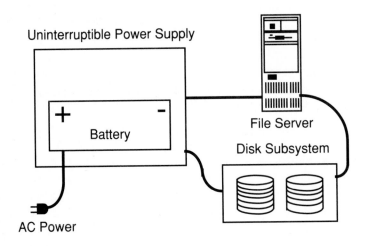

Figure 1-7: An uninterruptible power supply (UPS) protects the file server and disk subsystems from commercial power fluctuations.

The NetWare operating system includes a *UPS monitoring* capability. The file server must be set up so that the UPS can notify NetWare when a power failure occurs. Once notified by the UPS, the operating system sends word to any workstations that still have power that the server is on auxiliary power and that the users should log out. If power is not restored within a specified time period, the server automatically writes all memory buffers to disk, closes all open files, and shuts itself down.

External Bridges and Gateways. LANs can be joined together via bridges and gateways. In Novell terminology, an *external bridge* (or *router*) is a separate computer on the network that connects one LAN to another nearby LAN, a remote LAN, or a remote workstation. (Remember, internal bridging occurs when you have more than one network interface board inside the same file server.)

By contrast, a *gateway* connects a LAN to a disparate system, such as a minicomputer or mainframe. Usually, the other system does not communicate by the same protocols as the LAN, so the gateway must perform some type of protocol translation or conversion between the two systems.

A group of LANs connected by bridges or gateways is referred to as an *internetwork*, or internet. The NetWare operating system uses sophisticated dynamic routing algorithms to keep track of where servers and routers are on an internet at any given time.

NETWORK TOPOLOGIES AND PROTOCOLS

The flurry of networking topologies and protocols that existed in the early days of LAN technology has dwindled down to three: Ethernet, ARCnet, and Token-Ring. NetWare supports all of these, individually or in any combination.

To provide a background for our discussion of these networking schemes, let's look first at what types of cabling are available (the physical media), how the cable can be laid out (the LAN topology), and what methods are used to send data over the cable (the media access protocol).

The Physical Media

Three basic types of cabling can be used with NetWare LAN installations: coaxial, twisted pair, and fiber optic.

Coaxial Cable. Coaxial cable, or coax, is a popular cabling medium for connecting computers in a LAN. Coaxial cable consists of a center copper conductor surrounded by a layer of insulation, which is in turn surrounded by a braid or foil conductor and protected by an outer insulating jacket. The coaxial cable used for LANs resembles that used for cable TV. Because it is a metal-based cable, coax is susceptible to radio frequency (RF) and electromagnetic interference. Figure 1-8 illustrates coaxial cabling.

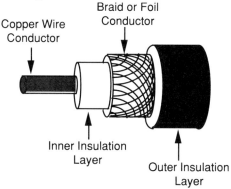

Figure 1-8: Coaxial cable has several layers surrounding a center copper wire.

Twisted Pair Cable. Twisted pair cable is the type of cabling used by the telephone company to hook up telephones. Twisted pair comes in shielded and unshielded varieties. *Shielded twisted pair* (STP) cable has pairs of wires twisted around each other, protected by a layer of foil insulation. This foil shielding makes STP cable more resistant to electrical noise.

Unshielded twisted pair (UTP) cable is the kind of wire used for telephones. It has one or more pairs of wires twisted together in twos, and the whole cable is surrounded by a layer of insulation (with no foil shield). Despite its high susceptibility to electrical noise, unshielded twisted pair has grown in popularity over the past several years. This acceptance is due in part to its low cost and easy handling (many buildings already have twisted-pair wiring in place). Figure 1-9 shows what twisted pair cabling looks like.

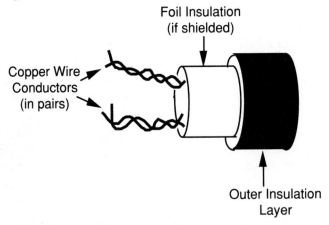

Figure 1-9: Twisted pair cable consists of one or more pairs of wires twisted together and encased in an outer covering.

Fiber Optic Cable. Fiber optic cable contains a glass or plastic core through which data is transmitted as pulses of light. Because it uses light to transfer information, fiber optic cable is immune to electrical interference. It also allows very high transmission speeds. Due to the skill and sophistication needed to install fiber optic cable, its use is limited to circumstances where speed or immunity to electrical noise is essential. Figure 1-10 shows a typical fiber optic cable.

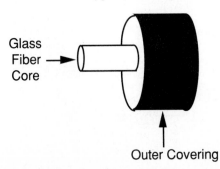

Figure 1-10: Fiber optic cable has a glass or plastic core surrounded by a protective outer covering.

Baseband and Broadband. You should also be aware of what is meant by baseband and broadband networks. A *baseband* network, regardless of the cabling type, provides a single data transmission path that allows only one set of signals to travel on the wire. In other words, the bandwidth of signals on a baseband network is the same as the data transmission rate the wire supports. Most local area networks are baseband networks.

A *broadband* network can transmit more than one set of signals on a single network wire. Besides multiple sets of network data, broadband networks can also carry telephone and video signals. Broadband is rarely used with PC LANs, except to provide the backbone for an internetwork. Broadband networks are common in the minicomputer and mainframe environments.

Physical LAN Topologies

Generally, there are three ways that LAN cabling can be physically strung between stations on the network: in a bus, a ring, or a star topology.

Bus Topology. In a bus topology, a single string of cable runs between network stations connected in a linear fashion. Figure 1-11 illustrates the linear bus topology.

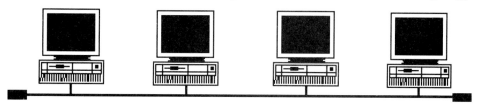

Figure 1-11: Network stations connected in a linear bus topology.

Ring Topology. In a ring topology, the stations are connected in a circular fashion. The cable begins at one station and makes a complete loop of the stations, ending up back where it started. Figure 1-12 illustrates the ring topology.

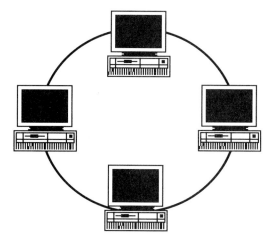

Figure 1-12: Network stations connected in a ring topology.

Star Topology. In a star topology, each network station is connected directly to a central server or hub. No cables are strung between stations. Figure 1-13 illustrates the star topology.

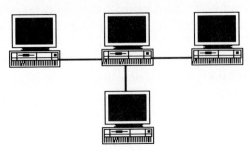

Figure 1-13: Network stations connected in a star topology.

In actual practice, star networks often resemble a string of stars. In this arrangement, a central hub is connected to one or more additional hubs, which may or may not have stations connected to them. The use of hubs extends the distance that can be covered in a star-topology network.

Media Access Methods

Various methods have been developed over the years to allow stations on a LAN to gain access to the physical medium (cable). Two dominant standards have emerged: Carrier Sense Multiple Access with Collision Detection (CSMA/CD) and Token Passing.

CSMA/CD. Carrier Sense Multiple Access with Collision Detection is the most common method of controlling medium access in bus topology networks. In this system, a station wanting to send data "listens" to see if anyone else is using the wire. If the network is not busy, the station sends its message.

Because all stations are contending for use of the wire, it is possible for two stations to attempt to send data on the wire at the same time. When this happens, a *collision* occurs and neither station's data will arrive at the intended destination. However, various means are provided for the stations to detect collisions and resend the data when the wire is not busy. Normally, collisions are very rare and do not impact the overall throughput of the network.

Token Passing. This media access method is commonly used in ring topology networks. With token passing, stations must wait their turn to get access to the network. A *token* (a specialized unit of data used to control access to the LAN) is sent around the ring from one station to the next. Initially, the token is marked "free." When a station needs to transmit data, it grabs the token, marks it as "busy," and sends the data along with the token. The "busy" token and accompanying data continue around the ring. When they reach the station the data is intended for, that station makes a copy of the data and passes the still "busy" token along. After circulating the entire ring, the token arrives back at the sender, which changes it back to a "free" token and relinquishes control of it. If the station wants to send additional data, it must wait for the token to come around again.

This rather complex arbitration scheme guarantees that only one station is transmitting at any given time, eliminating the possibility of collisions. On the other hand, passing the token adds a good deal of overhead to the network, which can slow down data transmission.

THE BIG THREE NETWORK SCHEMES

Now that we've seen what types of cable are available and looked at the two main ways of accessing the cable, let's see how these are implemented in the "big three" networking schemes.

Ethernet

The Ethernet networking scheme was originally invented at Xerox Corporation and eventually developed into a standard with the help of Digital Equipment Corporation and Intel. The current version is perhaps the most widely used system for connecting networks. Interfaces for the various versions of Ethernet are available for virtually any kind of desktop computer, as well as most minicomputers and mainframes.

The original Ethernet wiring scheme calls for a thick coaxial cable, which has come to be known as thick Ethernet cable. Following the classic bus topology, a single thick Ethernet trunk cable runs from one end of the network to the other. The stations are connected to the bus via transceivers and transceiver cables.

Most PC-based Ethernet networks use the thinner RG-58 coaxial cable, which has been dubbed thin Ethernet or "Cheapernet" cable. Stations are connected using a linear bus topology in which cable is strung from one station to the next. A T-connector is used to attach the cable to the network interface board at the back of each network station.

Recently, other wiring systems for Ethernet have been developed. For example, a number of vendors offer Ethernet systems that use twisted-pair cable in a star topology. These systems are easier to install and manage, but are usually more expensive than the coaxial-cable wiring schemes.

Ethernet uses the CSMA/CD medium access method and provides a transmission speed of 10 megabits per second (10Mbps).

ARCnet

The Attached Resource Computer network (ARCnet) system was originally devised by Datapoint Corporation. ARCnet interfaces are now available from many network vendors, including Novell with their RX-Net boards. ARCnet is the least expensive, and slowest, of the popular PC network connection systems.

The original (and still the most common) ARCnet connection scheme uses RG-62 coaxial cable connected in a star configuration. There is a central hub, and each node has a cable going from the node to the hub.

Alternative ARCnet schemes allow stations to be connected in a bus topology using either RG-62 coaxial cable or twisted pair.

ARCnet is a 2.5Mbps token-passing network that supports up to 255 stations. In ARCnet's implementation, the token is passed around in *logical* ring order. Stations are assigned addresses and control of the token moves from one address to the next in sequential order, independent of the physical ordering on the cable.

Token-Ring

Token-Ring is a network wiring system invented by IBM. Token-Ring interfaces are available for IBM-compatible microcomputers and for IBM mini-computers and mainframes.

Token-Ring normally uses shielded twisted pair wiring connected in a ring topology. The cable goes around from the first computer to the last, and a second wire returns in the other direction. Having two wires going between each pair of computers allows Token-Ring networks to continue to function (although at a reduced speed) if one of the wires fail.

The original Token-Ring specification offers a transmission speed of 4Mbps. Newer versions offer 16Mbps. Both use the token passing medium access method in which the token is passed in *physical* ring order.

Macintosh Wiring Schemes

For those who now have or plan to have NetWare for Macintosh running on their NetWare 286 networks, here's a quick rundown of Macintosh cabling topologies and protocols.

LocalTalk. LocalTalk is a network wiring scheme frequently used to connect Macintosh computers. Hardware is also available to connect IBM PC-compatible computers to LocalTalk networks; this hardware is primarily used when PCs and Macs are to be connected together in a single network. In the NetWare environment, LocalTalk can be used in connection with NetWare for Macintosh. Macintosh systems include the hardware needed to interface to LocalTalk, so no network interfaces are needed. PC-compatible computers must have a LocalTalk board, such as the Novell NL1000, installed.

The primary alternative for connecting Macintosh systems is Ethernet. This is much faster, but requires the purchase of network interfaces for the Macs.

LocalTalk is a CSMA/CD wiring system that operates at 230 kilobits per second (Kbps). This is much slower than the other common network wiring schemes (ten times slower than ARCnet, which is the next slowest system). LocalTalk wiring is very inexpensive, as it normally uses telephone-type wire.

AppleTalk. AppleTalk, also known as Apple File Protocol (AFP), is the network protocol most commonly used on Macintosh networks. It is usually run on LocalTalk wiring.

Current versions of NetWare do not support AFP directly. Instead, a gateway program runs as a set of value-added processes (VAPs) in the file server or in an external bridge. The VAPs translate between AFP and the NetWare communications protocol.

2 File Server Hardware

This chapter builds on the basic concepts introduced in the previous chapter. Because this book concentrates on the NetWare file server and its associated hardware and software, we'll take a closer look at the file server from the hardware standpoint.

THE FILE SERVER MACHINE

Because the file server is the heart of a NetWare 286 network, the personal computer chosen for use as the file server largely determines how well the network performs. The general guidelines given in the NetWare installation manuals state that a file server should be an IBM PC AT or compatible, or an IBM Personal System/2 (PS/2) Model 50 or above. However, because of the availability of numerous clones with varying degrees of IBM compatibility, the choice is not always an easy one.

File Server Suitability Factors

It is not our intent in this discussion to recommend any particular brand of computer over another. Rather, we include this information so that you will be aware of network problems that can be caused by improper selection of file server hardware. The basic issues you must consider when determining the suitability of a file server include the manufacturer, the CPU, the bus type, the ROM BIOS, the amount of RAM supported, and Novell certification.

Manufacturer. As a general rule, purchase the best computer you can afford from a reputable manufacturer. To skimp on the file server is to flirt with disaster. Evaluate your initial hardware investment in terms of the reliability you want to have over the long run. Your file server, like any other piece of electronic equipment, will need to be serviced from time to time. Consider the manufacturer's commitment to service and support of its products.

CPU. NetWare 286 requires that the file server have an 80286 or 80386 microprocessor. On these CPUs, clock speeds typically range anywhere from 8MHz to 33MHz. Naturally, a faster CPU and clock speed will yield better performance from the file server. If you want high performance, or if you plan to upgrade your network, get a 386-based machine. If your budget is tight, or if you expect to stay with NetWare 286, get a high-quality 286-based machine.

Another consideration is the number of wait states used to match the performance of the CPU with the rest of the file server hardware. The lower the number of wait states, the faster the server (0 wait states is best).

Bus Types. Three types of I/O buses are currently battling it out over their relative merits for file server use: standard AT bus, Micro Channel Architecture, and EISA.

The standard AT-style bus (often referred to now as the Industry Standard Architecture, or ISA, bus) is found in most IBM PC AT and compatible computers. Machines with an ISA bus accept standard 8- or 16-bit network and disk interface cards. The standard speed of the AT-style bus is 8MHz.

Micro Channel Architecture (MCA) is the type of bus design found in IBM's PS/2 Model 50 or above. These PS/2 computers will accept only boards that have been specifically designed for MCA. MCA cards will not work in standard AT bus machines. MCA offers higher data transfer speeds than the standard AT bus.

The Extended Industry Standard Architecture (EISA) was designed by a consortium of nine computer manufacturers as an alternative to IBM's proprietary Micro Channel Architecture. Most EISA-bus machines are very high performance computers specifically designed to be used as a network file server. As such, they are quite expensive compared to ISA or low-end MCA machines. Besides offering a high transfer speed, EISA has the added advantage of being able to accommodate cards designed for the AT bus as well as EISA-designed cards.

If you are thinking of upgrading to a different bus type, base your decision on the network's throughput requirements, the types and cost of interface boards you already have or intend to purchase, and the availability of software drivers for the boards. (Currently, NetWare drivers are available for only a small number of EISA-compatible network interface boards.)

ROM BIOS. On a personal computer, the ROM BIOS (Basic Input/Output System) contains basic instructions and procedures used by the CPU. The BIOS is the interface between the computer's hardware circuitry and the software (both the operating system and applications) running on the machine. Among other things, the ROM BIOS controls the computer's interaction with the monitor and the keyboard.

File servers with older ROM BIOS firmware can experience serious problems (such as the inability to boot, random crashing, and ABEND errors) when running nondedicated versions of NetWare. If you plan to run nondedicated NetWare 286, the ROM BIOS must be 100 percent IBM compatible.

Another consideration is whether your hard disk type (its number of heads and cylinders) is included in the ROM BIOS's setup tables. If it is not, you will have trouble getting the file server to recognize the disk when you run the SETUP routine.

If you have an older (pre-1985) computer, you can avoid many problems by updating the ROM BIOS. For IBM and Compaq computers, obtain the updated BIOS directly from an authorized dealer. For other PCs, a good updated BIOS is available from Award Software, Inc. (See Appendix C for address information.)

Memory. Novell installation manuals give the minimum random access memory (RAM) requirements for a file server as 1MB for dedicated NetWare 286 and 1.5MB for nondedicated NetWare. These absolute minimums are typically insufficient for most real-world implementations.

A more practical minimum for NetWare 286 is 2MB of RAM. The maximum amount of memory a file server can have is 16MB, but it is extremely rare for a server running NetWare 286 to require that much RAM. Except for the largest network installations, 4-8MB is usually sufficient. Adequate memory becomes especially critical when the server must service a large number of users, or when it has more than 70MB of hard disk storage space to keep track of. (See Chapter 26 for a more complete discussion of file server memory requirements.)

The memory you install in the file server should be configured as *extended* memory. NetWare cannot use expanded memory. You will be better off with a machine that provides an easy means for adding memory, either on the motherboard itself or through memory expansion cards.

Novell Certification. The safest route to take when purchasing a file server is to get one that is certified to run NetWare 286. Novell authorized resellers usually have access to a list of computers that have been approved by Novell for use as file servers. In order to make this list, the manufacturer must submit a machine to Novell, where it must pass a battery of compatibility tests.

A few caveats here: Novell charges a substantial fee for this testing, which is sometimes prohibitive for smaller PC manufacturers. A machine that is fully NetWare-compatible may not carry Novell's official stamp of approval simply because it was never submitted to Novell for testing. Your dealer should be able to help you determine the suitability of a particular brand or model. Be doubly certain that the computer is suitable for use as a file server, not just as a workstation.

NETWORK INTERFACE BOARDS

Not all network interface boards available for NetWare workstations are recommended for use in the file server. This section explains the factors that determine a network board's suitability for use in a file server.

8-bit, 16-bit, and 32-bit Boards

Most network interface boards are available in either 8-bit or 16-bit varieties. An 8-bit board moves data from the computer's I/O bus to the cable 8 bits (one byte) at a time; a 16-bit card moves data 16 bits (two bytes) at a time. Because of the higher performance of 16-bit cards, they are most often used in the file server, whereas the slower 8-bit cards are used in workstations on the LAN.

A 16-bit board has two edge connectors (one long and one short), so they will only fit in a 16-bit slot in the expansion bay of the computer. Make sure your file server has an adequate number of 16-bit slots available to accommodate the boards you must install.

Many 16-bit boards can use hardware interrupts 9 or above. This capability is important in avoiding hardware conflicts when the board must coexist in the same machine with other expansion boards that use the lower hardware interrupts.

If you have a 386-based file server, another option is to use one of the new 32-bit boards available for either Micro Channel Architecture or the EISA bus. These boards offer top-of-the-line performance for LANs that require it.

Hardware Settings

On most non-MCA and non-EISA boards, various hardware settings are made by manipulating jumpers or switch blocks on the board. A jumper refers to a group of metal pins sticking out of the board. You set the jumper by connecting certain pairs of pins with a jumper block. Figure 2-1 illustrates a typical jumper.

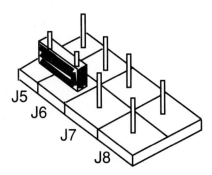

Figure 2-1: On some network interface boards, you make settings by altering jumper pin connections. In this figure, pins J5 and J6 are connected.

A switch block consists of a bank of DIP switches typically numbered from 0 up to 7 or 15. You make the setting by turning the DIP switches on or off in various patterns. Figure 2-2 illustrates a switch block.

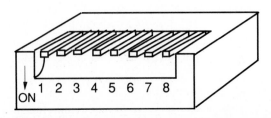

Figure 2-2: Some hardware settings are made by setting DIP switches on the network interface board.

Typical hardware settings include the hardware interrupt line (or IRQ, for Interrupt ReQuest line), the base I/O port address (or just I/O address), the base memory address (or RAM address), and the Direct Memory Access (DMA) line. On ARCnet cards, the station or node address is typically set via a switch block.

MCA and EISA cards allow these settings to be made through a software program that comes with the card. This procedure is much easier than having to pull out a board and mess with itsy-bitsy components that defy the agility of most human fingers. You may want to keep this in mind when selecting your network interface boards.

Availability of LAN Drivers

In order for a network interface board to function in a NetWare file server, there must be a corresponding LAN driver written for that board. Be aware that there is a difference between an *OS* LAN driver and a *workstation* LAN driver. An OS LAN driver is required for all file server boards.

Novell ships a core set of the most commonly-used LAN drivers (both OS and workstation) with the basic NetWare software package. The exact list varies from release to release, but a representative list is included in Appendix C. A number of less common drivers is also available separately from Novell.

Other network interface board manufacturers provide NetWare-compatible LAN drivers for their own hardware. If you are using third-party network interface boards, make sure the driver has been certified by Novell through the Independent Product Testing Program. Independent Product Testing Bulletins containing Net-Ware compatibility information can be downloaded from Novell's NetWire forum on CompuServe.

HARD DISKS AND CONTROLLERS

Hard disks are perhaps the most critical file server component, as they are responsible for storing the valuable data generated by the LAN users. Hard disks come in a wide variety of sizes and types that run off of different kinds of controllers. Here is a quick rundown of what you should know about disk hardware.

Hard Disk Terminology

The name "hard disk" is misleading, for a hard disk is usually made up of several thin, rigid disks stacked vertically. These disks, or platters, rotate around a spindle at speeds of nearly 3,600 revolutions per minute (that's 60 spins in one second). Some high capacity disk drives rotate at 5,400 rpm to provide very fast access times.

Most hard disks in IBM PC AT compatibles contain eight or more platters. Each platter is coated on both sides with a metallic substance that is highly responsive to magnetic fields. Older disks have a ferric oxide coating, which is fragile and tends to wear out over long periods of extensive use. Newer disks use a more durable plated cobalt alloy that offers increased storage capacity and improved reliability. Figure 2-3 shows the insides of a typical hard disk.

Electromagnetic read/write *heads* are attached to an arm mechanism that positions the heads above and below each platter, as shown in Figure 2-3. As these heads move in unison across the surface of the platters, they read and write data on the disk by manipulating or sensing the alignment of the magnetic particles.

Other mechanical parts of a hard disk shown in Figure 2-3 include the actuator, which pushes and pulls the arm mechanism to the precise track (cylinder) locations; the *spindle motor*, which turns the spindle at the specified number of revolutions per minute; and the PCB (printed circuit board or logic board), which controls all of the drive's components.

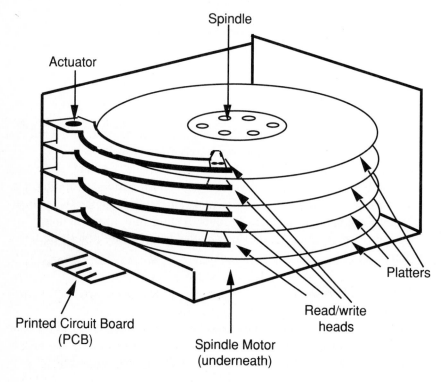

Figure 2-3: A typical hard disk consists of eight or more platters rotating around a spindle.

Data is stored on the surface of a platter in concentric circles or *tracks*. These tracks are very small—usually only a thousandth of a inch apart. Each platter has the same number of tracks. The tracks are further divided into wedge-shaped sectors. A sector is the smallest unit of storage on a hard disk. On a typical AT hard disk, the tracks are divided into either 17 or 26 sectors of 512 bytes each. Figure 2-4 illustrates tracks and sectors.

A *cylinder* is the set of corresponding tracks from each platter. For example, the set of all track 0's on each platter is called cylinder 0. Since the heads move in unison, all of the read/write heads will be positioned over the same track on each platter at any given moment. To save on excess head movement, as many pieces of a file as possible are stored in the same cylinder.

The two most common specifications given for hard disks are the seek time (in milliseconds) and the total storage capacity (in megabytes). *Seek time* measures how long it takes to physically locate and retrieve data from the disk. Typical seek times range from 55ms down to 15ms, while some of the fastest new disks claim seek times of 10ms. Several factors determine the total *storage capacity* of a disk: the number of platters, the coating material used, the number of heads, the number of cylinders (tracks per platter), and the sector size.

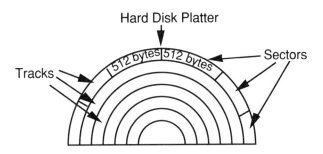

Figure 2-4: Each disk surface is divided into concentric tracks, which are further divided into 512-byte sectors.

Data Encoding Methods

Another factor that determines a disk's storage capacity is the format used to write data on the disk. Two data encoding schemes are used most often for PC hard disks: MFM and RLL.

MFM, or Modified Frequency Modulation, is an older data encoding method that formats the disk with 17 sectors per track. MFM drives typically have a storage capacity of less than 80MB. Most hard disks found in the IBM XT and early AT and PS/2 Model 50 computers are MFM drives. MFM is also the encoding method used on double density floppy diskette drives.

RLL, or Run Length Limited, employs a newer encoding scheme that allows data to be compressed more tightly on the disk. An RLL drive formats the disk to 26 sectors per track. The compactness of the data requires more precision in positioning the read/write heads, but the storage capacity of the disk can be larger than the 80MB supported by MFM. In fact, all drives over 100MB in size use some form of RLL technology.

Several enhancements to RLL technology provide a significant increase in the transfer rate and storage capacity possible. Foremost among these improvements are Advanced RLL (ARLL) and Enhanced RLL (ERLL), which allow formats of 53 or more sectors per track. Because of the increased precision required for disks using RLL encoding methods, these disks need a different controller interface than MFM disks. Controllers and controller interfaces will be discussed next.

Disk Controllers

A hard disk controller is a circuit board that translates operating system requests into the electronic pulses that the hard disk components can understand. It acts as the intermediary between the disk and the OS. Both internal and external hard disks must be connected to some type of controller board.

Disk controllers generally fall into three main categories, according to the type of interface they use: ST-506, SCSI, or ESDI. All three are recognized as standard interfaces, so they are used by a number of different manufacturers. Other disk controllers use their own proprietary interface. The SCSI and ESDI interfaces are most commonly used with NetWare file servers.

Disk controllers that adhere to the ST-506 design generally use the MFM encoding method, whereas others (labeled ST-506/RLL) use the RLL method. Disk drives attached to an ST-506/RLL controller must be rated for RLL.

The SCSI (Small Computer Systems Interface) standard was originally developed by Shugart Associates, who dubbed it SASI. The American National Standards Institute (ANSI) has since adopted this standard and renamed it SCSI. The main advantage of SCSI is its hardware independence, which is accomplished through two means: logical block-oriented addressing and "bus" technology.

The SCSI interface looks at data storage in terms of logical "blocks" of storage area, rather than physical sectors on the disk. Hence, any device that is block-addressable can be used with SCSI. Most hard disk and tape drives made for PCs are block-addressable.

Thanks to SCSI's bus implementation, you can attach up to seven additional controllers in a daisy-chain formation. The SCSI bus provides a "data highway," if you will, over which data is transferred from the controllers of the individual devices to the server. Normally, each controller controls one or two devices. The controllers are connected together via a 37- or 50-pin cable. Both ends of the SCSI bus must be terminated with a terminating resistor pack Figure 2-5 illustrates a typical SCSI bus configuration.

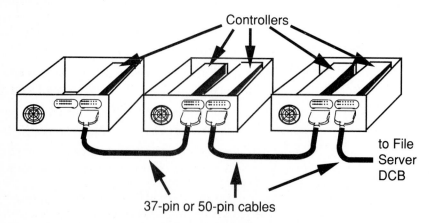

Figure 2-5: On a SCSI bus, several controllers can be daisy-chained together. The first and last controllers on the chain must be terminated with a terminating resistor pack.

Note that you connect device controllers to the SCSI bus, not the devices themselves. On some hard disks, the controller is built in to the disk housing rather than being an external board. These are called *embedded SCSI* drives. Due to this one-to-one controller/drive correspondence, you cannot attach a second drive to the controller in an embedded SCSI drive. However, embedded SCSI drives are generally more reliable because they require fewer cable connections. Since the drive and the controller are inseparable, the performance of embedded SCSI drives performance can been greatly optimized by the manufacturer.

The *ESDI* (Enhanced Small Device Interface) standard was introduced by Maxtor Corporation and was used by IBM in the PS/2 Models 60 and above. The ESDI interface transmits signals digitally and shifts the responsibility for clock timing from the controller to the disk. As a result of these and other enhancements, ESDI disks are able to access data faster and more efficiently. ESDI controllers typically support up to two disk drives.

NetWare-Compatible Controllers. A number of different kinds of disk controller boards are used in NetWare file servers. The most common ones are summarized below.

Internal hard disks in an IBM AT-compatible are most often run off a Western Digital-type MFM controller. Internal hard disks in the IBM PS/2 Model 50 also use an MFM controller. In the Model 60 and above, the PS/2s use an ESDI controller for the internal disk drives. (However, IBM recently announced some new PS/2 models that contain SCSI drives.)

To govern the activity of external hard disks, Novell designed a specialized disk channel controller called a *disk coprocessor board* (DCB). Novell has licensed its DCB technology to third-party manufacturers. As a result, a variety of DCBs are now available for use in both AT-compatible file servers and PS/2 MCA machines.

While technically not a SCSI controller, a DCB can control up to eight SCSI controllers on a SCSI bus. The SCSI controllers are typically located in separate boxes called *disk subsystems*, with each disk subsystem housing from one to four disk drives.

Availability of Disk Drivers

As with network interface boards, hard disks and controller boards need a specialized driver in order to run with NetWare. Drivers for the commonly-used controllers mentioned above are shipped with each copy of NetWare 286. Drivers for other types of disk drives and controllers are available as VADDs (value-added disk drivers) from various manufacturers.

BACKUP HARDWARE

You may as well face it now—you *will* lose data on *your* file server. It's Murphy's Law of Networking. To be prepared for this eventuality, every NetWare file server must have a means for its data to be backed up onto another storage medium and restored to the file server disks.

Traditionally, quarter-inch cartridge (QIC) magnetic tape systems have been the mainstay for file server backups. Their popularity is due mainly to their relatively low cost and availability in a variety of configurations. Recently, other backup options (such as 8mm tape, 4mm DAT, and optical disks) are becoming more and more popular.

As with other peripheral devices, tape drives and optical disk drives run off a controller board inside the file server. The device itself can be either internally mounted in a spare drive bay or externally located in a separate box.

Availability of Backup Device Drivers

The drivers for the Wangtek streaming tape backup drive included in some Novell-made file servers are offered only with SFT NetWare v2.1. Since Novell has been slowly phasing out hardware offerings, third-party backup solutions are more and more common. Many backup programs now allow DOS-addressable disks and SCSI-compatible devices to be used for backing up NetWare file servers.

UNINTERRUPTIBLE POWER SUPPLIES

As explained in Chapter 1, an uninterruptible power supply (UPS) provides battery backup power to the file server in case it loses commercial power. Like the other file server peripherals we have discussed, UPSes come in many different varieties. A list of Novell-approved UPS units is available from authorized NetWare resellers, consultants, or NetWare Centers.

The main concerns in selecting a UPS are determining how many amps you need, and deciding what network components (besides the file server) to protect with a UPS. Novell strongly recommends that every file server and *its attached disk subsystems* have UPS protection. (In fact, it is a requirement if you want Novell's service and support package.) It won't do you much good to keep the file server running if the disk drives lose power.

It is also a good idea to use a UPS with any value-added servers (print servers, archive servers, and so on) and with workstations that run key applications without a user present. Do *not* connect printers to a UPS. Some printers (especially laser printers) require more power than the typical UPS can provide, and all printer motors generate voltage fluctuations that can cause problems for the UPS.

To determine a sufficient power rating for the UPS, add up the individual wattage requirements for each piece of equipment that the UPS must supply power to. Then add about a 10 percent margin of safety to that total. Most manufacturers list the power consumption ratings in watts somewhere on the equipment itself or in its accompanying documentation. If you can only find the current (given in amps), multiply that by 120 (the standard voltage in the United States) to get the number of watts the equipment uses.

PRINTERS

The final type of hardware that can be attached to the file server is the network printers. NetWare 286 lets you connect up to five printers directly to the file server. Depending on the ports you have available on the file server PC, you can have two serial printers and three parallel printers, or any combination thereof. Over a serial interface, data is transferred sequentially one bit at a time, as opposed to eight or more bits in unison over a parallel interface. Hence, parallel printers usually print faster than serial printers.

Most any brand of printer can be used as a network printer. However, printer definitions (control commands and escape sequences) for some of the more popular printers have been predefined and included with NetWare. You may want to consider this when selecting your network printers. The exact list may vary from version to version, but here is a representative list from Advanced NetWare 286 v2.15c.

Apple Imagewriter II	Hewlett-Packard LaserJet I/II
Apple Laserwriter II/PlusIBM	ProPrinter 4201
Citizen 120-D	IBM ProPrinter II/XL
Citizen 20	NEC Spinwriter 2050/3050
Citizen 224	NEC Spinwriter 8810/8830
CItoh 310/315	NEC Pinwriter P-6
CItoh 600	Okidata Microline 192/193
Diablo 630	Okidata 290
Epson FX80/FX100	Okidata 390
Epson FX-800	Okidata Laserline 6
Epson FX86e/FX286e	Panasonic 1080/1080i
Epson LD-2500	Panasonic 1091/1091i
Epson LQ-800/LQ-1000	Star NX-1000
Epson LX-80	Star Gemini 10X
Epson LX-800	Toshiba P321

External Print Server Software

As of February 1990, Novell's external print server software is being bundled with NetWare 286 to give you a little more flexibility with network printers. For starters, you can have more of them—up to 16. And they need not be within printer-cable distance of the file server anymore. You can either dedicate a network workstation to act as a full-time print server and attach the printers to it, or you can attach printers to various workstations around the network and run them as part-time print servers. Best of all, you no longer have to bring the file server down and run NETGEN or ELSGEN to change the network printer configurations.

By bundling the print server software with the NetWare operating system, Novell has endorsed external print servers as the preferred mechanism for controlling network printers.

3 How NetWare Works

Okay, the easy part is over. In this chapter, we're going to dive head-first into the inner workings of that complicated, mysterious piece of software called NetWare. Knowing a little bit about what the NetWare operating system does and how it controls the file server can help a great deal when the time comes to figure out what's going wrong.

Don't worry if you didn't major in computer science with an emphasis on operating systems design. We'll try to keep this discussion within the visible spectrum. And we promise not to mention the OSI Reference Model even once.

THE NETWARE OPERATING SYSTEM

NetWare is not an application. It is an operating system, just as MS-DOS and OS/2 are operating systems. However, unlike DOS and OS/2 (which control just one computer at a time), NetWare is a *network* operating system. It was designed from the ground up to handle the unique requirements of a multiuser environment, where more than one user is vying for the system's resources.

Operating System Fundamentals

As a basis for our discussion of NetWare, let's look at some of the basic functions that any operating system performs. An operating system (or OS) is a set of software routines that control the execution of other software programs in a computer. Until the OS is loaded and running, the computer can do nothing.

One term you might hear in relation to an operating system is *kernel*. Don't let this term confuse you. The kernel is simply the core set of operating system functions, around which the other OS functions and routines are based.

The OS, in conjunction with the ROM BIOS, controls the basic *input/output* (I/O) functions that take place inside the computer. Input from the keyboard and other sources is handled by the OS, as is the output to the monitor, a printer, or other devices.

The disk and file management routines within the OS handle all *disk I/O*. These include creating, opening, closing, copying, deleting, and renaming files; reading from a file, writing to a file, and searching for files; and creating, deleting, and changing directories. Another important part of file management is the ability to lock part or all of a file to prevent more than one user from changing the same data at the same time.

The OS is also responsible for coordinating access to the CPU's computing resources and allocating memory for various applications. It provides a uniform method for initiating and terminating all other programs that run on the computer. The OS also has the capability to interpret and process commands typed at the file server keyboard (called the *console*).

The NetWare operating system performs all of these functions in the network environment. Network-aware applications take advantage of these services through the function calls and application program interfaces (APIs) that NetWare provides. NetWare is a multitasking, multithreaded operating system that is ideally suited to the distributed processing environment inherent to LANs. If that last statement leaves you bewildered, we'll next try to explain what all these terms mean.

Multitasking and Distributed Processing Terms. A *multitasking* operating system divides up the CPU's processing time among several tasks, giving the illusion that more than one program is running at the same time. A *task* is simply a discrete operation or subroutine within a parent program. For example, a database application could consist of a task that controls the user interface, another task that handles updates to the database, and another that resolves conflicts when two users are trying to update the same data simultaneously. The terms "task" and "process" are often used interchangeably; technically, however, a *process* can consist of one or more tasks.

In a network environment where many workstations are connected to a single file server, the file server's OS must handle tasks from all kinds of different applications running at the various workstations. For this reason, NetWare is also *multithreaded*, which means one task doesn't have to finish before the next one can begin. Think of a *thread* as a processing "channel" that the OS creates to service a given task. A *scheduler* process makes sure that each process gets its turn to use the CPU. NetWare assigns each task a priority level so that the most important tasks can be completed before the less critical ones.

In a multitasking system, the task or process that currently controls the computer's keyboard and display is running in the *foreground*. Other tasks that are running but do not have control of the keyboard and display are being executed in the *background*. Spooling print jobs to a queue is an example of a background operation in NetWare.

In certain instances, the processes or tasks currently running need to communicate with each other. Multitasking operating systems can use several means to accomplish interprocess or intertask communications: queues, semaphores, shared memory, messages, signals, and sockets. These terms will be explained later in their respective contexts.

Because a LAN consists of intelligent workstations, each with their own CPU, it forms the classic environment for *distributed processing*. The main idea behind distributed processing is to farm out the processing of various tasks, rather than have a central CPU do all the computing. In LANs, this is usually accomplished by having each workstation run applications locally, using its own CPU and desktop operating system (DOS, OS/2, or Macintosh). The workstations share the resources provided by the file server, such as program and data files and access to printers and other network services.

Two other terms are frequently used to describe how workstations interact with the server in a network: *client* and *server*. Workstations or programs that use network resources are called "clients," while the devices that provide the resources and service the clients are called "servers."

Services Provided by NetWare. Among the services administered by the NetWare operating system are:

- Internetwork communications
- File system services
- Fault tolerance
- Security
- Connection maintenance
- Printing
- Queue management
- Accounting
- Network management
- Application services

Let's look briefly at how these services are implemented in the NetWare operating system.

INTERNETWORK COMMUNICATIONS

One fundamental service that NetWare must provide is the ability for all stations on the network to communicate. If computers connected to a common cabling system can't talk to each other, you don't really have a network. To lay the groundwork for talking about internetwork communications, we need to define a few terms first.

Networks and Internetworks

To begin with, we must distinguish between a plain old network and an internetwork. The distinction between the two is not always clear, for in some contexts they are synonymous. In the context of NetWare, a *network* consists of all the computers running off a particular network interface board in a file server. An *internetwork* is a collection of interconnected networks.

You can form an internetwork in a number of ways. You could have both an Ethernet board and a Token-Ring board installed in the same file server, with each board controlling its own network. Or you could connect two or more networks through an external bridge (or router). Other methods involve gateways and remote asynchronous links. Whatever the method, the main idea behind internetworking is to make the services and resources on one network available to clients on other networks. The communication between disparate networks all happens behind the scenes, so to a client the internet looks like one big network. This transparency allows an Ethernet workstation to exchange information with a Token-Ring workstation, blissfully unaware that they are actually on different networks that use different media access protocols.

Internet Addressing

Each station on an internetwork is uniquely identified by an *internet address*. This address has three parts: the network address, the node address, and the socket number. The *network address* identifies a group of directly connected computers, as opposed to computers that must communicate through a bridge. The *node address* indicates a specific computer residing on the network. The *socket number* identifies a program running in the computer, or a process within a program.

This addressing scheme is often compared to the post office's address system. Think of a networked computer as an apartment building housing four apartments, located at 1535 Elm Street. The network address is analogous to the street name (Elm Street). The node address corresponds to the building number (1535). The socket number would be the apartment number within the building (#2, for instance). Network and node addresses are illustrated in Figure 3-1.

Network Addresses. In reality, a network address is a hexadecimal number containing from 1 to 8 digits. Each of the four possible network interface boards in a file server must have a unique network address assigned, even if they use the same type of cabling. For example, if you have two Ethernet boards in the same file server, they cannot share the same network address because they control physically separate Ethernet cabling systems.

The four boards in the server are identified internally as LAN A, LAN B, LAN C, and LAN D. Network addresses for LANs A through D are assigned in NetWare's installation program (NETGEN for SFT and Advanced NetWare 286, ELSGEN for ELS NetWare Level II, INSTALL for ELS NetWare Level I). The installation program checks to make sure you haven't duplicated network addresses in the same file server. However, if you have more than one file server on the internet, you must consider the network addresses set on the other file servers as well.

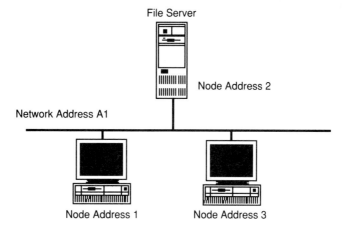

Figure 3-1: Network addresses identify a particular cabling system, or "street." Node addresses identify the locations of network interface boards attached to the cabling system, or "buildings" on the same street.

A common way to connect multiple file servers on an internet is to use a *backbone* cable. The backbone cable has only file servers and bridges attached to it, not workstations. In this case, the network interface boards that physically connect the file servers to the backbone cable must all have the *same* network address. Figure 3-2 illustrates proper network addressing with an internetwork configuration that employs a backbone cable.

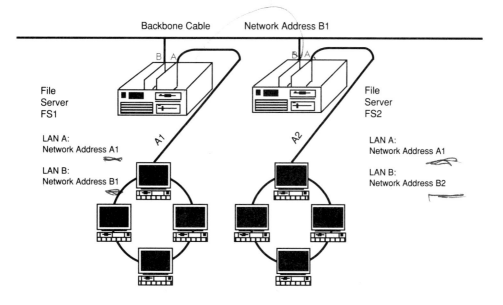

Figure 3-2: This internetwork has a backbone cable (network address B1) that connects only file servers. The network interface boards in each file server that attach to the backbone all have a network address of B1.

When NetWare's routing function requests a server's network address, the server returns only the address for LAN A. Thus, the address for LAN A is the one stored in the Server Information Table and copied to the file server bindery (as explained under "How Information Gets Around on the Internet" below).

Sometimes you might have a file server connected to the same network cabling system as other workstations, instead of to a backbone. In this case, the network interface board that connects the file server to this cabling system must share the network address of the cabling system. Figure 3-3 illustrates proper network addressing when you have a second file server attached to the same network cabling system as the workstations.

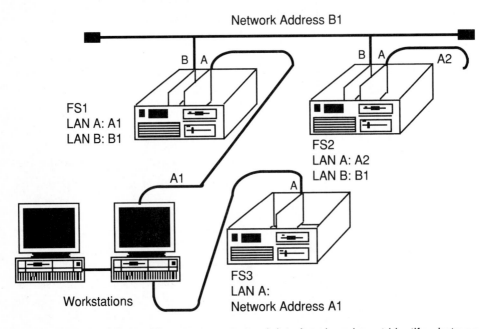

Figure 3-3: The network address set on a network interface board must identify whatever cabling system the board is physically attached to.

With nondedicated NetWare, you must also assign a network address to the DOS process within the file server (internally identified as LAN E). Think of the nondedicated DOS process as a separate "logical" network with only one workstation attached: the workstation side of the nondedicated file server. Like other network addresses, the address assigned to LAN E must be unique across the internet.

Node Addresses. A node address is also a hexadecimal number, but it can contain up to 12 digits. Each node address on the same network address must be unique. The node address is set on the network interface board itself, in one of three possible ways:

• Every Ethernet board is preset by the manufacturer to have a unique node address. In theory, you could hook up one gigantic Ethernet internetwork and no two boards would have the same node address.

• On some boards, such as ARCnet boards, the installer sets the node address by means of a switch block on the board. The installer must ensure that no two ARCnet node addresses are the same.

• Other boards, including Token-Ring boards, set their own unique node addresses when they are initialized on the network. These boards read the node addresses that already exist and configure themselves with a nonconflicting node address.

One clarification is helpful to understand node addresses for a file server. Used loosely, the term *node* usually refers to any workstation, bridge, or server on the network. Technically, though, a node is any juncture or point of connection within the network. A juncture occurs wherever the network cable connects to a network interface board. The node address, then, really identifies a particular network interface board on the network. Workstations typically contain only one network board, so a workstation's node address is also its station address. Because file servers and bridges can contain up to four network boards each, it is possible to have up to four node addresses in the same file server or bridge.

How Information Gets Around on the Internet

To get information where it needs to go on an internetwork, NetWare uses an adaptive routing mechanism based on Xerox Network System's datagram routing and transport protocols.

Packets. Rather than transmitting files all at once, NetWare splits a file's data into small chunks called *packets*. (Packets are called "frames" or "datagrams" in some protocols.) This division of data into packets makes the sharing of the network wire possible. If a user was allowed to transfer a large file all at once to the exclusion of all other network transmissions, the other users would be locked off the network for a long time.

A packet is like an envelope into which data is inserted prior to being sent. In addition to data, packets have a *header* that contains two sets of addresses: the source address (where the packet originated) and the destination address (where the packet must ultimately arrive). These addresses are complete network-node-socket internet addresses. Figure 3-4 shows the general format of an internet packet. The specific format will vary depending on the network protocol used.

Each packet contains Cyclical Redundancy Check (CRC) control codes in the header so that the receiver can make sure the packet arrives intact. If for some reason a packet is not received intact, the receiver asks the sender to resend the packet. Retransmissions are another area where splitting data into packets proves advantageous. Entire files do not need to be resent, only individual packets.

Routing. To get the packets of data where they need to go on an internetwork, NetWare incorporates a *routing process* in each NetWare file server and bridge. Each router tracks the other routers on the internet and retains their location and distance in a Routing Information Table. The router uses this information to forward packets along the shortest route to their final destination.

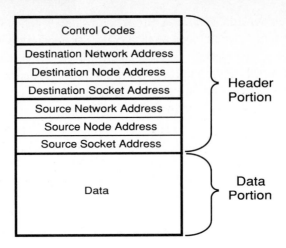

Figure 3-4: A typical internet packet consists of a header (which contains control codes, the destination address, and the source address) and the data itself.

NetWare's routing mechanism is designed to react quickly to changes in the internet configuration. When a new router comes up, it requests routing information from all other routers and builds its routing table from the responses it receives. When an existing router is shut down, it notifies all other routers so they can update their tables. If a router fails, the other routers ascertain that it is gone and search for alternate routes that bypass the nonfunctional router. This is called *adaptive routing*.

Service Advertising Protocol. The Service Advertising Protocol (SAP) is a mechanism by which information about servers is distributed throughout the internetwork. The SAP requires a server to advertise three pieces of information to the network every 60 seconds: the server's name, the type of server it is (for example, file server, print server, or archive server), and its address on the network. Each server sends this information out in SAP packets; other servers pick up the SAP information and store it in their Server Information Table.

Keeping track of server addresses is important because a potential client must know where a server is located before it can establish a connection with the server and use the services the server provides. To facilitate server address queries from potential clients, each server copies all the server names it knows about, along with their types and addresses, to a database called the *bindery*. A workstation desiring a particular service can query any bindery on the internetwork and find out the physical address of a server that can provide that service. Once the address is known, the client can establish a connection to the server. (The bindery is explained in more detail under "NetWare Security" on page 46.)

The SAP provides an efficient way of keeping track of the services available in a dynamic network, especially one in which servers appear and disappear sporadically. When a server knows that it is going down, it tells the SAP, and all binderies are updated to indicate that the server is unavailable. If a server stops advertising without advance notice, the SAP assumes after a time that the server is no longer available. Word of the server's assumed unavailability is spread throughout the internetwork by the SAP. Note that if a faulty connection or bad network board causes a server to come up and go down frequently, internet performance may become sluggish because the servers must continually update their routing tables.

NetWare's Interface Protocols

The native NetWare environment provides two general-purpose communication protocols—IPX and SPX—that serve as an interface between the various types of networks (ARCnet, Ethernet, or Token-Ring) and the NetWare operating system. NetWare also emulates IBM's NetBIOS interface to allow compatibility with applications written to this IBM standard.

IPX. The *IPX* (Internet Packet Exchange) protocol defines a "quick and dirty" method for conveying packets on an internetwork. By building packets according to the structure specified by the IPX protocol, NetWare workstations can send packets to and receive packets from any node on the internet, including other workstations. The combination of IPX and the routing services provided in NetWare servers and bridges makes the routing of packets between physically separate LANs largely automatic and transparent.

IPX makes a "best effort" to deliver all packets to their proper destination, but it does not guarantee delivery. Part of the reason IPX is so fast is that it doesn't wait for an acknowledgement from the destination that a packet has been received. Rather, it assumes that the packet arrived safe and sound when the response is received from the destination. IPX can get away with this for two reasons. First, the CRC codes in every IPX packet ensure 99.9999 percent accuracy. With a success rate that high, waiting for a "packet received intact" acknowledgment is not necessary. Second, IPX automatically resends the packet if the receiver does not respond within a certain amount of time. This covers the rare case when a packet does arrive damaged.

The other reasons for IPX's speed are that it doesn't worry about sending or receiving packets in any particular order, nor does it have to establish an actual connection between sender and receiver. Establishing a connection, sequencing the packets, and guaranteeing delivery are left to the higher-level SPX protocol.

SPX. The *SPX* (Sequenced Packet Exchange) protocol is an extension to IPX that provides guaranteed, sequenced delivery of packets. Internally, SPX offers a simple and functional connection-oriented interface. A sequencing protocol allows SPX to reliably exchange messages in a sequenced packet stream. In addition to the information in the IPX packet, an SPX packet contains extra connection control information. SPX also includes a flow control mechanism to reduce packet congestion during peak network loads.

NetBIOS. The *Network Basic Input/Output System* (NetBIOS) is IBM's standard application interface for peer-to-peer communications on IBM Token-Ring and IBM PC networks. Many applications have been and will be written to this standard.

Novell's NetBIOS emulator is a translation mechanism that offers complete compatibility for NetBIOS applications.

How LAN Drivers Work

LAN drivers are often called communication drivers because they make communication over the physical cable possible. LAN drivers provide the link between the operating system software and the network interface board. The network interface board, of course, is attached directly to the network cabling.

We've been talking about how data is sent over the wire in discrete packets that have a specific structure. A typical packet consists of a header and error checking codes as well as the actual data. The exact size and position of a packet's fields varies depending on the type of network (ARCnet, Ethernet, or Token-Ring). Because of these differences in packet structure, network interface boards can communicate only with other boards of the same type over a certain kind of cable.

To achieve hardware independence, NetWare itself does not make any protocol-specific assumptions. The NetWare operating system code was kept as generic as possible so that it could talk to a large number of devices operating under different protocols. The responsibility of actually forming the packets and sending them out over the wire is delegated to LAN driver software that is custom-written for each type of network interface board. For example, if the board is an Ethernet board, the driver performs actions necessary to create an Ethernet packet in the format that NetWare can understand. The LAN driver code is also responsible for receiving packets and checking them for internal consistency.

If the driver code is slow or inefficient, the performance of the entire system suffers. For this reason, LAN drivers are specific to particular boards. It is unlikely that a driver will work on a board other than the board for which it was designed. However, some manufacturers build boards with look-alike interfaces so that an existing driver can run them.

NetWare Core Protocols (NCP)

NetWare file servers accept requests expressed in the NetWare Core Protocol (NCP) service protocol. A service protocol defines the common "language" that must be spoken in order for computers to exchange information. Novell invented NCP because at the time there were no service protocols available that supported PC workstation operating systems.

NCP packets are usually those that contain requests for file services (disk reads and writes, directory searches, and so on). The bulk of packets that arrive at a NetWare 286 file server are NCP packets. The only process in the OS that can handle NCP request packets is called a *file service process* (FSP). Depending on how much memory is available within a certain segment of file server RAM, more than one FSP can be running at a time to handle file service requests.

THE NETWARE FILE SYSTEM

Another primary function of the NetWare operating system is to provide file services for network clients. File access is by far the most common request made of NetWare servers. In order to service file requests quickly and efficiently, Novell developed its own file system for NetWare. While in many respects this file system resembles the hierarchical file system used by DOS (a root at the top with directories, subdirectories, and files underneath), NetWare's file system is designed to handle the added rigors of multiuser access, built-in security, and intensive disk I/O required in the network environment.

The Hard Disk Communication Channel

A hard disk "channel" encompasses all of the hardware and software needed to read or write data on a hard disk. From the hardware standpoint, a disk channel includes the hard disk, controller board, cabling, connectors, a power supply, and all associated electronics. From the software end, many pieces of code work together to effectuate a disk read or write: request handling processes, caching and hashing algorithms, File Allocation Table indexes, elevator seeking queues, disk processes, and disk drivers. Figure 3-5 illustrates the major software pieces involved in a file server's disk communication channels.

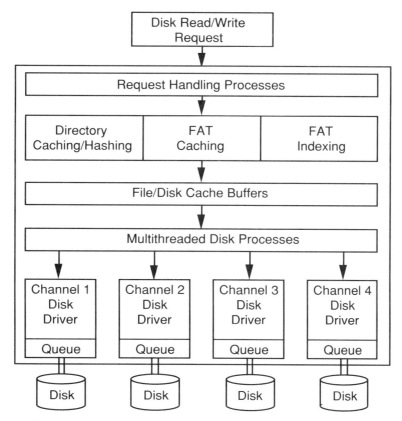

Figure 3-5: Many processes in the NetWare operating system work together to provide communication with network hard disks.

How Disk Drivers Work. Because NetWare supports a wide assortment of hard disk drives, both internal and external, a specialized disk driver is used to provide the communication link between a disk channel and NetWare. The disk driver software is responsible for initializing the channel and initiating channel operations. It also handles channel time-outs and services hardware interrupts from the controller.

Elevator Seeking. In a multiuser environment, a large number of unrelated disk I/O requests from various workstations can arrive at the server in a constant stream. The NetWare disk process that oversees access to network disk drives is multithreaded, meaning it can handle more than one request at a time. However, if these requests were serviced in first-come, first-served order, the disk would spend more time positioning and repositioning its read/write heads than it would in actually reading or writing data. This condition is called "thrashing."

To avoid disk thrashing, the disk process maintains queues in which disk operations are logically organized to optimize the use of the disk channel. Disk I/O requests are queued up in an order that allows the read/write heads to operate in a sweeping fashion from one edge of the disk to the other and back again, servicing each request when the heads arrive at the appropriate position—much like an elevator taking floor requests. This *elevator seeking* mechanism reduces wear and tear on the drive's mechanical parts, minimizes overall seek times, and significantly reduces disk head thrashing.

Disk Caching. Disk caching (or file caching) refers to storing data from the hard disk in memory to speed up access to the data. NetWare continually tracks which files or parts of files are accessed most often and stores them in RAM. Once a file is cached, it can be accessed significantly faster than it could be from the disk itself.

In response to a disk read request, NetWare's disk process retrieves the data from the disk in 4KB blocks. A client request may be for much less than that—for example, 512 or 1,024 bytes. The entire 4KB of data are stored in file server memory just in case the client issues another request for the same information or for data located in the same vicinity. These subsequent requests can be serviced from the cache, rather than waiting for the disk drive to supply the data again.

Write requests are also held in cache memory for a short time before the information is actually written to the disk. This delay serves two purposes. First, the delay allows the server to accumulate several small write requests and consolidate physical drive accesses. Second, it allows the client to move on to other things once the data is received by the server. The OS takes care of the actual write operation as a background process.

The size of the cache buffers used in NetWare 286 v2.1x is fixed at 4KB. Previous versions of NetWare allowed the buffer size to be configured to various sizes between 512 bytes and 4KB.

Directory Entry Tables and FATs. Once a hard disk is formatted for NetWare, it can be subdivided into volumes. On a NetWare disk, a *volume* corresponds to the root level on a DOS disk. It is the highest level in the directory structure hierarchy.

Every file server has at least one volume, always named SYS. The SYS volume and other volumes are set up on NetWare disks at installation time.

After the volumes are set up and the file server is operational, the network administrator can create additional *directories* and *subdirectories* beneath the volume level. As in DOS, *files* can be stored at any level of the directory structure (although placing files at the NetWare volume, or root, level is not recommended because users don't have rights there). A full directory path in NetWare would include the file server name and volume name in addition to the familiar directory/subdirectory specification used in DOS.

Because of the division of hard disk storage media into tracks and sectors, pieces of the same file are typically scattered all over the disk. In order to locate data on the disk, NetWare keeps two important tables: the Directory Entry Table and the File Allocation Table.

As its name suggests, the *Directory Entry Table* contains an entry for each directory and file in a NetWare volume. However, directory entries are also used to store other information such as directory trustee lists. NetWare uses the Directory Entry Table to piece together the logical hierarchy of the directory structure from the physical components stored randomly all over the disk.

The *File Allocation Table*, or FAT, serves a similar purpose, but at the file level. A FAT is a singly-linked list of pointers to the disk locations of specific files. When NetWare receives a request to read a file, it looks in the FAT to find out exactly where on the disk that file is located. If a file is larger than a single unit of disk storage space (usually a 4KB chunk called a block), the links between the various pieces of the file are stored in the FAT. Each FAT entry corresponds directly to a disk block (for example, FAT entry 3 corresponds to block number 3 on the disk). The OS scans down the list for a file and reads each piece in the order indicated by the FAT. Figure 3-6 shows the relationship between the Directory Entry Table and the FAT.

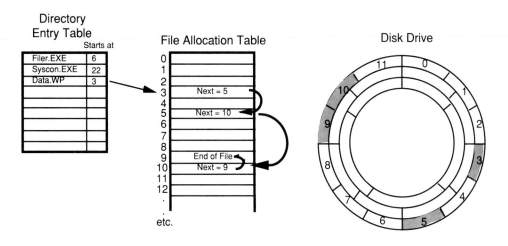

Figure 3-6: The Directory Entry Table lists file names and gives the first FAT entry for the file. The first FAT entry contains the location of the first part of the file and points to the next entry, which in turn points to the next entry, until the end of the file is reached.

FATs are singly linked, which means the operating system can only scan forward through the table. For sequential reads on relatively small files (under 2MB), forward scanning works very well.

FAT Indexing. As files become larger, the time required to scan the FAT to find all of its pieces increases proportionally. For example, to read information from offset 3,072,000 in a file, the OS first calculates that the offset is in the 750th 4KB block of that file ($3,072,000/4,096 = 750$). To get to the 750th block, the OS starts at the top of the FAT and scans down through the first 749 links before finding the 750th. Scanning takes only microseconds per link, so scanning even 749 links doesn't really take that long.

Now suppose the next read request is for block 700 in the file. The OS must go back to the top of the FAT and start scanning all over again until it finds block 700. You can see that when many non-sequential read requests occur in very large files (such as database files), the data access time could increase enough to noticeably degrade network performance.

To speed up FAT scans for large, non-sequential database files, NetWare provides a method of FAT indexing. Indexed FATs allow the OS to find data entries two to four times faster than with regular FATs. When a file is assigned the "Indexed" file attribute in NetWare, the OS reserves space in file server memory to build an index table to help it find specific FAT entries for that file. You can reserve a maximum number of indexed files during the NetWare installation procedure.

An analogy would be looking for a listing in a phone book, with each city representing a file. Phone books for small metropolitan areas often contain listings for several cities. If you know which city the person lives in, you can flip to that part of the phone book and start looking for the person's name. If you happen to live in New York City or Los Angeles, where it takes an entire phone book just for one city's listings, the looking gets harder. Think of FAT indexing as putting tabs on the phone book, taking you directly to the name you are looking for.

The operating system builds an entry index in memory for every file flagged as indexed. When a user makes a read request for that file, the operating system goes to the "tab" entry to find the physical disk block. This process allows the operating system to make quick jumps to data locations without having to scan through the FAT or even the index table.

Directory Caching and Hashing. To speed up access to the Directory Entry Tables, NetWare copies these tables into file server RAM. *Directory caching* refers to the caching of the Directory Entry Tables. Information stored in memory can be accessed and updated much faster than on the hard disk. And since the disk is accessed less, directory caching also helps eliminate some disk-related bottlenecks. You specify whether or not to cache a volume's directory tables as part of the NetWare installation procedure. FATs are always placed in memory.

Directory hashing refers to a method of indexing the directory structure by file, directory, and volume to allow more efficient file searches, especially when wild-card characters are used. Hashing is similar to the way dictionary entries are alphabetized so users can find an entry: they go initially to the first letter instead of scanning through the entire dictionary in a random order. Hashing occurs automatically for all volumes.

SYSTEM FAULT TOLERANCE

NetWare 286 presently offers two levels of system fault tolerance: SFT Level I, which includes redundant FATs and Directory Entry Tables, read-after-write verification, and Hot Fix; and SFT Level II, which includes all the features of Level I plus redundant hardware and the Transaction Tracking System.

Features of SFT Level I

The following basic aspects of fault tolerance are included in all versions of NetWare 286 (ELS, Advanced, and SFT).

Redundant FATs and Directory Entry Tables. Both the File Allocation Tables and the Directory Entry Tables are crucial to NetWare's ability to provide file services. If these tables were to become corrupted, the OS would no longer be able to locate files on the hard disk. To guard against this possibility, NetWare stores two copies of these tables in different areas on the disk.

When the file server is turned on, NetWare performs a self-consistency check. As part of this process, each set of tables is checked for internal consistency and then compared with the other copy. If a discrepancy is found, NetWare uses whichever set of tables is good and sends a warning message via the file server console that the two copies do not match. During normal operations, a process in the OS is charged with updating both sets of tables as directories and files are created, changed, or deleted.

Read-After-Write Verification. The OS routine in charge of overseeing disk read and write operations initiates a read after every write to see if the data just written to the disk can be read back accurately. The data is held in memory during this time so that the OS can verify that the disk data matches the data in memory.

Hot Fix. If the data written to a network disk cannot be read back, or if it does not match the original data still in memory, NetWare's Hot Fix function takes over. This corrective feature is called Hot Fix because it occurs while the server is running. When Hot Fix is installed on the disk, a small portion of the disk (usually about 2 percent of the total disk space) is reserved as the Hot Fix Redirection Area. Hot Fix assumes that if the read-after-write verification fails, the disk block that the OS was trying to write data to must be bad. Hot Fix takes the original data from memory and rewrites it to a good block in the Redirection Area. The faulty block is marked as bad and that location is added to the bad block table to prevent the OS from trying to write to that block again.

UPS Monitoring. The NetWare operating system includes a UPS monitoring process that can receive and act upon signals from the uninterruptible power supply attached to the file server. When the commercial power is interrupted, the UPS switches the file server its battery backup power and informs the OS that the battery is now on-line. NetWare broadcasts a message to any workstations that still have power and can receive broadcast messages, telling the users to log out because the server is on auxiliary power and will be going down soon.

If the UPS battery power becomes drained, the UPS sends a "battery low" signal to the OS. The OS proceeds to shut down the file server before the UPS battery power runs out. If commercial power is restored before this happens, the UPS switches the server back to regular power. The OS informs any users still connected that commercial power has been restored so they don't have to log out.

Additional Features of SFT Level II

SFT Level II includes all of the features of Level I, plus disk mirroring, disk duplexing, and the Transaction Tracking System. These features are available only with SFT NetWare 286, not in ELS or Advanced NetWare.

Disk Mirroring. While great strides have been made in improving the reliability of hard disk drives, disk drive failures still account for a large number of network problems. Recognizing this fact, Novell offers a *disk mirroring* capability in SFT NetWare 286. Disk mirroring employs redundant hard disks to guard against mechanical failures in the disk drives. With disk mirroring, two similar disks are paired together to form a single logical disk. NetWare writes the same data to both physical drives so that one is the "mirror image" of the other. The first disk in a mirrored pair is called the *primary* disk, while the second is referred to as the *mirror* disk.

If either disk drive fails, the OS can continue to use the good disk in the pair until the other disk can be repaired and remirrored. Figure 3-7 illustrates disk mirroring.

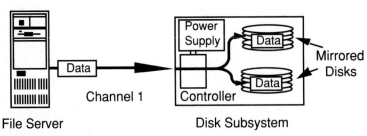

Figure 3-7: SFT NetWare's disk mirroring feature duplicates data on two physical disk drives to form one logical disk.

Disk Duplexing (Channel Mirroring). Disk mirroring only protects against failures in the disk drives themselves. A failure elsewhere along the disk channel could cause data to be lost even with mirrored disks. To guard against failures in disk controllers, cabling, DCBs, and power supplies, SFT NetWare allows an entire disk channel to be duplicated via *disk duplexing*. If a failure occurs anywhere along one disk channel, the duplicate channel keeps working. Naturally, disk duplexing requires a heavy investment in redundant channel hardware. For maximum protection, every channel component, from the DCB down to the power supply, must be duplicated. Figure 3-8 illustrates disk duplexing.

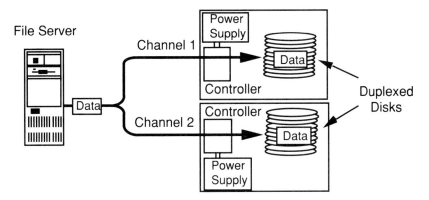

Figure 3-8: SFT NetWare's disk duplexing feature duplicates entire disk channels to protect against mechanical failures anywhere along the channel.

When the server has duplicate disk channels, the OS can perform *split seeks* by sending disk read requests to both channels. Whichever channel can respond the quickest is the one that services the request. If the OS receives multiple read requests to the same hard disk all at the same time, the requests are divided up among the redundant channels to speed up the request processing.

Transaction Tracking System (TTS). Partial updates to a database can be just as bad as, if not worse than, lost data. To ensure that database update transactions are either wholly completed or wholly backed out, SFT NetWare offers the Transaction Tracking System (TTS).

A *transaction* is a series of file updates that must be performed together. TTS tracks all of the updates in database files flagged as "Transactional." It stores each update to a separate area on a volume defined as the *transaction backout volume*, just in case something happens to the server before the transaction is completed. This transaction backout data is deleted only after the entire transaction is written successfully to disk. If something prevents a transaction from completing, the OS uses the transaction backout data to "roll back" the database to the way it was before the problem occurred. Users will have to re-enter the aborted transaction, but that is much preferable to trying to undo the effects of a partially completed transaction.

TTS can recognize a transaction either explicitly or implicitly. Applications that use NetWare's TTS function calls explicitly tell the file server when a transaction is beginning and when the application finishes a transaction. Other databases use TTS through implicit transactions, meaning that the server "implies" a transaction when an application performs a physical or logical record lock on a file or group of files. TTS implies the end of the transaction when the locks are released from the files.

NETWARE SECURITY

A particular strong point of NetWare is its security. Because NetWare allows network users to share applications and files across the network, it has a very sophisticated file protection method that is tied directly to NetWare's security features. It is the combination of these rights that determine which directories, files, and applications each user can access on the network.

User Level Security

Security begins with *user accounts* and *passwords*, which allow only authorized persons to log in to the network. Passwords are unique to individual users and are encrypted so that not even the network administrator can see what they are.

Once logged in to the file server, a user's access to directories (and, therefore, the files within those directories) is limited by *trustee rights* assignments. Trustee security is established through eight basic rights: Read, Write, Open, Create, Delete, Search, Modify, and Parental.

A combination of these rights is usually required to enable users to perform particular functions. For example, to run an application, users need at least Read, Open, and Search rights to the application's program files. The Read right lets you see what's in an existing, open file. You need the Open right to open the file in the first place. The Search right allows you to list the files within the directory.

In order to write to a file, users need Write, Create, Delete, Modify, and Search rights. You need the Create right to create a new file, and the Write right to add data to the new file or to change any file's contents. The Delete right will allow you to delete a file. The Modify right gives you the ability to flag a file. With the Parental right, you can create new subdirectories and control user access to these subdirectories through the basic rights.

You can also assign trustee rights to users in groups to control access to an application or directory. For example, if only four employees need to access the SYS:DATA/REPORTS directory containing accounting reports, you can create a group called "ACCTG" and give that group the necessary rights to the applications used to modify the report files. Then only those users who are a part of the ACCTG group will have access to SYS:DATA/REPORTS.

Directory Level Security

The eight basic rights can also be manipulated at the directory level through what is called the *Maximum Rights Mask*. The rights allowed in a directory's Maximum Rights Mask are coupled with trustee rights to give an added layer of security. The Maximum Rights Mask determines what rights any user may exercise in the directory and overrides individual users' trustee rights.

For example, suppose you give user JANE Read, Open, and Search rights in a directory and then restrict the directory itself to Open and Search rights in the Maximum Rights Mask. JANE will not be able to read any files in the directory, even though she has the Read right as a trustee assignment.

File Level Security

File attributes (or flags) are an effective means of preventing accidental changes or deletions of a particular file. A file may be flagged "Shareable" or "Non-shareable," "Read/Write," or "Read/Only." On-screen memos, for example, can be flagged "Shareable Read/Only" and shared by all office personnel.

Through the FILER menu utility, a file can also be flagged "Hidden" and "Execute Only." The "Hidden" flag hides the files from a directory listing, and "Execute Only" allows applications to be run or deleted, but not copied or renamed. Other file attributes are used for purposes not related to security.

The Bindery

NetWare stores the whole security picture—user security, group security, directory security, and file security—in a special-purpose database called the *bindery*. Each server maintains its own bindery containing the security information for all the users and groups defined for that server. As a result, NetWare access and security are file server-based.

To illustrate, suppose user Chris on file server A wants to run an application located on file server B. Chris must first attach to file server B under a user account defined in the bindery of file server B. That user account must have the necessary rights to access the application. File server B cannot go to server A's bindery and use the rights defined there for user Chris.

Each entry in the bindery is composed of an object and its associated properties. An *object* can be a user name, a group name, the name of a resource (such as a print queue), or any other entity (logical or physical) that has a name. The OS assigns a unique ID number to each object. An object's *properties* describe the information known about the object. For example, the properties for a user object would include the user's password, mail directory, trustee rights, a list of groups the user belongs to, and so on. A group's properties would consist of a list of the group's members and the group trustee rights. A property for a resource could be a list of users authorized to use the resource.

NETWARE SUPPORT SERVICES

In addition to file services, the NetWare Core Protocols provide a number of support services for other activities that take place on the network.

Connection Maintenance Services

In the client/server processing model, the client must establish a *service connection* to the server before it can pass its requests along for servicing. In most cases, each workstation takes up one service connection when it logs in to the file server. However, it is possible for a single client workstation to establish more than one service connection if a particular application warrants it. The OS treats each service connection as a logically distinct entity, regardless of which physical machine originated the connection.

NetWare's connection maintenance services provide the means to create, maintain, and terminate a connection. When the OS receives a request to create a connection, it first checks its list of service connections to see if a connection already exists with the specified client. If so, the OS uses that connection. Otherwise, the OS establishes a new connection and starts taking requests.

Several things can go wrong when packets are flying around on a busy network. Although it rarely happens, requests or responses can get lost, and packets can be corrupted through collisions or electrical interference. To infuse some kind of order into this seemingly chaotic system, NetWare has established various rules to govern the exchanges between client and server. A client is allowed to send only one request at a time on a given service connection. For each request, the client expects to receive only one response. The OS numbers each request and includes the request number in its response packet to the client. The OS keeps a copy of the last service response it sent to the client so that it can detect duplicate requests.

From the other end, it is up to the client to resend a given service request until it either receives an appropriate response or determines that the connection has somehow failed. These retry and timeout mechanisms are part of the NetWare shell loaded at every DOS workstation.

To help keep track of connections, NetWare has a *watchdog* process that periodically monitors file server connections. The watchdog process sends regular requests to each workstation to determine its status. If the workstation does not respond after 15 minutes, the watchdog process assumes the connection is no longer being used and terminates it.

Printing Services

Printing is another frequent activity on a normal network. NetWare provides a number of printing processes that allow clients to send printer-bound data to the file server. At the server, the print job is placed in a queue or spooled (temporarily held in memory) until a network printer is ready to print the data.

Spooling was the process used to collect print jobs in previous versions of NetWare. NetWare v2.1x introduced the more flexible *queueing* method. If the process in charge of submitting print jobs to queues is idle when a print job arrives at the server, another print process must activate the print job handling process. This print process activation happens at 15-second intervals, which explains why there is often a delay between the time a print job arrives at the server to the time it is serviced by the print queue.

Queue Management System

The NetWare operating system incorporates a Queue Management System (QMS) to act as a central dispatcher for various specialized servers. The most familiar type of queue is the print queue, but other types of queues can be created on the file server and then accessed and serviced by database servers, archive servers, batch servers, or any other type of value-added server.

Accounting Services

In the NetWare context, accounting doesn't refer to general ledgers, accounts payable, and invoices. Rather, the NetWare accounting system is a means of charging users for their use of file server resources. NetWare provides the ability to assign users an account balance and charge the user accounts for connect time, file server requests made, bytes read from disk, bytes written to disk, and disk storage space used. The *accounting* process is in charge of periodically updating charges to user accounts and deducting them from the account balances.

Network Management Services

Keeping tabs on everything that goes on within a NetWare file server involves monitoring, and providing access to, a large number of statistics. The NetWare Core Protocols provide a way to keep track of everything from the file server's internal clock setting to the current status of a connection. These network management services and statistics are available to any application through a number of NetWare function calls. All of these management functions and statistics are accessible through the NetWare FCONSOLE utility. Various third-party network management utilities now available are easier to work with than FCONSOLE's kitchen-sink approach. (See Appendix C for a list of third-party NetWare management products.)

Other Support Processes

Some of the other processes that are part of the NetWare operating system include an *error logging process* that writes system errors to the SYS$LOG.ERR file in SYS:SYSTEM, and a process that handles input from the file server keyboard.

NETWARE APPLICATION SERVICES

Another aspect of the NetWare file service protocols concerns the interaction between applications and the operating system. As we pointed out at the beginning of this chapter, an operating system is not in and of itself an application that people can use. The whole purpose of an operating system is to allow users to run applications that help them do their work. Ideally, the applications will be written to take advantage of the features the OS provides.

NetWare APIs

To enable software developers to write programs that can exploit NetWare's advanced file services, Novell offers a wide range of *application program interfaces* (APIs) for NetWare. These APIs are sets of function calls that applications can use to access a particular function within the OS. For example, when an application needs to know what trustee rights have been assigned in a certain directory, it uses the ScanDirectoryForTrustees function call provided with the NetWare APIs.

Data Access Synchronization

This is an elaborate term for the methods by which NetWare oversees access to files by more than one user at a time. NetWare offers both file locking and record locking to prevent two users from changing the same data at the same time.

File locking is a fairly basic way of managing multiuser access to data. When a workstation is using a file, it reserves access to the entire file. Nobody else can use the data until the workstation is finished with it. Depending on the application and the operation being performed, the file may be locked whenever data is being accessed, or only when data is being changed.

Record locking is a more powerful way of managing multiuser access to data, but it is more difficult to implement. With record locking, the application prevents access to only the part of the data that a user needs to protect at the time (perhaps a record that the user is changing). Other users can freely read and change other parts of the database.

Semaphores

As the name suggests, a *semaphore* is a "flag" or signalling mechanism that can be used to coordinate operations between different computers. Multiuser applications might use semaphores to keep a count of how many users are currently running the program. An application can set a semaphore to indicate that it is in possession of a resource. The same application can set the semaphore more than once (increasing the use count each time), but another application cannot set the semaphore until the use count decreases to zero.

The application can also give a value to the semaphore. This value indicates to other users how the resource controlled by the semaphore is being used.

Software Protection Services

The NetWare Core Protocols include various mechanisms that application programs can use to protect against copyright infringement or unlicensed use. Each copy of the NetWare operating system has a unique *serialization number* and *application number* that applications can use for their own serialization and verification purposes. By using semaphores, a program can keep track of how many users are currently running the program. This information comes in handy for restricting the number of concurrent users to the number specified by a site license.

VAP Interface

Multiuser applications are by far the most common types of programs run on a network. However, these applications run at the workstations, not at the file server. The designers of NetWare 286 v2.1x wanted to provide a way for specialized server-based applications to run in the file server as an extension to the OS. To this end, NetWare provides a *VAP interface*, or shell, that allows value-added processes (VAPs) to run in the file server.

VAPs written to use the support routines provided in the VAP interface have direct access to OS resources such as file services and RAM, without going through the usual client request channels. A number of specialized servers (database servers, print servers, and archive servers) have already been implemented as VAPs by third parties. Novell itself uses the VAP interface for its Btrieve database management services, for the new Streaming Tape Backup VAP, and for service protocol gateways.

SERVICE PROTOCOL GATEWAY

Although associated early on with MS-DOS clients only, NetWare was originally designed to be able to service many different types of clients. Software called a Service Protocol Gateway (SPG) can run on a NetWare bridge or file server to act as a translator between NetWare's protocols and some other protocol. Thus, an SPG could allow an entire non-NetWare LAN to become a NetWare client.

The best-known implementation of an SPG is NetWare for Macintosh. This product is a set of VAPs that, when loaded in a NetWare 286 v2.15 file server or bridge, translate requests from Macintosh workstations running the Macintosh operating system. Using their native AppleShare networking software and the Apple Filing Protocol (AFP), Macintosh users view and access NetWare file servers as if they were AppleShare servers. The SPG translates AFP packets into NCP packets.

Section 2

Maintenance

MANAGING THE NETWORK ENVIRONMENT

Managing a LAN is not a casual undertaking. To get your network running smoothly, keep it performing at its peak, and make it easy to maintain takes quite a bit of forethought and planning. It doesn't just happen by chance.

Unfortunately, many inexperienced installers and LAN administrators just don't take the time to really design the LAN at the outset. They overlook critical concerns like the server's directory structure and access security, not to mention the finer points of optimizing performance. Some of the manifestations of a poorly-planned LAN are:

• LANs strung together in piecemeal fashion, often mixing products from different vendors indiscriminately.
• Access control security poorly implemented, if implemented at all.
• Server directories laid out haphazardly, subdirectories piled ridiculously deep, many of them empty for no reason.
• Applications installed at random on the server, executable files mixed in with data files, conflicts between applications.
• User accounts created with abandon, little or no use of groups to simplify access to applications, overly complex login scripts.
• No consistent user interface, each user accesses the network differently using their own batch files or menus.
• Supervisor spends most of the day dealing with one user problem after another.

If any of these (or—perish the thought—all of them) describes your network, take heart. This section will help you assess where your LAN stands and offers some useful guidelines that you can adopt from now on to transform a trouble-prone LAN into a relatively trouble-free LAN.

• Chapter 4 gives some general tips and techniques for effective network management and will get you thinking along the lines of planning and simplification, the two keys to making a LAN easier to maintain and use.

• Chapter 5 offers suggestions for loading new applications onto the network with a minimum of pain for you and the people who will use the applications.

• Chapter 6 delves into the intricacies of NetWare security, describing the rights and restrictions that can be assigned at the user, directory, and file level.

• Chapter 7 gives hints for creating an effective directory structure on the server and establishing security at the volume, directory, and file level. It shows how to use various NetWare utilities relating to the file system.

• Chapter 8 looks at user and group management and the utilities you can use to create users, establish user and group security, and protect the network from intruders.

• Chapter 9 presents information on creating effective system and user login scripts, focusing on ways to make them as simple, generic, and trouble-free as possible.

• Chapter 10 discusses using the NetWare MENU utility to implement a front-end menuing system for the LAN.

• Chapter 11 addresses NetWare's resource accounting features and details how to set up charge rates for network usage.

• Chapter 12 explains how to accommodate diskless workstations that boot from the file server.

4 Network Management Tips and Techniques

Many new supervisors, when faced with the prospect of managing the mass of computers and cables known as a LAN, conjure up images of analyzing packets, counting collisions, and performing similar technical tasks. While these tasks are important, and sophisticated tools for doing them are readily available, the actual business of managing a LAN starts at a more fundamental level. Before you start peering into peripatetic packets, look at your LAN from an overall maintenance perspective: just how manageable is it?

This chapter helps you analyze your network, assess its current manageability, and take steps to make it even more manageable. The tips and techniques presented in this chapter represent proven methods used in managing real-life NetWare networks. While not all of these suggestions will apply to all networks, you will find many useful ideas that you can implement in your own LAN situation. This chapter also looks at one other important aspects of LAN management: protecting the network against computer viruses.

Because the topic of LAN management encompasses just about every aspect of the network, we can't include everything you need to know and give all the details in a single chapter. This chapter consolidates the general principles that apply on a higher level. Subsequent chapters will give more detail on how to actually implement these principles, using the NetWare utilities.

TAKING STOCK OF YOUR NETWORK

The first step toward making your LAN more manageable is to take stock of exactly what you're dealing with, in terms of both hardware and software. (In high-tech terminology, this assessment is called "configuration management.") It requires a remarkable memory to retain all the configurations, hardware settings, cabling information, user profiles, login scripts, and software versions for even the smallest of LANs. As the LAN grows and changes (as all LANs do), the chances of being able to remember everything dwindle in geometric proportion.

Documenting the LAN

Documenting your network is an absolute must, for the following reasons:

• You can't rely on the human brain to retain all the information you'll need about your network components. Written information is safer, more permanent, and makes it easier to access at will.
• Documenting hardware configurations saves you from having to perpetually pull the covers off computers to see what's inside.
• In the absence of the regularly appointed manager, another person must be able to handle the network's problems. A written record of configurations and settings will be of immense help to LAN "pinch hitters."
• In the event of a complete file server crash, documentation of all network configurations allows the network administrator to reconstruct the server, user accounts, login scripts, and so on.

What to Document. Hopefully, a good portion of network documentation was completed when your file server was installed. Novell installation manuals come with a set of preprinted worksheets for recording installation parameters and settings. If you don't have access to these, you can make your own forms. The important thing is to get the information written down.

You may prefer to enter information into a database for easier sorting and retrieval. Since you must usually collect the information away from your own computer and write it down on paper anyway, devise a worksheet to make data collection easier and to help you avoid overlooking key information.

Having the network's configuration, directory structure, security, groups, menu system, and batch files documented comes in handy when training a substitute administrator to step in while you're away. For these occasions, you should also document your day-to-day tasks, including the backup procedure. Detail the setup of each multiuser application and provide a map of the network cabling.

With this in mind, then, here's a quick list of the items you should record. This list can serve as the basis for your homemade worksheets. After the list, we'll show you how to obtain all this information.

Workstation Hardware

Brand and model of the computer (include CPU type and speed)
Type of floppy drive(s) installed (size and capacity)
Brand, model, and vendor of network interface board
Network address of the cabling system it's attached to
Node or station address
LAN driver and board configuration settings (IRQ, DMA, I/O addresses, memory addresses)
NetWare shell (IPX and NETx) versions
Contents of the SHELL.CFG file
Internal hard disk controller type and settings
Internal hard disk types (heads, cylinders, tracks/sector)
Internal hard disk capacities (megabytes)
Amount of RAM installed (conventional, expanded, extended)
Video board/monitor type and settings used
Number and configuration of serial and parallel ports
ROM BIOS version
Other internal hardware and settings (mouse, modem, etc.)
DOS version
AUTOEXEC.BAT and CONFIG.SYS files
Last drive letter used by local disk drives

Cable and Other Networking Hardware

Types of cable used (description and vendor)
Types of connectors, hubs, repeaters, and other hardware
Location of backbone cables, wiring closets, concentrators, and terminators
Layout of cable and numbering scheme used (if any)

Network Printing Setup

Brand, model, and vendor of each network printer
Type of printer interface (serial or parallel)
Communication settings for serial printers
Print queues serviced by each printer

UPS Information

Brand, model, and vendor
Maximum power rating (watts)
Type of UPS monitoring hardware and I/O address used
Configured UPS down time and wait time

File Server Hardware

Brand and model of the computer (include CPU type and speed)
Type of floppy drive(s) installed (size and capacity)
Internal hard disk controller type and settings
Internal hard disk types (heads, cylinders, tracks/sector)

Internal hard disk capacities (megabytes)
Amount of RAM installed (conventional, extended)
Number and configuration of serial and parallel ports
Brand, model, and vendor of network interface board(s)
Node address of each network interface board
Brand, model, and vendor of disk coprocessor board(s)
Video board/monitor type and settings used
ROM BIOS version
Other internal hardware and settings

File Server/OS Configuration
Type of NetWare operating system (include version and revision)
Serial number of NetWare OS
LAN drivers and board configuration settings (IRQ, DMA, I/O addresses, memory addresses)
Disk channel drivers and interface board configurations (IRQ, DMA, I/O addresses, memory addresses)
Network address assigned to each network interface board
Number of communication buffers

File Server Installation Parameters
File server name
Configured number of open files
Configured number of indexed files
Configured number of transactions
Transaction backout volume
Disk space limitation setting
Configured number of bindery objects

Hard Disk/Subsystem Information
Brand, model, and vendor of external disk subsystem
Brand, model, and vendor of hard disk controllers
Each disks's channel number, controller number, and drive number
Disk partition table information
Hot Fix logical size (in blocks)
Disk mirroring/duplexing information
NetWare volumes created on each disk

Volume Information
Volume name
Volume size (megabytes)
Configured number of directory entries
Directory cache setting (yes or no)
Physical disk the volume resides on (channel, controller, drive)

Directory Structure
Directories and subdirectories within each volume
Any changes to the default Maximum Rights Mask for each directory
User and group trustees assigned in each directory

Users and Groups
User login names, full names, and ID numbers
User password restrictions; station and time restrictions
User account restrictions
User trustee rights assignments
User security equivalences
User login scripts
Group names, full group names, and ID numbers
Group membership lists
Group trustee rights assignments

System Configuration Files
System login script
AUTOEXEC.SYS file
SERVER.CFG file

Value-Added Processes (VAPs)
VAPs installed in the file server
Configured VAP wait time

Application Software
Manufacturer, vendor, version, and revision numbers
Licensing agreements and limitations
Options chosen during install or setup (if any)
Directory or directories in which the application is installed
Mappings required in login scripts
Which users or groups have access
Amount of RAM required to run at a workstation
Any other unusual characteristics/configurations

That's quite a list—but don't despair. Thanks to FCONSOLE and SYSCON, most of this information is available at your fingertips. You may have to dig for some of the other information, but it's worth the effort. It will also be helpful to gather any hardware manuals, software documentation, and purchase records relating to your LAN. When you're ready with your pencils, worksheets, manuals, and records, read on.

Gathering Workstation Hardware Information

Accurate information on each workstation attached to the server is indispensable for effective file server management. In particular, you need the network and node addresses of workstations when you run the DOSGEN program for diskless workstations. Knowing the monitor types and DOS versions helps you set DOS environment variables in the system login script. If you know how many drives a workstation uses for DOS, you can avoid overlapping when you set up network drive mappings in the login scripts.

You can glean most of the hardware-specific information from the *Guide to Operations* or similar manual supplied with each computer. Keep the documentation for any graphics adapters, memory add-on boards, or serial/parallel port add-ons. This information will prove invaluable when you must deal with hardware conflicts in the workstation. Information about the network interface board and settings can be found either in the Novell installation supplements or in the documentation that came with the board.

A number of utilities (public domain, shareware, and commercial) will give you information about the CPU, DOS, and the ROM BIOS. An example is the ROMINFO utility available on CompuServe. The WPINFO utility that comes with WordPerfect 5.x will also give you listings of the AUTOEXEC.BAT and CONFIG.SYS files. The DOS VERSION command displays the version of DOS currently running in a workstation.

Note: A full version number typically includes a *major* version number, a minor version number, and a revision number or letter. For example, in SFT NetWare v2.15c, the major version is 2, the minor version is .15, and the revision is c.

You can obtain much of the NetWare software version information from the command line. Typing **NVER** at any workstation on a NetWare v2.15 network will give you the full version numbers for IPX/SPX, the shell (NETx.COM), the NetBIOS emulator (if loaded), and even DOS. It also displays the LAN driver used by the workstation and the configuration settings (IRQ, DMA, and so on). (NVER is not available for NetWare versions prior to v2.15. Watch the screen while the shell loads to obtain version numbers.) Typing the command **IPX I** at a workstation will also yield the LAN driver and configuration settings, but not the shell and NetBIOS versions. Another shortcut is to print out the CONFIG.DAT file containing the IPX configuration used to generate the shell. The SHGEN program saves this file on the SHGEN-1 diskette (or in the SHGEN-1 directory if you ran SHGEN from a hard disk).

To obtain the workstation's network address and node address, type **USERLIST /A** and look at the entry marked with an asterisk (*).

The AUTOEXEC.BAT and CONFIG.SYS files are DOS text files—you can print their contents using any word processor. The last drive setting will be indicated by the "LASTDRIVE=" setting in CONFIG.SYS; if there isn't one, NetWare assumes the last DOS drive (with DOS v3.x and above) is E:, making F: the first network drive. Wherever possible, keep the LASTDRIVE setting uniform for all DOS workstations on the network, even if it wastes a few drives on some workstations. Uniformity often makes troubleshooting easier.

Redirecting Screen Output to a File. To save you from having to write by hand everything displayed on the screen, use the DOS redirect parameter (>). When you add this parameter, followed by a file name, to a regular DOS or NetWare command, the output normally sent to the screen will be saved in a text file in the default drive. You can then print out the files later. To print the files out directly, type a command such as "TYPE CONFIG.SYS > PRN:" from the directory in which CONFIG.SYS resides. The contents of CONFIG.SYS will be sent to the printer defined as the DOS PRN: device (usually LPT1). See your DOS manual for further information.

Drawing Up the Network Floor Plan

While gathering information on cabling and other networking hardware is a good time to document the physical layout of the network if you haven't already done so. Every network, large or small, should have a floor plan showing exactly where backbone and drop cables run, along with the location of wiring concentrators, hubs, MAUs, repeaters, terminators, and the like. You should implement some type of identification scheme both on paper and on the cabling itself. Affixing a label at each end of a cable length will save you guesswork and frustration when troubleshooting cabling problems.

In addition, the floor plan should show the location of all servers, external routers (bridges), gateways, and other connecting points. Also include the location of shared network peripherals (printers, plotters, UPS units, and so on).

Gathering Printer and UPS Information

Printer maintenance goes more smoothly if you know the brand and model of all network printers. Printer definition files and most application setup routines identify printers by brand and model (for example, HP LaserJet Series II). Most printers can work with either a serial or a parallel interface. Printer settings are usually made via switches or control panel settings on the printer itself. Refer to the printer documentation for information about serial interface parameters (baud rate, word length, stop bits, parity, and handshake protocol).

Refer to the UPS documentation or look at the unit itself to obtain the brand, model, and vendor information and the maximum power rating in watts. The UPS monitoring hardware in an AT-compatible file server could be either a Novell standalone UPS interface board, disk coprocessor board (DCB), or keycard with UPS monitoring circuitry built in. The I/O address on the standalone UPS board can be set to either 240h or 231h; the address of a DCB depends on what channel the board is for; the address of the keycard is always 230h. Refer to the Novell documentation that came with the boards for information on UPS switch settings. In a PS/2-compatible server, the UPS monitoring is accomplished through the mouse port, so there is no I/O address setting.

The UPS down time and wait time are recorded in the SERVER.CFG file (v2.15) or CONFIG.UPS file (previous versions) located in the SYS:SYSTEM directory on the file server.

Gathering File Server Hardware Information

Refer to the *Guide to Operations*, or a similar manual for your file server, for information on brand, model, CPU type and speed, floppy drives, internal disk controller, RAM, and built-in ports. The video board and monitor come with their own documentation that should indicate the I/O addresses used (useful information when you're chasing down hardware conflicts). The ROM BIOS version is especially critical if you are running nondedicated NetWare. Bring up the server under DOS and use a utility such as ROMINFO (available on CompuServe) to identify the type of BIOS. Refer to the documentation that came with other internal hardware for information about its settings.

File server manufacturers often use disk drives from other vendors for internal hard disks. The documentation normally indicates what type of disks they are, their total storage capacity (in megabytes), and how many heads, cylinders, and tracks per sector they have. If this information is not readily available, go into the SETUP routine and make a note of which hard disk "type" number was selected for the disk. This usually indicates the number of heads and cylinders the disk has. (Be careful not to change the setup information when you exit.)

If you have external hard disks attached to the file server, they are usually controlled via one or more DCBs. (Up until recently, Novell sold its own line of DCBs while allowing third parties to develop and market their own DCBs as well. As of early 1990, Novell no longer sells DCBs directly—its DCB technology was licensed to ADIC Corporation, which now handles Novell's DCB product line.) Also record the brand, model, and vendor of all external disk subsystems.

You can find information about the network interface board and settings either in the Novell installation supplements or in the documentation that came with the board. It is important to know the node address of each network interface board as well. The node address is set in one of three ways, depending on the type of board:

• Some boards require the node address to be set manually by the installer. For example, on ARCnet boards, the node address is set via a switch block on the board itself and can range from 1 to 255 (decimal).
• On some boards (Ethernet, for example), the node address is encoded by the manufacturer into the firmware of the board and cannot be changed. Ethernet node addresses are centrally coordinated so that no two boards have the same address. Theoretically, you could hook up every Ethernet board to one huge network and not have any duplicate node addresses.
• Other boards automatically determine a valid node address when they are brought up on the network. The node address will change, depending on the board's location on the network. IBM Token-Ring boards use this node addressing scheme.

One quick way of obtaining node addresses for file server network interface boards is to type the CONFIG command at the server console while the server is operational. The display will show the node address of each board immediately to the right of the network address. You can also obtain this information through the "LAN Driver Information" option of FCONSOLE.

Gathering File Server/Installation Configuration Information

Speaking of FCONSOLE, all of the information listed under File Server/OS Configuration, File Server Installation Parameters, Hard Disk/Subsystem Information, and Volume Information in our list above is readily available through various options of the FCONSOLE utility. Here is a quick rundown of what you'll find under various menu options in FCONSOLE. Sublevels under the main menu options are indicated by a slash. For example, "Statistics/Channel Statistics" means choose "Statistics" from the "Available Options" menu, then "Channel Statistics" from the submenu that will appear.

"LAN Driver Information" Option
LAN drivers and board configuration settings
Network address assigned to each network interface board
Node address of each network interface board

"Statistics/Channel Statistics" Option
Disk channel drivers and interface board configurations

"Statistics/Disk Mapping Information" Option
Disk mirroring/duplexing information

"Statistics/Disk Statistics" Option
Brand and model of hard disk controllers
Each disks's channel number, controller number, and drive number
Hot Fix logical size (in blocks)
Number of heads, cylinders, sectors per tracks

"Statistics/Summary" Option
Number of communication (routing) buffers
Configured number of transactions
Configured number of open files
Configured number of indexed files
Configured number of bindery objects ("N/A" means disk space limit was set to "no")

"Statistics/Transaction Tracking Statistics" Option
Configured number of transactions
Transaction backout volume

"Statistics/Volume Information" Option
Volume name and number
Volume size (in 4KB blocks)
Configured number of directory entries
Directory cache setting (yes or no)
Physical disk the volume resides on

"Version Information" Option
Type of NetWare operating system (including version and revision)

The only remaining items are the serial number of the NetWare OS and the disk partition table information. For some reason, FCONSOLE does not give the OS serial number anywhere, but SYSCON does. To view the serial and application number of the OS, log in as SUPERVISOR, go into SYSCON and select "File Server Information," then choose your file server from the list of known servers. You can only see the serial number for servers on which you have supervisor rights.

Obtaining the disk partition table information is less simple. Of course, you'll only need this information if you have a non-NetWare partition on one of your *internal* hard disks. For example, a nondedicated file server often has a DOS partition set up for use by the workstation side of the file server computer. You can use the DOS FDISK utility to display the partitions set up on a disk (as long as the machine is running under DOS). To DOS, the NetWare partition will be listed as an unknown partition type.

To see the partition table from NetWare's point of view, go into the installation half of NETGEN and use the "Modify Partition Table" option. To do this, bring the file server down and start the NETGEN program. From the "Network Generation Options" menu, choose "NetWare Installation." After verifying that the list of disk drives is correct, you will see the "Installation Options" menu. Choose "Select Custom Installation Options." A "Modify Partition Table" option should appear in the "Custom Installation" menu. (If it is not there, your version of NetWare is using all available disk space for NetWare partitions by default.) Select this option and record the partition information displayed. Do *not* change anything! Press Escape when you are through and exit NETGEN by choosing "Continue Installation," answering "No" to the "Install Networking Software on File Server?" prompt, and "Yes" to the "Exit Installation and ABANDON Changes" prompt.

Documenting the Directory Structure

NetWare doesn't provide a utility that shows entire directory trees. With FILER you can move around from directory to directory, but you don't get an overall view of what the directory structure actually looks like. If you have a small network with one or two volumes, you can sketch out the directory tree on paper without much difficulty. For more complicated directory structures, you'll need additional tools.

Several utilities are available that create a visual listing of a DOS directory tree. One example is VTREE, a *PC Magazine* utility available on CompuServe or on the utilities diskette available from the magazine. Using VTREE and the DOS redirect parameter (>), you can dump the directory structure of a volume into a text file and print out the file for a hard-copy record of the volume's directories. Since NetWare's volume level is the same as DOS's root level, you'll have to repeat the procedure for each volume. Here's a quick example of how to perform the procedure.

Start by logging in at any network workstation as SUPERVISOR. Copy the VTREE.COM file to a work directory (for example, SYS:WORK). Then, using NetWare's MAP command, proceed to map a drive to the work directory (type **MAP F:=SYS:WORK**) and then map a drive to each volume on the file server. If you have three volumes—SYS, VOL1, and VOL2—you can map drive G: to SYS:, drive H: to VOL1:, and drive I: to VOL2:. (As long as you are attached to only one file server, you need not include the file server name in the map command.) Now, from drive F:, type **VTREE G: > SYS.DIR**. The directory tree for volume SYS will be copied to a file named SYS.DIR in the work directory. This DOS text file can be printed from most word processors. Repeat the command, substituting drives H: and I: and an appropriate file name each time. Print out the files using the NetWare NPRINT command. For example, to print out SYS.DIR, type **NPRINT SYS.DIR** from the directory containing the SYS.DIR file. (NPRINT also allows you to specify which file server and print queue you want to send the file to. See Chapter 17 for more information.)

Once you have a hard copy of each volume's directory tree, indicate on this copy whether any directories have a Maximum Rights Mask different from the default (the default is to allow all rights in the mask). You can check the Maximum Rights Mask in FILER by selecting each directory, one at a time, and choosing the "Current Directory Information" option, then highlighting "Maximum Rights Mask" in the list. Highlight "Trustees" to see a list of user and group trustees assigned in the directory.

Gathering User and Group Information

Use the SYSCON utility to assemble information on each user and group defined on the file server. Look at each user and group individually to gather all necessary information. This process can take some time if you have many users and groups. Here are a few hints to make it go faster.

If most user accounts are set up the same way in terms of account, password, station, and time restrictions, record the system default restrictions first; note deviations from the default only if there are any for the individual users.

Use the WHOAMI /A command to gather information on users' group membership, security equivalences, and trustee rights assignments. (See "Listing Information about a User with WHOAMI" in Chapter 8 for more information.)

Printing Out User Login Scripts. There is no easy way from within SYSCON to print a copy of a user's login script. However, the login script is stored as a text file in each user's mail directory. Each defined user has a subdirectory under SYS:MAIL. The name of a user's mail subdirectory is the user ID number shown in SYSCON. Within this mail subdirectory is a file named LOGIN, with no extension. That is the user's login script file. You can print the contents of the file using any word processor that can handle DOS text files, or with the NetWare NPRINT command.

Printing the System Configuration Files

You can use a similar technique to print out the system login script. The system login script is stored as a DOS text file named NET$LOG.DAT in the SYS:PUBLIC directory.

Two other configuration files used by the file server are the AUTOEXEC.SYS file and the SERVER.CFG file. (Prior to v2.15, the SERVER.CFG file was called CONFIG.UPS.) These text files, located in the SYS:SYSTEM directory, can be printed out in the same manner as any DOS text file.

Keeping Tabs on VAPs

Value-added processes (VAPs) are also stored in the SYS:SYSTEM directory on the file server. They usually have the extension .VAP or .VP?, where ? can be any digit from 0 to 9. Common VAPs found on file servers include the Btrieve VAP, the Keyboard Lock VAP, the Streaming Tape Backup VAP, and the Macintosh Service Protocol Gateway VAPs.

When the file server boots, it scans SYS:SYSTEM for any VAP files. If it finds any, the bootup procedure asks you if you want to load the VAPs. Loading VAPs is an all-or-nothing proposition. If you answer "Yes," they all load. If you answer "No," none of the VAPs load. Having a record of which VAP files are in SYS:SYSTEM will help you know exactly what you're getting into when you say you want to load all VAPs.

The configured VAP wait time is a line in the SERVER.CFG file (which, except for this parameter, is used for UPS configuration parameters) that indicates how long the file server waits for input to the VAP load prompt before it continues with the bootup procedure. It might be helpful to record this parameter along with the rest of the VAP information.

Gathering Information about Applications

Information about the various applications loaded on the file server could be the most difficult to assemble, yet could also prove the most valuable when it comes to maintaining the network. Since many conflicts and problems can arise from application software, the more you know about that software the better.

Consult the application's manuals for manufacturer, vendor, version and revision numbers. Especially note any site licensing or concurrent-number-of-user limitations associated with the application. List the options chosen in the application's install or setup procedure, including what directory or directories the program files were installed in. Also note what drive mappings (both regular and search drive mappings) users must have in their login scripts to run the application. Keep a list of which users or groups have access to each application.

Another useful piece of information to record is the amount of RAM each application needs in order to run. A common source of problems when running multiple applications on a network is not having enough RAM at the workstation. Older versions of the NetWare workstation shell take up a significant amount of workstation RAM. (The new DOS workstation shell v3.01 takes up less memory.) That, along with DOS device drivers, TSRs, and the like, can easily reduce a 640KB workstation to 512KB or less. Also make a note of any other unusual characteristics or configurations for each application.

Other Record-Keeping Tips

A few final tips on record-keeping: File all purchase orders, invoices, equipment lists, and software licenses so they will be available for review. Also, establish the habit of filling out and sending in the registration cards for all equipment and software. Proof of purchase date is often not enough to get quick service for equipment under warranty. Besides making warranty repairs less of a hassle, registering your purchases, in most cases, qualifies you for vendor support and keeps you informed of important software revision notices and new product information.

ASSESSING YOUR NETWORK'S MANAGEABILITY

Three main criteria distinguish a network that is easy to manage and expand: simplicity, consistency, and modularity. These three characteristics are very closely interrelated; usually, a LAN is at once simple, consistent, and modular, or it is none of these things. The absence of any one of these three ingredients can seriously affect the overall manageability of the LAN. As we go through and explain what we mean by each of these factors, evaluate how your network stacks up in each area.

Simplicity

Many LANs are unnecessarily complicated. Oddly enough, most of this complexity results when supervisors try to do what a LAN is best at: accommodate the varying needs of many users, each with different hardware and software requirements. Supervisors usually recognize the fact that if LAN use is made easy and intuitive for the users, they won't ask as many questions. However, to attain this goal, supervisors often tend to treat each user as a totally independent entity and set up separate batch files, menus, account restrictions, and security for each one. Such a program creates a heavy maintenance load for the supervisor, especially in light of what we'll call the First Law of LANs:

The First Law of LANs: A LAN never stays the same.

A network is a living, mutating thing. No matter how adequately you set up the LAN to begin with, you'll have to change something sooner or later. Technological advances render existing systems obsolete almost before they're installed; new applications or new versions of old applications arrive on the scene at a breathtaking pace; organizations double and triple in size practically overnight; old users get new hardware along with transfers or promotions—the list goes on and on. The simpler and more generic your network is, the easier it will be to accommodate changes in hardware, in software, and in the users themselves.

Consistency

Closely related to simplicity in measuring a LAN's manageability is the consistency with which the LAN is set up and configured. Obviously, if you set up each workstation and user differently, you effectively multiply your user support workload by the number of users on the network. True, different users have different needs—but that should not preclude establishing conventions and policies that apply across the board.

Structuring directories in a consistent manner not only promotes more effective data sharing, but also simplifies backups and software upgrades. Having a consistent pattern in naming users, groups, and file servers, for example, will cut down on the number of times you hear such questions as, "What's the name of that group again?" Having one central menu that covers the entire network is easier to maintain and troubleshoot—a statement which brings us to the Second Law of LANs:

The Second Law of LANs: The user interface is *the network.*

This law simply points out that users equate the LAN with whatever interface the LAN presents to them, whether it be a front-end menu system, a subset of a familiar computing environment (such as Windows or the Macintosh Desktop), or the stark command-line interface of DOS. Whatever type of interface you use on your network, it should be possible for users to log in at other workstations on the network and be greeted with the same interface as on their own machines.

Modularity

NetWare was designed to be a modular network operating system. For the most part, you can add on pieces here or take away pieces there, and still have a functional network. The easier it is to add on or modify pieces of the network, the better manageability score the network earns. That leads us to the Third Law of LANs, which you may have already experienced in your network:

The Third Law of LANs: A LAN always grows beyond initial expectations.

Many network experts advise that once you've determined your initial LAN needs as far as number of users supported, disk storage space, and so on, you should double or even triple your estimates to allow for the inevitable growth every LAN experiences. Networks that are easy to add on to not only are easier to manage, but better accommodate growth as well.

Modularity is especially important in the face of the network industry trend toward more and more decentralization of services. Novell is moving away from the "file server as center of the universe" philosophy, as evidenced by the capabilities starting with v2.1 to have value-added servers in addition to the file server on the network. For example, the recent bundling of print server software with NetWare 286 demonstrates that the preferred way to handle printing on a LAN is no longer to have the file server do it all. The ability to use any vendor's hard disks in an external disk subsystem is a real boon when the time comes to upgrade to a faster file server or add more disk space to an existing server. You need only attach the disk subsystems to the server.

MAKING THE NETWORK EASIER TO MANAGE

With simplicity, consistency, and modularity firmly in mind as our overriding principles, let's look at some specific suggestions for making a NetWare network easier to manage. Reworking a LAN so that it is easier for you to manage and easier for users to use—especially in the face of resistance to the LAN or in an environment not committed to computerization—requires special skills. You will have to be patient, diplomatic, and ready to improvise much of the time.

Do Your Homework

Before you make major changes in the file server setup, learn as much as you can about NetWare. Take classes and read books (like this one) that cover multiuser applications, network security, directory structure, user/group management, login scripts, backup strategies, and proper hardware and software selection for network expansion.

Automate as Much as You Can

Work to create tools that will simplify LAN use, especially for novice users. Effective use of batch files, login scripts, and menu systems is critical to a simple-to-use network. If you take the time to automate as many network procedures as possible, you'll save yourself time and maintenance difficulties over the long run.

Batch Files. The process of getting onto the network is an ideal place to start simplifying operations. Novice users should not have to deal with complex start-up procedures. The only input they should be required to give is a password; a batch file can take care of the rest.

If you haven't already done so, set up each user's AUTOEXEC.BAT file to automatically load the NetWare shell files, attach to the file server, and issue the LOGIN command. To do this, place the following commands in the AUTOEXEC.BAT file in the order shown:

IPX	;loads the NetWare IPX/SPX file
NET*x*	;loads NetWare's workstation DOS shell
NETBIOS	;include only if the user needs IBM NetBIOS compatibility
F:	;assumes that E: is the last drive used by DOS
LOGIN *file server name/user name*	

Replace the *x* in NET*x* with the major version number of DOS that the workstation is booting ("3" for DOS 3.x, "4" for DOS 4.x). The IPX.COM, NETx.COM, and NETBIOS.EXE files should be in the bootup directory accessible to DOS after a cold boot (usually in the same directory as COMMAND.COM and other DOS boot files on a hard disk). If you don't like to "pollute" a local hard disk's DOS directory with non-DOS files, place the network bootup files in a separate directory and include the directory in the DOS PATH command. If the workstation has no local hard disk, the files should be on the boot diskette.

Always include the file server name after the LOGIN command. This step eliminates problems that can occur on an internetwork when the shell initially attaches to a file server other than the desired one. After the user enters the correct password, the NetWare login scripts will take over.

Login Scripts. NetWare includes both a system login script and individual user login scripts; all the "universal" setup that applies to all users can happen in the system login script, leaving minor user differences to be handled in the personal login scripts. The bulk of the search drives, network drive mappings, and other environment settings can be handled in the system login script through the use of two key login script commands: the IF MEMBER_OF *group* command and the DOS SET command. The rationale behind these commands is summarized below; details on actual implementation is given in Chapter 9.

Besides the relatively few applications that all users must be able to access, such as E-mail and group productivity software, most network users run only one or two other applications on a daily basis. For example, users in an accounting department typically run a specialized accounting package and a spreadsheet program. In a typical publications group, the writers run a word processing program, the illustrators run a graphics program, and the layout people run the desktop publishing system. The point is that application usage on a network tends to be based on groups, rather than individuals, and any given group needs access to only a small number of applications. By setting up drive mappings according to group membership through the system login script, you can eliminate many drive mappings from individual users' login scripts.

Using a combination of DOS environment variables and the DOS SET command in the system login script, you can set up "generic" commands containing NetWare's identifier variables (%LOGIN_NAME, %P_STATION, %OS_VERSION, and so on). When a user logs in at a workstation, these variables in the system login script will be replaced with information applying to that specific user or workstation. This is a common technique for mapping users to the correct DOS directory when multiple versions of DOS are running on the same network. Its use can be extended to the menu system and batch files as well. For example, if you have the command **DOS SET USER="%LOGIN_NAME"** in the system login script, NetWare will store the user's login name in the workstation's DOS environment. You can then use the variable %USER% in any batch file or menu command; DOS will automatically substitute the appropriate login name for %USER%. Note that variables in DOS batch files have the "%" symbol as both the first and last character, while the identifier variables in NetWare login scripts only begin with "%." (See Chapter 9 for more explanation and examples.)

Likewise, you can set an environment variable in each workstation's AUTOEXEC.BAT file to identify the workstation's monitor type. Many applications require a different setup, depending on the type of graphics adapter/monitor (Hercules, EGA, or VGA, for instance). If you include a line such as SET MONITOR=VGA in the AUTOEXEC.BAT file, VGA is substituted for the %MONITOR% variable in any subsequent batch files or menu commands. (More complete explanations and examples are given in Chapter 10.)

Menu Systems. A front-end menuing system is another foundation of a simple-to-use system. Through a good menu system, you can shield users from enigmatic network commands. This book contains suggestions for using the MENU program included with NetWare. However, a number of superior menu systems that work with NetWare are available from third parties (consult Appendix C for some suggestions). Whichever menu system you choose, the following tips will apply.

The first principle of effective, easy-to-maintain menus is to make them as universal as possible. If every user has a separate menu script and batch files containing specific user, directory, and program names, changing one program or directory forces you to rewrite all the batch files and menu scripts. Using the DOS environment variables as explained above can save much of this rewriting.

In most business environments, you should set up menus for everyone, even advanced users. Novice users, usually the majority, need as much automation as possible. Even though working from menus is often frustrating to "power" users, they sometimes have an exaggerated opinion of their skills and can cause problems if given the option of operating from the command line. Once advanced users have proven their competence, however, they can usually work more effectively from the command line.

In an attempt to simplify network usage, network administrators often create one menu option per application and expect users to correctly set up directories and printers from within the application. A better way, however, is to create a separate menu option for each category of application usage. The following example demonstrates what we mean. When a user selects "Word Processing" from the main menu, the following submenu is presented:

```
————————Word Processing Options————————

1)   Letters Directory - Network Draft Quality Printer
2)   Letters Directory - Network Letter Quality Printer
3)   Reports Directory - Network Draft Quality Printer (Compressed Mode)
4)   Reports Directory - Network Laser Printer
```

Each of these submenu options loads the same word processing program, but with a slightly different setup. Directory and printer settings are normally handled either through command-line options or by means of a macro run when users enter the program. You will need to write a batch file containing the appropriate startup commands for each variation on the submenu. The advantage of this menu technique is that users do not need to understand directory structure, printer setup, or network commands to use the word processor. This approach also reduces training requirements and lessens the chance of operator error by automating keystrokes.

Keyboard macros are another useful tool that can supplement menu systems by automating keystroke sequences. Many programs have a built-in macro capability that lets you assign complex application functions to a single keystroke combination. For example, you could define Alt-S as a "save, print, and exit" macro. When users press Alt-S, the macro takes over and issues the commands necessary to save the file, send it to the printer, and exit the program.

Admittedly, implementing a detailed menu like this takes planning and work. You must think through what should happen when users select each option, and you must test every option thoroughly on each individual workstation. Novice users in particular are generally intolerant of network crashes. Try to catch problems before your users do, and get the bugs worked out beforehand.

Create Customized End-User Documentation

Another important aspect of the overall network interface is end-user documentation, both written and on-line if possible. Because each workstation on a network has a custom setup, the NetWare user manuals are of limited help to users. Even minor hardware dissimilarities can make a big difference in how NetWare "looks" to the user. Users need individualized reference manuals that detail their specific configurations, keyboard macro assignments for each application, and other pertinent information.

Custom On-Line Help Screens. You can use a keyboard macro program in combination with a memory-resident editor to create custom help screens for your menus and all network applications. The macros we talked about earlier are specific to their own applications. However, several terminate-and-stay-resident (TSR) keyboard macro programs, such as Prokey and Smartkey, work across multiple applications. (See Appendix C for third-party product availability information.)

You could use these keyboard macro programs to create a uniform help key that would be consistent across all applications. That way, users have to learn only one set of keystrokes to call up a customized help screen, no matter which application they are in. Each menu, submenu, option, and application can have a custom help file written for it. By pressing the assigned help-key combination (for instance, Shift-Ctrl-H), the user can get a help screen giving details about the current situation and options. Here is one way to set it up.

For each menu option, include a command in the batch file that changes the data file used by the keyboard macro program. For example, in the batch file for the main word processing option, assign a "word processing menu keystroke file" to the macro program. Then, when users press the predefined help-key sequence, the memory-resident editor loads the text file containing help instructions for the word processing submenu.

Useful as they are, keyboard macro programs can also be tricky. As with any memory-resident programs, they take up memory space and may conflict with keyboard assignments in some applications. Test the keyboard macro program with every application before you use it on the network.

Individualized Documentation. Lucid written documentation, tailored to your own network setup, will cut down on the number of questions you have to answer. This documentation should cover how to log in to the network, what to do if you forget your password, how to use the menu system, what printers are available, and how to use batch commands, network utilities, and applications.

One technique for creating individualized "manuals" is to create "print screen" documentation that walks the user, screen by screen, through the various activities specific to his or her environment. Use a memory-resident editor with screen-capture capability (such as Borland's Sidekick). Begin with the login screen. Use the editor to capture the screen, then add a couple of lines of explanation or comment. Enter the password, then capture the first menu and add comments. Proceed through each option, grabbing screens and making comments. The result is a complete step-by-step document that requires relatively little work to put together. You can use the same procedure to supplement documentation for each major application.

Another good idea is to keep a record of the questions your users ask and update your documentation regularly to incorporate the answers to these user questions. It's difficult to anticipate every single question users might have, so rely on user feedback to improve your documentation.

Provide User Training

Despite all your efforts to make using the LAN as simple and intuitive as possible, you will still need to provide some user training. Granted, training is expensive, disrupts the normal office routine, and reduces productivity for a few days. But don't fall into the trap of thinking that users can figure out everything on their own. Experience has shown that this is not the case. No matter how much work goes into simplifying a LAN, users—be they data entry personnel or "power" users—need training on networking in general and on each network application.

Group Training. Individual training is impractical, expensive, and less effective than group training. The best approach may be to institute your own classes before work, after work, or at lunch every other week or so. This way, everyone can attend and the office routine is not unduly interrupted. Another advantage to the group experience is the "bonding" that results as everyone learns and participates together. The technically proficient usually stand out in group training classes, and the rest of the group instinctively recognize who to go to for assistance.

Peer Group Support. As power users emerge (as they will in almost any group), enlist their help in providing user support. Let as many of these users as possible acquire "guru" status. If one user is proficient in advanced word processing, for example, you can refer user questions on the subject to that "guru" user. If another user is good at databases, refer database questions to the database "guru." These user experts have closer contacts with the other users on the network and do not intimidate novice users as much as you might.

PROTECTING THE NETWORK FROM VIRUSES

Over the past several years, computer viruses have come to represent one of the most serious threats known to LANs. While it is still debateable how much of the threat is real and how much is the result of media sensationalism, no competent network administrator can ignore the possibility of virus infection happening on his or her network. This section will look at how to recognize virus symptoms, what corrective action to take, and—most importantly—how to prevent the spread of viruses on your network.

Recognizing a Virus

A computer virus is a small program that propagates within a computer system by attaching to other software and reproducing itself. Many variations on the virus theme exist, known by equally repugnant names: bombs, worms, Trojan horses, diddlers, and so on. Knowing the distinctions between each variation is not as important as realizing that they are all spread by running infected programs. Just as a biological virus spreads by infecting its host first and then being passed to other hosts, a single execution of an infected program on a network can initiate an "epidemic" as the virus quickly spreads to other programs on the network.

Depending on the design of the virus and the intent of its author, its effects range from annoyances such as increasing system response time and displaying strange messages, to debilitating consequences such as modifying or destroying data, physically damaging computer hardware, or bringing the entire network down. Some strains begin their destructive work immediately upon infection; others lie dormant until they have replicated themselves sufficiently to trigger their destructive payload, or until some predetermined condition or date triggers the destructive mechanism.

Here are some typical warning signs of virus infection. This list is by no means all-inclusive; new strains are being produced at an alarming pace, and existing strains are being modified to produce different results.

- A noticeable slowdown in system response time that gets worse over time
- Programs that take up more and more RAM with every subsequent execution
- Abnormal behavior of screen display (cascading characters, screen filled with "snow," flippant or threatening messages appearing at random)
- Files mysteriously disappearing or listed on the screen as "not found"

Preventive and Corrective Measures

Here are some guidelines for preventing viruses. You should establish specific policies in your company advising users what to do if they think they have encountered a virus manifestation.

Limit Network Access. Preventing unauthorized access is a good first step toward controlling what enters the network. Only legitimate users should be allowed on the network. Enforce tight password security; require users to change passwords frequently. Implement the security features provided with the network operating system so that users have access to data on a need-to-use basis only. If users circumvent the rules, require them to work on a standalone machine instead of on the network.

Whenever possible, flag all executable files as "Read-Only" to prevent them from being written to. Grant only Read, Open, and Search rights in the directories in which application program files reside, except in rare instances where the application needs to write information back to the executable file or other system files. (See Chapter 5 for more information.)

Keep a log of all accesses or attempted accesses to the network. The log should record at least the time, date, and node address of each access. This information will help you pinpoint exactly when and where any illegal break-ins. Installing resource accounting and activating the "Intruder Detection/Lockout" option in SYSCON can help in this area. (See Chapters 6 and 11 for details.)

Carefully monitor how users boot up the network workstations. The most common way for a virus to enter a computer system is through a contaminated floppy disk. Always use a boot diskette that is known to be safe when booting floppy-based PCs. Never boot a hard disk system with a floppy disk—this only increases the chances of introducing a virus onto the system.

Precautions for New Software. To avoid acquiring contaminated software, purchase all software from reputable dealers. Make sure all diskettes are still in their original packaging. Never use pirated programs—they could harbor infection. If you order public domain, shareware, or freeware programs, make sure the supplier of those programs obtains the software directly from the authors and checks all diskettes for viruses before distributing them. If you are not sure where a program came from, contact the author and compare the creation date and file size with your version. Do not use any program that doesn't provide a contact address or phone number. Software of unknown origin is the most likely to contain viruses.

Thoroughly test all new software on an isolated system before uploading it to the network. There have been cases where even commercial software (and anti-virus programs themselves) contained viruses.

Make working copies of all original diskettes. Write-protect the originals (instructions are included with the diskettes) and store them in a safe place so that you always have uninfected masters available if virus contamination should occur.

Test All Software Regularly. Regularly check system programs, utilities, and applications for unusual behavior. In particular, watch for possible symptoms of viruses at work: unexplained size changes in executable files, a change in the number of hidden files on a disk, files with unusual creation dates and times, inordinately large or small files, and files with unconventional names or extensions.

To help you compare files, maintain a hard copy of all directories and their contents. Include a check sum or cyclic redundancy check on all systems and utility software. A check sum is a unique number derived by running files through a data compression program such as ARC or ZIP (see Appendix C for availability information); the check sum is almost certain to differ between two files that are not exactly identical.

Remove any suspicious programs with a utility that completely overwrites the disk space formerly occupied by the deleted files. Do not use the DOS DEL or ERASE commands. These commands do not actually remove files from the disk until the space is needed for other files.

Use Anti-Virus Utilities. Use anti-virus programs as part of your total security scheme. Numerous kinds exist—it is best to use a combination of virus detection and removal utilities, like Antitoxin or Disinfectant, with preventive programs such as Vaccine or GateKeeper. (Disinfectant, Vaccine, and GateKeeper are available from on-line services or through users' groups.) Understand how these programs work and don't expect them to provide 100% protection.

Back Up Regularly. Make frequent backup copies of all program and data files. If a virus does destroy your data, you can restore that data from a backup copy. Be aware, however, that some viruses lie dormant for a time, so it is possible for them to be copied onto your backup disks.

Other Virus Prevention Tips. Stay current on the latest developments. Participate in public virus forums or join a users group. Offer classes on viruses for all system users so they will be aware of the risks involved and be better able to avoid them. The National Computer Security Association has published a book called *Computer Viruses* which contains information on 145 known viruses. The book also details ways to detect, remove, recover from, and prevent viruses on microcomputers.

Encrypt data whenever possible, especially when the data is sent over telephone lines or other transmission media. This security measure discourages unauthorized tampering with data during transmission. Don't overlook hardware protection options. A combination of hardware and software protection provides the safest defense. Many external devices are available to positively identify users. Examples include handheld "smart cards" that initiate dialogue with the user, biometric devices that scan the user's retinas or sense their fingerprints, and dial-back systems that identify the user, break the connection, then call the user back before granting access. This prevents unauthorized external access to a WAN.

5 Managing Network Applications

This chapter gives some guidelines for installing and maintaining application software on the network. In a very real sense, applications are the only purpose for which the network exists. Without powerful, network-aware, multiuser application programs, LANs are just an expensive way for isolated users to share disk storage and printers. Rather than being an afterthought, then, putting applications on the network should be the overriding basis for all network setup and maintenance decisions. Ultimately, everything relates to what applications you are running and how you set them up:

> • The file server's directories must be structured to accommodate the various requirements of the applications.
> • Network security exists mainly to protect the applications and their data.
> • Users and groups are given trustee rights and drive mappings expressly for the purpose of running applications.

A surprising number of LAN problems are related to the improper or careless installation of application software. Most network-aware applications are fairly easy to install on the file server; others (especially sophisticated client/server programs) are not so easy. And there are always those few stragglers (most often custom programs written in-house) for which a network version is not yet available. This chapter will give some tips to consider when installing applications so that they will be easier to work with, maintain, and upgrade when new versions come out.

GETTING THE BIG PICTURE

In general, you must include the following steps when loading an application on the network:

- Determine the application's level of NetWare compatibility
- Plan where the application will fit in the file server's directory structure
- Install the application according to the documentation
- Flag the program's .EXE files "Shareable Read-Only" (in most cases)
- Set up drive mappings in NetWare login scripts
- Assign users appropriate trustee rights to the application directories

Here are some suggestions for accomplishing each of these steps.

Determining an Application's NetWare Compatibility

Not all applications run equally well on a NetWare network. To determine the degree of NetWare compatibility, look at the following major characteristics of the application.

Single-User vs. Multiuser Applications. In the early days of LANs, existing single-user applications were simply modified to run in a multiuser environment. These revamped applications, typically word processors, spreadsheets, and single-user databases, did not take advantage of the distributed processing capabilities inherent in NetWare LANs; rather, they relied on basic file locking to prevent more than one user from getting at the same data at the same time.

Eventually, true multiuser applications emerged. These applications were network-aware; they began to more fully utilize distributed processing. Current multiuser applications allow several workstations to access and alter the same data files at the same time. Physical or logical record locks synchronize multiuser access. Each workstation loads the application into its own memory and processes all data locally. The file server acts as the source of shared files that the applications (running at the workstations) access through file reads and writes. A multiuser database is a prime example of this type of application.

Server-Based Applications. With the advent of NetWare v2.1, server-based applications became possible. In this type of application, the workstations become "clients" of a "server" that performs services other than the usual file services of the traditional file server. The services provided by a server-based application can either be something the workstations cannot do for themselves (usually the functions of a print server, CD-ROM server, or communications gateway involving specialized hardware not locally available to the client) or something the workstations could do for themselves but not as efficiently as the server (as is usually the case with database servers and batch job servers).

Multiple Defaults and Setup Files. A common difficulty with applications that aren't very network-aware lies in the way they handle user preferences for defaults, configurations, and setup options. Most true multiuser applications provide a way for users to save their preferences in their personal network directories so that they don't overwrite other users' preferences. Even if an application doesn't allow for individual user preferences, however, there are still ways to circumvent this problem and have the application work on the LAN. (Refer to the hints for installing non-network-aware applications later in this chapter.)

NetWare-Specific Features. The slickest applications to install are those that have a version designed specifically for NetWare. These types of programs recognize and use NetWare search drives, print queues, and security information. Being able to specify a network printer in the setup routine is a big plus, for it eliminates a lot of "spooling" around with the NetWare CAPTURE command.

License Agreements. Know the terms of the application's software license agreement. Multiuser software is usually sold with one of three basic licensing schemes: a site license, a per-server license, or a number-of-users license.

Software issued with a *site* license allows an unlimited number of users to run the application simultaneously as long as they are at the licensed site.

With a *per-server* license, one copy of the software is loaded onto the file server; that copy can be used by any number of users attached to that server. Some companies offer network user add-on packages that contain the manuals, but no software. However, if you want to load the program on another file server, you must purchase a new copy or get a multiple server license.

Under a *number-of-users* license agreement, you purchase a version of the software tailored for a specific number of simultaneous users (four-user version, eight-user version, and so on). This type of software might include a mechanism that keeps track of how many users are currently using the program to prevent more than the maximum number of users from using the program at the same time. Sometimes, though, the only policing mechanism is the old-fashioned honor system.

In another scenario, your site might have three or four licensed copies of a single-user program. Obviously, you don't want duplicate copies of the same program cluttering up the file server. Some single-user licenses are tied to the user who bought the application; other licenses don't specify who may use the application so long as only one person at a time uses it. Single-user applications are not necessarily protected from having more than one user accessing them at one time. If there isn't a network version of your favorite single-user application, you can protect your site against license infringement by using a software metering product to limit the application to only those users who have a legitimate copy of the application.

Note: Some companies may not want their single-user programs to run on a network at all. Don't take risks with license infringements. The legal consequences are dire. If you have any questions about whether or not you can use a single-user application on the network, call the vendor and ask if they have a network copy of the program in question. If they don't, try to work something out with the vendor directly.

Fitting the Application into the Directory Structure

Find out what kind of directory structure the application requires. Some require that all program files go into a single directory; with others, only certain files go into a main directory, and the rest go into nested subdirectories. As you consider where to put the application directories in the overall directory structure, let three principles be your guide.

First, keep applications separated from other types of software on the network, including the NetWare utilities in SYS:PUBLIC and SYS:SYSTEM and any other network utilities that aren't actually application programs. Upgrading NetWare on the file server becomes tedious when you have a zillion non-NetWare utilities mixed in with the NetWare directories. NetWare comes with so many utilities that it's hard to keep track of what is NetWare and what isn't. So to be safe, make a separate directory or directories for useful, non-NetWare network utility programs.

Second, separate applications from each other. Obviously, you wouldn't want WordPerfect 4.2 and WordPerfect 5.1 installed in the same WORDPERFECT directory. That would cause many kinds of conflicts and confusion. By the same token, don't mix Microsoft Word in with WordPerfect, either. Don't even mix WordPerfect enhancement utilities with WordPerfect. As a general rule, make a separate directory for each application or version of the same application on the network. This setup simplifies batch files and drive mapping assignments, and makes it much easier to upgrade an application or delete it from the network entirely if it's no longer needed.

Third, install application *program* files (the files needed to run the program) in a different branch of the directory tree, on a different volume, or even on a different physical hard disk than the *data* files users work with from within each application. There is a very fundamental reason for keeping applications and data separated, and it has to do with backing up. Typically, the application program files are static; you load them on the network and they don't change until you upgrade the application or modify it in some way—not an everyday occurrence. Data files, on the other hand, may change several times a day. If the program files are in another directory branch or on another volume or disk, it is easier to exclude them when you perform your daily backup of what was modified that day. It is a waste of backup media space to continually back up program files that rarely change. Backing those up once a week or even once every two weeks should be sufficient.

Figure 5-1 illustrates a directory structure that reflects these three principles of setting up application directories.

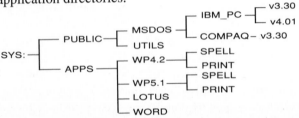

Figure 5-1: This directory structure separates applications from utilities, separates applications from each other, and groups all utilities and applications under the SYS volume.

Following the Directions

To paraphrase a common aphorism: *Before* all else fails, read the directions. Always follow the installation instructions provided with the application. If the application has both standalone and network directions, use the network directions. Otherwise, problems can crop up later, and tracking down software troubles resulting from incorrect installation is very difficult.

It is risky to assume that all you have to do is copy the files from the diskettes to a directory somewhere on the server. Many companies today compress program files so they'll fit on fewer diskettes. These files are decompressed as part of the install procedure. Often, the program needs to be specially configured for your file server hardware. Even more tricky are those applications that store users' monitor, mouse, and printer types in a user-specific setup or configuration file. (Some tips for handling multiple users' preferences are given later in this chapter.)

Flagging Program Files

The Novell manuals say that you should flag all program files "Shareable Read-Only" (SRO) with the NetWare FLAG command after you have installed them on the file server. This file flagging is generally the best route to take, as it prevents users from writing over the program files even if they have Write rights in the directory. Be careful, though—if a user has Modify rights in the directory, he or she can alter the file attributes and turn "Read-Only" files into "Read-Write" files. Flagging executable files "Read-Only" also helps prevent viruses from attaching themselves to the files.

Flag only .EXE and .COM files "Shareable Read-Only." Most overlay and configuration files must be written to, so they should be flagged "Read-Write." Some applications that are not NetWare-friendly must write information to the .EXE or .COM files at various times while the program is running. In this case, the executable files must be flagged "Shareable Read-Write" (SRW) in order for the application to run properly. Again, carefully follow the installation instructions for each application to learn how the files are to be flagged.

Shareable vs. Nonshareable. Much confusion surrounds the use of the Net-Ware "Shareable" and "Nonshareable" file attributes, mostly stemming from the fact that they do not actually make files behave as their names suggest. New files copied to or created on the network are flagged "Nonshareable/Read-Write" by default. You would think that you'd have to flag the file "Shareable" in order for more than one user to access the file. Technically, however, "Nonshareable" does not mean that only one user can access the file at a time. All it does is prevent two users from having the file open at the same time. After one user has opened a "Nonshareable" program file long enough to load it into the workstation's memory, another user can come along and open the file as well. Data files, on the other hand, can be kept open for long periods of time, if necessary. A NetWare-aware application can tell the OS through the appropriate function calls that it wants to let multiple users share a "Nonshareable" data file, and NetWare will allow it. The application prevents data corruption through file and record locks.

Execute-Only. The Read, Open, and Search rights normally granted to users to allow them to run applications are also sufficient to allow them to copy the program files. If you are concerned about users making unauthorized copies of applications on the file server, you can protect executable files (those with .EXE or .COM extensions) by flagging them as "Execute-Only" files. Once a file is flagged "Execute-Only," you can only do two things with it: run it or delete it. It cannot be copied or modified in any way (a useful barrier to virus infection). "Execute-Only" protects the file regardless of what other file attributes are assigned to the file or what rights you have in the directory (even if you have all rights as SUPERVISOR). Even with Modify and Parental rights, you cannot remove the "Execute-Only" attribute.

For this reason, you should assign Execute-Only with extreme caution. Make sure, before you do anything, that you have the original copy of the executable file on a diskette; NetWare won't allow "Execute-Only" files to be archived, so if anything corrupts a file flagged "Execute-Only," your only recourse is to delete the file and reinstall it from the original diskette.

Applications that need to write information back to the executable file or read data from it cannot be flagged "Execute-Only." WordPerfect's WP.EXE file is this way. Other applications will try to open the .COM or .EXE file before executing it; if such an application is marked "Execute-Only," nothing will happen. You may have to install the application, flag the file "Execute-Only," and see if it runs. Also, don't use the "Execute-Only" flag with applications that let you install only a specified number of copies of the application. If such an application is marked "Execute-Only" and won't run, you won't be able to uninstall the program and save your installation markers.

One last thing about the "Execute-Only" flag: you cannot assign it or even see it with the FLAG utility at the command line. You must go into FILER to see and assign this flag.

Conserving Drive Mappings

In order for a user to work with a given application on the network, the following logical drive mappings must be correctly set up through the NetWare login scripts:

- A search drive mapping to the application's program directory
- Regular drive mappings to the application's data directories

The exact commands used to establish both search drive mappings and regular drive mappings are detailed in Chapter 9.

Certain applications require more than one search drive mapping to function properly. Often, one search drive must be mapped to the directory containing the actual program files, and another must be mapped to a directory containing user-specific configuration or setup files. Some MHS-compatible E-mail programs (such as *The Coordinator* from Action Technologies) require four or five search drive mappings.

As the network grows and users need access to more and more applications, the temptation is to dole out drive mappings and trustee rights as if they were commodity items in unlimited supply. But such is not the case. Each user is limited to a maximum of 26 drive mappings (A through Z). DOS usually takes the first five (A through E), and only 16 of the 26 can be search drive mappings. Figure 5-2 illustrates these drive mapping limitations.

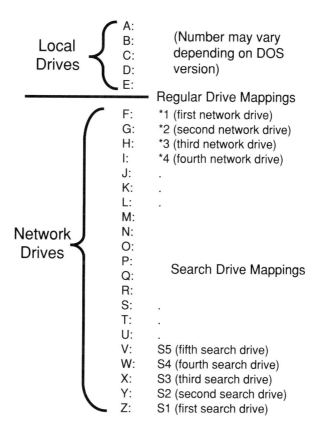

Figure 5-2: Of the 26 possible drive letters, DOS usually takes the first five (A through E). A workstation can have up to 16 NetWare search drive mappings, starting with drive Z and working backwards through the alphabet.

As you can readily see, users can soon run out of drive mappings. Filling up all 16 search drives also adds significant overhead, as NetWare must look through all 16 directories to find a file in the last search directory.

Finally, every drive mapping users establish takes up 16 bytes of file server memory. While this may not seem like a lot, it can add up fast when your server supports a large number of users having 26 network drive mappings each.

Changing Drive Mappings in Batch Files. One highly effective way of conserving the total number of drive mappings required is to use the concept of "generic" drive mappings in the login script. With this technique, you set up a single search drive mapping that can be manipulated by various batch files to start specific applications. The idea is to set up a "generic" search drive mapping for the most commonly used application in the system login script. Then, when necessary, a batch file can temporarily redefine the existing generic drive mappings, run a different application, then restore the original mappings when the user exits the program.

Here's an example of a batch file that redefines the third search drive mapping (drive X) for a program named TEST.EXE located in FS1/SYS:APPS/TEST. Suppose drive X is normally mapped to the WordPerfect directory. The data files are located in a TEST subdirectory under each user's home directory (SYS:USERS/*username*/TEST). Drive F is normally mapped to the home directory.

```
@echo off
cls
map x:=fs1/sys:apps/test < y.fil
map f:=fs1/sys:users/%USER%/test
f:
test
map x:=fs1/sys:apps/wp < y.fil
map f:=fs1/sys:users/%USER%
f:
```

This batch file first disables the echoing of commands to the screen and clears the screen. Then it remaps drive X to the test directory and drive F to the user's TEST data subdirectory. We used the full path names, including file server name, in case there is more than one file server on the network.

The Y.FIL file is a one-character text file containing the letter Y. It is necessary because when you remap an existing drive in NetWare, you get the following confirmation prompt:

```
Drive X: is used by the following search map:
SEARCH3:
Do you want to change it?(Y/N) Y
```

Since we don't want users to have to enter "Y" in the middle of the batch file, we use the DOS "pipe" symbol (<) to respond to the prompt automatically. With this pipe technique, the contents of Y.FIL (the letter Y) will be fed to DOS in response to the prompt and the batch file can continue. Place Y.FIL in a shared UTILS directory to which there is also a search drive mapping.

Note the %USER% variable used in the map command for drive F. This is a DOS environment variable set through the command **DOS SET USER=%LOGIN_NAME** in the system login script. NetWare will substitute the user's login name in place of %USER% in the batch file.

The batch file next places the user in the TEST data subdirectory and starts the TEST program. When the user exits TEST, the batch file restores the original "generic" drive mappings in the same way it changed them earlier. The user ends up back in his or her regular home directory.

You can avoid having to pipe the "Y" response in the batch file if you use "map s3:=fs1/sys:apps/test" instead of "map x:= ...." This variation of the MAP command doesn't initiate the confirmation prompt shown above when you are changing an existing search drive mapping. Just make sure that the third search drive mapping is always drive X.

An alternative method for temporarily changing search drive mappings in a batch file is to use the MAP INS variation. MAP INS causes a search drive mapping to be inserted into the list without overwriting existing mappings. For example, consider a batch file similar to the following:

```
map ins s3:=fs1/sys:apps/test
test
map rem s3:
```

This batch file would insert a search drive mapping to SYS:APPS/TEST as the third search drive, bumping the existing third search drive to the fourth, the fourth to the fifth, and so on. After the TEST program is done, the batch file removes the temporary search drive mapping, and the former mappings move back up to their former positions in the list.

Another technique is to designate a spare drive as a "save" drive and use it to store a current drive mapping while you reassign it. The batch file would look something like this:

```
map q:=f:
map f:=fs1/sys:users/%USER%/test
map ins s3:=fs1/sys:apps/test
f:
test
map del s3:
map f:=q:
map del q:
f:
```

Here, drive Q is used to save the current mapping to drive F before reassigning it for the TEST program.

Assigning Trustee Rights for Applications

To run most applications, users need at least Read, Open, and Search rights in the application's program directory. These three rights come up by default when you make trustee assignments in the NetWare v2.15 versions of SYSCON and FILER. (In previous versions, you must manually select all rights.) For those few programs that must write to the executable files, users will also need Write privileges.

In a directory where shared data files are stored, users need at least Read, Open, Search, Write, Create, and Delete rights. Assign Parental and Modify rights only if there is a real need for users to grant other users rights to the directories and subdirectories, or to change the directory and file attributes.

Keep in mind, as you mete out trustee assignments, that every five user trustee assignments takes up one directory entry in the volume's directory entry table. A maximum number of directory entries is set at installation for each volume, although this number can be increased if absolutely necessary. Again, since directory entry tables are stored in file server RAM, increasing the size of the table eats into the memory available for other network operations. It is much preferable to assign group trustees, because they count as only one trustee assignment regardless of the number of members in the group.

TIPS FOR INSTALLING NETWARE-AWARE APPLICATIONS

With the big picture now clearly drawn, here are some suggestions for installing applications designed to run on a LAN. Getting straightforward NetWare-aware programs to run on the network is usually not difficult. Thousands of NetWare-compatible applications programs are on the market. Some are easier to install correctly than others, but if you plan ahead and follow the instructions, you will have no major difficulties. As more and more complex applications arrive on the scene (particularly client/server and distributed applications), you will need more skill to install them.

Test New Applications Rigorously

Before you initiate a new application on the network, make sure it works with your particular arrangement of server hardware, network interface cards, printers, and workstations. Making printers work correctly is particularly troublesome. As a last resort, issue a CAPTURE command to redirect the output of either LPT1 or LPT2 to the file server, then set up the application to print to the LPT port you have CAPTUREd. Be prepared to change the directory structure, access rights, login scripts, user groups, batch files, and search paths if necessary.

Bring Up Applications One at a Time

You should bring up applications on the LAN one at a time, starting with the easiest programs. It's a mistake to give novice users immediate access to the full range of network applications. Before you can get them adequately trained, some users will start exploring new applications on their own. These adventurous users will either fail miserably, concluding that the skills needed are beyond their capabilities, or they will run into problems and demand your immediate help. Once the easy applications are installed and running smoothly, install the more complex ones, such as groupware programs and server-based data managers.

Restrict Use of Complex Applications

If an application is complex or specialized, restrict its use to a few knowledgeable users. For instance, not every user should have access to desktop publishing software. Users may assume that since they can access the program, they are supposed to be able to run it. Such a tacit demand can be intimidating, especially for novice users, and they will desire training on the subject. This training isn't always a good idea: It takes less time and money to confine novices to word processing and have them forward their files to a desktop publishing specialist for special publishing skills.

TIPS FOR INSTALLING NON-NETWORK APPLICATIONS

For almost all commercial single-user software packages, the license agreement expressly forbids the use of the software on more than one personal computer. Even loading the licensed copy on the file server and running it on only one workstation on the LAN can be construed as a violation of the license agreement. More than one user simultaneously using the single copy on the file server is unquestionably *illegal*. Don't do it. Get a network version of the software, or contact the vendor and work something out.

In the case of non-commercial software programs (ones written in-house, for example) that are not network-aware, there are quite a few traps to watch out for to run them on a LAN. The biggest danger is that there is no built-in protection for multiple users accessing the same data file at the same time. If two users are working in the same database, for instance, the first user could change a record and save it, only to have the second person who made different changes to the record save it and write over the first user's changes. Also, these programs may have user-specific configuration or setup files that reflect a single user's preferences for screen colors, printer ports, monitor type, and other hardware. If allowances are not made on the LAN, each user who accesses the application will write over the previous user's preferences.

With the exception of these two areas, most software that will run on standalone IBM-compatible personal computers will work on a NetWare LAN. Here are some suggestions for installing the software on the network in a way that works around its single-user idiosyncrasies.

Controlling Multiple User Access to Files

Single-user applications use several different methods of opening and closing data files. Most likely, the program uses at least some crude form of file locking that holds the file open from the time it is read into memory until the time it is saved. If another user tries to access the data file during this time, the user will be denied access. Some, like standalone versions of spreadsheet programs, hold a worksheet file open only when it is actually being written to or read from disk. The rest of the time, other users are free to open the file and access the same worksheet on their workstations. Other applications hold data files open the entire time a user is working on them, not closing the files, even after they are saved, until the user exits the program altogether.

One way to control access to users' data files is to make sure users keep their own data files in their personal directories. Since no other network users have rights in a user's home directory, the user can work on private data free from impingement by other users. This approach, however, defeats the fundamental purpose of a LAN: sharing data between users. But it is a workable solution for spreadsheet and word processing applications where users seldom need to be in the same file at the same time.

Another solution is to use a software metering program to grant only one user at a time access to the application. This even more completely defeats the purpose of a LAN, as it reduces the network to serving as a large disk storage repository for a single user. However, until you can convince your in-house programmers to convert the program to a LAN version, you must run with what you've got. LANSMITH offers a Net-Aware utility that can help in making single-user applications into networkable programs (see Appendix C for availability information).

Handling Hardware-Specific Configuration Files

For programs which use configuration files to store information about the type of monitors, pointing devices (mice), or printer configurations, you can install the application several times on the file server and use DOS environment variables to allow a workstation to find its particular version of the program.

Some applications allow you to give the configuration files any names you choose. For example, Lotus 1-2-3 lets you have a HERC.SET file for a Hercules graphics adapter, a VGA.SET file for a VGA adapter/monitor, and so on. For other programs, like Microsoft Windows, the configuration file must always have the same name (WIN.INI, for example).

Let's look at the multiple-name case first. You would have to install the application several times in the same directory, each time specifying a different set of options that represents one of the possible hardware combinations on the users' workstations. Then you would name the configuration file so that you can identify it later, and repeat the installation routine using a different set of options. When you are finished, you'll have a number of differently-named configuration files in the same directory as the program files.

Suppose your single-user program requires you to specify the desired configuration file as part of the program's startup command (for example, TEST VGA or TEST EGA). In the AUTOEXEC.BAT file on each workstation's boot diskette, include a line such as **SET MONITOR=VGA** to identify the hardware configuration. Then, in the batch file for the menu option that starts the program, use the %MONITOR% variable identifier. DOS will substitute the appropriate value for %MONITOR% in the command. In our example, the TEST %MONITOR% command in the batch file would be interpreted as TEST VGA when the batch file was run from the workstation.

To handle programs such as Windows that have a fixed configuration file name, create subdirectories for each configuration under the primary application directory. As you create each different configuration file, copy it to the appropriate subdirectory. You'll have to provide two search drive mappings: one for the configuration subdirectory and one for the application itself. Make sure the drive mappings appear in that order in the login script so that the correct configuration file will be loaded before the application files. Again, you can use an environmental variable to identify the workstation configuration.

For example, suppose our TEST program was installed in SYS:APPS/ TEST and the configuration files were installed in subdirectories identified by the physical station number (node address) of the various workstations. This allows us to use NetWare's P_STATION variable identifier in the system login script. So, the configuration file for the workstation with node address 5B (in hexadecimal notation) would be stored in SYS:APPS/TEST/5B. The system login script would then contain the following lines:

```
IF P_STATION="000000005B" THEN MAP S3:=SYS:APPS/TEST/"P_STATION"
MAP S4:=SYS:APPS/TEST
```

When a user logs in at the workstation with node address 5B, the search drive mappings will be correctly set up to run TEST on that workstation hardware.

Of course, you'll need an IF...THEN line for each node address on the network to make the system login script work for all users. In this case, it might be wise to save all of these IF...THEN commands in a separate DOS text file in the SYS:PUBLIC directory. Access the text file from the system login script via the INCLUDE login script command. (See Chapter 9 for details.)

It's a good practice to set the configuration variables by workstation rather than by user name. That way, a user can run the same program from a different workstation on the network and the program will use the configuration for that workstation. The application might lock up or behave erratically if it tries to use the wrong configuration file.

USING GROUPS TO SECURE APPLICATIONS

Using groups to control rights is much easier than giving individual rights to directories and applications. Through groups you can control access to an application and keep your site within the vendor's license agreement. You also minimize your network maintenance workload.

Let's look at how this can be done at the hypothetical company named Stats, Inc., that wants to run three applications: WordPerfect 5.1, Microsoft Excel, and What's Best!, a statistic analysis program.

Before networking the PCs, Stats had three copies of the What's Best program and four copies of single-user Excel. They have purchased a network version of WordPerfect, including manuals for each user. According to the license agreements, everyone on the network can use WordPerfect; however, only those who purchased What's Best! can use that application. Excel's license states that it can be used by a single user on a standalone computer or by a single person on a personal computer network. For two or more users, a company must buy a manual pack (at about three-quarters of the single-user cost) for each additional user. Since Stats already has four copies of Excel, they have chosen not to buy the add-on pack. As a result, only four people can use the spreadsheet program at a time. However, seven users need to access the company's spreadsheets from time to time.

Through groups (and a software metering utility for the Excel situation), controlling application access at this installation is simple. The first thing to do is to create the directory structure and security so that the applications are copy protected. Stats' file server has a directory called APPS under the SYS volume. No one has rights in SYS:APPS. It's just a convenient directory for grouping all applications together in the directory structure. Under the APPS directory are the

WORDPERF, EXCEL, and BEST directories. After installing the programs in their respective directories, the network supervisor flags all the program files "Shareable/ Read-Only." Then, to prevent users from copying the application files, he flags all the .COM and .EXE files "Execute-Only" (except WP.EXE, which won't work as an "Execute-Only" file). Figure 5-3 illustrates this directory structure.

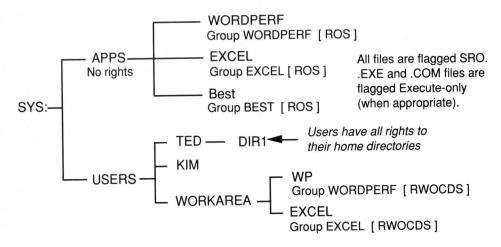

Figure 5-3: The directory structure and security set up for the hypothetical company Stats, Inc.

With the application directories created and applications properly flagged, Stats creates the following groups in SYSCON: WORDPERF, BEST, and EXCEL.

Since everyone at Stats will be using WordPerfect, all users are made members of the WORDPERF group. The group is then assigned Read, Open, and Search rights to the SYS:APPS/WORDPERF directory. The supervisor could have used the group EVERYONE instead of creating another group with all users as members; the problem with this approach, however, is that user GUEST will also have access to WordPerfect, probably forbidden by the license agreement.

Only those users with copies of the original What's Best software are made members of the BEST group. This group is assigned Read, Open, and Search rights in SYS:APPS/BEST.

Stats makes all seven spreadsheet users members of the EXCEL group and gives the group rights to the EXCEL directory. To remain within the four-user license agreement, they obtain a software metering program that limits the number of active sessions of an application—in this case, to four simultaneous users. If a fifth user tries to start up Excel, that user will be denied access. Examples of software metering products are Integrity Software's SiteLock or Connect Computer's Turnstyle.

For the shared spreadsheets and word processing data files, Stats set up a workgroup directory in addition to each user's personal directories. The supervisor adds a group trustee assignment giving Read, Write, Open, Create, Delete, and Search rights to the appropriate shared data directory so that all users in a group can create and store files that must be shared within that group.

With the directories and groups in place, the only task remaining is to go into the system login script (via SYSCON) and map drives according to group membership. For example, to map the drives necessary for Excel users, the network supervisor includes the following lines:

```
if member of "EXCEL" then begin
   map ins s4:=sys:apps\excel
   map g:=sys:users\work_area
end
```

This series of commands maps a search drive to the application directory and a regular network drive to the work area for easy file sharing within that group.

When the supervisor designates groups to specific search drives, users who are a part of that group won't have to set up their own search drives. When a new employee is hired, all the supervisor has to do is to add the new user to the appropriate group. When that user logs in, he or she will automatically receive the necessary mappings and rights to use the application.

With the group structure in place, users at Stats will have access to only those directories and applications they need to do their jobs. When a user no longer needs access to a particular application, the supervisor simply drops him or her out of the group that accesses that application.

6 Understanding NetWare Security

NetWare provides security management at four basic levels: the login/password level, the user (trustee) level, the directory level, and the file level. Think of these as four "doors" through which a user must pass to get to the ultimate goal—the valuable data contained in files on the network. If the user lacks the proper keys at any one of the four doors, he or she is effectively barred from the data. With a little knowledge and planning, you can combine all four levels of security to keep your network data safe from unauthorized access.

This chapter explains the basics of login and password security, the eight access rights in NetWare 286 and how they are used in various combinations to form trustee and directory level security, and how attributes or "flags" figure in to the mix at both the directory and file level. We'll also talk about plugging up potential security holes with the SECURITY utility. Lastly, we'll give some general tips for preventing unauthorized access to the network.

LOGIN AND PASSWORD SECURITY

Login and password security are often lumped together because they are so closely connected. These two forms of security provide the first line of defense in securing the file server. In order to log in to a NetWare file server, a person must correctly enter a valid user name (unique to each user on the network), followed by the correct password for that user account. If the person enters either one or both of these items incorrectly, he or she is denied access to the file server.

Login security, then, determines how secure this login process is. Password security is actually a subset of login security, since it affects how secure the password part of the login process is. In SYSCON, the implementation of login security is divided among three "User Information" options:

- "Account Restrictions" (which includes password restrictions)
- "Time Restrictions" (which determines when a user can log in)
- "Station Restrictions" (which limits a user to logging in only at specific workstations)

Most of these restrictions can also be set in the MAKEUSER and USERDEF utilities when you need to create users in bulk. The discussion in this chapter is oriented towards how the restrictions are presented in SYSCON, but the same principles apply to the other user-creation utilities as well.

Account Restrictions

SYSCON provides several login-related restrictions that can be placed on a user's account. These restrictions are accessed via the "User Information" sub-menu that appears after you select a user account.

Account Disable. For one, NetWare allows you to disable a user account. This ability to temporarily invalidate an account without deleting it altogether is useful when you have ascertained that an intruder has been trying to log in using that account.

Expiration Date. You can also set an expiration date on any user account. Academic networks use this feature to render user accounts invalid after the end of a term or semester.

Limit Concurrent Connections. To keep users from logging in all over the network and taking up file server connections unnecessarily, you can limit the number of concurrent logins a given user can perform. If you set the maximum number of connections to one, the user can log in on only one workstation at a time.

Password Restrictions

Passwords are a critical component of the overall NetWare security system. To preserve the confidentiality of passwords, NetWare does not allow them to appear on the screen, either when a user is logging in or when the user changes the password in SYSCON or SETPASS. Not even the network supervisor can see users' passwords, although you can change them if necessary. In addition, you have several other options to increase the effectiveness of passwords.

Requiring Passwords. You can either require users to have passwords or not. Requiring passwords is recommended for any network where security is a concern at all. For maximum security, every user account (including GUEST) should be required to have a password.

Minimum Password Length. You can define the minimum length of passwords as well. Passwords should be short enough to remember, yet unusual and difficult to guess. To be secure, passwords should be at least five or six characters long. Allowing passwords shorter than five characters increases the chances of someone "cracking" a password and illegally entering the network.

Allowing Users to Change Passwords. Another option allows users to change their passwords. Most network supervisors do allow users to select and change their own passwords because it is more user-friendly than assigning preset passwords that users cannot change. Assigned passwords often have no meaning to users and are bothersome to remember, especially if changed frequently. Users often resort to writing down frequently changed, hard-to-remember passwords and posting them near their workstations—thus defeating the whole purpose of a password.

In some cases, certain users should not be able to change their passwords. For example, when temporary employees need limited access to the network's applications and you don't want to deal with assigning and reassigning permanent names and passwords for them, you can set up an account named TEMP with the proper access to the needed applications. Users of these types of accounts shouldn't ever need to change the password.

Requiring Periodic Password Changes. You can also have passwords expire after a certain period of time. When a user's password expires, the user receives a message during the next login attempt indicating that the password has expired. Users don't have to change their expired passwords on the spot. They can go ahead and log in with the old password—as long as you have allowed a certain number of "grace" logins (explained below). If a user exceeds the maximum number of grace logins without changing his or her password, the user will be locked out of the system until you clear the user's account.

The length of time between forced password changes depends on the type of business or work your organization is engaged in. Typically, network users should change their passwords every 30 to 60 days. However, in environments (such as banking and government work) where data is extremely sensitive, passwords should be changed more frequently.

Unique Passwords. You can also require users to come up with a new, unique password every time their old one expires. Users are sometimes tempted to alternate between the same two or three passwords so they can remember them more easily, but this practice compromises password security. NetWare tracks up to eight previous passwords for each user, as long as the user keeps each new password for at least one day. A user who is aware of this could circumvent the unique password requirement by changing his or her password eight times in a single day, then reusing the original password that expired that day.

"Grace" Logins. Whenever you require passwords to be changed periodically, you can set the number of times a user can log in with the expired password before changing it. The default is six times. You can allow an unlimited number of grace logins, but this defeats the whole purpose of forcing password changes.

Password Expiration Date. Another option you have is to invalidate passwords on a specific date. For example, if you know an employee is leaving, you can set the password to expire on the employee's last work day.

Time and Station Restrictions

With time restrictions, you can limit the hours of the day when users can access the network—for example, from 7 a.m. to 6 p.m. Users can log in only during these hours. You can also prevent users from logging in on certain days of the week. For instance, if you don't want anyone using the network over the weekend, you can restrict logins on Saturday and Sunday. One good use for time restrictions is to make sure no users log in during time reserved for performing system backups.

Station restrictions allow a user to log in only from a specific workstation on the network. If you set a station restriction on a user, NetWare checks the network and node address of the workstation the user is trying to log in from. If the addresses don't match those specified in the station restriction, the user won't be allowed to complete the login process.

Setting System-Wide Login Restrictions

SYSCON also allows certain of these login restrictions to be set up so they apply universally across the network. The "Default Account Balance/Restrictions" window under "Supervisor Options" in SYSCON allows you to:

- Set a common expiration date for all accounts
- Set system-wide minimum password length
- Force periodic changes on all user passwords
- Establish the number of days between these forced password changes, the number of grace logins, and the unique password requirement

Likewise, you can use the "Default Time Restrictions" option to set login time restrictions that will apply to everyone on the network.

THE EIGHT ACCESS RIGHTS IN NETWARE 286

Once users make it past the first door and get on the network, security at the user and directory level comes into play. Both user-level security and directory-level security rely on various combinations of NetWare 286's eight rights: Read, Write, Open, Create, Delete, Parental, Search, and Modify. These rights affect what users can do with an application or data file residing on a NetWare 286 file server.

Rights in NetWare v2.15

The basic meaning of the eight rights is explained below. After this brief listing, we'll get into some of the nitty-gritty technicalities of how the rights interrelate and depend on each other.

Note that the functions allowed by the Create, Delete, Parental, and Modify rights changed slightly between NetWare 286 v2.12 and v2.15. The explanation below applies to *all* v2.15 versions of NetWare. For information about rights for previous versions, see "Rights: The Way They Used to Be" later in this chapter.

Read. The Read right allows a user to read files in a directory. "Read" in this context means to view the contents of a text file, to see single or multiple records in a database file, or to be able to run the commands in an executable file.

Write. The Write right allows a user to change the contents of files in a directory. That could mean adding, moving, modifying, or deleting portions of a text file, recording new or modified records in a database file, or writing configuration information back to an executable file.

Open. The Open right, true to its name, allows a user to open (not necessarily read from or write to) an existing file in a directory.

Create. The Create right allows a user to create new files or subdirectories in a directory.

Delete. The Delete right allows a user to delete existing files or subdirectories in a directory.

Parental. This right's functions are not as obvious from its name. The purpose of the Parental right is twofold: it allows users to change their own access rights to the directory and its subdirectories, and it allows users to control other users' access to the directory and its subdirectories either through altering the Maximum Rights Mask or through explicit trustee assignments.

Search. The name "Search" is a bit misleading, mainly because in other computer applications, searching usually implies looking for some kind of match. However, in NetWare, the Search right is required in order for users to "see" what files are in a directory. Without the Search right in a directory, a user who invokes a directory listing command (such as the DOS DIR command or NetWare's NDIR command) will see "No files found," even if the directory is full of files.

Modify. The Modify right, again, has a slightly misleading name. This right allows a user to modify, not the file contents, but just about anything else associated with the file: its name, its attributes, and extended information such as the last accessed date and time—provided, of course, that the file is flagged with the Read-Write attribute (more about file attributes later).

Looking More Closely at the Eight Rights

At first glance, the eight rights seem simple enough to understand. However, no single right really does very much by itself. It is only when you combine the access rights in various ways that any real work can be done in a given directory. Let's go through the rights again to get a better feel for how they act in combination.

Interplay between Read, Write, Open, and Search. Both DOS and NetWare require a file to be *opened* before you can read from it or write to it. The only prerequisite for opening a file is that the file must exist before it can be opened.

So, in NetWare 286, the Open right is *always* required in conjunction with either Read or Write. If you give a user the Read right in a directory without the Open right, the user won't be able to actually read anything because the files have to be opened first. Same goes for Write—users can't write to files unless they have both Write and Open rights. Furthermore, an application must be able to find a file before it can open it and read or write in it. Therefore, to read files in a directory, you actually need Read, Open, and Search rights; to write to files, you must have Write, Open, and Search rights in the directory.

Rights work a little differently when you are creating a *new* file. New files are automatically opened when they are created. The Open and Search rights are not required in this case.

More about Create and Write. The Create right by itself does not allow a user to do anything further with the newly created file. In order to add some contents to the file (write to it), the user needs the Write privilege as well.

If the user has only Create and Write privileges, with no Open or Read rights, the user can create a file, place data in it, and close it. Once the new file is closed, the user cannot reopen the file, and therefore cannot read or change the data. This is the principle behind a "drop box" directory in which all users with Create and Write rights can deposit a file (typically a mail message) in the directory, but only a user with Open and Read rights in addition to Write and Create can read the messages.

The Parental and Modify Rights. Users need both of these rights to rename a directory and alter the extended information (such as the creation date and time) for any of the subdirectories.

Some applications need to update a file's attributes after reading from or writing to the file. These types of applications will not function properly unless the user has the Modify right in the file's directory.

A Strange Thing about Delete. DOS workstation users need the Delete right to copy a file to a directory where a file of the same name already exists. This is because before you can put the new file in, you have to get rid of the old one. The Macintosh OS does not require Delete privileges to overwrite a file with a file of the same name.

Rights: The Way They Used to Be

Prior to v2.15, NetWare's Create, Delete, Modify, and Parental rights behaved a little differently. The Create and Delete rights applied mainly to files, not subdirectories. To create and delete subdirectories in a directory, a user needed the Parental right in addition to Create and Delete rights.

The Modify right allowed users to modify file attributes and rename files. To rename subdirectories, however, a user had to have both Parental and Modify rights.

Rights Needed to Perform Tasks in a Directory

The chart in Figure 6-1 lists the possible tasks or capabilities a user can have concerning files in a directory, the directory itself, and subdirectories of the directory. The rights required (both in NetWare v2.15 and prior versions) to perform each task are also shown. Italics highlight the differences between versions.

Task/Capability	————Rights Required————	
	v2.12 and below	**v2.15**
List files	Search	Search
Read files	Read+Open	Read+Open
Write to files*	Read+Write+Open	Read+Write+Open
Create files	Create	Create
Delete files	Delete	Delete
Rename files*	Modify	Modify
Modify file attributes	Modify	Modify
Rename directory	Modify	Modify
Assign trustee rights in directory	Parental	Parental
Modify Maximum Rights Mask of directory	Parental	Parental
Alter extended info of the directory	Supervisor**	Supervisor**
Set directory attributes	*N/A*	*Modify*
Create subdirectories	*Parental+Create*	*Create*
Delete subdirectories	*Parental+Delete*	*Delete*
Rename subdirectories	*Parental+Modify*	*Modify*
Assign trustee rights in subdirectories	Parental	Parental
Modify Maximum Rights Mask of subdirectories	Parental	Parental
Alter extended info of subdirectories	Parental+Modify	Parental+Modify

*Files must be flagged Read-Write
**Only the supervisor can do this

Figure 6-1: The rights needed to perform various tasks in NetWare directories.

USER-LEVEL SECURITY

At the user level, you provide access to a directory by assigning users a combination of the eight rights to that directory. These are called trustee rights, because you are in essence making the user a trustee over the files in the directory. What users can actually do with those files depends (in part) on what rights you grant them.

You can assign trustee rights using either SYSCON, FILER, or GRANT. SYSCON and FILER are menu-driven utilities, while GRANT is a command-line utility. GRANT provides a "quick and dirty" method for granting trustee rights. SYSCON and FILER give a clearer picture of what you're doing, because they can show you what rights the users already have.

Assigning Trustee Rights

You can assign trustee rights in a directory to a user or a group. When deciding what rights to give a user or group, consider what kind of files the directory contains and what actions the user or group needs to perform on the files. In a directory containing only executable program files, users need only Read, Open, and Search rights. In a directory containing data files, users need at least Read, Write, Open, Create, and Search rights.

When you have programs and files on your network that are intended for use by a subset of all users, you can limit access to those programs and files by using group trustee assignments. For example, only the members of the Payroll department should have access to on-line employee payroll records. You can define a group called PAYROLL and make only the payroll clerks members of the group. Then, instead of assigning rights to the payroll records individually to each clerk, you can simply give a trustee assignment to the group PAYROLL in the appropriate directories.

The Trickle Effect. To assign trustee rights effectively, you need to understand this basic concept:

Trustee rights flow down to any subdirectories of the directory in which you originally assigned the rights, until they are redefined at a lower level.

To illustrate, consider the directory structure shown in Figure 6-2.

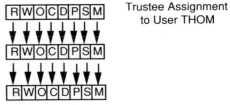

SYS: USERS/THOM

SYS: USERS/THOM/WORK

SYS: USERS/THOM/WORK/OCT90

Trustee Assignment to User THOM

Figure 6-2: Due to the trickle effect, trustee rights assignments made in one directory also apply to any subdirectories.

Suppose you assigned user Thom all rights in SYS:USERS/THOM (his "home" directory). Because trustee rights assignments trickle down to subdirectories, Thom would also have all rights to SYS:USERS/THOM/WORK, SYS:USERS/THOM/JUNK, and any other subdirectories down that branch of the directory tree. In most cases, that is the desired effect. As in the example of a user's home directory, you wouldn't want to have to reassign rights at every subdirectory. That would use up a lot of trustee rights assignments in a hurry, and every five trustee rights assignments take up one directory entry in the server's directory entry table.

In some cases, you won't want a users rights at one directory level to flow down to all subdirectories. For example, consider the directory structure shown in Figure 6-3.

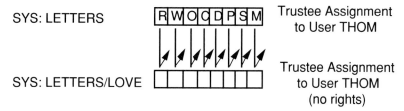

SYS: LETTERS

SYS: LETTERS/LOVE

Trustee Assignment
to User THOM

Trustee Assignment
to User THOM
(no rights)

Figure 6-3: To stop the trickle effect, you must reassign trustee rights at a lower directory level.

Suppose you also assigned Thom all rights to SYS:LETTERS. The LETTERS directory contains a subdirectory named LOVE. To keep Thom from accessing the delicate data stored in SYS:LETTERS/LOVE, you would have to reassign his trustee rights at the SYS:LETTERS/LOVE level. In this case, you would probably want to reassign him with no rights, which in essence cancels the trickle effect.

By changing the trustee rights assigned in a given subdirectory, you can revoke some or all of a user's rights to that subdirectory. The user retains the rights assigned in the parent directory.

How User and Group Rights Interact. At first, being able to grant trustee rights to both users and groups seems fairly straightforward. However, when a user has rights to a directory and is also a member of a group that has a trustee assignment in that directory, things can get confusing. NetWare keeps track of user and group rights separately, but adds the two together when a user has both individual rights and rights as a member of a group.

To clarify, suppose Thom is a member of the group WRITERS. This group is assigned Read, Write, Open, Create, and Search rights in SYS:LETTERS. This allows all writers to work with the letter files in that directory, but not delete any of them. User Thom, however, has all rights (including Delete) as a result of his user trustee assignment in SYS:LETTERS. Consequently, he *will* be able to delete files in the LETTERS directory.

Now throw in the trickle effect. Remember that we didn't want Thom to be able to access the data in SYS:LETTERS/LOVE, so in that subdirectory we gave him a "no rights" trustee assignment. But Thom is also a member of WRITERS, and that group's trustee assignment (RWOCS) in SYS:LETTERS trickles down to SYS:LETTERS/LOVE. As a result, even though as a user Thom has no rights in LOVE, by virtue of his membership in WRITERS he can exercise Read, Write, Open, Create, and Search rights. Figure 6-4 illustrates this complex scenario.

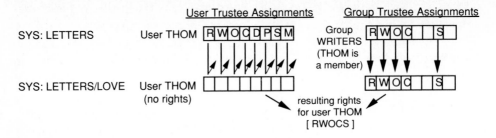

Figure 6-4: When determining what rights a user can exercise in a directory, NetWare considers both the user's individual trustee rights assignment and the rights the user has as a member of a group.

Guidelines for Assigning Trustee Rights. To help you keep trustee assignments to users and groups straight and avoid situations like the one just described, observe the following guidelines when you assign trustee rights.

Never grant trustee rights at the NetWare volume (root) level. Because of the trickle effect, every directory and subdirectory in the entire volume would inherit those rights assignments. Granting rights at the root makes it impossible to devise secure access schemes like the earlier Payroll department example.

Inexperienced network supervisors often grant rights at the root level because they feel it's too hard to figure out security on a directory by directory basis. Assigning rights at the root is especially dangerous on the SYS volume of a NetWare file server because most supervisor-only utilities and files reside in SYS:SYSTEM. All users require access to the SYS:PUBLIC directory, but few users, if any, should have access to the SYS:SYSTEM directory. Appropriate access to the PUBLIC directory is provided for at installation when the group EVERYONE is created and given Read, Open, and Search rights to SYS:PUBLIC.

Granting rights at the root of the SYS volume can be a greater breach of security than you might suspect. For example, all the mail directories reside on the SYS volume. When you grant rights at the root, users then have sufficient rights to go browsing in other users' mail directories and read each other's mail. If you revoked rights at the root level for all users to put a stop to all this snooping, no one would be able to do any work. Also, most applications are installed somewhere on SYS, and you will have just revoked their rights to those applications. Without sufficient rights, users get a "Bad command or file name" error message whenever they try to run an application.

The best policy is to grant trustee rights to each user one directory at a time, according to that user's needs. You should grant rights for each user at the lowest level of the directory tree that will allow that user access to the programs and data files he or she needs. At the same time, you should be careful not to grant a user rights to a directory in which he or she doesn't need rights.

Better yet, assign most of the access to applications and shared data directories through groups. Leave individual user trustee assignments for home directories and other non-shared data areas.

Security Equivalences

One last thing needs to be mentioned about user-level security. NetWare allows you to make two users "security equivalent" to each other. For example, if user Frankie was made security equivalent to user Johnny, Frankie would be able to exercise whatever rights Johnny had (either through individual or group trustee assignments), and vice versa.

While security equivalences seem useful enough, in practice they are seldom used except to give one user temporary access to the applications and data normally used by another user. Since users often keep personal data in their home directories, be careful when you assign security equivalences between two users. Nothing can prevent one from snooping into the private affairs of the other as long as they have equivalent rights.

Note, however, that when you make a user a member of a group, NetWare assigns the user a security equivalence to the group. If you look at a user's security equivalences in SYSCON, you will see the list of groups that user is a member of.

It is generally not a good practice to create "backup" supervisors by making a regular user security equivalent to the user SUPERVISOR. The only user account on the file server that should be security equivalent to SUPERVISOR is the officially designated network supervisor. If you are going to be gone, you should entrust the password for the SUPERVISOR account to a reliable user. Be sure to change the SUPERVISOR password as soon as you get back.

DIRECTORY-LEVEL SECURITY

At the directory level, you can establish a restriction on which of NetWare's eight rights any user can exercise in a given directory. This is accomplished through manipulating the directory's Maximum Rights Mask. In addition, you can assign certain attributes to a directory that further restricts access.

The Maximum Rights Mask

Every directory created on a NetWare file server has a *Maximum Rights Mask*. This directory mask limits what rights can be exercised within that directory. The Maximum Rights Mask supersedes any trustee rights assigned at the user level and applies to all users except the supervisor. By default, the rights mask allows all trustee rights to be exercised in the directory. You can change a directory's Maximum Rights Mask using FILER.

You will seldom have to bother with Maximum Rights Masks. They should be changed only in rare circumstances when you are sure that you don't want any user except SUPERVISOR to be able to exercise a given right in a directory. Note that the trickle effect does *not* apply to Maximum Rights Masks. The restrictions effected by removing rights from a directory's Maximum Rights Mask apply only in that directory. They do not flow down to subdirectories.

When you delete one or more rights from a directory's Maximum Rights Mask, you are essentially preventing any user from exercising those rights in that directory, even if they have been given the rights through a user or group trustee assignment. For example, if you removed the Parental right from a directory's Maximum Rights Mask, that would prevent any user (except SUPERVISOR) from assigning trustee and directory rights in that directory or its subdirectories.

Determining a User's Effective Rights

In NetWare, the rights that a user can actually exercise in a directory are called *effective rights*. You can determine a user's effective rights as follows:

- Write down the rights a user has from an individual trustee assignment. If the user has no trustee assignment in that directory, look at the directories above that one to see if any have trickled down from a higher level assignment.
- Add any rights the user has from a group trustee assignment. Remember to consider the trickle effect here too.
- Add any rights the user may have as a result of a security equivalence with another user.
- Cross out any rights that are not listed in the directory's Maximum Rights Mask.
- What you have left are the user's effective rights in the directory.

An easier way for users to check their effective rights in a directory is through FILER. When a user chooses the "Current Directory Information" option from FILER's main menu, a submenu appears containing the "Current Effective Rights" option. Selecting that option will display the user's effective rights in the directory indicated at the top of the screen.

An even quicker way to check a user's effective rights from the command line is to type **RIGHTS** at the DOS prompt. This utility will display which rights the user can exercise in the current directory. You can add a directory path specification to the command to see a user's effective rights in any directory on the file server. For example, typing **RIGHTS SYS:LETTERS** at a user's workstation will display that user's effective rights in the SYS:LETTERS directory.

Directory Attributes

Starting in NetWare v2.15, you can assign various flags or attributes to a directory. These *directory attributes* include Normal, Private, Hidden, and System. While these attributes were implemented primarily to support Macintosh workstations, they are a great boon to PC users as well. For example, if users have directories containing sensitive material, they can assign Hidden or Private flags to them using the FLAGDIR utility. NetWare's directory attributes are explained briefly below.

Normal. This is the default directory attribute, indicating that no attributes have been set. It corresponds to the public folder in the Macintosh world.

Private. Corresponding to a grayed-out folder on the Macintosh, the "Private" directory attribute prevents users from seeing the contents of a directory (its files or subdirectories) unless they have the Search right in that directory. The directory name will still appear in a DOS DIR listing. Users who know the correct path can access subdirectories even though they are not listed.

Hidden. The "Hidden" directory attribute prevents a directory from showing up in the directory listing. Again, users who know the directory is there can access it.

System. This directory attribute should only be used to flag a directory used for the system to function. A directory flagged "System" will not appear in a directory listing.

FILE LEVEL SECURITY

The fact that users have all eight rights in a given directory doesn't necessarily mean that they can do whatever they want to the files in that directory. File attributes security forms another variable in the user access rights formula. Security enforced by file attributes applies even to the supervisor. That is, even though the supervisor has all rights in all directories, he or she cannot write to a file that is flagged for reading only.

Security-Related File Attributes

You can assign the following attributes to protect files on a NetWare server: "Read-Only," "Read-Write," and "Shareable." The "Nonshareable" attribute is in effect by default whenever a file is *not* flagged "Shareable." You can manipulate these file attributes with either the FLAG or the FILER utilities.

Read-Only. The "Read-Only" file attribute prevents users from writing to the file, renaming it, or deleting it regardless of whether they have Write, Modify, or Delete rights in the directory. However, a user with Modify rights (or the network supervisor) can change the file attribute to "Read-Write" and then write to, rename, or delete the file.

Most executable files and other files that are never to be written to should be flagged "Read-Only." If you ever need to delete these files, you'll have to flag them "Read-Write" first.

Read-Write. This file attribute allows users to change the contents of (write to) the file. It also allows them to rename the file.

All data files and other files that must be written to should be flagged "Read-Write." Files that are newly created or copied onto the file server are flagged "Nonshareable/Read-Write" (NRW) by default.

Shareable. Files that aren't flagged "Shareable" only work properly for one user. For example, suppose you flagged an often-used data file as "Nonshareable." The next time several users try to access this file simultaneously, each of their workstations will lock up except for the first user's workstation. You should always flag data files that will be used by more than one individual at once as "Shareable/Read-Write" (SRO). By the same token, flag all utilities and program file "Shareable/Read-Only" (SRO).

Other NetWare File Attributes

The FLAG command manipulates only the file attributes mentioned above. In FILER, however, you can assign other file attributes: "Hidden," "System," "Indexed," "Transactional," and "Execute-Only." Another attribute, "Modified Since

Last Backup," can be manipulated in FILER as well. Since this chapter is on security, we'll explain the "Execute-Only" attribute here and save the rest of these attributes for Chapter 7.

The *Execute-Only* file attribute can only be assigned to executable files (those having .EXE or .COM extensions) via the FILER utility. Once a file is flagged "Execute-Only," the only two things anyone (including the supervisor) can do with it are execute it and delete it. (Users would need the Delete right to delete the file, however.) The main use of the "Execute-Only" flag is to prevent users from making unauthorized copies of application program files on the server.

Be very careful when assigning the "Execute-Only" attribute: it can be risky. You should have another copy of the file on a floppy diskette somewhere, because NetWare won't allow that file to be archived. If anything happens to corrupt a file flagged "Execute-Only," you must delete the file and reinstall it from your original diskette.

CHECKING FOR POTENTIAL SECURITY HOLES

To inspect your file server for potential holes in your network security setup, you can run the SECURITY utility located in SYS:SYSTEM. This utility checks through the file server bindery and identifies any security problems it finds. The bindery is a specialized database maintained on every NetWare file server. It contains information about each object defined on the server (objects can be users, groups, or other named entities). All user and group names are stored in the bindery as objects, along with their corresponding passwords, rights, and other security information.

Running the SECURITY Utility

SECURITY is easy to run. Go to the SYS:SYSTEM directory and type **SECURITY**. Or, if you want the output placed in a file for easier reference, type **SECURITY >** *FileName*.

The following are the possible network security deficiencies that SECURITY checks for.

Objects with No Password Assigned. To be secure, you should assign passwords for all user accounts defined on the file server—especially those that don't correspond to real users. For instance, the GUEST account is created automatically (without a password) on every file server. If you don't assign a password for GUEST, anyone can log in to the server as GUEST and have access to SYSCON, FILER, and other network utilities. Through SYSCON, the person could obtain a list of all users on the file server (valuable information to potential intruders). With FILER, a person can peruse the entire directory structure. Even without Search rights, anyone can see the directory and subdirectory names (unless they are flagged "Hidden"). An intruder can deduce a lot about where information is stored just by looking at the skeletal structure of directories.

Objects with Insecure Passwords. SECURITY checks all passwords on the file server, compares them to the corresponding user names, and reports any that are the same. SECURITY also checks the account restrictions and identifies the following weaknesses:

- Users that aren't required to have passwords at least five characters long
- Users that aren't required to change their passwords at least every 60 days
- Users that have an unlimited number of grace logins after their password expires
- Users that aren't required to use unique passwords when they change passwords

Objects with Security Equivalence to SUPERVISOR. As we explained earlier, no one besides the designated supervisor should have a supervisor equivalence. Assigning additional supervisor equivalences could open the door for a knowledgeable hacker to attack without anyone ever knowing an intruder has been on the network.

Consider this method commonly used by hackers trying to break in to a network. Through various means, the hacker discovers that a user is supervisor equivalent. The hacker then replaces one of the executable files that user runs often with a counterfeit version. When the user runs the bogus program, it appears normal but is actually doing something devious like changing all users' passwords or saving them somewhere for later use by the hacker. The lesson to be learned is simple—don't assign supervisor equivalences.

Objects That Have Rights at the Volume Level. SECURITY notes any objects that have trustee rights at the NetWare volume (root) level. We have already seen how this practice essentially gives users rights in every directory on the volume, unless the rights are reassigned lower in the directory structure. Even so, if users have the Parental right at the root, they can reassign themselves rights anywhere on the volume.

Objects without a Login Script. SECURITY reports users that do not have a login script as a security hole for the following reason. User login scripts are stored in the users' mail subdirectories in SYS:MAIL. The group EVERYONE has Write and Create rights to SYS:MAIL to provide the "drop box" capability we discussed earlier. Any user can create a file in another user's mail subdirectory; they just can't reopen the file once it's in there. If a user does not have a login script, an intruder could create a login script file and dump it in that user's mail subdirectory. The next time that user logs in, all kinds of things could happen, depending on what was in the intruder's file.

Objects with Excessive Rights in Certain Directories. Users should have only Read, Open, and Search rights in SYS:LOGIN and SYS:PUBLIC, Write and Create rights in SYS:MAIL, and no rights in SYS:SYSTEM. SECURITY will report any deviation from this norm.

PREVENTING UNAUTHORIZED ACCESS

As you can see, security holes may lurk in places you'd never think to look. In addition to the recommendations made by the SECURITY utility, here are some further suggestions for preventing unauthorized access to your file server.

Using Effective Passwords

While NetWare's password restrictions and the SECURITY utility can help shape password security on the network, the most important aspect of password protection cannot be enforced by NetWare itself. Rather, it hinges on the users' willingness to create and use effective passwords. Stress to your users the importance of keeping passwords confidential. If passwords are not kept confidential or if they are easy to guess, the file server is not secure.

The most common way for an intruder to enter a network illegally is by somehow discovering a user's password. Such an intruder would have access not only to that user's personal files, but to all of the network directories and applications that user has rights to. Depending on the trustee assignments and security equivalences on the account, the entire network could be at risk. With information theft and computer viruses becoming more and more prevalent the LAN environment, you can't afford to be lax in password security.

To help in this area, here are some simple techniques for creating effective passwords that you can pass on to your network users.

A good password should be easy for a user to remember but difficult for someone else to guess. Avoid using "obvious" passwords like the names of spouses, children, and pets. Even spelling these names backwards is too easy to guess. Encourage users to break out of the word-oriented password mode. With NetWare, you can use any character on the keyboard, upper or lowercase, as part of a password, including numerals, spaces, and special keys. Here are some ideas to get the creative juices flowing.

Join unrelated words with a dash, space, or other symbol: for example, pig*carpet. If a user speaks a foreign language, words in that language might be useful as passwords. Other password ideas are the names of famous artists, writers, or sports teams.

Combine letters with numbers for good passwords. For example, users could combine a familiar name with an easy-to-remember number ("HAL2001," for instance). Using the first letters of the words in favorite phrases also makes a good password because they form no recognizable words. For instance, all piano players are familiar with "Every Good Boy Does Fine," the mnemonic device for remembering the name of lines of the treble staff. To make the password doubly secure, the user could add a number to "EGBDF," resulting in a password such as "EGBDF400."

Another method for making a password hard to guess but easy to remember is key shifting. You simply choose a phrase or word, such as "IBM-PS/2," and shift one key to the left as you type it to get "UVN-OA/1." Character replacement is another scheme in which you replace letters with digits. For example, if you replace the vowels A, E, I, O, and U with 1, 2, 3, 4, and 5, the word "security" becomes "S2C5R3TY."

Intruder Detection and Lockout

NetWare includes a rudimentary system for detecting attempted access by unauthorized users. It is based on the number of unsuccessful login attempts made from a single user account. After a person makes a certain number of login attempts using the same user account name but supplying an incorrect password, NetWare will assume that person is an intruder and disable that user account, displaying the message "Intruder detection has disabled this account" on the screen. That account will remain locked for however long you specify (15 minutes is the default).

This intruder detection feature prevents a hacker from methodically trying all the commonly-used or obvious password possibilities in the hopes of stumbling onto the correct password. The trick is to establish an appropriate threshold so that you don't lock out legitimate users who may have forgotten their exact passwords or who have trouble typing accurately. A reasonable threshold is around six or seven retries (seven is the default NetWare provides). You set up the threshold and the length of time the account remains locked through the "Intruder Detection/Lockout" option under the "Supervisor Options" in SYSCON's main menu. You should set the length of the lockout period long enough to deter hackers from waiting it out and trying again. The lockout period can be as long as 40 days, but 15 to 20 minutes should be sufficient.

If a legitimate user does manage to get locked out accidentally, go into SYSCON, choose "User Information" from the main menu, and select the user's name from the resulting list. Then unlock the account by selecting the "Intruder Lockout Status" option in the "User Information" submenu.

Suppose some misguided hacker (or even a curious employee) tries to log in repeatedly using the name SUPERVISOR. If the user manages to exceed the intruder detection threshold, NetWare will lock the SUPERVISOR account just like it would any other user account. If this happens, go to the file server console keyboard (this can't be done in FCONSOLE) and type **ENABLE LOGIN**. Since the file server should be kept under lock and key, only the supervisor should be able to get to it. ENABLE LOGIN will unlock the supervisor account, but not any locked user accounts. You must go into SYSCON to clear any other locked accounts.

Zero-Byte Login Scripts

Some users may not need an individual login script, especially if the system login script handles all the setup and drive mappings. One way around the problem of users with no login scripts is to create an empty login script. Login scripts are simple DOS text files named LOGIN (with no extension) and placed in the subdirectory under SYS:MAIL that corresponds with the user's ID number. In SYSCON, look under "Other Information" for each user to get the ID number. The ID number tells you what subdirectory of SYS:MAIL to place the empty login script text file. Go to that subdirectory and type **COPY CON LOGIN**. Press Enter, then type Ctrl-Z and press Enter again. The screen should tell you that one file has been copied. If you do a DIR command, the file "LOGIN" will appear in the subdirectory as a file containing zero bytes of data.

Securing the File Server

NetWare offers a number of commands that can be issued at the file server itself. These are called *console commands*. The ENABLE LOGIN command mentioned earlier is an example; others include MONITOR, DISK, CLEAR STATION, and DOWN. These last two are potentially dangerous commands if used improperly. Any time a user connection is severed or the file server goes down unexpectedly, data can be lost.

Novell offers a Keyboard Lock VAP that will lock the file server console keyboard to anyone who doesn't know the keyboard password. This protection is only partially effective if the server is located out in the open. No software can prevent people from turning off the computer or yanking out the power cord.

For this reason, you should keep the file server out of the reach of unauthorized hands. A locked room is the safest place for the file server. Only the supervisor should have access to the key to the server room. Keeping the file server locked up is especially critical in light of the recent publication in several books and magazines of a step-by-step method for recovering the supervisor password using DISKED. While this information was intended only for supervisors, its widespread dissemination means it could also fall into the wrong hands. Any reasonably knowledgable person could use this procedure to change the password for SUPERVISOR, then log in as SUPERVISOR and gain full access to the file server.

7 Managing Volumes, Directories, and Files

This chapter looks at the NetWare file system and at ways to manage volumes, directories, and files on the file server. We'll look at what makes an effective directory structure and show how to use various NetWare utilities to implement this structure.

THE NETWARE FILE SYSTEM

Simply put, the NetWare file system encompasses those parts of the operating system that deal with reading and writing files on network hard disks. While that may sound simple at first, a large part of what you usually think of as NetWare itself—volumes, directories, trustee assignments, rights masks, and file attributes—all fall under the domain of the file system.

Because disk reads and writes are by far the most common operation performed by a file server, NetWare was designed from the beginning to perform heavy disk I/O efficiently. That is why Novell came up with its own file system, complete with partitions, volumes, File Allocation Tables (FATs), Directory Entry Tables, and so on.

Partitions and Volumes

Most versions of NetWare 286 support the partitioning of a disk for use by more than one operating system. In addition to the NetWare partition (which is required on every NetWare disk), you can set up other partitions for use by DOS or UNIX. Although good reasons for dividing up a disk in this way are rare, it is possible to do.

NetWare can set up its volumes only in that portion of a disk designated as the NetWare partition. As far as NetWare is concerned, the rest of the disk does not exist. Likewise, the operating system controlling another partition cannot use any of the disk space in the NetWare partition.

Figure 7-1 illustrates how the major divisions of a NetWare-compatible hard disk—partitions and volumes—fit together and relate to each other.

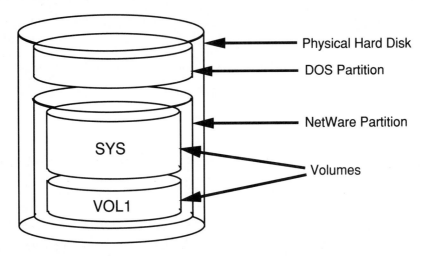

Figure 7-1: A NetWare hard disk is divided into partitions, which are further divided into volumes. A disk can have both a DOS partition and a NetWare partition.

Caveats Regarding Hard Disk Partitions. Back when a 10MB hard disk was considered a lot of storage space, DOS partitions were scarcely a consideration. DOS as an operating system could only recognize and address up to 32MB of disk space. DOS versions prior to v3.3 made no allowances for disks much larger than that. However, as 20MB, 40MB, 80MB, and larger disks became prevalent, the 32MB address ceiling became an issue. DOS v3.3 provided a solution of sorts: it could handle a disk larger than 32MB, but only if the user created a *primary DOS partition* out of the first 32MB of disk space and set up the rest as an *extended DOS partition*.

Novell, meanwhile, recognized that shared disks on a LAN would normally need to be much larger than 32MB. As a result, NetWare 286 was designed with no partition size limitation. However, there was one important stipulation: the NetWare partition had to start at the beginning of the disk, at cylinder 0.

This is all well and good—until you try to put both a primary DOS partition (using DOS v3.3) and a NetWare partition on the same disk. If the disk is larger than 32MB, DOS requires you to locate the primary DOS partition somewhere in the first 32MB of disk space. Since the NetWare partition must start at cylinder 0, you must cram both the NetWare partition and the primary DOS partition into that first 32MB. All you can do with the rest of the disk is create extended DOS partitions.

Figure 7-2 illustrates the partition limitations when combining NetWare v2.1x and DOS v3.3. (Note that the 32MB DOS partition boundary is removed in

DOS v4.0 and above. NetWare 386 eliminates the cylinder 0 starting requirement and other limits for NetWare partitions.)

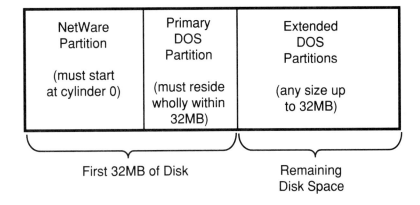

Figure 7-2: With DOS v3.3, a primary DOS partition must reside within the first 32MB of storage space. Since the NetWare partition must start at cylinder 0, both the NetWare partition and the primary DOS partition must squeeze into the first 32MB of the hard disk.

Programmers and VAP developers might need both DOS and NetWare partitions for testing purposes. For most network environments, though, the only time you might want both a DOS and a NetWare partition on the same hard disk is when you're running nondedicated NetWare and you want the workstation side of the file server to have some local hard disk storage available to it. The file server operating system (NetWare) could use only that part of the disk allocated to the NetWare partition, and the workstation operating system (DOS) could use only the space in the DOS partition. However, this arrangement has a number of drawbacks that should be enough to discourage its use.

For example, NetWare and DOS partitions don't always coexist well on the same disk. NetWare reserves about two percent of its partition space at the end of the NetWare partition for data that must be redirected to circumvent bad blocks on the disk. This space is called the Hot Fix Redirection Area. In earlier versions of NetWare, the Hot Fix feature did not always strictly observe the boundary between the end of the NetWare partition (where the redirection area is) and the start of the DOS partition. NetWare v2.15 revision C amended Hot Fix so that it doesn't spill over into the DOS partition.

The disk I/O performance of both the server side and the workstation side of a nondedicated file server suffers as well. While NetWare uses its elevator-seeking mechanism to access the disk more efficiently, whenever a disk read or write request comes from the workstation side, DOS takes over with its slower disk access mechanism. Besides interfering with each other, these differing methods of controlling disk access cause increased wear and tear on the disk's mechanical components.

Unless you have a very good reason, don't bother with any other partitions on a NetWare hard disk. Just use the whole disk for NetWare. If you must use nondedicated NetWare and want the workstation side to have local disk storage, install two disks and set up one for NetWare and one for DOS.

Limitations for NetWare Volumes. While NetWare places no restrictions on the size of a NetWare partition, it does place a limit on the size and number of NetWare volumes created within that partition. There is also a limit on the total number of volumes a file server can support. The following list summarizes the volume restrictions in NetWare 286:

Maximum number of volumes per file server	32
Maximum number of volumes per partition	16
Maximum size of a NetWare volume	255MB
Minimum size of a NetWare volume	10MB

As long as your disks are less than 255MB in size, Novell recommends that you set up only one volume per physical hard disk. Keeping track of which volumes are on which disk will be easier, especially when you are mirroring drives. You will gain no security advantages by splitting a disk into more than one volume; NetWare security is implemented at the directory level, not at the volume level.

On disks larger than 255MB, you must create more than one volume due to the 255MB limit on volume size. For example, if you had a 300MB disk, you could divide it up in one of several ways:

- One 255MB volume and one 45MB volume
- Two 150MB volumes
- Three 100MB volumes
- Sixteen 19MB volumes (roughly)

You'd probably never want 16 little volumes on a hard disk. NetWare must "mount" each volume when you boot the file server (it could take a long time to mount 16 of them), and you'd need enough memory in the server to cache the directory entry tables for all 16 volumes. Choosing among the other three options is largely a matter of looking at your file size needs. If you have a 200MB database file, for instance, you should go with a volume spread similar to option one (a 255MB volume and a 45MB volume). The database wouldn't fit in a 150MB or a 100MB volume.

Keep in mind also that NetWare 286 volumes are fixed in size and cannot extend over more than one physical hard disk. When a hard disk is first installed on a NetWare 286 file server, all of the storage capacity in the NetWare partition (usually the whole disk) must be allocated to NetWare volumes. That leaves no room for one volume to grow without encroaching on another volume's space. You can't leave extra, undefined space on the disk to draw upon in case a volume fills up. If you ever need to change the size of a volume, you must back up all data in all volumes on the disk, shuffle the volume sizes around, and restore the data to the newly rede-fined volumes. (NetWare 386 allows you to increase the size of a volume, as well as extend a volume over several physical hard disks.)

How NetWare Stores Data on a Hard Disk

On most hard disks, the smallest physical unit of storage space is the sector. These sectors, which usually hold 512 bytes of data each, are arranged in concentric tracks on the surface of each disk platter. Tracks are numbered consecutively, starting with track 0. When you put together all the tracks with the same number on each platter, you have what is called a cylinder. (See Chapter 2 for more details.)

NetWare 286 divides up physical disk storage space into logical 4,096-byte chunks called blocks. For example, a 40MB hard disk would be divided up into roughly 10,000 blocks of 4KB each. Since the sector size on most NetWare-compatible disks is 512 bytes, a block can hold 8 sectors of information (8 x 512 = 4,096).

Like DOS, NetWare stores a file in the first sectors it finds available, which may or may not be contiguous sectors on the disk. As a result, a single file may be scattered all over a hard disk in hundreds of different sectors.

To keep track of where all the pieces of a file are physically located on the disk, NetWare uses a *File Allocation Table* (FAT) system similar to the one used by DOS. The FAT is essentially a linked list of pointers that tell the operating system which disk blocks contain the pieces of a particular file. Each entry in the FAT corresponds directory to a physical block on the disk; hence, the larger the disk, the larger the FAT. As shown in Figure 7-3, the OS scans down the list of pointers to find where the requested data is located on the disk. Each link in the chain leads to the next block that contains more of the file, until the end of the file is reached.

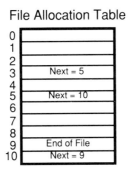

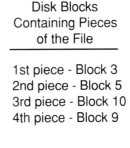

Figure 7-3: To locate all the pieces of a file, NetWare starts at the top of the FAT and reads one block at a time until the end of the file is reached.

NetWare also uses the FAT to determine where the next free locations are when writing new files to the disk.

The *Directory Entry Table* contains an entry for each directory and file on the disk. Every five trustee assignments take up a directory entry as well.

Figure 7-4 summarizes the various tables stored on each NetWare volume and shows how the storage space on the disk is divided up in NetWare 286.

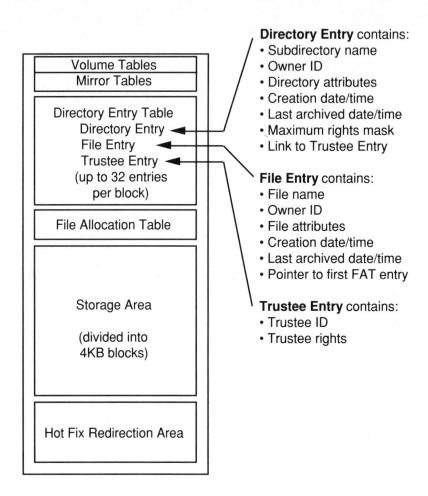

Figure 7-4: NetWare 286's file system keeps file and disk information in several tables.

MANAGING NETWARE VOLUMES

To establish new NetWare volumes or make changes to existing ones, you must use the appropriate installation utility—NETGEN or ELSGEN (INSTALL for ELS Level I). Here is a list of what you can do at the volume level with these utilities:

• Create a new volume
• Change an existing volume's parameters (name, number of directory entries, caching)
• Change the size of an existing volume

The first two tasks are fairly easy to accomplish. You must create a new volume whenever you add a new hard disk to the file server. (A new hard disk, in this instance, means one that has never been used as a NetWare hard disk before.) When users start getting error messages involving running out of file handles, it is time to increase the size of the directory entry table for the volume in question by increasing the number of directory entries for that volume.

The third task—changing a volume's size—is very difficult, but you should not have to do it very often. As explained earlier, you can't change the size of one volume without affecting all the other volumes on the same disk. On most types of hard disks, changing the size of one volume would obliterate all of the data in all volumes. To avoid this problem on a two-volume disk, for example, you would have to back up both volumes, redefine both of their sizes, then restore the data to each volume. If a disk contains only one volume, there is no way to change the size of that volume except to reduce it, which doesn't make sense.

Again, these volume-related tasks involve rerunning NETGEN, ELSGEN, or INSTALL and are usually performed in conjunction with adding, removing, or reinitializing hard disks on the server. The exact procedures for defining volumes on a new hard disk, changing the parameters of an existing volume, and changing the size of an existing volume are explained in Chapter 20.

Utilities for Managing NetWare Volumes

NetWare provides utilities (VOLINFO and CHKVOL) that don't require you to bring down the file server in order to work with volumes. Any user, regardless of rights, can run these two utilities.

The VOLINFO Utility. This NetWare menu utility displays the following information about all volumes on a file server:

- The volume name
- The total disk space on the volume (in kilobytes)
- How much free disk space is remaining on the volume (in kilobytes)
- The total number of directory entries configured for the volume
- How many available directory entries are left on the volume

The main use of VOLINFO is to see how close your volumes are to filling up or running out of directory entries. If either number in VOLINFO's "free" column is blinking, it means that the volume is dangerously close to capacity.

What to Do When a Volume Is Full. A volume represents a fixed amount of space on the disk. Once that space is full, users will get file creation errors when they try to save new files or directory creation errors when they try to create additional directories. Your only immediate recourse is to remove existing information from the volume to make room for the new data. Use either or both of the following suggestions:

- Have users delete all their unneeded files from the volume.
- Use NDIR to see which files have not been changed in a while and archive those files to floppy diskettes or some other archive medium. (NDIR is explained later in this chapter.)

As explained earlier, making the volume bigger requires much effort in NetWare 286; try to find other solutions to full volume problems.

What to Do When a Volume Runs Out of Directory Entries. This problem is more difficult to remedy. The only way to increase the number of directory entries is to bring the server down and rerun NETGEN. If that will take too long and users need to continue working on the volume, have them delete or archive any unnecessary files or directories on the volume to free up some entries.

Note: The DOS DELETE and ERASE commands do not immediately remove references to files from NetWare's Directory Entry Tables. This is why you can bring back a deleted file with the SALVAGE command. However, this also means that if your volume has run out of directory entries and users are deleting files with DELETE or ERASE to make room for more files, you must issue the PURGE command after deleting the files before you can actually reuse the disk space occupied by the deleted files. PURGE removes references to deleted files from the Directory Entry Tables.

Remember that every directory, DOS file, and list of up to five trustee assignments takes up an entry in the directory entry table. If you have Macintosh workstations attached to the file server, each Macintosh file takes up two directory entries—one for the data fork and one for the resource fork. Using group trustee assignments wherever possible will help conserve directory entries, because a group assignment counts as only one trustee assignment no matter how many users are in the group.

The CHKVOL Command. This NetWare command is analogous to the DOS CHKDSK command. Always use CHKVOL instead of CHKDSK to make a quick check of the status of a NetWare volume. Type CHKVOL from any drive mapped to the volume you want to check, or append a volume path to the end of the CHKVOL command. The screen will display information similar to this listing:

```
Statistics for fixed volume SLASHER/SYS:
    21170176 bytes total volume space,
    17274880 bytes in 446 files,
     3858432 bytes remaining on volume,
     3858432 bytes available to user SUPERVISOR,
         119 directory entries available.
```

Most of this information is self-explanatory. Note that in CHKVOL the figures are given in bytes, whereas in VOLINFO figures are given in kilobytes. The byte-kilobyte-megabyte conversions can be confusing until you get used to them. In the CHKVOL display above, for example, the 21170175 bytes of total volume space corresponds to roughly 21 megabytes (you must mentally add the commas yourself). A kilobyte is technically 1,024 bytes, although the approximation of 1,000 bytes is often used for simplicity. By the same token, a megabyte is actually 1,048,576 bytes or 1,024 kilobytes. That's part of the reason why a 20MB hard disk does not translate into an even 20,000,000 bytes of storage space.

You can set up the disk space limitation feature in NETGEN to limit the total number of kilobytes of disk space a user can use. If you do, both the number of bytes remaining and the number of bytes available will reflect that limited space for a given user, not the actual space on the entire volume. NetWare never informs users that their disk space utilization is being curbed in this way. (Of course, if the actual remaining disk space is less than the maximum available to the user, the actual space left is displayed.)

HINTS FOR AN EFFECTIVE DIRECTORY STRUCTURE

Once you go below the volume level in the NetWare directory structure, creating directories, subdirectories, and files works the same as it does for a hard disk in DOS. Use the same general principles of directory organization.

General Principles of Directory Organization

No book or manual can dictate exactly how you should set up your directory structure. The needs of every organization differ, and the directory scheme ideally should reflect those needs. However, there are some general guidelines that can be applied in most situations. Adhering to these guidelines will help simplify backing up and maintaining directories and files on your file server.

Keep It Simple. Above all else, a directory structure should be simple, uncluttered, and logical. By looking at the skeletal outline of the structure, you should be able to decide what types of files should go where. In most cases, a directory exists solely to hold a certain set of files that belong together: all of the program files for an application, for example, or all chapters of a book. The only purpose for an empty directory is to act as an "umbrella" level under which you can group related sub-directories.

Some of the signs that identify an illogical directory structure are:

• Directories thrown onto the server with no rhyme or reason—some applications over here, others there, data files everywhere
• An inordinate number of useless subdirectories that contain few or no files
• Executable files mixed in with data files in the same directory
• Parts of the same report or chapters in the same book located in different directories for no apparent reason
• Ridiculously long directory paths, such as SYS:DATA/ACCTG/ PAYABLES/ REPORTS/1990/MAY90/PAST_DUE

Avoid Files at the Root Level. You should never store files directly at the volume (root) level in NetWare, for one simple reason. You would have to grant users rights to the files, and granting rights at the root level essentially allows those rights to be exercised anywhere on the entire volume.

Don't Go Too Deep. Besides being hard to type in when you have to map NetWare drive pointers to directories, long directory paths can cause problems in applications not designed to handle them. Some programs provide relatively short fields in which to enter file names along with their complete directory path. If the full path is too long to fit in the field, you cannot access the file.

Another consideration is the workstation operating environments your file server supports. Even though NetWare allows a directory path to be up to 255 characters long (including delimiters), DOS, for example, is limited to 127 characters. The Apple Macintosh has completely different directory and file-naming conventions.

NetWare Directory Path Name Conventions

To maintain compatibility with the way DOS handles directory paths, NetWare requires a colon to separate the volume level from the subsequent directory level. (To DOS, a colon indicates the root level.) For example, on a DOS hard disk a directory path like WORK/LETTERS would appear something like this:

C:WORK/LETTERS

The same directory path on a NetWare hard disk would have the file server and volume name in place of the "C" disk identifier:

STATS/VOL1:WORK/LETTERS

To specify a full directory path in NetWare, then, use the following convention:

File server name	followed by a slash (/)
Volume name	followed by a colon (:)
Directory name	followed by a slash (/)
Subdirectory name	followed by a slash (/)
.	
.	
.	
File name	(optional)

Note that while DOS recognizes only the backslash (\) as a directory delimiter, NetWare is more flexible, allowing either a backslash or a forward slash (/).

Standard File Server Directories

Every NetWare file server must have a SYS volume. Four directories are automatically created in this volume at installation:

• SYS:SYSTEM, which contains the NetWare operating system itself and NetWare utilities and data files intended for use by the supervisor
• SYS:PUBLIC, which contains most of the other NetWare utilities and data files intended for general use by everyone on the network
• SYS:LOGIN, which contains the NetWare utilities needed for logging in
• SYS:MAIL, which contains "mailbox" subdirectories for each defined user

Although the SYS:MAIL directory was originally designed for use by NetWare's proprietary Electronic Mail System (EMS), which is no longer offered by Novell, the structure still must be there. User login scripts and print job configurations are stored in the mail subdirectories. Besides, some other NetWare-compatible mail programs use the SYS:MAIL directories.

In addition to these standard directories, several other directories are often useful on NetWare file servers. Setting up similar directories on all file servers helps reduce the overall maintenance workload and provides familiarity when a new supervisor takes over a file server. These directories are explained below.

Application Directories. Each shared network application should be installed in a separate directory on the file server. This separation helps eliminate conflicts between executable file names (two word processors that both have a WP.EXE file, for instance) and makes it much easier to upgrade or remove applications later. One standard practice is to create an umbrella directory named APPS or PROGRAMS in the SYS volume and locate each application in a subdirectory underneath it. That makes it easier to single out all applications at once when you are backing up the server. (Most application program files rarely change and do not need to be backed up as often as data files that change frequently.)

It is helpful, especially when you have several versions of the same program, to include the version number in the application's directory name. For example, if you have both WordPerfect v4.2 and v5.1 on your file server, you can name the directories WP.42 and WP.51, or WP4.2 and WP5.1. (NetWare allows you to include one period in a directory name. DOS consider the period as the start of the extension part of the directory name.)

DOS Directories. Having a copy of DOS on the file server makes life easier for DOS workstation users because they don't have to keep inserting a DOS system diskette when they want to execute a DOS command or when they exit an application. DOS is generally treated like any other application, with the following exceptions:

DOS directories are generally placed under SYS:PUBLIC so that you need not assign rights separately to every DOS user. (The group EVERYONE has Read,

Open, and Search rights in SYS:PUBLIC, which trickle down to any subdirectories as well.) A DOS directory traditionally follows this naming convention:

SYS:PUBLIC/*MachineName*/MSDOS/*DOSVersion*

The *MachineName* is a character string set in the workstation's SHELL.CFG file to identify the type of workstation: IBM_PC (the default machine name), COMPAQ, or ACER, for example. The machine name can be no more than six characters long. *DOSVersion* is a string that represents the version of DOS the workstation is running—for example, V3.30 or V4.01. Adhering to this convention lets you put the following generic search drive mapping in the system login script to give all users access to the appropriate DOS version:

```
MAP S2:=SYS:PUBLIC/%MACHINE/%OS/%OS_VERSION
```

This convention is also used by the default template in USERDEF. As long as the workstation's SHELL.CFG file specifies the correct machine type with the LONG MACHINE NAME parameter, it will map to the correct DOS directory. (The OS and OS_VERSION parameters are read automatically by the shell.)

If you don't plan to use USERDEF's default template to create users, you can safely eliminate the empty "MSDOS" directory level in the DOS directory path. This directory level is a holdover from the early days of NetWare, before MS-DOS became firmly established as a workstation operating system.

Non-NetWare Utilities Directory. If you have accumulated several useful .COM, .EXE, or .BAT files, or macros used frequently by a large number of network users, put these all in a single directory instead of spreading them out all over the network or putting them in SYS:PUBLIC. Name the directory UTILS or NETU-TILS or something similar. Then give users access to these utilities by including a search drive mapping to the UTILS directory in the system login script.

User Home Directories. No matter how much file sharing takes place on the LAN, there is almost always a need for each user to have a secure, private place for his or her own personal files. A standard practice is to create a separate "home" or personal directory for each user on the file server. You usually assign a user all rights to his or her home directory. Home directories also serve as a convenient place for applications such as WordPerfect to create their temporary files. Users can store personal setup and configuration files in their home directories as well.

Shared Data Directories. Databases, word processing documents, spreadsheets, and other work files shared by users should be grouped under common directories. These common directories can be segregated either by department or by project. For example, you might group all reports and spreadsheets used solely by the accounting department under an ACCTG directory. If several departments work together on a project, group the files associated with that project under an identifying directory such as CATALOG.

UTILITIES FOR DIRECTORY AND FILE MANAGEMENT

The main NetWare utility intended to be helpful in directory and file management is called FILER. Other utilities can also be useful: for example, NDIR, LISTDIR, RENDIR, and FLAGDIR at the directory level, and HIDEFILE, SHOW-FILE, FLAG, SALVAGE, and PURGE at the file level. FILER is the only menu utility in the group; the rest run from the command line.

The FILER Utility

FILER is not just a supervisor utility. With FILER, users can manage their own files and directories, while supervisors manage the ownership and trusteeship of file server volumes, directories, and data. File management is especially important to supervisors of file servers with a large amount of disk storage attached. When it comes to maintaining this disk storage—building and altering directory structures, moving files, searching for files, and managing directory information—DOS is sometimes limited. FILER is designed to do some things that DOS can't do.

For example, DOS won't allow you to delete an entire directory structure; you must delete all files in each subdirectory and then remove the subdirectories one at a time. FILER, on the other hand, will delete an entire directory structure, including all subdirectories and their files, with one command. (Details on this procedure will be given later.)

FILER's main menu contains the following options:

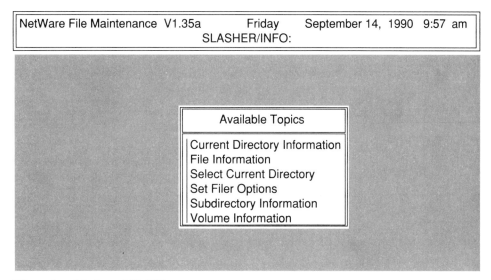

```
NetWare File Maintenance  V1.35a        Friday      September 14, 1990  9:57 am
                                    SLASHER/INFO:
```

```
                          Available Topics

                     Current Directory Information
                     File Information
                     Select Current Directory
                     Set Filer Options
                     Subdirectory Information
                     Volume Information
```

Tips for Using FILER

All activity in FILER centers around the "current directory" named in the header at the top of the screen. FILER treats the current directory as the equivalent of a DOS root directory and any directories within the current directory as subdirectories, although it doesn't actually place you in the directory you select. When you exit FILER, you'll be in the same directory in which you started it, regardless of which directory you selected as the current directory in FILER.

Selecting the Current Directory. Once you select the current directory, you can use FILER's maintenance functions to perform operations on that directory's files and subdirectories. If you have supervisory rights, you can change some directory and file attributes.

Select the current directory by choosing the "Select Current Directory" option from FILER's main menu. FILER will display a window in which you can type the full NetWare path of whatever directory you want as the current directory. Pressing Enter causes FILER to use your entry as the current directory.

If you don't want to type the NetWare directory path in the text window, you can use the Insert key instead. Pressing Insert when the text window is open causes FILER to display directory, volume, or file server names (according to the hierarchical status of the current directory) in a pop-up menu. Selecting a file server, volume, or directory name from the pop-up listing causes FILER to place that item in the text window, just as if you'd typed it in yourself.

FILER's Selection Options. Looking for files or directories on a large NetWare volume can be like looking for a needle in a haystack. Selection patterns are FILER's way of making the selection process easier. Using FILER's selection patterns, you can throw away 95% of the "hay" before you start searching for the "needle."

To set up a selection pattern, choose "Set Filer Options" from the "Available Topics" menu. FILER will display the following "Filer Options Settings" menu:

```
┌──────────────────────────────────┐
│       Filer Options Settings      │
├──────────────────────────────────┤
│ Confirm Deletions                 │
│ Confirm File Copies               │
│ Confirm File Overwrites           │
│ Directories Exclude Pattern       │
│ Directories Include Pattern       │
│ File Exclude Pattern              │
│ File Include Pattern              │
│ File Search Attributes            │
└──────────────────────────────────┘
```

The first three items on the menu allow you to turn confirmation on or off for deletions, file copies, and file overwrites. For example, selecting "Confirm Deletions" means that FILER will prompt you with a "Yes or No" prompt every time you try to delete something.

The next four options are for setting up FILER selection patterns. FILER can select two kinds of objects: directories and files. FILER, therefore, allows you to set both file selection patterns and directory selection patterns. FILER always selects the directory first, and the files within that directory second. For example, once FILER finds a directory and you make that directory the current one, FILER limits its file searches to files within that current directory. The final option lets you see files that are flagged "System" or "Hidden" when you list files in FILER.

Inclusion and Exclusion. FILER gives you two ways to refine what you see in a listing of either directories or files: inclusion and exclusion. An include pattern is similar to using a wildcard search pattern with the DOS DIR command (as in DIR *.EXE). Only those files or directories that match the include pattern will be listed. An *exclude* pattern works the same way except that all directories or files that match the exclude pattern will *not* appear in the listing.

For example, choosing to exclude objects with the pattern "*.EXE" causes FILER to ignore all files with the extension ".EXE" as long as that pattern is active. To set up this type of exclude pattern, choose "File Exclude Pattern." The "Exclude File Pattern" window appears, listing all current exclude patterns. If you have no patterns activated, the "Exclude File Pattern" window will be empty. To add a file exclusion pattern, press Insert. FILER will present you with a new window containing the text "New Pattern:." Enter your file exclusion pattern, "*.EXE," and press Enter. The characters "*.EXE" will appear in the "Exclude File Patterns" window. To add another pattern, press Insert once more and type in the new pattern.

You can set up multiple selection patterns for each object, or combinations of selection patterns. Furthermore, you can mix and match selection patterns that include objects with selection patterns that exclude objects. You can, if you wish, set up selection patterns for both files and directories. An exclusion pattern takes precedence over an inclusion pattern if a file matches both include and exclude patterns.

Include and exclude patterns remain in effect until you exit FILER. When you re-enter the utility, you will have to set up the patterns all over again to re-use the same ones.

Including Hidden and System Files. Normally, FILER does not display names of files flagged "Hidden" or "System." If you need to see these files, you can cause FILER to include "System" files, "Hidden" files, or both in its listings. Unless you specify "System File" or "Hidden File" with the "File Search Attributes" option, FILER will ignore files with system or hidden attributes, regardless of the include or exclude patterns in effect at the time.

Tagging Multiple Files and Directories. Whenever FILER presents a list of directories or files, you can use the NetWare "Mark" key (F5 on most keyboards) to tag a subset of those directories or files for operations that can be performed on more than one object.

For example, if you want to delete a group of files, choose "File Information" from FILER's main menu. When FILER displays the list of files, highlight each file in turn and press F5. After you've marked as many as you want to delete, press Delete. FILER will delete all of the marked files.

When you mark more than one file or directory, FILER sometimes presents menus that are slightly different from the single-object FILER menus. For example, when you highlight a single file in the Files window and press Enter, FILER displays the following "File Information" menu, containing nine items:

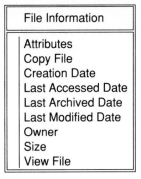

```
File Information
──────────────────
Attributes
Copy File
Creation Date
Last Accessed Date
Last Archived Date
Last Modified Date
Owner
Size
View File
```

However, if you mark more than one file in the Files window using F5, FILER displays the following "Multiple File Operations" menu:

```
Multiple File Operations
──────────────────────────
Set Attributes
Set Creation Date
Set Last Accessed Date
Set Last Modified Date
Set Owner
```

This menu doesn't allow you to view file information; it only allows you to change file information and attributes. Whatever changes you make will affect each file in exactly the same way.

Routine Maintenance with FILER

FILER's maintenance functions have the word "information" in their menu option names. "Current Directory Information," "Subdirectory Information," "File Information," and "Volume Information" are all maintenance functions.

Current Directory Maintenance. From the "Current Directory Information" menu, you can perform the following maintenance tasks for the current directory:

- Change the directory's creation date and time
- Change the directory's Maximum Rights Mask
- Change the directory's owner
- Change the directory's trustee assignments

Creation Date and Time. You'll rarely need to change a directory's creation date and time. About the only reason to make such a change would be to include an older directory in a backup program that keys off creation date. To change the creation date and time, select "Creation Date" from the "Current Directory Information" menu. FILER will display the current directory creation date and time in an inset. Only the supervisor can change the date and time shown.

Maximum Rights Mask. The Maximum Rights Mask restricts what effective rights users can exercise in the directory. The mask allows all rights by default. If you want to prevent all users (regardless of their trustee rights in the directory) from exercising a certain right in the directory, you must delete that right from the Maximum Rights Mask. To do this, select "Maximum Rights Mask" from the "Current Directory Information" menu. FILER will display a "Maximum Rights" window listing the possible rights for the current directory. Highlight the right you want to delete and press Delete. You can add a right back into the mask by pressing Insert. Manipulating the Maximum Rights Mask is not a supervisor-only function; users who have the Parental right in a directory can change the Maximum Rights Mask for the directory in this same way.

Owner. To see who the owner of the current directory is, select "Owner" from the "Current Directory Information" window. FILER will display the login name of the directory's owner. Only supervisors can change a directory's owner by typing in a different user name. Or, you can press Insert to have FILER display a list of user names from which to select.

The exact meaning of "owning" a directory is not clear in NetWare. Being listed as a directory's owner doesn't give a user any privileges above and beyond those determined by the user's effective rights. All it means is that the user created the directory in the first place. Why, then, should you be concerned about a directory's owner? One reason is to more accurately determine how much disk space a users' directories take up. The NDIR command includes an option whereby you can list directories by owner and see the total number of bytes those directories occupy.

Note: One quirk of the DOS XCOPY command and some other non-NetWare utilities is that when a user copies directories from one place to another on the file server, XCOPY changes the owner of all directories copied to the user who did the copying. This person may or may not be the actual, original owner of the directories. If you still want to use NDIR to produce reports of directory usage by owner, you might have to check all directories moved with XCOPY and change the owner back to the original creator to get an accurate report. Or use NCOPY instead of XCOPY (you'll have to copy directories one at a time with NCOPY).

Trustees. Supervisors (or any user with the Parental right in the current directory) can add or remove trustees in the current directory. To do so, choose "Trustees" from the "Current Directory Information" menu. FILER will display a list of defined trustees for the current directory.

To add a trustee, press Insert. FILER will display a list of trustees. Highlight the name of the user or group you want to add and press Enter. The default rights of Read, Open, and Search will be automatically granted to the new trustee. If you want to grant additional rights, press Enter and then Insert to get a list of other available rights. Mark the ones you want to grant, then press Enter.

To remove a user or group as a trustee for the current directory, highlight the name of that user or group and press Delete. Users without the Parental right won't even see the "Trustee" option listed in the "Current Directory Information" window.

Subdirectory Maintenance. You can perform similar maintenance chores on subdirectories of the current directory by going back to FILER's main menu and selecting "Subdirectory Information." Selecting this option causes FILER to display a list of subdirectories within the current directory.

Here's what you can do to these subdirectories:

- Change a subdirectory's creation date and time
- Change a subdirectory's Maximum Rights Mask
- Change a subdirectory's owner
- Change a subdirectory's trustee assignments
- Rename a subdirectory
- Create a subdirectory
- Delete a subdirectory

The first four tasks work exactly the same as in the "Current Directory Information" menu. You simply select a subdirectory to get an identical menu, but without the "Current Effective Rights" option. From this menu, supervisors can change a subdirectory's creation date, maximum rights, owner, and trustees. Users can view these items, but cannot change them.

Renaming a Subdirectory. To rename one of the subdirectories, highlight it and press the NetWare "Modify" key (F6 on most keyboards). An inset will appear containing the current subdirectory name. Type in the new name and press Enter.

Be careful when renaming subdirectories. If users have drive mappings to these directories in their login scripts, they must change the mappings to reflect the new subdirectory name. The same is true of mappings in the system login script.

Creating a Subdirectory. To create a new subdirectory, press Insert while viewing the subdirectory list. Type in a name for the new subdirectory and press Enter. You can then assign trustees to the new subdirectory in the same way as for any other subdirectory in the list.

Deleting a Subdirectory. To delete a subdirectory in the list, highlight it and press Delete. FILER gives you a choice between deleting only the files in that subdirectory and all subsequent subdirectories down the tree (leaving the structure itself intact), or deleting the entire subdirectory structure—files, subdirectories, trustee rights assignments, and all—from that point down in the directory tree.

File Maintenance. With FILER, you can work only with the files in the current directory. Selecting the "File Information" option from FILER's main menu produces a list of files located in the current directory. If you have specified any selection patterns earlier, only files that match those selection patterns will appear in the list.

At this point, you can rename or delete any of the files in the list. To rename a file, highlight the file name and press F6. The current file name will appear in an inset. Type in a new name for the file and press Enter. To delete a file, highlight the file name in the "Files" window and press Delete. Answer "Yes" to the confirmation prompt (unless you have disabled delete confirmation).

You can perform the following tasks on a single file that you select from the "Files" list:

- Change the file's attributes
- Copy the file to another directory
- Change the file's creation date and time
- Change the file's last accessed date, last archived date, and last modified date
- Change the file's owner
- View the size and contents of the file

Changing File Attributes. The first "File Information" option, "Attributes," allows you to view the NetWare file attributes of the selected file. The possible file attributes you can manipulate in FILER are: "Read Only," "Shareable," "Indexed," "Transactional," "System," "Hidden," "Execute Only," and "Modified Since Last Backup." Supervisors (and users with the Modify right in the current directory) can add or remove any of these attributes from a file.

Copying a File. To copy the selected file to another directory anywhere on the file server (or even to another file server), choose "Copy File" from the "File Information" menu. FILER will display a "Destination Directory" window where you can type the full directory path (from file server name on down) of where you want FILER to copy the file to.

Changing Various Dates and Times. Three of the next four items—"Creation Date," "Last Accessed Date," and "Last Modified Date"—are fairly self-explanatory. Supervisors can change any of the above items; users can only view them.

For example, when you select "Creation Date," FILER displays the date and time the file was created. By backspacing and typing a new date in the window, you can change a file's "creation" date. The "Last Accessed Date" and "Last Modified Date" items are functionally similar to the "Creation Date" item.

The "Last Archived Date" item was reserved for the exclusive use of archive server software. At the time NetWare v2.1 was being developed, Novell was also working on an Archive Server product of its own that used the "Last Archived Date." The Novell Archive Server product was never released—this option, therefore, is essentially useless. If you select it, FILER will return a "not archived" error message.

Changing a File's Owner. You can change the owner of a file in much the same way as you change the owner of a directory. Select the "Owner" option in the "File Information" menu. FILER displays the login name of the file's owner. Only supervisors can change the ownership of the file by backspacing over the owner's name and typing another user name in the File Owner window. If you're lazy, you can simply press Insert to get a list of defined users from which to choose.

The same problem exists with file ownership as with directory ownership. While the owner name usually identifies the person who first created the file, XCOPY and some other utilities will change the owner name when copying the files. You must use this option in FILER to change the owner name back to that of the original user.

Viewing a File's Size and Contents. Selecting "Size" from the "File Information" menu displays how big the file is in bytes. This size cannot be changed in FILER. The only way to change a file's size is to modify the file from an application.

To view the file's contents, select "View File." FILER will show any displayable ASCII characters in the file. This option works well for DOS text files, batch files, and some word processing documents. However, if you try to view the contents of an executable file, database file, spreadsheet, or any other file in a non-DOS format, the display will be virtually unreadable.

For example, FILER handles WordPerfect v4.2 documents fairly well, although it displays only the straight ASCII characters—no fancy WordPerfect bolding, underlining, or formatting. FILER's display is similar to that you obtain by using the DOS TYPE command. However, FILER cannot handle the printer information and other data stored in WordPerfect v5.x headers. When you try to view a WordPerfect v5.x document from FILER, you'll see only a few readable characters and a lot of gibberish.

Volume Information. The last item on FILER's main menu, "Volume Information," returns information about the NetWare volume that holds the current directory, but doesn't allow you to change any of that information. When you select "Volume Information," FILER displays the name of the file server, the name and type of the volume, bytes available, and directory entry information.

The FLAGDIR, RENDIR, and LISTDIR Utilities

These three command line utilities are useful when you must work with directories from the DOS prompt. Use FLAGDIR to set directory attributes, and RENDIR to rename directories. LISTDIR lists basic subdirectory information.

Flagging Directories with FLAGDIR. In NetWare v2.15, you can assign certain attributes to directories as well as to files. These directory attributes are "System," "Hidden," and "Private." You can view or change directory attributes from the command line with FLAGDIR.

Only directories used solely by the operating system should be flagged as "System" directories. This flag prevents these directories from showing up in a DOS DIR command listing. If a directory contains sensitive data and you want to keep it from showing up in a DIR listing, you can flag the directory "Hidden." A "Private" directory does show up in a DIR listing, but only the directory's owner can see the files in that directory.

To flag a directory, use the following command format:

```
FLAGDIR Path Option
```

Specify the full directory path in place of *Path*, and for *Option* use either "S" for System, "H" for Hidden, or "P" for Private. You can assign only one of these directory attributes to a given directory. For example, to make SYS:ADMIN/ BONUSES a hidden directory, type **FLAGDIR SYS:ADMIN/BONUSES H**. Make sure you keep track somewhere of what directories you hide. You'll need to know the exact directory name in order to unhide it with a future FLAGDIR command.

To check a directory's attributes, leave off the option letter. For example, to make sure that the BONUSES directory was properly hidden, type **FLAGDIR SYS:ADMIN/BONUSES**. NetWare will show you the directory's attributes.

Renaming Subdirectories with RENDIR. RENDIR offers a quicker way to rename a directory than using FILER. The format for this command is:

```
RENDIR OldSubdirectoryName TO NewSubdirectoryName
```

Substitute the appropriate old and new names for the subdirectory you are renaming. Remember to amend accordingly any login script mapping references to the directory.

Listing Subdirectory Information with LISTDIR. The main use of LISTDIR is to list the subdirectories one level down from your default directory or from any other directory you specify. However, you can also use it to view the following information:

- The entire directory structure from the default directory on down, including all subdirectories and their respective subdirectories
- The Maximum Rights Mask of all subdirectories beneath the directory
- The creation date and time of all subdirectories beneath the directory.

To view all this information for every lower subdirectory, type the command as **LISTDIR /A**. Replace /A with /R if you want to see only the Maximum Rights Masks, /D to see only the creation dates and times, or /S to just see all subdirectories. (NetWare versions prior to v2.15 may not include all of these options.)

You can redirect the output to a file using the DOS redirect symbol (>) and specifying a file name. For example, by going to the root level and typing **LISTDIR /A >** *FileName*, you can quickly produce a complete report of LISTDIR's subdirectory information for the entire volume, then print out the file using NPRINT or a word processor.

Managing Directories and Files with NDIR

NDIR is the NetWare counterpart to the DOS DIR command. NDIR works only with network drives, not local drives. Because it is NetWare-aware, NDIR can give much more network-specific information about files and directories than DIR can. NDIR has more than 30 options that you can combine in an almost infinite number of ways when you execute the command. We'll look only at the most useful variations for maintaining files and directories. As always, you can redirect the output of NDIR to a text file (using the > symbol) and use it to create customized reports.

A Few NDIR Basics. First, let's cover some of the basics for using NDIR. In its simplest form, you can use it just like the DOS DIR command. Valid variations would include:

```
NDIR
NDIR *.EXE
NDIR SYS:PUBLIC
```

The first variation (NDIR) would simply list all files and subdirectories in the default directory (the one you are in when you execute NDIR). The output would typically look something like this:

```
INFO:
File Name      Size     Last Modified      Accessed    Created  Flags         Owner
 
DIRSTAMP SYS   630784   8-21-90  7:09a     6-21-90     3-19-90  [WSM-HS--]    SUPERVISOR
ACRONYMS        44253   5-30-90  9:52a     6-22-90     4-10-90  [W-M-----]    FREDDY
LETTERS  LAW    12745   7-13-90  1:37p     7-13-90     7-13-90  [W-M--S--]    JASON
RESUME          62453   7-14-90  8:44a     7-15-90     7-12-90  [W-M--S--]    NORMAN
STEPS    NUM    77333   6-28-90  3:33p     9-12-90     1-02-90  [W-M--S--]    MICHAEL
BODYDUMP       102756   8-18-90  9:56p     9-14-90     7-13-90  [WSM-HS--]    SUPERVISOR


Directory Name   Created           Max Rights    Eff Rights   Owner
 
MASKS            3-21-90   5:44p    [RWOCDPSM]    [RWOCDPSM]   JASON
HORRORS          3-26-90   8:37p    [RWOCDPSM]    [RWOCDPSM]   FREDDY
FSBOOK           6-18-90   1:59p    [RWOCDPSM]    [RWOCDPSM]   MICHAEL
BADTIMES         4-02-90   5:37p    [RWOCDPSM]    [RWOCDPSM]   SUPERVISOR
RECORDS          4-26-90  10:17a    [RWOCDPSM]    [RWOCDPSM]   NORMAN
           5 subdirectories found
```

In addition to DIR's usual listing of file name, size, and last modified date and time, NDIR also shows the creation date, the last accessed date, the owner, and the file attributes for each file. For any subdirectories in the default directory, NDIR shows you the creation date, the Maximum Rights Mask, your effective rights, and the owner name. Like DIR, NDIR shows you the total number of files listed and the number of bytes they occupy. Unlike DIR, NDIR also totals how much actual disk space is used (in bytes and in blocks) by whatever is listed on the screen.

The second variation, NDIR *.EXE, would show similar information, but only for files having a .EXE extension. No subdirectories would be shown. This variation is one example of using the "NDIR *FileName*" command format shown in Novell manuals.

The third variation, NDIR SYS:PUBLIC, illustrates how to use the "NDIR *Path*" command format. Instead of a file specification, you give NDIR the full path up to and including the directory you want to look at. This particular example would list all files in the SYS:PUBLIC directory, no matter what directory you are in when you type the command.

NDIR Selection Options. By adding options to basic NDIR commands, you can select which directories and files you see based on certain criteria. For files, these criteria include file name, size, owner, creation date, last accessed date, and last modified date. For directories, they include owner and creation date only.

When you add any of these options to NDIR, you must include a directory path before the option: either type the entire path or enter the drive letter corresponding to a directory path. In most cases, you can use the shortcut symbols "\" for the root level, "." for the current directory, or ".." for the immediate subdirectory. The "SUB" option includes all subdirectories in the scope of the NDIR command. The following list summarizes NDIR's file and directory selection options.

To see only files that:	Include this NDIR option:
Match a certain pattern	FILENAME=*FileName*
Are larger than a certain size	SIZE GR *Bytes*
Are smaller than a certain size	SIZE LE *Bytes*
Belong to a certain user	OWNER=*UserName*
Were created before a certain date	CREATE BEF *Date*
Were created after a certain date	CREATE AFT *Date*
Have not been not accessed since a certain date	ACCESS BEF *Date*
Have been accessed after a certain date	ACCESS AFT *Date*
Have not been modified since a certain date	UPDATE BEF *Date*
Have been modified after a certain date	UPDATE AFT *Date*

To see only directories that:	Include this NDIR option:
Belong to a certain user	OWNER=*UserName*
Were created before a certain date	CREATE BEF *Date*
Were created after a certain date	CREATE AFT *Date*

The variable *FileName* can be a specific file name or a file pattern using the * and ? wildcard characters.

Replace *Bytes* with a number representing the number of bytes (not kilobytes or megabytes) you want for the breakoff boundary. For example, to see all files larger than 50KB on the volume, you would type **NDIR \ SIZE GR 50000 SUB**.

For *UserName*, substitute a valid user account name that exists on your file server. You cannot use wildcard characters with the Owner option.

For *Date*, NDIR accepts the following date formats:

> MM-DD-YY (for example: 09-25-90)
> Month Day, Year (for example: September 25, 1990)

You can use slashes, commas, or periods in place of the hyphens in the first format. You can abbreviate the month name down to the first three characters (Jan, Feb, Mar, Apr, May, Jun, Jul, Aug, Sep, Oct, Nov, and Dec). If you leave off the year, NDIR assumes you mean the current year.

If you want to negate any of these options, insert the word NOT into the option. For example, to see all files that do *not* have the extension .EXE, you could type **NDIR \ FILENAME NOT=*.EXE SUB**.

NDIR File Attribute Options. You can list all files having a particular file attribute or combination of file attributes with NDIR. Here are the appropriate abbreviations:

To see files with this attribute:	Include this NDIR option:
Read-Only	RO
Read-Write	RW
Shareable	SHA
Nonshareable	NOT SHA
Indexed	I
Transactional	T
System	S
Hidden	H
Execute-Only	EO
Modified Since Last Backup	M

For example, to see all Hidden files on the volume, type **NDIR \ H SUB**. To see all files flagged Shareable/Read-Only, type **NDIR \ SHA RO SUB**.

Again, you can see all files that do *not* have a particular file attribute or combination of file attributes by inserting the word NOT before the appropriate option (as in the "NOT SHA" example for seeing files that are not Shareable).

NDIR Sorting Options. NDIR allows you to sort the listings it displays by file name, by owner, by size, or by creation date, last accessed date, or last modified date. File name and owner sorts can be either alphabetical or reverse alphabetical (but why reverse?); numerical sorts can be either ascending or descending.

To sort the display:	Include this option:
By file name (alphabetically)	SORT FILENAME
By owner (alphabetically)	SORT OWNER
By size (smallest to largest)	SORT SIZE
By size (largest to smallest)	REVERSE SORT SIZE
By creation date (oldest to newest)	SORT CREATE
By creation date (newest to oldest)	REVERSE SORT CREATE
By last accessed date	SORT ACCESS
By last accessed date	REVERSE SORT ACCESS
By last modified date	SORT UPDATE
By last modified date	REVERSE SORT UPDATE

NDIR Archive Options. Only one of NDIR's archive-related options is at all useful for most popular NetWare backup systems. BACKUP, ARCHIVED DATE, CHANGED, TOUCHED, and WIDE all deal with the last archived date reserved exclusively for use by Novell's aborted archive server product. You can use them with NDIR, but all they will show you is a last archived date of 0-00-80 at 0:00am, which is useless information.

The ARCHIVE BIT option, however, deals with the "Modified Since Last Backup" file attribute. The DOS equivalent of this NetWare file attribute is the archive bit. When a file is backed up by any DOS-aware program (including the DOS BACKUP command), the archive bit of that file is turned off. The next time the file is changed (either written to or renamed), the archive bit is set again to indicate that the file contains new information that must be backed up the next time you run the program. Whenever DOS sets the archive bit, NetWare also sets the "Modified Since Last Backup" attribute on the file.

Using NDIR's ARCHIVE BIT option produces a list of files that have the archive bit set (and hence have the "Modified Since Last Backup" attribute). For example, to see a list of files on a volume that need to be backed up (according to the DOS archive bit), type **NDIR \ AB SUB**. (AB is the NDIR abbreviation for the ARCHIVE BIT option.)

Miscellaneous NDIR Options. A few last options are sometimes helpful in NDIR commands:

Option	Abbreviation	Effect on NDIR Command
Files Only	FO	Restricts NDIR to listing only files that match all other selection criteria
Directories Only	DO	Restricts NDIR to listing only directories that match all other selection criteria
Brief Listing	BR	Reduces the NDIR display to show only the size and last modified date for files (similar to the standard DOS DIR listing)
Macintosh Files	MAC	Restricts NDIR to listing only files created on Macintosh workstations (otherwise, Macintosh files are identified by an *)
NDIR Help Screens	HELP	Displays the possible options you can use with NDIR. This option cannot be used with any other option.

Some Practical Management Uses for NDIR

Here are some specific examples of how to use NDIR in the everyday management of the file server.

Relieving Full Volumes. When volumes begin to fill up, you might want to see which users are taking up the most room on the volume so they can remove their unnecessary files. To find out how many directories and files on a volume belong to a specific user, type the NDIR command as follows (assume the user name you want is TDUNCAN):

```
NDIR \ OWNER=TDUNCAN SUB
```

Another way to make more room on an almost-full volume is to identify which files haven't been changed or even accessed for a long time and either delete them or archive them to some other storage medium. For example, if the date is September 1, 1990, and you want to see which of TDUNCAN's files have not been accessed in the past six months, type:

```
NDIR \ OWNER=TDUNCAN NOT ACCESS AFT Mar 1 SUB FO
```

Remember that if you leave off the year, NDIR uses the current year.

Finding Lost Files. Suppose you copy a file to a directory somewhere and then forget where you copied it. If you know the file name is LOST.EXE, for example, you can find it by typing:

```
NDIR \ FILENAME=LOST.EXE SUB
```

It might take NDIR a while to search through every directory in a large volume. NDIR will say "Scanning directory . . . please wait" while it is searching.

If you don't remember the exact name of the file except that it starts with "L" and is an .EXE file, use this variation:

```
NDIR \ FILENAME=L*.EXE SUB
```

Printing Custom Reports. By combining various options in a single NDIR command and redirecting the output to a file, you can produce useful and informative reports that will help you manage the files and directories on your file server. For example, if you want a report of volume utilization directory by directory, sorted by owner, excluding .EXE files and .COM files, type the following NDIR command:

```
NDIR \ FN NOT=*.EXE FN NOT=*.COM SORT OWNER SUB > VOLUME.RPT
```

The output will be redirected to the file VOLUME.RPT, which you can later format and print out using a word processing program.

The HIDEFILE and SHOWFILE Utilities

To hide and unhide files from the command line rather than in FILER, use HIDEFILE and SHOWFILE. HIDEFILE.EXE and SHOWFILE.EXE are both in the SYS:SYSTEM directory so only supervisors can run these utilities.

A Few Warnings about Hidden Files. Hiding files is an activity best left only to a knowledgeable NetWare supervisor. You should hide only files that truly must be hidden. Never hide executable files or any other files necessary for an application to run. Even though the files are still there, a hidden file cannot be executed until it is unhidden. For this and other reasons, you should assign the Modify right, which allows users to hide files, with caution—*never* in a directory containing executable files.

NetWare hides files by setting the DOS Hidden and System file attributes. Once these attributes are set, the file cannot be deleted or overwritten by a file with the same name. The file can still be backed up and restored with most backup software, and you can type the contents of the file by using the DOS TYPE command (provided you remember the file name). Oddly enough, even though hidden files do not show up in a DOS directory search (using the DOS DIR command), they do show up in an NDIR search.

Hiding Files with HIDEFILE. To hide a file, type **HIDEFILE** *FileName*, replacing *FileName* with the name of the file you want to hide. Use wildcard characters to hide a group of similar files all at once. Remember the names of the files you hid, or write them down somewhere, so you can unhide them if necessary.

Unhiding a Hidden File with SHOWFILE. To unhide a hidden file, go to the directory where the file resides and type **SHOWFILE** *FileName*, replacing *File-Name* with the name of the file you want to unhide. You can use SHOWFILE on only one hidden file at a time.

If you forget the name of a hidden file, you have two options. One is to use NDIR in the hidden file's directory; the file will be listed in the NDIR display. The other option is to go into FILER and set the "File Search Attribute" option to include "Hidden" files. Then you can make the directory FILER's current directory and select "File Information." The hidden file will appear in the list.

Setting File Attributes with the FLAG Utility

FLAG lets you view and set file attributes from the command line. However, the only file attributes you can affect with FLAG are "Shareable/Nonshareable," "Read-Only/Read-Write," "Indexed," and "Transactional." For the rest ("Hidden," "System," "Execute Only," and "Modified Since Last Backup"), you must use FILER (or HIDEFILE/SHOWFILE for "Hidden" files).

FLAG recognizes the following abbreviations for file attributes:

S	Shareable
NS	Nonshareable
RO	Read-Only
RW	Read-Write
SRO	Shareable Read-Only
NRW	Nonshareable Read-Write
N	Normal (same as Nonshareable Read-Write)
I	Indexed
T	Transactional

For example, to change all files in a directory from "Nonshareable Read-Write" (the default attributes assigned when files are first created or copied to the network) to "Shareable Read-Only," type **FLAG *.* SRO**. If you want to flag all .EXE files in the default directory and in all subdirectories as "Shareable Read-Only," type **FLAG *.EXE SRO SUB**.

To view the file attributes set for files, use the FLAG command without any attribute abbreviations. For instance, to check attributes for all files in the default directory, type **FLAG *.***.

The SALVAGE and PURGE Commands

Every now and then, a network user accidentally deletes a file or two. With the DOS DELETE or ERASE command, files are not immediately wiped off the disk; rather, the directory entry for the file is removed from the Directory Entry Table. To the user, it appears that the file is gone, but it is still on the disk.

You or any network user can use the SALVAGE command to bring back an accidentally deleted file or group of files, as long as the following conditions are met:

- You don't execute a second DELETE or ERASE command
- You don't execute the PURGE command
- You don't log out or lose your file server connection

In other words, the instant you realize you have accidentally deleted a file, don't type *anything* except the SALVAGE command. If you are at the command line, don't even do a DIR command. If you have used wildcards to delete a group of files with a single DELETE command, you will be able to recover all files in that group. If you have been deleting a number of files one at a time, however, you will be able to recover only the last one deleted. If you are in an application, don't exit the application; shell out to DOS from within the program and issue the SALVAGE command before you do anything else. Utility programs designed to recover lost files on standalone systems (such as the Norton Utilities or PC Tools Deluxe) are generally not able to do the same for network disks.

From the standpoint of being able to recover accidentally deleted files, it's good that NetWare doesn't actually remove the file from the disk following the DELETE command. On the other hand, there are times when you want the file to be completely removed from the disk. This is where the PURGE command comes in. Typing PURGE at the command line after a deletion will cause NetWare to actually remove the deleted file from the disk.

As previously mentioned in this chapter, you can run into problems if the directory entry table is completely filled up and you are trying to delete some old files to make room for new ones. In this situation, you must use the PURGE command before the directory entries will actually be freed up for use by new files.

8 Managing Users and Groups

Managing a typical LAN requires a fair amount of time, more than a few pages of documentation, and enough experience to know the needs of network users. Because the number of network users and their needs seldom remain static, one of the most frequent network management activities is the creation and manipulation of user accounts. This chapter talks about creating, deleting, and changing users and groups on your file server. We'll first give some pointers on setting up user accounts in general, then look at the various NetWare utilities used to create and manage users and groups.

CREATING USERS

Creating a fully functional user account on a NetWare network involves much more than simply adding a new user name to the list of defined users. New users need rights in order to run applications and work with shared data on the file server. They should have home directories for their personal files and user-specific setup and configuration files. They need personal login scripts to set up drive mappings and environmental variables not provided in the system login script. They must have the appropriate login, password, and account restrictions to preserve the file server's security. And they should be organized into groups wherever possible to ease your user maintenance workload.

This section gives general information regarding user accounts and groups. We'll look at some conventional practices for naming users and groups, some shortcuts you can take by using groups, and some suggestions for implementing security at the user and group level.

The User Account

To log in to a NetWare file server, a person must provide a valid user name and the corresponding password. Every person authorized to use the file server should have a user name defined in the bindery of that file server. Here are some useful things to know about user names:

• The user name must be unique; no two user names can be identical on the same file server
• The user name can be from 1 to 47 characters in length
• The user name is also referred to as the login name, login ID, or user account

Tips for Assigning User Names. Each user account name should uniquely identify its authorized user. Establishing a consistent naming scheme will help you and your users keep track of who's who on the file server. An intuitive naming scheme makes it easier to send broadcast messages or E-mail to specific network users, because you won't have to look up their user names first. Some common conventions are to use people's first names, first initial and full last names, or the first initial and the first six characters of the last name.

Using first names is all right for small networks; the chance of users having the same first name is remote. However, first names tend to go in and out of vogue generation by generation, while some (like Michael and Mary) are perpetually popular. Your chances of having two users named Michael, even on the smallest LAN, are greater than you might think. Then you are faced with such problems as who to make MICHAEL and who to make MIKE—or do you use MICHAEL1 and MICHAEL2? Adding the last-name initial is not a very good solution, either, as the resulting word may have undesired overtones. For example, Mike Young may not like being known as MIKEY on the network.

Using a person's first initial and full last name results in less likelihood of duplication—or so it would seem. In actuality, given the large number of common last names like Smith and Johnson, you may stand an even greater chance of having identical user names. For example, under this scheme, Chris Smith, Carol Smith, and Craig Smith would all need the user name CSMITH. You'd have to come up with some contrived variations to work around these types of duplications: CHSMITH, CASMITH, and CRSMITH don't work very well as intuitive identifiers. Also, last names (especially foreign ones) can sometimes be long and difficult to type accurately; for example, imagine making a first initial-last name user name for Kris Kristofferson or Bahgwan Mahareesh.

The third method—using the first initial of the first name and the first six characters of the last name—seems to work best in most organizations. It has the advantages of keeping user names short (under eight characters) and being fairly intuitive for users to remember. It is also the naming convention standardized by IBM for their mail naming system. However, you still have the problem of what to do with Chris, Carol, and Craig Smith. In these cases (hopefully rare), the convention stipulates that you append a digit to the username, resulting in CSMITH1, CSMITH2, and CSMITH3 for our three Smiths. Somehow you'll have to make it clear to all users which one is which.

Whatever user naming system you come up with, consider the length factor carefully. Although a user name can be 47 characters long, long names are unadvisable for several reasons. First, it's hard to type long names accurately. Second, and most importantly, user's home directories are typically named with the user account names. DOS limits directory names the same as file names to eight characters—unless you insert a period, after which you can add three more characters. Keeping your user names to eight characters or less makes it much easier to create and map to home directories automatically, using the LOGIN_NAME identifier in the login script.

Accounts for Special-Purpose Users. Sometimes you must create a user account that doesn't necessarily correspond to a single authorized user. For example, if your organization employs temporaries or part-time help, you can set up an account specifically for them to use. More than one person can log in under the same user account and use the network. This allows you to set up, for instance, a TEMP account for all temporaries to use.

Another useful special-purpose account is a backup account. If someone other than the network supervisor does the regular system backups, rather than giving that user supervisory rights you can set up a BACKUP user account. When the time comes to do the backups, the designated backup person logs in as BACKUP instead of using his or her regular user name. You can then assign the "user" BACKUP the rights necessary to back up the system. Password security will prevent other users from logging in as BACKUP.

User Names on Multiple File Servers. Until the recent announcement of the NetWare Name Services, Novell did not provide any way to propagate user names and other setup information from one file server to another. If you want a user account set up on more than one file server, you have to create that user and all associated trustee rights on each file server individually. When you do this, it is generally advisable to use the same user name on each file server. User names must be unique only on a single file server. Identical user account names can exist on every file server on the internet, if necessary. However, a user can only be attached to a maximum of eight servers at a time.

You don't necessarily have to create a separate user account in order to allow users to access another file server's resources or services. Users can attach to other file servers under a different user name (such as GUEST or TEMP). Then the users can do whatever GUEST or TEMP can do on the additional file server.

When a person has identically named user accounts on several file servers, NetWare allows that person to have the same password on each file server. That makes it easier to attach to the other servers through commands in the login script. It is not necessary to have the same user name to have the same password. As long as your password is the same everywhere, you can synchronize the password for all user names you use on the internet. When the user's password expires on one file server and the user changes it, NetWare's password synchronization feature automatically changes the passwords on all attached servers if the user so specifies.

(Password synchronization works only with NetWare v2.15; previous versions do not offer users the ability to automatically synchronize passwords.)

Setting Up a User Account

In most network situations, every user account should be set up with:

• A valid user name (eight characters or less)
• A full name (a longer character string identifying the authorized user of the account)
• An *initial* password (generally used only the first time the user logs in, whereupon the user changes it)
• Appropriate account restrictions (account expiration date, limit on concurrent connections)
• Secure password restrictions (allow user to change password, require passwords at least five characters long, force password changes at least every 60 days, limit the number of grace logins after password expires, require new passwords to be unique)
• Login time and station restrictions, if appropriate
• A login script that provides only drive mappings and commands not included in the system login script
• Membership in appropriate groups to provide access to applications and network services
• A home or personal directory where the user has all rights
• Trustee rights assignments to other applications and data directories as needed.

If you have set up the OS to be able to limit the amount of disk space each user can use on the file server, you will also need to specify the maximum disk space for each user account.

If you have installed NetWare's accounting option (see Chapter 11), each user account will also need:

• A sufficient beginning account balance
• An appropriate credit limit (specifying how far, if at all, a user can go in the hole after the initial account balance is depleted).

You can designate certain users (those you want to become involved in helping you manage the file server) as File Server Console Operators. This designation gives them the ability to use most of the options in the FCONSOLE utility (except downing the file server and deleting user connections).

UTILITIES FOR CREATING USERS

Novell originally provided the SYSCON utility as the sole means for creating user accounts and setting them up with everything users need to function on the network. Therefore, you can perform all user setup tasks listed above from within SYSCON—but on only one user account at a time.

To answer the need for dealing with user accounts in bulk, Novell came up with two additional user-creation utilities: MAKEUSER and USERDEF. Of the two, MAKEUSER is much more difficult to master; it is based on writing fairly complex *scripts* containing keywords that correspond to various user options in SYSCON.

After receiving many complaints from users about MAKEUSER's high learning curve, Novell introduced USERDEF. This simplified utility, originally developed for ELS NetWare Level II (v2.12 and v2.15) but since included with SFT and Advanced NetWare v2.15, acts as a front end to MAKEUSER. USERDEF allows you to develop any number of *templates* that define how you want to set up users. When you're ready to create the user accounts, USERDEF calls MAKEUSER automatically to accomplish the actual work of creation.

The sections below give the overall process for creating and setting up user accounts with SYSCON, USERDEF, or MAKEUSER. You can use any of these utilities that meet your particular needs at a given time. After you create user accounts in bulk with either USERDEF or MAKEUSER, you can use SYSCON to make individual alterations to the bulk user setup. Note also that any system-wide default restrictions that you set up in SYSCON *will not* apply to users created with USERDEF or MAKEUSER.

One final note: The ability to create groups is a function relegated solely to SYSCON. You can assign users to *existing* groups in USERDEF or MAKEUSER, but you can only create *new* groups with the "Group Information" option in SYSCON.

Creating Users with SYSCON

SYSCON is a menu utility with many functions other than creating user accounts. Most of the user-related functions are grouped, appropriately enough, under the "User Information" option of SYSCON's main menu. A few, such as setting up default restrictions that apply to all users and assigning console operators, are accessed via the "Supervisor Options" menu selection.

In general, then, to create a new user in SYSCON, select "User Information," press Insert to add a new user account to the list of defined users, then select the newly defined account to arrive at the "User Information" submenu for that account:

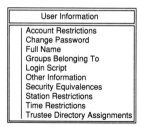

User Information
Account Restrictions
Change Password
Full Name
Groups Belonging To
Login Script
Other Information
Security Equivalences
Station Restrictions
Time Restrictions
Trustee Directory Assignments

After that, simply go down the menu, selecting each item in turn and filling in the appropriate information. You can skip over "Other Information"; it is a display-only option. Note that SYSCON doesn't automatically assign an initial password to new user accounts even if passwords are required; you must do that with the "Change Password" option. If you do require passwords but don't set an initial password for users, they can log in the first time without a password.

Setting Up Default Restrictions. There are a few tricks you can use in SYSCON to make your job easier. First of all, if you want the same account and password restrictions to apply to all users (or even most users with a few exceptions), set up those restrictions first, using the "Default Account Balance/Restrictions" and "Default Time Restrictions" options under "Supervisor Options." Unless you establish some system defaults in SYSCON, each user account you create will initially have no expiration date, no connection limitations, no password restrictions, no disk space limits, and no login time restrictions; you will have to set these all up individually for each user account. It's much easier to establish common restrictions—and then refine them on a user-by-user basis as the need arises—than it is to set up almost identical restrictions for each user account separately. Note that system default restrictions apply only to users created *after* the defaults are established. They have no effect whatsoever on user accounts already set up.

Using the "Default Account Balance/Restrictions" option in SYSCON, you can set up defaults in the following areas:

- *Account expiration date*. A system-wide default here is especially useful in academic environments when you want all users' accounts to run out the last day of the term or semester.
- *Concurrent connections limit*. This restriction is useful when the number of connections is critical on your file server. For example, in ELS NetWare Levels I and II, which limit you to four or eight users total, you don't want one user logging in at two or three different workstations.
- *All password restrictions*. Global password restrictions are useful for security-critical file servers when you want the user passwords to be as secure as possible.
- *Initial account balance and credit limits*. When you install the accounting option, every user must have an initial account balance in order to use the file server. Using a default here is much easier than assigning a separate balance for each user.
- *Disk space limit*. Enabling the disk space limit option in NETGEN or ELSGEN is only half the battle against disk hogs. You must also "turn on" the option in SYSCON and specify a maximum disk space (in kilobytes) for each user account. If you want each user to have an equal amount of disk space available, this option is much easier to set up as a system default.

Using the "Default Time Restrictions" option, you can block out certain hours or days and prevent all users from logging in during that time. Remember, though, that if you've already created users with different individual time restrictions or none at all, the default time restrictions will not apply to those users. As with all default restrictions, if you create a user after you set up the default time restrictions and then change the time restrictions just for that user account, the individual restrictions will take precedence over the system-wide restrictions.

Creating Directories in SYSCON. You might not think of using SYSCON to create directories. Nevertheless, it is possible in SYSCON to create a new directory and assign to it user or group trustees all at once. This approach is most useful when you are creating a new user for whom you want to set up a home directory. Here's how to do it.

After you have inserted the new user account name and set up all other security restrictions in the "User Information" submenu, select the "Trustee Assignments" option. You will see a list (initially empty) of the user's trustee assignments. Press Insert and specify the directory in which you want to assign the user trustee rights. SYSCON will allow you to specify a nonexistent directory here. For example, if you have other users' home directories as subdirectories under SYS:USERS and you want to create a home directory for new user JSMITH, type "SYS:USERS/JSMITH." SYSCON will check the directory structure; if that directory doesn't exist, you'll see a prompt asking you to confirm the creation of a new directory. Answer "Yes" to the prompt; then proceed to assign trustee rights in the usual manner.

Creating Users with USERDEF

The USERDEF utility was designed with the entry-level network supervisor in mind. By automating the creation of user accounts and the installation of DOS directories on the file server, USERDEF helps you get the network ready for use more quickly. USERDEF works by making some general assumptions about the needs of a typical network user: for instance, that the user will need a DOS directory on the file server, a home directory, basic account and password security restrictions, a login script with rudimentary NetWare drive mappings, and access to some basic print job configurations. These assumptions are arranged into a *template* you can use as a boilerplate when creating users. USERDEF provides a default template suitable for use in small networks, but you can create your own, more sophisticated templates for larger network needs.

Here's a summary of the user account setup tasks that USERDEF and its templates will accomplish for you:

  • Read a workstation's machine type and DOS version, and create a corresponding DOS directory on the file server if one doesn't already exist
  • Upload the appropriate DOS system files to the new DOS directory
  • Create a user name, full name, and initial password based on the person's first and last names
  • Create home or personal directories to which the users have all rights
  • Copy print job configurations previously set up for some other user via PRINTCON to the new user accounts (this is a feature unique to USER-

DEF—with SYSCON and MAKEUSER, you have to do this from the PRINTCON utility itself)

• Assign users as members of up to six already-existing groups on the file server

• Assign users an initial account balance and low account limit (if the accounting option has been installed on the file server)

• Establish concurrent connections limits and password restrictions that will apply to all users created with the template

• Set a maximum disk space usage amount (if the Limit Disk Space option was enabled in NETGEN or ELSGEN)

• Provide users with a login script containing at least search drive mappings to SYS:PUBLIC and to the appropriate DOS directory, and a network drive mapping to the appropriate home directory.

As you can see, USERDEF provides for just about everything users need to get up and running on the network. The only account restrictions you cannot set in USERDEF that you can set in SYSCON are the account expiration date and the limit on grace logins.

Be aware that USERDEF's default template may not set things up the way you would normally do it. For example, using the default template will create users' home directories directly under the SYS volume (SYS:BILL, SYS:TED, and so on). If you have created an umbrella directory, such as SYS:USERS or SYS:HOME, you'll need to make a custom template and use it to create your users.

Getting Help in USERDEF. USERDEF provides on-line help screens throughout the utility. The screens are particularly helpful during work on the template parameters. As in all NetWare menu utilities, the help screens explain each of the options in the current menu or the fields in a given screen. If you are uncertain about what a particular field means, position the cursor within that field and press the Help key (F1 on most keyboards). The resulting help screens will describe what types of entries are acceptable for that particular field.

Creating DOS Directories with USERDEF. One of the most tedious tasks every network supervisor faces is creating a network environment conducive to each user's workstation operating system (usually DOS). When you have some workstations using IBM PC-DOS v4.0, some using COMPAQ DOS v4.0, and others still using MS-DOS v3.3, setting up directories for each version on the file server can be tricky. Usually, you must create a directory and copy DOS files such as COMMAND.COM, CHKDSK.COM, and FORMAT.COM into that directory. Then you must set each user's login script to map a search drive to that directory. The USERDEF utility streamlines this whole process by taking care of DOS directories automatically.

The first time you run USERDEF from a particular workstation, the utility reads the machine name specified in workstation's SHELL.CFG file (if there isn't one, it uses the default of IBM_PC) and the DOS version from the ROM BIOS. Then USERDEF checks on the file server to see if there is a directory that matches the conventional DOS directory name for this combination. For example, if you run the utility on a COMPAQ workstation running COMPAQ's version of MS-DOS v4.01, USERDEF will check to see if the directory SYS:PUBLIC/COMPAQ/MSDOS/ V4.01 exists on the file server. If it does, you get the main menu (explained below). If such a directory does not exist, USERDEF will create it and then prompt you insert the appropriate diskettes so it can copy the workstation's DOS files to the directory.

Important: USERDEF's default template assumes that you follow the conventional naming scheme for DOS directories. The user login scripts created from the default template will include the generic search drive mapping MAP S2:=SYS:PUBLIC/%MACHINE/%OS/%OS_VERSION. It also contains the appropriate COMSPEC command (COMSPEC= S2:COMMAND.COM) to direct the workstation applications to the appropriate DOS command processor. If you have already set up DOS directories under a different naming scheme, running USERDEF could result in superfluous DOS directories being created on your file server. To avoid this, answer "No" to USERDEF's initial prompt to load DOS.

USERDEF requires this DOS directory initialization only once for each workstation/DOS version combination on the network. When you subsequently run USERDEF from that workstation, it presents you with the "Available Options" main menu:

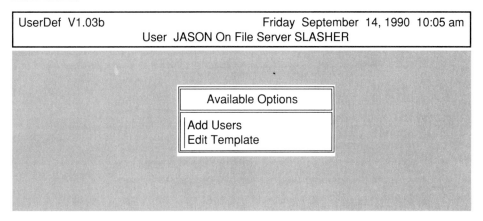

```
UserDef  V1.03b                        Friday  September  14, 1990  10:05 am
                      User  JASON On File Server SLASHER
```

```
              Available Options

            Add Users
            Edit Template
```

The process for creating users is the same whether you use the default template or your own template. The following section describes how to create users with the default template.

Adding Users with USERDEF's Default Template. Select the "Add Users" option. USERDEF produces a list of available templates for creating network users; choose the default USERDEF template from this list. USERDEF will show a list all currently defined user names on the file server. (USERDEF refers to user names as login names.) Press Insert and type in a new person's full name (first and last). Then press Enter.

After you enter each full name, USERDEF suggests a login name for that user, normally the person's first name. If the person's first name is the same as an existing user name, USERDEF adds a number to the name to make it unique. You are free to edit the suggested name, shorten it, or change it completely. Press Enter to accept the login name.

USERDEF places the new login names, in alphabetical order, into the list of user login names defined on the server. USERDEF indicates in the right-hand column which users are "new," meaning their user accounts are not yet defined. Press Insert to add another new name to the list, and repeat the above process. When all the users you want to create appear as "new" users in the list, press Escape. USERDEF asks you if you want the new user's accounts created using the default template. Answer "Yes" to the prompt.

USERDEF's default template requires passwords for users; USERDEF suggests an initial password for each new user. The suggested initial password is the user's first name. If the user's first name is not as long as the minimum field length required by the template (five characters in the default template), the utility doubles the user name until the password length requirement is either met or surpassed. For example, for the user name JIM the suggested initial password would be JIMJIM. Again, you are free to edit or replace each of the suggested passwords.

Once the password issue is taken care of, USERDEF creates the new users' accounts by invoking the MAKEUSER utility, NetWare's standard tool for bulk user creation. USERDEF creates the new accounts without any further input from you and reports the results when it is finished.

If there's a problem with the creation of any new user account, USERDEF lets you know what the problem is and how it's been handled. For example, suppose you delete the group EVERYONE through the SYSCON utility. MAKEUSER assumes that all users will be created as a member of the group EVERYONE. Since USERDEF creates users by invoking MAKEUSER, an error message, "User created, but unable to create as a member of group EVERYONE," will be returned to USERDEF to indicate that the user accounts were created, but the users were not made members of the group EVERYONE.

USERDEF returns you to the list of defined users, indicating that the new users are now officially created.

Creating Your Own USERDEF Template. If you need to create a customized template to meet the requirements of particular workgroups on your file server, you can create your own USERDEF templates through the "Edit Template" option. Here's how.

Select "Edit Template" from the main USERDEF menu. The utility presents a list of available templates. The first time you run USERDEF, the default template will be the only template to appear. By pressing Insert, you can enter the name of a new template, then define that template.

There are two parts to a USERDEF template: the template parameters and the login script. A menu appears containing the two options "Edit Login Script" and "Edit Parameters."

Editing the Login Script in USERDEF. Choose "Edit Login Script" to modify USERDEF's default login script. In USERDEF, the default login script gives each user two search drives. The first one is mapped to SYS:PUBLIC for access to the NetWare user utilities; the second is mapped to the appropriate DOS directory. The default login script also sets COMSPEC (a command that tells the workstation where the COMMAND.COM file is) to this DOS directory. The first available network drive is set to the user's default directory.

You can change these search drives, add more search drives, or include any other option that would appear in a regular login script. If the SYS:PUBLIC, DOS directory, and home directory mappings are taken care of in the system login script, you can delete them from the USERDEF login script template. Every user must have a search drive mapped to SYS:PUBLIC, however. Don't delete this mapping from the template unless you're sure it is provided through the system login script.

Editing the USERDEF Template Parameters. The "Edit Parameters" option allows you to edit the NetWare environment parameters that will define each user created with this template. The parameters are presented as various fields on the screen:

```
┌─────────────────────────────────────────────────────────────────────┐
│                    Parameters for Template DEFAULT                    │
├─────────────────────────────────────────────────────────────────────┤
│  Default Directory:      SYS:                                         │
│  Copy PrintCon From:   (see list)                                     │
│  Groups Belonging To:  (see list)                                     │
│  Account Balance:                              1000                   │
│  Limit Account Balance:                        No                     │
│         Low Limit:                                      0             │
│  Limit Concurrent Connections:                 No                     │
│         Maximum Connections:                   8                      │
│                                                                       │
│  Require Password:                             Yes                    │
│         Minimum Password Length:               5                      │
│  Force Periodic Password Changes:              Yes                    │
│         Days Between Forced Changes:           90                     │
│  Require Unique Passwords:                     Yes                    │
│  Limit Disk Space:                             No                     │
│         Maximum Disk Space (in KB):            79448                  │
└─────────────────────────────────────────────────────────────────────┘
```

The first field indicates the directory path to the user's new default or home directory. In USERDEF, the default path is to the root directory on volume SYS. If you have a different directory for this (such as SYS:USERS or SYS:HOME), change the default path to reflect your situation.

The next field is "Copy PRINTCON From." When you highlight this field and press Enter, USERDEF brings up a list of all users who currently have print job configurations defined through the PRINTCON utility. PRINTCON gives each user a database of ways for the NetWare CAPTURE and NPRINT commands to print files on a network printer. For example, a print job configuration might specify normal print output on network printer 0, or compressed printing. You can choose the user from which you want to copy these configurations. If no one has a PRINT-CON database set up, "none" will be the only entry in the list. USERDEF will still create users, but those users will have no print job configurations available. You can set them up later with PRINTCON if it becomes necessary.

Next is the "Groups Belonged To" field. Pressing Enter in this field brings up a list of groups you want the users to be made members of. EVERYONE appears in the list by default. Press Insert to get a list of other defined groups on the server. You can either select individual groups from the list, or you can mark desired groups with the Mark key (F5 on most keyboards). Press Enter after you have made your selection. The result is a list of groups the new users will belong to after they are created with this template. You can select as many as six groups with the USERDEF template. (The six-group limitation is a characteristic of USERDEF, not a NetWare limitation.) Later, you can grant individual users membership to any additional network groups through SYSCON if necessary.

If the file server has been established as an accounting server through SYSCON, the USERDEF template will include an entry for the user account balance. The units used in determining the account balance are called "charge units" in NetWare. Charge units can be dollars, cents, pesos, francs, or any other appropriate monetary unit.

You also have the option of granting a low limit for the user account balance. The low limit amount must be smaller than the account balance. If the low limit is a positive number or zero, the users will not be able to go into the hole. You can enter a negative number to make a type of "credit account" allowing users to continue to accrue charges after depleting their account balance.

The next field lets you specify a limit on the number of concurrent connections users can have. This can be an important designation in the ELS environment. Because ELS NetWare Level II allows for no more than eight concurrent connections to the file server, it may be wise to permit each network user to log in at only one workstation at a time. This lowers the probability of a user being turned away for lack of connections because a user somewhere else on the LAN has logged in at more than one workstation.

The USERDEF template also lets you establish the standard password restrictions offered in SYSCON.

The fields dealing with limited disk space appear only if the "Limit Disk Space" option was enabled in NETGEN or ELSGEN. "Limit Disk Space" allows you to establish a limit on the amount of disk storage space available for use by each user. NetWare allocates disk space in 4KB blocks. The disk space is designated in kilobytes (KB); you should round to the nearest 4KB when allocating disk storage space limits to the user, or at least keep in mind that the file server will round down to the amount of disk space allotted to the next lower 4KB increment.

After you have set up the template parameters, press Escape to exit the window. USERDEF will ask if you want to save the changes you have made. Answer "Yes" to this prompt. From this point on, your new template will appear as one of the template choices when you select USERDEF's "Add Users" option. You can create as many templates as you need. To actually create users using a custom template, you need to select "Add Users," choose the custom template (not DEFAULT), and go through the name-entering process described above for the default template procedure.

Creating Users with MAKEUSER

Although far more complex than USERDEF, MAKEUSER is much more powerful once you learn how to use it. MAKEUSER is designed to create users in larger quantities than you could normally use USERDEF for. For example, some schools routinely set up hundreds of student user accounts at a time. These are typically generic accounts that don't carry specific people's names, but rather account numbers assigned to individual students. MAKEUSER is the ideal tool for this type of bulk user needs. On the other hand, using MAKEUSER to create five or six users is a great deal of work that would more easily be handled by USERDEF.

How MAKEUSER Works. MAKEUSER works by processing script files that contain certain keyword commands arranged in such a way as to be meaningful to the MAKEUSER utility (not necessarily to humans). Of course, these keywords are unique to MAKEUSER, and there are dozens of them you need to learn. Keyword functions range from setting account restrictions to specifying a login script to actually creating or deleting a user. MAKEUSER assists you by scanning your user file first and reporting any syntax errors it finds. Once you get a workable user script file, you can usually use it over and over, making only slight modifications each time.

MAKEUSER script files are simple DOS text files. You can create and edit them with any text editor or from within the MAKEUSER utility itself. When saved, these files are given a .USR extension—hence the nickname "USR files." You can process USR files either within MAKEUSER or from the DOS command line. MAKEUSER, then, is both a menu utility and a command-line utility.

Structure and Syntax of USR Files. A USR file consists of one or more lines setting general parameters for users, and then one or more lines creating the users themselves. Every line in both these areas is based around a keyword, which is a specific word in a specific form, followed by values that you specify (such as a certain login script, or a user's name). A keyword is identified by the "#" symbol as its first character (for example, #CREATE and #RESET).

The order of the keywords is extremely important in MAKEUSER. In general, any keywords that precede the #CREATE keyword apply to all user accounts specified in the create commands. If you are setting up all users exactly the same, you simply group all the restrictions in the first part of the script file and all of the create commands at the end. If some users need different restrictions and parameters than others, you need to divide the users into sets. Put the keywords that apply to one set of users in front of the create commands for that set. Use the #RESET keyword to clear the slate so you can set up completely different restrictions for the next set of users.

Regardless of how many of these keywords you select, the overall procedure remains the same: In the USR file, you specify what rights and restrictions a set of users will have, then you specify the commands to create that set of user accounts. You then have MAKEUSER process the file—and your new set of users is ready to go.

MAKEUSER Keywords. The MAKEUSER keywords and their functions are summarized below. For more details on each keyword, refer to Novell's supervisor manuals.

Use the following keywords to set up default restrictions that will apply to all users created in the same script file:

#ACCOUNT_EXPIRATION *Date*   Sets a common date when all the user accounts will expire.

For *Date*, substitute a valid date in either MM-DD-YY format (as in 10-31-90) or Month Day, Year (as in October 31, 1990) format. If you do not include this keyword, the accounts will have no expiration date.

#CONNECTIONS *Number*   Limits all users to the specified number of concurrent connections.

Replace *Number* with the number of connections you want users to be able to establish. If you do not include this keyword, users will be able to log in using the same account from any number of workstations (up to the maximum number of connections supported on the file server).

#PASSWORD_REQUIRED   Requires all users to have a pass word. None of the other password keywords can be used without this one being entered first.

If you do not include this keyword, the users can choose whether or not to have a password.

#PASSWORD_LENGTH *Length*   If passwords are required, this keyword establishes the minimum length they can be.

Replace *Length* with the minimum number of characters you want passwords to have. If you do not include this keyword, the program will use the default minimum password length of five.

#PASSWORD_PERIOD *Days*   If passwords are required, this keyword forces users to change their passwords at the specified frequency.

Days can be any number between 1 and 365. If you do not include this keyword, passwords will never expire.

#UNIQUE_PASSWORD

If passwords are required and a password period is established, this keyword requires replacement passwords to be unique (not one of the previous eight passwords the users have set).

If you do not include this keyword, users can reuse a previous password when the current one expires.

#ACCOUNTING *Balance,LowLimit*

If the accounting option is installed, this keyword establishes an initial account balance for all users and sets a limit on how low the balance can go before it is invalidated.

The number you specify for *Balance* must be larger than the *LowLimit*. If you do not include this keyword, users will be assigned a default initial account balance of 1,000 charge units with no low limit.

#MAX_DISK_SPACE *NumberKB*

If the server is set up to limit user disk space, this keyword establishes a maximum amount of disk space available for all users.

Replace *NumberKB* with the maximum number of kilobytes of disk space you want available to each user. (Since NetWare divides disk space into 4KB blocks, the OS will actually round your number down to the nearest multiple of 4 if it is not evenly divisible by 4.) If you do not include this keyword, users will not be limited in the amount of disk space they can use.

#RESTRICTED_TIME *Day,Start,End*

Restricts the days and hours during which users can log in. You can specify more than one *Day,Start,End* combination; separate them with a semicolon with no spaces in between.

Day means day of the week (Sun, Mon, Tue, and so on). You can type "everyday" to mean every day of the week. The *Start* time must be earlier in the day than the *End* time. Include "am" and "pm" designations in the times specified, and round to the nearest half-hour increments. If you do not include this keyword, users may log in any day of the week, any time.

> **#HOME_DIRECTORY** *DirectoryPath*   Specifies the parent directory for all users' home subdirectories.

The directory you type for *DirectoryPath* must already exist on the file server. In this directory, MAKEUSER will create subdirectories having the same name as the user name specified in the individual #CREATE keywords. Each user automatically gets all rights to his or her home directory. If you do not include this keyword, the home directories will be created directly under the SYS volume.

> **#GROUPS** *GroupName*   Makes all users in the set members of the specified group.

You can specify more than one *GroupName*; separate multiple group names with a semicolon with no spaces in between. If you do not include this keyword, users will become members of the group EVERYONE by default.

> **#LOGIN_SCRIPT** *FileSpec*   Assigns a common login script to each user account in the set.

For *FileSpec*, type the full directory path up to and including the file name. The login script file must already exist on the file server and contain generic commands that will work for all users. If you do not include this keyword, the users will have no personal login script.

> **#STATIONS** *Network,Station*   Restricts the actual workstations from which users can log in.

Replace *Network* with the actual network address of one of the network interface boards in the file server (up to eight hexadecimal digits). Replace *Station* with a valid station or node address (up to twelve hexadecimal digits) on that network address. You can include more than one station address per network address—separate multiple station addresses with a comma. You can use "all" to indicate any station on a given network address. To include an additional *Network,Station* combination, insert a semicolon with no spaces between the entries. If you do not include this keyword, users will be able to log in from any workstation on the network.

Use this keyword with caution, because the station restrictions will apply equally to all user accounts specified in subsequent #CREATE keywords. If you specify only one network and station address, for example, you are requiring every user to log in from the same physical workstation.

MAKEUSER's Functional Keywords. The following keywords have specialized functions in MAKEUSER:

#CREATE *UserName;FullName;*
   Password;Group;
   TrusteeDirectory [Rights]
	Specifies what a user account's name, password, and trustee rights should be, as well as what existing groups that user is to be made a member of.

UserName is the only required variable; the rest are optional. Keep the username to eight characters or fewer, because MAKEUSER also uses it for the name of the user's home directory.

The *FullName* cannot contain commas. If you don't specify a full name, the user won't have one.

Password is an initial password for the account. You must specify a password if the #REQUIRE_PASSWORD keyword appears before the #CREATE keyword in the script (without a #CLEAR or #RESET in between). If you specified a minimum length with the #PASSWORD_LENGTH keyword, the password must be at least that long.

Group specifies what group the user should be made a member of. You need not specify the group EVERYONE in the #CREATE command. If you want the user to be a member of more than one group, separate the group names with a comma. The groups must already be defined on the file server.

If you don't specify any trustee assignments in #CREATE, the user by default will have only one trustee assignment: all rights in the home directory. To assign the user trustee rights in another directory, type the full directory path in place of *TrusteeDirectory*. For *Rights*, either type "ALL" for all rights or the first letters of the rights you want (for example, "RWOCS" for Read, Write, Open, Create, and Search). If you don't specify *Rights*, the program uses the default of ROS (Read, Open, and Search rights). You can include more than one directory-rights combination in the same #CREATE keyword—separate the entries with a comma.

#CLEAR	Clears all keywords and allows you to start a new set of keywords in the same USR script file
#RESET	Same as #CLEAR
#REM	Allows you to insert comments or informational remarks in the script file

Keywords for Deleting Users. The following keywords delete user accounts from the file server. Since the current discussion concerns creating users, we will explain these two later in this chapter (see "Deleting Users in Bulk").

#PURGE_USER_DIRECTORY
#DELETE

MAKEUSER/SYSCON Comparison Charts. If you are already familiar with setting up user accounts in SYSCON, the following comparison charts might be useful. They show which keywords in MAKEUSER correspond to the various options in SYSCON.

Option in SYSCON	Corresponding MAKEUSER Keyword
Default Account Balance/Restrictions	
Account Has Expiration Date: Date Account Expires:	#ACCOUNT_EXPIRATION *Date*
Limit Concurrent Connections: Maximum Connections:	#CONNECTIONS *Number*

Require Password:
  Minimum Password Length:
Force Periodic Password Changes:
 	
  Days Between Forced Changes:
  Limit Grace Logins:
    Grace Logins Allowed:
Require Unique Passwords:
	#PASSWORD_REQUIRED
	#PASSWORD_LENGTH *Length*
	Assumed Yes if you use
	#PASSWORD_PERIOD
	#PASSWORD_PERIOD *Days*
	Not Available in MAKEUSER
	Not Available in MAKEUSER
	#UNIQUE_PASSWORD

Account Balance: Allow Unlimited Credit: Low Balance Limit:	#ACCOUNTING *Balance,LowLimit*
Limit Disk Space: Maximum Disk Space (in KB):	#MAX_DISK_SPACE *NumberKB*
Default Time Restrictions	#RESTRICTED_TIME *Day,Start,End*
User Information	
Account Restrictions Change Password Full Name Groups Belonged To Login Script Other Information Security Equivalences Station Restrictions Time Restrictions Trustee Assignments	Set with individual keywords #CREATE ...;*Password*;... #CREATE ...;*FullName*;... #CREATE ...;*Group*;... #LOGIN_SCRIPT *FileSpec* Not Applicable Not Available in MAKEUSER #STATIONS *Network,Station,Station* #RESTRICTED_TIME *Day,Start,End* #CREATE...;*TrusteeDirectory [Rights]*

MAKEUSER/USERDEF Comparison Chart. If you are already familiar with setting up user accounts with USERDEF, the following comparison chart might be helpful. It shows which keywords in MAKEUSER correspond to the parameters you can set in a USERDEF template.

USERDEF's Template Parameters	Corresponding MAKEUSER Keyword
Default Directory:	#HOME_DIRECTORY *DirectoryPath*
Copy PrintCon From:	Not available in MAKEUSER
Groups Belonged To:	#GROUPS *GroupName;GroupName*
Account Balance:	#ACCOUNTING *Balance,LowLimit*
Limit Account Balance:	
Low Limit:	
Limit Concurrent Connections:	#CONNECTIONS *Number*
Maximum Connections:	
Require Password:	#PASSWORD_REQUIRED
Minimum Password Length:	#PASSWORD_LENGTH *Length*
Force Periodic Password Changes:	Assumed Yes if you use
	#PASSWORD_PERIOD
Days Between Forced Changes:	#PASSWORD_PERIOD *Days*
Require Unique Passwords:	#UNIQUE_PASSWORD
Limit Disk Space:	
Maximum Disk Space (in KB):	#MAX_DISK_SPACE *NumberKB*

Rules for MAKEUSER Keywords. Here are some general rules to remember about MAKEUSER's keywords:

- Every USR script must contain at least one #CREATE keyword. All other keywords are optional.
- Each keyword must start on a separate line in the script.
- If the same keyword (except #CREATE) appears more than once in the same script file, only the parameters in the last keyword will be processed.
- If necessary, you can continue long entries on the next line by typing a plus sign (+) at the end of the line.
- With all keywords, use semicolons to separate the fields in a line.
- With keywords that require multiple fields (such as #CREATE), if you skip a field include a semicolon to hold that field's place.
- To terminate a multiple-field keyword before you get to the last field, put a caret (^) as the last character on the line.

Before going further into MAKEUSER and USR files, you should also be aware of three important prerequisites:

• Any groups you are going to assign users to must already exist.
• Any path you specify for creating users' home directories in must already exist (only the parent directory must exist, not the home directories themselves).
• Any login scripts you intend to use must already exist.

As in other NetWare utilities, on-line help is available in MAKEUSER via the Help key (F1). Frankly, the MAKEUSER help screens are not very helpful. No on-line help even mentions the possible keywords you can use in a script file. Persistent use of the Escape key will get you out of virtually any situation within MAKEUSER, with no harm done.

Creating a USR File in MAKEUSER. After you start the MAKEUSER utility, the following "Available Options" menu appears on your screen:

```
Available Options

Create New USR File
Edit USR File
Process USR File
```

To write a new MAKEUSER script file, choose the first option, "Create New USR File." The resulting screen is your blank slate for creating a USR script file. Below is a sample script file for creating several accounts for students in a computer science lab.

```
#REM Script for Creating Lab Students
#GROUPS jets;publishers
#PASSWORD_REQUIRED
#PASSWORD_LENGTH 3
#RESTRICTED_TIME Monday,10:00 pm,11:59 pm
```

So that you and others can more easily tell later what the script file does, it's a good idea to include some informational remarks in the file. The sample USR file begins with such a remark. The keyword for a remark is #REM, followed by a space and the remark, "Script File for Lab Students."

Remember, in MAKEUSER you start with the keywords that represent parameters that apply to all users, then add the create keywords. In our sample file, the next line sets the groups that all lab students will be members of: JETS and PUBLISHERS.

The next two keywords, #PASSWORD_REQUIRED and #PASS-WORD_LENGTH 3, specify that users created by this file must have passwords and those passwords must be at least three characters long.

To restrict the network access times for all lab students, the file includes the keyword #RESTRICTED_TIME followed by the day and time spans during which users may not log in. Note that the start time (10:00 pm in the sample .USR file) must be earlier than the end time (11:59 pm in the sample).

The first #CREATE line creates the account for the lab's teaching assistant. Remember to type two consecutive semicolons wherever you have an empty field. Note the use of the caret at the end of the second and third #CREATE lines to indicate that although there are other possible fields in the line, no values will be given for them; the lines are finished. The last line of the sample USR file shows how to assign groups user by user, rather than all at once via the #GROUPS keyword. In this case, Norman Bates will become a member of the group PSYCHOS as well as JETS and PUBLISHERS.

Saving and Processing the USR File. After setting all the parameters and #CREATE keywords for all users, press Escape. MAKEUSER asks if you want to save your file. Answer "Yes" to the prompt, then give MAKEUSER an eight-character or less file name for your USR file. You do not have to include the .USR extension after the file name; MAKEUSER automatically adds it.

You are now back at the opening menu, where one of the available options is "Process USR File." Highlight that option with the cursor keys and press Enter. MAKEUSER prompts you to enter a file name. If you just finished creating a USR file, the prompt will display that file name.

Press Enter to start processing the file. If you want to specify some other USR file to process, press Insert and select from the list of all USR files in the default directory (the one from which you started MAKEUSER). You can also process a USR file outside MAKEUSER by entering "MAKEUSER *FileName*.USR" at the DOS prompt.

Whichever method you use to specify the USR file, MAKEUSER first scans the file and reports any errors. To correct errors from within MAKEUSER, choose "Edit USR File" from the "Available Options" menu, enter the offending file's name, and make the necessary corrections. Then save and process the file as you did when you first created it. If you processed the .USR file from the command line, go into MAKEUSER or a text editor to correct the file. Then save and process the .USR file again.

After successfully processing a .USR file, MAKEUSER places a report of the results in a file with the same file name as the .USR file, but with an .RPT extension. The .RPT file reports which users were created successfully. You can use the DOS TYPE command to look at this report file, or print it out for future reference if you want.

Reprocessing a USR File. Should you wish to create more users with a previously processed .USR file, simply pull up that file either in MAKEUSER or with a text editor, then enter the keywords and user names required. Save and process the USR file again, then check the report file. You'll see that only the new creations or deletions were processed; MAKEUSER doesn't re-create already existing users.

This characteristic of MAKEUSER does lead to one of its quirks: If you make changes to the parameters in an already processed USR file, those changes will apply only to new users created in the file's reprocessing. MAKEUSER does not alter previously created user accounts; their parameters remain whatever they were the first time the file was processed (or however they have been modified since then).

Where to Store USR and RPT Files. MAKEUSER.EXE is located in the SYS:PUBLIC directory, although you must be supervisor to run it. This makes it possible to run MAKEUSER from any directory on the file server. MAKEUSER saves all .USR and .RPT files in the same directory in which they were created. It can only process *.USR files in the current directory. If you anticipate needing several USR files, consider creating a specific directory for them and their accompanying report files. Then do all MAKEUSER creating, processing, and editing within that directory.

UTILITIES FOR MANAGING USERS

If you define managing users as anything you can do to user accounts after they are initially created, then the list of user management tasks is virtually endless. Altering user account and login restrictions, changing the password or password restrictions, modifying the user login scripts, assigning new trustee security, even deleting user accounts—all fall under the user management umbrella.

You'll perform most of these day-to-day user tasks with SYSCON. Deleting users in bulk is best left to MAKEUSER (you cannot delete users in USERDEF). NetWare provides a few other utilities that can help out as well: USERLIST and WHOAMI.

Managing Users with SYSCON

In general, SYSCON allows you to change anything about a user account in basically the same way as you set it up in the first place. You can also use SYSCON to change any restrictions or characteristics set up for user accounts created in bulk with USERDEF or MAKEUSER.

Here are a few potential problems to be aware of as you maintain user accounts in SYSCON. First, the changes you make to a user's account in SYSCON may not take effect until the next time the user logs in. So, for example, if you go into SYSCON and assign a user trustee rights in a directory, the user will have to log out and log back in before exercising the newly assigned rights.

When you delete user accounts in SYSCON, the user name is not removed from the trustee lists of the directories where that user had rights assigned. Nor are the user's home directory and mail subdirectory deleted. You can clear all this excess baggage after deleting a user by running the SECURITY utility.

Deleting Users in Bulk

The #DELETE keyword in MAKEUSER allows you to get rid of users in bulk as easily as you created them. You can create and delete users within the same .USR file, although you cannot create and delete the same users within one file.

To delete users' home directories and mail subdirectories at the same time as you delete the user accounts themselves, you need to use the #HOME_DIRECTORY and #PURGE_USER_DIRECTORY keywords along with #DELETE. For example, to delete users STUDENT1 and STUDENT2 with MAKEUSER, include the following lines in a .USR file (assume you created home directories under SYS:USERS):

```
#HOME_DIRECTORY SYS:USERS
#PURGE_USER_DIRECTORY
#DELETE student1, student2
```

The two student user accounts, along with their home and mail directories, will be deleted when you process the .USR file with MAKEUSER.

Listing User Information with USERLIST

The USERLIST utility displays the users that currently have an active connection on your file server, along with their connection (station) numbers and the date and time they logged in. For example, when you type **USERLIST**, you see a display similar to this one:

```
User Information for Server SLASHER
Connection  User Name       Login Time
----------  ------------    ----------
        1   PRINTSERVER     8-30-1990  7:54 am
        2   APPLETALK       8-30-1990  7:54 am
        3   APPLETALK       8-30-1990  7:54 am
        4   APPLETALK       8-30-1990  7:54 am
        8   APPLETALK       8-30-1990  7:54 am
       19   JASON           9-11-1990  8:54 am
       20   MICHAEL         9-11-1990  8:53 am
       22   FREDDY          9-11-1990  9:23 am
       23 * SUPERVISOR      9-11-1990  8:13 am
```

Here are a few technicalities having to do with the connections displayed by USERLIST. Notice that, in addition to the people logged in to the file server, USERLIST shows the connections used by print servers and other VAPs as well. In the sample display above, connection 1 is a print server VAP connection. Connections 2, 3, 4, and 8 are used by NetWare for Macintosh VAPs.

Connection numbers are not permanent assignments. Whenever a workstation or VAP establishes a connection with the file server, NetWare assigns that entity the next available connection number in its connection tables. (In the case of some VAPs, NetWare may assign several connections.) When a connection is terminated, that connection number goes back into the pool of available connection numbers to be reassigned to someone else.

The important thing to remember about connection numbers is that a user can be logged out and still be taking up a connection on the file server. As long as the NetWare shell remains loaded on the workstation (regardless of whether the user is logged in or out), the connection remains active in the server's connection table. In a connection-critical network such as ELS Level I or II, you must make sure that users not only log out but also unload the workstation shell to completely terminate the connection. In the past, users had to cold boot their PCs to unload the shell. However, the latest versions of the NetWare's DOS workstation shell (v3.01) allow users to unload the shell without rebooting the machine by typing **NET3 U** or **NET4 U** from the workstation's boot drive.

Network and Node Addresses with USERLIST /A. If you add the /A option, USERLIST will display network addresses and node addresses in addition to the regular user connection information.

```
User Information for Server SLASHER
Connection  User Name      Network      Node Address      Login Time
_____  _____      _____      _____      _____

    1       PRINTSERVER   [BA5EBA11] [    1B032BE2]     8-30-1990   7:54 am
    2       APPLETALK     [BA5EBA11] [    1B032BE2]     8-30-1990   7:54 am
    3       APPLETALK     [BA5EBA11] [    1B032BE2]     8-30-1990   7:54 am
    4       APPLETALK     [BA5EBA11] [    1B032BE2]     8-30-1990   7:54 am
    8       APPLETALK     [BA5EBA11] [    1B032BE2]     8-30-1990   7:54 am
   19       JASON         [BA5EBA11] [    1B052D17]     9-11-1990   8:54 am
   20       MICHAEL       [BA5EBA11] [    1B035F59]     9-11-1990   8:53 am
   22       FREDDY        [   CAB1E] [    1B20E8E2]     9-11-1990   9:23 am
   23       * SUPERVISOR  [   CAB1E] [    1B03551C]     9-11-1990   8:13 am
```

A full NetWare internetwork address consists of a network address, a node address, and a socket number. NetWare routers use these addresses to see that packets arrive at their proper destinations.

The network address is a number assigned at installation time to uniquely identify the cabling system attached to each of the network interface boards in the file server. In the sample display above, the workstations Jason and Michael are using are physically connected to network BA5EBA11. The workstations used by Freddy and Supervisor are connected to separate cabling system identified as CAB1E.

The node address identifies the network interface board within the workstation. Some boards, like ARCnet boards, have their node address set with switches. Others, like Ethernet boards, have a built-in node address that is unique for every board made. Using both the network number and the node address, NetWare can uniquely identify every workstation and file server on an internetwork.

Notice that the USERLIST /A command does not show socket numbers. This is because a number of processes can be running in the same physical machine, as in node 1B032BE2 above. Conceivably, a single node or workstation could have many open sockets, although most workstations have only two or three sockets in use at a time.

Using Wildcards with USERLIST. USERLIST always sorts its display by ascending connection numbers. On a file server with many users, you may want see only a subset of all users. USERLIST accepts the wildcard characters * and ? in the command. The question mark wildcard (?) stands for a single character, whereas the asterisk wildcard (*) can stand for any number of characters, including zero.

For example, to see only users whose names start with "A," you could type **USERLIST A***. To see only users whose names end in "A," you could type **USERLIST *A**. To see only users whose names have the letter "A" anywhere in them (including those that start and end with A), you could type **USERLIST *A***.

USERLIST Information for Other Attached Servers. USERLIST can also display the same user information for any file server you are attached to. To see this display, specify a file server name before anything else after the USERLIST command. For example, to see the full information on active users on file server RIPPER, type **USERLIST RIPPER//A**. Note that you must put a slash after the file server name.

Listing Information about a User with WHOAMI

The NetWare WHOAMI (Who Am I) utility can display a variety of information about one user account at a time. The most frequent use of this command is when users type **WHOAMI** to see what user accounts they are using on each file server they are currently attached to. For each file server, WHOAMI shows the user name on that file server, the version of NetWare running on the server, and the date and time the user logged in or attached to the server. For example:

```
You are user JASON attached to server SLASHER connection 19.
Server SLASHER: SFT NetWare 286 TTS V2.15 Rev. C (080989)
Login Time:  Thursday  September 9, 1990  10:37 am
```

By adding various options to the basic WHOAMI command, you can cause the display to show additional information relating to that user. The possible variations of the WHOAMI command are:

WHOAMI /G   Display the groups the user is a member of
WHOAMI /S   Display the security equivalences the user has
WHOAMI /R   Display the user's effective rights in all directories
WHOAMI /A   Display all of the above

To see the user information for just one of the file servers the user is attached to, specify the server name before the option (as in WHOAMI SLASHER /A).

Typical output resulting from using the WHOAMI /A command looks like this:

```
You are user JASON attached to server SLASHER connection 19.
Server SLASHER: SFT NetWare 286 TTS V2.15 Rev. C (080989)
Login Time:  Thursday  September 9, 1990  10:37 am
You are security equivalent to the following:
    EVERYONE (group)
    WORDPERF (group)
    BEST (group)
You are a member of the following Groups:
    EVERYONE (group)
    WORDPERF (group)
    BEST (group)
You have the following effective rights:
    [ W C   ]  SLASHER/SYS:MAIL
    [RWOCD SM]  SLASHER/SYS:MAIL/BB31033B
    [R O   S ]  SLASHER/SYS:PUBLIC
    [RWOCDPSM]  SLASHER/SYS:USERS/TED
    [RWOCDPSM]  SLASHER/SYS:USERS/TED/TEST1
    [R O   S ]  SLASHER/SYS:APPS/BEST
    [R O   S ]  SLASHER/SYS:APPS/WORDPERF
    [RWOCDPSM]  SLASHER/SYS:USERS/WORK_AREA/WP
```

Notice that NetWare makes a user a member of a particular group by assigning that user a security equivalence to the group. That is why each group is listed twice, once under security equivalences and once under groups.

Uses for the WHOAMI/A Command. A user's overall NetWare security profile can become a rather tangled web to unweave. To ascertain exactly which directories on the file server a user has effective rights in and what those rights are, you must take into account the user's rights as an individual, as a member of various groups, as a result of any security equivalences to other users, and as a result of the trickle effect. (The term "trickle effect" refers to the way trustee rights assigned in any given directory flow down and are effective in all subdirectories of that directory; see Chapter 6 for more information.)

The WHOAMI /A command provides a convenient way to compile this information quickly for each user on your file server. This quick WHOAMI /A check is especially useful after you have changed user or group rights assignments, and you want to make sure you haven't inadvertently given rights where they shouldn't be. It may startle you to see which directories users have rights to, either through the trickle effect or through membership in a new group. Be particularly wary when users routinely attach to other file servers as GUEST. Since GUEST is by default a member of the group EVERYONE (and may possibly be a member of other groups as well), the GUEST account will have access rights wherever its corresponding groups have rights.

Here's how to produce a printed report of each user's effective rights in all directories on all attached file server, plus group and security equivalence information. Have all your users log in as themselves, just as they normally do. Then have each user type the following command:

```
WHOAMI /A > LPT1:
```

Usually output destined to LPT1 is rerouted to a network printer via the CAPTURE command. If a CAPTURE command is in effect, the WHOAMI information will be printed on a network printer. If the user has a local printer attached to port LPT1 on the workstation, the WHOAMI information will be printed on that printer. Check over the printed copies; then file them in your network log or notebook.

Another possibility for collecting WHOAMI information is to include the following line in the system login script:

```
#WHOAMI /A > SYS:USERS/RIGHTS/%LOGIN_NAME.LST
```

This command automatically writes the output of the WHOAMI /A command to files in the SYS:USERS/RIGHTS directory. Don't leave this command in the system login script permanently. Include it only when you want to update the user information for your network logbook.

UTILITIES FOR MANAGING USER-LEVEL SECURITY

User-level security consists mainly of trustee rights assignments in various network directories. Trustees can be either users or groups. You can always make and change trustee rights assignments for both users and groups through SYSCON. If you prefer working from the DOS prompt, NetWare also provides command-line utilities to manipulate user and group trustee assignments. These include RIGHTS, TLIST, GRANT, REVOKE, and REMOVE.

Viewing Effective Rights with RIGHTS

The RIGHTS command shows users what effective rights they have in a given directory. If users are having trouble seeing or working with files in a particular directory, have them type **RIGHTS** from that directory. The display will be similar to this one for a user on file server SLASHER:

```
SLASHER\SYS:PUBLIC\UTIL
Your effective rights are [ROS]
You may Read from Files.(R)
You may Open existing Files.(O)
You may Search the Directory.(S)
```

RIGHTS automatically figures all aspects of the effective rights equation: the user's individual rights, group rights, security equivalences, and the directory's Maximum Rights Mask.

However, effective rights do not take into account file attributes security. If users have Write and Open rights in a directory but get errors when trying to write to certain files, it's probably because the files are flagged Read-Only. Type **FLAG *.*** in the directory to check the file attribute settings on all files.

Viewing the Trustees of a Directory with TLIST

The TLIST utility shows you which users and groups are trustees of a particular directory and what rights they have as trustees. Users must have the Parental right in the directory in order to use TLIST. Supervisors have all rights in all directories, so they can type TLIST in any directory.

TLIST displays the trustee list in a format similar to this one:

```
SYS:USERS/JASON
User trustees:
  JASON                [RWOCDPSM]   (Jason Voorhees)
  MICHAEL              [R O   S ]   (Michael Myers)
  —
Group Trustees:
  SHRINKS              [RWOCD SM]   (Psychiatrists)
```

The listing shows the user and group names, the trustee rights they have, and then the full name (if one is assigned).

Manipulating Trustee Rights with GRANT, REVOKE, and REMOVE

Briefly, GRANT allows you to give rights to a single user or to a group within a given directory. REVOKE allows you to take away some or all of the rights already granted to a user or group in a directory. REMOVE allows you to completely remove a trustee from a directory, rights and all.

These three utilities can be a little confusing. To better understand how these utilities work together, let's review how trustee rights assignments work. In SYSCON, when you select a user and choose the "Trustee Assignments" option from the "User Information" submenu, you see a list of directories and the rights which that user has already been assigned in those directories. Normally, you can either change some of the rights listed for an existing directory, or you can insert a new directory and assign rights to it. These activities correspond to what you can do with the GRANT command.

It is also possible in SYSCON to delete some or all of the rights the user can exercise in the directory without deleting the directory assignment itself. This ability to delete rights corresponds to the function of the REVOKE command. Even if you revoke all rights, NetWare still considers the user or group a trustee of a directory—and, more importantly, the assignment still takes up a slot in the volume's directory entry table. (Actually, every five trustee assignments take up one directory entry.)

The only time you need to have a user or group assigned as a trustee in a directory without any rights is to cancel out an unwanted trickle effect situation. In Chapter 6, we gave the example of user Thom and the SYS:LETTERS/LOVE directory. Thom had all rights to SYS:LETTERS, and because of the trickle effect has all rights to the LOVE subdirectory as well. To prevent that, you would have to reassign Thom as a trustee of SYS:LETTERS/LOVE, but not give him any rights. Redefining rights at a lower level like this is the only way to stop the flow of trustee rights down a directory tree. Using TLIST, you can easily spot a no-rights trustee in a directory, like Michael Myers in the following example:

```
User Trustees:
  JASON                  [RWOCDPSM]   (Jason Voorhees)
  MICHAEL                [         ]   (Michael Myers)
  ──

Group Trustees:
  SHRINKS                [RWOCD SM]   (Psychiatrists)
```

The REMOVE command corresponds to what SYSCON does when you delete the whole directory and rights entry altogether. NetWare deletes the user or group from the trustee list of the directory; a little more space is freed up in the directory entry table, and the user or group no longer shows up in a TLIST listing.

Assigning Rights with GRANT. You can actually use GRANT to both grant and revoke rights. If the user or group you specify isn't already a trustee of the directory, GRANT makes that user or group a trustee and assigns the appropriate trustee rights. If the user or group already has a trustee assignment in the directory, whatever rights you specify in the GRANT command will overwrite the existing rights. If the new list includes more rights than they used to have, you have granted rights; if less, you have revoked rights.

The command formats for using GRANT are slightly different, depending on whether you are working with an individual user or with a group. To assign a user rights in a certain directory, use this format:

```
GRANT RightsList FOR DirectoryPath TO UserName
```

To assign a group rights in a certain directory, use this format:

```
GRANT RightsList FOR DirectoryPath TO GROUP GroupName
```

Adding the qualifier GROUP will ensure that NetWare knows which entity you mean when a user and a group have the same name.

For *RightsList*, type either the whole name or just the first letter of each right you want to grant. Or, you can substitute any of the following variations:

ALL	All eight rights
ALL BUT *Right*	All of the eight rights except the one named
NO RIGHTS	None of the eight rights

The last variation, NO RIGHTS, retains the user or group a *trustee* of the directory, but doesn't give that user or group any actual rights in the directory. This has the same effect as revoking all rights with the REVOKE command, normally used to cancel out an unwanted trickle effect situation as explained above.

You can leave out "FOR *DirectoryPath*" in the command if you issue the command in the directory you want to affect. Otherwise, type a full directory path, starting with the volume.

Taking Rights Away with REVOKE. The REVOKE command works very much like GRANT, except that (obviously) you cannot revoke rights from a user or group not already a trustee of the directory. The command formats for using REVOKE are slightly different, depending on whether you are working with an individual user or with a group.

To revoke rights from a user trustee in a certain directory, use this format:

```
REVOKE RightsList FOR DirectoryPath FROM UserName
```

To revoke rights from a group trustee in a certain directory, use this format:

```
REVOKE RightsList FOR DirectoryPath FROM GROUP GroupName
```

Again, adding the GROUP qualifier will ensure that NetWare knows which entity you mean when a user and a group have the same name.

For *RightsList*, type either the whole name or just the first letter of each right you want to grant. Or, you can substitute ALL to revoke all rights in the directory.

As with GRANT, you can leave out "FOR *DirectoryPath*" in the command if you issue the command in the directory you want to affect.

Removing Trustees with REMOVE. The REMOVE command also works much like GRANT and REVOKE. The command formats for using REMOVE are slightly different, depending on whether you want to remove an individual user or a group from the trustee list.

To remove a user trustee from a certain directory, use this format:

```
REMOVE UserName FROM DirectoryPath
```

To remove a group trustee from a certain directory, use this format:

```
REMOVE GROUP GroupName FROM DirectoryPath
```

Again, adding the GROUP qualifier will ensure that NetWare knows which entity you mean when a user and a group have the same name.

As with GRANT and REVOKE, you can leave out "FROM *DirectoryPath*" in the command if you issue the command in the directory you want to affect.

9 Creating Effective Login Scripts

This chapter describes the three types of login scripts offered by NetWare: the *default login script*, the *system login script*, and the *user login script*. It explains how to set up a system login script that applies to all users logging in to your file server. We'll look at specific commands that can be used in either system or user login scripts, and present some ideas for making the system login script as generic (and therefore as maintenance-free) as possible. The chapter winds up with an example of a real-life system login script and gives some suggestions for managing user login scripts.

THREE TYPES OF LOGIN SCRIPTS

When a file server is first installed, the users SUPERVISOR and GUEST are automatically created. The first time you log in as SUPERVISOR to create the other user accounts, a *default login script* runs, giving you the bare essentials to work with. This default login script is documented in the NetWare *Supervisor Reference* manual. Essentially, the default login script maps a search drive to SYS:PUBLIC so you can use the NetWare utilities there; for SUPERVISOR, it maps a search drive to SYS:SYSTEM as well.

Normally, you create a *system login script* to set up global NetWare drive mappings and other environmental variables that apply for all users. To handle any drive mappings or other set up procedures that apply to individual users, you create a *user login script* for each user. The system login script runs first, then the user login script. If you don't create a system login script, or create a login script for each user, the default login script remains in effect for everyone who logs in.

A user can have a separate login script on every file server he or she normally uses. However, only the user login script on the primary file server is run. The primary file server is the one the user logs in to with the LOGIN command. When a user attaches to another server with the ATTACH command, no login script is run, even if one exists for that user on that server.

The system login script is saved in a DOS text file called NET$LOG.DAT located in the SYS:SYSTEM directory. A user login script is saved to a text file called LOGIN located in that user's mail subdirectory that NetWare creates under the SYS:MAIL directory. The default login script is hard-coded into the LOGIN.EXE file.

WORKING WITH THE SYSTEM LOGIN SCRIPT

The system login script allows you to set up an initial NetWare environment for everyone who uses your file server. A login script is similar to a batch file, in that it consists of a series of commands that are automatically executed in sequence when a user logs in to a file server. As explained above, the system script runs before users' personal login scripts. Alternatively, you can have the system login script exit directly to a menu system and bypass user login scripts altogether.

Accessing the System Login Script

To access the system login script, type SYSCON at the network prompt. From the "Available Topics" menu, select "Supervisor Options." (You must be supervisor or equivalent to view the options under the "Supervisor Options" selection.) Select "System Login Script" from the submenu that appears. The existing system login script, if any, appears in a window. If no system login script has been created yet, the window will be empty.

Moving Around in the Login Script Window

Type the commands you want in the login script window. To move the cursor around, use any of the following keys:

Key	Function
Up arrow	moves the cursor up one line
Down arrow	moves the cursor down one line
Right arrow	moves the cursor one character to the right
Left arrow	moves the cursor one character to the left
Ctrl-Right	moves the cursor one word to the right
Ctrl-Left	moves the cursor one word to the left
End	moves the cursor to the end of a line
Home	moves the cursor to the beginning of the line
PgUp	moves the cursor to the top of the present screen

PgDn	moves the cursor to the bottom of the present screen
Ctrl-PgUp	moves the cursor to the top of the login script
Ctrl-PgDn	moves the cursor to the bottom of the login script
Backspace	deletes one character to the left
Delete	deletes one character to the right

Each line in the login script can contain up to 150 characters; however, the script will be more readable if you limit the length of lines to under 78 characters (the width of the login script window in SYSCON). Type only one command per line and press Enter after each line. Commands can be typed using either uppercase or lowercase letters.

You can use the Mark key (F5) to mark a block of text. Move the cursor to where you want to start the block and press F5; then move the cursor to the end of the block and press Delete. Pressing the Insert key will reinsert the block of text somewhere else. For example, to delete a block of text, press F5 at the beginning of the first line you want to delete, then press the Down arrow key to include the rest of the lines to delete. Press Delete to remove the blocked text. If you want to place the deleted block of text somewhere else in the script, move the cursor to where you want to insert the text and press Insert.

SYSCON holds the most recently deleted block of text in a temporary buffer until you exit the utility. Blocking text and pressing Delete fills the login script buffer with the highlighted information; pressing Insert places the information back in the script at the cursor position. Using this technique, you can copy pieces of one login script to another one. (See "Copying Pieces of Other Login Scripts" later in this chapter.)

Saving the System Login Script

After you have typed in the appropriate commands or made any changes to the system login script, press Escape. Answer "Yes" to the "Save Changes" prompt. You will return to the "Supervisor Options" menu. Exit SYSCON in the usual manner.

LOGIN SCRIPT COMMANDS

This section contains a list of login script commands, divided into two parts: the MAP commands as they function in the system login script, and the other login script commands. Each explanation shows how to use the particular command— you can draw from these examples when creating your own system login script.

MAP Commands in the System Login Script

The following lines from a sample system login script illustrate some of the most common uses of the MAP command:

```
MAP DISPLAY OFF
MAP ERRORS OFF
MAP S1:=SYS:PUBLIC
MAP S2:=SYS:PUBLIC/%MACHINE/%OS/%OS_VERSION
COMSPEC=S2:COMMAND.COM
MAP INS S16:=SYS:PUBLIC/UTIL
MAP *1:=VOL1:USERS/%LOGIN_NAME
MAP DISPLAY ON
MAP ERRORS ON
DRIVE F:
MAP
PAUSE
```

MAP DISPLAY ON/OFF. The MAP DISPLAY ON command shows users their drive mappings as they are being created; the MAP DISPLAY OFF command prevents users from seeing their drive mappings being created. The default is ON. If you place MAP DISPLAY OFF at the top of the system login script and MAP DISPLAY ON at the bottom, before the MAP command itself, users won't see the login script process the drive mapping commands. By placing the MAP command at the end of the system login script commands, you allow users to see the resulting drive mappings at the end of the login process—unless, of course, you take the users directly into a menu system.

MAP ERRORS ON/OFF. With MAP ERRORS ON (the default setting), NetWare will display any errors encountered while the login script processes its MAP commands. If you include the MAP ERRORS OFF command in the login script, users won't see any login script errors or hear any beeps that denote error messages.

Allowing users to see mapping errors may hurt your reputation as a system supervisor, but the advantage is you'll be better able to ascertain why MAP commands didn't work. Since the login script defaults to MAP ERRORS ON, you need not place MAP ERRORS ON in the login script unless you include the MAP ERRORS OFF command early in the script and want to reverse the effect at the end of the script. One reason including MAP ERRORS ON at the end of the system login script is to allow users to view any mapping errors in their personal login scripts.

Commonly Used Drive Mappings. The next five lines in the sample login script illustrate how to implement some of the most commonly used NetWare drive mappings. NetWare offers both regular drive mappings and search drive mappings. Users can have up to twenty-six total drive mappings, one for each letter in the alphabet.

Regular drive mappings begin with the first drive letter after those reserved for use by DOS. With DOS 3.x and above, the first network drive is usually drive F:. You can specify regular drive mapping commands in the system login script in two ways. First, you can use the wildcard method, which consists of an asterisk (*) followed by a number, such as MAP *1:= VOL1:PERSONAL/%LOGIN_NAME. The *1 finds the first available drive letter for the first drive mapping. The next drive mappings use the next number specification, such as *2, *3, *4, and so forth.

The second way to place drive mappings in the system login script is to use the actual drive letters: for example, MAP F:=VOL1:PERSONAL/%LOGIN_ NAME. If you use drive letters in the system login script, users will always see the same drive mappings, no matter which workstation they use. This method works fine as long as users do not overwrite the system login script mappings in their personal login scripts.

If you or users modify the "last drive" parameter in the workstation's CONFIG.SYS file to something different from the DOS default (E: for DOS 3.0 and above), use the DRIVE F: command in the login script. This guarantees that users will enter the network in their home directories (unless they change to a different directory path in their personal login script).

Search drives begin with drive letter Z: and work their way backwards through the alphabet. If NetWare can't find an executable file in a user's current directory, the OS begins looking through the search directories (S1, S2, S3, and so forth) until it finds the designated file. Users can have up to sixteen search drives mapped at a time. However, the network response time may be adversely affected when NetWare must look in sixteen different directories to find a file. To keep the network running as quickly as possible and to conserve file server memory, it is best to keep the number of drive mappings to a minimum whenever possible.

Search Drive Mapping for SYS:PUBLIC. The line "MAP S1:=SYS:PUBLIC" maps the first NetWare search drive to the file server's SYS:PUBLIC directory. (The "S" stands for search drive, and the "1" stands for the first search drive.) Access to the NetWare commands and utilities stored in SYS:PUBLIC is essential for all users on the network. Make sure you include this line in the system login script, because creating a system login script and saving it nullifies the default NetWare login script.

Search Drive Mapping to a DOS Directory. The next two lines, "MAP S2:=SYS:PUBLIC/%MACHINE/%OS/%OS_VERSION" and "COMSPEC=S2: COMMAND.COM," give all users access to the appropriate DOS directory on the file server. This example uses a number of login script *identifiers*, or variables. (A complete list of login script identifiers is included later in this chapter.) If workstations on the server run different DOS versions for different computer types, you can load those DOS versions in different directory paths and use the %MACHINE, %OS, and %OS_VERSION variables to map to the correct directory.

For example, suppose you are using IBM PS/2s and Compaqs as workstations; you are running both IBM PC-DOS v3.3 and Compaq's version of MS-DOS v4.01. Under SYS:PUBLIC, you create two directories, one named IBM_PC and another named COMPAQ. These directory names correspond to the long machine name represented by the %MACHINE variable. Under each of these directories, create a subdirectory named MSDOS. This name corresponds to the %OS identifier variable (NetWare v2.1x recognizes only MSDOS for the %OS identifier). Under the IBM_PC/MSDOS directory, create a directory named V3.30 to hold the actual DOS system files from the IBM PC-DOS v3.30 diskettes. Create a similar directory named V4.01 under the COMPAQ/MSDOS directory for the Compaq DOS v4.01 diskettes. The %OS_VERSION variable corresponds to this level of the directory structure.

When the MAP S2:=SYS:PUBLIC/%MACHINE/%OS/%OS_VERSION command is interpreted at a PS/2 workstation running IBM DOS v3.30, the workstation substitutes "IBM_PC" for %MACHINE, "MSDOS" for %OS, and "V3.30" for %OS_VERSION. The resulting DOS search drive mapping for that workstation will be to SYS:PUBLIC/IBM_PC/MSDOS/V3.30.

Following this naming pattern, you can create as many directories as you have DOS types on the network. For example, if you are running PCDOS versions 3.3 and 4.01 on workstations, create two directories—V3.30 and V4.01—under the IBM_PC/MSDOS directory. If you are running MSDOS versions 3.2 and 3.3 on the Compaqs, create two subdirectories—V3.20 and V3.30—under the COMPAQ/MSDOS directory. Be sure to copy the appropriate DOS files (including COMMAND.COM) into their respective directories.

Setting the COMSPEC command to S2:COMMAND.COM tells DOS to look on search drive 2 whenever it needs to reload the DOS command processor (called COMMAND.COM). This way DOS calls up the command processor from the network rather than from a workstation's boot diskette or hard disk.

Search Drive Mapping for Non-NetWare Utilities. The next line, "MAP INS S16:=SYS:PUBLIC/UTIL," provides a search drive mapping to a directory containing other utilities that you think users will find helpful. It is best to create a UTIL directory under SYS:PUBLIC to hold these utilities. Some supervisors prefer to dump all third-party utilities into the SYS:PUBLIC directory; however, this practice can make it difficult for users (and supervisors) to ascertain which programs are NetWare utilities and which are not. Upgrading the server later on also becomes more difficult.

Including "INS" in the MAP command inserts the drive mapping in front of the next drive mapping. Rather than overwriting existing mappings, the inserted drive mapping bumps subsequent search drive mappings down one notch in the list. A special case of this usage is "MAP INS S16:=", which tells NetWare to insert the search drive mapping after the last existing search drive mapping without overwriting any other search mappings. Use this variation for non-critical drive mappings that can go at the end of NetWare's list of search paths. If you do not use MAP INS, and you specify in a MAP command a drive letter already used by another drive mapping, only the last drive mapping specifying that drive letter will be in effect.

Do not use the MAP INS to insert drive mappings before S3, as S2 normally designates the DOS directory which the COMSPEC command uses as a reference. *If you do move the DOS directory mapping, move the COMSPEC accordingly.*

Drive Mapping to Users' Home Directories. The "MAP *1:= VOL1:USERS/%LOGIN_NAME" command maps a drive to a personal directory for each user who logs in to the server. Depending on your file server security scheme, it is usually a good idea to give users a home directory where they have enough user rights to save personal files (these rights include Read, Write, Open, Create, Delete, and Search rights). If you want users to maintain their own personal directory structures, give the users Parental rights as well. However, starting with NetWare v2.15, granting users Create and Delete rights to their personal directory also allows the users to create and delete subdirectories.

The %LOGIN_NAME variable substitutes the user's login name for the subdirectory name. For example, if a user logs in as TIM and you have created a home directory called TIM in the VOL1:PERSONAL directory, user Tim will receive a drive mapping to the VOL1:PERSONAL/TIM directory. By your using the %LOGIN_NAME parameter, NetWare will map a drive for each user for whom you create a corresponding home directory name. This saves you time and the labor of personally creating user login scripts with a drive mapping to their home directories. Make the first drive mapping the user's personal directory, for this will be the directory where each user ends up after the system and personal login scripts run their course.

DRIVE. The DRIVE F: command in the login script designates the drive letter that determines the default drive your users will have after the system login script runs its course. The DRIVE command accepts either a drive letter designation (such as DRIVE F:) or a wildcard designation (such as DRIVE *1), but using the wildcard designation in the system login script can cause problems. If you leave out a default drive command, NetWare will default to the first drive letter specified by the LASTDRIVE parameter in CONFIG.SYS and designated in the MAP *1:=VOL1:USERS/%LOGIN_NAME command. However, if users wish to have a different default drive mapping when they come out of the login script (and you permit them to have personal login scripts), they can include the "DRIVE *DriveLetter*" command in their personal login scripts.

MAP and **PAUSE**. The command "MAP" in a login script causes NetWare to display the drive mappings at that point in the execution of the script. If you want users to be able to read the mappings before the login script continues, add the "PAUSE" command. This command stops the execution of the script until the user presses a key.

Other MAP Command Variations. There are other ways to use MAP commands in the login script; the above examples only show some preferred methods. For more MAP examples, consult the NetWare *Command Line Utilities* manual.

Other Login Script Commands

NetWare comes with many other commands that you can place in the system login script for setting up your users' NetWare environment. These commands are listed below in alphabetical order:

ATTACH
BREAK
COMSPEC
DISPLAY or FDISPLAY
DOS BREAK
DOS SET
DOS VERIFY
EXIT
(EXTERNAL PROGRAM EXECUTION)
FIRE PHASERS
INCLUDE
MACHINE NAME
PAUSE
PCCOMPATIBLE
REMARK
WRITE
IF...THEN

We will explain each command and give you an example of how to use it. After explaining all the commands, we'll show you how to use the commands in a sample system login script.

ATTACH. To attach certain users to other servers when necessary, place an ATTACH command in the system login script. The format for this command is:

```
ATTACH ServerName/UserName; Password
```

If you couch this command in an IF...THEN statement that checks for membership in a group, then NetWare will attach only members of a specific group to the specified server.

For example, suppose members of the group RECORDS need to access Lotus 1-2-3 and a spreadsheet directory on server ADMIN. Set up the following commands in the system login script:

```
IF MEMBER OF "RECORDS" THEN BEGIN
   ATTACH ADMIN/REC;ACCORD
   MAP INS S3:=ADMIN/SYS:APPLIC/LOTUS
   MAP N:=ADMIN/VOL1:RECORD/SPREAD90
END
```

In this example, those users who are members of the group RECORDS will attach to server ADMIN under the user name "REC." The semicolon followed by the password (ACCORD) allows the ATTACH command to proceed without every member of the group having to know (and remember) the password for REC. For this particular setup to work, you or the supervisor on server ADMIN must create a user called REC and give REC the password ACCORD, as well as Read, Open, and Search trustee rights to the LOTUS directory and Read, Write, Open, Create, Delete, and Search trustee rights to the SPREAD90 directory. Then, as users belonging to group RECORDS log in to their default server, they are automatically attached to server ADMIN with two additional network drive mappings on that server.

Be sure to use the ATTACH command before you designate any drive mappings on another server. For all attached servers, include the server name in the map designation (you do not need to type in the server name for the default server). Some applications lock the directory as well as the file, making it possible for only one person in the group to call up Lotus from the SPREAD90 directory. One way around this problem is to have members of group RECORDS start Lotus from their home directories and then change to the SPREAD90 directory.

You can also put in the ATTACH command without any name; NetWare will then ask for a user name and the password (if you have given one to user REC). Only after users enter the correct user name and password will they be mapped to server ADMIN's directories. However, this procedure can be awkward for users who attach to more than one server during the login procedure.

A better way to handle passwords on multiple servers is to use NetWare's password synchronization feature. If you or your users have the same username on more than one server and you have synchronized the passwords across the servers, you won't be asked for your password when you attach to those servers in your login script.

BREAK ON/OFF. This command determines whether or not users can break out of the login script by pressing Ctrl-Break. The default is BREAK OFF, which prevents users from breaking out of an executing login script. If you want users to be able to interrupt the login script if necessary, add the BREAK ON command at the beginning of the login script.

COMSPEC. Some applications remove DOS from memory while they run so they can use more memory. The COMSPEC designation tells DOS where to find the command processor (COMMAND.COM) so it can reload it after these applications are exited. The format for the COMSPEC command is:

```
COMSPEC DirectoryPath/FileName
```

You normally use COMSPEC in conjunction with the DOS directory mapping. See the explanation under "Search Drive Mapping to a DOS Directory" above for more details.

DISPLAY. The DISPLAY command allows you to display a message from a text file on the screen when users are logging in. Use this command to call up a text file containing login messages for users, instead of writing the messages directly in the system login script with the WRITE command. That way, you can change the text file from time to time as needed, with no need to rewrite the login script every time you want to change the message. The format for this command is:

```
DISPLAY    DirectoryPath/FileName
```

When you use DISPLAY, write out the full directory path; drive letters won't work. If NetWare can't find the directory path or the file, it ignores the command altogether and users won't see your message.

The FDISPLAY variation stands for a "filtered" display. Use FDISPLAY if you save the file in a word processor format (DISPLAY assumes the file is a straight ASCII text file). Since FDISPLAY cannot correctly display files created by all word processors, you may have to save the file as a DOS text file.

As an example, suppose you have an important meeting coming up and you want everyone to attend. You can create a little text file using DOS's COPY CON command in one of your regular directories, such as SYS:SYSTEM. For example:

```
COPY CON MEETING.TXT
As you all know, we are having a general meeting to discuss RAISES!
If you don't attend, we shall assume you aren't interested, or are
overpaid already. The meeting is Thursday at 2 pm sharp. Be there!
^Z
```

Press Enter after each line. The last line (^Z), which you create either by pressing Ctrl-Z or the F6 key, signals the "End of File" and causes the file to be saved under the name MEETING.TXT.

In the system login script, enter the following commands:

```
IF DAY_OF_WEEK <= "THURSDAY" AND HOUR24<"14" THEN BEGIN
    DISPLAY SYS:SYSTEM/MEETING.TXT
    PAUSE
END
```

Every time users log in before Thursday at 2:00 p.m., NetWare will find the MEETING.TXT file in SYS:SYSTEM, display the contents of the file, and pause for users to read the message. When the users press a key, the system login script will continue.

You may want to maintain a separate login message file for different groups of users. For example, you can ensure that only members of group ADMIN see your message. Replace the first line in the example above with "IF MEMBER OF 'ADMIN' AND DAY_OF_WEEK <= 'THURSDAY' THEN BEGIN."

DOS SET. The DOS SET command lets you set up DOS environment parameters for use by programs that everyone is running on the network. While the AUTOEXEC.BAT file is a better place to invoke most of DOS's SET commands, there are still some universal SET commands you can use in the system login script to make life easier for users on the network.

For example, you can use the DOS SET command when you load such programs as WordPerfect so users won't have to type in their initials every time they go into the network version of WordPerfect. You can do this by placing the following command in the system login script:

```
DOS SET WP="/u-%LOGIN_NAME"
```

Every time your users type "WP" at the DOS prompt, WordPerfect will accept the first three letters of their login name as their initials. This can be a problem if more than one user name has the same first three letters; WordPerfect may assign only one backup file to both names. To avoid backup file overlap and other WordPerfect conflicts, place the "DOS SET WP=" command in users' personal login scripts along with their individual initials. Train users to start WordPerfect from their home directories, and have them each designate a different directory path location for backup files through the WordPerfect Setup function (Shift-F1).

If you are running The Coordinator and your users' Coordinator names are the same as their login names, you can place the following in the system login script:

```
DOS SET usr="%LOGIN_NAME"
DOS SET pwd=""
```

If you have set up your system so that users' login names are the same as their Coordinator names, they will go directly into the opening menu—provided that the users have not given themselves Coordinator passwords. Application startup parameters may change from one product release to the next. Consult each product's documentation for the correct parameters to use with the SET command.

You can also put **DOS SET PROMPT="\$P \$G"** in the system login script to have the DOS prompt show entire directory paths, or you can put this prompt command in everyone's AUTOEXEC.BAT files. Using the system login script is less laborious, and users can override this prompt setting with their own prompt command in their individual login scripts.

Another useful SET command that may have universal appeal is adding color to the DOS prompt if your users have color monitors. Be sure to place an ANSI.SYS driver in the CONFIG.SYS file of each workstation if you plan to use DOS's color capabilities.

As you add more and more DOS environment variables, you may have to expand the size of the DOS environment in CONFIG.SYS as well; see your DOS manual for more information on color and environment variables.

DOS VERIFY ON/OFF. NetWare performs an automatic read-after-write verification of all files you copy from one network directory to another network directory through DOS's COPY or NetWare's NCOPY command. However, NetWare does not verify files that are copied to local drives. Set the DOS VERIFY command to ON if you wish to verify that files are written correctly when copied locally. Otherwise, users will have to add the "/V" parameter in their DOS COPY command to copy files locally.

EXIT. The EXIT command terminates the execution of the login script so you can run a particular program, such as a batch file or menu system. Specify the batch file or program you want to exit to according to the following format:

```
EXIT "FileName"
```

After EXITing, NetWare does not come back to the login script, so be sure to place this command at the end of the login script.

Placing the EXIT command at the end of the system login script also prevents users' personal login scripts from running. For example, to keep users from executing their personal login scripts and have them come up in a menuing system such as MENU, type EXIT "MENU MAIN" at the bottom of the system login script.

There is no sure way within NetWare to prevent users from breaking out to DOS before they get into Novell's MENU program. If you do not want users to access the DOS command line, purchase a third-party menuing system that can prevent users from breaking out, or one that logs users out automatically if they break out of the menu.

A number of applications allow users to "shell out to DOS" while remaining in the application. For example, you can go to DOS from within WordPerfect by pressing Ctrl-F1. Some third-party menu programs may be able to prevent even this method of accessing the DOS command line.

The EXIT command places the command inside the quotation marks directly into the keyboard buffer. If the EXIT command doesn't work for a particular workstation, that workstation may have a BIOS that is not fully IBM PC-compatible. Try inserting the PCCOMPATIBLE login script command before the EXIT command. Even with PCCOMPATIBLE, the EXIT command may not work correctly.

EXTERNAL PROGRAM EXECUTION (#). To execute a DOS or NetWare command from within the system login script, use the pound sign (#) followed by the command (include the directory path where the command is located). It is a good idea to place external command calls after the MAP assignments in the login script so that NetWare can use the NetWare drive mappings to help execute the command.

For example, suppose you want to set up a CAPTURE command for everyone who logs in to server PLANT1. Include the line "#CAPTURE S=PLANT1 Q=GENERAL NT NB NFF TI=5" in the system login script. This command captures all print jobs and sends them to print queue GENERAL on server PLANT1; the CAPTURE options specify no tabs, no print banner, no form feeds, and a timeout of five seconds. (Refer to Chapter 17 for more information about the CAPTURE command.)

Once you have a general CAPTURE command in place, you can then specify a specific queue for those users who are a part of a group that uses a different printer. For example, if the group SALES needs to access print queue SALES which is serviced by Printer 2, you can put in the following lines:

```
IF MEMBER OF "SALES" THEN BEGIN
    MAP INS S4:=SYS:PUBLIC/APPLIC/MONEY
    #CAPTURE S=PLANT1 Q=SALES NT NB NFF TI=15
END
```

With #, you can run .COM files, .EXE files, and batch files. You may sometimes need to write out the entire directory path in order for the # command to work. Add DOS command line flags after the filename. To run batch files, be sure to run COMMAND.COM with the "/C" parameter after the batch file name. (The "/C" parameter returns control to the login script after the batch file is finished.)

For example, suppose you want to run a batch file called CLEAR.BAT that clears the workstation screen before displaying the MAP commands. Create the batch file in a directory that everyone has access to and that does not change due to additional group mappings. (This example assumes the batch file is in SYS:PUBLIC, which is mapped to drive Z:.) To create the batch file, change to the SYS:PUBLIC directory and type:

```
COPY CON CLEAR.BAT
CLS
^Z
```

Then in the system login script, type:

```
#Y:COMMAND /C Z:CLEAR
```

The Y: designates where COMMAND.COM is located (the DOS directory), and Z:CLEAR is the drive letter mapped to SYS:PUBLIC along with the CLEAR.BAT filename.

You don't need a batch file to clear the screen, however; typing "#Y:COMMAND /C CLS" in the system login script will accomplish the same thing. If you are presenting messages before the clear-screen command, put in a PAUSE command before you clear the screen. You may also wish to follow the clear-screen command with a MAP command.

Do not use the # command to load terminate-and-stay-resident (TSR) programs. Workstations initially load COMMAND.COM, IPX, and NET3 programs into memory for as long as the workstation is on. The workstation then loads the LOGIN utility, which takes up memory for only as long as it is run; then LOGIN is discarded. Loading a TSR program from the login script will lock the TSR into memory above the LOGIN program, creating a hole when LOGIN is removed from memory. This memory hole cannot be accessed by any other software. Instead of the TSR taking up 4KB of memory, it effectively takes from 30KB to 70KB, which may not leave enough for users to run large applications.

FIRE PHASERS. If you want to accentuate a certain condition in the system, you can use the FIRE PHASERS command to generate a sound like the laser noises you hear in old science fiction movies. The format for this command is as follows:

```
FIRE PHASERS n TIMES
```

Replace *n* with the number of times you want the phasers to fire.

For example, if a particular volume is running out of room and you want to alert users when they log in to get rid of unnecessary files, type the following lines in the system login script:

```
FIRE PHASERS 6 TIMES
WRITE "VOL1 is almost out of disk space and file handles."
WRITE "I have the volume backed up three times for safe keeping."
WRITE "Please delete all files you have not accessed in"
WRITE "the last three months. If you need help, call me."
PAUSE
```

INCLUDE. The INCLUDE command allows you to place parts of the login script in a file kept outside of the NET$LOG.DAT file. By doing this, you can unclutter the system login script by removing IF/THEN statements that you only occasionally use to a separate file. The format for the INCLUDE command is as follows:

```
INCLUDE   DirectoryPath/FileName
```

For example, suppose you want to set up certain supervisory network drive mappings apart from the regular system login script. You don't use these extra mappings all the time—only when you type the word "SUPE" after your login name when you log in. (See "Using Command Line Parameters When Logging In" at the end of this chapter for details.) To make this work, first place in the system login script (or your personal login script) the following commands:

```
IF "%2" = "SUPE" THEN BEGIN
   INCLUDE SYS:SYSTEM/SUPE
END
```

If the second parameter you type in after the LOGIN command is the string "SUPE" (as in "LOGIN PLANT/ED SUPE"), the login script will run the extra commands you have placed in the SUPE file located in the SYS:SYSTEM directory. The SUPE file could contain such commands as:

```
ATTACH ADMIN/SUPERVISOR
MAP INS S16:ADMIN\SYS:PUBLIC\UTIL
MAP INS S4:=PLANT\SYS:APPLIC\BRIEF
```

```
IF "%2" == "SUPE" THEN BEGIN
    SET BFILE="SLD.RST"
    SET BFLAGS=""
    SET BBACKUP="."
    SET BPATH="W:\\APPLIC\\BRIEF\\MACROS"
    SET BHELP="W:\\APPLIC\\BRIEF\\HELP"
    SET DIRSTACK = "PLANT\\VOL1:PERSONAL\\ED"
    SET USR="ED"
END
IF "%2" == "SUPE" THEN BEGIN
    MAP INS S3:=SYS:APPLIC/REMOTE
    MAP M:=VOL1:DATABASE
END
```

You can create and edit the SUPE file with any text editor or word processor, but save the file in DOS text form. You can nest other INCLUDE commands within the SUPE file to call up other files and execute the commands contained therein. You can nest up to ten levels deep if you wish (although that's a bit extreme).

The INCLUDE command is different from the DISPLAY command. While you can display messages with either command, messages are easier through DISPLAY.

MACHINE NAME. Some programs written to run under NetBIOS need a MACHINE NAME variable set in the DOS environment. You can set this variable in the system login script using the following format:

```
MACHINE NAME=Name
```

Replace *Name* with a character string up to fifteen characters long. Those certain NetBIOS programs will then accept the string you type as the machine name for the application. You could also use each workstation's physical node address (via the NetWare %P_STATION variable) as the machine name. To do this, type the command as follows:

```
MACHINE NAME="%P_STATION"
```

You need to use this command only if an application's installation instructions tell you to do so.

PAUSE or **WAIT**. These commands allow you to put a pause in the login script, as shown in the FIRE PHASERS example above. You can also use the PAUSE command when you write a long text for the DISPLAY command. Users will see the "Strike a key when ready..." message at the point where you invoke PAUSE; when the users press any key, the rest of the login script will execute.

PC COMPATIBLE. When you run the EXIT command, NetWare takes advantage of the workstation's BIOS to place the command you designate into the keyboard buffer. However, some workstations that are not 100 percent IBM-compatible do not have type-ahead keyboard buffers and can lock up when the EXIT command starts stuffing data into the keyboard buffer. To prevent this from happening, NetWare checks the workstation's BIOS to see if it is IBM-specific.

For those workstations whose Short Machine Name setting in the SHELL .CFG file is anything other than "IBM," type PCCOMPATIBLE before you type the EXIT "*filename*" command. This command allows computers using a machine name other than "IBM" to use the EXIT command as well. For example, if you are using Compaq computers as workstations and you want to run the MENU program from the system login script, type PCCOMPATIBLE (or just COMPATIBLE) on one line and EXIT "MENU *MenuName*" on the next line.

REMARK. Use the REMARK command to make a comment to yourself inside the system login script. Text you type after the word REMARK is not displayed on the screen. Alternatives to using the full word "REMARK" include the abbreviation "REM," an asterisk (*), or a semicolon (;). An example of each type of remark is shown below:

> REMARK Be sure everyone has access to this file
> REM Be sure that all of SALES can write to this directory
> * Check on progress of backup
> ; Assign all users ROS rights to this directory

The WRITE Command

The WRITE command allows you to write short login messages that will appear on the screen of everyone who logs in. The command can accept two basic parameters: literal text strings and identifier variables that NetWare recognizes. Throughout the login script examples shown above, you have seen some of the text string capabilities as well as some of the login script identifiers.

Using Text Strings with WRITE. When you write literal text strings (without identifiers), place the text itself inside quotation marks. In the FIRE PHASERS example shown above, you saw the following text strings:

```
WRITE "VOL1 is almost out of disk space and file handles."
WRITE "I have the volume backed up three times for safe keeping."
WRITE "Please delete all files you have not accessed in"
WRITE "the last three months. If you need help, call me."
PAUSE
```

NetWare login scripts recognize four symbols known as super-characters that can help you write out text strings. These super-characters and their functions are:

\r	Places the cursor at the beginning of the present line
\n	Places the cursor on the next line
\"	Allows you to embed quotation marks within the text
\7	Sounds a beep

The WRITE command automatically moves the cursor down to the next line when one line is full, so you need only use the "\r" or the "\n" super-characters when you want to break the text string in a different place. The login script is indiscriminate—it will break lines right in the middle of a word. Lines more than 128 characters long can produce error messages. The "\r" super-character moves the cursor only to the far left of your current line, so if you want to break a sentence, place the "\n" between the words you wish separated. Do not break a line by pressing Enter unless you place quotes at the end of the line and begin the next line with a new WRITE command, as in the FIRE PHASERS example.

In addition to super-characters, newer versions of NetWare allow a number of operators for creating compound strings. These operators include:

;	Concatenate	%	Modulo
*	Multiply	+	Add
/	Divide	-	Subtract

The operator you will use most often is the semicolon. With the semicolon, you can join or concatenate two text strings together on one line. For example, to join the literal text string "Hello," with a user's login name, enter this WRITE command:

```
WRITE "Hello, "; LOGIN_NAME
```

When user JASON logs in, the output of this WRITE command would be:

```
Hello, JASON
```

The next section explains more about using NetWare's identifier variables in WRITE commands.

Using Identifier Variables with WRITE. The login script recognizes a number of identifiers to let you call information from the NetWare workstation shell or from the OS itself. These identifiers allow you to write variable information: for example, which workstations users are on, their login names, the DOS operating system they are using, and the file server date and time. When you use identifier variables within WRITE commands, precede the identifier with a percent sign (%) and type the identifier in all capital letters. Enclose the entire string following the WRITE command in quotation marks.

Here's a list of the identifiers you can use in the login script, along with what NetWare will display in place of the each variable when the login script is executed.

Identifiers	What You See on the Screen
MONTH	Month as a number (01 to 12)
MONTH_NAME	The name of the month (April, June, ...)
DAY	Day of the month as a number (01 to 31)

DAY_OF_WEEK	Day of the week (Wednesday, Friday, ...)
NDAY_OF_WEEK	Day of the week as a number (1 to 7; Sunday is 1)
YEAR	Year in full format (1990, 1991, ...)
SHORT_YEAR	Year in short format (90, 91, ...)
HOUR	Hour of the day or night (1 to 12)
HOUR24	Hour of the day or night in 24-hour time (00 to 23)
MINUTE	Minutes (00 to 59)
SECOND	Seconds (00 to 59)
AM_PM	Either "a.m." or "p.m." depending on time
GREETING_TIME	"Morning," "Afternoon," or "Evening," depending on time
LOGIN_NAME	The user's login name
FULL_NAME	The user's full name (as defined in SYSCON)
STATION	Workstation's connection number
P_STATION	Physical station number or node address (12 hex digits)
NEW_MAIL	Shows if new mail has arrived ("YES" or "NO").
SHELL_TYPE	Shell type number (0, 4, 26, ...)
OS	MS-DOS
OS_VERSION	DOS version (such as V3.20)
MACHINE	Long machine name in SHELL.CFG (up to six characters, default is "IBM_PC")
SMACHINE	Short machine name (up to four characters, default is "IBM")
ERROR_LEVEL	"0" if no errors, any other number if errors

Here's an example of how you could use these identifiers for listing a greeting time, the user's full name, the day of the week, month, year, hour, and whether it is in the morning or afternoon.

```
WRITE "Good %GREETING_TIME, %FULL_NAME,"
WRITE "it's %DAY_OF_WEEK, %MONTH_NAME %DAY, %YEAR"
WRITE "at %HOUR:%MINUTE:%SECOND %AM_PM."
WRITE "You are on workstation %P_STATION, running %OS %OS_VERSION."
```

Through this particular **WRITE** command, users will see:

```
Good afternoon, James R. Brown,
it's Friday, September 7, 1990
at 1:23:14 pm.
You are on workstation 0000D800F53E, running MS-DOS V4.01.
```

As explained earlier, you can use the concatenate operator (a semicolon) to join text strings, in which case you type all identifiers in lower case and enclose only literal text strings in quotation marks. The semicolon method works well for small strings, but becomes unwieldy in longer string sets. You must be more careful about where you insert spaces with the semicolon method than with the percent sign method. Experiment and see if you like the semicolon method as an alternative. Here's another example of using the semicolon method:

```
IF MEMBER OF "SALES" THEN BEGIN
    WRITE "Good "; greeting_time;  " ; sales report due on Friday."
END
```

Users who belong to group SALES will see the following message when logging in after twelve o'clock noon:

```
Good afternoon; sales report due on Friday.
```

On smaller text lines, allow the login script to handle the line breaks for you. Experiment with the different WRITE variables and see which method you like. If you don't get the syntax quite right, the login script will generate an error message upon execution (not while you write it or even when you save it). Watch where these error messages occur when the login script runs, for they occur at the place where you used the wrong syntax.

There are many different ways to use super-characters, operators, and identifiers. This chapter has covered only a few of them. Take these concepts, apply them to your particular network, experiment a little, and you'll begin to see how the login script can make your life easier.

Using IF...THEN Statements in Login Scripts

Using IF...THEN statements lets system supervisors set up login script commands that execute based on a certain condition. For example, you can test for membership in a group and set up drive mappings for all members of that group, rather than having to set up specialized login scripts for each individual user. In IF...THEN statements, you can use everything you have learned up to this point, including all the WRITE command super-characters, operators, and identifiers.

The format for a simple IF...THEN statement is:

```
IF Condition... THEN Command
```

When the condition specified in the IF statement is true, the login script executes the command(s) following THEN. The three dots after Condition mean you can specify more than one condition at once. Since IF statements are conditional, you can present this conditional relationship as equal, not equal, greater than, less than, greater than or equal to, and lesser than or equal to. The possible ways to specify equals and not equals relationships include:

Equals	Not Equals
IS	IS NOT
=	!=
==	<>
	#
EQUALS	DOES NOT EQUAL
	NOT EQUAL TO

Specify other conditional relationships, such as greater than, less than, greater than or equal to, and less than or equal to either by writing them out all in caps or by using the symbol that stands for the conditional:

Writing Out the Condition	Using the Symbol
IS GREATER THAN	>
IS LESS THAN	<
IS GREATER THAN OR EQUAL TO	>=
IS LESS THAN OR EQUAL TO	<=

You can test for two conditions using the logical operators "AND" and "OR." Two conditions separated by the word "AND" must both be true in order for the commands after THEN to be executed. With "OR," the commands will be executed if one or the other condition is true.

Below are four examples of how to use conditional relationships with IF...THEN statements in the system login script.

Example 1: Testing for Group Membership. Groups are the best way to assign drive mappings in the system login script. If you have not already set up groups on your network, do so now; it will save you time in the future. (See Chapter 8 for more information.) Rather than setting up individual search drive mappings in each user's login script, you can set up the majority of them in the system login script based on group membership. For example:

```
IF MEMBER OF "WP51" THEN MAP INS S4:=SYS:APPLIC/WP51
```

In this example, all users who belong to the group WP51 will have their fourth search drive mapped to the SYS:APPLIC/WP51 directory.

Example 2: Commands Based on Login Name. You can set up login script commands to run for only certain users, or for everyone who is not a certain user (using a "not equals" conditional). Here's one way to do it:

```
IF "%LOGIN_NAME" == "SUPERVISOR" THEN BEGIN
    MAP INS S3:=SYS:APPLIC/REMOTE
    MAP M:=VOL1:DATABASE
END
```

In this example, when you log in as SUPERVISOR, search drive 3 will be mapped to the SYS:APPLIC/REMOTE directory and network drive M: will be mapped to the VOL1:DATABASE directory.

This example also shows how to use BEGIN and END if you need multiple commands in the IF...THEN statement. If you don't include "BEGIN" after the word "THEN," you must place the whole IF...THEN statement on one line, as in the previous WP51 example. The END parameter tells NetWare where the end of the IF...THEN statement is.

Example 3: Attaching to Other Servers. We've already seen this example in our discussion of the ATTACH command:

```
IF MEMBER OF "RECORDS" THEN BEGIN
    ATTACH ADMIN/REC;ACCORD
    MAP INS S3:=ADMIN/SYS:APPLIC/LOTUS
    MAP N:=ADMIN/VOL1:RECORD/SPREAD90
END
```

Users who are members of the group RECORDS attach to the ADMIN server under the user name "REC" with the password of "ACCORD." Their third search drive is mapped to the LOTUS directory and drive N: is mapped to the SPREAD90 directory.

Example 4: Commands Based on Date or Time. Using the date and time identifiers, you can have certain messages display only on a certain day of the week or at a certain time of the day. Consider the following examples:

```
IF DAY_OF_WEEK="WEDNESDAY" AND HOUR24<"10" THEN BEGIN
    WRITE "\7MEETING WITH SALES AT 10:00!"
END
IF DAY_OF_WEEK="FRIDAY" AND HOUR24<"09" THEN BEGIN
    WRITE "\7CONFERENCE MEETING AT 9:30. BE THERE!"
END
```

The first IF...THEN statement says, "If the day of the week is Wednesday and it is any time before than 10:00 a.m. (1000 hours), then beep once (\7) and write the message concerning the sales meeting at 10:00." When users log in after 10:00 a.m. on Wednesday or on another day of the week, they won't see the message. This example also illustrates the use of "AND" to test for two conditions.

The second example is similar to the first DAY_OF_WEEK example, but points out an important note relating to numbers. When referring to a number that is less than 10, put a zero (0) before the number, as in 09. Otherwise, NetWare might misinterpret what you mean. For example, suppose you wanted the login script to do something every day between the ninth and the twentieth of the month. You typed the following in the system login script:

```
IF DAY >= "9" AND DAY <="20" THEN ...
```

NetWare would misinterpret this to mean "If the day is greater than or equal to 9 but less than or equal to 2, then perform something"—in which case nothing will be performed. Include a "0" in front of the 9 to make the conditional work.

These examples only begin to scratch the surface of what you can do with IF...THEN statements in the system login script. With a little experimentation, you can come up with some fairly inventive ways to make the system login script work most effectively for your network.

Fixing Errors in Login Scripts

SYSCON doesn't check for syntax errors or invalid commands when you type in the login script text. However, if the login script contains an invalid command or a wrong syntax, you will receive the following message upon logging in:

```
Illegal identifier ... Remainder of login script ignored.
WARNING: Due to a serious error in your LOGIN script, further
initialization of your network environment can not be accom-
plished successfully. Drive F: has been mapped to the SYS:PUBLIC
directory to give you access to the network utilities. Use the
SYSCON menu utility to fix the error in your script (as indi-
cated above) and then run LOGIN again.
```

As the message says, drive F: is mapped to SYS:PUBLIC so you can go back into SYSCON and rectify the problem.

SAMPLE SYSTEM LOGIN SCRIPT

Here is a sample of a real-life system login script that shows how to use the login script features in combination. You can use those parts of this example script that best fit your particular needs.

```
REM preliminary greeting
MAP DISPLAY OFF
WRITE "Good %GREETING_TIME, %LOGIN_NAME."
WRITE "Welcome to server SLASHER."
WRITE "You are logged in as connection number %STATION."

REM basic NetWare environment setup
MAP INS S1:=SYS:PUBLIC
MAP INS S2:=SYS:PUBLIC/%MACHINE/%OS_VERSION
COMSPEC=S2:COMMAND.COM
SET PROMPT="$P$G"
DOS SET MV=SLASHER/SYS:

REM supervisor mappings
IF "%LOGIN_NAME" = "SUPERVISOR" THEN BEGIN
     MAP Q:=SYS:SYSTEM
     MAP *1:=SYS:
     MAP *2:=VOL1:
     DRIVE Q:
END

REM user's home directory mapping
MAP *1:=VOL1:USERS/%LOGIN_NAME

REM mappings for e-mail
MAP INS S10:=VOL1:MHS/EXE
MAP INS S11:=VOL1:ATC/EXE
```

```
REM mappings for network applications
IF MEMBER OF "WP42" THEN
    MAP INS S3:=SYS:APPS/WP42
IF MEMBER OF "WP51" THEN
    MAP INS S3:=SYS:APPS/WP51
IF MEMBER OF "DBASE" THEN BEGIN
    MAP INS S16:=SYS:APPS/DBASE
    MAP INS S16:=VOL1:USERS/%LOGIN_NAME/DBASE
    MAP *2:=VOL1:DATA/DATABASE
END
IF MEMBER OF "POWER_USERS" THEN
    MAP INS S16:=SYS/PUBLIC/UTILS


REM printer settings by group
IF MEMBER OF "PRINT0" THEN
    #CAPTURE Q=PRINTQ_0 NB NFF TI=5
IF MEMBER OF "PRINT1" THEN
    #CAPTURE Q=PRINTQ_1 NB NFF TI=5


REM display daily and monthly login messages
IF NDAY_OF_WEEK = "1" AND HOUR24 < "09" THEN
    DISPLAY SYS:PUBLIC/MON.MSG
IF NDAY_OF_WEEK = "2" AND HOUR24 < "09" THEN
    DISPLAY SYS:PUBLIC/TUES.MSG
IF NDAY_OF_WEEK = "3" AND HOUR24 < "09" THEN
    DISPLAY SYS:PUBLIC/WED.MSG
IF NDAY_OF_WEEK = "4" AND HOUR24 < "09" THEN
    DISPLAY SYS:PUBLIC/THURS.MSG
IF NDAY_OF_WEEK = "5" AND HOUR24 < "09" THEN
    DISPLAY SYS:PUBLIC/FRI.MSG
IF DAY <= "31" AND HOUR24 < "09" THEN BEGIN
    WRITE "/n/7 End of the month again."
    WRITE "Please archive old mail messages and other unnecessary files"
    WRITE "and delete them from the file server./n"
    PAUSE
END


REM display drive mappings
MAP DISPLAY ON
MAP
PAUSE


REM exit to menu program
EXIT "MENU MAIN"
```

SETTING UP PERSONAL LOGIN SCRIPTS

With the system login script, you can satisfy 90% of user needs. Supervisors can cut down on their day-to-day user support workload by planning out group and directory access. Before setting up personal login scripts, outline the system login script, including the groups you will have, the users who will make up the groups, the applications and directories the groups will access, and the trustee assignments each group will have.

Since this is a troubleshooting and maintenance book, let's work from the assumption that the network is already running and you have taken care of all the general features in the system login script, such as drive mappings to the SYS:PUBLIC directory, DOS directory, application and utility directories, and a user home directory (depending on your security scheme). Your next step is to assess the effectiveness of the present system login script. Sit down with each user and find out where the system login script is falling short. From this feedback, you may see where you need to add a new group or another generic command.

Adding Drive Mappings to User Login Scripts

The main reason for personal login scripts is to create drive mappings specific to each user. For example, user Bill wants two extra drive mappings to MAY and JUNE directories that lie beneath his VOL1:PERSONAL/BILL directory path. User Bill also wants to set up a personal search drive mapping and place some PopUp utilities that he purchased in that directory. Bill also wants his default drive to be the JUNE directory instead of his PERSONAL/BILL directory.

To avoid overwriting mappings from the system login script, first see what drive mappings Bill presently has. Before going into SYSCON, have Bill type MAP at the DOS prompt and note the drive mappings presently being used. Suppose drive letters G: and H: are unused. Go into SYSCON, select "User Information," choose "BILL" from the list of users, then select "Login Script." Add the following mappings to Bill's login script:

```
MAP G:=VOL1:PERSONAL/BILL/MAY
MAP H:=VOL1:PERSONAL/BILL/JUNE
MAP INS S16:=VOL1:PERSONAL/BILL/POPUP
DRIVE H:
```

The "MAP INS S16" command will place the POPUP directory in the next available search drive mapping. To save the changes, press Escape. Answer Yes to the "Save Changes" prompt.

Copying Existing Login Scripts to New Users

If you are creating a new user and you know of a generic personal login script prototype, you can copy that generic login script for the new user. For example, if Bill has a very generic login script and Frank is a new user that you just created on the system, select FRANK from the "User Name" list (accessed by selecting "User Information" from SYSCON's main menu), then choose the "Login Script" option. You will see the "Login Script Does Not Exist" message, along with a box that says "Read Login Script From User: FRANK." Backspace over FRANK and type "BILL" in the box. NetWare copies Bill's personal login script to Frank; from there, you can modify the login script to suit Frank's needs. To save Frank's new script, press Escape and answer "Yes" to the "Save Changes" prompt.

Copying Pieces of Other Login Scripts

Suppose there are no generic login scripts that meet Frank's needs. You can copy pieces from one login script and place those pieces in another login script. For example, suppose Bill's script has three lines you need for Frank's login script. Go into Bill's login script and press F5 at the beginning of the lines you wish to copy. Then press the Down arrow key until all the lines you need are highlighted. Press Delete to put the lines into SYSCON's buffer, then press Insert to restore the lines to Bill's login script. SYSCON's login script buffer still holds a copy of the three lines you highlighted.

Exit Bill's login script and return to the "User Names" window. Select FRANK, then select Frank's "Login Script" option. Position the cursor where you want to place the lines from Bill's login script. Now press Insert. The three lines from Bill's login script are now in Frank's login script, where you can modify them if necessary to fit Frank's needs.

IF...THEN Statements in User Login Scripts

Users can set up their personal login scripts to run certain programs only if some condition is met. In the following example, the environment necessary to run the Brief program will be set up only if the user logs in from a specific workstation. This example uses NetWare's %P_STATION identifier.

```
IF "%P_STATION" == "0000D729F1AB" THEN BEGIN
    set bfile="sld.rst"
    set bflags=""
    set bbackup="."
    set bpath="W:\\applic\\brief\\macros"
    set bhelp="W:\\applic\\brief\\help"
    set dirstack = "plant\\vol1:personal\\bill"
    set usr="bill"
END
```

When user Bill logs in from node address 0000D729F1AB, his Brief environment will be set up. Note that since the login script reserves the backslash character to identify its own operators, you need to put in two backslashes in the SET command to designate a single slash. If Bill logs in from another workstation, he will not have automatic access to his Brief environment. He could enter all of the SET commands by hand to construct the environment if he wants to use Brief on that workstation.

Using Command Line Parameters When Logging In

Adding parameters after the LOGIN command at the command line allows users to call up applications as they initially log in, as well as call up different network environments. The parameters themselves are pointers which, depending on their placement, can denote a different environment or application. Users can add as many as nine parameters, which are names or keywords to designate the options they wish to use. The first parameter (%1) is always the user's login name. The following parameters (%2, %3, and so on) can be whatever the user chooses—the name of a directory, the name of a program, or an abbreviation of a program name.

For supervisors, setting up command line parameters in the system login script may not be worth the trouble, since they are specific to what the user types. However, you may need to familiarize yourself with how they work in case you need to help someone.

For example, suppose user Bill wants to use a menu called FROG whenever he attaches to server LAP. Bill can add the word "FROG" as the second parameter when he logs in and set up the menu environment at the end of his personal login script:

```
IF "%2" == "FROG" THEN BEGIN
    ATTACH LAP/BILL
    MAP INS S16:=LAP/SYS:MENUS
    EXIT "MENU FROG"
END
```

Once Bill sets up these parameters in his personal login script, he can type LOGIN PLANT/BILL FROG to attach to the LAP server and invoke the FROG menu.

The next example maps a search drive based on the second parameter and designates the name of the directory that Bill wants to set up in the search drive:

```
IF "%2" = "REPORTS" THEN MAP S16:=PLANT/VOL1:PERSONAL/BILL/%2
```

When Bill logs in and adds "REPORTS" after his login name, NetWare will set up a search drive to the REPORTS directory if that directory is found at the end of the PERSONAL\BILL directory path. Again, you will need to experiment to find out how you can best use command line parameters.

PRINTING OUT LOGIN SCRIPTS

It is a good idea to keep a hard copy of the system login script and each user login script in your network logbook. These hard copies are easier to refer to when you are diagnosing a problem with login scripts or overlapping drive mappings.

Printing the System Login Script

As mentioned at the beginning of this chapter, the system login script is saved in a DOS text file called NET$LOG.DAT located in the SYS:PUBLIC directory. You can print this with any word processor that handles DOS text files. Or you can type the following NPRINT command at your workstation:

```
NPRINT SYS:PUBLIC/NET$LOG.DAT Q=PRINTQ_0 NB NFF
```

This command will send the file to print queue PRINTQ_0, with no banner and no form feed. (You must be logged in as supervisor or equivalent to access the system login script file.)

Printing User Login Scripts

Each user's login script is saved to a text file called LOGIN, located in the user's mail subdirectory under the SYS:MAIL directory. To find out which mail subdirectory belongs to which user, go into SYSCON and look at each user's ID number. Select "User Information" from the main menu, then choose a user name from the resulting list of users. Select "Other Information" and write down the 8-digit number displayed as the user ID. Do the same for each user account.

Now exit SYSCON and change to the SYS:MAIL directory. Type **LISTDIR**; you'll see that there are several subdirectories with numbers for names. NetWare removes any zeros at the beginning of the 8-digit user ID number when it forms the subdirectory name for the user. For example, if user Bill's ID number is "0024b0af," his mail subdirectory will be SYS:MAIL/24B0AF. The file named "LOGIN" in this subdirectory contains Bill's personal login script. If you or Bill make any changes to the login script, a file named "LOGIN.BAK" will also appear. This file contains the former version of the login script as it existed before the most recent changes.

Print out each LOGIN file in the same manner in which you printed the system login script file. Make a note on each hard copy of whose login script it is; file the copies in your network log book.

10 Using the NetWare MENU System

An effective menu system is a key part of an easy-to-manage network. A well-designed menu can reduce an overwhelming number of network applications and commands to a manageable number of discrete options that users need to do their work. The menu shields users from the complexity of the command line, reduces command syntax errors, and demands less user training on your part.

A number of popular menu systems will work on a NetWare network. Novell's offering is the MENU command, which lets you create customized menus to suit your network's needs. This chapter discusses some general principles for good menus, then explains how to implement those principles in designing an effective menu script for use with the NetWare MENU command.

PRINCIPLES OF EFFECTIVE MENUS

We touched on some of the principles of effective menus in Chapter 4. To recapitulate some of these, you should strive to make a single menu work for all users on the network. Having one master menu cuts down on the amount of time you have to spend modifying individual menu scripts and batch files. If your network has a definite segregation of novice and advanced users, it might work better to create two separate menus and tailor them to the users' level of computer sophistication.

The hierarchy of menus should be simple, logical, and intuitive for users to move through. Most systems start with a main menu containing a relatively small number of general options. Each of these main menu options leads to an appropriate submenu containing more specific options. Select the wording of menu options carefully so that they provide a succinct yet accurate indication of what will happen when the user selects the option.

A good place to start in designing a menu system is to look at the applications you have on the file server. Analyze the various tasks that users perform regularly within each application. Determine which DOS and NetWare commands they use and how frequently they use them. Note any other utilities or batch files that need to be run on a regular basis. From within the NetWare MENU system, you can run any program, utility, or batch file that works from the command line—*except* terminate-and-stay-resident (TSR) programs.

Group similar applications, utilities, and commands under the same menu option. For example, if you had WordPerfect, WordStar, and Microsoft Word on the same network, you'd probably arrange these three applications under a single "Word Processing" option in the main menu. Instead of having just one option per application, provide a separate submenu option for each discrete function that users perform every day. Batch files or keyboard macros are especially useful here. Organize any infrequently used DOS or NetWare command-line commands into a single submenu. Then users can go to this submenu and select the appropriate command, complete with correct syntax, rather than having to constantly look up the proper format and parameters to include.

The more advance planning you put into your menu system, the easier it will be to implement with the NetWare MENU command. For each menu and submenu option, it is helpful to write down the exact commands you would have to type from the DOS prompt in order to accomplish each task.

How NetWare's MENU System Works

The NetWare MENU command interprets a menu script file that contains commands formatted in a way meaningful to MENU. These script files are DOS text files that you create and edit with any text editor or word processor. Menu script files are identified by a .MNU extension. NetWare comes with a prewritten menu script file named MAIN.MNU.

The MENU system is actually composed of two executable files located in the SYS:PUBLIC directory. MENU.EXE is a small program (just over 10KB) that works in conjunction with the larger MENUPARZ.EXE program. MENUPARZ contains the code that handles windowing, user interaction, and the interpretation of the lines in the menu script file. MENU.EXE executes the actual commands in the script file by spawning DOS's COMMAND.COM command processor. MENU.EXE calls MENUPARZ.EXE once when you first issue the MENU command, and then again after each command is executed. MENU is a multiuser program; more than one user can use MENU at the same time.

Limitations of NetWare's MENU System. MENU was originally designed by Novell engineers who at the time were working on NetWare v2.0. These engineers needed a general-purpose control program that could execute other programs and be easily configured. The resulting rudimentary menu system was released with the v2.0 operating system almost as an afterthought. Although it was never actually intended to be used by the general LAN public, network supervisors quickly latched on to MENU and used it extensively to create menu systems for their users. Novell made a few enhancements and fixed a few bugs for the v2.1x release of MENU, but has made no further refinements since then.

As simple and flexible as it is, the current version of MENU is not without its limitations. We already mentioned that you cannot call TSR programs from within MENU. This limitation is due to the way MENU executes commands by spawning another copy of COMMAND.COM in memory. Calling a TSR creates all kinds of serious memory allocation problems and will most likely cause the workstation to hang.

Perhaps the major limitation of MENU is the fact that, starting with v2.1x, you cannot call a menu script file from within a batch file. In other words, an AUTO-EXEC.BAT file similar to this one would not work:

```
F:
LOGIN
MENU MAIN
LOGOUT
A:
```

The idea behind this type of batch file is to shield users completely from breaking out of MENU to the DOS command line. Most programs, when called by a batch file, return control to the batch file when they are terminated. In the above batch file, when users exited MENU they would be logged out of the network automatically. This process won't work with MENU. If you load MENU from a batch file, the first time you try to run another batch file from within MENU, that batch file returns control to the original batch file instead, aborting the whole MENU program.

Other complaints about MENU are that it is slow, that it is not very secure (users can easily break out of it to access the DOS prompt), and that it still has a few bugs in it. As long as these potential problems are not a great concern to you, go ahead and use MENU.

Advantages of NetWare's MENU System. All problems aside, MENU does have its advantages. For one, the menus it produces look and behave just like the other NetWare menu utilities such as SYSCON and FILER. Thus, NetWare presents the same outward face to the users no matter which utility they are in. You can create menu options so that even NetWare's command-line utilities have a familiar menu interface.

MENU scripts are fairly simple to create and use, and the program is designed for multiuser access. Because MENU is included with every copy of NetWare, using it doesn't incur any extra expense.

Structure of a MENU Script File

Again, a MENU script file is a DOS text file. In this text file, you can build a simple menu according to the following pattern:

Lines in Menu Script File	Resulting Menu

%Menu Title,*Row,Column,Color*
First Menu Option
   Command or *SubmenuTitle*
Second Menu Option
   Command or *SubmenuTitle*
Third Menu Option
   Command or *SubmenuTitle*
... and so on, until the
Last Menu Option
   Command or *SubmenuTitle*

```
           Menu Title
 ┌──────────────────────────┐
 │ First Menu Option        │
 │ Second Menu Option       │
 │ Third Menu Option        │
 │ . . .                    │
 │ Last Menu Option         │
 └──────────────────────────┘
```

Menu Titles. MENU interprets whatever follows a percent sign (%) as a menu title. The character string following the % will appear at the top of the resulting menu. This string can contain uppercase and lowercase letters and spaces. Optionally, you can indicate what row and column position you want the menu centered on (*Row* and *Column*), and what color palette you want the menu to use (*Color*). If you don't specify a row and column, MENU defaults to 0,0 (the center of the screen). If you leave off the color palette indicator, MENU will use the standard NetWare color palette used by the other menu utilities. When you use a number for *Color*, you must set up a corresponding color palette for your menus by using the NetWare COLORPAL utility, as explained later in this chapter.

Option Names. List the options you want to appear in a particular menu as character strings starting at the left margin. These character strings can contain both uppercase and lowercase letters, as well as spaces. MENU automatically adjusts the width of the screen box to accommodate the longest string. The MENU utility will allow up to 72 characters per line, beginning at column 1. Spaces between letters count as a character. (MENU limits text strings enclosed in quotation marks to 40 characters maximum.)

Commands or Submenu Titles. Directly underneath each option name, indent at least two spaces (or use a Tab) and specify either the command you want to execute when that option is selected (*Command*) or the title of the submenu you want to call from that option (*SubmenuTitle*).

   Command can be any valid NetWare or DOS command, the name of a batch file, or the startup command for an application. It cannot be a command that loads a TSR program. The *SubmenuTitle* you specify must appear later in the script file, preceded by a "%" and followed by its own set of options and commands.

The MAIN.MNU File. As an example of a simple, one-level menu to help you get started, NetWare includes a sample menu script file called MAIN.MNU. Below are the lines in the MAIN.MNU file and the resulting menu as it appears on the screen.

%Main Menu,0,0,3
1. Session Management
        Session
2. File Management
        Filer
3. Volume Information
        VolInfo
4. System Configuration
        SysCon
5. File Server Monitoring
        FConsole
6. Print Queue Management
        PConsole
7. Print Job Configurations
        PrintCon
8. Printer Definitions
        PrintDef
9. Logout
        !Logout

```
┌─────────────────────────────────┐
│            Main Menu            │
├─────────────────────────────────┤
│ 1. Session Management           │
│ 2. File Management              │
│ 3. Volume Information           │
│ 4. System Configuration         │
│ 5. File Server Monitoring       │
│ 6. Print Queue Management       │
│ 7. Print Job Configurations     │
│ 8. Printer Definitions          │
│ 9. Logout                       │
└─────────────────────────────────┘
```

Although not very complicated, the MAIN.MNU file does illustrate several useful MENU tricks. For one, MENU automatically alphabetizes the options in a given menu, no matter what order you insert them in the script file. If you want your options in a different order, use numbers in front of the options to order them numerically.

Each option in the "Main Menu" (except the "Logout" option) calls a NetWare menu utility. The wording of the option names is meant to indicate intuitively what each utility is for. For example, "File Server Monitoring" is much more descriptive than "Run FCONSOLE" would be for a novice user.

The "Logout" option is a special case in MENU. Since a user choosing this option is essentially logging out while the script file and MENU.EXE file are still open on the file server, a special version of the logout command called !LOGOUT is needed so that MENU can close the files and exit gracefully. If you want to include a logging-out option in your own script file, use !LOGOUT rather than the regular LOGOUT command.

Creating Your Own MENU Script Files

Unlike MAKEUSER, MENU does not provide a way to create and edit the script files from within the utility itself. Therefore, you have to use a separate text editor or a word processor that can handle straight ASCII text files. The basic procedure is simple: you enter the text editor or word processing program, start a new file, type in the menu script in the appropriate format, then save the file as a DOS text file with the .MNU extension. When MENUPARZ sees an .MNU extension, it recognizes that file as a menu script. It is best to store menu files that all users need access to in SYS:PUBLIC. That way, you don't have to worry about rights or search drive mappings.

The command format to start up MENU with your custom menu script file is:

```
MENU MenuFile.MNU
```

You don't necessarily have to type the .MNU extension. Remember, you cannot include this command in an AUTOEXEC.BAT or any other batch file. If you want users to automatically come up in the menu system, put the following command last in their personal login scripts:

```
EXIT "MENU MenuFile.MNU"
```

If you put this command as the last entry in the system login script, no user login scripts will be run. The EXIT command in a login script terminates all further login script execution in favor of the command specified after the EXIT keyword.

As explained earlier, MENU.EXE executes a companion program, MENUPARZ.EXE, which looks for *MenuFile* and uses that file as a script for building the menu.

Playing with Menu Positions

The system MENUPARZ uses to position its menus on the screen is confusing because it differs from the standard X-Y coordinate system. Setting *Row* and *Column* to 0,0 does place the menu in the center of the screen, but that's where any resemblance to a standard coordinate system ends. MENUPARZ uses the *Row* and *Column* values you specify as the center point for the entire menu box. MENU-PARZ assumes a 24 row-by-80 column screen display. So, for example, if you specified 10,10 for the position parameters, the center of the resulting menu box would be at the intersection of the 10th row and the 10th column on the user's monitor.

The best way to understand MENU's coordinate system is to play around with it. Create the following Spacing Test Menu to get a feel for how the row and column coordinates affect the menu's placement.

```
%0_0 Spacing Test Menu,0,0,0
1. Open Menu at 10,10
        %10_10 menu

%10_10 menu,10,10,0
1. Open Menu at 20,20
        %20_20 menu

%20_20 menu,20,20,0
1. Open Menu at 20,60
        %20_60 menu
```

```
%20_60 menu,20,60,0
1. Open menu at 10,70
        %10_70 menu

%10_70 menu,10,70,0
1. Dummy item
   Nothing
```

The Spacing Test Menu produces a main menu and four submenus, for a total of five menus. Each menu has different screen location parameters. The first line causes MENUPARZ to create the main menu, name it "0_0 Spacing Test Menu," and place it at 0,0 (the center of the screen). This main menu has only one option: "This option opens a menu at 10,10." Selecting that option causes MENUPARZ to open the "10_10 menu" centered at row 10, column 10; and so on through the other submenus. When all options have been chosen, the screen will look like this:

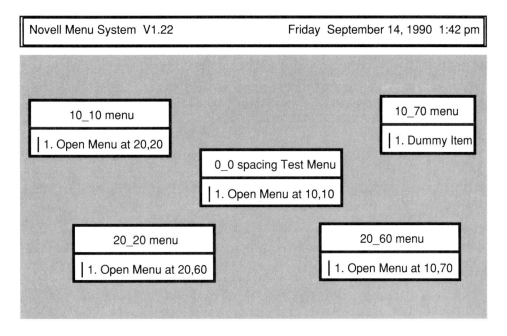

Note that menu boxes can overlap each other, so you must be careful to place your submenus so that they don't obscure any vital information in a previous menu.

Including Variables in MENU Commands

MENU will accept user input from variables that you define with the "at" symbol (@). When MENUPARZ interprets a command that contains an @ character, it initializes a variable and opens a window in which the user can enter a character string for the variable. For example, look at the command in these script lines:

```
%User List Menu,0,0
List Network Users
    USERLIST @"Enter Name or Pattern"
    pause
```

The @"Enter Name or Pattern" part of the third line causes MENUPARZ to open a window in which the user can enter a character string for the @ variable. The window will contain the text between the quotation marks as a prompt for what to enter, like this:

```
Enter Name or Pattern:
```

The value assigned to the @ variable will be whatever name or pattern the user types. After the user enters a character string, MENUPARZ passes control back to MENU, which executes USERLIST with the appropriate name or pattern value. For example, if the user enters "F*" for the @ variable, MENU executes USERLIST F* and displays a list of all users whose names begin with F. If the user entered "FDOBBS," the resulting USERLIST display would list only the information for user FDOBBS. The "pause" command works the same way as in a standard DOS batch file: it displays the text "Strike any key when ready..." and waits for the user to press a key on the keyboard before continuing.

Since USERLIST has an optional "/A" flag that lists network and node addresses in addition to users and their connection numbers, you could enhance the above User List Menu as follows:

```
%User List Menu,0,0
1. List Network Users
        userlist @"Enter Name or Pattern"
    pause
2. List Network Users and Addresses
        userlist @"Enter Name or Pattern" /A
    pause
```

The first option executes USERLIST so that it lists only users. The second option adds the "/A" flag, which causes USERLIST to list the appropriate addresses as well. Including optional command flags in this way allows users to run variations of the same command without having to remember the exact syntax for each variation.

Defining Multiple Variables in the Same Command. You can define more than one variable for a single command. For example, if you want to set up a menu option for using the NetWare NCOPY command to copy files from one directory to another, set up one variable for the source directory and file name, and a second variable for the destination directory:

```
%NetWare Commands,1,10
Copy Files from One Directory to Another (NCOPY)
   NCOPY @1"Enter Source Drive and Filename" @2"Enter Destination"
   pause
```

The resulting menu option will prompt the user first for the source drive and file name and store whatever the user types in variable @1. Then the user will be prompted for the destination directory, and the user input will be stored in @2. For example, if user CARRIE typed "F:*.DOC" for @1 and "SYS:USERS/CARRIE/ DOCFILES" for @2, the resulting NCOPY command would be executed as:

```
NCOPY F:*.DOC SYS:USERS/CARRIE/DOCFILES
```

All of the files with the .DOC extension in Carrie's F: drive would be copied to the DOCFILES subdirectory under her home directory.

When you use multiple @ variables in the same command, the variables must all appear on the same line in the script. You can reuse the same variables further down in the script if you want.

Empty Variables. If a user presses the Enter key without typing anything in response to an @ variable prompt, that variable is ignored when the command is executed. For example, look at these script lines for the NetWare MAP command:

```
%NetWare Commands,1,10
Display NetWare Drive Mappings (MAP)
   MAP @"Enter Drive Letter or 'Enter' for All Mappings"
   pause
```

If the user types a drive letter such as G:, the MAP G: command will be executed. If the user types Enter, the MAP command will run as normal, displaying all current drive mappings. Notice that if you want to include something in quotes within a prompt, you must use single quote marks. Also, don't use @, %, or a comma (,) inside the double quotes. MENU will get confused because these characters have a specialized meaning to the program.

Incorporating Batch File Commands in MENU

Generally, any batch command or construct that works from the command line will work when MENU invokes it. This is also true for valid *.BAT files. You can use all standard DOS batch file commands in your MENU script.

A particularly useful one is the IF *Condition* GOTO *Label* instruction. This DOS batch file instruction checks for a certain *Condition*. If the *Condition* is true, DOS skips to the line specified by *Label*. Otherwise, DOS simply continues through each line in the batch file.

The condition is usually the "error level" results from an instruction or the value of a variable set in the DOS environment. DOS returns "errorlevel=0" every time it successfully executes a command or an .EXE utility (such as NDIR, SLIST, ATTACH, and so on). If DOS can't complete the instruction, it returns "error-level=1" instead. DOS environment variables are those established with a DOS SET command, such as DOS SET STATION=P_STATION in a login script. These environment variables are displayed when you type SET at the DOS prompt.

You can use IF *Condition* GOTO *Label* to create an "intelligent" MENU script. Consider the following example for attaching to a server and mapping a drive to a directory on that server:

```
%New Menu,0,0,0
Attach to Server "FUN"
    ATTACH FUN/@1"Enter your login name"
    IF errorlevel 1 GOTO offline
    MAP @1"Enter an available network drive":=FUN/SYS:GAMES
    GOTO online
    :offline
    CLS
    ECHO Server FUN is down.
    PAUSE
    :online
```

Upon selecting this option, the user is prompted to enter a login name. The ATTACH command tries to attach the user to file server FUN using that login name. If server FUN isn't available, the script skips to the label ":offline" and displays the message "Server FUN is down." If server FUN is up, the script prompts the user for an available network drive letter and maps that drive to the directory FUN/SYS:GAMES.

Constructing Submenus with MENU

You can assemble a sophisticated MENU system by using submenus. Suppose, for example, that you have several word processing programs on your file server. You might make an item for each word processor on your main menu, as in this menu script:

```
%New Menu,0,0,0
1. WordPerfect
        WP
2. WordStar 2000
        WS
3. MS Word
        WORD
```

However, placing everything on the primary menu might overburden users with too many options. A more elegant solution would be to create a word processing submenu from which users can execute their word processor of choice:

```
%New Menu,0,0,0
1. Word Processing
   Word Processing Menu
```

```
%Word Processing Menu,20,20,0
1. WordPerfect
   WP
2. WordStar 2000
   WS
3. Microsoft Word
   WORD
```

This sample script presents the user with New Menu, which has one item: "Word Processing." When the user selects "Word Processing," MENU opens up the submenu named "Word Processing Menu," containing three options: "WordPerfect," "WordStar 2000," and "Microsoft Word."

Alternatively, you could call another submenu from each option on the Word Processing Menu. These submenus could call the respective word processing program using various command line flags or initial directory/printer setups. (See the example in Chapter 4.)

You can nest submenus as deeply as you need to in MENU. However, don't get carried away. Users shouldn't have to go down more than about three or four levels to get to the option they want.

COLORING YOUR MENUS WITH COLORPAL

The NetWare COLORPAL utility lets you design your own color scheme or "palette" for your menus. The number following the row and column position designations in a menu title signifies the color palette MENU will use when displaying the menu. For example, the menu title specification "%New Menu,0,0,5" will display New Menu, located at the center of the user's monitor, using color palette 5. If no number is specified for the color palette, MENU uses NetWare's default color palette 0. (With this default, your menus have the same color scheme as SYSCON, FILER, and the other menu utilities.)

If your users don't have color monitors, it's best not to change the color palettes. However, some types of PCs (most notably the AT&T 6300 and certain Compaq machines) typically have a monochrome monitor attached to a composite color adapter. On these types of workstations, users might have trouble seeing option names once they are highlighted on the screen. To resolve this problem, copy the SHELL.CFG file from the NetWare DIAGNOSTICS diskette to the workstation's boot disk. (Refer to Novell's documentation for more details.)

Creating Your Own Color Palette

COLORPAL comes with five palettes already defined. These palettes are:

Palette	Defines Colors Used For:
0	Lists, menus, and normal text
1	Screen header and background
2	Help screens
3	Error messages
4	Exit and alert portals

NetWare's menu utilities all use these predefined color palettes, so you should not change them. You can define your own color scheme starting with palette number 5.

Running COLORPAL. To set up colors for palette 5, first copy the IBM$RUN.OVL file from SYS:PUBLIC to your menu work directory containing your menu script file. Since this overlay file contains all color palette definitions for all IBM-type machines on the network, you don't want to risk losing them if something goes wrong. Once you test your new color scheme, you will copy the file back out to SYS:PUBLIC so all users will have access to the new menu colors.

Change to the work directory where you just copied IBM$RUN.OVL and type **COLORPAL**. The first screen lists the palettes that are already defined. Press Insert to add "Color Palette 5" to the list. Now select "Color Palette 5" from the list. You will see an "Edit Attribute" menu listing five attributes: "Background Normal," "Background Reverse," "Foreground Intense," "Foreground Normal," and "Foreground Reverse."

The following chart summarizes exactly what screen elements each color attribute affects.

Color Attribute	Affects:
Background Normal	The background area of the screen on which menu boxes are displayed.
Foreground Normal	Menu titles, option names, and menu box borders.
Foreground Intense	Menu titles and menu box borders of the currently active menu.
Foreground Reverse	Text covered by the highlight bar.
Background Reverse	The highlight bar itself.

To help you see how your colors will look before you save your changes, the "Current Palette" window shows you how any changes you make affect normal text, intense text, and reverse text.

Select the color attribute you want to edit. COLORPAL presents a list of possible colors for that attribute. The possible foreground colors are different than the possible background colors.

Select the color you want from the list. You will then return to the "Edit Attribute" window, where you can select the next color attribute you want to change. After changing the color attributes, press the Escape key twice. You will see a prompt asking if you wish to save the changes. Answer "Yes," then press the Escape key again and exit COLORPAL.

Your new color palette 5 is now saved in the IBM$RUN.OVL file in the menu work directory. Try out your menu by starting it from the work directory. If the new colors don't suit you, repeat the COLORPAL process to edit the colors for palette 5. When you are satisfied, copy the IBM$RUN.OVL file back into the SYS:PUBLIC directory.

Make sure you include the new color parameter ("5" in this case) in each menu title description of your menu script file. Otherwise, the MENU system will simply use the default palette 0.

11 Managing NetWare's Resource Accounting

NetWare's resource accounting feature tracks file server usage and allows you to charge users for various services provided by the file server. Don't confuse this feature—often referred to as simply "Accounting"—with a full-fledged accounting software package with debits and credits and ledgers. Novell's accounting system serves a completely different purpose. Installing Accounting on your file server is actually only the first step in implementing a comprehensive system for charging and billing users. NetWare resource accounting accumulates usage data and records it in chronological order in various data files on the file server. But you'd need a third-party program that incorporates NetWare's Accounting APIs to interpret all this data and use it to actually bill users.

Not all networks need the resource accounting feature. This chapter first discusses what types of situations warrant its use on the file server. Then we'll explain how to install resource accounting in SYSCON and assign appropriate charge rates for file server services. We'll show you how to use NetWare's two accounting-related utilities (PAUDIT and ATOTAL) to maintain the audit files generated by the resource accounting function. And finally, we'll explain how to remove resource accounting from your file server should you determine that you no longer need it.

WHEN TO USE RESOURCE ACCOUNTING

As we just said, some NetWare LANs have no need for resource accounting. For others, the resource accounting features may be indispensable. Still others may need only a few resource accounting features. As a network supervisor, you must determine when and how to implement resource accounting on your file server.

In some organizations, the need for resource accounting is obvious. Computer labs at universities, for example, are excellent candidates for resource accounting. At these facilities, each student is typically assigned a temporary account and must pay an initial balance at the beginning of the term or semester. The student's use of the LAN is charged against this initial balance, and if it runs out before the term is over, the student must pay for extra time or services.

Another good use for resource accounting is to facilitate chargebacks on a LAN where a single file server services more than one department in the same company. For instance, suppose department A and department B have separate budgets. Department A buys a storage subsystem and makes space on it available to department B. For internal reporting purposes, department A can use NetWare's resource accounting features to track department B's use of the server and charge department B's budget for the appropriate usage.

Avoid assigning limited account balances to users who use the LAN as part of their everyday work; you might unintentionally be reducing their productivity. For example, if workers know that they have a limited amount in their account balance, they may limit certain activities to "save up" for a major task they know they must perform in the future. It is a waste of capital and manpower to limit access to network resources when those resources are plentiful. NetWare is designed to empower users, not to limit them; if you've got the resources, and they've already been justified in the budget, make them available without limit to your users.

NetWare's resource accounting features are tailored to those LANs whose resources are limited. In this situation, careful and concise accounting of network usage can encourage your users to be more efficient consumers of the file server's resources.

Resource accounting can be an invaluable tool for justifying future hardware upgrades or the purchase of additional resources on the LAN. You can install accounting on your server and have it track usage without actually charging users. In this way, you will be able to collect solid data to support your case for additional resources, without affecting user productivity.

In some cases, the decision whether to use resource accounting is blurry at best. Usually, where there are no clear indicators or where there are conflicting indicators, LAN resources are used unevenly. You may, for example, have several key resources that are constantly in use, while other resources sit mostly idle. If your users tax some file server resources more heavily than others, you may want to implement only that part of resource accounting that deals with the heavily used resources.

One last consideration: Even if you don't need to charge users for file server usage, if you're concerned about keeping track of logins and logouts, install accounting anyway. One basic function of the accounting option is to record the date and time of every login and logout attempt made on the file server; this function works even if you don't activate any of the charging options. The resulting login audit trail could prove useful if you suspect that unauthorized users are trying to break into your file server.

INSTALLING RESOURCE ACCOUNTING

Once you've agonized over whether or not to install Accounting and you've decided to go ahead, activating the Accounting feature on your file server is simple. Access SYSCON and choose "Accounting" from the main menu. SYSCON will ask if you want Accounting installed. Just answer "Yes" to the prompt, and the "Accounting" submenu will pop up:

```
┌─────────────────────────────────┐
│          Accounting             │
├─────────────────────────────────┤
│ Accounting Servers              │
│ Blocks Read Charge Rates        │
│ Blocks Written Charge Rates     │
│ Connect Time Charge Rates       │
│ Disk Storage Charge Rates       │
│ Service Requests Charge Rates   │
└─────────────────────────────────┘
```

If you've already installed Accounting on the file server, choosing "Accounting" from SYSCON's main menu takes you directly to the submenu shown above.

Two things happen when you initially install Accounting. First, SYSCON automatically defines your file server as an "accounting server." If you select the "Accounting Servers" option, you will see your file server name listed as a server currently authorized to charge for its services. You can also authorize other types of servers (such as print servers and database servers) to charge your file server users for their specialized services. However, you are only *authorizing* these charges; you must perform the actual mechanics of setting up charge rates in a separate application written using NetWare's Accounting APIs.

The second thing that happens when you install Accounting is that from this moment on, NetWare will record an audit file entry each time a user logs in or out of the file server. These login and logout entries, as well as any other entries generated by the accounting option, are placed into a new file called NET$ACCT.DAT kept in the SYS:SYSTEM subdirectory.

No user charges are associated with Accounting's default login and logout tracking function; in fact, the file server won't automatically charge users for anything until you set up charge rates with the other options in the "Accounting" submenu.

Deciding What Services to Charge For

As you can see from the options in the "Accounting" submenu, a file server can charge for five different services: disk reads (in blocks), disk writes (in blocks), connection time, disk storage, and file service requests. You can charge either for one service at a time (such as for connect time only) or in any combination.

Block Reads. The first of the charges, Block Reads, allows you to charge users for every workstation request for the file server to read a block of data from a network disk. A block is equal to 4,096 bytes, or 4KB. Charging for blocks read is extremely useful when your file server provides an information service, such as a commercial database. In most other situations, however, charging for blocks read is not a good idea; it may unfairly penalize users who must load large applications from the server. Users will certainly change their work habits to lessen the charges; perhaps your users will check their E-Mail less frequently, for example.

Block Writes. Next is the Blocks Written service. As with Blocks Read, you can charge users for every 4KB block the file server writes to disk for their workstations. This isn't a charge for storage so much as a charge per disk write request. This type of charge is appropriate for some applications, such as word processing, in which data is processed mostly at the workstation and saved to the file server less frequently. But charging by blocks written is inadvisable if you are running applications that write to disk continually, as database applications do. Also, charging users for writing data to the server may discourage them from saving their work frequently.

Connect Time. Connect Time is a familiar concept to those who have worked with electronic bulletin boards or who come from a mainframe environment. In NetWare, users can be charged for every minute they remain on the file server from login to logout. Users may respond to a connection time charge in unexpected ways. For example, they may view it as an implied command to work quickly, which may or may not be a problem. If you want your users to work more slowly and accurately, charging them for connect time probably isn't appropriate for your file server. Again, in most business environments, giving employees only so much time to do what they must do doesn't make much sense.

Disk Storage. The next possible charge is for disk storage space used. Unlike the other types of charges, which are based on a certain number of services or minutes, NetWare charges for disk storage in block-days. Once per day, NetWare will check to see how much disk space (in blocks) each user is listed as the owner of. Each user will be charged for that number of blocks for that day.

Resist the temptation to use resource accounting solely for the purpose of limiting each user's amount of network disk space. NetWare offers a better way to do that through the "Limit Disk Space" option in NETGEN or ELSGEN and its counterpart option in SYSCON. When you set up the file server to charge for disk storage space used, you must deal with the administrative details of setting initial account balances for users, calculating the appropriate charge rate for disk usage, and so on. The SYSCON alternative is much cleaner and easier to maintain.

You can charge for disk storage in addition to using the "Limit Disk Space" feature. Definitely use both features if you plan to audit users' disk storage during a peak period for your file server. As you can well imagine, it takes a good deal of server CPU time to go through each directory and file, check the owner, and tabulate the total number of disk blocks each owner is using; if you enable the "Limit Disk Space" feature first, however, the server keeps a running total of each user's disk space and the tabulation process doesn't require nearly as much CPU time. If you set the disk storage audit time for 2:00 a.m. or some other period when server usage is low, you don't necessarily need to enable the "Limit Disk Space" option.

Charging users for disk space might encourage users to keep their personal directories cleaned out and refrain from indiscriminately dumping files onto the server. However, it could also encourage users to store important files on floppy diskettes or on a local hard disk where they cannot be shared by other network users. Carefully consider the types of applications you are running on the server and the amount of user access of shared data files. Make sure your users understand that they will be charged only for directories and files for which they are listed as the owner.

If you do set up the server to charge users for disk storage, you should be aware that the DOS XCOPY command, and some other non-NetWare file-managing utilities, change the owner of any files copied to the person who did the copying. If you as SUPERVISOR use XCOPY, for instance, to move a whole branch of a directory tree to some other location on the file server, the owner of all the moved directories and files will be changed to SUPERVISOR. The original owners of the data will no longer be charged for the disk space used unless you change the owner back with FILER (see Chapter 8).

Service Requests. Assign service request charges with care, as almost everything users do on the network is a service request. Don't charge for service requests and for blocks written or blocks read, since they are essentially the same thing. Logging in, reading files, writing files—all involve service requests. NetWare's service request charging works on the same principle as most lawyers: Every time users talk to the server, they will be charged.

Charging by service requests is not generally recommended, unless the server is extremely overworked and you want to reduce the number of service requests. However, if LAN users are to be truly productive, they must make service requests to the file server continually.

DETERMINING APPROPRIATE CHARGE RATES

By now you should have a good idea of what you want to charge for on your file server. Now the question is, what should you charge? You probably know your LAN better than anyone else, so most of the time it will be your decision. You'll probably have to do some experimentation, though, to arrive at the ideal accounting charge rates for your server.

Preliminary Decisions and Research

Before you actually set the charge rates for resource accounting in SYSCON, you must make a few preliminary decisions, and you must do some research on how your file server is actually used.

Step 1: Define the Unit of Charge. First of all, you must understand that NetWare's resource accounting doesn't deal in dollars, pesos, or marks. It deals in user-definable *charge units*. A charge unit can represent whatever you like; for instance, you can decide that one charge unit equals one dollar, one penny, or one hundred dollars. It doesn't matter, as long as you are consistent across all charged services. You can't claim, for example, that a charge unit equals a dollar for disk

storage charge rates and a penny for connection time charge rates.

In the United States, it's probably easiest to set one charge unit equal to one penny, since that is the smallest monetary denomination. Whatever equivalence you choose, you'll have to make the appropriate conversions from charge units to real money. NetWare won't do it for you.

Step 2: Decide How Much You Need to Recover. You'll also need to decide how much money you must recover from the users for each charged service. For example, suppose a company wants to recoup $24,000 over the next two years to help justify the cost of installing a LAN. That means that the company must collect $1,000 a month from users by charging them for file server usage. The LAN supervisor might apportion this $1,000 in a number of ways. If you decide that half of that amount should come from connect time charges and half from disk storage charges, then the company must charge enough to make $500 per month from each category.

Step 3: Measure Actual File Server Usage. The only variable left in the equation is to find out how much each service is used on your file server. Use SYSCON for this research. In SYSCON, set charge rates for all services for which you intend to charge to the ratio of 1/1 (as explained below); then let your file server run for two or three weeks of normal LAN activity. During this trial period, the accounting feature will tabulate and record usage data in the NET$ACCT.DAT file in SYS:SYSTEM.

At the end of the trial period, use the ATOTAL utility to total up all the accounting data. (On a heavily used file server, ATOTAL can take a long time to run, so don't be concerned if it takes a while.) ATOTAL.EXE is in the SYS:SYSTEM directory. Go to that directory and type ATOTAL > USAGE.TST. This command will direct ATOTAL to dump its output to a text file in SYS:SYSTEM named USAGE.TST. Afterwards, you can print out the USAGE.TST file, using NPRINT or a word processor that works with DOS text files.

The USAGE.TST file will contain daily totals for each day of the trial period, and weekly totals similar to these:

```
Totals for week:
   Connect time:      7346     Server requests:    8081302
   Blocks read:     563278     Blocks written:           0
   Blocks days:          0
```

The average of the weekly totals will give you a representative figure for how much a given service is used on your file server in a week.

Step 4: Compute the Charge Rate Ratios. Now get out your pocket calculator—you're in for a bit of arithmetic. The Novell *Supervisor Reference* manual gives the following equation for calculating the charge rate:

$$\frac{\text{Total amount you want to charge for a service}}{\text{Estimated total usage of the service}} = \frac{\text{Multiplier}}{\text{Divisor}}$$

If it's been a while since you studied fractions, don't worry about what "multiplier" and "divisor" mean. All you need to know is that when you divide the total amount of money you want to recoup for a given service in a week (see Step 2 above) by the average total usage of the service in a week (see Step 3 above), you get a certain fraction, or ratio. This ratio represents how much you should charge (in charge units) for each unit of service (each block read, or each minute of connect time).

Connect Time Example. Here's a sample calculation of an appropriate charge rate for connect time. Suppose you determine that you must take in $600 a week in connect time charges. Assuming a one-cent charge unit, that's 60,000 charge units a week. Over a two-week evaluation period, the combined users' totals of connect time, as figured by ATOTAL, is 240,000 minutes. Divide this number by two to get the average for one week: 120,000 minutes.

Plugging these figures into the above formula, you get:

$$\frac{60{,}000 \text{ charge units per week}}{120{,}000 \text{ minutes of connect time per week}} = \frac{1 \text{ charge unit}}{2 \text{ minutes}}$$

So, you need to charge users one charge unit (1 cent) for every two minutes they are connected to the file server. To implement this charge rate in SYSCON, set the multiplier to "1" and the divisor to "2."

While this textbook example works out to a nice even ratio (1/2), your real-life figures probably will not. If you use a calculator to do the division, you will end up with some number like 0.37465. SYSCON will only let you enter whole numbers up to five characters long, with no decimal points. Use the following table to round off your calculator result to the nearest whole fraction. It's much easier to work with 1 as the multiplier, but it doesn't have to be 1.

Decimal Figure	Fraction
1.0000	1/1
0.9000	9/10
0.8750	7/8
0.8000	4/5
0.7500	3/4
0.7000	7/10
0.6250	5/8
0.6000	3/5
0.5000	1/2
0.4000	2/5
0.3750	3/8
0.3333	1/3
0.3000	3/10
0.2500	1/4
0.2000	1/5

0.1666	1/6
0.1428	1/7
0.1250	1/8
0.1111	1/9
0.1000	1/10
0.0500	1/20
0.0400	1/25
0.0333	1/30
0.0250	1/40
0.0200	1/50

Setting the Charge Rates in SYSCON

Setting the charge rates works the same for all but the "Disk Storage Charge Rates" option. Here's how you would set the connection time charge rate at one charge unit for every two minutes of connect time, as in the above example.

Choose the "Accounting" option from SYSCON's main menu. Then select "Connect Time Charge Rates." A window will open containing a time and day grid, as shown below:

		Sun	Mon	Tue	Wed	Thu	Fri	Sat
Connect Time Charge Rates	8:00am	1	1	1	1	1	1	1
	8:30am	1	1	1	1	1	1	1
	9:00am	1	1	1	1	1	1	1
Sunday	9:30am	1	1	1	1	1	1	1
8:00 am To 8:29 am	10:00am	1	1	1	1	1	1	1
	10:30am	1	1	1	1	1	1	1
Rate Charge Rate Charge	11:00am	1	1	1	1	1	1	1
1 No Charge 11	11:30am	1	1	1	1	1	1	1
2 12	12:00pm	1	1	1	1	1	1	1
3 13	12:30pm	1	1	1	1	1	1	1
4 14	1:00pm	1	1	1	1	1	1	1
5 15	1:30pm	1	1	1	1	1	1	1
6 16	2:00pm	1	1	1	1	1	1	1
7 17	2:30pm	1	1	1	1	1	1	1
8 18	3:00pm	1	1	1	1	1	1	1
9 19	3:30pm	1	1	1	1	1	1	1
10 20	4:00pm	1	1	1	1	1	1	1
(Charge is per minute)	4:30pm	1	1	1	1	1	1	1

You can define different charge rates for each half-hour period if you want. SYSCON tells you what day and time period you are currently working with on the left side of the screen. The middle left side of the screen shows you what the currently defined charge rates are. Initially, all time periods in the grid are set to Rate 1, which is set for "No Charge."

To define a charge rate, you must first block out the times and days you want the new charge rate to apply to. To specify Monday 8:00 am to Friday 5:00 pm, for example, position the cursor at the 8:00am row of the Mon column. Press the Mark key (F5) to mark the beginning of the block. Then move the cursor to the 5:00pm row of the Fri column. The entire block of time will be highlighted.

Press Enter. A "Select Charge Rate" list will pop up. Select "Other Charge Rate" from this list to get the "New Charge Rate" window, asking you for a multiplier and a divisor:

```
                                      Sun Mon Tue Wed Thu Fri Sat
   Connect Time Charge Rates      8:00am   1   1   1   1   1   1   1
                                  8:30am   1   1   1   1   1   1   1
                                  9:00am   1   1   1   1   1   1   1
   Sunday                         9:30am   1   1   1   1   1   1   1
   8:00 am To 8:29 am            10:00am   1   1   1   1   1   1   1
                                 10:30am   1   1   1   1   1   1   1

   Rate   ┌─────────────────────┐     ┌──────────────────────┐   1   1   1
     1   N│   Select Charge Rate │     │   New Charge Rate     │   1   1   1
     2    │                      │     │                       │   1   1   1
     3    │  1   No Charge        │     │  Multiplier      1    │   1   1   1
     4    │  Other Charge Rate    │     │  Divisor         1    │   1   1   1
     5              15            └──────────┘                  1   1   1   1
     6              16            2:00pm   1   1   1   1   1   1   1
     7              17            2:30pm   1   1   1   1   1   1   1
     8              18            3:00pm   1   1   1   1   1   1   1
     9              19            3:30pm   1   1   1   1   1   1   1
    10              20            4:00pm   1   1   1   1   1   1   1
         (Charge is per minute)   4:30pm   1   1   1   1   1   1   1
```

The multiplier and divisor determine the amount that will be charged to the user's account each minute, as the bottom left side of the screen tells you. To charge one cent for every two minutes (as in our example above), leave the multiplier at 1 and set the divisor to 2. Press Escape twice. The 1's in the highlighted portion of the grid are now 2's, and the charge rate associated with the number 2 is displayed as 1/2 on the left.

For more information about setting charge rates in SYSCON, refer to the NetWare *Supervisor Reference* manual.

Assigning User Account Balances

As soon as you define a charge rate other than "No Charge" for a service in SYSCON, the file server begins keeping track of how much each user account uses that service. The charges accrued are not actually subtracted from a user's account balance until that user logs out. Unless you specified otherwise, each user is created with a default account balance of 1000 charge units. Depending on the charge rate you set, that amount may not last very long and will need to be replenished often.

Important: When you set a credit limit on user accounts, have your users check their account balances each time they prepare to log out. If a user's account balance reaches or surpasses the established credit limit, that user will not be able to log in again until his or her account balance is replenished. He or she will see the message "Attempting to login after account balance has dropped below the minimum." Warn users also that if they ever receive a message from the file server to log out because their account balance is low, they should save their files and log out immediately. Otherwise, NetWare's watchdog function will automatically log them out and they will lose any data they have not saved. Before they can log in again, you will have to go into SYSCON and give them a new account balance.

If you are actually collecting money from users for their account balance, you will have to make the necessary conversion from charge units to monetary units. With a one-cent charge unit, for instance, if a user pays $25 for an account, you should assign 2,500 charge units for that account balance. You can set up default account balances under "Supervisor Options" from the main menu in SYSCON to give all new users the same starting balance.

If you are assigning charge rates to see how much a particular service is used on your server without actually charging money for the services, you must still give each user an account balance. In this case, though, you should give users unlimited credit to avoid locking them out of the server when their account balance drops below 0.

If you aren't sure what to assign for an account balance, give users unlimited credit for a month or two, then check the figures on system use. Based on those figures, you can formulate charges that reflect real-life file server usage. After you set the actual account balance, establish an appropriate credit limit.

MAINTAINING THE ACCOUNTING AUDIT FILES

While you can use SYSCON to view charges, account balances, and other accounting parameters, the actual accounting data is stored in two data files in SYS:SYSTEM. One file—NET$ACCT.DAT—contains raw accounting data in machine code that only NetWare can comprehend. The other file, NET$REC.DAT, is used to translate this raw data into language humans can understand. As NetWare continually appends data to these files, they grow larger and larger. To save on storage space, all the data in the audit file is appended in condensed format.

Two supervisor command line utilities—ATOTAL and PAUDIT—help you work with the network usage data stored in these two files. ATOTAL, as we have already seen, goes through the NET$ACCT.DAT file and totals every posted transaction. The resulting output shows daily and weekly usage totals for each service being charged for on the file server. PAUDIT uses the information in the NET$REC.DAT file to interpret the contents of NET$ACCT.DAT and print these contents to the screen.

Monthly Audit File Maintenance Procedure

It is a good practice to keep a printed "audit trail" of activity on your file server. An audit trail, according to accountants, is a series of records that document individual transactions in the sequence in which they occurred. Different from a SYSCON account balance, which is a summary record, an audit trail shows every transaction separately and sequentially.

You can develop your own audit trail by running ATOTAL and PAUDIT to get a detailed summary record of network usage. You do this by periodically archiving contents of NET$ACCT.DAT to a DOS text file on another storage medium (such as floppy diskette or tape backup). Once the data is safely archived, delete NET$ACCT.DAT from the SYS:SYSTEM directory. When you delete NET$ACCT.DAT, the file server simply starts a new file. (*Never* delete the NET$REC.DAT file, however. This file is needed by PAUDIT and won't be automatically recreated if you accidentally delete it. You'd have to restore it from a backup.)

Even though data is stored in a compressed format in the NET$ACCT.DAT file, after a month or so the file can become unmanageably large. Deleting the file every month and starting over will also help keep the accounting data file down to a manageable size.

Here's the recommended procedure to follow at the end of each month to clear out the NET$ACCT.DAT file and produce a printed audit trail.

Total the Monthly System Usage with ATOTAL. Before archiving and deleting NET$ACCT.DAT at the end of the month, total its postings with the ATOTAL utility. The resulting monthly file server usage report may prove useful when you must readjust charge rates to reflect changes in file server usage patterns.

To run ATOTAL, change to the SYS:SYSTEM directory. Type **ATOTAL > *FileName.*** This will put the results into the indicated file rather than outputting them to the screen.

ATOTAL ferrets out the raw data in the NET$ACCT.DAT file and compiles totals for every posted transaction. While ATOTAL is working, it displays the message "Processing accounting records . . ." on your computer screen. If you haven't set up any charge rates, ATOTAL will have very little to process; but if you have been charging for services, ATOTAL shows you what the actual charges are based on and how much they amount to.

A typical ATOTAL report has seven daily records grouped together, followed by a "Totals For Week" record. This daily/weekly total format continues, covering every week contained in the current NET$ACCT.DAT file. Here is a sample of ATOTAL's output:

```
8/29/1990:
   Connect time:           46    Server requests:        1302
   Blocks read:             0    Blocks written:            0
   Blocks days:            78

8/30/1990:
   Connect time:            1    Server requests:         490
   Blocks read:             0    Blocks written:            0
   Blocks days:            40'

Totals for week:
   Connect time:           47    Server requests:        1792
   Blocks read:             0    Blocks written:            0
   Blocks days:           118
```

ATOTAL will compile and report totals for as many charges as you have defined in the SYSCON utility. In the sample above, the file server was set up to charge for connect time, disk storage (as indicated by "Blocks days"), and server requests.

ATOTAL can take a long time to run. Just how long, of course, depends on the size of the NET$ACCT.DAT file. You cannot abort ATOTAL—once started, the utility must run its course and should not be interrupted.

Print the Audit Trail File with PAUDIT. Whereas ATOTAL generates a summary of the audit file totals, PAUDIT generates a detailed, entry-by-entry report of NET$ACCT.DAT's contents. Because the NET$ACCT.DAT file is typically quite large, PAUDIT may take several hours to read and transcribe the entire contents of the audit trail file.

PAUDIT normally prints its output to the screen. The PAUDIT output contains an entry for each accounting-related event on the file server: logins, logouts, and charges made to each user. These events are arranged in strict chronological order. PAUDIT itself does not sort the information by user or type of charge; however, several utilities are available that will do this. Check with your local NetWare users group or bulletin board service.

To obtain a permanent record of PAUDIT's output, redirect the output into a DOS text file by including the DOS redirect symbol (>) in the PAUDIT command and specifying an appropriate file name for the output.

For example, to save PAUDIT's output into a DOS text file named 990AUDIT.TXT, type the PAUDIT command as **PAUDIT > 990AUDIT.TXT** from the SYS:SYSTEM directory. Here is a sample of PAUDIT's output:

```
09/14/90 17:11:27  File Server PUBLISHER1
   NOTE: about User ED during File Server services.
   Logout from address 0000F00D:0000D800353B.
09/14/90 17:11:36  File Server PUBLISHER1
   NOTE: about User VINCE during File Server services.
   Logout from address 0000ACE2:0000000000FD.
```

```
09/14/90 18:02:49  File Server PUBLISHER1
   NOTE: about User KEN during File Server services.
   Logout from address 0000ACE2:0000000000FB.
09/15/90 7:20:20  File Server PUBLISHER1
   NOTE: about User VINCE during File Server services.
   Login from address 0000ACE2:0000000000FD.
09/15/90 7:42:59  File Server PUBLISHER1
   NOTE: about User ED during File Server services.
   Login from address 0000F00D:0000D800353B.
09/15/90 8:04:11  File Server PUBLISHER1
   NOTE: about User ED during File Server services.
   Logout from address 0000F00D:0000D800353B.
```

Each entry includes the date, time, and file server on which the event took place. The NOTE indicates which user account and which services were involved. The third line in each entry identifies the event itself (login, logout, accounting charge, and so on). PAUDIT also records an entry each time NetWare detects an intruder trying to log in to the file server, and whenever the file server's system time is changed.

Although ATOTAL must run to completion, you can stop PAUDIT at any time by pressing Ctrl-C.

When PAUDIT finishes, the contents of NET$ACCT.DAT will be contained in the indicated text file. Because this file is composed entirely of ASCII text, you can manipulate the data with almost any standard word processor or database manager—for example, you could import the contents into a database or spreadsheet.

UNINSTALLING ACCOUNTING

Understandably, running the resource accounting feature adds a certain amount of overhead to the NetWare operating system. Where resource accounting is truly needed, the slight drop in performance is offset by the usefulness of the feature. If you don't need resource accounting on a permanent basis, you can uninstall it at any time.

The procedure for deactivating and removing the resource accounting feature from your file server depends on your version of NetWare 286.

For all NetWare 286 versions 2.12 and higher, you must first delete all authorized accounting servers (including your file server). Go into SYSCON, choose "Accounting" from the main menu, then choose "Accounting Servers." Highlight the name of your file server in the list of authorized accounting servers and press Delete. Answer "Yes" to the confirmation prompt. If any other servers are listed, delete them in the same manner. Now press Escape. SYSCON will ask you "Do you wish to remove accounting?" Answer "Yes," and the job is done.

For SFT and Advanced NetWare 286 v2.11, you must cancel all charge rates before you can delete the file server as an authorized accounting server. Go into each charge rate option and set the entire time grid back to No Charge. Then follow the procedure indicated above for NetWare v2.12 and above.

For SFT NetWare v2.1, you must obtain a separate program from Novell to deactivate the resource accounting feature.

12 Supporting Diskless Workstations (DOSGEN)

Diskless workstations are becoming more and more popular as a practical, cost-effective means of adding nodes to a LAN. These scaled-down PCs have no local floppy or hard disk drives, making them not only less expensive than full-fledged PC workstations but also more secure. Without access to a local disk drive, users cannot download sensitive information from the LAN, nor can they upload potentially destructive files containing viruses. However, they cannot boot up locally, either.

NetWare v2.1x supports diskless workstations through a feature called Remote Reset. Remote Reset allows workstations to boot from a file in the SYS:LOGIN directory on the file server. This file contains an exact image copy of what would normally be on a boot diskette. A specialized chip called a *boot ROM* in the diskless workstation takes over when the machine is turned on or reset and handles the bootup procedure.

A supervisor utility called DOSGEN creates the boot image files in the SYS:LOGIN directory. We've included this chapter on Remote Reset and DOSGEN (even though it deals mainly with workstations) in this file server book because the DOSGEN procedure is for supervisors only and the boot files are stored and maintained on the file server.

This chapter starts with a fairly technical overview of exactly how Remote Reset works. Although understanding these technicalities is not necessarily a prerequisite to running DOSGEN, it is often helpful to know what is supposed to be happening in case you run into trouble with the boot image files on your file server. After the overview, we'll discuss how to run DOSGEN and create the files necessary for your file server to support diskless workstations.

One other note before we start: although the information in this chapter applies primarily to diskless workstations, any workstation can be set up to use Remote Reset—provided it contains an appropriate boot ROM. Some regular PC workstation users may prefer booting from the file server because of its convenience. Since boot diskettes are frequently misplaced or damaged, users may prefer not to rely on a boot diskette in order to boot their workstations. Others may simply prefer the easier and faster bootup provided by Remote Reset.

HOW REMOTE RESET WORKS

To understand how NetWare's Remote Reset feature (booting workstations with boot ROMs) works, let's compare it with what happens when you boot a regular DOS workstation.

The Normal Workstation Bootup Sequence

When you boot or reset a regular workstation, the machine's ROM BIOS first initializes the DOS interrupt vectors. (Interrupt vectors are pointers to the addresses of routines that service hardware and software interrupts.) Then the BIOS scans for the presence of boot ROMs. If no boot ROMs are found, the BIOS executes the boot interrupt (INT 19). This interrupt routine loads the information contained in the boot sector of the floppy diskette in the workstation's diskette drive. The boot sector instructs the machine to load DOS into memory from the floppy diskette, then passes control to DOS. DOS, in turn, initializes the DOS Services interrupt (INT 21), executes the commands in the CONFIG.SYS file, and then processes the AUTOEXEC.BAT file, if there is one.

On most NetWare LANs, each workstation has an AUTOEXEC.BAT file that contains the commands to load the NetWare shell (IPX.COM and NET3.COM) and log in to the file server. IPX.COM loads the internetwork communication part of the shell, while NETx.COM establishes a logical connection between the workstation and the file server. (Throughout this chapter, when we refer to NETx.COM, we mean NET2.COM, NET3.COM, or NET4.COM, depending on which version of DOS the workstation is running.) The LOGIN command logs the user in and executes the commands in the user's login script. The user is now ready to work on the network.

Figure 12-1 summarizes the normal procedure for booting a workstation from a floppy diskette.

The Bootup Sequence with Boot ROMs

In order for a workstation to boot from a remote file, it must contain a boot ROM chip. This chip is sometimes called a boot PROM (for Programmable Read Only Memory), because it is the kind of chip that can have executable code programmed into it. Once the code is programmed on the chip, it can be only read. You cannot write to or change the programs on a boot ROM chip.

Instructions for installing boot ROM chips and enabling Remote Reset on a workstation's network interface board are included in Novell's installation

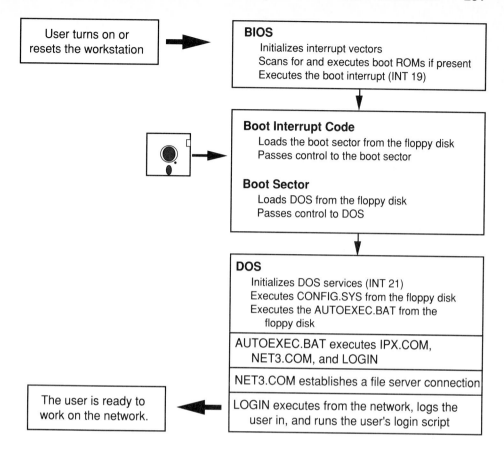

Figure 12-1: The normal bootup sequence when booting a workstation from a floppy diskette.

supplements. The workstation must have at least 256KB of memory in order for Remote Reset to work (640KB for IBM Token-Ring workstations).

In a machine containing a boot ROM chip, the same bootup information must be loaded into memory. But instead of reading the boot sector and loading DOS from a local disk, the boot ROM takes over and reads the information from an image copy of a boot diskette stored in the SYS:LOGIN directory on the file server. This remote boot image file is an exact replica of the boot diskette. It not only contains the *files* that would normally be on the boot diskette (COMMAND.COM and the DOS system files, CONFIG.SYS, AUTOEXEC.BAT, IPX.COM, and so on), but also the *structural* information found on an actual DOS diskette: system sectors (including the boot sector), file allocation tables, a directory, and a directory structure. It is as if you took the boot diskette itself and copied it, sector by sector, into the boot image file (which is precisely what DOSGEN does).

When this type of workstation is started up, the BIOS initializes the interrupt vectors as usual. This time, when it scans for a boot ROM, it finds one. Novell-supplied boot ROMs first look to see if a boot diskette is present in drive A:. If so, that boot diskette will *always* be used. If not, but the workstation has a local hard disk, the boot ROM checks to see if boot files exist on the disk. If so, the bootup procedure will ask the user whether to boot from the hard disk or from the network. Only when there is no boot diskette and no boot files on the local hard disk does Remote Reset automatically go to the file server to boot up. When this is the case, the boot ROM takes over the boot interrupt vector (INT 19) and substitutes its own routine for the standard BIOS boot routine.

The boot ROM knows it must go outside the workstation and find the boot image file in SYS:LOGIN on the file server. Hence, the first thing its INT 19 routine does is to initialize the network interface board and issue a Get Nearest Server function call to establish a connection to the nearest file server. The boot ROM code opens the boot disk image file on the server and then takes over the workstation's disk interrupt (INT 13). This is the interrupt DOS normally uses to talk to a local disk.

The boot ROM next loads the boot sector from the boot disk image file and passes control to it. The boot sector instructions load DOS into the workstation's RAM from the boot disk image file and pass control to DOS. Since the boot ROM has taken over the disk interrupt, DOS thinks it is talking to a local disk drive. The boot ROM code intercepts the diskette sector and track read requests and redirects them to the file server as network file read requests.

DOS, oblivious to all this interrupt redirecting, initializes the DOS Services interrupt as usual, executes the CONFIG.SYS file (from the boot disk image file), and then processes AUTOEXEC.BAT from the same source. Just as in a normal workstation, the AUTOEXEC.BAT in the boot disk image file contains the commands to load IPX.COM and NETx.COM. NETx.COM establishes a connection with the desired file server (not necessarily the nearest one that the boot ROM routine connected with before), replaces the disk interrupt, and terminates the boot ROM's connection. The LOGIN command logs the user in and executes the user's login script; at that point, the user is ready to work on the network.

Figure 12-2 summarizes this modified bootup procedure.

A list of boot ROMs certified for NetWare 286 v2.1*x* is included in Appendix C. If you have boot ROMs for IBM Token-Ring or IBM PC Network II workstations, or for 3Com's 3Station, you should be aware that these behave a little differently than other boot ROMS. IBM-supplied Token-Ring boot ROMs require a diskette drive (if present in the workstation) to be physically disconnected. When the BIOS addresses these boot ROMs, the system calls a specialized boot ROM driver. This driver is contained in a file named TOKEN.RPL located in the file server's SYS:SYSTEM area. The BIOS downloads the TOKEN.RPL file to the workstation just as if the file was programmed into a boot ROM on the workstation's network interface board.

Here's the tricky part. You can't just copy the TOKEN.RPL file into SYS:SYSTEM. After you copy the file into SYS:SYSTEM, you have to bring the file server down and reboot it. Only then will workstations be able to read the TOKEN.RPL file and boot from the file server properly.

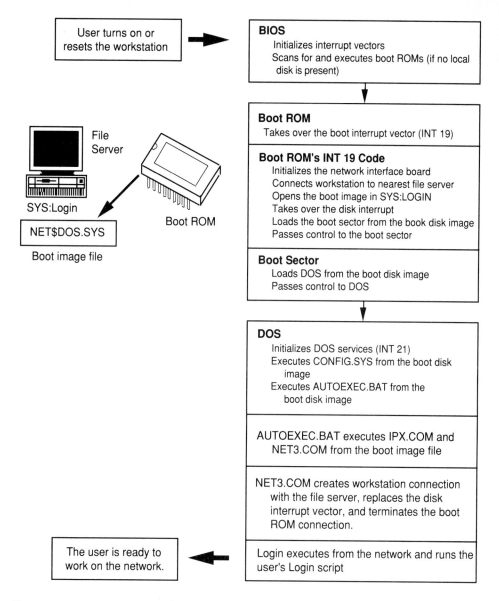

Figure 12-2: The bootup procedure for a workstation with a remote boot ROM installed.

CREATING THE BOOT IMAGE FILE WITH DOSGEN

Obviously, the boot image file is as critical to booting Remote Reset workstations as a boot diskette is to booting regular PC workstations. Workstations can boot from a boot ROM only after you have run the DOSGEN utility to generate the correct boot image file on the file server. DOSGEN.EXE is located in the SYS:SYSTEM directory reserved for supervisor utilities; you must, therefore, be supervisor equivalent to run DOSGEN.

Create the Boot Diskette First

Before you run DOSGEN, you must create a boot diskette for the diskless workstation, just as though it could boot from a floppy disk. To do this, go to a workstation that has a floppy disk drive and either copy or create from scratch the appropriate boot diskette. Format the diskette as a bootable DOS diskette (containing COMMAND.COM and the two hidden DOS system files—IBMBIO.COM and IBMDOS.COM). The boot diskette must contain the correct IPX.COM file generated for the network interface board in the diskless workstation. Copy also the NET3.COM file (and NETBIOS.EXE and INT2F.COM if necessary). Then either create or copy the appropriate CONFIG.SYS and AUTOEXEC.BAT files onto the diskette. Remember, you'll need everything on this boot diskette that you would normally have if you were going to boot the workstation with it.

One important condition applies to a Remote Reset boot diskette that does not apply to normal boot diskettes. Normally, including an AUTOEXEC.BAT file is a matter of choice and convenience; however, the AUTOEXEC.BAT file is required for Remote Reset and must contain at least the IPX.COM and NETx.COM command in order to load the appropriate shell. The AUTOEXEC.BAT file can also contain any other instructions normally used in these files.

If this is the only workstation that will boot from the file server, follow the instructions below for creating a single boot image file. If you have several diskless workstations, each with different boot file requirements, you must create a boot diskette for each as described above. Then follow the instructions for creating multiple boot image files on the next page.

Creating a Single Boot Image File   *Map F:=sys:system*

You must run DOSGEN from a workstation that has a floppy disk drive. DOSGEN creates a sector-by-sector copy of the diskette in drive A and places this copy in the SYS:LOGIN directory on the file server. The default name for the boot image file is NET$DOS.SYS.

Once you are logged in as supervisor, map drive F to SYS:SYSTEM and drive G to SYS:LOGIN. DOSGEN.EXE is in SYS:SYSTEM, and you want the boot image file to end up in SYS:LOGIN. Since DOSGEN will create the boot image file in the default directory, change to drive G (SYS:LOGIN).

Now type **F:DOSGEN**. DOSGEN automatically reads the diskette in drive A and copies it to the default NET$DOS.SYS file in SYS:LOGIN.

There's one final step: you must flag NET$DOS.SYS Shareable and Read-Write (SRW). Type **FLAG NET$DOS.SYS SRW**, and you're finished.

From now on, when the diskless workstation is booted, its boot ROM will go out to SYS:LOGIN and use NET$DOS.SYS as the remote boot image file. Since the file is flagged Shareable, more than one diskless workstation can access it. However, the second workstation must have identical bootup requirements. If it requires a different IPX.COM, AUTOEXEC.BAT, or a slightly different CONFIG.SYS file, you'll have to create a separate boot image file for it. Here's how.

Creating Multiple Boot Image Files

Typically, users have different boot requirements on a LAN. While some users are satisfied with fairly generic CONFIG.SYS and AUTOEXEC.BAT files, others prefer to load all kinds of device drivers and fancy TSRs before they log in to the LAN. Hardware differs from workstation to workstation as well; for example, every workstation may not have the exact same network interface board with the exact same configuration setting.

When these workstations are diskless workstations that must boot from the file server, you are faced with the problem of creating more than one boot image file on the server and then matching each boot file with the appropriate workstation.

Fortunately, the v2.1x version of DOSGEN and the boot ROMs certified for NetWare v2.1x are able to handle multiple boot image files. All they need is a little help from a file named BOOTCONF.SYS that you create and store in SYS:LOGIN along with the remote boot image files. The BOOTCONF.SYS file contains the network and node addresses of each Remote Reset workstation and the name of the corresponding boot image file.

Here's an example of how you would go about setting up multiple boot image files. Suppose you have two new users—Jim and Tammy—on your file server. Tammy has a diskless PC-style workstation containing an NE-1000 Ethernet network interface board. Jim has an IBM PS/2 workstation with an NE/2 board and a local hard disk. Jim likes to load Fansi-Console and other TSRs in his CONFIG.SYS file. Because Tammy has a diskless workstation, she has to use Remote Reset to boot. Jim, although you have already made him a boot diskette, decides that he also wants to use Remote Reset.

Obviously, Jim and Tammy cannot both boot from the same boot image file. And there's another diskless workstation on the network that already boots from the default NET$DOS.SYS file in SYS:LOGIN. You, the network supervisor, confront the dreadful reality that you're going to have to run DOSGEN again to create two more boot image files.

Jim already has a boot diskette for his workstation. Sit down at his workstation and log in as supervisor. Map drive F to SYS:SYSTEM and drive G to SYS:LOGIN as usual for DOSGEN. Insert Jim's boot diskette in drive A. Change to drive G and type the DOSGEN command as follows:

```
F:DOSGEN A:  JIMBOOT.SYS
```

Be sure to leave a space between the A: and the name for the new remote boot image file. You can name the file anything you want, but ideally, the name should identify whose workstation the file is for. DOSGEN will copy the boot diskette in drive A to a file named JIMBOOT.SYS in SYS:LOGIN. Flag the new JIMBOOT.SYS file Shareable/Read-Write by typing FLAG JIMBOOT.SYS SRW. That takes care of Jim.

For Tammy, you need to create a boot diskette for her workstation first. Go back to your own workstation that has a floppy drive and log in as supervisor. Format a diskette using the DOS FORMAT /S command (this makes it a DOS-bootable diskette). Run SHGEN to generate the IPX.COM file for an NE-1000 board. Then download that IPX.COM to the newly formatted diskette. Copy NETx.COM as well. Create a standard CONFIG.SYS and AUTOEXEC.BAT file for Tammy's workstation and place these on the diskette as well.

Map drives F and G to SYS:SYSTEM and SYS:LOGIN, respectively, and change to drive G. Now, with Tammy's new boot diskette in drive A, type the DOSGEN command as follows:

```
F:DOSGEN A:   TAMYBOOT.SYS
```

DOSGEN creates yet another boot image file in SYS:LOGIN. This one is named TAMYBOOT.SYS. Flag the file SRW as before.

Creating the BOOTCONF.SYS File. The BOOTCONF.SYS file contains the network address and node address for each workstation that needs a boot image file. The boot ROM routine will scan this file if it exists and look for its own network and node address. If it finds it, the boot ROM uses the boot image file indicated for that node. If not, the boot ROM uses the default NET$DOS.SYS boot image file.

With a text editor or word processor, create a DOS text file in SYS:LOGIN and name it BOOTCONF.SYS. In our sample scenario, this file would contain the following lines:

```
0x1,d8000f9a=jimboot.sys
0x1,d8002dc5=tamyboot.sys
```

Both Jim and Tammy's workstations are on network address 1. Jim's workstation has node address D8000F9A, while Tammy's node address is D8002DC5. Both network and node addresses are in hexadecimal notation, indicated by the "0x" at the beginning of each line. The node addresses are set on the Ethernet boards themselves. Usually the node address is also stamped on the board or printed on a label affixed to the board. You can verify the network and node addresses by typing **USERLIST /A** from any workstation while Jim and Tammy are both logged in.

Now both Jim and Tammy are all set to boot their workstations from the file server. Their boot ROMs will find the appropriate network and node address in BOOTCONF.SYS and run the boot image file listed for that address.

If you don't know the node address of a diskless workstation, you can't use the USERLIST /A command to view the network and node addresses. (The workstation must be booted up and have established a file server connection before it will show up in the USERLIST listing.) One possible recourse is to alter the boot files temporarily so that the workstation can boot from the default NET$DOS.SYS file. Once the workstation is active on the network, use USERLIST /A to obtain its network and node address.

Remote Booting in a Multiple File Server Environment

An additional consideration is necessary when a network contains workstations that use boot ROMs. When these workstations are on a network that has multiple file servers, you have no way of telling which server is going to respond to a workstation's first broadcast for file service.

Recall that when the user boots the workstation, the workstation issues a request to find the closest file server. The workstation will attach to whichever file server responds first. When more than one file server exists, one server is usually faster. Thus, the workstation will usually attach to the same one. However, the fast server may be down or may be busy servicing a disk request, allowing another server to respond first. Because of the method a workstation uses to find a server, you must place a copy of all the boot information for that workstation on any server that may respond.

TROUBLESHOOTING REMOTE RESET

To troubleshoot a problem with a boot image file or DOSGEN, use the following checklist:

• Are you logged in to the network as supervisor?

• Is the workstation from which you are running DOSGEN using the same version of DOS that the Remote Reset workstation will use?

• Did you create a boot diskette containing all the files the workstation would normally need to log in to the file server, including an AUTOEXEC.BAT file that at least loads IPX.COM and NET3.COM and runs the LOGIN program?

• Is the Control-Z at the end of the AUTOEXEC.BAT file on a line by itself? (It should be, to signal the end of the file.)

• Does the boot diskette contain the correct version of IPX.COM for the Remote Reset workstation's network interface board and settings?

• Did you insert this boot diskette in drive A before you ran DOSGEN?

• Did you have drive F mapped to SYS:SYSTEM and drive G mapped to SYS:LOGIN?

• Did you type the DOSGEN command correctly, including the A:, a space, and the file name for the boot image file with the extension .SYS?

• Have you created the BOOTCONF.SYS file in SYS:LOGIN with correct network and node addresses and boot image file names for each Remote Reset workstation? Is each line preceded by "0x" to indicate hexadecimal notation?

• If you have more than one file server to which the Remote Reset workstation could possibly attach, did you copy the same remote boot image files and BOOTCONF.SYS file to the SYS:LOGIN directory of each file server?

If a Remote Reset workstation is having trouble booting from the file server, double-check all of the above points before you start to suspect the hardware (boot ROM chip, network interface board, and so on). Sometimes if you just delete all the remote boot files and start over with DOSGEN, you'll resolve a problem that was due to a small oversight the first time you ran DOSGEN.

If everything on the software side checks out and the workstation still won't boot, start replacing hardware components one by one until, by the process of elimination, you have isolated the faulty component. Swap the boot ROM first, then the network interface board if necessary. If possible, add a floppy drive to the workstation temporarily and try booting from diskette to verify the hardware setup.

CONTROLLING NETWORK PRINTING

Even in the standalone environment, printing is one of the most essential yet problematic functions that computers offer. Few applications are truly useful unless you can print out a hard copy of the reports, documents, or spreadsheets they produce. On a NetWare network, setting up and maintaining printers can be an arduous task, especially if users don't clearly understand how the NetWare operating system handles printing. Ideally, once printing is set up correctly, users should be able to print to network printers as easily as they can to locally attached printers.

This section introduces the basic concepts involved in printing on a NetWare network and serves as a guide to NetWare's printing utilities and console commands. It also contains information about printing-related error messages.

• Chapter 13 discusses network printing in general and summarizes the steps involved in getting a printer to work on a NetWare LAN. This chapter also talks about other options for setting up printers, including print servers. The information in this chapter forms a foundation for the next four chapters on using the NetWare printing utilities.

• Chapter 14 explains how to use the NetWare PRINTDEF and PRINTCON utilities to set up the printer definitions, print modes, forms, and print job configurations that will be used on the network.

• Chapter 15 tells how to use the NetWare PCONSOLE utility to maintain network printers and print queues. It also offers some suggestions for setting up print queues to make network printing easier and more flexible for users.

• Chapter 16 explains how to control network printers and print queues from the file server console itself. It lists and discusses what to do about printing-related error messages that may appear on the console screen.

• Chapter 17 shows how to use other NetWare printing commands to print files outside of network applications. These commands include CAPTURE/END-CAP and NPRINT. This chapter also explains how to use the PSTAT command to view the status of network printers.

13 Network Printing Overview

This chapter gives an overview of the NetWare printing environment. First, we'll show how network printing differs from printing on a standalone machine. We'll define the elements involved in printing on the network (print servers, print queues, and so on) and show how they work together. Then we'll discuss how to set up a network printer.

HOW PRINTERS WORK

On the surface, printing seems like a simple operation. You create something on the screen, press a few keys, and the results are printed out on paper. Underneath, however, producing printed output is a fairly complex process involving a series of interactions between the computer, the operating system, and the printer hardware. It helps to have a basic understanding of this process, especially when a problem arises with an existing printer or during the installation of a new printer. One way to better understand the network printing process is to compare it with the standalone printing process.

Printing on a Standalone Computer

On a standalone computer with a printer attached locally, a number of players get involved in printing data from within an application. These include the application software, the computer's operating system, the BIOS, the I/O bus, the printer port, the printer interface cable, and the printer itself. Figure 13-1 illustrates the standalone printing process.

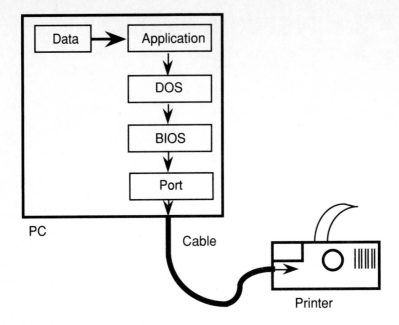

Figure 13-1: The printing process on a standalone computer system. The application sends data to DOS, which uses the BIOS to send the data through the printer port, over the interface cable, and to the printer.

First, the application sends the operating system a file to be printed. The internal process used is fairly standard across all types of applications: the application issues a software interrupt to the OS, signalling that it needs to use the print service routine included in the operating system. The OS's print service routine attempts to establish a connection with the requested DOS print device (LPT1 or COM1, for instance) by issuing a call to the BIOS to "open" the device. If the print device does not respond, the OS sends a "Printer Timeout" or "Printer Not Online" error back to the application. It is up to the application to handle these types of error messages. If the device does respond, a printer connection is established and the OS signals the application to send the data. The OS passes the data to the BIOS, which sends it to the proper printer port over the computer's I/O bus.

At this point, the hardware takes over; the software no longer has control of the data. The port collects the data in an input buffer, then transfers it one character at a time to another buffer, where the data waits until the printer is ready to accept it. The process of the port and the printer assuring each other they are ready to transfer data is called a "handshake."

After the handshake, the port sends the data one character at a time to the printer over the printer cable. This cable connects the computer and the printer's interface circuitry, literally joining them into one circuit. Each pin on the port corresponds to a specific signal line on the cable. For example, a parallel printer connection involves fifteen main signals. Eight of the signal lines carry the actual data, while the other lines carry such control signals as Acknowledge, Busy, Ground, On Line, and Paper Out.

The printer holds incoming data in yet another buffer, where the data waits to be sent to the print head. Data containing control characters (usually in the form of escape sequences) causes the printer to perform a particular function, such as switching to compressed mode or to letter-quality output. The data itself is printed in whatever mode the control codes dictate.

Printing on the Network

With network printing, the paths travelled by data to be printed are quite different from those on a standalone PC. The main difference in network printing is that the information to be printed is rerouted through the network cabling to a print queue on the file server before being sent to the printer. Understanding this difference is vital for troubleshooting a printing problem on a network.

Figure 13-2 illustrates how the various printing players interact on the network. Notice that some of these players work the same as in the standalone scenario (for example, the application software and the printer interface cable); others are specific to network printing (the shell and print queue, for instance).

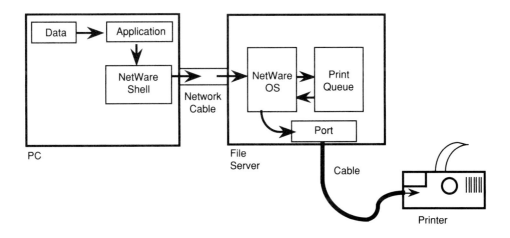

Figure 13-2: The printing process on a NetWare LAN. The workstation shell intercepts data to be printed and sends it out over the network cabling to the file server. There, the OS places the data in a print queue until it is ready to send it out the file server port to the printer.

The complexity of network printing depends on the design of the application. Some applications are designed to print only to a local printer; to these applications, the network is non-existent. Many NetWare-specific applications take advantage of the NetWare OS printing features; these applications establish intricate printer interfaces through the network. The following description of network printing may not apply to network-aware applications that set up printing through NetWare's printing APIs.

As you can see in Figure 13-2, NetWare (meaning the workstation shell, the network cabling, and the NetWare operating system in combination) takes over the printing functions that DOS and the BIOS usually handle in a standalone scenario.

Before running an application, a user issues the NetWare CAPTURE command. CAPTURE tells the shell to intercept all DOS print commands destined for the local printer port (usually LPT1) and send them to the file server. When the application issues the interrupt to DOS to request print services, the NetWare workstation shell (which is memory-resident on the PC) snatches the interrupt and tells the application that network printing services are available and ready to receive print data. The shell encapsulates the data into a network packet and sends it out over the network cabling to its destination—the print queue on a file server.

Once the packet reaches its destination and the sending PC receives an acknowledgement, the NetWare OS takes over. The data is stripped from each packet and stored in a print queue file on the server until all the information to be printed is received: the time required for this process creates the delay between the time the application starts sending data and the time the network printer actually begins to output that data. Several print jobs can arrive at the server at the same time; the jobs are held in the print queue in the order of their arrival until the printer can service them.

The print server code built in to NetWare (or some external print server software) coordinates the transfer of data to the printer. The print server code sends data through the printer port on the file server or print server computer to the printer in much the same manner as in the standalone printing process.

ELEMENTS INVOLVED IN NETWORK PRINTING

The previous discussion mentions several network printing elements that we must define more precisely: the print queue, the print job, and the print server.

What Is a Print Queue?

Conceptually, a print queue is a holding mechanism in which print jobs are accumulated prior to being printed. Technically, these print queues correspond to subdirectories in the SYS:SYSTEM directory on the file server. When you create a print queue, NetWare assigns it an ID number just like for any other named bindery object (yes, a print queue is a bindery object). NetWare also creates a subdirectory in SYS:SYSTEM having the print queue's ID number as its name. Print queues are always defined on the file server, not on the printers themselves.

NetWare automatically creates one print queue for each file server port you spool a printer for in NETGEN/ELSGEN. The default names for these print queues are PRINTQ_0 for printer 0, PRINTQ_1 for printer 1, and so on. Using NetWare's PCONSOLE utility, you can create additional print queues, as well as delete or rename the default print queues.

What Is a Print Job?

When users send data to a print queue for printing, the data becomes known as a "print job." Print jobs are stored as files in the print queue's subdirectory in SYS:SYSTEM. Print job file names start with "Q$" and include the last four digits of the print queue ID number as the rest of the file name, plus the job number as the extension. For example, print job number 854 in queue TEST (ID number 02020109) would be Q$0109.854. Print jobs are also referred to as print requests or print queue entries.

Each user has control over his or her own print jobs in the queue. As supervisor, you can reorder, edit, or delete jobs from the queue and modify the status of the queue. You can also assign certain users as *queue operators* so that they can help you deal with all print jobs in a given print queue. You perform these types of functions in the PCONSOLE utility.

What Is a Print Server?

A print server is software that takes jobs from the print queue and sends them to the printer. Until recently, Novell provided the print server software as a process built in to the NetWare OS itself. However, NetWare v2.1x has always provided for third-party print servers through its Queue Management Services and the VAP interface. As of February 1990, Novell's own print server software, originally offered only with NetWare 386, was bundled with all NetWare 286 operating systems.

External print server programs, running on a workstation, can log in to the server and service print jobs from queues defined on that file server. A print server, therefore, does not have to be part of the file server. Several third-party vendors have written print servers that take advantage of this ability. Other print server programs run as a VAP in the file server.

External print servers offer several advantages over the built-in NetWare print server code. If a print server is running at a workstation, the printer does not have to be connected to or even close to the file server. With a dedicated print server, print queue-to-printer mappings traditionally performed at the file server console can be performed at the print server. This transfer of functionality to the print server makes it more practical to keep the file server locked away safely in a separate room.

With Novell's external print server software, each print server can support up to sixteen printers, which allows you to have more than the five printers you are limited to with the OS's built-in print server code. To further expand the number of printers available, a network can support more than one print server. For example, a network might have three print servers running, each with four or five printers attached. A print server need not be tied to a single file server; it can attach to several file servers (up to eight maximum) and service jobs from each of them. As supervisor, you can specify which print servers can service which print queues, and which printers can print the jobs in each queue.

Another advantage of many print servers is that they allow the supervisor to charge for print services through NetWare's accounting system. (The print server software must have the ability to charge written into it.)

INSTALLING A NETWORK PRINTER

Now that you know how network printing works, it's time for some hints on installing a new printer on the network.

Your first decision is which type of printer to use. A wide variety of printers are currently available, ranging from the most basic dot matrix printers to the most sophisticated color laser printers. Of course, you must match the printer to its projected use and to your new equipment budget. A color laser printer is probably not necessary to print out everyday accounting reports.

The two most commonly cited printer specifications—print speed (in pages per minute) and print quality (in dots per inch)—are important to consider, but there are others that are just as important. For example, printer purchasers should look at the *duty cycle* rating (the length of time a printer can be operated continually before needing a rest) and the *mean time between failure*, or MTBF (how long the printer should operate before requiring service). Another rating worthy of consideration is the *mean time to repair* (the average time required to repair a printer when it fails).

Choosing Between Serial and Parallel Printers

Deciding between a serial or a parallel printer interface can be difficult, because each interface has its advantages and disadvantages. Parallel interfaces are generally faster because they allow eight or more bits to be sent simultaneously across the cable, whereas with a serial interface, the bits must be sent one at a time in sequential fashion. Most high-speed printers use a parallel interface. If the printer will be located closer than 25 feet from the computer, a parallel connection is probably the best choice.

However, parallel printer interfaces have two main disadvantages. First, parallel interfaces usually require more wires and connections than do serial interfaces, which increases the possibility of cable problems. Second, the further the parallel printer is from its host computer, the greater the chance of "crosstalk" between the wires within the cable. Crosstalk confuses the signals between the computer and the printer, causing corrupt data to be transmitted and printed. Shielded cable can help prevent crosstalk and other types of signal interference. Using shielded cable also allows you to extend the distance between the computer and the parallel printer.

The main advantage serial interfaces have over parallel interfaces is that the printer can be located farther from the computer without as much chance of data corruption. Due to the relative slowness of transmitting characters one bit at a time, however, serial interfaces are unsuitable for many high-speed printers. Because serial interfaces operate under the RS-232C standard, configuring the interface cable can also be tricky. The RS-232C standard is not intended for interfacing with printers, so NetWare must set up its own criteria for communication with serial printers (baud rate, word length, number of stop bits, parity, and so on). Essentially, the trick is finding a combination of lines and jumpers that lets the printer and the host computer make the required handshake. A good text on RS-232C is must reading for anyone who will be installing and troubleshooting serial printers.

Printer Installation Procedure

The following procedure applies only when you are using the built-in print server process within NetWare. This setup requires that you attach printers directly to printer ports in the file server. (If you are attaching printers to an external print server or workstation, follow the installation instructions provided with the print server software.)

If you already have printers connected to the file server's built-in printer ports, you must install an add-on printer port expansion board in the file server to make more printer ports available. If the board uses an interrupt, make sure the interrupt does not conflict with those used by the network interface boards and other hardware in the server. Bring down the file server and install the add-on board according to its accompanying documentation.

Next, run NETGEN or ELSGEN to tell NetWare it will have a new printer. You do this in the "NetWare Installation" half of the program by selecting the "Printer Maintenance" option in the "Miscellaneous Maintenance" menu. Make sure you specify the correct port and make a note of the printer number you assign to the printer. For a serial printer, note the communication settings you specify (baud rate, word length, stop bits, and so on).

Set up the printer, following the instructions provided by the manufacturer. Run the printer's self-test, if there is one, to ensure that the printer is defect-free. If the printer passes the self-test, you are ready to establish the printer's connection to the server.

Connecting a standard parallel interface cable between the file server and printer is fairly straightforward. Simply connect one end of the cable to the appropriate parallel port at the back of the file server, and connect the other end to the parallel input on the printer.

As long as the cable supplied with a serial printer is already configured for the proper handshake between your particular printer and server, connecting a serial printer should be no problem either. If the cable is not correctly configured, you may have to use a break-out box to establish a good handshake. Information on break-out boxes, printer pin-outs, and serial printer configurations for a variety of printers is available through Novell authorized dealers, from NetWire, or by calling Novell's customer support group.

Testing the New Printer

Once you make the physical connection between the server and the printer, the new printer is ready for testing on the network. Reboot the file server and log in to the network from any workstation. Use the CAPTURE command to redirect printing to the file server. Be sure to specify the print queue defined for the new printer as an option in your CAPTURE command. NetWare automatically defines a default print queue for new printers; if the new printer is defined in NETGEN/ELSGEN as printer 3, the default print queue will be named PRINTQ_3. (See Chapter 17 for details on using the CAPTURE command.)

Once you issue the CAPTURE command, the workstation shell should reroute all data destined for the workstation's LPT1 port to the server instead. To test your setup, type **DIR** at the command line to display some information on the screen. Now hold down the Shift key and press the PrtScr (Print Screen) key. If you installed the printer correctly, the new printer should print out the directory information shown on the workstation's screen.

Troubleshooting Printer Problems

If the captured data isn't reaching the printer, start troubleshooting with the printer itself and work your way back to the file server. First, make sure the printer is plugged in and turned on. Check the printer for an off-line or a fault condition. If the printer checks out, move on to the interface cable. Incorrectly configured or faulty interface cables are the source of most printing problems. Try swapping the cable with an identical cable that you know works.

If that doesn't solve the problem, boot the file server with DOS and see if you can print directly to the printer as if the server was a standalone machine. Enter a DOS command, such as **TYPE A:CON-FIG.SYS > LPT2:** (assuming you have a CONFIG.SYS file on the DOS boot diskette and that you connected the new printer to the LPT2 port). If the contents of CONFIG.SYS are printed on the new printer, you know the problem lies either with the network cabling or at the workstation.

Check to make sure that the network interface boards and cabling are properly installed and that the network addresses are correct. If you suspect the problem is at the workstation end, double-check the status of the CAPTURE command by typing **CAPTURE SH** at the workstation; you may have inadvertently redirected data to a different network printer or to a file. The NetWare CAPTURE command can redirect output destined for LPT1, LPT2, or LPT3, even if the workstation has no physical LPT ports installed; however, you cannot redirect output destined to a serial port with CAPTURE. Be sure you match the DOS print device specified in the application to the device being captured by the shell.

If you are sure you executed the CAPTURE command properly and you still can't print to the network printer, type **ENDCAP** to cancel the capturing. Attach a printer to the workstation and check whether the workstation can print locally. Perhaps the workstation or the application you were trying to print from is set up incorrectly.

SETTING UP ADDITIONAL PRINTER FUNCTIONALITY

NetWare's printing defaults provide the bare minimum of what is needed in order for users to print to the new printer, without setting up any special options. The group EVERYONE is automatically assigned as a queue user for the print queue NetWare creates for the new printer. The user SUPERVISOR is initially assigned as the only queue operator.

You may want to change the NetWare printing defaults or set up additional functionality for the new printer. The following chapters explain how to enhance network printing capabilities by using the NetWare printing utilities.

14 Setting Up Printing with PRINTDEF and PRINTCON

Although NetWare's PRINTDEF and PRINTCON are separate utilities, they are closely interrelated; neither can offer much that is worthwhile without the other. In PRINTDEF, you define the printers, forms, and basic printing options available on the network's printers. In PRINTCON, you use the printer definitions created in PRINTDEF to set up complete print job configurations for specific print jobs. Users can then include these print job configurations with the NetWare CAPTURE, NPRINT, and PCONSOLE commands to tell the printer how to print files from outside an application. Note that this is the *only* use for PRINTDEF and PRINTCON. If you never use CAPTURE, NPRINT, or PCONSOLE to print from outside network applications, you need not worry about PRINTDEF or PRINTCON.

This chapter explains how to use the PRINTDEF utility to establish basic print definitions, then shows how to use these definitions when creating print job configurations in PRINTCON.

ESTABLISHING PRINT DEFINITIONS WITH PRINTDEF

Most network applications handle all printing functions for you. However, you may encounter a situation in which a printer does not reset properly after certain jobs are printed. Or, a printer may have additional functionality that an application does not address. In situations like these, the NetWare PRINTDEF utility allows you to create a customized printing environment for network users.

Specifically, you use PRINTDEF to define the network printers as print *devices*. Associated with each device is a set of functions and output *modes* that you define according to the types of print jobs the users need. One essential mode is the "reinitialize" mode to reset the printer. With PRINTDEF, you can also define the *forms*, or types of paper, each network printer will use. These definitions are stored in a special PRINTDEF database named NET$PRN.DAT, located in the SYS:PUBLIC directory of the file server.

Setting up devices, functions, modes, and forms involves some work on your part. However, PRINTDEF provides some versatile tools for making the process as painless as possible. You should also be aware that, starting with SFT and Advanced NetWare v2.15 and ELS NetWare Level II v2.12, Novell provides predefined printer functions for thirty commonly used printers. If you have one of these printers, much of the work in PRINTDEF is already done for you; you can import these predefined functions into the PRINTDEF database on your file server. Check the list of printers in Chapter 1 to see if your printer is included.

Running PRINTDEF

To start PRINTDEF, log in as SUPERVISOR or equivalent and type **PRINTDEF** at the command line. The "PrintDef Options" menu appears on screen, containing the "Print Devices" and "Forms" options:

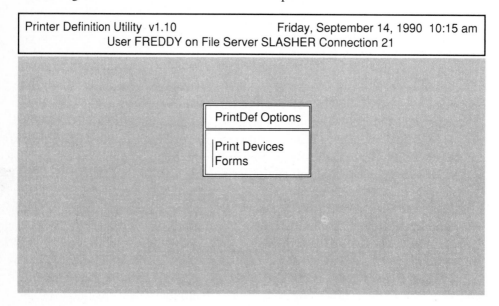

```
Printer Definition Utility  v1.10                Friday, September 14, 1990  10:15 am
              User FREDDY on File Server SLASHER Connection 21
```

```
                            PrintDef Options

                            Print Devices
                            Forms
```

The basic steps involved in running PRINTDEF are:

1. Define each network printer as a print device, giving it a logical name.

2. Define the functions for each device. A *function* is a sequence of escape codes that form an instruction that the printer understands (for example, reset, eject page, set fixed spacing, and so on).

3. Define the modes for each device. A print *mode* is a series of functions that define how you want a job to be printed (for example, reinitialize, draft mode, letter quality mode, and so on).

4. Define the forms for each device. A print *form* corresponds to a certain type of paper: letter size bond, continuous feed checks, wide green bar paper, and so on.

You can define print devices in any of three ways:

    • Copy NetWare's predefined print device definitions for one or more of the thirty common printers.

    • If print device definitions are already set up on another file server on the internetwork, copy them to your file server.

    • Set up your own print device definitions where they don't already exist.

Begin by selecting "Print Devices," then follow the appropriate instructions below.

Copying Predefined Print Definitions

Choose "Import Print Device" from the "Print Device Options" menu. A "Source Directory" box will appear. Type in "SYS:PUBLIC" and press Enter. A list of available printer definition files (.PDFs) appears, from which you can choose the one that corresponds to your print device.

Once the PDF is imported, check to see which functions and modes are included for the device. To see the functions and modes already defined, select the device name from the list produced when you choose "Edit Print Devices." If you want to create additional functions or modes, do so as described under "Creating Your Own Print Definitions" below. Otherwise, press Escape until you return to the main menu. You're now ready to define forms, as explained under "Defining the Print Forms" below.

Importing Existing Print Definitions

You can copy only one print device definition at a time from another file server's NET$PRN.DAT file. Since the database may contain several device definitions, first export the one you want into a .PDF file; then you can import this .PDF file into your server's NET$PRN.DAT file.

Attach to the other file server as SUPERVISOR (using the NetWare ATTACH command). Start PRINTDEF and select "Print Devices" from the main menu. Choose "Export Print Device" from the "Print Device Options" menu. Select the device definition you want to copy to your file server; then, for the "Destination Directory," type the directory path to your file server's SYS:PUBLIC directory (for example, SLASHER/SYS:PUBLIC). Press Enter to leave the "Destination Directory" box. In the "Export File Name" box, type a valid name for the file you are exporting (the name must be no more than eight characters long, with no extension) and press Enter. Then press Escape to return to the "Print Device Options" menu.

Now choose "Import Print Device" from the "Print Device Options" menu. A "Source Directory" box will appear. Type in the full path ("SYS:PUBLIC") and press Enter. The .PDF file you just exported should be included in the list of available printer definition files. Select it. Check to see which functions and modes are included for the device. To see the functions and modes already defined, select the device name from the list produced when you choose "Edit Print Devices." If you want to create additional functions or modes, do so as described under "Creating Your Own Print Definitions" below. Otherwise, press Escape until you're back at the main menu. You're now ready to define forms, as explained under "Defining the Print Forms" below.

Creating Your Own Print Definitions

Choose "Edit Print Devices" from the "Print Device Options" menu. You will see a list of "Defined Print Devices" on the current file server. You can select a printer from this list by highlighting the name and pressing Enter, or you can add a new print device by pressing Insert. For example, suppose your LAN has three network print devices: an IBM ProPrinter and two Hewlett-Packard LaserJet printers. The names assigned to these print devices in PRINTDEF are "IBM Proprinter," "LaserJet1," and "LaserJet2." (Print device names must be unique and cannot be over 32 characters long.)

Select a printer name from the list of available printers. To define the device functions, choose "Device Functions" from the "Edit Device Options" menu. Remember, print functions are a series of control code sequences that the printer can interpret as commands or instructions. These control codes, or *escape sequences*, are usually documented in the printer's manual.

With PRINTDEF, you define each function once and save those definitions for use by all current (and future) users. To define a new function, press Insert from the printer "Functions" window. The following form appears, containing two fields:

```
┌─────────────────────────────────────────────┐
│                                               │
│           Function Definition Form            │
│                                               │
├─────────────────────────────────────────────┤
│                                               │
│                                               │
│     Name:                                     │
│                                               │
│     Escape Sequence:                          │
│                                               │
└─────────────────────────────────────────────┘
```

The first field is for the name you give to the function. In the second field, you type the escape sequence codes that instruct the printer to perform this particular function. Here's where PRINTDEF provides you with a versatile and powerful tool: the PRINTDEF delimiters.

Understanding PRINTDEF's Delimiters. Printer manufacturers do not subscribe to a common standard in establishing escape sequences for their printers. An escape sequence that means one thing to one type of printer may mean something entirely different to another printer. To make matters worse, many printers use extended ASCII set characters to build their escape sequence strings.

PRINTDEF handles the problem of entering extended ASCII characters by using *delimiters*. Delimiters allow you to group a string of characters into a single control character that both PRINTDEF and the printer will understand. The delimiters "<" and ">" say to PRINTDEF, "Any characters within these two delimiters represent one byte or ASCII character of the printer's escape sequence." For example, PRINTDEF interprets the string "<SOH>" as a single character with the ASCII value of 1. The mnemonic SOH, which stands for "Start Of Header," represents the Ctrl-B control character (see Figure 14-1).

PRINTDEF's delimiters allow you to enter printer control codes in whatever format you are used to. People with previous experience in defining printers, using font editors, or creating special batch files may have diverse methods for representing control code sequences. Some people are accustomed to using numbers; others prefer ASCII mnemonics; still others prefer to use control characters. PRINTDEF will understand any of these methods, as long as the instructions appear within the PRINTDEF delimiters "<" and ">". PRINTDEF's delimiters alleviate the need for you to learn new commands in order to define network printers for NetWare.

Although PRINTDEF portrays control symbols in mnemonic form, you may enter them in most any manner you wish. PRINTDEF also accepts two other types of delimiters to designate an ASCII character: a carat (^) followed by a character, or a backslash (\) followed by a decimal number value. For example, a Ctrl-U (^U) is the equivalent of the ASCII NAK (Negative Acknowledge) character that has a decimal value of 21. Figure 14-1 lists ASCII/control character equivalences and their delimiter acronyms.

Delim Mnemonic	ASCII Value	Ctrl Char	Delim Mnemonic	ASCII Value	Ctrl Char
<NUL>	0		<DC1>	17	^Q
<SOH>	1	^A	<DC2>	18	^R
<STX>	2	^B	<DC3>	19	^S
<ETX>	3	^C	<DC4>	20	^T
<EOT>	4	^D	<NAK>	21	^U
<ENQ>	5	^E	<SYN>	22	^V
<ACK>	6	^F	<ETB>	23	^W
<BEL>	7	^G	<CAN>	24	^X
<BS>	8	^H	<EM>	25	^Y
<HT>	9	^I	<SUB>	26	^Z
<LF>	10	^J	<ESC>	27	
<VT>	11	^K	<FS>	28	
<FF>	12	^L	<GS>	29	
<CR>	13	^M	<RS>	30	
<SO>	14	^N	<US>	31	
<SI>	15	^O	<SP>	32	
<DLE>	16	^P	<DEL>	127	

Figure 14-1: ASCII/control character equivalences and their corresponding delimiter mnemonics.

If you need additional help with PRINTDEF delimiters, a full explanation is provided in the utility's help screens. Highlight the "Escape Sequence" field and press Enter, then press the Help key (F1) to access the on-line help.

Defining New Functions. You must name and define each new function in the fields shown on the screen. Name the function according to the list in the printer manual. You have some leeway, as discussed above, in entering the escape sequences for each particular function. Insert as many escape sequences as needed in the "Escape Sequence" field. When both fields contain the desired information, press Escape to add the new entry to the list of functions.

After inserting all necessary functions for the printer, press Escape to leave the "Functions" window and return to the "Edit Device Options" menu. Now you're ready to combine the print functions into print modes.

Defining Print Modes. The new list of printer functions defined above allows you to set up the modes of operation for entire print jobs. Depending on the capabilities of the printer, common modes include a "reinitialize" mode that resets the printer to its default state, a "draft quality" mode for printing draft copies of long files quickly, a "letter quality" mode for printing the final output copy, and a "condensed" mode for printing spreadsheets or other reports with lots of columns.

Suppose you want to set up a mode for printing spreadsheet files. Select "Device Modes" from the "Edit Device Options" menu. First enter a name for the mode, for example, "spreadsheet." A list of the functions that you will associate with that mode appears, initially empty. Press Insert to display the list of all available functions. You can choose from this list by highlighting multiple functions and pressing the Mark key (F5). After marking the functions you require, press Enter to move those functions into the new list for the "spreadsheet" mode.

Note that the functions you moved appear in alphabetical order. Some modes of operation require that the functions take place in a particular order. For instance, some printers allow you to have the "emphasized" and the "compressed" functions in that order, so that you get text that is both emphasized and compressed. But if you list the compressed function before the emphasized function, you will get only the compressed capability.

For these situations, re-order the entries in this way: delete, one at a time, any entry that appears out of order by highlighting that entry with the cursor keys and pressing Delete. As you delete an entry, it reappears in the list of available functions. Highlight the entry that the deleted function should be in front of and press Insert. Next, select the previously deleted function from the "Available Functions" list. PRINTDEF will insert it into the appropriate place in the new list, rather than appending it to the end of the list.

Once the functions for the "spreadsheet" mode are complete and in the correct order, save the mode by pressing Escape. Move on to define the next mode.

The Reinitialize Mode. The reinitialize print mode is an important element to include in every network printer's definition. Not all applications are courteous enough to leave the printer in the same state in which they found it. For this reason, it's a good idea to define and use a reinitialize mode for each network printer. Your users will thank you.

For some printers, such as the HP LaserJet, the function is as simple as the escape sequence "<ESC>E" (note the PRINTDEF delimiters). Other printers, however, don't include a reset function. In this case, instruct the printer to cancel any functions that may have been set by other applications or modes. Here is an example for the IBM ProPrinter:

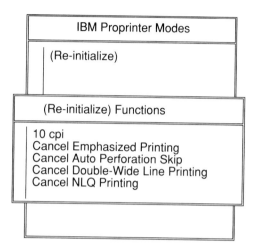

Defining the Print Forms. You should define a print form for each type of paper that could possibly be loaded into your network printers. Common types of paper include letter size bond paper, continuous feed paper, address labels, preprinted checks/invoices/statements, and so on.

NetWare identifies forms by the name and number you assign to each. When a user sends a print job that requires a certain form, the server will wait until that form is mounted on the printer before printing the job. Printing on different forms is much easier if you stick to only one form per printer. For instance, have one printer dedicated to printing checks, and leave the preprinted check paper loaded in that printer all the time. Use another printer for printing out letters and other reports on letter-size paper. That way, your users need not stop between print jobs to load the correct type of paper.

Important: If you define several forms for the file server with PRINTDEF, make sure you provide your users a list of valid forms and form numbers. Designating an invalid form number in a NetWare printing command halts all printing in the specified print queue and requires the server to be rebooted before printing will resume. For example, suppose you define forms 0 through 2, but a user includes the "form=3" option in a CAPTURE or NPRINT command to send a print job to queue PRINTQ_0. As a result of this command, print jobs will back up in PRINTQ_0 indefinitely, waiting for the nonexistent form 3 to be loaded. Even if you subsequently run PRINTDEF to define a form 3, NetWare won't recognize the new form until after you have rebooted the server. To avoid this problem, train your users on the proper selection of forms in NetWare printing commands. (See Chapter 17 for more information about the CAPTURE and NPRINT commands.)

To define a print form, select "Forms" from PRINTDEF's main menu. Press Insert to bring up the "Forms Definition Form" box. You define each form in terms of a name, number, length (lines per page), and width (characters per line).

Form Name and Number. The name of a form can be up to 12 characters long. The first letter must be alphabetic, and the name cannot contain spaces. The form number can be any number between 0 and 255. Assign form number 0 (the default) to the most commonly used type of paper.

Form Length. The length of a form defines how many lines there are per page. The number depends on how many lines per inch the printer is set to print. For a printer set at six lines per inch, for example, a sheet of paper 11 inches long would contain 66 lines per page. The maximum length is 255.

Form Width. The width of a form defines how many characters can be printed on a full line from one edge of the paper to the other. The number depends on how many characters per inch (cpi) the printer is set to print. For a printer set at 10 cpi, a sheet of paper 8.5 inches wide could have 85 characters per line.

Press Escape to leave the form definition box. Answer "Yes" to the "Save Changes" prompt. Repeat the above procedure for each form. Keep a record of which form number you assign to which type of paper so you can refer to it when changing paper in the printers.

Saving the New PRINTDEF Database. When you have defined all the modes and forms you need for your network print devices, press Escape until you see the "Exit PrintDef" prompt. Answer "Yes" to this prompt. Then choose "Save Data Base, then EXIT" to save your new print definitions into the NET$PRN.DAT file.

At this point, the printer definitions are complete. The database file is saved and the forms are defined. The next step is to go into PRINTCON, where you combine the modes and forms into print job configurations that users can use with CAPTURE, NPRINT, and PCONSOLE.

CREATING PRINT JOB CONFIGURATIONS WITH PRINTCON

NetWare's CAPTURE, NPRINT, and PCONSOLE printing utilities have many possible options. When using these utilities to print files, users can specify which printer they are sending the job to and which server that printer is on. They can also specify what type of paper to use and whether the job requires a form feed after each page. All these possibilities (and more) are part of a print job's "configuration" that specifies how and where files are printed.

Frequently, users prefer a particular configuration, but they find it difficult to type all the options every time they want to print a document. They may also forget to reconfigure the printer for their job after a previous user's print job is finished. The PRINTCON (PRINT job CONfiguration) utility permits you to predefine commonly used print job configurations so users can more easily set the options available in the CAPTURE, NPRINT, and PCONSOLE utilities. You can make the configurations defined with PRINTCON available to your users as standard choices. Users can then choose the configuration that fits a particular document without wasting time specifying the individual print command options.

PRINTCON stores its data in a file called PRINTCON.DAT, stored in each user's mail directory on the primary server that user logs in to. Users can connect to other servers, but the directory with their PRINTCON data remains on that primary server.

Relationship Between NetWare Printing Utilities

Although CAPTURE, NPRINT, and PCONSOLE are separate utilities, they can all recognize and use the print job configurations you establish with PRINTCON. The CAPTURE utility redirects output destined for a workstation's LPT1 port to the network for printing. NPRINT is a command-line utility to print a document from outside an application. By specifying various options in either CAPTURE or NPRINT, users can indicate which printer and queue they want to send files to, whether they want banners, form feeds, timeouts, and so on. If these options are compiled into a print job configuration with PRINTCON, users can simply specify "Job=*ConfigurationName*" in the command rather than specifying each option individually. Thus, PRINTCON's print job configurations provide a time-saving way to specify these options in CAPTURE and NPRINT. (See Chapter 17 for more information on using CAPTURE and NPRINT.)

The PCONSOLE utility has its own set of defaults for printing jobs. However, if print job configurations are defined with PRINTCON, these configurations will be available for users to select when printing a file from within PCONSOLE. (See Chapter 15 for more information about using PCONSOLE.)

A key benefit of using the NetWare printing utilities to print files from outside of applications is that users can automatically reinitialize the printer between every print job. By using the "reinitialize" mode you set up in PRINTDEF, which defines the starting command sequence the printer will use during initialization, users won't leave the printer in an odd state; the printer will reinitialize itself. For example, if most of your users run WordPerfect, your print job configurations can have the network printer reinitialize itself and set itself up for WordPerfect files after every print job. When a renegade Lotus user comes along and prints a compressed sideways spreadsheet, you don't need to worry about how the "compressed sideways" settings may affect later printing of the WordPerfect documents. After the printer has printed the spreadsheet, it will revert to the printer definition settings suitable for WordPerfect files that you defined in PRINTDEF.

Since PRINTCON uses the print devices and modes defined in PRINTDEF, you should run PRINTDEF first. Also, you should already have the network printers set up with print queues on the file server (see Chapter 15).

Starting PRINTCON

Now that you know how the different NetWare printing utilities can use PRINTCON's print job configurations, you're ready to run PRINTCON.

To start the PRINTCON utility, type PRINTCON at the network prompt. PRINTCON's "Available Options" menu appears:

```
Configure Print Jobs V1.11b          Wednesday September 19, 1990  8:23 am
                    User SUPERVISOR On File Server SLASHER


                      Available Options

                  Edit Print Job Configurations
                  Select Default Print Job Configuration
                  Supervisor - Copy Print Job Configurations
```

Creating a New Print Job Configuration

Select the "Edit Print Job Configurations" option. If this is the first time you have run PRINTCON, the resulting screen will be blank because you haven't yet defined any configurations.

Press Insert to indicate that you want to define a new printer configuration. Type a name for the print job configuration in the "Enter New Name" box. Give each configuration a unique, descriptive name. Users should be able to infer the purpose of a print job configuration from its name. As an example, suppose you want to define a general-purpose configuration that users can select for most print jobs; type the name "Normal" in the "Enter New Name" box and press Enter.

The "Edit Print Job Configuration" Window. An "Edit Print Job Configuration" window appears on the screen. This window is the main workspace in PRINTCON. Each field in the "Edit" window has a default setting already entered (see the sample screen below). These default settings are suitable for a wide variety of situations, but you can change them as you see fit.

```
┌─────────────────────────────────────────────────────────────────────────┐
│           Edit Print Job Configuration "Normal"                          │
├─────────────────────────────────────────────────────────────────────────┤
│                                                                           │
│   Number of copies:     1          Form name:       (None defined)        │
│   Suppress form feed:   No         Print banner:    No                    │
│   File contents:        Byte stream Banner name:                          │
│   Tab size:                        Banner file:                           │
│                                                                           │
│                                                                           │
│   Local printer:        1          Enable timeout:  No                    │
│   Auto endcap           No         Timeout count:                         │
│                                                                           │
│   File server:          SLASHER                                           │
│   Print queue:          PRINTQ_0                                          │
│   Device:               (None)                                            │
│   Mode:                 (None)                                            │
│                                                                           │
└─────────────────────────────────────────────────────────────────────────┘
```

To move around in PRINTCON's "Edit" window, use the arrow keys to take you from field to field. Or you can use the Tab key to go from item to item. There are two columns of settings; start in the upper left corner of the edit window, tab to the upper right corner, and then down to the next row of parameters. Position the cursor in a field and press the Help key (F1) to see on-line help for each entry.

Number of Copies. We'll begin with the first entry on the screen, "Number of copies." For most print jobs (including our "Normal" example), you'll want only one copy printed. However, if you always need three copies of a certain report, type in the number "3" and press Enter.

Form Name. The "Form name" field allows you to specify which type of paper to use in the printer—legal size or white letterhead, for example. If you didn't define any forms with the PRINTDEF utility, the field will indicate "(None defined)" and the print jobs will use whatever paper is currently loaded in the printer. If you did define forms in PRINTDEF, pressing Enter in the field will bring up a list of these forms; select the form you want from this list.

Suppress Form Feed. The next option is "Suppress form feed." Setting this option to "Yes" means that the printer will not eject a blank page at the end of the print job. "No" causes a blank page to be ejected at the end of the job. Select "No" only if you have trouble with one user's job starting to print on the last page of the previous user's job. Otherwise, you're wasting one sheet of paper for every job printed.

Print Banner Options. Three options for print banners are located on the right side of the edit window immediately below the "Form name" option: "Print banner," "Banner name," and "Banner file."

Setting "Yes" for the "Print banner" option will cause a banner page to be printed as the first page of the print job. The banner identifies the document and the user who printed the document. NetWare has a default banner format that includes the user's login name and the name of the file being printed. If you say "No" for "Print banner," NetWare won't print a banner page.

The other banner options allow you to customize the banner. For example, if you are logged in as SUPERVISOR, you may want to change the name on your banner from "SUPERVISOR" to your name, thus differentiating you from other users that might log in as SUPERVISOR. If you want some other text to replace the file name on the banner, enter up to 12 characters in the "Banner file" field.

File Contents. The "File contents" option offers two choices: "Byte stream" or "Text." "Text" assumes you are dumping plain ASCII characters—no proprietary control codes—to the printer, as when you print a DOS text file. "Byte stream" assumes that you are printing a file that was formatted within an application, such as WordPerfect. "Byte stream" is the most common setting.

Tab Size. The "Tab size" option applies only if you chose "Text" as your "File contents" setting. The number you enter determines the size of tabs in the printed output. NetWare will change tabs into the specified number of spaces when the file is sent to the printer.

For CAPTURE Only. The settings thus far have been for options used by PCONSOLE, CAPTURE, and NPRINT. The parameters listed in the middle section of the "Edit Print Job Configuration" window apply only to the CAPTURE utility.

Local Printer. The "Local printer" option specifies which LPT device on the workstation (LPT1, LPT2, or LPT3) will be redirected by CAPTURE to a network printer. CAPTURE can intercept output destined for any LPT port even if the workstation has no parallel port actually installed.

Auto Endcap. The "Auto endcap" option partly determines when the file will actually be sent to the printer. Setting this option to "Yes" causes captured data to print when you exit the current application. Setting it to "No" delays the printing of captured data until the user issues the ENDCAP command. "Yes" is the most common setting.

Timeout Options. The "Enable timeout" option determines when captured data will be printed in a subtly different manner from the "Auto endcap" option. Setting "Enable timeout" to "Yes" causes captured data to be printed automatically after a certain time period has elapsed, beginning with the last time printing occurred. Thus, you can print captured data without having to exit the application.

If you set "Enable timeout" to "Yes," also set the "Timeout count" by entering a number from 1 to 1000. The "Timeout count" is the number of seconds before captured data is automatically sent to the printer. With Timeout enabled, captured data will be printed when the Timeout Count is up, regardless of what you are doing in your application.

If both "Auto endcap" and "Enable timeout" are set to "No," nothing will print until the user exits the application and runs ENDCAP. If both "Auto endcap" and "Enable timeout" are set to "Yes," data sent to the printer will be printed either when the user exits the current application, after the Timeout Count has expired, or when the user runs ENDCAP.

Precautions for the CAPTURE Options. In some cases, you should not use timeouts to print captured data. Printing initiated by a timeout, and then interrupted by the current application, usually produces unacceptable hard copy. Typically, these cases occur when the current application interrupts its own printing process. For example, in WordPerfect 5.x, if you start to print a job and then go into layout mode, printing will stop for the entire time you are in layout. In WordPerfect, this problem is unavoidable because the printing and layout functions share common code.

Don't use Auto Endcap or Timeout when you are using CAPTURE to save screen dumps from applications to a network file that you plan to print later. If you are capturing to a file and a timeout occurs, CAPTURE closes the file and sends subsequent output to the network printer—whether you want it to or not. If you want to capture screens from several applications to a file and Auto Endcap is enabled, CAPTURE closes the file and sends subsequent output to the network printer after you exit the first application.

Each case—applications that interrupt their own printing process and users that capture to a file instead of printing immediately—causes the same basic problem. At some point, the shell decides that the capture is complete and sends it to the printer; but the capture isn't complete, and the result is unacceptable hard copy.

Specifying Print Queues, Devices, and Modes. At the bottom of PRINTCON's edit screen are the "File server," "Print queue," "Device," and "Mode" options.

File Server. The "File server" option allows you to specify which file server's print queues you want to print to. (Remember, print queues are defined on the file server, not on the printers.) Position the cursor in this field and press Enter to view a list of current file servers. Choose the file server you want from this list.

Print Queue. Once you have chosen a file server, you must choose a queue. A queue is a physical location on the server where print jobs are stored until the printer is ready for them. Highlight the "Print queue" field and press Enter to display a list of available queues on the selected file server. Select the appropriate one. (It helps to assign descriptive names to your print queues, such as "Dot_Matrix" or "Laser_Jet.")

Device. The "Device" option allows you to select a printer from those authorized to service the specified queue on the specified server. This print queue-printer authorization is established in PCONSOLE, while the device names are defined in PRINTDEF. Position the cursor in the field and press Enter to get a list of print devices. Choose the type of printer you want for this configuration. Leaving the field set to "(None)" will allow any printer authorized to service the print queue to print your job.

Mode. The "Mode" option can help you eliminate instances where users disrupt each other's printing. A mode is a specific kind of printing output defined in PRINTDEF—compressed mode, for example. Position the cursor in the field and press Enter to view the list of modes defined in the selected file server's PRINTDEF database. If you leave this field set to "(None)," the job will be printed in whatever mode the printer happens to be in at the time.

Saving the New Configuration. Your "Normal" configuration is now complete. Press Escape and answer "Yes" to the prompt asking if you want to save this configuration.

Use the same procedure for creating other configurations. For example, if you use Lotus 1-2-3, you might wish to create a configuration called "Lotus" for printing spreadsheet files with CAPTURE, NPRINT, or PCONSOLE.

Designating the Default Configuration

PRINTCON designates one configuration as the default. The default configuration is simply the set of print options that NPRINT, CAPTURE and PCONSOLE will use whenever users fail to specify another configuration. The first configuration you create is automatically designated as the default.

You can change the default configuration by choosing "Select Default Print Job Configuration" from PRINTCON's main menu. When the default print job window appears, select the configuration that you want for the default.

PRINTCON will not allow you to delete the default configuration. You can change the default, and delete the old default, but there must always be one default configuration.

Copying Configurations for Users

Once you've defined print job configurations for yourself, you'll want to make them available to your users. You can do this by selecting "Supervisor -Copy Print Job Configuration" from PRINTCON's main menu. Copying print configurations in this way saves a lot of time. If you (or another user on the file server) set up PRINTCON configurations that other users want to use, PRINTCON can send any user's already-defined configurations to any other user's mail subdirectory, where they will be accessible to that user.

Choose "Supervisor - Copy Print Job Configuration" from the main menu. You will be prompted to select a source user and a target user. For the source user, type the name of the user whose print job configurations you want to copy. The target user is the user you are copying the configurations to. You're essentially packaging the source user's PRINTCON file and sending it to the target user.

If the target user already has something defined in PRINTCON, your copying over it will destroy it. Check with your users, therefore, before you copy a PRINTCON configuration file over a particular user's own configuration file.

SPECIFYING CONFIGURATIONS IN NETWARE UTILITIES

When users issue the NPRINT command without specifying a configuration, NPRINT reverts to the default configuration specified in PRINTCON. But if they include the print job configuration option in the command (as in **NPRINT File-Name j=lotus**, for example,) NPRINT goes to PRINTCON and runs that specific configuration ("Lotus" in this example).

The CAPTURE command works with PRINTCON just as NPRINT does. If users type only "CAPTURE," any printing uses the default printer configuration.

However, if they include the print job configuration option in the command (as in **CAPTURE j=lotus copies=5**, for example), CAPTURE uses that particular configuration for printing. There is no need to specify such things as tab settings, forms, or banners unless you want to change a parameter. In the example above, typing "copies=5" from the command line temporarily changes the "Number of copies" parameter in the "Lotus" configuration to 5.

From PCONSOLE, you can also assign different print configurations to jobs that are in the queue. First select "Print Queue Information" from the main menu. Then select the appropriate print queue and choose "Current Print Job Entries." Press Insert to add a job to this queue. Specify the directory of the file you want to print, then select that file. PCONSOLE will list your PRINTCON configurations and let you choose from them as well.

15 Controlling Printing with PCONSOLE

The NetWare PCONSOLE (Printer CONSOLE) utility allows you to work with print queues and print servers on the network. This chapter explains how supervisors can use PCONSOLE to help manage network printing. Through PCONSOLE, you can create new print queues on your file server, rename existing print queues, and manage jobs in the print queues. You can also control the queue status and designate the print queue operators, print servers, and users. Use PCONSOLE as well to define external print servers and authorize them to service the print queues on your file server.

STARTING PCONSOLE

To start the PCONSOLE utility, type **PCONSOLE** at the command line. The "Available Options" menu offers three options:

```
NetWare Print Console v1.02a        Friday    September 14, 1990  10:20 am
              User FREDDY On File Server SLASHER Connection 21


                              Available Options

                          Change Current File Server
                          Print Queue Information
                          Print Server Information
```

CHANGING THE CURRENT FILE SERVER

The "Change Current File Server" option allows you to attach to other file servers from within PCONSOLE so you can set up print queues and servers on any file server on the internet. This option works the same as in SYSCON and other NetWare menu utilities. You select "Change Current File Server" and either select a file server you are already attached to, or press Insert to attach to a new file server. See the Novell *Menu Utilities* manual for further details.

Any print queue or print server information you see in PCONSOLE's other two options will be based on the currently selected file server. For example, if you change to file server SLASHER and then choose "Print Queue Information" from the main menu, you will see only the print queues defined on file server SLASHER.

WORKING WITH PRINT QUEUES

When you select the "Print Queue Information" option from PCONSOLE's main menu, you first see a list of the print queues that have been defined on the currently selected file server. For example, the following screen shows the three print queues automatically defined for the three printers attached to file server SLASHER:

```
┌─────────────────────────────────┐
│         Print Queues            │
├─────────────────────────────────┤
│  PRINTQ_0                    │  │
│  PRINTQ_1                    │  │
│  PRINTQ_2                    │  │
└─────────────────────────────────┘
```

As supervisor, you can do any of the following tasks at this point:

• Create a new print queue
• Rename an existing print queue
• Delete an existing print queue

A little advance planning is helpful, however, before you start playing with the default print queues. First, you should realize that if you change *anything* about these default print queues, you will invalidate the automatic print queue-printer mappings established by NetWare when the file server is booted up. You must then either re-create the print queue-printer mappings you want every time you reboot the file server, or place the appropriate commands in the file server's AUTOEXEC.SYS file. (More on that later.)

There are several reasons why you might want to change the default print queue setup. First, the default queue names chosen by NetWare are ugly and difficult to type. (The underscore character is not one of the most accessible characters on a computer keyboard.) By renaming them, you make it easier for yourself and your users to add the "Queue=*QueueName*" option to CAPTURE and NPRINT commands. Furthermore, the default names do not indicate intuitively what types of jobs users can send to the queue. Since users tend to associate a queue with a certain printer (even though the queue is defined on the file server, not on the printer), you can rename the queue to help users identify its purpose. For example, naming a print queue "LASERJET" lets users know that jobs sent to this queue will be printed on the LaserJet printer.

Second, you may want to establish a separate print queue for each type of print job your network printers support. For example, if one printer has continuous-feed payroll checks loaded all the time, you wouldn't want users sending a 57-page word processing document to that printer. You could create a separate print queue named "CHECKS" just for the payroll check printer and not allow anyone except the payroll department to use that queue. Another possibility is to have one queue for high-priority "rush" print jobs and another queue for lower-priority jobs. You could assign only upper management as users of the "rush" queue, while everybody else uses the regular print queue.

As you can see, setting up print queues is rather flexible. Each printer can be set up to service more than one print queue, or a single queue can feed jobs to more than one printer. You can set this all up in PCONSOLE.

Creating a New Print Queue

To create a new print queue, select "Print Queue Information" from PCONSOLE's main menu. Press Insert when you see the list of defined print queues. Type in the name you want for the new print queue and press Enter. The new queue name will appear in the list, but you're not finished yet. You must also assign one or more printers to service the queue. This, unfortunately, you cannot do in PCONSOLE. You must go to the file server console and use the PRINTER console command (see Chapter 16). Save the new printer-print queue mapping in the AUTOEXEC.SYS file if you want it to be permanent.

As an example, suppose you had a laser printer (printer 0) and a dot matrix printer (printer 1) attached to your file server. At various times, users need output from both printers (perhaps from the laser printer for word processing and from the dot matrix for wide spreadsheets). Sometimes they just want whichever is fastest.

In this case, you could create three print queues and name them something like LASER, DOT, and DONT_CARE. At the file server console (and later in the AUTOEXEC.SYS file), type the following commands:

```
PRINTER 0 ADD QUEUE LASER
PRINTER 1 ADD QUEUE DOT
PRINTER 0 ADD QUEUE DONT_CARE
PRINTER 1 ADD QUEUE DONT_CARE
```

Users submit print jobs to queue LASER or DOT if they have a preference. A user who wants a job printed as quickly as possible submits it to queue DONT_CARE. A print job in DONT_CARE is printed by whichever printer can get to it first. You could even include the "AT PRIORITY" clause in your printer mappings so the laser printer would take the jobs in LASER before (or after) jobs in DONT_CARE.

This method works well as long as the printers are located close together. It may not save any time for users if they have to walk back and forth between two printers at opposite ends of the building to find out which one printed their "rush" job.

Renaming a Print Queue

To rename a print queue, highlight it in the list produced when you select "Print Queue Information" from the main menu. Then press the Modify key (F3). A "Rename Print Queue To" box will appear. Delete the old name and type in a new one, then press Enter.

Remember to change the name of the queue in any permanent mapping commands set up in the AUTOEXEC.SYS file. You'll also have to change any print job configurations you set up in PRINTCON to reflect the new queue name. Although print queue names can be up to 47 characters long, we suggest you keep them short and easy to type.

Deleting a Print Queue

To delete a print queue, highlight it in the list produced when you select "Print Queue Information" from the main menu. Then press the Delete key. Answer "Yes" to the "Delete Print Queue" confirmation prompt. Remember to edit any print job configurations in PRINTCON that referred to that print queue.

Assigning Print Queue Users

By default, NetWare assigns the group EVERYONE as a queue user for all newly created print queues. However, you may want to limit access to certain queues to a select group of users (as in the example of the payroll department above). Here's how to explicitly decide who gets access to a print queue.

Select "Print Queue Information" from PCONSOLE's main menu and choose the queue you want to work with from the resulting list of queues. From the "Print Queue Information" menu, choose "Queue Users." A list similar to this one following will be displayed:

Queue Users	
BADBOYS	(Unknown Type)
EVERYONE	(Group)
NITEMARE	(Group)

To delete a user or group from the list, highlight it and press Delete. Then press Insert to get a list of all defined users and groups on the file server. Highlight the one you want, or mark several with the Mark key (F5), and press Enter. Press Escape to leave the "Queue Users" list.

Assigning Print Queue Operators

By default, NetWare assigns only the user SUPERVISOR as a print queue operator for a newly created print queue. If you want another user to help you manage print jobs in the queue (but you don't want to assign that user a supervisor equivalency), you can make that user a print queue operator. That user will then be able to:

- Change the sequence of print jobs in the queue
- Put an operator hold on any print job in the queue
- Edit some of the print job parameters
- Delete any print jobs in the queue (even the one currently printing)
- Disable the queue so that no one can submit jobs to it
- Temporarily stop all print servers from servicing the queue
- Allow or not allow print servers to attach to the queue

To make a user a print queue operator, select "Print Queue Information" from the main menu and choose the queue you want to make the user an operator for from the resulting list of queues. Select "Queue Operators" and then press Insert to add a user to the list of operators. Highlight the user you want in the list and press Enter. Press Escape to leave the "Queue Operators" list.

Other Print Queue Information Options

Here's a brief explanation of the other options in the "Print Queue Information" menu.

Current Print Job Entries. Select this option to work with the print jobs currently in the selected print queue. You'll see a screen similar to this one:

Seq	Banner	Name	Description	Form	Status	Job
1	FREDDY		LPT1 Catch	0	Active	713

From left to right, this display shows the sequence number of each print job, the banner name, a description of the job, the form number the job needs, the current status of the job, and a job number. NetWare updates the information in this window every five seconds.

Here are some interesting things to note about the print job listings.

• The sequence numbers range from 1 to however many jobs are in the queue. As the top job is finished, all lower jobs move up one notch in the sequence. Queue operators and supervisors can change the sequence number of a print job by highlighting the job and pressing Enter to bring up extended information about the queue entry. Then highlight the "Service Sequence" field and change the number to the desired position in the queue.

• The banner name column usually displays the login name of the user who submitted the job. However, the default banner name can be changed in PRINTCON.

• The description shown is either the name of the file being printed or "LPT1 CATCH" if CAPTURE is being used to redirect printer output on the network. You can change the description by highlighting the queue entry and entering different text in the "Description" field.

• The "Status" column will display one of five possibilities: Adding, Ready, Active, Held, and Waiting. "Adding" means the job is still being put into the queue. "Ready" means the job is ready to print. "Active" means the job is being printed. "Held" means either the user or a queue operator has put a hold on the job. "Waiting" indicates that the job is waiting to be printed at a later date and time. You can check what that date and time is by highlighting the queue entry and pressing Enter.

By highlighting any queue entry and pressing Enter, you will see a window similar to this one:

```
┌─────────────────────────────────────────────────────────────────────────┐
│                       Print Queue Entry Information                       │
├───────────────────────────────────────────────────────────────────────────┤
│ Print Job:              846              File Size:              4811      │
│ Client:                 FREDDY(46)                                         │
│ Description:            LPT1 Catch                                         │
│ Status:                 Ready To Be Serviced, Waiting For Print Server     │
│                                                                            │
│ User Hold:              No               Job Entry Date:      July 13, 1990│
│ Operator Hold:          No               Job Entry Time:      10:26:20 am  │
│ Service Sequence:       1                                                  │
│                                                                            │
│ Number of copies:       1                Form:                0            │
│ File contents:          Text             Print banner:        No           │
│ Tab size:               8                Banner name:                      │
│ Suppress form feed:     Yes              Banner file:                      │
│                                                                            │
│ Defer printing:         No               Target date:                      │
│                                          Target time:                      │
│ Target server:          (Any Server)                                       │
└───────────────────────────────────────────────────────────────────────────┘
```

You can edit any of the fields that become highlighted as you move the cursor down the screen. Most of the fields are self-explanatory. If you need additional help, highlight a field and press the Help key (F1). Some of the fields ("Number of copies," "File contents," and so on) are the same as those you have seen in the PRINTCON utility.

Deleting a Print Job from the Queue. Delete a print job from the queue by highlighting it in the list of print jobs and pressing Delete. Answer "Yes" to the confirmation prompt.

Adding a Print Job to the Queue. By pressing Insert in the list of print jobs, you can submit a file to be printed in that queue. You will see a "Select Directory to Print From" box, in which you can enter the directory path of the directory containing the file you want to print. Once the desired directory path appears in the box, press Enter to get a list of "Available Files" in that directory. Select the file you want from this list.

PCONSOLE then presents a list of possible print job configurations you can use to print the file. If you haven't set up any in PRINTCON, the "(Pconsole Defaults)" configuration will be the only one shown. Choose the appropriate configuration and press Enter. The "New Print Job to be Submitted" window will appear, looking very much like the window for an existing queue job shown above. PCONSOLE will print the file according to the configurations shown unless you change them here. Press Escape to submit the job to the queue.

Current Queue Status. This option allows supervisors and queue operators to change the status of the queue. The three possibilities are to disable or re-enable the queue, allow or disallow all print servers to service jobs in the queue, and allow or disallow print servers other than the one currently attached to service the queue.

These options are useful when you are having trouble with a particular print server or printer. You can disable the queues serviced by the troublesome printer until you get the problem fixed. The queue operator can stop jobs from being submitted by users and can stop jobs in the queue from being serviced. If the operator stops jobs from being serviced, users can still submit jobs, but those jobs won't be printed until the operator changes the "Servers Can Service Entries" flag back to "Yes." When you stop jobs from being submitted, PCONSOLE informs a user who tries to submit a job that the queue has been closed down.

Currently Attached Servers. This option shows what print servers are presently attached to the queue. You cannot change this information; you can only view it.

Print Queue ID. This option displays the ID number NetWare assigned to the print queue. NetWare uses this number to identify the print queue in the bindery, and a corresponding subdirectory is created in the SYS:SYSTEM directory on the file server.

Queue Servers. Use this option to authorize external print servers to service the queue (if you are using external print server software). NetWare's internal print server is automatically listed as a queue server, using the file server name as its queue server name. Refer to the print server documentation for details on authorizing external print servers to service queues.

WORKING WITH PRINT SERVERS

PCONSOLE's "Print Server Information" option is used to create, delete, or rename external print servers. Refer to the print server documentation for instructions on how to use this option.

Once a print server is created, you need to go back into the "Print Queue Information" option, choose a queue, and select "Queue Servers" to authorize the new print server to service that print queue.

SUGGESTIONS FOR USING PCONSOLE

This section contains some suggestions for using PCONSOLE to handle some of the day-to-day problems you may encounter when printing on the network. Training your users and print queue operators in these techniques can save you a good deal of time in managing print jobs.

Deferring Large Print Jobs

PCONSOLE lets users delay the actual execution of a print job to a time when it may be more convenient to print. For example, suppose a user has a 100-page inventory report that he generates once a week and that takes several hours to print. It's not a high-priority item that he needs right away. To keep that user from tying up the printer when other users need to use it, have him submit the print job, then go into PCONSOLE and find the job in the list of queue entries for the appropriate queue. Highlight the job and press Enter. Set the "Defer Printing" option to "Yes," then specify the date and time the job should be released for printing. The print job will wait patiently in the queue until its appointed hour (preferably after regular working hours). Make sure there is plenty of paper in the printer if the job will print unattended.

Overriding Print Job Configurations

Show your users that if they can get to a job in the queue before it prints, they can override some of the settings specified in PRINTCON's print job configurations. For example, if a user sends a job to a queue and then realizes that she wants five copies instead of just one, she can go into PCONSOLE, find the job in the queue, and change the "Number of copies" field to 5. You can also use this feature to change the job's form, banners, and other options any time up until the start of printing.

Creative Uses of Print Queues

PCONSOLE's flexibility in defining print queues can be put to great use in a busy network. For example, suppose you have only one printer. Most of the print jobs on the network fall into two basic types: one type, sent by mail to customers, is a low-priority print job; the other type, used in-house, must be printed quickly. How can you make sure the high-priority jobs are printed first, but still get all the lower priority jobs out as quickly as possible?

Using PCONSOLE, create two queues: one called FAST and the other SLOW. Then, at the file server console (and later in the AUTOEXEC.SYS file), type the following commands:

```
PRINTER 0 ADD QUEUE FAST AT PRIORITY 1
PRINTER 0 ADD QUEUE SLOW AT PRIORITY 10
```

This setup will cause jobs from queue FAST to be serviced before jobs from queue SLOW. The priority can be from 1 to 10. If you have more than two queues, you can have several different priorities.

To prevent users with low-priority jobs from putting them into the FAST queue, remove those users from the list of queue users for the FAST queue. If a user should be submitting jobs to the SLOW queue only, make that person a queue user for SLOW but not for FAST. Unauthorized users will no longer be able to slow down the fast queue with their jobs.

Using Print Servers to Advantage

There are also creative ways to set up print servers on the network. For example, you could set up a print server to service all the jobs requiring a certain form before making a form change. Imagine a queue with 50 jobs; the odd-numbered jobs need form 0, while the even-numbered ones need form 1. That queue would normally require 50 form changes. But a print server can service all the jobs of one form type before switching to the other form, necessitating only one form change.

16 Using the Printer Console Commands

NetWare includes a number of console commands used exclusively for controlling network printers and print queues from the file server console. These commands work only with the printers physically attached to the file server. This chapter explains what you can do with these commands and gives several examples of how they are used. Where applicable, we'll indicate how you can perform the same task from a workstation, using PCONSOLE or some other NetWare printing utility.

The command formats given in this chapter are intended to be less confusing than those shown in the Novell manuals. Therefore, we show only one way of entering the command. After you become familiar with this one way, you can check the Novell documentation to see how you can abbreviate some of the keywords and leave out others to make the commands shorter and easier to type.

CONTROLLING PRINTERS WITH THE PRINTER COMMAND

The PRINTER console command and its variations are used for a number of tasks involving both printers and print queues. We have grouped these tasks below according to general functionality. (The keyword "PRINTER" can be abbreviated as "P" in all of the command formats shown in this section.)

Viewing Information About Network Printers

You must know the printer numbers assigned to each network printer in NET-GEN/ELSGEN in order to use any but the simplest variation of the PRINTER console command. These printer numbers range from 0 to 4 in sequence, with printer 0 being the first printer to be defined. Refer to the installation worksheets or, better yet, keep a list next to the file server console for ready reference.

Viewing the Status of the Printers. To see the status of all printers attached to the file server, which form is currently mounted, and how many queues each printer is servicing, type the following command at the console:

```
PRINTER
```

The console screen will display the printer status information in the following format:

```
SLASHER is configured for 2 printers:

  Printer 0:  Running On-Line   Form 0 mounted    Servicing 2 Queues
  Printer 1:  Running On-Line   Form 0 mounted    Servicing 1 Queues
```

This information is useful when you are troubleshooting a printing problem. If a printer is not printing jobs, use this command as a quick check to see if the printer has stopped running or is off-line for some reason.

You can get similar information from a workstation by using the PSTAT command explained in the next chapter.

Viewing the Queues Serviced by a Printer. To see what queues a network printer is set up to service, type the following command at the console:

```
PRINTER n QUEUES
```

Replace *n* with the printer number of the printer you want. The console screen will display the queues in the following format:

```
  Printer 0:  Running On-Line   Form 0 mounted    Servicing 2 Queues

  Servicing PRINTQ_0 at priority 1

  Servicing NEW_QUEUE at priority 1
```

The display indicates the name of each print queue and its priority level, with 1 being the highest priority. NetWare defaults to priority 1 if no other priority is assigned.

Setting Up Printer-Print Queue Relationships

You can also use the PRINTER console command to have a printer start servicing a new queue, to remove a queue from a printer, or to reroute a queue from one printer to another. You cannot perform any of these tasks through any other NetWare utility.

Assigning a Queue to a Printer. To add a queue to the list of queues serviced by a printer, type the following command at the console:

```
PRINTER n ADD QUEUE QueueName
```

Replace *n* with the printer number and *QueueName* with the name of the print queue you want it to service. The print queue can also be serviced by other printers. NetWare will assume you want the queue serviced at the highest priority (priority 1) unless you add a different priority to the command, as in:

```
PRINTER n ADD QUEUE QueueName AT PRIORITY xx
```

The number you substitute for *xx* can be from 1 to 10, with 1 being the highest priority and 10 being the lowest.

If you want this new print queue assignment to be permanent, add this command to the AUTOEXEC.SYS file (accessed through "Supervisor Options" in the SYSCON utility).

Removing a Print Queue Assignment. To remove a print queue from the list of queues serviced by a printer, type the following command at the console:

```
PRINTER n DELETE QUEUE QueueName
```

Replace *n* with the printer number and *QueueName* with the name of the print queue you want to remove from its service list.

This command does not delete the print queue itself; it only severs the relationship between the printer and the print queue. Any print jobs in the queue at the time you enter the command will remain in the queue, and users can continue to submit jobs to the queue. These print jobs will not be serviced, however, until you reroute the queue to another printer or reassign it to the same printer at a later time.

Rerouting a Queue to Another Printer. If you have more than one printer on the file server, you can reroute a queue normally serviced by one printer to another printer. This is useful when one printer goes down with several print jobs left in its queue. Remove the queue from the bad printer and add it to a good printer until you can get the bad printer fixed.

For example, if printer 1 goes down and you want to reroute its queue, PRINT-Q_1, to printer 0, enter the following PRINTER commands:

```
PRINTER 1 DELETE QUEUE PRINTQ_1
PRINTER 0 ADD QUEUE PRINTQ_1
```

You can specify a priority, as in the ADD QUEUE example above. This print queue assignment will remain in effect until you either remove the queue from the printer (as explained above) or reboot the file server.

Controlling Printers

You can control the operation of the printer itself with the PRINTER console command. These control functions include stopping the printer, restarting the printer, and reprinting some of the pages in an interrupted print job. No corresponding commands exist in any other NetWare utility.

Stopping a Printer. To temporarily stop a printer when you need to change a ribbon, load new paper, realign continuous-feed forms, and so on, type the following command at the console:

```
PRINTER n STOP
```

Replace *n* with the printer number of the printer you want to stop. The printer will stop as soon as the printer buffer is empty. The status of the printer will say "Halted at Console" when you type **PRINTERS** at the console.

The console commands to rewind the printer or change forms (explained below) automatically stop the printer and restart it when the operation is completed, so you do not need to use the STOP and START commands with these commands.

Restarting a Printer. The proper way to put a printer back into service after it has been stopped with the "PRINTER *n* STOP" command is to type the following at the console:

```
PRINTER n START
```

The printer will resume printing exactly where it left off. The printer status will again say "Running" when you type **PRINTERS** at the console.

Reprinting Pages of an Interrupted Print Job. From time to time, paper will jam in the printer, the toner will run out, or something else will happen to render several pages of a print job unusable. If this occurs while you are close enough to the console to do something about it, stop the printer with the STOP command. Fix whatever is wrong with the printer, and count the number of pages affected. Then type the following command at the console:

```
PRINTER n REWIND x PAGES
```

Replace *n* with the printer number and *x* with the number of pages you want reprinted. The maximum number you can specify is 9. For example, if three pages were affected, you would substitute "3" for *x*. If you specify "0" pages, printing will resume at the top of the current page. If you don't specify any number (by leaving off the "*x* PAGES" part of the command), printing will start over from the beginning of the job.

Use the START command to restart the printer when you are ready. If you forgot to stop the printer with the STOP command, the REWIND command will automatically stop and restart the printer.

Many applications will let you resend a certain number of pages in a document. This method of reprinting bad pages is preferable for users, since they don't normally have access to the file server console.

Changing Forms on a Printer

The final three variations of the PRINTER console command help you in changing the forms, or paper types, mounted on the printer. The forms are defined by name and number in the PRINTDEF utility. It might be helpful to keep near the console for reference a list of what types of paper correspond to what form numbers. The PRINTER console command is the only way to tell NetWare that you have changed the form number a printer is set to print on.

Changing the Paper Type on a Printer. When NetWare encounters a job in a print queue that requires a different form number than the one currently mounted on the printer, it sends a message to the file server console indicating that you need to change the form. The status line of the PRINTER console command output will also indicate if a form needs to be changed and what form is currently mounted in the printer. Printing will halt until you physically change the paper and then tell the file server you have done so by typing the following command at the console:

```
PRINTER n FORM xxx MOUNTED
```

Replace *n* with the printer number and *xxx* with the form number (between 0 and 255) corresponding to the paper type you just mounted on the printer.

Checking the Alignment of a Form. With continuous-feed forms, you should check the top-of-page alignment after you load the paper on the printer. Type the following command at the console:

```
PRINTER n MARK TOP OF FORM
```

The printer will print a row of asterisks to show where it thinks the top of the form is. If necessary, readjust the paper in the printer and type the command again until the asterisks print on the top line of the form. Use the FORM FEED command explained below to advance to the top of the next blank form, then restart the printer with the START command.

The MARK TOP OF FORM command works even if a printer has been stopped with the STOP command. If the printer has trouble keeping the output aligned from page to page, stop the printer and use the MARK TOP OF FORM command to readjust the positioning. You can use the REWIND command to reprint misaligned pages.

Advancing to the Top of the Next Form. To advance continuous-feed paper to the top of the next page, type the following command at the console:

```
PRINTER n FORM FEED
```

Replace *n* with the printer number. This command works even if the printer has been stopped with the STOP command. However, if the printer is off-line when you enter this command, you will get an error message at the console.

CONTROLLING QUEUES WITH THE QUEUE COMMAND

The QUEUE console command and its variations are used for a number of tasks involving print queues and print jobs in those queues. Each task is explained below, along with the corresponding option in PCONSOLE. If you have trouble typing the keyword "**QUEUE**," you can abbreviate it as "**Q**" (a valid abbreviation recognized by NetWare).

Viewing All Print Queues Defined on the File Server

To see a list of all print queues defined on your file server, type the following command at the console:

```
QUEUE
```

The names of the print queues will be listed, along with the number of jobs in each queue and the number of printers servicing each queue, as in this sample output:

```
SLASHER Print Queues:

PRINTQ_0                7 queue jobs     serviced by 1 printers
PRINTQ_1                0 queue jobs     serviced by 1 printers
```

This is a more concise summary of print queue status than PCONSOLE gives you. When you run PCONSOLE from a workstation, choose "Print Queue Information" from the main menu to get a list of print queue names. You must select each print queue individually and choose "Current Print Job Entries" to see the number of jobs in the queue. You cannot tell how many printers are servicing the queue in PCONSOLE; you can see only what print *server* is controlling the printers.

Note that QUEUE does not show you which printers are servicing the queues, either. To better keep track of which printers are servicing which queues on your file server, record all printer-print queue assignments in your network logbook.

Creating a New Print Queue

To create a print queue from the file server console, type the following command:

```
QUEUE QueueName CREATE
```

Replace *QueueName* with a valid name for the new print queue. The name can be up to 47 characters long, but we suggest you keep it short and easy to type. NetWare automatically assigns the group EVERYONE as a queue user and the user SUPERVISOR as a queue operator. The built-in print server code is authorized to attach to the queue.

To put the new print queue into service, assign it to one or more printers for servicing (see "Assigning a Queue to a Printer" above). For example, if you wanted to create a queue named "NO_RUSH" to handle low-priority print jobs and have it serviced by both printer 0 and printer 1, type the following commands:

```
QUEUE NO_RUSH CREATE
PRINTER 0 ADD QUEUE NO_RUSH AT PRIORITY 10
PRINTER 1 ADD QUEUE NO_RUSH AT PRIORITY 10
```

If you want these new print queue assignments to be permanent, enter the two PRINTER commands in the AUTOEXEC.SYS file (accessed under "Supervisor Options" in the SYSCON utility).

PCONSOLE lets you create a print queue by choosing "Print Queue Information" from the main menu, then pressing Insert from the list of queues that appears and typing a new queue name. However, you must still assign the queue to a printer with the PRINTER console command and put the commands in the AUTOEXEC.SYS file to make them permanent.

Deleting a Print Queue

Deleting a print queue is a permanent thing. Proceed only if you are sure you don't want the print queue around anymore. You won't be able to recover any of the jobs in the queue. If you want to delete print jobs in a queue without destroying the queue itself, use the DELETE JOB variation of the QUEUE command described below. To remove a queue from the service list of a particular printer without destroying the queue altogether, use the PRINTER command for removing a queue as explained above.

To completely wipe out a print queue and any print jobs it contains, enter the following command at the console:

```
QUEUE QueueName DESTROY
```

Replace *QueueName* with the name of the print queue you want to obliterate. The queue will be removed from all printers that were servicing it. Any jobs that were in the queue are permanently lost. The only way to bring back the queue is to re-create it from scratch. There is no way to bring back the jobs that were in the queue. Users will have to resubmit jobs to the newly re-created queue.

PCONSOLE lets you delete a print queue by choosing "Print Queue Information" from the main menu, highlighting a queue in the resulting list of queues, and pressing Delete.

Working with Print Jobs in a Queue

The final four variations of the QUEUE console command allow you to manipulate the print jobs in a queue. All of these tasks can also be accomplished in PCONSOLE (see Chapter 15 for details).

Listing the Jobs in a Print Queue. To see what print jobs are currently in a print queue, type the following command at the console:

```
QUEUE QueueName JOBS
```

Replace *QueueName* with the name of the print queue whose jobs you want to see. The jobs will be displayed in this format:

```
Jobs currently in Print Queue PRINTQ_0:

    Priority    User        File         Job      Copies
    ---------   ---------   -----------  ------   ------
      *1        JASON       WORDPERFECT   15        1
       2        MICHAEL     WORDPERFECT   16        1
       3        JAMIE_LEE   WORDPERFECT   17        2
```

The asterisk marks the job currently printing. For "File," the console lists the application that the print job was sent from, if known.

To see similar information in PCONSOLE, choose "Print Queue Information" from the main menu, select a print queue, and then select "Current Print Job Entries."

Changing the Sequence of a Job in a Print Queue. From the console, you can change the sequence order of print jobs in a queue. Type the "QUEUE *Queue-Name* JOBS" command first to see the current sequence order of jobs (the sequence is indicated in the "Priority" column). Then type the following command:

```
QUEUE QueueName CHANGE JOB nn TO PRIORITY xx
```

Replace *QueueName* with the print queue the job is in, *nn* with the job number listed under the "Job" column, and *xx* with the new sequence number ("Priority" column) you want for the job. Type the "QUEUE *QueueName* JOBS" command again to make sure you did it correctly.

To change the sequence number of a job in PCONSOLE, choose "Print Queue Information" from the main menu, select a print queue, and then select "Current Print Job Entries." Highlight the job you want to change and press Enter. Type in a new sequence number in the "Service Sequence" field. Then press Escape to leave the job information window.

Deleting a Job from a Print Queue. To delete one print job from a print queue at the file server console, type the "QUEUE *QueueName* JOBS" command first to get the job number (listed in the "Job" column). Then type the following command:

```
QUEUE QueueName DELETE JOB xx
```

Replace *QueueName* with the print queue the job is in and *xx* with the job number listed under the "Job" column. Type the "QUEUE *QueueName* JOBS" command again to make sure you did it correctly. If the job was being printed at the time you enter the command, printing will stop when the printer buffer has emptied. All other jobs will move up one notch in the sequence order of the queue.

To delete a job in PCONSOLE, choose "Print Queue Information" from the main menu, select a print queue, and then select "Current Print Job Entries." Highlight the job you want to delete and press Delete. Answer "Yes" to the confirmation prompt.

Deleting All Jobs from a Print Queue. When a printer malfunctions, you sometimes need to delete the jobs from the print queues it services. To delete all of the print jobs from a print queue, type the following command at the console:

```
QUEUE QueueName DELETE JOB *
```

Replace *QueueName* with the print queue whose jobs you want to delete. Deleting the jobs in a queue does not affect the print queue itself or its relationship with a printer. Users will still be able to submit new jobs to the queue.

If you want to keep the jobs in the queue but reroute the queue to another printer while you fix the malfunctioning printer, see "Rerouting a Queue to Another Printer" above.

To delete all jobs in a queue from PCONSOLE, you must delete them one at a time. Choose "Print Queue Information" from the main menu, select a print queue, and then select "Current Print Job Entries." Highlight the job you want to delete and press Delete. Answer "Yes" to the confirmation prompt. Repeat until all jobs are deleted.

WORKING WITH SPOOLER MAPPINGS

Spooler mappings originated in the days of NetWare v2.0x, when network printing was handled by a print spooler. The spooler served a function similar to that of a print queue in that it rerouted print jobs to a temporary storage area until the printer was ready for them. NetWare v2.1x introduced print queues into the network printing picture.

To maintain compatibility with older versions of NetWare and some applications, NetWare v2.1x automatically assigns spooler mappings to the default print queues created at installation. When you create new print queues or rename the default ones, you should reassign spooler mappings along with the new print mappings, both at the console and in the AUTOEXEC.SYS file. NPRINT and CAPTURE need the spooler mappings to be in place in order to handle some of their options correctly.

Tasks involving spooler mappings are accomplished only through the SPOOL console command. These tasks are explained below.

Viewing the Current Spooler Mappings

To see a list of the current spooler mappings, type the following command at the console:

```
SPOOL
```

The console screen will display the spoolers and the print queues they are mapped to as follows:

```
Spooler 0 is directed into queue PRINTQ_0
Spooler 1 is directed into queue PRINTQ_1
```

The spooler numbers correspond to the printer numbers. Spooler 0 is created for printer 0, and so on.

Changing a Spooler Mapping

To change a spooler mapping when you rename a print queue or create a new one, type the following command at the console:

```
SPOOL n TO QUEUE QueueName
```

Replace *n* with the spooler number (same as the printer number) and *QueueName* with the name of the print queue to which you want to map the spooler.

As an example, suppose you use PCONSOLE to rename the default print queue for printer 1 (PRINTQ_1) to NEW_QUEUE. You would type the following commands at the console:

```
PRINTER 1 ADD QUEUE NEW_QUEUE
SPOOL 1 TO NEW_QUEUE
```

To make these new assignments permanent, include them in the AUTO-EXEC.SYS file (accessed under "Supervisor Options" in SYSCON).

PRINTER-RELATED CONSOLE ERROR MESSAGES

The following error messages related to network printing may appear at the file server console. Some of the messages may be preceded by the word "Abend" (*ab*normal *end*). Abend messages always halt the operation of the file server.

Configured printer not found.

Explanation. The file server is unable to recognize a printer or printer port in its printer configuration tables.

Severity. Warning—the file server will continue to function, but will not be able to service all attached printers until you resolve the problem.

Possible Causes. You attached a new printer to the file server or removed an old printer without rerunning NETGEN/ELSGEN to update the printer configuration tables.

Possible Solutions. Run NETGEN/ELSGEN whenever you add or remove printers to update the file server's printer configuration tables. Do this in the NetWare Installation part of the program under "Miscellaneous Maintenance." After changing the printer configuration tables, reinstall the new OS on the file server.

Invalid printer definition table. Run NETGEN to fix it.

Explanation. The file server could not use the printer definition table during bootup because the table is either corrupt or missing.

Severity. Fatal—the file server bootup will not be able to proceed.

Possible Causes. The error may be caused by a memory failure in the file server. Memory failures can be caused by hardware failure, poor power line conditioning, or a corrupted operating system file.

Possible Solutions. Run the "NetWare Installation" part of NETGEN/ELSGEN and set up the printer definition table again. Reboot the file server. If the error persists, check the file server's memory and power line conditioning. Repair or replace any faulty components.

Network Spooler Error: (probably out of space on SYS volume)

Explanation. The NetWare v2.0x print spooler encountered a fatal error and could no longer continue. NetWare v2.1x supports print spooling to maintain compatibility with previous versions. When a print job is sent to a file server for printing, the spooler creates a temporary spooler file on the SYS volume. The print job is sent to the printer from this temporary file.

Severity. Warning—the file server will continue to operate, but you must resolve the problem as quickly as possible, as more serious errors could result.

Possible Causes. There is not enough disk storage space on the SYS volume for the temporary spooler file. An off-line printer could also cause this error.

Possible Solutions. Free up space on the SYS volume by deleting or archiving unnecessary files. Make sure that the printer the job is being spooled to is on-line. Don't spool huge files all at once; break them up into smaller pieces for printing.

Printer *n* not in system.

Explanation. The printer number specified in a console command is not found in the printer configuration table.

Severity. Warning—the console command will not be processed.

Possible Causes. You used a variation of the PRINTER console command, but typed an invalid printer number.

Possible Solutions. Check the valid printer numbers by typing PRINTERS at the console. Retype the original command, using a valid printer number. Keep a list of printers and their corresponding printer numbers next to the console.

SPOOLER ERROR—PRINTER NOT FOUND

Explanation. The internal consistency check performed when the print spooler is activated as a task in the file server has failed.

Possible Causes. This error has nothing to do with printer hardware. Somehow the spooler process has been purged from the file server's RAM. This error could result from faulty memory chips or other internal memory problems in the file server, or from running software on the file server that interferes with the normal file server resources.

Possible Solutions. Bring down the server and then reboot it. If the error persists, run a diagnostics test on the file server's memory. Replace any bad chips or boards.

WARNING — CANNOT CREATE SPOOL FILE!!!

Explanation. NetWare is unable to create the temporary print spooler file.

Severity. Warning—print spooling on the file server will not work correctly until space is available on the SYS volume and the file server has been rebooted.

Possible Causes. This error could result from an insufficient amount of work space or an insufficient number of directory entries on the SYS volume. NetWare needs a minimum of 2 to 3 megabytes of free workspace and 20-40 free directory entries in the SYS:SYSTEM directory.

Possible Solutions. Use VOLINFO at a workstation to examine the free disk space and number of directory entries available on the volume. Run the NetWare Installation half of NETGEN/ELSGEN to allocate more directory entries on the SYS volume, or delete or archive unnecessary files from the SYS volume.

ERRORS PRINTED OUT AT THE PRINTER

The following errors are printed out, along with a banner page, by a network printer if the printer encounters a problem when printing a job:

***** SPOOLER ERROR ***** Error attempting to open the file

Explanation. This message notifies the user that a problem occurred when the spooler attempted to open the file for printing.

Severity. Warning—some users may be prevented from accessing network printing resources.

Possible Causes. The file may have been locked by another user when the printer tried to open it for printing. This error can also be caused by a break in the network cabling, with one file server on either side of the break.

Possible Solutions. Check the file lock status, using the "File/Lock Activity" option in FCONSOLE. Resend the job after the file lock has been cleared. Check for breaks in the network cabling between file servers.

***** SPOOLER ERROR ***** File is empty

Explanation. This message notifies the user that the selected file was not printed because it contained no printable data.

Severity. Warning—the operation of the server is not affected.

Possible Causes. The file may be corrupted or it may have been saved without any valid data.

Possible Solutions. The user should check the file and try printing it again if it contains valid data.

17 Using Other Printing Commands

This chapter explains how to use the other NetWare printing commands, including CAPTURE/ENDCAP, NPRINT, and PSTAT.

USING THE CAPTURE COMMAND

The NetWare CAPTURE command takes the place of the v2.0x SPOOL command for printing on the network. The CAPTURE command gives supervisors and users alike the ability to redirect output originally destined for a workstation's LPT ports to network printers, queues, or files. CAPTURE can redirect the output of up to three LPT ports (LPT1, LPT2, and LPT3) to various print queues or files at the same time. CAPTURE recognizes these three LPT devices as logical connections; the workstation need not have the actual LPT ports installed. By redirecting LPT ports with CAPTURE, you can print to network printers from applications that are not designed to run on a network.

CAPTURE is not usually necessary to print from applications designed to run on NetWare. With a network version of an application, the application sends print jobs directly to the network printers, rather than requiring NetWare to "intercept" jobs intended for a local printer. For example, you can set up the network version of WordPerfect so that users can select network printers as easily as if the printers were attached directly to their workstations. Network applications typically offer faster printing, increased font and formatting options, and easier printer management. Use network versions of applications whenever possible to avoid having to use CAPTURE.

There are cases, however, when you can use CAPTURE even with network versions of applications. CAPTURE offers a convenient way for users to print on a different file server than the server they initially log in to. When you use an external print server–for example, to service print jobs on more than one file server–you can use various CAPTURE commands to redirect print jobs to the appropriate printer. By using CAPTURE, the users can redirect all print jobs to the server and printer most convenient for them to use. See "Using CAPTURE with Network Applications" below for other examples.

CAPTURE's Options

The CAPTURE utility offers quite a number of options (twenty, to be exact) that you can add to the basic command. With these CAPTURE options, you can specify which file server, print queue, print job configuration, or printer you want to use. You can also set printing specifics, such as number of copies, tabs, banners, text names, form feeds, autoendcaps, and timeouts.

Here is a brief explanation of each CAPTURE option. With the exception of the "SHow" option, you can include more than one option in the same CAPTURE command. The order of the options is not important.

Specifying Where Data Will Be Printed. The following CAPTURE options allow you to specify which file server, printer, and print queue the captured data will be sent to.

Queue. Most of the time, it is sufficient to specify only the print queue you want your captured data sent to by including "Q=*QueueName*" in the CAPTURE command. By default, data will be sent to PRINTQ_0, the print queue NetWare automatically creates for network printer 0 (if it exists).

Printer. If you know the printer numbers assigned to the printers physically connected to the file server, you can send data directly to one of those printers by including "P=*n*" in the CAPTURE command. The printer number *n* can be 0, 1, 2, 3, or 4, depending on how many printers are installed. The default is setting is "P=0." Don't include the "P=*n*" option if you have already specified a print queue in the command.

Server. Include "S=*ServerName*" in the CAPTURE command if you want to send data to a print queue or printer attached to a file server other than your default file server.

Local. Include "L=*n*" in the CAPTURE command to indicate which "logical" LPT port you want to redirect data from. Replace *n* with 1, 2, or 3 (the default is 1). With CAPTURE, you can redirect data destined to LPT1, LPT2, or LPT3 even if your workstation does not have any parallel ports physically installed.

Determining When Data Will Be Printed. The following options help determine when captured data will actually be sent to the printer. Normally, the LPT port remains captured and NetWare holds all redirected data until you issue the ENDCAP command. Only then is the data delivered to the print queue to be printed.

Autoendcap. When this option is enabled, CAPTURE will automatically end the capture without waiting for an ENDCAP command—but not until you exit an application. Every time you invoke the application's print commands, CAPTURE collects the data to be printed and holds it at the file server. When you exit the application, Autoendcap signals the file server to release all collected data and send it to the specified network print queue or printer.

Autoendcap is enabled by default. If you do not want to wait until you exit the application for files to be printed, include "NA" (for NoAutoendcap) in the CAPTURE command. To re-enable Autoendcap, include the "A" option in a subsequent CAPTURE command.

Timeout. If Autoendcap is disabled, you can use the Timeout feature to tell CAPTURE how long to wait after you issue a print command within an application before the print job is closed and sent to the print queue. The default setting is "TI=0," or TImeout disabled. You can specify anywhere from 1 to 1,000 seconds for the Timeout count; for example, "TI=30" causes CAPTURE to wait 30 seconds before sending the job to the print queue to be printed.

When printing from within an application, it is generally best to set Autoendcap off and enable a timeout count appropriate for the particular application. For most applications, a short timeout of about 5 or 10 seconds should suffice. Desktop publishing applications like Ventura Publisher and PageMaker often need time to download fonts or format text before files are ready to be printed. To produce complicated reports, database applications might have to sort a large number of records before the report is ready to be printed. In cases like these, set a relatively long timeout count—30 seconds or more. A long timeout gives the DTP program time to format files properly and gives the database time to sort records between printing reports. If the timeout count is too short, you might get only part of your print job printed. You may need to experiment with various timeouts to find the right setting for your applications.

Keep. This option ensures that the file server will keep all redirected data even if your workstation hangs or loses power before closing the capture. You should include the "K" option whenever you plan to capture data over a long period of time (an hour or more). If your workstation does lose its file server connection before properly closing the capture, the server will wait fifteen minutes, then send any partial data received to the specified print queue.

If you do not include the "K" option, the file server will discard any partially captured data fifteen minutes after the workstation connection is lost.

Determining How Data Will Be Printed. The following options help determine how the captured data will be printed.

Job. If you have set up print job configurations in PRINTCON, you can avoid having to specify the various CAPTURE options individually by including "J=*ConfigurationName*" in the CAPTURE command. Replace *Configuration-Name* with the name of the PRINTCON print job configuration you want to use.

Copies. By including "C=*n*" in the CAPTURE command, you can specify how many copies of the job you want to print. The number of copies (*n*) can be from 1 to 256. The default is C=1.

Tabs. Most applications have a print formatter to handle margins, tabs, and other format parameters. If your application does not have a print formatter, you can include the "T=*n*" option in the CAPTURE command. The number you specify indicates how many spaces you want each tab converted to when the file prints. The number *n* can be from 0 to 18; the default is 8.

If you don't want tabs converted to spaces, include the "NT" (No Tabs) option in the CAPTURE command.

Banner Options. By default, CAPTURE inserts a banner page at the beginning of each print job. The top section of the banner page indicates the login name of the user who sent the print job, the file name and directory path, a description of the job, the date and time the job was sent, and the print queue and server that serviced the job. This information is followed by a large login name and a large banner description, as shown in this sample banner page:

```
*************************************************************
* User Name: ED                           Queue:  PRINTQ_0   *
* File Name: REPORT.SEP                    Server: SLASHER    *
* Directory: SLASHER/VOL1:USERS/ED                            *
* Description: REPORT.SEP                                      *
* Date: 9/14/90                            Time: 16:58:03     *
*************************************************************
*                                                             *
*                                                             *
*   EEEEE   DDDD                                               *
*   E       D   D                                             *
*   E       D    D                                            *
*   EEEE    D    D                                            *
*   E       D    D                                            *
*   E       D    D                                            *
*   EEEEE   DDDD                                               *
*                                                             *
*************************************************************
*                                                             *
*                                                             *
*   L        SSSSS    TTTTT                                    *
*   L        S          T                                     *
*   L        S          T                                     *
*   L        SSSSS      T                                     *
*   L            S      T                                     *
*   L            S      T                                     *
*   LLLLL    SSSSS      T                                     *
*                                                             *
*************************************************************
```

If you don't want a banner page printed, include "NB" in the CAPTURE command. If you do want a banner page, you can specify a different login name by including "NAME=*Name*" in the CAPTURE command. Replace *Name* with the user name you want to appear in large letters on the banner page. You can change the default "LST" string in the banner by including "B=*Banner*" in the CAPTURE command. Replace *Banner* with any text string up to twelve characters long. The string cannot contain spaces; use an underscore character to represent a space between words (for example, JOB_ONE).

Form Feed. By default, CAPTURE enables a form feed after each print job. Enabling form feed causes the printer to eject the final page of a print job, readying itself to begin the subsequent job at the top of the next form.

Some applications automatically eject the last page of a printed document, in which case CAPTURE's form feed will cause a blank page to be ejected after each document. To avoid wasting this extra sheet of paper, disable form feed by including "NFF" (No Form Feed) in the CAPTURE command. To re-enable form feed, include "FF" (Form Feed) in a subsequent CAPTURE command.

Form. If you have defined more than one form in the PRINTDEF utility, you can specify which form on which you want captured data printed by including "F=*n*" in the CAPTURE command. Replace *n* with a valid form number. Alternatively, you can include "F=*FormName*" if you know the name assigned to the form.

Important: Do *not* specify a form that has not been defined in PRINTDEF. If you do, all printing in that print queue will halt and you'll have to reboot the file server (thus losing all jobs in the queue) to resume proper operation of the print queue.

Capturing Data to a Network File. At times, you may want to save captured data to a file on the network, rather than sending the data directly to a printer. The "CR=*FileName*" option will create a file and save data to that file; replace *FileName* with a full directory path and file name, or just a file name if you want the file to be in your default directory.

The only other options you can include with "CR=*FileName*" are Autoendcap, No Autoendcap, TImeout, and Local. If you plan to save data from several applications to the same file, don't specify any Timeout, and disable Autoendcap by including "NA" in the CAPTURE command. Use the ENDCAP command to signal the end of the data capturing session.

For example, to save a series of screen dumps to a file so you can include them in your customized user documentation, issue the following command before entering the application:

```
CAPTURE CR=SCREENS.CAP NA
```

Enter the application. When the desired information appears on the screen, press Shift-PrtScr. CAPTURE will create the file SCREENS.CAP in your default directory (the directory you were in when you typed the CAPTURE command) and save the contents of the screen to that file. You can save as many screens as you want to the same file. When you are finished, exit the application and type ENDCAP at the network prompt. The SCREENS.CAP file created is a DOS text file; you can print it out using either NPRINT or a word processor that handles DOS text files.

Viewing the Current CAPTURE Status. By including the "SHow" option, you can see the current settings used by the CAPTURE command. Typing CAPTURE SH will display information similar to this:

```
LPT1:   Capturing data to server SLASHER queue PRINTQ_0 (printer 0)
        Capture Defaults:Enabled    Automatic Endcap:Enabled
        Banner  :LST:               Form Feed      :Yes
        Copies  :1                  Tabs           :Converted to 8 spaces
        Form    :0                  Timeout Count  :Disabled

LPT2:   Capturing Is Not Currently Active.

LPT3:   Capturing Is Not Currently Active.
```

You cannot include any other CAPTURE options with the "SH" option.

Using CAPTURE with Network Applications

CAPTURE lends itself to some interesting printing capabilities, especially when you mix those capabilities with network applications. Because network applications such as WordPerfect have their own network printing capabilities, you don't need CAPTURE, but it's good to know what options CAPTURE and network applications have to offer.

First, you must know which LPT port your application plans to print to. Some applications, which we'll call "dumb" applications, print only to LPT1, which is also where the Shift-PrtSc keyboard command prints to. "Smart" applications have a SETUP or INSTALL program that allows supervisors to designate which LPT port to send print jobs to. Any application that allows you to designate a printer port can be called a smart application. The network version of Lotus is an example of a smart application.

If an application does print to a port other than LPT1, you must make certain that the CAPTURE command intercepts data at the correct port. If you change an application to print at an LPT port other than LPT1, be sure to execute the correct CAPTURE parameters so that CAPTURE knows where to pick up that application's print jobs.

Network applications that take advantage of the NetWare environment can set up their own printing without having to use CAPTURE. Figuring out what application ought to print where can get pretty messy for supervisors. Most users just want the network to work, without hassles and without having extra things to do. To alleviate some of the extra work, here's an example of how CAPTURE and a network application, such as WordPerfect 5.1, can work together on a network.

Suppose that supervisor Kim has two file servers, PURCHASE and ADMIN, to look after. Suppose also that user GREG logs in to server PURCHASE and often captures screen dumps into a file for a manual he is working on. Greg belongs to a group named ADMIN that prints to an HP LaserJet Plus printer defined as printer 0 on server ADMIN.

Kim has set up a capture command in the system login script for group ADMIN so they can use printer 0 on server Admin:

```
if member of "ADMIN" then begin
    #capture L=1 p=0 s=admin nb ti=3
end
```

With this setup, when Greg captures his screen dumps by using Shift-PrtScr (which automatically sends the contents of the screen to LPT1), he will lose his LPT1 connection to printer 0 on ADMIN.

With network applications such as WordPerfect 5.1, this type of printer port conflict is not an issue. If Greg's screen dump command conflicts with the CAPTURE command set up by his supervisor, he can reconfigure WordPerfect to do the bulk of his printing through another LPT port. Then he can set up a macro and a batch file to go back to LPT1 to capture the screen dumps. Through a WordPerfect macro, all of Greg's regular print jobs can be sent to printer 0 on server ADMIN. Greg can then use LPT1 to create a file in which to put the screen dumps. He does this by typing "CAPTURE LPT1 CR=MANUAL1.SCR" at the command line. If screen dumps are more than an occasional event, Greg may wish to put this command into a batch file or his login script.

There are several different ways to handle the above scenario. For example, you could use a smart application, which can print jobs to another LPT port, such as LPT2 (COM port designations won't work with CAPTURE). A CAPTURE of LPT2 can then redirect data destined for LPT2 and send it to the proper printer.

Take time to experiment with CAPTURE. It's quite versatile and can present some interesting solutions.

USING THE ENDCAP COMMAND

When you type ENDCAP at your workstation, whatever printer port redirection was in effect at your workstation will be canceled and the ports will be returned to their normal status. Users might want to end CAPTURE in order to print to a locally attached printer for a while.

If you have set up an elaborate printing environment using CAPTURE commands in batch files or login scripts, train your users not to use ENDCAP indiscriminately. Many users will be unable to understand why they suddenly can't print on the network anymore.

USING THE NPRINT COMMAND

NPRINT is a network printing command, similar to the DOS PRINT command. NPRINT allows you to send files to network printers without being in an application. Most of the time, you'll use NPRINT to print only DOS text files. Novell's documentation states that you can also use NPRINT to print files already formatted within an application for the printer you are sending them to. However, this does not work for very many of today's applications. Enhancements made to both printers and printing capabilities (soft fonts, PostScript fonts, and so on) over the past several years require print format codes too complex for NPRINT to handle correctly.

NPRINT's Options

NPRINT offers fourteen different options that you can add to the basic command. All but one of these options are the same as for CAPTURE. The duplicate options include:

> Queue=*QueueName*
> Printer=*n*
> Server=*ServerName*
> Job=*ConfigurationName*
> Copies=*n*
> Tabs=*n*
> No Tabs (NT)
> B=*Banner*
> NAME=*UserName*
> No Banner (NB)
> Form Feed (FF)
> No Form Feed (NFF)
> Form=*n* or *FormName*

NPRINT also offers a "Delete" option. Including "D" in the NPRINT command will automatically erase the file after it is printed.

Here's an example of how to use NPRINT to print the system login script. The system login script is stored as a DOS text file called NET$LOG.DAT in the SYS:PUBLIC directory. To send the file to queue PRINTQ_0 serviced by printer 0 on the file server, type the following command at your workstation:

```
NPRINT SYS:PUBLIC\NET$LOG.DAT Q=PRINTQ_0 NB NFF
```

The system login script will be printed by printer 0 with no banner (NB) and no form feed (NFF) at the end of the job.

USING THE PSTAT COMMAND

NetWare's PSTAT command gives you a quick check of the status of printers connected to your file server. The display is similar to that obtained when you type the PRINTERS command at the file server console (see Chapter 16).

To use PSTAT, type PSTAT at the command line of a workstation. The screen will display printer status information similar to the following:

```
Server SLASHER : Network Printer Information
Printer    Ready      Status       Form: number, name
———————    ——————     ———————      ——————————————————————
0          On-line    Active        0, unknown name
1          Off-line   Stopped       1, labels
```

If you take a printer off-line, the information displayed in the "Ready" column will not change to "Off-line" until someone sends a job to that printer. Only then does the file server detect that the printer is off-line.

MAINTAINING THE FILE SERVER

A smoothly running file server is essential to a healthy LAN. Since LANs are constantly changing and growing, the day-to-day maintenance of the file server is an ongoing concern for network supervisors. This section covers various aspects of maintaining a NetWare 286 file server using the FCONSOLE utility, the NETGEN/ELSGEN installation program, and the NetWare console commands. It also covers other subjects of interest for NetWare servers: TTS, VAPs, and UPSes.

- Chapter 18 explains how to use the NetWare FCONSOLE utility to control the file server and view static configuration information about the network.

- Chapter 19 explains how to use the NetWare FCONSOLE utility to monitor factors that influence the file server's performance. This chapter briefly describes some of the more esoteric statistics presented by FCONSOLE, but concentrates on those that really make a difference to network supervisors.

- Chapter 20 provides an overview of NetWare's installation programs and gives insights into what happens behind the scenes when you run NETGEN or ELSGEN. It gives tricks and traps to watch out for in these programs. This chapter explains how to perform the most common maintenance tasks in these programs, and gives hints for some of the less common tasks as well.

- Chapter 21 discusses how to use NetWare console commands (those that you enter at the file server console) to send messages to users, view file server information, monitor file server activity, and control various file server functions.

- Chapter 22 explains the NetWare DISK console command, the commands for mounting and dismounting removable disks, and the commands for controlling disk mirroring. It also lists and explains what to do about error messages that can occur when using these commands.

- Chapter 23 discusses how to maintain the SFT NetWare Transaction Tracking System and use the SETTTS utility to set transaction thresholds. It also tells how to install value-added processes (VAPs) on a NetWare file server and give some tips about maintaining VAPs.

- Chapter 24 discusses the installation and use of Uninterruptible Power Supplies (UPSes) to protect the file server and its attached peripherals from power fluctuations and outages. It also explains how to configure a UPS to work with NetWare's UPS monitoring feature.

18 Controlling the File Server with FCONSOLE

The FCONSOLE (File server CONSOLE) utility, introduced with NetWare v2.1*x*, is a useful tool for troubleshooting and maintaining NetWare 286 file servers. FCONSOLE displays pertinent file server information, not only for supervisors, but for a new breed of system manager—the file server console operator. One winning feature of FCONSOLE is that it allows you to access server information and perform certain console tasks without being at the console. Supervisors and users with console operator privileges can log in to other file servers and view their information as well.

Basically, FCONSOLE displays two kinds of information: information for supervisors about the network server, and information for programmers about file locking and connection information. While some of the programming information may assist the system supervisor, this handbook is primarily aimed at the supervisor and will not go into great detail about the programming aspects.

This chapter looks at the options in FCONSOLE that allow you to actually control the file server. Essentially, that group includes all but the "LAN Driver Information," "Statistics," and "Version Information" options. The options under "Statistics" help you monitor and troubleshoot file server performance. We will discuss these performance-related options in Chapter 19. The "LAN Driver Information" and "Version Information" options are explained in this chapter.

ACCESSING THE FCONSOLE UTILITY

Although users can access FCONSOLE and look at some of the information presented, the full power of the utility can be tapped only by supervisors and designated console operators. To access the FCONSOLE utility, type **FCONSOLE** at the DOS prompt. You will see a screen similar to this one:

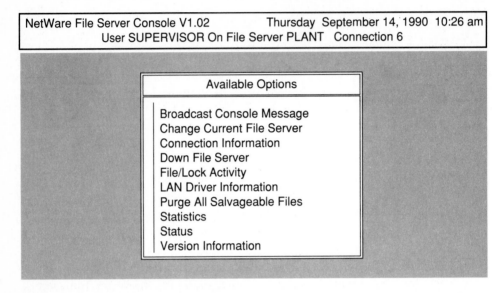

```
NetWare File Server Console V1.02        Thursday  September 14, 1990  10:26 am
              User SUPERVISOR On File Server PLANT   Connection 6
```

```
                        Available Options

                  Broadcast Console Message
                  Change Current File Server
                  Connection Information
                  Down File Server
                  File/Lock Activity
                  LAN Driver Information
                  Purge All Salvageable Files
                  Statistics
                  Status
                  Version Information
```

Getting Around in FCONSOLE

You get around in FCONSOLE the same way as you do in other NetWare menu utilities. To highlight options, use the Up/Down arrow keys to move the cursor up one line or down one line, or the PgDn key to move to the bottom of a window and the PgUp key to move to the top of a window. You can also type in the first few characters of the option you wish to select. Once you highlight the desired option, press the Enter key to select the option and move into the next level. Pressing Escape backs you out one level. Alt-F10 will bring you to the "Exit FConsole" prompt, no matter how many levels deep you are.

BROADCASTING MESSAGES

FCONSOLE's "Broadcast Console Message" option allows you to broadcast a message to every user who is logged in or attached to the server. (Users who have issued the CASTOFF command with the "/C" flag at their workstations will not receive messages broadcast in FCONSOLE). "Broadcast Console Message" is already highlighted when you enter FCONSOLE, so to activate the option, simply press Enter. A "Message" window appears, allowing you to type in a fifty-five character message to the users on the server. For example, if you need to bring the server down for one of those quick five-minute fixes, type "The server will be down for 5 minutes—log out NOW!" and press Enter. The message is then sent to everyone attached to or logged in to the server who is not running "CASTOFF /C."

To check the progress of everyone logging out, choose "Connection Information" from the "Available Options" menu. This option shows you who is still connected to the server and gives you the opportunity to broadcast another message or clear their connections (more on clearing connections after we explain the "Change Current File Server" option).

CHANGING FILE SERVERS IN FCONSOLE

If you have supervisor or console operator equivalence on other servers, you can attach to them and view their information. The "Change Current File Server" option in FCONSOLE works exactly the same as the similar option in SYSCON and FILER. When you select the option from the main menu, you see the servers you are currently attached to and the user name you used to attach to each server. By choosing another server from this list, you can view information about that file server. You will be returned to the "Available Options" menu, and the second line in the FCONSOLE header will change to reflect the different server name and user name if you are attached to that server under a different name. Again, you must have supervisor or console operator privileges to see anything of importance. You can also attach to other servers from the "File Server/User Name" window by pressing the Insert key and entering the requested information.

WORKSTATION CONNECTION INFORMATION

Every file server maintains a connection table to keep track of all connections to the server. These connections are usually workstations, but they can also be VAPs or value-added servers. When you select the "Connection Information" option from the main menu, you see a list (updated every two seconds) of all current connections to the file server.

When you select a connection from this list, you see eight options in the resulting "Connection Information" submenu:

```
┌─────────────────────────────────┐
│      Connection Information      │
├─────────────────────────────────┤
│  Broadcast Console Message       │
│  Clear Connection                │
│  Logical Record Locks            │
│  Open Files/Physical Records     │
│  Other Information               │
│  Semaphores                      │
│  Task Information                │
│  Usage Statistics                │
└─────────────────────────────────┘
```

From these options, you can get several kinds of information about how the workstation locks the files it is using, the workstation's physical address, when the workstation attached to the server, and how many bytes the workstation has read and written to the server since establishing this connection. We will explain this information in more detail after we talk about the first two options: sending messages and clearing connections.

Sending Messages to Connections

To send a message to one connection at a time, select the connection from the list produced when you choose "Connection Information" from the main menu. Then choose "Broadcast Console Message" and type the message you want to send in the resulting "Message" box. Press Enter to send the message on its way.

To work with several connections at once, mark a number of connections in the list with the Mark key (F5). You can then send a private message to the selected workstations only. For example, suppose that after you send a general "Logout now" broadcast message to all connections, several connections remain active. Mark them all with F5, then press Enter. Only two options appear in the resulting "Connection Information" menu: "Broadcast Console Message" and "Clear Connection." Select "Broadcast Console Message," type a second warning such as "Last chance to log out before I clear your connection!" and press Enter.

Clearing Connections

To clear a file server connection, you must have supervisor rights on the file server. Clearing a workstation's connection while the workstation still has files open on the server can result in data loss, so use this option carefully. Generally, you should clear a connection only if the workstation has hung anyway, or after sending repeated warnings to save files and log out of the server.

To clear a single connection, select "Connection Information" from the main menu and choose the connection from the resulting list. Then select the "Clear Connection" option from the "Connection Information" submenu. Answer "Yes" to the "Clear Connection" prompt.

To clear a number of connections all at once, follow the same basic procedure, except that you mark several connections with the F5 key and press Enter. You will see a prompt that asks if you want to "Clear All Marked Connections," with the "Yes" option highlighted. If you have included the workstation you are currently on, pressing Enter will display another prompt that says "Clear This Station's Connection," with the "No" option highlighted. Pressing Enter clears the workstation connections except the station that you are running FCONSOLE. If you answer "Yes" to the last prompt, your connection will be cleared as well and you will have to log back in to the file server.

Other Connection Options

Briefly, here's what the other options in the "Connection Information" submenu mean. (Most of this information is useful only to programmers trying to debug a network applications.)

Logical Record Locks. This option shows you which *logical* record locks the selected connection is using, which task is using the lock, and the status of the lock. While this information is not of much use to most system supervisors, you can learn a little bit on how logical record locking works.

Applications use logical record locks to control the number of users who can be in the application at one time. A logical lock (as opposed to physical lock) uses a naming convention to lock each record, or section of data, in the file. The application locks the name only when it accesses the data. When another application that recognizes the naming convention (or the same application being run by another user) tries to access the locked record, the application waits until the record is no longer locked before accessing it.

The information you see on the screen includes the name of the logical record lock and the number assigned to the task that is using the logical record. Applications can lock records in a number of ways, as indicated by the four possible messages:

• *Record is not locked.* This indicates that no logical locks are being used by the connection.

• *Record is locked shareable.* Shareable record locks allow other connections to read data at the same time as the workstation connection.

• *Record is locked exclusive.* When the connection is ready to write data to a record, that record is marked with an exclusive lock so that no other workstation can lock that record during that time.

• *Record is being held by the Transaction Tracking System.* While NetWare waits for a transaction to be written to disk, it places exclusive locks on all records in the transaction. If something were to happen during the transaction update, the server could then back out of the transaction and the records would be protected.

Records that are read as part of a set will be shown as "logged" or as "not logged." Logged records are locked as a set so other stations won't compete for one of the records or for the entire record set.

To get out of the "Logical Record Locks" window, press the Escape key.

Open Files/Physical Records. This option shows you which files the chosen connection presently has open, along with the task number DOS has assigned to the task that is using the files themselves. Select one of the file entries, and you will see the "File/Physical Records Information" menu containing the "File Status" and the "Physical Record Locks" options.

The "File Status" option shows you how the operating system currently views the file's status. You can see any number and combination of the status statements that explain the file's status. The status possibilities include:

• *File Is Open.* The workstation has the file open, but not as a shareable file.

• *File is Open In Share Mode.* The workstation has the file open and the file is a shareable file.

• *Open For Read Only.* The workstation opened the file to read from it, but not to write to it.

• *Open For Write Only.* The workstation opened the file to write to it, but not to read from it.

• *Open For Read And Write.* The workstation can read from the file and write to it.

• *Allow Reads And Writes From Other Stations.* This workstation will allow other workstations to read from and write to the file.

• *Deny Reads, But Allow Writes From Other Stations.* Other workstations cannot read from the file, but can write to the file.

• *Allow Reads, But Deny Writes From Other Stations.* Other workstations can read the file, but not write to it.

• *Deny Reads and Writes From Other Stations.* Other workstations cannot read or write to the file.

• *Locked By File Lock.* A file lock has locked this file.

• *File Is Logged.* The workstation has marked the file as logged, meaning the file will be locked with several other files.

• *File Is Not Open.* The file is either locked or logged as part of a set, but is no longer open by the workstation.

• *Locked By Shared File Set Transaction.* The file is locked as part of a shared file set transaction.

• *File Is Detached.* The file was locked as part of a shared file set, but is not unlocked. The workstation must relock the file in order to access it.

• *File Detach Is Being Held By The Transaction Tracking System.* The SFT NetWare Transaction Tracking System (TTS) is holding the file open until the transaction ends.

• *Transaction Will Be Tracked By The Transaction Tracking System.* The file has been flagged as "Transactional" so that TTS can ensure that changes to the file are tracked in case the transaction fails.

• *File Is Being Held Open By the Transaction Tracking System.* The workstation has closed the file, but TTS is holding the file open until it can complete the transaction.

• *TTS Holding Lock.* The workstation has released the lock, but now TTS is holding the lock until it completes the transaction, at which time it will release the lock.

• *Explicit Transaction Tracking In Progress.* The file has been flagged as "Transactional" and a transaction has begun but has not ended.

• *Implicit Transaction Tracking In Progress.* The file has been flagged as "Transactional" and a transaction has begun because of a physical or logical record lock. The transaction ends when the workstation unlocks the record.

The "Physical Record Locks" option shows you if there are any physical record locks on the file you are viewing. A physical record lock differs from a logical record lock in that it physically locks a range of bytes to prevent other workstations access to the byte range. Once locked, other workstations cannot access the data until the physical lock is removed. Since the physical record list is updated every two minutes, you may not see physical record locks as they go through the locking procedure.

The top of the physical record lock screen shows you the directory path where the file is stored, along with the file name itself. The other information you see on the screen includes the physical record's name and the task that is using the physical record. This information is essentially the same as the information shown in the "Logical Record Locks" option. The lock status can be either shareable, exclusive, held by TTS, or not locked. Records that are read as part of a set will be shown as logged or as not logged.

Some supervisors use the file locks and file status information to see how open files are flagged and how NetWare responds to those flags, but that is not reason enough to look at file status. If you are having problems accessing an application, or if the application is having problems accessing information, use the file locking and file status information to see why a file is behaving the way it is. You can then talk a little more intelligently with the application vendor or a Novell technician. Press the Escape key until you return to the "Connections Information" window.

Other Information. This option shows you miscellaneous information about the connection, including the object name, object type, full name, login time, and the network and node address. The "Object Name" is the login name used by the connection. Objects can be users, print servers, or whatever else can log in to the server. The "Object Type" displays what type the object is. Users are type 1; other objects have different type numbers. The "Full Name" entry shows the user's full name if the supervisor defined one in SYSCON. The "Login Time" shows when the user or object last logged in to the file server. "Network Address" shows both the network and node address of the connection. These addresses identify the physical address of the connection.

Semaphores. This option shows you how the connection is using semaphores. Supervisors can look at semaphore information to see an application's status on resource sharing, but the information is useful mostly to programmers. Programmers use semaphores to limit the number of tasks that can use a resource within an application, or to limit the number of workstations that can access an application at one time. What you see in the semaphore window for each semaphore is the name of the semaphore, the task that opened the semaphore, all of the tasks or connections (workstations) that have the semaphore open, and the semaphore's current value.

A positive number in the "Value" column indicates the number of resources available at this time. A value of 0 means that there are no resources available and that there are no workstation waiting for the resource. When the value is a negative number (such as -1), it means that there is a workstation waiting for the resource. The workstation will wait a certain amount of time for a resource to free up; if the resource does not free up, the application will tell the workstation that there are no available resources, either for the task to be performed or for the workstation to run the application.

To exit the semaphore information screen, press Escape.

Task Information. This option is more of a programming tool rather than a supervisor tool. When you select "Task Information," you see two windows containing information about the status of the connection itself and the tasks running within that connection. The "Connection Status" window tells you if the connection is waiting for a semaphore or a lock, while the "Active Tasks" portion of the screen shows you which tasks the connections in the "Connection Status" window are using.

The "Connection Status" window can display the following types of messages:

- *Connection Is Not Waiting.* The connection is not waiting for a semaphore or a lock.
- *Connection Is Waiting On A Physical Record Lock.* The connection is trying to lock a physical record, but must wait for another station to unlock that record first. You will see the byte range of the record to be locked.
- *Connection Is Waiting On A File Lock.* The connection is trying to lock a file, but must wait for another station to first unlock that file. You will see the name of the file to be locked.
- *Connection Is Waiting On A Semaphore.* The connection is trying to use a resource limited by a semaphore, and that resource is currently being used by another connection.

The "Active Tasks" window can display the following types of messages:

- *Normal.* The task is using network files, locks, and semaphores normally.
- *Explicit Transaction In Progress.* The task just issued an explicit begin transaction, which means TTS will track updates to the file in case something happens and TTS has to back out of the transaction.
- *Implicit Transaction In Progress.* The task locked a file, causing a transaction to begin. TTS will track the file updates in case something happens and TTS has to back out of the transaction.
- *Shared File Set Lock In Progress.* As a shared file set transaction begins, all logged files within that file set are locked (TTS is not tracking changes).
- *Explicit Transaction And Shared File Set Lock In Progress.* In this instance, TTS is tracking changes as the task issues a begin shared file set transaction call in addition to an explicit TTS call.
- *Implicit Transaction And Shared File Set Lock In Progress.* In this instance, TTS is tracking changes as the task issues a begin shared file set transaction call in addition to an implicit TTS call.

To return to the "Connection Information" submenu, press Escape.

Usage Statistics. This option shows you how many resources this particular connection has used since the workstation has logged in or attached to this server. Specifically, the "Connection Usage Statistics" window shows you how long this particular connection has been established with the server and the number of requests the server has received since this connection was established. The "Disk Bytes Read" entry shows you how many bytes of information the workstation has read from the server disks, and the "Disk Bytes Written" entry shows you how many bytes of information the workstation has written to the server disks.

To return to the "Connection Information" submenu, press Escape.

Exiting "Connection Information"

To exit the "Connection Information" window, press the Escape key. If you want to see connection information about another workstation, choose one of the other connections in the "Current Connections" list. While some of this information can give you a better idea of how workstations are handling files, most of the information is aimed at programmers debugging an application rather than a system supervisor troubleshooting a network.

DOWNING THE FILE SERVER

Through FCONSOLE, you can shut down a file server just as if you were at the console typing the DOWN command. (Only a system supervisor can down the server from FCONSOLE; a console operator cannot.)

To bring down the currently selected file server, choose "Down File Server" from FCONSOLE's main menu. You will see a "Down File Server *ServerName*" prompt with the "No" option highlighted. Highlight "Yes" and press Enter. If there are files still open on the server, you will see another prompt that says "Server Has Open Files, Force Down Server"—again with the "No" option highlighted. To go ahead and down the server, highlight "Yes" and press Enter. The server will shut down and you will lose your connection, as will any other user who did not log out. FCONSOLE generates a message at the file server console indicating that the server has completed the "DOWN" sequence. You can then go to the server and physically power it down for repairs or whatever you need to do.

VIEWING FILE AND RECORD LOCKING ACTIVITY

The "File/Lock Activity" option is better suited for programmers than for supervisors, for it gives information about how NetWare uses locks, files, and semaphores. As a supervisor, however, you might use the "File/Lock Activity" option if you are having problems with an application and want to see how NetWare is handling the file locking for that application. You can trace down the files the application has open and report the file, record, and semaphore status to the vendor; the vendor may have suggestions as to why the applications is having problems.

When you select the "File/Lock Activity" option from the main menu, you see the following "File/Lock Activity" submenu:

```
┌─────────────────────────────────────┐
│           File/Lock Activity         │
├─────────────────────────────────────┤
│ Current Transactions                 │
│ File/Physical Records Information    │
│ Logical Lock Information             │
│ Semaphore Information                │
└─────────────────────────────────────┘
```

(You will not see the "Current Transactions" option if you do not have TTS installed.)

Viewing Current Transactions

The "Current Transactions" option shows you which transactions TTS is presently tracking. In the "Conn/Task" window, you can see the connections and the tasks that are performing the transactions. Transactions are either written completely to the disk or are not written to the disk at all.

The "Transactions In Progress" entry shows you which transactions are currently in progress; if a workstation is performing the transaction, you will also see the station's connection and task number. The "New Transactions" entry shows you which transactions have begun in the last second, keeping you appraised of the situation. The "Total Transactions" entry shows how many transaction have transpired since the last time the server was brought up.

Viewing File and Physical Records Information

This option displays the same information about file status and physical record locks as the "Connection Information" option, but you approach it by file name rather than by user name. To look at a particular file, choose "File/Physical Records Information" and enter the full directory path of the file in the "Directory Path" box. Either type the directory path in from memory, or press Insert to build the path from the lists NetWare will present. When the correct directory path appear in the box, press Enter to see the "File Name" box. Either enter the file name or press Insert again to see a list of files from which you can select the file name you want. Pressing Enter on the file name brings you to another "File/Physical Records Information" window with two options: "File Status" and "Physical Record Locks."

The "File Status" option has the following options in two windows:

• *Use Count*. This entry shows you how many connections are using the file (by having the file either open, logged, or locked).

• *Open Count*. This entry shows you how many connections have the file open.

• *Open For Read*. This entry shows you how many connections have the file open for read access.

• *Open For Write*. This entry shows you how many connections have the file open for write access.

• *Deny Read*. This entry shows you how many connections, while opening the file, have prevented other workstation read access to the file.

• *Deny Write*. This entry shows you how many connections, while opening the file, have prevented other workstation write access to the file.

• *Status*. You can see three entries in the "Status" field: "Not locked," "Locked by file lock," or "Locked by share file set transaction." You will see the latter message when the connection locking the file displays a list of connections using the file.

• *Connection Number and Task Number*. These entries show the number of the connection using the file, as well as the task number within that connection.

• *Status*. The second "Status" field shows you how the file is locked: whether it is locked exclusively, locked by a shared lock set, not locked at all, or whether TTS is holding the lock.

The "Physical Record Locks" option shows you which connections have any physical record locks on the file. The information you see in the physical record lock screen include the byte range that is being locked, how many connections are using that byte range, and the lock status.

Viewing Logical Lock Information

The "Logical Lock Information" option lists the connections that are using a logical record lock, as well as the status of the lock. Selecting the "Logical Lock Information" option brings up a "Logical Record Name" window. Here you must know the logical record name in order to view the file's lock information. The NetWare *Supervisor Reference* manual suggests that if you don't know the logical record name, you might try examining the connection that is using the logical record lock.

Once you enter the record lock name, you will see a screen showing the following entries:

- *Use Count*. This entry shows you how many connections are using that logical record.
- *Share Count*. This entry shows you how many connections have the logical record lock and are using the lock in a shareable fashion.
- *Status*. You can see three entries in the "Status" field: "Not locked," "Locked exclusive," and "Locked shareable."
- *Connection Number and Task Number*. These entries indicate the number of the connection and task within that connection that is using the logical record lock.
- *Status*. This entry shows you how the file is locked: whether it is locked exclusively, locked as part of a shared lock set, not locked at all, or whether TTS is holding the lock.

Viewing Semaphore Information

The last option in the "File/Lock Activity" submenu is the "Semaphore Information" option, which shows you if a semaphore is in use and the status of the semaphore. If you don't know the name of the semaphore you want to examine, try examining the connection that is using the semaphore (using the "Connection Information" option).

Once you enter the semaphore name, you will see a screen showing the following entries:

- *Open Count*. This entry tells you how many connections are using the semaphore.
- *Value*. This is a positive number if resources are available at this time. A value of 0 means that there are no resources available, and that there are no workstation waiting for the resource. When the value is a negative number (such as -1), it means there is a workstation waiting to use the resource. The workstation will wait a certain amount of time for the resource to free up; if the resource does not free up, the application will tell the workstation that there are no available resources, either for the task to be performed or for the workstation to run the application.

• *Connection*. This entry shows you the connection number of the workstation using the semaphore.

• *Task*. This entry shows you the task number within the workstation connection using this semaphore.

Press the Escape key until you exit from the "File/Lock Activity" window and return to the "Available Options" menu.

LOOKING AT THE SERVER'S LAN DRIVERS

You can configure SFT and Advanced NetWare file servers to have up to four network interface boards; ELS NetWare allows only one network interface board in the file server. Each board requires a corresponding LAN driver to be chosen and linked into the NetWare operating system. The LAN driver/network interface board combination allows for asynchronous communication in an event-driven environment. As you install the NetWare operating system, or as you later bring up the operating system, the OS initializes the drivers to the network interface board for packet reception and administration.

To see the information about a particular driver, select "LAN Driver Information" from the main menu. Choose that LAN driver from the "Select LAN Driver" list. (If you have only one network interface board linked into the operating system, you will not see the "Select LAN Driver" window; you will go directly to the configuration screen.) Note that nondedicated NetWare lists a configuration for LAN E. LAN E represents a "network" of one workstation: the workstation side of the file server. The OS communicates with workstation side of the file server through LAN E.

For each LAN driver, FCONSOLE displays a configuration screen similar to this one:

LAN A Configuration		
Network Address:	BA5EBA11 Node Address: 00001B032CBD	
LAN Board Type:	NetWare Ethernet NE2000 With AppleTalk V3.00EC (890915)	
Configuration: 0		
Hardware Option:	IRQ = 3, I/O Base = 300h, no DMA or RAM	

Essentially, the LAN configuration information shows you the network address of the physical cable attached to this network interface board, the node address for the network interface board, and the physical board settings that you chose during NETGEN/ELSGEN. Here is a little more detail on the entries.

Network and Node Addresses

The first two entries show the network interface board's network and node address. The "Network Address" is the address that you or an installer selected for the board during NETGEN/ELSGEN. The network address can be up to eight digits long and uses a hexadecimal notation (meaning you can use numbers 0 through 9 and letters A through F in the address).

The "Node Address" is the physical address of the network interface board you have installed in the server. Some network interface boards come with the node address manufactured permanently into the board. Some boards give themselves a node address when they attach to the network; this node address may change, depending on where the station is located, each time it attaches to a server. Other boards come with dip switches you can set to ensure that no two network interface boards have the same node address on a physical network.

For instance, suppose you are using ARCnet as your LAN A topology physically connecting the workstations to the server. The server's network interface board (and driver) that services LAN A must have a different node address from all other network interface boards in the workstations. IPX packets use network, node, and socket addressing for sending packets to the correct server process. All workstations physically connected to the LAN A ARCnet cabling must have the same network address, but different node addresses. Two boards with the same node address on the same physical network will cause major networking difficulties.

LAN Driver Configuration

The "LAN Board Type" entry shows the type of network interface board you are using for the LAN connection. The "Configuration" entry shows the configuration option selected for the board in NETGEN/ELSGEN. The "Hardware Option" entry shows the interrupt, DMA, I/O address, and memory address settings that correspond to the configuration option. FCONSOLE reads these text strings from the LAN driver, not from the board itself. The settings displayed here should match the settings physically made on the network interface board and must not conflict with any other hardware in the file server.

To see another LAN driver configuration, press Escape to return to the "Select LAN Driver" window, then choose a different driver.

PURGING SALVAGEABLE FILES

When users delete files from the file server, the server temporarily keeps the deleted files to allow users to recover files using the NetWare SALVAGE utility. If users accidentally erase a file, for example, they can use the SALVAGE command to recover the file as long as they adhere to the following SALVAGE stipulations:

• The user cannot perform any file modification, such as running DEL or ERASE or creating any files since deleting the files. Such actions make it impossible to retrieve those files.

• The user cannot log out, log in again, and then run SALVAGE to retrieve files deleted in the previous server connection. The user must run SALVAGE at the same workstation from which the files were deleted.

• The user must not run the NetWare PURGE command before running SALVAGE.

Teach your users the proper way to get accidentally erased files back if the need arises.

When users don't need their erased files, use the "Purge All Salvageable Files" option to free up some disk space. But as you can see by the stipulations of the SAL-VAGE command, these files do not stay in the system for long. If you need more disk space, either have users delete files they have not accessed for the last three months or add another disk.

To use the option, select "Purge All Salvageable Files" from the main menu and answer "Yes" to the prompt. The OS will purge any salvageable files and return you to the "Available Options" menu.

CHANGING THE SERVER STATUS

The "Status" option on the main menu allows you to set the following file server status items from within FCONSOLE: the current date and time, login enabling or disabling, and Transaction Tracking System enabling or disabling.

When you choose the "Status" option, you will see the following window:

```
+-----------------------------------------------------------+
|                    File Server Status                     |
+-----------------------------------------------------------+
| Server Date:      September 14, 1990     Time:  8:59:47 am |
| Allow New Users To Login:        Yes                       |
| Transaction Tracking:            Enabled                   |
|                                                            |
+-----------------------------------------------------------+
```

Setting the File Server Date and Time

The first entry highlighted is the "Server Date." If the date is inaccurate, type in the correct month, day, and year. The "Time" field will then be highlighted. If the time is inaccurate, type in the correct time. The new time will overwrite the old time.

Disabling and Enabling Logins

At times—for example, when you are performing maintenance or installing new software on the file server—you don't want users to be able to log in. To disable the login process, highlight the "Allow New Users To Login" entry and type the letter "Y" in the field. Press Enter to activate your choice. Users currently logged in to the server will remain logged in, but no new users will be able to log in until you set the field back to "Yes."

The entry toggles between "Yes" and "No," so when you want to enable logins again, highlight the entry, type the letter "Y," and press Enter.

Disabling and Enabling TTS

If the SFT NetWare Transaction Tracking System is not installed on your server, you will see "Not Available" in the "Transaction Tracking" field. If TTS is installed, you can disable the service by highlighting the field, typing "D," and pressing Enter. The server itself will automatically disable TTS if the volume where the server stores the TTS backout files (the "transaction backout volume") runs out of space or becomes damaged.

After you fix the problem, enable TTS by highlighting the field, typing the letter "E," and pressing Enter. For more information about transaction tracking, see Chapter 23.

LOOKING AT THE NETWARE VERSION

Like other NetWare utilities, FCONSOLE shows you which version of NetWare software that server is running. To view the software version, choose the "Version Information" option from the "Available Options" menu. The information displayed includes the NetWare version, the software version's creation date, the company that sold the NetWare copy, the type of NetWare, the system fault tolerance level, and availability of transaction tracking support. (ELS versions may not indicate the type of NetWare, the fault tolerance level, or the TTS support.)

To return to the "Available Options" menu, press Escape. The rest of FCONSOLE's options are explained in the next chapter.

19 Checking Performance with FCONSOLE

Perhaps the best place to check on the performance of your file server is FCON-SOLE's "Statistics" option. The suboptions under "Statistics" display information on caching, disk drive channels, logical-to-physical disk mappings, disk drives, the file system, LAN I/O, transaction tracking, and volumes. A "Summary" suboption gives you a quick overview of the most relevant statistics from all areas.

This chapter goes through each of these "File Server Statistics" options and explains what all the numbers mean and which numbers are significant to you as the system supervisor. Where appropriate, the explanation includes a brief summary of the concepts behind what you see on the screen. Chapter 3 contains a fuller explanation of the inner workings of the NetWare operating system.

FCONSOLE'S "STATISTICS" OPTION

To access FCONSOLE's "Statistics" suboptions, enter the utility by typing **FCONSOLE** at the DOS prompt. Select "Statistics" from the main menu, and you'll see the following list of options:

```
┌─────────────────────────────────────┐
│        File Server Statistics        │
├─────────────────────────────────────┤
│  Cache Statistics                    │
│  Channel Statistics                  │
│  Disk Mapping Information             │
│  Disk Statistics                     │
│  File System Statistics              │
│  LAN I/O Statistics                  │
│  Summary                             │
│  Transaction Tracking Statistics     │
│  Volume Information                  │
└─────────────────────────────────────┘
```

Since TTS is an exclusive feature of SFT NetWare, the "Transaction Tracking Statistics" option appears only if the file server is running SFT NetWare 286 v2.1x.

The list comes up with the "Summary" option already highlighted, because that is the option you will probably use the most to analyze file server performance. We'll discuss this option first.

THE STATISTICS "SUMMARY" OPTION

The most pertinent information about a file server is found under the "Summary" option of the "File Server Statistics" submenu. When you select this option, you will see a screen similar to this one:

```
┌─────────────────────────────────────────────────────────────────────┐
│                      File Server Statistics Summary                   │
├─────────────────────────────────────────────────────────────────────┤
│  File Server Up Time:     14 Days  1 Hour  58 Minutes  23 Seconds     │
│  Number of File Service Processes:      4    Current Server Utilization:   7%   │
│  Disk Requests Serviced From Cache:  90%    Packets Routed:             0   │
│  Total Packets Received:        4,388,221   File Service Packets:       10   │
│  Total Number of Cache Buffers:      817    Dirty Cache Buffers:         0   │
│  Total Server Memory:         6,289,408     Unused Server Memory:  2,048     │
│                                                                       │
│                        Maximum       Peak Used       Currently in Use │
│  Routing Buffers:         150            81                 0         │
│  Open Files:              244            35                24         │
│  Indexed Files:             0             0                 0         │
│  Transactions:             90            10                 0         │
│  Bindery Objects:         N/A           N/A               N/A         │
│  Connections:             100            27                22         │
│  Dynamic Memory 1:     16,800         6,226             4,736         │
│  Dynamic Memory 2:     26,812         5,516             4,986         │
│  Dynamic Memory 3:     47,104         1,842               822         │
└─────────────────────────────────────────────────────────────────────┘
```

Summary Statistics: The Top Half

The top half of the "File Server Statistics Summary" screen shows eleven statistics relating to the current operation of the file server. These statistics serve as a barometer to indicate how the server is performing over a period of time. Some of these statistics (such as the "Total Packets Received") can reach a maximum displayable limit and start over at zero if the server is kept running over a long period of time. Generally, the statistics that do roll over are strictly informational, "gee whiz" numbers that give no real indication as to how your server is performing (other than to indicate that the server has not gone down for a long time).

Here is a brief explanation of each statistic in the top half of the screen. (The more important ones will be explained in more detail later.)

The "File Server Up Time" entry shows how much time has elapsed since the server was last booted up. The time, shown in days, hours, minutes, and seconds, is updated once a second.

More than one file service process can be going on at the same time in a file server. The "Number Of File Service Processes" available depends on the LAN and disk drivers that were linked in with the NetWare operating system, as well as other features that you defined during NETGEN/ELSGEN. Chapter 34 is devoted to file server processes.

"Current Server Utilization" shows, as a percentage, how busy the CPU was in the past second. You can also find this information at the top of the MONITOR screen at the file server console.

The "Disk Requests Serviced From Cache" entry shows the percentage of requests that are serviced from the cache buffers in file server memory. The service request percentage gives you an idea how well the file server disk caching is working, and when to add extra memory to provide more cache buffers.

"Packets Routed" is a count of packets received on one LAN board within the server and routed through another LAN board to the network address specified by the packet. This entry shows the number of packets routed in the last second, giving you current network routing traffic information. "Total Packets Received" is a count of the file service requests and IPX socket-based request packets the server has received since it was brought up. "File Service Packets" indicates the number of file service requests serviced each second.

The "Total Number Of Cache Buffers" shows the number of cache buffers the file server presently has, based on how much memory is left after the OS has allocated file server RAM for other network features. With NetWare v2.1x, each cache buffer is 4KB in size. The number of cache buffers will increase when you add more memory to the file server. "Dirty Cache Buffers" are buffers that contain updated information from workstations that needs to be written to the server's disk drives. The information in these cache buffers is written to disk every three seconds or as soon as the buffers are full.

"Total Server Memory" shows the amount of memory currently on the file server. For nondedicated NetWare, the total memory you see does not include the amount of memory that DOS uses. "Unused Server Memory" shows how much of the total memory, after the server initializes, is left over in fragments too small to be used. It is normal to have a small amount of fragmented memory. The close to 2KB of unused memory shown in our sample screen is typical of most file servers.

The Bottom Half of the Summary Screen

The bottom half of the summary screen contains statistics on various file server parameters, arranged into three columns. The "Maximum" column shows the ceiling set for each parameter. "Peak Used" indicates the highest value achieved for each parameter since the server was brought up. "Currently In Use" shows the value of each parameter at the present time. The entries from "Routing Buffers" down through "Bindery Objects" are configurable parameters set during NETGEN/ELSGEN. You can use these numbers to determine if there is a need to rerun NETGEN/ELSGEN and raise or lower the maximums.

The "Routing Buffers" entry indicates the number of communications buffers designated during NETGEN/ELSGEN. These are buffers that the file server uses to hold incoming and outgoing packets until the OS is ready to deal with them.

Depending on the topology you use, routing buffers can range from 576 bytes to 1,088 bytes in size.

The "Open Files" entry corresponds to the "Number of Open Files" parameter set in NETGEN/ELSGEN's "System Configuration" screen. This number represents the maximum number of files that can be open at the same time by the server, by applications, or by users.

"Indexed Files" corresponds to the "Number of Indexed Files" set in NETGEN/ELSGEN. With NetWare v2.1x, the server can build an index to the FAT of large files and keep this index in memory along with the FAT. Through this index, the server can quickly locate the file's data on the disk. You can access a database larger than two megabytes two to four times faster by setting it up as an indexed file (setting the "Indexed" file attribute in FILER). The number shown under the "Maximum" column represents the maximum number of indexed files for which the server has reserved memory.

"Transactions" indicates the number of transactions that can be active (tracked by SFT NetWare's Transaction Tracking System, or TTS) at a given time. TTS guarantees data integrity by ensuring that related information (for example, a debit and a corresponding credit in an accounting system) is either completely written to the disk or not written at all. You will see ten fewer transactions in the "Maximum" column than the number specified as the maximum number of transactions in NETGEN. Don't be alarmed—the file server uses ten transactions for purposes other than tracking active transactions, and this usage is reflected in the number on the screen. If your server isn't running SFT NetWare, you will see "N/A" in the columns for "not applicable."

The number of "Bindery Objects" is also selected during NETGEN/ELSGEN, but only if the "Limit Disk Space" option has been enabled. Bindery objects can be the names of users, groups, file servers, and other entities the file server's bindery keeps track of. If you did not enable the disk resource limitation feature during NETGEN/ELSGEN, you will see "N/A."

Except for the Dynamic Memory 2 pool, the rest of the parameters are fixed within the operating system and cannot be changed during installation. The "Connections" entry shows the number of logical connections the file server can support at the same time. SFT and Advanced NetWare support 100 connections, ELS Level II supports eight, and ELS Level I supports four.

In a server running NetWare 286, dynamic memory is divided into three memory pools, each of which the OS uses for something different. The final three parameters show how much of the server's dynamic memory (in bytes) is being used in each memory pool. The "Dynamic Memory 1" entry shows the amount of memory being used for disk drive mappings and servicing file server requests (much more on Dynamic Memory 1 in Chapter 34). "Dynamic Memory 2" shows the amount of memory set aside to track open files, file locks, and record locks. The size of this second pool is controlled partly by the number of open files designated during installation. "Dynamic Memory 3" shows the amount of memory being used to track other file servers, routers, and bridges on the internetwork. It is normal for the amount of memory shown under "Peak Used" and "Currently In Use" to be much less than the amount shown in the "Maximum" column.

What to Look For in the Summary Statistics

Depending on the type of network you are running, the following general guidelines for monitoring your system may not apply to your specific environment. If yours is a small, static network with few users and limited potential growth, you may be able to adjust some of the file server's configurable parameters to correspond more closely to actual network throughput. Larger, dynamic internetworks with rapidly expanding growth must be monitored more closely. Dynamic networks have enough variables that effective tweaking may not be possible. Supervisors must plan ahead for growth so they won't have to run NETGEN/ELSGEN each time another user is added to the network.

Here are the areas in the statistical summary screen that are of most interest to supervisors.

Checking Up on File Service Processes. The "Number Of File Service Processes," a key statistic for NetWare 286 file servers, depends on the way your operating system is configured. A fully-loaded server with three or four network interface boards may have only two or three processes for file server processing (the maximum is ten). If the server must also support a large number of high-capacity disk drives, the number of file service processes could drop to one. Depending on the type of work the server does, low numbers can hurt network performance. This is especially true for servers that do a great deal of heavy database access and retrieval. Having fewer than two file service processes is a signal that you need to do some reconfiguring.

When the OS doesn't have enough file service processes available, it puts extra service requests in the communications (routing) buffers until the requests can be serviced. Check this by pressing Escape to get out of the "File Server Statistics Summary" window, then choosing the "LAN I/O Statistics" option under "File Server Statistics." The "LAN I/O Statistics" screen has a "File Service Used Route" entry that shows how many times file service requests have used the routing buffers for storage. You will have to watch this statistic for a while to get a feel for your network.

It is normal to have a few file service requests stored on routing buffers over a ten-minute period. Networks routing many packets will also see more file service requests stored in routing buffers. But if the number of file service processes are four or five, and the service requests stored in routing buffers are changing faster than once every five seconds, consider splitting up your LAN by moving part of your LAN cabling and applications to another server. Other solutions to low file service processes are detailed in Chapter 38.

The statistics for "Dynamic Memory 1" are closely related to file service processes because this is the memory pool the OS uses for servicing file service request packets (among other things). If the "Peak Used" number is approaching the "Maximum" amount of memory in Dynamic Memory 1, you may need to take some of the steps outlined in Chapter 34 to free up some of this memory pool.

Checking Server Utilization. Applications such as databases interact with the server through various data retrieval mechanisms, such as file/record locking and semaphoring. Much of the file server's time is spent in file locking and coordinating user access when retrieving data. Continually high server utilization (over 80 percent) can mean that you should either add more memory to the server or split the network and dedicate a server to a specific database.

Checking Up on Disk Caching. Look first at the percentage of "Disk Requests Serviced From Cache." If this percentage is below 80 percent, it may indicate that you need more cache buffers. Then look at the number of "Dirty Cache Buffers" and compare it to the "Total Number Of Cache Buffers." The number of dirty buffers should not exceed 50 percent of the cache buffers on the file server. When it does, it's time to add more memory to the file server to increase the number of cache buffers. Each megabyte of memory you add to the file server will yield 256 more cache buffers.

Checking the NETGEN/ELSGEN Configurables. Typically, installers set the "System Configuration" parameters in NETGEN/ELSGEN to their default settings. These defaults are designed to work adequately for the majority of file servers. However, it is a good idea to let your system run for a week or two and watch the relationship between the "Maximum" and "Peak Used" columns. If the "Peak Used" numbers start closing in on the maximums, you may have some adjusting to do. But before rushing headlong back into NETGEN or ELSGEN, sit down and plan out your network's growth. NETGEN and ELSGEN are not programs you'll want to run often, since you have to bring the file server down to run them.

Routing Buffers. As you can see from the information in this chapter, routing buffers do more than just hold packets to be routed. Depending on the size of your internetwork and the amount of traffic on the file server, you may want at least 15-20 buffers over the number shown in the "Peak Used" column. If you plan to add more workstations in the near future, adjust the number of routing buffers accordingly now so you need not run NETGEN/ELSGEN again.

Open Files. The number of open files affects the size of the Dynamic Memory 2 pool: the more open files are allocated, the more memory is made available in Dynamic Memory pool 2. You can use the dynamic pool numbers as a thermometer for your number of open files. Networks with only a few users can get a tight ratio between the "Maximum" open files and the "Peak Used" column. However, with only a few users, the ratio doesn't matter as long as the network is running smoothly.

A rule of thumb for adjusting the number of open files per new user is to divide the "Peak Used" column by the number of workstations on the network, giving you an average of open files. Add in that average number for each new user you plan to add to get an appropriate total open files number. The open files ratio also depends on which applications your network users run. Database applications can use a lot more open files than word processing applications. Plan accordingly.

Transactions. The number of transactions is tricky to adjust because it depends on the internetwork, the bindery, and the database size. All updates to the bindery are tracked by TTS, so if you have the memory, set the transaction maximum to 200. The extra transactions will help the file server during initialization as well as during bindery updates. If you need to conserve memory for other things, set the transaction maximum to 50. Transaction tracking works even after it hits the "Maximum" ceiling; it just takes longer to process the transactions.

THE "CACHE STATISTICS" OPTION

FCONSOLE's cache statistics show how the file server's disk caching is currently operating. Chapter 3 explains the concepts behind disk caching. Here is a quick review of important points to remember.

NetWare's disk caching feature is designed to optimize disk access by acting as a buffer between user requests and disk drive access. When a user requests data from a network disk, NetWare copies the entire block of data from the disk into a cache buffer, with the idea that more requests will likely occur in the same vicinity as the original request. Retrieving full blocks of data cuts down on the number of requests that have to go to disk. Since the server can access data in memory around 100 times faster than it can from the hard disk, overall performance of the network is dramatically improved.

In NetWare 286 v2.1x, cache buffers are fixed at 4KB in size (previous versions allow you to vary the size). This large buffer size works best for most networks, since larger cache buffers generally mean fewer disk I/Os. Each disk block is also 4KB in size. A disk block is divided into eight sectors, with each sector 512 bytes in length. Cache reads are done in 4KB blocks; cache writes are done in 512-byte sectors.

To speed up disk writes from the user application's end, NetWare essentially lies to the application, telling it that data has been written to disk when NetWare has merely placed the data in cache memory. The application can then move on to other things while the OS coordinates the write requests in the background.

Getting to the "Cache Statistics" Screen

If you are not already in FCONSOLE, type **FCONSOLE** at your workstation. Choose "Statistics" from the main menu. Once you are in the "File Server Statistics" submenu, choose the "Cache Statistics" option. FCONSOLE will display a screen similar to the one on the following page.

Some of this information is similar to information shown in the statistics "Summary" option. However, the summary screen shows a little of everything, while the "Cache Statistics" screen gives you a complete picture of disk caching. Most of the information on the screen is not relevant for a network supervisor, but it does provide some idea of what is happening in this function of file service. Following the pattern we've established, we'll explain each statistic briefly before concentrating on those that are the most important to you as the network supervisor.

Cache Statistics			
File Server Up Time: 14 Days 1 Hour 59 Minutes 16 Seconds			
Number of Cache Buffers:	817	Cache Buffer Size:	4,096
Dirty Cache Buffers:	0		
Cache Read Requests:	3,456,740	Cache Write Requests:	423,147
Cache Hits:	3,512,404	Cache Misses:	371,074
Physical Read Requests:	364,318	Physical Write Requests:	36,257
Physical Read Errors:	0	Physical Write Errors:	0
Cache Get Requests:	3,546,978		
Full Write Requests:	332,909	Partial Write Requests:	90,238
Background Dirty Writes:	4,592	Background Aged Writes:	30,749
Total Cache Writes:	35,371	Cache Allocations:	371,053
Thrashing Count:	0	LRU Block Was Dirty:	21
Read Beyond Write:	57	Fragmented Writes:	886
Hit On Unavailable Block:	2,767	Cache Blocks Scrapped:	0

What the Cache Statistics Mean. When you bring up the file server, all memory not used for other NetWare services is made into caching buffers. The "Number Of Cache Buffers" and "Cache Buffer Size" entries give you an idea of how much memory is used for caching. Multiplying the number of cache buffers by 4KB (the fixed size of cache buffers in NetWare 286) will show you how much memory is currently being used for caching.

Cache buffers that contain updated data not yet written to disk are marked as "dirty." An algorithm in the OS writes the data to disk either as soon as all sectors in the cache buffer have been updated, or after three seconds have passed. In other words, if the buffer is completely full before three seconds have elapsed, the buffer is written to disk; otherwise, it is written to disk every three seconds. This "aging" of write requests for up to three seconds before writing the data to disk allows the OS to combine multiple small writes into one larger write request, thereby cutting down on the number of actual hard drive accesses.

"Cache Read Requests" shows a cumulative total number of requests made to the file server in order to read data from the disk. When a user makes a read request, the caching software first looks to see if the requested data is already in memory. Finding the data in memory is called a "Cache Hit"; not finding the data in memory is called a "Cache Miss." In the case of a cache miss, the caching software performs a physical read request to read the data from the disk into cache memory for future reference. Hence, "Physical Read Requests" are "missed" cache reads for which the caching software had to go to the disk for the data. The number of physical read requests indicates how many read requests are made to the disk driver for data stored on the disks. "Physical Read Errors" counts the number of times a read request couldn't be completed due to a failure reported by the disk driver.

Similarly, "Cache Write Requests" shows the total number of requests the file server has received to write data to network disks. Cache write requests come in two flavors: full and partial. "Full Write Requests" are those writes that contain a full 512-byte sector of data. When a full 512 bytes of data are written to cache, the caching software tells the application that the write has been performed. "Partial Write Requests" add one more step to the writing process. If a user updates only a portion of a sector (for example, 200 bytes), NetWare reads the original disk block into a cache buffer (if it's not already in cache), writes the updates to the specified sector, and copies that sector out to disk through the dirty buffer algorithm. Hard disk drives can accept only writes containing complete sectors of data.

"Physical Write Requests" represents the total number of times the caching software made a request to the disk drivers to write a block of data back to the hard disks. This figure is the sum of the "Total Cache Writes" and the number of "Fragmented Cache Writes." Total cache writes are writes in which the entire buffer is written to disk; fragmented writes occur when new data is written to some, but not all, sectors of the cache buffer so that each group of sectors must be written to disk separately. "Background Dirty Writes" indicates the number of times a full cache block of new data (marked as "dirty") was written to disk. "Background Aged Writes" indicates how many times a block only partially filled with new data was written to disk because the three-second aging limit had elapsed. "Physical Write Errors" counts the number of write requests that couldn't be performed due to a failure reported by the disk driver.

The total of all cache read requests and cache write requests is indicated by the number of "Cache Get Requests." The number of "Cache Allocations" indicates how many times the OS had to allocate a new cache buffer to handle read or write requests for data that was not currently held in cache memory.

The "Thrashing Count" indicates how many times the server couldn't allocate a new cache buffer when one was needed because all available buffers were in use and no more memory was available to create any new cache buffers. When there are not enough cache blocks available for allocation to a particular caching function, a condition known as "thrashing" occurs. Thrashing means that the server spends more time unallocating and reallocating cache buffers than actually reading and writing data on the disk.

NetWare keeps track of how often information is accessed in each cache buffer. When the OS has to reallocate cache buffers, it starts with the one that has been used the least. This is called the least-recently-used (LRU) buffer. The "LRU Block Was Dirty" entry counts the number of times a read or write request needed a buffer allocated to its function and the LRU buffer was marked as dirty (it contained data that needed to be written to disk). The number of "Cache Blocks Scrapped" indicates how many times the following (rare) scenario occurs: Process A is put on hold while waiting for NetWare to write the LRU block to disk. While process A is on hold, process B requests information in the same disk block that process A wants. Somehow process B gets a cache buffer allocated to it first, so when process A comes back from hold and needs the same block of information, process B must scrap its cache block allocation and use the buffer allocated to process A.

"Hit On Unavailable Block" indicates how many times a desired cache block was not available because it was being read from or written to the disk at the time. The requesting application had to wait until the disk I/O was completed before it could access the information. "Read Beyond Write" indicates how many times, while a 4KB disk block was being written into a cache buffer, a read request came in for part of the data in that disk block that had not yet been written into memory. In this case, the OS reads the data from the disk instead of waiting for it to appear in the cache buffer.

What to Look For in the Cache Statistics

The "Cache Statistics" screen contains only a couple of statistics that are really useful to supervisors.

How Is Your Disk Caching Doing? From FCONSOLE's disk caching statistics, you can get a fairly clear picture of the overall effectiveness of disk caching on your file server. You should check regularly to make certain that you have an adequate number of cache buffers and that the number of cache hits is significantly more than the number of cache misses. Calculate the hit rate by dividing "Cache Hits" by the total of "Cache Hits" plus "Cache Misses." Another good way to monitor caching is to look at the percentage of disk requests serviced from cache (this percentage is displayed in the "File Server Statistics Summary" screen). If the percentage of disk requests serviced from the cache is below 80 percent and performance is noticeably slower, add more memory to your server.

It might be interesting, when analyzing how your file server is used, to keep track of the number of read requests versus write requests for your file server over a period of time. Database applications typically generate more writes compared to word processing and spreadsheet programs. You might notice that the number of physical write requests is actually much less than the total number of cache write requests. In our sample "Cache Statistics" screen, "Cache Write Requests" is eleven times greater than "Physical Write Requests." This is due to NetWare's aging of write requests in a background process so that more sectors can be updated in a cache block before it is written to disk. Since caching keeps the most currently used data in memory, much of the data requested for reading is already found in memory. Take a look at the number of physical read requests versus cache read requests. You can see that disk caching buys you even more on read requests than write requests. In our sample screen, the number of read requests serviced from cache is nine times more than the number of requests actually read from disk.

Early Warning Signs. Increasing numbers of "Physical Read Errors" and "Physical Write Errors" are an early warning that something may be wrong. Thanks to NetWare's automatic retries and Hot Fix feature, it is unlikely that any data has actually been lost due to these read or write errors, but you should save your data and make a backup copy just in case. Next, check the cabling all along the disk channel for bad connections. Also, check the seating of your disk controller boards and disk coprocessor boards. The problem may be a simple bad connection, so make sure all connectors are tight. If you are getting a large number of errors, you may need to reformat the drive with COMPSURF. Be sure to back up all drives before you run COMPSURF.

Watch the "Thrashing Count" closely. Thrashing seriously degrades server performance. If the thrashing count begins to increase, it's time to get more memory for the file server. A related warning statistic is the "LRU Block Was Dirty" count. If this number is on the rise, add more memory to accommodate the number of allocation requests on your file server.

THE DISK CHANNEL STATISTICS

A disk channel is the communications path that the file server uses to read and write information on the network disk drives. Think of each channel as a single lane in a multi-lane highway. You can have up to five disk channels in a NetWare 286 file server: four external channels controlled by disk coprocessor boards (DCBs) and one internal channel controlled by an AT-type controller.

The "Channel Statistics" option in FCONSOLE shows you a disk channel's operational status as well as its configuration. You can also see if the channel has failed. To look at the channel statistics, select "Channel Statistics" (accessed from the "Statistics" option in the main menu). After choosing a particular disk channel, you will see a screen similar to this one:

```
┌─────────────────────────────────────────────────────────────┐
│                      Disk Channel  0                          │
├─────────────────────────────────────────────────────────────┤
│ File Server Up Time:     14 Days  2 Hours  0 Minutes  6 Seconds │
│ Status:  Channel is running.                                  │
│ Sychronization:  No process is using the channel.             │
│ Driver Type:  104.   Plus Impulse Multiple Channel Adapter/AT │
│ Driver Version:  1.24                                         │
│ IO Addresses:  0170h  to  0178h  and  0376h  to  0377h        │
│ Shared Memory Addresses:  C800000:0000h  to  C801FF:000Fh     │
│ Interrupts Used:  0Bh                                         │
│ DMA Channels Used:                                            │
│ Channel Configuration:  0  =  170-178,  INT  =  11,  BIOS  =  C8000-C9FFFI │
└─────────────────────────────────────────────────────────────┘
```

The "Disk Channel" screen displays two kinds of entries: dynamic and static. "Status" and "Synchronization" are dynamic entries, giving you real-time operational information about the disk channel. The rest of the entries ("Driver Type" through "Channel Configuration") display static information about the controller or DCB that supports the disk channels. This static information can help you identify which channel has become nonfunctional so you can service it without disturbing other boards in the file server.

Checking the Status of a Disk Channel

The "Status" entry informs you of the disk channel's current condition. You can receive any of the following current status messages:

• *Channel is running.* This is the status message you'll see under normal conditions.

• *Channel is being stopped.* This message indicates that NetWare is in the process of shutting down the disk channel to try to fix a problem. For example, suppose a write error has occurred on one of the drives. When this happens, the SFT recovery code takes control of the channel, shutting down all normal requests. If a request is still in progress, the SFT code lets the request complete and displays this message in the meantime.

• *Channel is stopped.* This message appears after SFT has stopped the channel. With the channel stopped, the SFT recovery code initiates the Hot Fix feature that redirects data from the bad block area to another area on the disk and performs a read-after-write verification. The recovery code then records the block in the bad block table. If there are no other errors, you will again see the "Channel is running" status message. (These messages happen in fractions of seconds, so you probably will never see a Hot Fix occur.)

• *Channel is non-functional.* This message usually means there is a hardware problem. You get this message if the disk driver can no longer read or write to the disk drives on the channel. The trouble may just be a bad connection, so check all cabling for possible bad connections and make sure all connectors are tight. Also, check the seating of the disk controller board and DCBs. This message usually means that the controller board or disk drive has gone bad and needs to be replaced.

Checking Channel Synchronization

The "Synchronization" entry applies only when the channel is being shared by non-NetWare processes and must therefore be synchronized. The synchronization process is analogous to having a traffic cop watch over a busy intersection, ensuring that there are no collisions. The best example of the need for synchronization is a nondedicated file server with both NetWare and DOS partitions on a disk drive.

Another example of a situation in which channel synchronization is used would be a value-added process (VAP) that archives data from a NetWare volume to a tape drive. When the VAP needs to access disk drives and uses the channel that NetWare is also using, then synchronization will come into play to mediate access to the channel.

When a channel is running in synchronized mode, you will see messages detailing the channel's current state. The following description of the possible synchronization states uses the NetWare/DOS scenario.

• *No one is using the channel*. Channels that are not shared will always display this message (even though NetWare is actually using the channel).

• *NetWare is using the channel*.This message is displayed on a shared channel whenever NetWare is using the channel and DOS doesn't want it.

• *NetWare is using the channel, someone else wants it*. When DOS makes a channel request and NetWare is using the channel, DOS changes the channel's state to this message and goes to sleep.

• *Someone else is using the channel*. You see this message when NetWare has finished its process and wakes up DOS so DOS can perform its request.

• *Someone else is using the channel, NetWare needs it*. When NetWare makes a channel request while DOS is using the channel, this message is displayed. NetWare doesn't go to sleep, but sets a bit telling the "current state" engine that it needs to access the disk channel and goes on to something else.

• *The channel has been released, NetWare should use it*. When DOS finishes its request, the channel state changes to this message. NetWare does not talk to the disk driver until this state occurs, at which time NetWare makes its channel request.

Channel synchronization has been a part of NetWare ever since nondedicated NetWare. To DOS, this channel synchronization happens invisibly; DOS doesn't even know channel sharing is going on.

Checking the Disk Driver Configuration

The "Driver Type" entry shows the name of the disk driver preceded by its selection number. Disk drivers are selected during NETGEN prior to the network operating system generation. The drivers are then linked in and become a part of the operating system. The "Driver Version" entry simply shows you the driver's version number.

Disk drivers and their associated controller boards can use any of four common means of coordinating information exchange between the disk controller board or DCB and the host computer: I/O addresses, shared memory addresses, interrupt request lines, and direct memory access (DMA) channels.

The "I/O Addresses" entry shows the address settings the driver uses to talk with the controller or DCB. I/O addresses are paths the host's CPU can use to check and set the controller's hardware status. The CPU also uses I/O addresses to exchange data. The host CPU opens communications to the I/O addresses, then writes data from memory to the designated address. Where this data goes depends on which device is listening to that address line. What you see in the sample screen above are the I/O addresses the host CPU uses to talk to the Novell DCB.

"Shared Memory Addresses" are used by some drivers to talk with the controller or DCB for a given channel. The shared memory is a block of memory that the host computer shares with the coprocessor on a board. The memory usually resides on the coprocessor board rather than in the host's memory. The shared memory becomes a mailbox between the host CPU and the controller board. The mailbox is a pivot point where the controller board puts information and the host then gathers and distributes that information. This mailbox can be used for request exchanges as well as data exchanges.

Interrupts signal the host CPU that something has happened, and provide a way for the controller or DCB to signal the host CPU that a process is completed. Such a signal is especially important for operations that take some time to perform. The interrupts used by the disk driver (if any) will be displayed in the "Interrupts Used" entry.

DMA channels allow the host CPU to move data without getting the controller's or DCB's processor involved. This is done through special chips that set up a direct memory access connection between two points (typically between the controller board and the file server's memory). Once the two points are established, data is sent without processor involvement. Direct memory access frees up the processor to do something else if it has more than one process to perform.

If any of these four entries are blank, it means that the disk driver doesn't use that particular method of sharing information. For example, Novell's DCBs use programmed I/Os to move data from the board's memory to the file server's memory. The DCBs also use interrupts to tell the file server's CPU that jobs are completed. They do not use shared memory or DMA channels.

The "Channel Configuration" entry summarizes the information shown in the four previous entries. The text strings displayed here come from the driver itself. The same strings are displayed when you select the driver configuration in NETGEN. If you haven't already done so, record the channel configuration in your network logbook for future reference. This configuration information can help you avoid hardware conflicts when you are reconfiguring your operating system or adding another controller to the file server.

THE DISK MAPPING OPTION

FCONSOLE's "Disk Mapping Information" option gives you certain information on your server disk drives, such as physical and logical disk count, pending disk I/Os, and the NetWare system fault tolerance (SFT) level your file server is using. While most of this information is geared towards disk mirroring in SFT NetWare, the option can help you troubleshoot a faulty disk drive in any version of NetWare.

To get into the "Disk Mapping" option, start FCONSOLE and choose "Statistics" from the main menu. From there, choose the "Disk Mapping Information" option from the "File Server Statistics" menu.

Checking Statistics for All Versions of NetWare

Only three of the statistics shown in the "Disk Mapping Information" screen are useful to non-SFT versions of NetWare.

The "SFT Support Level" entry shows how much system fault tolerance is supported by the version of NetWare running in the file server. These levels range from 0 to 2. Level 0 means you have duplicate directories and duplicate FAT table information; Level 1 includes Level 0 and also has Hot Fix and read-after-write

```
┌─────────────────────────────────────────────────────────────────────┐
│                      Disk Mapping Information                         │
├─────────────────────────────────────────────────────────────────────┤
│  File Server Up Time:     14 Days  2 Hours  0 Minutes  59 Seconds     │
│  SFT Support Level:        2            Pending I/O Commands:  0       │
│  Logical Disk Count:       2            Physical Disk Count:  4        │
│  Disk Channels:  0) Unused   1) Active   2) Unused   3) Unused   4) Unused │
│                   Logical Disk to Physical Disk Mappings              │
│          Primary Mirror               Primary Mirror        Primary Mirror │
│    0)    0      2              11)                    22)              │
│    1)    1      3              12)                    23)              │
│    2)                         13)                    24)              │
│    3)                         14)                    25)              │
│    4)                         15)                    26)              │
│    5)                         16)                    27)              │
│    6)                         17)                    28)              │
│    7)                         18)                    29)              │
│    8)                         19)                    30)              │
│    9)                         20)                    31)              │
│   10)                         21)                                     │
└─────────────────────────────────────────────────────────────────────┘
```

verification (bad block redirection capabilities). All versions of NetWare 286 v2.1x include at least up to SFT level 1. Level 2 is what SFT NetWare v2.1 is all about—disk mirroring and disk duplexing. Level 2 includes Level 0 and Level 1.

The "Pending I/O Commands" entry shows how many disk write requests are waiting in the disk driver queues to be performed. The requests are logically organized through an elevator-seeking method that accesses the information closest to the disk head first, then goes on to the next request in the direction the head is traveling. This way, the disk heads answer requests in a sweeping fashion across the disk. When the disk heads reach the end of the disk, the heads start in the other direction, picking up the disk write requests along the way.

The "Disk Channels" line can show one of three status messages for each disk channel: Unused, Active, or Failed. "Unused" means that the channel was not configured into the operating system at installation. The "Active" status means that the channel was configured into the OS and currently has disk drives that are being used. "Failed" means that the OS cannot communicate with the disk drives due to a disk channel failure. This is most likely the result of a physical failure, such as a faulty disk channel board or cabling to the disk drives. You will have to bring down the file server and perform repairs before using the disk channel again.

Checking the Status of SFT NetWare Disk Mirroring

The rest of the "Disk Mapping Information" entries apply mainly to SFT NetWare's disk mirroring and duplexing features. When you set up disk mirroring (possible only with SFT NetWare), the data on one disk, called the "primary" disk, is duplicated on another "mirror" disk. Once the mirrored pair is established in NETGEN, NetWare treats the two physically distinct disks as one logical disk drive. Identical volumes are created on both disks. As the server writes information to the primary disk, the same information is written to the mirrored disk.

The "Physical Disk Count" shows the physical number of attached disk drives. In our example, there are four actual physical disks. These four disks have been combined into two mirrored pairs, as indicated by the "Logical Disk Count" entry. To end users, it appears as if the file server has only two disks attached.

The "Logical Disk To Physical Disk Mappings" shows exactly how the physical drives are mirrored together. Notice that there are 32 possible entries, numbered from 0 to 31. SFT and Advanced NetWare 286 support up to 32 physical disk drives per server. These numbers (0 to 31) represent the disk numbers used in Net-Ware's disk information table to identify each physical disk. Each entry in the screen has two headings: "Primary" and "Mirror." These two headings show which physical drive in the pair is the primary disk and which is the mirrored disk. In our example, logical drive 0 consists of two physical drives, 0 and 2, while logical drive 1 consists of physical drives 1 and 3. If you are not running SFT NetWare on the server, or if you are running SFT NetWare but have not set up any mirrored pairs, the primary drives are the same as the logical drives and the "Mirror" column will indicate "None." If you think two drives should be mirrored and "None" is displayed for the drives, you need to go back into NETGEN and take another look at how you set up the mirror tables.

Checking on REMIRROR Status in FCONSOLE

The "Mirror" column can also show one of two other possible status messages: "Disabled" and "Remirroring." The "Disabled" status message appears when you issue the UNMIRROR command from the console or when a disk failure of some sort occurs.

When you use the UNMIRROR and REMIRROR console commands to affect mirrored disks (see Chapter 22), the status of these commands is displayed in the "Disk Mapping Information" screen. For example, you may need to unmirror two disks temporarily to repair one of them. When you use REMIRROR to re-establish the mirrored pair, the "Disk Mapping Information" screen will show the actual remirroring taking place. When this happens, the "Logical Disk To Physical Disk Mappings" line disappears and you see one of the following messages:

• *Initializing Remirror For Disk* nn. This message is displayed while Net-Ware checks what information needs to be copied to bring the new disk up to date. Bringing the new disk up to date can happen in one of two ways. Whenever you run the mirroring software, the file server sets up mirroring tables to keep tabs on which data it needs to update. If a drive has been mirrored before and you run UNMIRROR and REMIRROR, the file server first looks at the mirroring tables and updates only necessary data. For new drives, drives that have not been mirrored before, or drives whose data has been excessively modified, the file server copies all data over to the new drive.

• *Remirror Of Disk* nn *Copying Block* nn *of* nn. As information transfers to the new disk, you will see "Remirror Of Disk 01 Copying Block 23 of 28739" or some similar message. The display will continue to update the block numbers until all the information on the primary disk is transferred, whether that information fills part or all of the disk. The second block number on the display shows the disk's total block number. If the primary disk is only half full of information, the total block number won't be reached.

THE DISK STATISTICS OPTION

The "Disk Statistics" option gives information about the disk drives you have on your file server. For each disk, this option shows the drive type, the disk channel it's attached to, the size of the drive, the cylinder and sector count, the I/O error count, and Hot Fix table information.

From the "File Server Statistics" submenu (accessed by selecting "Statistics" from FCONSOLE's main menu), choose the "Disk Statistics" option. FCONSOLE will list the physical disks on the file server by number. Choose the one about which you want to view information. (If you have only one drive, you will not see this prompt.) The disk information is shown in a screen similar to this one:

```
                              Physical Disk 0

File Server Up Time:      14 Days  2 Hours  1 Minute  31 Seconds
Disk Type:   1. Impulse  80MB
Non-Removable Drive
Disk Channel:   0        Controller Number:  0        Drive Number:   1
Controller Type:  104.
Drive Size:  (less hot fix area): 81,371,136
Drive Cylinders: 965    Drive Heads: 10         Sectors Per Track:  17
IO Error Count:     0
Hot Fix Table Start:      19,866       Hot Fix Enabled
Hot Fix Table Size:       640 blocks   Hot Fix Remaining:  634 blocks
```

Identifying Disk Drives

The "Disk Type" entry shows the name and model number of the disk. This identification string comes from the information programmed into the DCB if the drive is on an external disk channel. You choose drive types in the DISKSET portion of NETGEN. For internal disk drives in IBM AT-compatible servers, you choose the drive type when you run the SETUP or similar program to program the CMOS memory on the system board. You set the drive types for PS/2s during the configuration procedure using the IBM "Reference" diskette. Entering the drive type sets the information on the "Reference" diskette and then write it to the PS/2's CMOS memory. (PS/2 disk drives also have the disk type written on top of the drive.)

The line below the "Disk Type" entry indicates whether the drive is removable (like a Bernoulli box) or non-removable (like most hard disks).

The next line identifies the disk by its channel, controller, and drive number. Disk channels are controlled by either DCBs or internal hard disk controller boards. Internal AT disk channels show a "0" for the "Disk Channel" number. Since you can install up to four DCBs for external disk channels, they can be numbered from 1 to 4. The "Controller Number" entry tells you to which controller the physical disk is attached. The controller number entry is the same as the controller address; controller addresses are set from 0 to 7 when the controllers are installed. The "Drive Number" is either 0 or 1, depending how the drive is attached to the controller board.

The "Drive Size" entry shows the size of the data portion of the drive (in bytes). The data area represents the total size minus the part of the disk reserved for the Hot Fix Redirection Area. To get the total size in bytes, multiply "Drive Cylinders" by "Drive Heads" by "Sectors Per Track" by 512 (the sector size). If you multiply the "Hot Fix Table Size" (in blocks) by 4,096 (to convert blocks into bytes) and add that to the "Drive Size" number, you should get the same result.

"Drive Cylinders" and "Drive Heads" will show either the numbers specified for the drive type or a zero if the drive type chosen does not match the actual number of cylinders and heads.

Checking for Disk Errors

The "I/O Error Count" entry displays the number of errors that have occurred on the disk since the server was last brought up. If the error count is going up slowly, you should look into what could be causing the errors on the drive. You may also want to back up data on that drive more often.

Checking the Hot Fix Status

The "Disk Statistics" option gives you an overview of how NetWare's Hot Fix feature is functioning. Hot Fix works in conjunction with read-after-write verification. After writing a block to the disk, NetWare looks to see if what is written to the disk matches the copy of the block still held in memory. If it doesn't match, Hot Fix steps in and writes that block of memory to a reliable part of the disk (within the Hot Fix Redirection Area). Hot Fix records the defective area's address in the disk's bad block table so the OS won't try to write data there again.

The "Hot Fix Table Start" entry shows where the Hot Fix Redirection Area begins on the disk. The screen also reports the Hot Fix status as either "Enabled" or "Disabled." If Hot Fix is functioning properly, the status is "Enabled." If the disk is bad, or if the OS has experienced a number of failures writing to the disk, you will see "Disabled." The "Hot Fix Table Size" shows how many blocks are set aside for redirection purposes. Every time a block is redirected, you will see one less block in the "Hot Fix Remaining" entry.

Using the "Disk Statistics" Information

The "Disk Statistics" option shows you information that was set up when the operating system was generated with NETGEN/ELSGEN. Here, you can find basic information about your drives. The option can also help you keep an eye on Hot Fix information. If your "I/O Error Counts" are growing and your "Hot Fix Remaining" blocks are diminishing, plan ahead to rectify the disk media problem. Don't wait until you run out of room in the Hot Fix Redirection Area.

If you haven't kept good records of your physical drive locations, you can use the channel, controller, and drive number entries to find this information. Suppose, for example, that you look at FCONSOLE's "Disk Mapping Information" option and see that primary drive number 1 is "Dead." You know that the primary disk number is also the physical disk number, so you can then select the "Disk Statistics" option, choose "Physical Disk 1," and see to which disk channel the disk is attached.

If the disk channel is 1, you know the drive is attached to DCB 1 and therefore you know which SCSI bus to look for. Here is where it is advantageous to arrange controllers in order along the SCSI bus. For example, if the controller number is 2, and you have set the controllers in both logical and physical order, you can simply trace along the SCSI cable to the second controller to find controller number 2. The drive number (0 or 1) will tell you if the disk is the first or second drive on the controller.

Another helpful hint for keeping track of disk channels is to take a marker and mark each disk channel number on the metal bracket that shows through the file server cover. You could also number the expansion slots, starting with the one nearest the floppy disk, then install your internal controller boards and DCBs in slot order. That way, the internal controller would be in slot 0, DCB 1 would be in slot 1, and so forth. Another way is to color-code your connections, a method which can be very useful if your subsystem is away from the server.

THE "FILE SYSTEM STATISTICS" OPTION

The "File System Statistics" option lets you look at the statistics for open files, File Allocation Tables (FATs), and indexed files on the file server.

From the "File Server Statistics" submenu (accessed by selecting "Statistics" from FCONSOLE's main menu), choose the "File System Statistics" option. A screen similar to this one will appear:

```
                        File System Statistics

File Server Up Time:       14 Days  2 Hours  2 Minutes  41 Seconds
Configured Max Open Files:        244    Peak Files Open:              35
Open Requests:                 82,008    Currently Open Files:         24
Read Requests:              4,680,209    Write Requests:          108,885
FAT Sector Writes:              1,773    Dirty FAT Sectors:             0
FAT Write Errors:                   0    Fatal FAT Write Errors:        0
FAT Scan Errors:                    0
Configured Max Indexed Files:       0    Peak Indexed Files Opened:     0
Active Indexed Files:               0    Attached Indexed Files:        0
```

Adjusting the Number of Open Files

The "Configured Max Open Files," "Peak Files Open," and "Currently Open Files" entries show the same information as the "Open Files" entry on the "File Server Statistics Summary" screen. The "Configured Max Open Files" entry shows the maximum number of files the server can have open at one time, as configured in NETGEN/ELSGEN. If the "Peak Files Open" is getting close to this maximum, you may want to increase the number of open files by rerunning NETGEN/ELSGEN.

The maximum number of open files your server needs depends on the number of users and the types of applications they run. For example, database applications can use many more file handles than word processing applications. Workstations running multitasking operating systems, such as DESQView and Windows, require more than the usual number of open files. OS/2 workstations running more than one application should be counted as an extra workstation for each "virtual machine" OS/2 has open.

One rule of thumb for determining an appropriate open file maximum is to divide the "Peak Files Open" column by the number of workstations on the network. This gives you an average number of open files per workstation. (Be sure to count each virtual machine in your OS/2 workstations as a separate workstation.) When you add new users to the network, look at the types of applications and workstation operating system they will use, and at the current status of peak open files versus maximum open files. If necessary, increase the maximum number by adding the average number of open files you calculated for each new workstation. Keep in mind that the number shown for the "Peak Files Open" entry is dynamic—it is updated anytime the number of "Currently Open Files" surpasses the previous peak number.

When you need everyone off the server, you can check here to see if files are currently open on the server. If so, go into the "Connection Information" option in FCONSOLE's main menu. The "Current Connections" list will show you which connections are currently active. Use the Mark key (F5) to mark the connection entries, then press Enter. You can then either send a broadcast message telling these users to log out, or (if you're desperate) you can clear their connections by selecting the "Clear Connection" option.

Open, Read, and Write Requests

The "Open Requests" entry shows the total number of requests the server has received to open a file since it was last brought up. Similarly, "Read Requests" indicates the number of requests the server has received to read a file, and "Write Requests" shows the number of requests to write to a file. You can use this information to analyze the ratios between reads and writes on your file server.

File Allocation Table Information

Chapter 7 explains how NetWare uses a file allocation table (FAT) scheme to link logical data addressing to physical data blocks. NetWare relies on this table to find files on the disk, and keeps two copies of the FAT in file server memory. Five of the entries in the "File System Statistics" screen deal with FAT usage.

The "FAT Sector Writes" entry shows how many times the server has written sectors containing FAT information to disk. Whenever users add, extend, or delete files, the FATs in the file server memory are changed accordingly. The changed FATs are then written to disk to keep disk FAT data current with the data in memory. The "Dirty FAT Sectors" entry shows how many changed FAT sectors are currently waiting to be written to disk. The OS writes FAT sectors to disk sequentially, starting with the first dirty FAT sector and continuing until all dirty sectors are written to disk.

"FAT Write Errors" occur when FATs have been changed and are being written to disk, but during this process there is a disk media failure. NetWare keeps two copies of each FAT on the disk to ensure against a total loss of data if such a media failure occurs. If a disk failure occurs and one FAT copy is lost, the OS automatically switches to the other FAT copy. Since all versions of NetWare 286 use Hot Fix to prevent data from being written to bad blocks on the disk, you shouldn't see FAT write errors unless the disk experiences so many errors that the OS disables Hot Fix.

"Fatal FAT Write Errors" occur when the OS can't write reliably to either FAT table on the disk. Although these errors are labeled as "fatal," the file server will continue to function, using the FAT kept in memory. Go into "Supervisor Options" in SYSCON and check the system error log file to see which volume is affected by the FAT error. Back up all data on this volume before you bring the server down to repair the disk problem.

Both types of FAT write errors can result not only from disk media failure, but also from faulty controllers, cables, or power supplies. Don't wait for disk problems to get worse; if these errors occur, check all disk-related hardware and replace any defective components.

"FAT Scan Errors" occur during an internal consistency check that the OS performs on FAT data. Novell engineers use this error count to debug a problem. You will probably never see this entry incremented, but if you do, call Novell.

Information About Indexed Files

Novell sometimes uses the term "Turbo FATs" to refer to NetWare's FAT indexes. Briefly, these indexes are used with large database files (over 2MB) to help the OS find data entries more quickly. You reserve file server memory space for a certain number of FAT indexes in NETGEN/ELSGEN. Then, when you flag large files as "Indexed" in the FILER utility, NetWare builds an index in memory to that file's FAT entries. (Chapter 3 explains the FAT indexing in more detail.)

The last five entries in the "File System Statistics" screen deal with indexed files. If you are not using the FAT index feature, these entries will all show zero. The "Configured Max Indexed Files" entry shows the maximum number of indexed files provided for in NETGEN/ELSGEN. This entry, along with "Peak Indexed Files Open" and "Active Indexed Files" entries, show the same information as the "Indexed Files" entry in the "File Server Statistics Summary" screen. Again, the peak number of indexed files is updated whenever the current number of indexed files exceeds the previous peak number. "Active Indexed Files" are those files currently indexed. Unless you plan to create more large database files on the server, you don't need more indexed files than you have database files to use them.

The "Attached Indexed Files" is an interesting entry. When a user opens an indexed file, NetWare builds the FAT index for that file. When the file is closed, NetWare retains the FAT index in memory, calling it an "attached index file." By keeping FAT indexes around in this way, NetWare doesn't have to rebuild the index when that file is reopened. The operating system drops the least-recently used index only when all FAT indexes are either attached or are currently being used and a new indexed file is opened.

As an example, say you have six database files, but you have specified only five indexed files in NETGEN/ELSGEN. If all five indexes are either actively used or attached when a request is received to open the sixth database, the operating system will drop the least-recently used attached FAT index and build a new FAT index for the sixth database. However, if all five FAT indexes are active, the sixth database will not get a FAT index.

Chapter 20 explains how to adjust the number of indexed files in NETGEN/ELSGEN. Remember that you also must flag the database files as "Indexed." To flag a file as indexed, go into the FILER utility as supervisor or equivalent, select the directory containing the file as the current directory, then choose the "File Information" option. Select the appropriate file name from the resulting list of files. In the "File Information" window, choose the "Attributes" option. Press the Insert key and select "Indexed" from the list of possible file attributes. Then exit FILER.

LOOKING AT LAN I/O STATISTICS

The "LAN I/O Statistics" option gives you statistics concerning NetBIOS broadcasts, connection information between workstations and file servers, workstation requests, and file service requests.

From the "File Server Statistics" submenu (accessed by selecting "Statistics" from FCONSOLE's main menu), choose the "LAN I/O Statistics" option. You will see a screen similar to this one:

```
                              LAN I/O Statistics

  File Server Up Time:      14 Days  2 Hours  2 Minutes  41 Seconds
  Total Packets Received:    4,389,019      Packets Routed:           235,403
  File Service Packets:      3,657,125      NetBIOS Broadcasts:             0
  Packets With Invalid Slots:        0      Invalid Connections:            1
  Invalid Sequence Numbers:          0      Invalid Request Types:          0
  Detach With Invalid Slot:          0      Forged Detach Requests:        19
  New Request During Processing:     0
  New Attach During Processing:      0      Ignored Duplicate Attach:       0
  Reply Canceled By New Attach:      0
  Detach During Processing Ignored:  0
  Reexecuted Requests:             243      Duplicate Replies Sent:       210
  Positive Acknowledges Sent:        9      File Service Used Route:      145
  Packets Discarded Because They Crossed More Than 16 Bridges:    0
  Packets Discarded Because Destination Network Is Unknown:       0
  Incoming Packets Lost Because Of No Available Buffers:          0
  Outgoing Packets Lost Because Of No Available Buffers:          0
```

Packet Information

The "Total Packets Received" entry shows you the total number of service requests packets, routing packets, and IPX socket packets that the file server has received since the last time the server was brought up. The "Packets Routed" entry monitors NetWare's routing services, showing the number of packets sent to other networks on the internet. "File Service Packets" are the packets containing requests for file services that the file server receives from workstations on the internetwork.

NetBIOS Information

NetBIOS is IBM's high-level networking protocol. To maintain compatibility with NetBIOS applications on NetWare LANs, Novell provides a NetBIOS emulator for workstations.

If you are running NetBIOS applications on your network, the "NetBIOS Broadcasts" entry needs some attention. NetBIOS supports a virtual circuit connection by establishing a session between two points—usually two workstations. When an application must establish a session with a NetBIOS partner, NetBIOS must do two things. First, NetBIOS sends a general broadcast packet across the internet to tell everyone that a workstation wants to establish a session. The broadcast includes a name by which that session will be known. The application must add this name to the residing NetBIOS node's local name table. The calling node does this by sending a name claim request to all other nodes speaking NetBIOS in order to get the name registered. If another node says it is using that name, the requesting node must try other names until if finds a name that no other node is using. The new session must register using a name that is not currently in use.

Once the application registers the name, each requesting node writes the new name in its local name table where it can find the names quickly. Applications can then use names from the name table when they wish to communicate. As a session begins, the calling node looks for a node with the designated name and sends a connect request to that node, who sends an answer back. Only the session interested in such a connection responds. When the partner responds, the session becomes a point-to-point connection and the global broadcasting stops.

The "NetBIOS Broadcasts" entry, then, shows how many global NetBIOS broadcast packets the file server has rebroadcasted to other networks on the internetwork. Originally, NetBIOS ran on one LAN and its global broadcast was of trivial concern. On a single LAN, NetBIOS doesn't even have to involve the file server when establishing a session with another workstation. But multiple networks involve bridging, and through bridging NetWare provides a routing mechanism for NetBIOS to travel across the internetwork. Such global broadcasts can take a toll on a network's performance.

Workstation-to-Server Connections

The next six entries, from "Packets With Invalid Slots" to "Forged Detach Requests," all have to do with server and workstation connection validation.

The "Packets With Invalid Slots" entry shows the number of times the file server has received a packet containing an illegal connection number. Each file server maintains a connection table containing all of the connection entries possible. For SFT and Advanced NetWare 286 v2.1x, the table has 100 allowable connection entries. Each workstation, file server, or bridge that attaches to the file server takes one of these connection entries. The "Packets With Invalid Slots" entry increases when a packet has become corrupted and tries to pass an invalid connection number (such as 110 on a 100-maximum connection table) to the file server.

The "Invalid Connections" entry shows the number of times a workstation tries to connect to the file server but the file server says the workstation's connection is no longer valid. You will see this error if the file server has been shut down and has come back up again without the workstation shell knowing the file server went down in the first place. The workstation would try to reattach to the old connection number, which is now invalid.

You can also see this error if you clear a workstation connection, which means the workstation will have to reestablish its connection. If the workstation (call is WS1) does not reestablish its connection, another workstation (WS2) may log in and use WS1's connection slot. If this happens, you will also get an increase in the "Forged Detach Requests" entry. A "Forged Detach Request" occurs when WS1 tries to log out and re-establish its connection by sending a detach request to the file server. The only problem is WS2 now occupies that connection slot, and since WS1 cannot log out WS2, you get an increase in this entry.

NetWare keeps track of requests by sequence number so it can tell if it receives the same request over again. The "Invalid Sequence Numbers" entry increases when a file server receives a request from a workstation that is out of sequence. For example, suppose a workstation sends a request packet (request 1) to the file server. The server processes the request and the workstation sends another (request 2). The server then services request 3, request 4, and so on. But if request 4 is followed by request 6, the "Invalid Sequence Numbers" count will be incremented.

"Invalid Request Types" occur when a packet contains an unknown NetWare Core Protocol (NCP) request. A number of request types perform services in the file server—some examples would be Open a File and Close a File. This count is increased whenever the file sever receives a request type it cannot recognize.

The "Detach With Invalid Slot" entry is similar to the "Packets With Invalid Slot" entry, but in this case the workstation is trying to detach itself from its connection. An increase in the detach count will also affect the packets count.

Workstation Request Processing

The "New Request During Processing" entry means the file server is processing a request from a workstation and receives another request before it can finish the first request. This entry can also involve retries. When a workstation sends a request and does not receive a reply (the shell determines the actual time), the workstation will re-issue the same request to the file server. If the file server is still working on the original request, the "New Request During Processing" entry is incremented. The server will disregard the re-issue request and complete the initial request.

The "New Attach During Processing" entry increases if the workstation reboots and reattaches to the file server while the server is still processing that workstation's last request. The "Ignored Duplicate Attach" entry means the server received a request connection packet while it was servicing a request to the old connection. In this case, the file server will cancel the reply to the old connection request.

The "Detach During Processing Ignored" entry means the file server is still working on a request for a workstation and the server receives a request to terminate that connection. The server ignores the termination request until it finishes the request for that connection.

The file server and workstations go through quite an elaborate acknowledgement process. In order for NetWare to maintain its speed on request completions, the shell waits a predetermined amount of time for any network call and then resends the request. The "Reexecuted Requests" entry shows the times the server reexecuted the same request for the workstation. The server sends a reply, but that reply gets lost in the network and the workstation resends the request. Sometimes the workstation reissues the request just as the file server is sending a reply, in which case the file server will reexecute the reply from its memory.

The "Duplicate Replies Sent" entry shows how many times the file server was asked to resend a request, but the previous reply was still in memory so the server did not have to reexecute the reply. Because requests are very dynamic in nature, certain job windows cannot be duplicated. As the FCONSOLE help screens state, "Some types of file server requests cannot be reexecuted (like find the next file, or get the next queue job)." As a file server completes a request, the server retains the request in memory until the next request. The server does this to make sure the workstation does not ask for a resend when the job window is already passed.

The "Positive Acknowledges Sent" entry shows the number of times a workstation reissues a request while the file server is finishing up that request. The file server sends a "work in progress" reply when it is working on a request and receives a resend from the workstation. This packet lets the workstation know that the request was not lost and that the server is working on the reply.

The "File Service Used Route" entry counts the number of times a file service request had to be placed in a routing buffer because all of the file service processes were busy. The file server has no more than ten file service request handlers (processes). A file service request handler is a process that takes a NetWare core protocol (NCP) request to its given destination.

One way to visualize this concept is to think of the file server as a great mansion and the file service request handlers as butlers. Inside the mansion are many different rooms: one room may be the Open File room, another the Read File room, and another the Write File room. At the door of the mansion stands a doorman (the MUX process), waiting for NCP requests. When the doorman receives a service request, he passes the request on to a butler. NetWare butlers are pretty efficient; they quickly usher requests to the proper room for processing, wait until the processing is completed, and then escort the requests out.

If all of the butlers are busy servicing requests and the doorman receives another NCP request, the doorman will put the request in a waiting room (routing buffer). When a butler becomes available, he first checks the waiting room to see if there are any waiting service requests before approaching the doorman for a new request.

Packet Routing Errors

NetWare uses an adaptive routing scheme. If a file server comes up on an internetwork, the other file servers and bridges broadcast their routing tables and insert any new additions. As file servers and bridges come and go on the internet, the routing tables adapt to the situation, updating the number of "bridge hops" between one router and another and the best route for a packet to travel.

If a file server is downed ungracefully from carelessness or from a power failure, there's a small window in which a routing loop can occur. A routing loop means packets get caught on the internet without a way to get to their proper destination. In NetWare, a packet that gets looped among 16 bridges is considered lost and is discarded. That's what you see in the "Packets Discarded Because They Crossed More Than 16 Bridges" entry.

The "Packets Discarded Because Destination Network Is Unknown" entry is similar. This entry increases because a workstation, file server, or value-added server sends packets to a network or file server that is unknown and therefore no longer available by the present routing tables. Such packets are simply discarded.

The "Incoming Packets Lost Because Of No Available Buffers" and "Outgoing Packets Lost Because Of No Available Buffers" entries both occur because there are no available routing buffers. This condition happens when the file server is kept busy with NCPs. In both instances, the packets are lost. If you see this happening, run NETGEN/ELSGEN and increase the number of communication buffers in the file server (see Chapter 20).

What to Look For in the LAN I/O Statistics

Admittedly, the "LAN I/O Statistics" screen contains a lot of statistics that you simply can't do much about. Except for the "Total Packets Received," "Packets Routed," "File Service Packets," and "NetBIOS Broadcasts" (if you use NetBIOS), the rest of the entries should all be zero. Occasionally you may see one or two errors reported in some of the entries, but this is no cause for concern unless the errors continue to increase over an extended period of time.

You can use some of these statistics to assess how busy your file server is and how much of its resources are taken up by internal routing of packets not destined for the server. The "File Service Packets" number should be considerably greater than the "Packets Routed" number. If your server becomes noticeably sluggish and you observe a significant increase in the number of "Packets Routed," it could indicate that most of the file service processes are being taken up by heavy internal bridging. If this internal bridging is mostly routing information to other file servers, you may want to add an external bridge to offload some of the routing burden from your file server.

However, if most of the network traffic is destined for your file server, adding an external bridge might not help because it puts the load on one bridge board instead of the two or three in the file server. Know where your traffic is going. If all your traffic is destined for one file server, find out why this server is so important. If the server is supporting two unrelated databases, put one database on one server and the other database on another server.

Another approach to the file service requests and performance issues would be to get a 386-based file server instead of a 286-based server. You won't gain more butlers, but the butlers you have will be a lot faster!

THE TRANSACTION TRACKING OPTION

If your file server is running SFT NetWare 286 with TTS (Transaction Tracking System), the "Transaction Tracking Statistics" option will appear in FCONSOLE. TTS protects data transactions by tracking all updates to a database in a separate file until all changes are made. If something goes wrong before the transaction is complete, TTS rolls back the database to the state it was in before the transaction started. Users will have to re-enter the entire transaction, but at least the database and its related files remain internally consistent. (See Chapter 3 for more details on TTS.)

The "Transaction Tracking Statistics" option tells you whether TTS is enabled, which volume TTS is using to track changes, how many transactions are configured and how many are in use, how much disk space transactions use, and what changes files flagged "Transactional" might experience.

To get into the "Transaction Tracking Statistics" option, type **FCONSOLE** at the command line prompt and choose the "Statistics" option. From the "File Server Statistics" menu, choose the "Transaction Tracking Statistics" option. FCONSOLE will display a screen similar to this one:

Transaction Tracking Statistics		
File Server Up Time: 14 Days 2 Hours 2 Minutes 41 Seconds		
Transaction Tracking Status: Enabled		
Transaction Tracking Volume: SYS		
Configured Max Transactions: 90	Peak Transactions:	10
Current Transactions: 0		
Transactions Performed: 1,424,243	Transactions Written:	1,342
Requested Backouts: 0	Unfilled Backout Requests:	0
Current Used Disk Space: 40,960	Total File Extensions:	0
Total File Size Changes: 338	Total File Truncations:	167

Checking Up on How TTS Is Configured

The first entry, "Transaction Tracking Status," indicates whether the TTS feature is currently enabled or disabled. You can enable or disable transaction tracking at the file server console by typing **ENABLE** (or **DISABLE**) **TRANSACTIONS**. If you have supervisor rights, you can also go into the "Status" option in FCONSOLE and enable or disable TTS there (see Chapter 18). TTS will disable itself if the server runs out of disk space on the backout volume during a large transaction.

The next two entries, "Transaction Tracking Volume" and "Configured Max Transactions," are set in NETGEN. The "Miscellaneous Maintenance" menu in the NetWare Installation half of NETGEN allows you to set various "System Configuration" options when the file server is installed. The "Transaction Tracking

Volume" is known as the "Transaction Backout Volume" in NETGEN. By default, NETGEN sets up the SYS volume as the transaction backout volume. This is the volume on which NetWare maintains the files necessary to back out of the transaction if it needs to.

The maximum number of transactions is also set in the "System Configuration" option under NETGEN's "Miscellaneous Maintenance" menu. The number of transactions can be configured anywhere between 20 and 200 (20 is the default). The *SFT NetWare 286 Maintenance* manual suggests that you set roughly twice the number of transactions as you have users on the network that are using TTS. That way users can have one transaction reserved for the current transaction and another for a previous transaction that is being finalized.

The "Configured Max Transactions," "Peak Transactions," and "Current Transactions" show the same information as on the "File Server Statistics Summary" screen. When the "Peak Transactions" starts to close in on the "Configured Max Transactions," it may be time to increase the maximum number of transactions for the file server.

If your server has enough memory, set the maximum transactions as high as you need to (up to the maximum of 200). Since all updates to the bindery are automatically transaction tracked upon initialization, the extra transactions will help the file server during initialization and when updating bindery transactions.

If your server is short on memory and you need more transactions than 20, set the transaction maximum to around 50. As we explained earlier, TTS continues to work even if it hits the maximum number of transactions; it just takes longer to process the transactions. Keep an eye on the "Current Transactions" entry. If it starts to get close to the configured maximum transactions again, you may want to configure more transactions.

Checking Up on How TTS Is Working

The "Transactions Performed" entry displays all the transactions that TTS has kept track of since the file server was brought up. The "Transactions Written" entry shows the number of transactions written successfully to disk since the file server was last brought up.

"Requested Backouts" come from three events: a failed workstation, a failed network, or an explicit request from an application. If a workstation using TTS fails and the file server logs that workstation out, TTS will back out of the transaction. Applications using explicit commands can also request that a backout be performed. The "Unfilled Backout Requests" entry is incremented when the transaction tracking volume has been disabled for some reason and either an application or TTS requests a backout. The backout cannot be performed because TTS is disabled.

The "Current Used Disk Space" entry shows how much disk space (in bytes) is being used on the Transaction Tracking volume for storing backout data. Since there is no limit to the size of a transaction (other than the size limit of the volume itself), the disk space entry can expand to meet transactional needs. This also means you are stuck with the highest transaction size as the disk space entry until you reboot your file server. Keep that in mind when deciding which volume to make the transaction tracking volume. Also keep in mind that TTS will be disabled if the volume runs out of disk space.

TTS File Size Information

The last three entries all have to do with the size of TTS files. If a file flagged as "Transactional" grows beyond its original size and needs a new disk block allocated to it, the "Total File Extensions" entry is incremented. This also means TTS will need to deallocate that disk block if a transaction backout is requested. The "Total File Size Changes" entry shows the number of times a file that is being tracked has changed in size. The "Total File Truncations" entry shows how many files have shrunk in size while being tracked.

Database programs treat files differently. One database may have a number of files that are updated each time you create a record. For example, a database may have an .EXE file, a .KEY file, an index file containing record parameters, and several files that contain the actual data, such as *.LNK or *.DBM files. When you create a new record within the database, you set up the record name (which is stored in the index file) and information about that record (which is stored in the data files).

Some index files hold the parameters of where a record's information is stored in the data files. Other indexes only tell you where the initial record information can be found. Then as users retrieve a record, the data retrieved from one database file will end with the location of the next piece of requested data. Thus the record parameters are chained together within the database files themselves instead of in the index files.

Never flag .EXE files or any key or index files as "Transactional." Flag only the main database file itself. There is a very important reason for this: In the implicit transaction mode, TTS begins a transaction at the initiation of a physical or logical record lock, and ends the transaction at a record unlock sequence. A key file, if flagged "Transactional," may initially lock itself, signaling TTS to implicitly begin a transaction. That key file may unlock itself later on, but TTS may not recognize that it has done so. To TTS, the file is still locked and remains locked until you exit the program. At that point, all of your work is released as a single transaction, and you stand more at risk of experiencing a transaction backout rather than a transaction update.

To avoid this problem, use the SETTTS command to set the logical and physical lock threshold for any given application. Then TTS ignores any logical or physical record locks that occur before the number you specify. (See Chapter 23 for more details on SETTTS.)

LOOKING AT VOLUME INFORMATION

The "Volume Information" option shows you such basic information as a volume's name, hashing and caching statistics, size, number of directory entries, and mirrored status. Where more pertinent information for managing volumes is available through other NetWare utilities, we will indicate it in the explanation below.

From the "File Server Statistics" submenu (accessed by selecting "Statistics" from FCONSOLE's main menu), choose the "Volume Information" option. If you have more than one volume on the server, you will see a list of the available volumes. Choose the volume you want to examine. FCONSOLE will display a screen similar to this one:

```
                            Volume Information
_____

  File Server Up Time:     14 Days  2 Hours  4 Minutes  12 Seconds
  Volume Name:             SYS            Volume Number:              0
  Volume Mounted:          Yes            Volume Removable:  No
  Volume Hashed:           Yes            Volume Cached:       Yes
  Block Size:              4,096          Starting Block:             4
  Total Blocks:            19,862         Free Blocks:            8,397
  Maximum Directory Entries:      5,504
  Peak Directory Entries Used:    1,194
  Current Free Directory Entries: 4,312
  Logical Drive Number:    0
  Volume Mirrored:         No
  Primary Disk Number:     0              Mirror Disk Number:  N/A
```

Identifying the Volume

The "Volume Name" entry indicates which volume's information is displayed on the screen. The "Volume Number" entry is the number the file server assigned to the volume when that volume was activated, or mounted, during initialization.

The "Volume Mounted" entry shows if that volume is currently activated. All volumes on fixed (non-removable) disks are automatically mounted. Volumes on removable disks can be mounted and unmounted with the MOUNT and DISMOUNT console commands (see Chapter 22). For these types of disks, the "Volume Removable" entry will indicate "Yes." If the volume is non-removable and "Volume Mounted" indicates "No," chances are the drive containing that volume has gone bad.

Hashing and Caching

Hashing and caching are two techniques used by NetWare to speed up data access on the network hard disks. The OS automatically hashes the directory and file names on a volume to speed up directory searches. Caching is where the OS keeps a copy of the directory entry table in cache so it doesn't have to read it from the disk each time. (Chapter 3 explains these features in more detail.)

The "Volume Hashed" entry shows you if the volume is hashed. The only reason it wouldn't be hashed is if the file server has insufficient or faulty memory. The "Volume Cached" entry displays "Yes" if you designated caching on that particular volume during NETGEN/ELSGEN. If your file server is short on memory, however, NetWare won't be able to cache all volumes even if it was configured to do so.

Volume Size and Directory Entry Table Information

The "Block Size" entry shows 4,096 bytes as the block size, since that is the fixed block size for NetWare v2.1x. The "Total Blocks" entry shows the total size of the volume in blocks. To figure out what the size is in bytes, multiply the "Total Blocks" entry by 4,096. The "Starting Block" entry shows you which block number on the disk this particular volume begins. The "Free Blocks" entry displays how many blocks aren't currently being used. To figure out how many bytes of free space that represents, multiply "Free Blocks" by 4,096.

During the NetWare Installation half of NETGEN/ELSGEN, when you gave the volume a name and determined its size, you also assigned a certain maximum number of directory entries for the volume. The operating system uses these directory entries to store file names, salvage files, trustee rights entries (each trustee entry can hold up to five trustee rights assignments), and directory names for that volume. The "Maximum Directory Entries" displays the total number set in NETGEN/ELSGEN. Unlike other FCONSOLE peak statistics, the "Peak Directory Entries Used" shows you the highest directory entry *number* used by the volume. This does not necessarily reflect the highest number of directory entries ever used since the file server was last booted. If you've just deleted a number of files, the peak number will probably stay about the same as it was, even though there are actually more entries available now. The "Current Free Directory Entries" shows how many directory entries are currently available.

A much easier way to check up on a volume's free space and number of directory entries is to use the NetWare VOLINFO utility. Typing **VOLINFO** at the command line shows you the volume names for every volume on the server, the volume sizes in kilobytes, and the maximum number of directory entries per volume. You will also see how many directory entries and kilobytes are currently free. The operating system updates this information every five seconds, so VOLINFO is a better source for current information on volume size and directory entries.

Volume Mirroring Information

The next entry, "Logical Drive Number," shows the logical disk drive number upon which this particular volume is located. A logical disk could actually be two physical disk drives if it is part of an SFT NetWare mirrored pair. Disk mirroring allows SFT NetWare to continue to function if one of the physical disks in a mirrored pair should fail. To see how your drives are mapped, press Escape to exit the "Volume Information" window and select the "Disk Mapping Information" option.

The "Volume Mirrored" entry shows you whether or not this volume is mirrored on two physical disks. The "Primary Disk Number" displays the number of the physical disk drive being used as a primary drive, and the "Mirror Disk Number" shows the number of the physical drive used to mirror this volume. If the drive is not mirrored, you will see "N/A" in the "Mirror Disk" entry. Primary drives are also the logical drives if you are not running SFT software or if you did not set up disk mirroring during NETGEN.

If something unusual happens to the disk or disks containing this volume, you may see one of three status messages in the "Volume Mirrored" entry:

• *Warning: Mirroring is disabled.* This message indicates that you have disabled mirroring with the UNMIRROR command at the console or that mirroring has been shut down due to a disk failure.

• *Warning: Volume shut down.* This message means the volume is no longer accessible because of a drive failure. This condition does not last long, for the file server will most likely dismount the volume soon.

• *Volume Dismounted.* When the file server can no longer access the drive or drives that a volume is on, the server will issue its own DISMOUNT command and shut down the drives.

These conditions are usually due to a faulty disk drive, disk controller board, disk channel board, or cabling. You should repair or replace any defective components as soon as possible. When you reboot the server, it should be able to mount the volumes affected by the faulty hardware and re-establish disk mirroring.

20 Reconfiguring the File Server with NETGEN/ELSGEN

Like most software installation programs, Novell's NETGEN or ELSGEN programs are also used to reconfigure the software after it has been initially installed. NETGEN is the installation/maintenance program for SFT and Advanced NetWare 286 v2.1x; ELSGEN is its counterpart for ELS NetWare Level II; and INSTALL is a scaled-down version for ELS NetWare Level I. Whenever you need to change anything involving the NetWare operating system—LAN and disk drivers, network addresses, communication buffers, number of open files, number of indexed files, NetWare volume parameters, and so on—you must rerun the appropriate installation program.

Novell's installation programs are not the easiest in the computer industry to run. They require a considerable amount of networking knowledge and expertise. As a result, NetWare installation is a task generally best left to dealers, consultants, or other knowledgeable installers. Yet, a supervisor can perform a substantial number of the most common NetWare maintenance tasks—those usually falling within the domain of the network supervisor—only by rerunning NETGEN or ELSGEN.

To help the average network supervisor more effectively use NETGEN and ELSGEN to maintain the file server, this chapter first gives a technical overview of how these programs work. We'll then give step-by-step procedures for performing the most common file server maintenance tasks, and finish off the chapter with some tips for the less frequent, more complicated tasks you can do in these programs.

NETWARE INSTALLATION PROGRAMS UNVEILED

Like most installation programs, NETGEN and ELSGEN can be run either from floppy diskettes or from files loaded from the diskettes onto a local hard disk. Two other methods were made available starting with v2.11: a RAM disk method (which allows you to use extended memory to reduce the number of times you have to swap floppies) and a network drive method (which allows you to load the diskettes onto another file server on an internet and run the programs from there). The INSTALL program for ELS Level I, which is basically a simplified variation of ELSGEN, is run only from floppy diskettes.

One important step, whether you are running NETGEN/ELSGEN from either floppy diskettes or from a hard disk, is to make working copies of the original NetWare diskettes. This precautionary step is a sensible one to take prior to installing any software, but it is doubly important for NetWare due to the large number of diskettes that come with each OS. Floppy diskettes are not 100 percent reliable; you are likely to experience a read error at least once. Always, always, always copy the NetWare diskettes and use the working copies when you run NETGEN/ELSGEN. If one of your working floppies goes bad, you can make a new copy from the original. If the original goes bad and you have a good working copy, you're still covered. If the original goes bad and you don't have a copy, you're sunk.

It's helpful to have an overall understanding of exactly what is going on "behind the scenes" in the NetWare installation programs. This section will help you see the entire program as a series of five distinct phases. These phases apply mostly to NETGEN; however, ELSGEN and INSTALL are both based on these same basic procedural phases. For ease of reference, we'll use NETGEN/ELSGEN to refer to all three in a generic sense. Where the procedure is markedly different, we'll use the specific utility name.

Overview of the NetWare Installation Procedure

Procedurally, the process of turning a normal personal computer into a NetWare file server can be divided into five distinct phases, as shown in Figure 20-1.

Think of NETGEN and ELSGEN as composite programs that oversee and control the operation of several different installation utilities. Indeed, that is precisely what they are. With the NetWare v2.0a file server installation procedure, you had the GENOS utility to configure and generate the operating system, the COMPSURF utility to format the hard disks, the DISKSET utility to program the disk coprocessor board, and the PREPARE utility to set up the disks for SFT mirroring. Finally, you ran the INSTALL utility to actually install the NetWare operating system on the file server.

In NETGEN/ELSGEN for NetWare v2.1x, however, the functions of Phase 1 are handled by a program called NCONFIG.EXE. Phase 2 is overseen by the NETGEN/ELSGEN control program itself, but it uses a separate linking utility called NLINK.EXE. Phase 3 isn't really a software phase; it is this stage during which you actually install the hardware in the file server. The Phase 4 utilities, COMPSURF and DISKSET, are still separate utilities, but they are callable from within NETGEN or ELSGEN. Phase 5 combines the old PREPARE and INSTALL

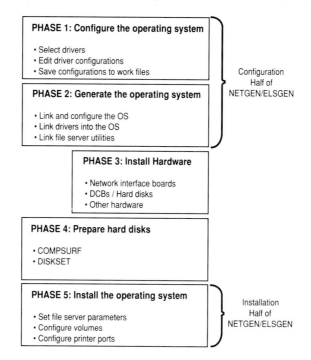

Figure 20-1: The five phases involved in running Novell's NETGEN or ELSGEN installation program.

utilities into a general-purpose installation and maintenance program called IN-STOVL.EXE.

Even though NCONFIG.EXE, NLINK.EXE, and INSTOVL.EXE have the .EXE extension, you cannot run them separately from the DOS command line. They rely on various overlay files, work files, and data files that are part of NETGEN/ELSGEN. You can, however, run DISKSET.EXE and COMPSURF.EXE separately from outside of NETGEN/ELSGEN.

If you are an experienced installer and you know how to avoid hardware conflicts, you can set the boards first and insert them into the file server before Phase 1. That way, you don't have to stop in the middle of NETGEN/ELSGEN to install the hardware. If you do it this way, make sure you match the configuration settings in NETGEN/ELSGEN with the actual settings on the boards.

The following sections explain in more detail what goes on in each phase of NETGEN/ELSGEN.

Phase 1: Configuring the OS. The first phase involves the "configuration half" of NETGEN/ELSGEN. In this configuration phase, you are in essence describing your file server hardware. You tell NETGEN/ELSGEN what kind of file server you have and what kind of network and disk interface boards you will use by selecting resource sets, LAN drivers, disk drivers, and other peripheral drivers. This is also the point at which you resolve hardware conflicts by arriving at an acceptable hardware configuration for each driver.

When you've finished selecting and configuring resources and drivers, NETGEN/ELSGEN saves all your selections and configurations back to disk in the form of work files. The program uses these work files during Phase 2, but nothing is actually installed on the file server itself.

Phase 2: Linking the OS. Programmers are familiar with the process of linking object files to produce a finished executable file. For non-programmers who desire some understanding of how this amazing transformation takes place, here's a quick course in generating executable files.

Most computer programs are written in a programming language such as BASIC or Pascal. NetWare is partly written in the "C" programming language and partly in assembly language. If you could look at the source code for the NetWare operating system, you would see a long list of complicated instructions that don't make much sense to non-programmers. These instructions tell the microprocessor what to do to run the NetWare OS.

Of course, Novell doesn't give out the source code for NetWare. Instead, the core of the OS is provided on the NetWare diskettes as an "object" file (with the .OBJ extension). This OS object file is generic—it's the same on every batch of NetWare diskettes. However, since the core functionality differs between, say, SFT NetWare 286 and SFT NetWare 286 with TTS, or between dedicated and nondedicated Advanced NetWare 286, a separate .OBJ file is provided for each variation of the OS. LAN drivers, disk drivers, and other drivers are also provided as object files.

You can't type the name of an object file at the DOS prompt and expect anything to happen other than the "Bad command or file name" response. However, two or more object files can be combined to form one big "executable" file (with the .EXE extension). This process is called *linking*. Once a file is linked and given the .EXE extension, you can run the program from DOS.

Novell includes its own Linker program on the NetWare diskettes. The work files you create in Phase 1 tell the Novell Linker which .OBJ files to link together to form your own custom version of the NetWare operating system. Another part of the linking process is *configuring* the .EXE file. This lets the executable file know what interrupts, DMA channels, I/O addresses, and memory addresses will be used for communicating with the drivers that have been linked in with it. The resulting executable file is usually named NET$OS.EXE, but larger OS files are sometimes broken up into two pieces named NET$OS.EX1 and NET$OS.EX2 in order to fit on 360KB floppy diskettes.

In addition to the OS file itself, NETGEN also links and configures various file server utilities that must talk to the server hard disks through the disk drivers you select in Phase 1. These utilities are COMPSURF, VREPAIR, and DISKED. A fourth "utility," called INSTOVL, is actually not a utility, but is the Installation Overlay used for the NetWare installation phase—Phase 5. (Since ELS NetWare uses only internal hard disks, these utilities come already generated and don't need to be linked at installation time.)

It is important to realize that the OS and these utilities are specially generated just for your particular file server. You cannot take your OS file and use it to boot up another file server that is set up differently. Nor can you run your customized version of COMPSURF or VREPAIR on any other file server. COMPSURF and VREPAIR are diagnostic programs that run from DOS; they cannot be run while the server is up. For this reason, you should always download the generated files to the working copies of your NetWare diskettes. Then, when the time comes to boot the server or run these utilities, you will have them readily available. Label all working copies specifically so you don't mix different versions.

Phase 3: Installing the Hardware. This phase involves putting together the physical elements of your file server, in much the same way as you put together the software elements in Phases 1 and 2. Phase 3 is not really part of NETGEN/ELSGEN. You must exit the program and save what you've generated in Phase 2 to disk. Eventually you will write the OS and the NetWare utilities to the file server disks, but that comes later (in Phase 5). For now, go to the file server itself, turn everything off, and pull the cover off the file server. Then you can safely set your boards, insert them into the expansion slots, and wire everything up.

Phase 4: Preparing the Hard Disks. For a hard disk to function on a NetWare file server, it must be low-level formatted in a certain way. NetWare 286 cannot use a disk that is formatted only for DOS. Since Novell designed its own file system differently from the one used by DOS (although it looks very similar to DOS from the users' perspective), various tables that NetWare needs must exist on the disk before NetWare can use it. File server disks must also be tested more thoroughly than disks used by DOS or OS/2. NetWare assumes that the drive has been extensively tested and that any bad blocks will be taken care of by the Hot Fix feature. This eliminates a lot of error-detection overhead from NetWare when it stores data to the hard disk. This low-level formatting and extensive surface testing are the role of Novell's COMPSURF utility.

When you use disk coprocessor boards (DCBs) to add external disk subsystems to the file server, you must program each DCB to recognize the number and types of disks that are attached to it. To do this, use the DISKSET utility.

Phase 5: Installing the Operating System. It is only after you have inserted all hardware and prepared the hard disks that you can actually install the NetWare operating system on the file server. The fifth phase includes such procedures as installing Hot Fix, setting up disk mirroring (SFT NetWare only), creating and naming volumes, copying the customized NetWare operating system to the file server, copying over the NetWare system files and utilities, and defining printers.

Anything done in Phase 5 during initial installation, you can modify later by rerunning NETGEN/ELSGEN and making the appropriate changes. In fact, there is even an option named "Miscellaneous Maintenance". Although the wording of this option is confusing at initial installation, the name makes sense every subsequent time you run NETGEN/ELSGEN to maintain the file server.

FACTORS THAT DETERMINE HOW NETGEN RUNS

Part of the reason NETGEN or ELSGEN is so complicated to run is that the program itself behaves somewhat differently, depending on a number of factors:

- Whether you are running the program from 5.25" diskettes or from 3.5" diskettes
- Whether you run the program from floppies or from a hard disk
- Whether you choose the Default or Custom level of the program
- How far along you are in the program

Diskette Size Differences

Because of the difference in storage capacity between 5.25" and 3.5" diskettes, Novell made a slightly different variation of NETGEN/ELSGEN for each size. On the surface, the two variations appear to run exactly the same. The differences are all down at the data file level. NETGEN keeps several data files that tell the program where to look for the files it needs. The 3.5" version, for example, doesn't have a SUPPORT diskette. All of the files on the 5.25" SUPPORT diskette are included on the 3.5" AUXGEN diskette.

You cannot mix diskettes from the two sizes when you run NETGEN. Further, if you have a set of 5.25" diskettes for one file server and a set of 3.5" diskettes for another file server, and you upload the diskettes to a hard disk, you cannot lump them all together in the same directory. You must upload the 5.25" diskettes into a different parent directory than the 3.5" diskettes.

Dynamic Menus

NETGEN and ELSGEN use what Novell calls "dynamic" menus. That is, the options you see in a particular menu come and go, depending on where you are in the program. The intent is two-fold: to eliminate confusion by showing only those options that are valid at a particular stage of the program, and to guide you along by having the highlight bar move to the next option you should select. However, going where the highlight bar takes you may not always lead to the proper choice when you are maintaining the file server with NETGEN or ELSGEN. Knowing what goes on behind the scenes to make each option appear and what each option is for will help you figure out when to follow the highlight bar and when not to.

The main menu in NETGEN and ELSGEN is called the "Network Generation Options" menu. All of the possible options in NETGEN's main menu are shown below. Some of these options will never appear in ELSGEN, for reasons explained later.

```
┌─────────────────────────────────────────┐
│          Network Generation Options       │
├─────────────────────────────────────────┤
│    Select Network Configuration           │
│    Link/Configure NetWare Operating System│
│    Configure NetWare Operating System     │
│    Link/Configure File Server Utilities   │
│    Configure File Server Utilities        │
│    Link/Configure "Other" Utilities       │
│    Configure "Other" Utilities            │
│    Configuration Utilities                │
│    Analyze Disk Surface                   │
│    NetWare Installation                   │
│    Exit NETGEN                            │
└─────────────────────────────────────────┘
```

Phase 1 corresponds to the first option, "Select Network Configuration." Selecting this option takes you into the NCONFIG utility, where you select resources and drivers and choose how you want them configured.

Phase 2 encompasses all of the "Link" and "Configure" options. "Link/Configure NetWare Operating System" both relinks and reconfigures the OS after you add or delete drivers in Phase 1. "Link/Configure File Server Utilities" relinks and reconfigures COMPSURF, VREPAIR, DISKED, and INSTOVL, whereas "Link/Configure 'Other' Utilities" does the same for Novell's internal streaming tape BACKUP and RESTORE utilities. The options that say "Configure" instead of "Link/Configure" only reconfigure an already-linked OS or utility. Use these options when you change the switches on a network interface board or disk interface board to use a different hardware configuration.

To do Phase 3, of course, you must use "Exit NETGEN" to get out of the program. A prompt will appear, asking you if you want to download files to floppy diskettes. Whenever you make a change in Phase 1 and regenerate anything in Phase 2, you should download the latest files to your working copies.

As far as Phase 4 is concerned, you access COMPSURF through the "Analyze Disk Surface" option and DISKSET through the "Configuration Utilities" option. These options are like little circular loops that take you into the appropriate utility and then bring you back to the main menu when you're finished.

Phase 5 is the "NetWare Installation" option. When you choose this option, the first thing NETGEN does is try to talk to all of the disks it knows about through the disk driver information contained in the INSTOVL.EXE file. Remember that INSTOVL was one of the "utilities" generated in Phase 2. If you try to use the wrong INSTOVL.EXE, NETGEN usually blows up and you never make it all the way into the installation half.

About NETGEN's Levels

You can run NETGEN on two levels: Default and Custom. As the names imply, the Default level of NETGEN assumes that you want to use the default settings for all configurations and parameters. Use the Custom level, on the other hand, if you need customized, non-default settings.

Generally, when you are rerunning NETGEN to change the way something is configured, you want more control over the configuration settings. Therefore, you should run NETGEN at the Custom program level. You specify which level you want either when you type the NETGEN command (explained below) or in the first window that pops up when you start NETGEN.

The options you see in NETGEN's dynamic menus are also influenced by the level you choose. For example, if you choose the Default level, none of the Linking or Configuring options appear in the main menu. These functions all happen automatically when you exit the configuration part.

The "NetWare Installation" option leads you to another menu called the "Installation Options" menu. If you start NETGEN at the Custom level (by typing **NETGEN -C**), this menu contains the following options:

```
┌─────────────────────────────────────────┐
│         Installation Options             │
├─────────────────────────────────────────┤
│  Select Default Installation Options     │
│  Select Custom Installation Options      │
│  Continue Installation                   │
└─────────────────────────────────────────┘
```

If you start NETGEN at the Default level (by typing **NETGEN**), only "Select Default Installation Options" will appear in this menu. Choosing this option takes you through a default installation sequence that shows you the default that NETGEN is setting for each configurable parameter. In order to get at the "Custom Installation" menu and the "Miscellaneous Maintenance" option, you must choose "Select Custom Installation Options."

With ELSGEN, the configuration half behaves as if you had selected the Default level to begin with (there is no initial Default or Custom level option for ELSGEN). ELSGEN chooses everything for you, but does allow you to change its default settings if you want to. The installation half runs as if you had selected the Custom level in that you are given the choice of selecting default or custom installation options as shown above.

NETGEN's Four Run Methods

The other choice you must make before actually getting into the NETGEN or ELSGEN program itself is whether you're going to run the program from floppies or from a hard disk.

Under the floppy diskette category, you can either use the Standard Floppy Disk method or the RAM Disk method. Running NETGEN or ELSGEN from floppy diskettes is renowned throughout the industry as great exercise for the hand and wrist. Be prepared to have to swap diskettes in and out *constantly* for long periods of time if you choose this method. If you have access to a PC with enough extended memory, the RAM Disk method might be preferable because it is faster and cuts down on the number of times you have to shuffle floppies in and out of the drive.

NETGEN offers two variations on hard disk installation as well. The Hard Disk method allows you to load the NetWare diskettes onto a machine with a local hard disk and then use this hard disk as your "NETGEN" disk from which to run the program. However, you can't run the installation half of NETGEN from the hard disk. You must download everything at the end of the configuration half, and then run NETGEN from floppies on the file server itself to actually install NetWare. A better way, if you have more than one file server on the network, is to load the NetWare diskettes onto a network drive. That way, you can run the entire NETGEN program from the file server itself by booting it initially as a workstation, logging in to the other file server, and mapping a drive to the NETGEN directory.

Either one of the hard disk methods is infinitely preferable to either of the floppy disk methods for the configuration half of NETGEN.

Tricks and Traps with the RAM Disk Method. NETGEN's RAM Disk option is rather meticulous. If you have tried to run NETGEN by using the RAM Disk method and received an error message saying your RAM disk is unusable, you probably don't have your RAM disk set up properly. NETGEN expects the RAM disk to be in *extended* memory, not expanded memory. You also must have enough extended memory to hold one low-density diskette's worth of information: 360KB for 5.25" diskettes, or 720KB for 3.5" diskettes.

Set up the RAM disk by using the DOS VDISK.SYS driver in the PC's CONFIG.SYS file. For example, if you have an AT-compatible machine with 1MB of extended memory and a 5.25" disk drive, put the following line in CONFIG.SYS:

```
device=VDISK.SYS 360 512 16 /E
```

Be sure you include the /E parameter so the RAM disk will be created in extended memory. If you're running on a PS/2 or other machine with a 3.5" drive, substitute "720" for the "360" in the command.

The RAM Disk method is useful only when you are running the configuration half of NETGEN. It will do you absolutely no good when you are running the installation half.

Tricks and Traps with the Hard Disk Method. The Hard Disk method for running NETGEN is most useful if you have a spare workstation or standalone PC with a local hard disk. Uploading the NetWare diskettes takes up about 8MB of disk space, so the disk will need at least that much free space.

Novell designed NETGEN to have as many "generic" diskettes as possible. The 5.25" SUPPORT diskette from one OS package, for example, is interchangeable with the 5.25" SUPPORT diskette from any set of NetWare diskettes. However, this is true only when they first come out of the box. As you run the configuration half of NETGEN, the program creates work files and data files on various diskettes. These work and data files contain information unique to the file server configuration you define; the diskettes are no longer generic. That set of diskettes can be used only for that file server from now on, unless you write over the work files with new ones.

When you run NETGEN using the Hard Disk method, you essentially dupli-cate the diskettes in the NetWare OS package on the hard disk. The directory struc-ture on the hard disk reflects the names and contents of the floppy diskettes. For example, with 3.5" diskettes you have an AUXGEN subdirectory, an OSEXE-1 sub-directory, a UTILEXE subdirectory, and so on. Each subdirectory is named exactly the same as its corresponding diskette and contains the same files.

Suppose you want to upload the NetWare diskettes to a hard disk and then use that hard disk to run NETGEN for more than one file server. This method is a common practice for dealers and technical support people who must often configure NetWare operating systems for a number of file servers. In this situation, every time you run NETGEN from the same hard disk subdirectory, NETGEN will save what-ever changes you make to the work files in the hard disk subdirectories as well as downloading them to floppies. The next time you start NETGEN, the previous configuration will still be intact (unless you specify the "-N" flag at the command line). This configuration might not be the one you want for the file server you are currently working on.

Be careful also of NetWare serialization when you have a GENDATA sub-directory on the hard disk. The files on the GENDATA diskette are *not* inter-changeable from file server to file server, because they control (among other things) how the OS is serialized at initial installation. To keep the correct serialization intact for each file server's OS, you should delete the GENDATA subdirectory from the hard disk. If NETGEN can't find a subdirectory on the hard disk, it will prompt you to insert the appropriate floppy diskette to get the files it needs. With no GENDATA subdirectory on the hard disk, you can insert the correct GENDATA diskette for whichever file server you are working on at the time.

You can't run the installation half of NETGEN using the Hard Disk method. The "NetWare Installation" option won't even show up in the main menu. You must go to the file server itself and start NETGEN from your floppies. It is theoretically possible, if you have a DOS partition and a NetWare partition on the same hard disk, to run NETGEN from the DOS partition and have it install to the NetWare partition. Avoid using this setup, however; it is extremely risky and wasteful of disk space.

Since you can't run the "NetWare Installation" part of NETGEN from a local hard disk, you don't need to upload any of the SYSTEM, PUBLIC, or INFO diskettes into subdirectories. The files on these diskettes are copied over to the file server at the end of the installation half. You'll have to load these files from the floppies.

Here's a little-known fact about the Hard Disk method (which also applies to the Network Drive method). If you start NETGEN or ELSGEN from a hard disk that already has the NetWare diskettes uploaded, choosing the "Standard Floppy Disk Method" will use the hard disk subdirectories, not the floppies. So, if you type **NETGEN -SC** from the command line, you'll skip over both introductory screens and go directly into the Custom level of the program, using the hard disk subdirec-tories.

Tricks and Traps with the Network Drive Method. The Network Drive method has all the advantages of the Hard Disk method, without some of the disadvantages. You can run NETGEN all the way through using the Network Drive method, and you can upload the SYSTEM, PUBLIC, and INFO files so NETGEN will copy them directly over from the network instead of from floppies. This is a big plus, especially with the 5.25" format, which includes eight PUBLIC diskettes (nine in v2.15c).

You must make the file server bootable as a workstation on the network, and you must be able to log in and map a drive to the other file server with the NETGEN directories on it. That means you'll need a boot diskette for the file server, complete with a NetWare shell.

You must be extra careful when you run NETGEN from a network drive for more than one file server. You could end up copying the wrong OS to the file server. The best trick is to delete the GENDATA subdirectory and use the diskette. Always double-check the current configuration before you select the "NetWare Installation" option. If you have the wrong disk driver selected for the file server on which you are running NETGEN, you'll get the following error message when you try to enter the installation half:

```
Abend: Invalid process id passed by interrupt procedure to kernel.
```

The file server will be hung. After this error, you'll have to completely reboot the machine and start over.

NETGEN/ELSGEN Command Line Flags

NETGEN includes some flags that you can add after the command in order to skip over the preliminary menus for selecting the program level and the run method.

Typing the command as **NETGEN -N** tells NETGEN that you are starting a new operating system generation. The program will save any previous configuration data files with the .BAK extension, then clear everything out so you can start over from scratch. Use the -N flag only when necessary; usually when you do maintenance with NETGEN, you don't want to start all over.

The flags for selecting the Default and Custom levels are "-D" and "-C" respectively. Adding the "-S" flag selects the Standard Floppy Disk run method for you. There isn't a flag for any of the other run methods, although if you start the program from a disk drive directory containing the NetWare installation subdirectories and use the "-S" flag, the program will run from the hard disk instead of from floppies.

ELSGEN doesn't have a Default or Custom level option, so the -D and -C flags do not apply.

Other Prerequisites for Running NETGEN/ELSGEN

To run either NETGEN or ELSGEN, the PC must have at least 640KB of conventional memory. It must be booted with DOS v3.3 or above (DOS 4.x will work) and a CONFIG.SYS file that contains the lines "FILES=20" and "BUFFERS=15." The files parameter can be set to a higher number, but it must be at least 20 to run NETGEN.

COMMON MAINTENANCE TASKS IN NETGEN/ELSGEN

Here are step-by-step procedures for performing some of the most common maintenance tasks in NETGEN or ELSGEN. We'll treat each task as if that is the only thing you will be doing in the program. If you must perform more than one of these tasks at the same time, stay in the NETGEN or ELSGEN program until you've completed them all. Then exit as instructed.

Resetting Network Addresses

You must reset network addresses whenever your file server or an external bridge (router) reports an error such as one of these:

```
ERROR! Address collision with ServerName.
!!!ROUTER CONFIGURATION ERROR!!! Router NodeAddress claims LAN A
is NetworkAddress!
WARNING!!! MULTIPLE ROUTERS WITH SAME INTERNET ADDRESS!
```

Network addresses must uniquely identify separate cabling systems on an internetwork. Generally, you set a different network address for each file server network interface board connected to the internet. However, if you have an internetwork backbone cable connecting several file servers, or any situation where you have more than one file server connected to the same cabling system, the network boards that connect to the common cabling system must have the same network addresses. Figure 20-2 illustrates some possible cases where this network address rule would apply.

Once you know the correct network addresses to set, follow these steps to change the appropriate network addresses. (You must bring the file server down before running NETGEN or ELSGEN.)

Changing Network Addresses in NETGEN. Here is the procedure for changing network addresses in NETGEN. (The process is similar for ELSGEN, but different enough that we've included a separate set of steps for ELSGEN.)

1. Go into NETGEN and choose "Select Network Configuration" from the main menu.

2. Choose "Configure Drivers/Resources" from the "Available Options" menu.

3. Now choose "Enter Server Information." The "Network Information" window will appear, showing the currently selected network addresses.

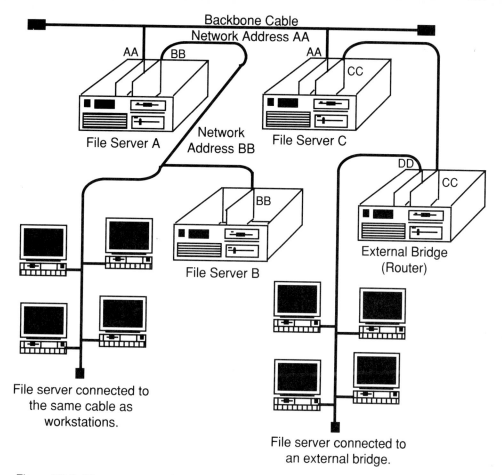

Figure 20-2: Whenever more than one file server is connected to the same cabling system, the network boards must have the same network address.

4. Highlight the network address you want to change and press Backspace to delete the old address. Then type in the new network address and press Enter.

5. Press Escape to leave the "Network Information" window. Keep pressing Escape until you see the "Continue Network Generation Using Selected Configuration?" prompt. Answer "Yes" to this prompt.

6. Since you have changed something about the NetWare OS, you must now regenerate the OS file. If you're running the Custom level of NETGEN, choose "Configure NetWare Operating System" from the main menu. If you're running the Default level, the OS will be reconfigured automatically. Insert any diskettes the program asks for.

7. If your file server runs the Advanced NetWare nondedicated OS, exit NETGEN and download the new OS to your OSEXE-1 and OSEXE-2 working diskettes. Use these diskettes the next time you boot the file server.

8. If your file server runs a dedicated version of NetWare and you boot it from the system disk, choose "NetWare Installation" from the main menu. NETGEN will analyze the disks and present a list of those it finds. After verifying that the list is correct, choose "Drive List Is Correct."

9. Choose "Select Custom Installation Options" from the "Installation Options" menu.

10. Choose "Miscellaneous Maintenance" from the "Custom Installation" menu.

11. Choose "Load Operating System" and answer "Yes" to the "Set Flag for Operating System Load?" prompt. This will signal NETGEN to write the new OS to disk when you exit.

12. Press Escape until you get back to the "Installation Options" menu. Then choose "Continue Installation." Answer "Yes" to the "Install Networking Software on File Server?" prompt.

13. NETGEN will load a new cold boot loader, then prompt you for the floppy diskette(s) containing the new OS (unless you are using the Network Drive method). After NETGEN successfully loads the OS, press a key as prompted.

14. Back at the main menu, choose "Exit NETGEN." Answer "Yes" to the download prompt and insert your working copies of the diskettes indicated.

15. When you reboot the file server, the new OS will assign the new network addresses; the routing errors should not reappear.

Changing Network Addresses in ELSGEN. Here's how to change network addresses in the ELSGEN program:

1. Go into ELSGEN and choose "Operating System Generation."

2. Choose "Generate Operating System" from the "Available Options" menu. The "File Server Information" window will appear, showing the currently selected network addresses.

3. Highlight the network address you want to change and press Backspace to delete the old address. Then type in the new network address and press Enter.

4. Press Escape to leave the "File Server Information" window. Keep pressing Escape until you see the "Continue Network Generation Using Selected Configuration?" prompt. Answer "Yes" to this prompt.

5. Since you have changed something about the NetWare OS, ELSGEN will automatically regenerate the OS file. Insert any diskettes the program asks for.

6. If your file server runs the ELS NetWare Level II nondedicated OS, exit ELSGEN and download the new OS to your OSEXE-1 and OSEXE-2 working diskettes. Use these diskettes the next time you boot the file server.

7. If your file server runs the ELS NetWare Level II dedicated OS and you boot it from the system disk, choose "NetWare Installation" from the main menu. ELSGEN will analyze the disks and present a list of those it finds. After verifying that the list is correct, choose "Drive List Is Correct."

8. Choose "Select Custom Installation Options" from the "Installation Options" menu.

9. Choose "Miscellaneous Maintenance" from the "Custom Installation" menu.

10. Choose "Load Operating System" and answer "Yes" to the "Set Flag for Operating System Load?" prompt. This will signal ELSGEN to write the new OS to disk when you exit.

11. Press Escape until you get back to the "Installation Options" menu. Then choose "Continue Installation." Answer "Yes" to the "Install Networking Software on File Server?" prompt.

12. ELSGEN will load a new cold boot loader, then prompt you for the floppy diskette(s) containing the new OS. After ELSGEN successfully loads the OS, press a key as prompted.

13. Back at the main menu, choose "Exit ELSGEN." Answer "Yes" to the download prompt and insert your working copies of the diskettes indicated.

14. When you reboot the file server, the new OS will assign the new network addresses; the routing errors should not reappear.

Changing the Number of Communication Buffers

Communication buffers are temporary storage areas in file server memory for incoming packets that haven't yet been processed. These buffers are also used for routing information across an internet; packets are received on one LAN board within the file server and routed through another LAN board to the LAN address specified by the packet. "Communication buffers" and "routing buffers" are the same thing; we'll use the term "communication buffers" because that's what NETGEN and ELSGEN call them.

There are a number of basic rules for determining how many buffers your operating system needs. Novell manuals recommend at least forty in an SFT or Advanced NetWare file server, plus one buffer for every workstation attached to the file server. For ELS NetWare, the minimum is fifteen, plus one per user.

Another formula you can use to get a more accurate number is:

```
  2 buffers per active user
+ 10 for each network board in the file server
+ 10 for routers directly connected to the file server

= total number of communication buffers needed
```

Note that the first line relates to *active* users, not *defined* users. If 150 users are defined on a file server, but only ten of those actively use the network at a time, you need only twenty buffers for this network. Directly connected routers are those that do not pass through another file server or bridge to communicate with your file server.

As an example of how you would use this formula, look at the sample internetwork shown in Figure 20-3:

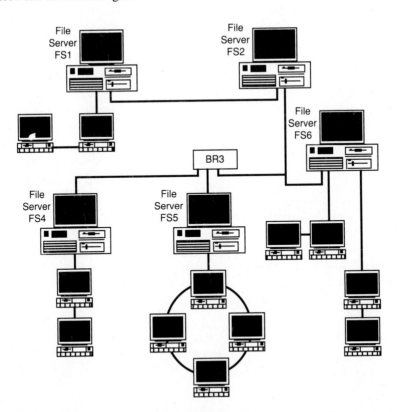

Figure 20-3: Sample internetwork to illustrate how to calculate an appropriate number of communication buffers.

Suppose file server FS1 has twenty active users. The file server has two network boards and has three direct router connections—file servers 1 and 6, and bridge 3. File servers 4 and 5 are connected through bridge 3, so they are not direct router connections. In this situation, you'd need:

```
   40 buffers for 20 active users
 + 20 buffers for the two network boards
 + 30 for routers directly connected to the file server
 _____

 = 90 communication buffers total
```

Suppose file server FS6 has thirty active users. From the figure, we can see that FS6 has four network boards and two direct router connections, to FS2 and bridge 3. In this situation, you'd need:

```
   60 buffers for 30 active users
 + 40 buffers for the four network boards
 + 20 for routers directly connected to the file server
 _____

 = 120 communication buffers total
```

Unless you have a very small network, such as an ELS network, you should always have a minimum of forty communication buffers. On the other side of the scale, the maximum number you can configure is 150 (250 in v2.15c). You probably won't ever need more than the maximum number of communication buffers, no matter how big your network is.

You can check the adequacy of your communication buffers in FCON-SOLE. The "File Server Statistics Summary" screen shows the configured maximum number of routing buffers, the peak number of buffers ever used at one time, and the number currently in use. (Note that FCONSOLE calls them routing buffers instead of communication buffers.) If the "Peak Used" number equals the "Maximum" number, you probably need more buffers.

Double-check by going into the "LAN I/O Statistics" option and looking at the "Incoming Packets Lost Because Of No Available Buffers" and "Outgoing Packets Lost Because Of No Available Buffers" entries at the bottom of the screen. If either number is greater than 0, your file server is losing packets because there are no available routing buffers. If you see this happening, you definitely need to increase the number of communication buffers.

On the other hand, if you see in FCONSOLE that you have a surplus of communication buffers, you can reduce the number in order to eke out more file server memory for other things. Each buffer takes about 500 bytes of RAM. If you reduce the number of buffers from 90 to 80, for example, you will free up about 5KB of memory in the file server.

Once you've determined how many communication buffers to set, follow these steps to change the number in the OS. (You must bring the file server down before running NETGEN or ELSGEN.)

Changing the Number of Communication Buffers in NETGEN. Here is the procedure for making this change in NETGEN. (The process is similar for ELSGEN, but different enough that we've included a separate set of steps for ELSGEN.)

1. Go into NETGEN and choose "Select Network Configuration" from the main menu.

2. Choose "Configure Drivers/Resources" from the "Available Options" menu.

3. Now choose "Enter Server Information." The "Network Information" window will appear, showing the current number of communication buffers.

4. Highlight the "Communication Buffers" field and press Backspace to delete the old number. Then type in the new number you want and press Enter.

5. Press Escape to leave the "Network Information" window. Keep pressing Escape until you see the "Continue Network Generation Using Selected Configuration?" prompt. Answer "Yes" to this prompt.

6. Since you have changed something about the NetWare OS, you must now regenerate the OS file. If you're running the Custom level of NETGEN, choose "Configure NetWare Operating System" from the main menu. If you're running the Default level, the OS will be reconfigured automatically. Insert any diskettes the program asks for.

7. If your file server runs the Advanced NetWare nondedicated OS, exit NETGEN and download the new OS to your OSEXE-1 and OSEXE-2 working diskettes. Use these diskettes the next time you boot the file server.

8. If your file server runs a dedicated version of NetWare and you boot it from the system disk, choose "NetWare Installation" from the main menu. NETGEN will analyze the disks and present a list of those it finds. After verifying that the list is correct, choose "Drive List Is Correct."

9. Choose "Select Custom Installation Options" from the "Installation Options" menu.

10. Choose "Miscellaneous Maintenance" from the "Custom Installation" menu.

11. Choose "Load Operating System" and answer "Yes" to the "Set Flag for Operating System Load?" prompt. This will signal NETGEN to write the new OS to disk when you exit.

12. Press Escape until you get back to the "Installation Options" menu. Then choose "Continue Installation." Answer "Yes" to the "Install Networking Software on File Server?" prompt.

13. NETGEN will load a new cold boot loader, then prompt you for the floppy diskette(s) containing the new OS. After NETGEN successfully loads the OS, press a key as prompted.

14. Back at the main menu, choose "Exit NETGEN." Answer "Yes" to the download prompt and insert your working copies of the diskettes indicated.

15. When you reboot the file server, the new OS will reserve memory for the new number of communication buffers. You can check the number of buffers in FCON-SOLE's "Summary" option (accessed by choosing "Statistics" from the main menu).

Changing the Number of Communication Buffers in ELSGEN. Here's how to make this change in the ELSGEN program:

1. Go into ELSGEN and choose "Operating System Generation."

2. Choose "Generate Operating System" from the "Available Options" menu. The "File Server Information" window will appear, showing the currently selected network addresses.

3. Highlight the "Communication Buffers" field and press Backspace to delete the old number. Then type in the new number that you want and press Enter.

4. Press Escape to leave the "File Server Information" window. Keep pressing Escape until you see the "Continue Network Generation Using Selected Configuration?" prompt. Answer "Yes" to this prompt.

5. Since you have changed something about the NetWare OS, ELSGEN will automatically regenerate the OS file. Insert any diskettes the program asks for.

6. If your file server runs the ELS NetWare Level II nondedicated OS, exit ELSGEN and download the new OS to your OSEXE-1 and OSEXE-2 working diskettes. Use these diskettes the next time you boot the file server.

7. If your file server runs the ELS NetWare Level II dedicated OS and you boot it from the system disk, choose "NetWare Installation" from the main menu. ELSGEN will analyze the disks and present a list of those it finds. After verifying that the list is correct, choose "Drive List Is Correct."

8. Choose "Select Custom Installation Options" from the "Installation Options" menu.

9. Choose "Miscellaneous Maintenance" from the "Custom Installation" menu.

10. Choose "Load Operating System" and answer "Yes" to the "Set Flag for Operating System Load?" prompt. This will signal ELSGEN to write the new OS to disk when you exit.

11. Press Escape until you get back to the "Installation Options" menu. Then choose "Continue Installation." Answer "Yes" to the "Install Networking Software on File Server?" prompt.

12. ELSGEN will load a new cold boot loader, then prompt you for the floppy diskette(s) containing the new OS. After ELSGEN successfully loads the OS, press a key as prompted.

13. Back at the main menu, choose "Exit ELSGEN." Answer "Yes" to the download prompt and insert your working copies of the diskettes indicated.

14. When you reboot the file server, the new OS will reserve enough memory for the new number of communication buffers. You can check the number of buffers in FCONSOLE's "Summary" option (accessed by choosing "Statistics" from the main menu).

Changing the Number of Open Files, Indexed Files, or Transactional Files

From time to time, check the "File Server Statistics Summary" screen in FCONSOLE to see how the other NETGEN/ELSGEN-configurable parameters are doing. These parameters include the maximum number of files the file server can have open at a time (Open Files), the maximum number of large database files that can be flagged Indexed (Indexed Files), and the maximum number of files that can be flagged Transactional (Transactions). The transactional entry applies only if your file server runs SFT NetWare with TTS.

For each of these items, FCONSOLE gives the configured maximum, the peak number ever used at one time, and the number currently in use. If the "Peak Used" number equals the "Maximum" number, you need to adjust the configured maximum accordingly.

All three of these parameters are set in the "NetWare Installation" half of NETGEN/ELSGEN. Here's how to change them:

1. Start up NETGEN or ELSGEN and choose "NetWare Installation" from the main menu.

2. NETGEN/ELSGEN will analyze the system and present a list of the disks it finds. After verifying that the list is correct, choose "Drive List Is Correct."

3. Choose "Select Custom Installation Options" from the "Installation Options" menu.

4. Choose "Miscellaneous Maintenance" from the "Custom Installation" menu.

5. Choose "System Configuration" from the "Miscellaneous Maintenance" menu. A window will appear showing the current settings for "Number of Open Files," "Number of Indexed Files," "Transaction Backout Volume," and "Number of Transactions," along with the file server name and the "Limit Disk Space" option. (The two transaction-related options appear only if your file server is running SFT NetWare with TTS.)

6. Highlight the field you want to change and press Backspace to delete the current number. Then type in the number you want and press Enter.

7. Press Escape until you get back to the "Installation Options" menu. Then choose "Continue Installation." Answer "Yes" to the "Install Networking Software on File Server?" prompt.

8. NETGEN/ELSGEN will load a new cold boot loader (if appropriate), then write the new OS to disk. After the program successfully loads the OS, press a key as prompted.

9. Back at the main menu, choose "Exit NETGEN" or "Exit ELSGEN." Answer "Yes" to the download prompt and insert your working copies of the diskettes indicated.

10. When you reboot the file server, the new OS will use the new system configuration settings. You can check them in FCONSOLE's "Summary" option (accessed by choosing "Statistics" from the main menu).

Enabling the Limit Disk Space Option

If your file server was not installed with the ability to limit the amount of disk space each user can use, here's how to enable this feature with NETGEN/ELSGEN. If you're not sure whether the disk space limitation feature is enabled or not, go into FCONSOLE and look at the "File Server Statistics Summary" screen. If the "Bindery Objects" entries all say "N/A," that means the option is not enabled. If there are numbers in these entries, the option is enabled from the OS side. You must establish individual disk space limits in SYSCON (starting with Step 11 below).

1. Start NETGEN using the Custom level, or start ELSGEN the normal way. From the main menu, choose "NetWare Installation."

2. NETGEN/ELSGEN will analyze the system and present a list of the disks it finds. After verifying that the list is correct, choose "Drive List Is Correct."

3. Choose "Select Custom Installation Options" from the "Installation Options" menu.

4. Choose "Miscellaneous Maintenance" from the "Custom Installation" menu.

5. Choose "System Configuration" from the "Miscellaneous Maintenance" menu. A window will appear showing (among other things) the current settings for "Limit Disk Space" and "Number of Bindery Objects." These two options work together.

6. To enable "Limit Disk Space," highlight that field and type "Y," then press Enter.

7. The "Number of Bindery Objects" field will now show a default number. When you limit disk space for users (which are objects in the file server's bindery, along with groups, print servers, backup servers, and so on), NetWare must establish a ceiling on the number of objects in the bindery so it can reserve enough memory to track the amount of space allocated to each user. You can choose between 500 and 5,000. In almost all cases, the default number of 500 will suffice.

8. Press Escape until you return to the "Installation Options" menu. Then choose "Continue Installation." Answer "Yes" to the "Install Networking Software on File Server?" prompt. The necessary changes are made to the control sectors on the hard disk, so loading a new operating system is not required.

9. Back at the main menu, choose "Exit NETGEN" or "Exit ELSGEN." Answer "Yes" to the download prompt and insert your working copies of the diskettes indicated.

10. Reboot the file server. The OS will now have the capability to track and limit the disk space each user is using.

11. Log in as supervisor and go into the SYSCON utility.

12. In SYSCON, you must specify the actual number of kilobytes you want available for each user already created on your file server. Choose "User Information" from the "Available Topics" menu and select the individual user whose disk space you wish to limit.

13. Select "Account Restrictions" from that person's "User Information" menu. Then highlight the "Limit Disk Space" field at the bottom of the window and type "Y."

14. In the "Maximum Disk Space" field, type in the total number of *kilobytes* you want that user to be able to claim as owner on the file server. For example, if you want to limit a user to 2MB of disk space, type "2048" in the field. Since NetWare divides disks into 4KB blocks, any number you type will be rounded to the nearest multiple of four when you exit.

15. For future users that you will create, you can set a default maximum disk space using the "Default Account Balance/Restrictions" option under "Supervisor Options" in SYSCON. Setting this default will not affect the disk space limit for existing users.

It's possible that a user is already using more disk space than the limit you just set. The next time that user logs in and tries to create or append information to files for which that user is listed as owner, he or she will get an "Out of Disk Space" error. The user must either delete some unneeded files or archive them to floppies to free up disk space.

The "Limit Disk Space" option is totally transparent to the users. It appears to them as if the disk is only as big as the space to which they are limited. For example, when users type DIR or CHKVOL at the DOS prompt, the available disk space will reflect only the amount they have been allotted. When users run out of disk space, they will receive an "Out Of Disk Space" error message. This means that users can read and open files in their directory, but unless they delete some files or convince the supervisor to give them more disk space, they will not be able to create new files or extend files they have already created.

Changing Volume Information

Volumes represent a physical amount of disk space on a NetWare hard disk. The size of a volume is fixed when the disk is initialized for use by NetWare. In addition, the installer names the volume, sets the maximum number of entries in the volume's directory entry table, and decides whether or not the directory entry table should be cached. A supervisor can change these volume-related settings only by rerunning NETGEN or ELSGEN. (If necessary, review the information about the NetWare file system and volumes in Chapter 7.)

This section first explains how to change the volume parameters (name, number of directory entries, and caching option). Then we'll describe how to change a volume's size.

Changing a Volume's Parameters. You should change a volume's parameters only if absolutely necessary. Rename a volume only if the existing name conflicts with the name of another volume or is too long or hard to type. Remember that you must change all drive mappings in login scripts to reflect the new volume name.

The directories for volumes should always be cached. Directory caching is a crucial part of file server performance; if a volume's directory isn't cached in file server memory, NetWare will have to read the directory from the disk every time a user wants to read a file on that volume—and disk access is significantly slower than memory access. If you're in dire need of file server memory, however, you may be able to get away with not caching the least-used volume. *Always* cache the SYS volume's directory.

Periodically, use the VOLINFO utility to check the number of directory entries left on your volumes. If the number of "Free" directory entries is blinking, you need to increase the number.

Decreasing the Number of Directory Entries. If, on the other hand, you have more than enough directory entries for now and the foreseeable future, you can decrease the number if you need to squeeze out more memory for your file server. Each directory entry takes 32 bytes of file server RAM. If you reduce the number by 100, for example, you'll free up just over 3KB of memory.

Do not decrease the number of directory entries, however, until you check to see how many you can safely manipulate without the risk of losing data from the volume. Go into FCONSOLE, select "Statistics" from the main menu, then select the "Volume Information" option. Choose the appropriate volume from the list of volumes to get the "Volume Information" screen. Now, subtract the "Peak Directory Entries Used" from the "Maximum Directory Entries" shown. The resulting difference is the maximum number of free directory entries that you can safely eliminate via NETGEN/ELSGEN. Reducing the number of directory entries by more than this number will result in lost files on that volume. (See Chapter 34 for more information about manipulating directory entries.)

Here's how to change the name, the number of directory entries, and the caching option for an existing NetWare volume. None of the data in the volume should be affected by any of these changes, but you should have a backup of the volume just in case.

1. Start NETGEN using the Custom level, or start ELSGEN the normal way. From the main menu, choose "NetWare Installation."

2. NETGEN/ELSGEN will analyze the system and present a list of the disks it finds. After verifying that the list is correct, choose "Drive List Is Correct."

3. Choose "Select Custom Installation Options" from the "Installation Options" menu.

4. Choose "Miscellaneous Maintenance" from the "Custom Installation" menu.

5. Choose "Volume Information" from the "Miscellaneous Maintenance" menu. If you have more than one volume on the file server, a list of volumes will appear. Highlight the volume you want and press Enter.

6. Highlight the field you want to change and type in the new information. (Remember, you can't rename the SYS volume.)

7. Press Escape until you get back to the "Installation Options" menu. Then choose "Continue Installation." Answer "Yes" to the "Install Networking Software on File Server?" prompt. The necessary changes are made to the volume information tables on the system disk, so loading a new operating system is not required.

8. Back at the main menu, choose "Exit NETGEN" or "Exit ELSGEN." Answer "Yes" to the download prompt and insert your working copies of the diskettes indicated.

9. When you reboot the file server, the new volume parameters will take effect.

Watch the bootup messages to make sure all the volumes you want to cache are indeed being cached. If the server doesn't have enough memory to cache a volume's directory, you will get a message saying "Not enough memory to cache volume *nn*." Make a note of which volume number is not being cached.

If the performance in reading from that volume is unacceptable, you have two choices: either add more extended memory to the file server (the preferred solution), or uncache the directory of another, less-used volume.

Changing a Volume's Size. Since all network disk space is assigned to volumes of fixed sizes at installation, changing the size later is not an easy matter. If you have only one NetWare volume per hard disk, as recommended, you cannot make the volume any bigger. You can make the volume smaller and create a second volume on the disk, but usually you're concerned about a volume's size only when the volume is full.

If you do have more than one volume on a disk and you absolutely must make one of the volumes larger, you can do it—but only at the expense of making the other volumes smaller to compensate. As long as there is enough unused room in the other volumes, you can make a volume bigger as follows:

1. Back up the data in all volumes on the disk. This is extremely important. *All data on all volumes will be destroyed* when you change the volumes' sizes.

2. Bring down the file server and start up NETGEN or ELSGEN. Choose "NetWare Installation" from the main menu.

3. NETGEN/ELSGEN will analyze the system and present a list of the disks it finds. After verifying that the list is correct, choose "Drive List Is Correct."

4. Choose "Select Custom Installation Options" from the "Installation Options" menu.

5. Choose "Reinitialize a Disk" from the "Custom Installation" menu. A list of all initialized disks will appear.

6. Highlight the disk you want to reinitialize. The disks are identified by channel, controller, and drive number. Press Enter to confirm your selection.

7. The program will show you which NetWare volumes currently exist on the disk. *All* data on *all* of these volumes will be lost when you reinitialize the disk. If you're sure you want to continue, answer "Yes" to the "Continue With Reinitialization?" prompt.

8. Recreate your NetWare volumes by pressing Insert in the "Volume" window. Specify the same names you had before, but enter the new sizes you want. Accept the default number of directory entries shown and the default of "Yes" for the caching option. Press Escape after you respecify each volume.

9. When the "Volume" window shows the appropriate volume information, press Escape and answer "Yes" to the "Create Volume?" prompt. Press Escape until you are back to the "Miscellaneous Maintenance" menu.

10. If your file server boots from the system disk and you have reinitialized the SYS volume, you must reload the operating system and the NetWare system and public files. Set both the "Load Operating System" option and the "Load System & Public Files" option to "Yes."

11. Press Escape until you are back in the "Custom Installation" menu. Choose "Continue Installation" and answer "Yes" to the "Install Networking Software on File Server?" prompt. The new volume information will be written to the disk. If you set the OS load flag, follow the prompts to load the cold boot loader and OS diskettes.

12. Back at the main menu, choose "Exit NETGEN" or "Exit ELSGEN." Answer "Yes" to the download prompt and insert your working copies of the diskettes indicated.

13. When you reboot the file server, the new volume sizes will take effect, but the volumes will be empty. Restore the data from your backups to the appropriate volumes.

Changing the Hot Fix Parameters of a Disk

Here's another interesting procedure for you. If you start getting error messages that mention the Hot Fix feature on a network disk, you may need to increase the size of the Hot Fix Redirection Area.

Normally, about two percent of a disk's space is reserved for redirecting data from bad blocks elsewhere on the disk. NetWare's Hot Fix feature uses read-after-write verification to make sure that whenever a block of data is written to the disk, it can be read back the same as it was written. If not, NetWare marks that block as unreliable and redirects the data to a good block in the Hot Fix Redirection Area. If the Hot Fix area starts filling up quickly, it could be a signal that the disk surface is wearing out or that the disk is having some other problem.

First, check FCONSOLE's "Disk Statistics" option (accessed by choosing "Statistics" from the main menu) to see whether Hot Fix is still enabled on the disk, how big the Hot Fix Table was configured to be, and how many free blocks are remaining in the Hot Fix Table. If the number shown after "Hot Fix Remaining" at the bottom of the window is low, that means the Hot Fix Redirection Area is almost full. Increasing the size of the Hot Fix Table (Redirection Area) may buy you some time, but eventually you must replace a worn-out disk.

Another reason why you might need to adjust the Hot Fix size of a disk is if you want to mirror two disks with different storage capacities. SFT NetWare can mirror two disks as long as they have the same logical size. If the disks are close enough to being the same physical size, you can make them the same *logical* size by adjusting the size of the Hot Fix Redirection Area appropriately.

Here's how to change the Hot Fix size in NETGEN or ELSGEN:

1. Back up the data in all volumes on the disk. This is extremely important. *All data on all volumes will be destroyed* when you change the Hot Fix sizes.

2. Bring down the file server and start up NETGEN or ELSGEN. Choose "NetWare Installation" from the main menu.

3. NETGEN/ELSGEN will analyze the system and present a list of the disks it finds. After verifying that the list is correct, choose "Drive List Is Correct."

4. Choose "Select Custom Installation Options" from the "Installation Options" menu.

5. Choose "Modify Hot Fix Redirection Tables" from the "Custom Installation" menu. A list of all drives identified by channel, controller, and drive number will appear.

6. Highlight the disk whose Hot Fix Redirection tables you need to modify. Make sure you are choosing the right disk. Press Enter to confirm your selection.

7. The program will show you the current physical and logical size of the disk (in 4KB blocks). The physical disk size cannot be changed, for it reflects the total amount of storage space available on the disk. To make the Hot Fix Redirection Area *bigger*, you need make the logical disk size *smaller*. (Logical disk size is what's left over when you subtract the Hot Fix area from the total disk space.) Type in the new logical disk size you want.

8. If the disk was part of a mirrored pair, you will get a list of options for handling the mirrored Hot Fix size change. You can either change the Hot Fix size on the mirrored drive as well (the preferred option), unmirror the drives and use the second drive for other volumes, or cancel the Hot Fix size change. (Two mirrored disks must have the same logical disk size.) Respond to the prompt as you see fit.

9. If you have changed the Hot Fix size on the disk containing the SYS volume and you boot the file server from the system disk, you must reload the operating system and the NetWare system and public files. Set both the "Load Operating System" option and the "Load System & Public Files" option to "Yes."

10. Press Escape until you return to the "Custom Installation" menu. Notice that the "Initialize a Disk" option appears in the menu. You must select this option and set up the volumes again, just as if the disk were brand new to the system. When you're finished, press Escape until you return to the "Custom Installation" menu.

11. Choose "Continue Installation" and answer "Yes" to the "Install Networking Software on File Server?" prompt. The new Hot Fix information will be written to the disk.

12. Back at the main menu, choose "Exit NETGEN" or "Exit ELSGEN." Answer "Yes" to the download prompt and insert your working copies of the diskettes indicated.

13. When you reboot the file server, the new Hot Fix sizes will take effect, but the volumes on the disk will be empty. Restore the data from your backups to the appropriate volumes.

LESS COMMON NETGEN/ELSGEN MAINTENANCE TASKS

NETGEN and ELSGEN have many other rarely used options. Some are performed in the configuration half, while most involve the "Custom Installation" and "Miscellaneous Maintenance" menus in the installation half.

Tasks in the Configuration Half

As we discussed earlier in this chapter, the purpose of the configuration half of NETGEN/ELSGEN is to establish and generate a NetWare operating system with no conflicts between hardware components in the file server. In addition to LAN and disk drivers, you can bring into the picture what Novell calls "resource sets" to prevent conflicts with other types of hardware in the file server.

Working with Resource Sets. NETGEN/ELSGEN allows you to define and select resource sets for any hardware in your file server not directly related to the network: for example, a clock-calendar card or a floppy disk controller. A *resource set* is a software definition of your file server's hardware characteristics. This definition is called a resource "set" because it consists of one or more individual *resource* definitions. Resource sets, when they are included in the network operating system configuration process, ensure that NetWare will be able to communicate with the server's processor, bus, and other expansion cards.

Novell provides standard resource set definitions for most common hardware used in file servers. For example, if you are using an IBM PC AT-compatible machine for a file server, you could use Novell's predefined resource set for an AT-compatible file server. If you have a Compaq DeskPro 386 machine, you can create your own resource set to define hardware peculiar to the Compaq.

Whenever you select a resource set or driver in NETGEN/ELSGEN, the program holds all possible configurations in memory until you choose a configuration. If you select too many resource sets and drivers without specifying a configuration for any of them, NETGEN could run out of memory and start deselecting things for you. In the worst case, you could get a memory error that forces you to reboot and start NETGEN all over again. If you run the Custom level of NETGEN, you can edit the resource sets to specify only one configuration for a given resource, thus freeing up memory space for NETGEN to make further selections.

If conflicts exist among resources and drivers that you need, or if Novell has failed to supply a predefined resource or driver that you need, you can create your own. Or you can edit existing resources so they suit your needs.

Creating a new resource set involves naming the resource or driver, naming and defining configuration options for that resource or driver, grouping one or more defined resources into a resource set, and selecting that new resource set or driver for linking as part of your NetWare operating system, if necessary. Most resource sets don't need to be linked in; they are used to eliminate possible conflicts with other driver configurations.

Creating a Resource Definition. NETGEN/ELSGEN can define several configuration options for each resource (just like it does for drivers). A single configuration option contains several configuration settings, each individual setting corresponding to a DIP switch, jumper setting, or some other physical characteristic of the hardware being defined.

By selecting "Edit Resource List" in the Custom level of NETGEN, or "Select Resource Set Options" in ELSGEN, you can define or redefine the component resources that make up a resource set. For each resource, you can change the elements of an existing configuration option, or you can create a new configuration option. After you select "Edit Resource List," NETGEN/ELSGEN produces a list of defined resources. You can edit an item from the list, delete items from the list, add new items to the list, or change the name of an item on the list.

To create a new resource, press Insert. A box for entering the resource name will appear. Type a name and press Enter. The new name will appear in the list of resources available for editing.

Each resource should have a separate configuration option for each possible way you can set the hardware's I/O addresses, shared memory addresses, interrupt lines (IRQ), or Direct Memory Address (DMA) lines. To define a configuration option for a piece of hardware, select that resource in the "Resources" window. The "Resource Configurations" window will appear, initially containing no information because you have yet to define any resource configurations.

Press Insert to bring up a window for naming the configuration you want to assign to the new resource. The *286 Installation* manual describes a useful convention for naming a resource's configuration options. Each configuration option name, according to the manual, should begin with a number and a colon. The option with the lowest number at the beginning of its name will be the default configuration. A configuration name beginning with "0:" will always be the default configuration setting for that resource. NETGEN/ELSGEN automatically choose the default configuration whenever possible, unless you manually select another configuration.

After naming the configuration option, you must define it. Highlight the name of the configuration option; then press Enter. In the resulting "Configuration Information" window, you can define the settings for I/O addresses, memory addresses, interrupt lines, and DMA lines. You can also specify whether the hardware works with the standard AT bus, the Micro Channel Architecture, or both. When all configuration option settings are correct, press Escape. NETGEN/ELSGEN will save the settings for you. Repeat the option-defining procedure for each possible combination of settings.

Creating a Resource Set. NETGEN/ELSGEN allows you to select only resource sets, not the resources themselves. Therefore, you must group each defined resource into a resource set. To do this, select "Edit Resource Sets." A list of defined resource sets will appear. Press Insert to add a new resource set to the list. Type a name for the resource set in the resulting box; then press Enter.

Now highlight the new resource set name and press Enter. A list of "Selected Resources" will appear, initially empty. Press Insert to obtain a list of all defined resources. The new resources you defined will appear in this list, along with NETGEN/ELSGEN's predefined resources. Select each resource, one by one, that you want to add to the resource set.

Whenever you make changes to resource or resource set definitions, you will see a "Save New Resource Set Definitions?" prompt when you exit NETGEN/ELSGEN. Answer "Yes" to this prompt to save your new definitions permanently.

Most NETGEN/ELSGEN users, fortunately, will never have to create or edit resources and resource sets. But, while NETGEN/ELSGEN's resource editing procedures are complicated and arcane, they ability they provide to edit resource configurations means that NetWare should work with any industry standard hardware—and even with some non-standard hardware—provided you define the resource configurations properly.

Adding, Changing, or Deleting Drivers. If you want to add, change, or remove network interface boards in your file server, see Chapter 27 of this book. To add, replace, or remove hard disks, see Chapter 28 of this book.

Tasks in the Installation Half

In NETGEN only (not ELSGEN), you can modify the hard disk partition tables from the "Custom Installation" menu accessed by choosing "Select Custom Installation Options" from the "Installation Options" menu. You should never modify any partitions unless you have a very good reason. Be sure you have a full system backup, both of data in the NetWare partition and of data in the other partition(s) as well. Changing a disk's partition table effectively wipes out all data in all the partitions. It also wipes out Hot Fix, mirroring, and everything else. After repartitioning the disk, you must initialize it again just as if it were a brand-new disk. See Novell's *286 Installation* and *286 Maintenance* manuals for details.

With SFT NetWare, you can unmirror and remirror drive pairs through NETGEN's "Modify Mirror Tables" option. This option is also found under the "Custom Installation" menu. You should do this in NETGEN only if you want the drives to stay permanently mirrored or unmirrored. NetWare has an UNMIRROR console command that allows you to undo a mirrored pair without bringing down the file server. The REMIRROR console command allows you to reestablish the mirrored pair. See Chapter 22 of this book, and Novell's *Console Reference* manual, for details.

If your file server has disk drives that support removable media, NETGEN has some options specifically for handling those types of drives. Since the volumes on such drives are not fixed, they are referred to as "removable volumes." See Novell's *286 Installation* and *286 Maintenance* manuals for details on how to install and maintain removable volumes. Removable volumes are not supported in ELS NetWare.

21 Using the NetWare Console Commands

Since the earliest versions of NetWare, Novell has offered a group of commands that can be executed only at the file server console. "Console" is Novell's term for the keyboard and monitor attached to the file server computer. These commands are thus referred to as console commands. They allow the supervisor to control the file server's resources (such as disks and printers), send messages to workstations, set the file server clock, monitor file server activity, and perform similar tasks.

This chapter explains the general-purpose console commands for sending messages, viewing file server information, and monitoring network activity. Subsequent chapters in this section of the book explain the console commands for maintaining hard disks, TTS, and VAPs. The console commands related to printing are explained in Chapter 16.

The FCONSOLE utility introduced with NetWare v2.1 is touted as a *virtual console* utility. In theory, a virtual console allows the network supervisor to execute the same commands from a workstation that he or she can execute from the file server console itself. In practice, FCONSOLE provides most, but not all, of the same capabilities as the console command set. FCONSOLE is a NetWare menu utility, so its interface is completely different from the file server console interface. Throughout this chapter, we will note what option in FCONSOLE, if any, corresponds to the console command we are discussing.

NETWARE'S CONSOLE COMMAND INTERFACE

The user interface at the file server console is peculiar to NetWare. It is a rather stark, unforgiving command-line interface, quite different from the DOS command-line interface that many supervisors are used to.

Instead of the familiar DOS prompt (usually F:> or something similar), the network console prompt is a colon (:). You must use the proper syntax in typing the console commands. If you type the command incorrectly, the console will respond with "??? UNKNOWN COMMAND ???." You'll then have to retype the full command—no F3 key shortcuts here. Since the file server runs NetWare, not DOS, you can't access TSRs or other tools that make life easier at the DOS command line. Even on a nondedicated file server, you must switch to the console mode before you can issue console commands. (Later in this chapter, we will explain commands for switching between console and DOS modes.)

NetWare security does not apply to the running of console commands. NetWare assumes that since you are at the file server console, you are authorized to service the network, and therefore allows you to run any console command. The danger here is that an unauthorized user who gains access to the file server console could also run these commands. If security is a concern in your network, keep the file server locked in a separate room to which only the network supervisor has the key. As an added level of console security, Novell offers a VAP that will lock the file server keyboard via a password. Only the person who set the password will be able to unlock the keyboard by entering the correct password.

To make typing console commands easier for the supervisor, NetWare allows you to abbreviate many of the keywords in the commands. However, there is no consistent pattern for when and how they are abbreviated. The safest way to learn is to type the words out in full until you get the command down pat. Then check the Novell *Console Reference* manual for ways to abbreviate the commands and leave out unnecessary words.

SENDING MESSAGES TO USERS FROM THE CONSOLE

One of the basic features of NetWare is the capability to send short messages around the LAN. This capability is most useful when you must quickly tell users to log out because you're going to bring down the file server for backups or other maintenance activities. You can also use this messaging capability for simple cable diagnostic purposes: for example, to broadcast a message to see which workstations on the network receive it. Those that don't are probably affected by some sort of cabling or communication channel problem. You can also use a broadcast message to warn users about problems or diagnostic activities that may affect them.

There are two commands you can use to send messages from the file server console itself: BROADCAST and SEND. Use the SEND command-line utility to send messages from any workstation.

The BROADCAST Console Command

The BROADCAST console command sends a message to every workstation that is either logged in or logically attached to the file server. Remember, as long as the NetWare shell is loaded at a workstation, that workstation has a logical attachment or connection with the file server.

The message can be up to 60 characters long and needn't be enclosed in quotation marks. For example, you could inform users to log out by typing the following command:

```
BROADCAST Please log out. File server going down in 2 minutes.
```

Workstations will receive this message on the twenty-fifth line of their monitors so that it doesn't block anything currently on their screens. The instruction "CTRL-ENTER t⌐ clear" is added at the end to tell users how to get rid of the message after they've read it.

If a user has entered the CASTOFF command at a workstation, that workstation will still receive messages you send via the BROADCAST console command. However, users can enter CASTOFF ALL to block even messages from the file server console.

The FCONSOLE counterpart to BROADCAST is found under the "Broadcast Console Message" option in the main menu.

The SEND Console Command

This command works the same from the console as it does from a workstation, except that you must know the users' station or connection numbers. You can't SEND a message from the console to a specific user name or even a group.

You can type the USERLIST command from your workstation to see all currently attached users and their connection numbers. However, unless your file server console is right next to your workstation, it's easier to use the SEND command from your workstation.

If you're simply sending a follow-up message from the console to those users who haven't yet logged out, you can use the MONITOR console command to check which station numbers are still active. (We will explain MONITOR later in this chapter.)

The format for SEND is slightly different from that for BROADCAST. With SEND, the message must be enclosed in quotation marks and cannot exceed forty characters in length. For example, to send a message to the users at workstations 2, 5, and 6 who haven't yet logged out, type:

```
SEND "Last chance to log out, you guys!" TO 2,5,6
```

If you leave off the list of station numbers, SEND will assume that you want the message to go to all currently attached workstations.

FCONSOLE has a "Broadcast Console Message" option, accessed from the "Connection Information" submenu. You can use this option to send messages to selected users rather than all users.

The CLEAR MESSAGE Console Command

Use the CLEAR MESSAGE command to clear any messages from the line just below the MONITOR display when it is active (the MONITOR display is explained later in this chapter). The rest of the console screen display will remain as it was.

VIEWING FILE SERVER INFORMATION
FROM THE CONSOLE

Several console commands let you view configuration information about the file server. These include NAME, VER, CONFIG, and TIME.

The NAME Console Command

Normally, the file server console display does not identify the file server. Even when you type MONITOR, the file server name does not appear. Therefore, Novell provided the NAME console command to display the file server name on the screen. NAME could prove useful if you have a bank of file server consoles all together on a rack and you can't remember which keyboard and monitor go with which file server.

FCONSOLE, like most NetWare menu utilities, displays the file server name in the header at the top of the screen. There is no direct FCONSOLE counterpart to the NAME console command.

The VER Console Command

To see which version of NetWare is running on the file server, type VER at the file server console. The console screen will display the full NetWare version, including revision and date of release. For example:

```
SFT NetWare 286 TTS V2.15 Rev. C  08/22/89
```

This undocumented console command is useful when you are talking with service technicians or support personnel, and they ask you for the full version of NetWare the file server is running.

To view the NetWare version in FCONSOLE, select "Version Information" from the main menu.

The CONFIG Console Command

CONFIG lists the current number of file service processes available on the file server, along with information about the network interface boards installed in the file server.

The "Number of Service Processes" displayed by CONFIG is the same as the number of "Number Of File Service Processes" shown in FCONSOLE's "File Server Statistics Summary" window. A file service process (FSP) is a task running in the file server that handles NetWare Core Protocol (NCP) requests from workstations. NCP requests are typically disk read and write request packets. A file service process is the only type of process that can handle these packets, but the server usually has more than one FSP available. Three to seven FSPs is considered good (ten is the maximum). Two is adequate, but any less than two could hurt network performance. (For a full discussion on file service processes, see Chapter 34.)

For each network interface board in the server, CONFIG also displays the network and node address, the "Hardware Type" (a character string that actually identifies the LAN driver linked in for that board), and the "Hardware Settings." CONFIG reads these settings from the LAN driver linked in with the OS, so they do not necessarily reflect the actual settings on the board. However, if your file server is currently up and running, you can assume that the software settings match the hardware. (Otherwise, the network board would not function properly.)

This information is useful when you are installing additional file servers or bridges (routers) and you want to make sure you're not duplicating the network addresses. It's also helpful when you are adding a board to an existing file server or trying to diagnose a LAN board problem. Keep in mind that sometimes NetWare can continue to function even though one or more of the specified network boards are not installed or are dead. The file server does read node addresses from the boards themselves. If the file sever cannot read the node address, it can display anything from zeros to a string of garbage (which sort of looks like a unique serial address for some boards, so be sure to keep a record of your network board configurations). An incorrect node address reported by CONFIG could mean one of three things: either no board is installed, the board is installed but it is not seated or configured correctly, or the board is dead and needs to be replaced.

You can see the same information about each network interface board in the file server from FCONSOLE's "LAN Driver Information" option.

The TIME Console Command

Use the TIME command at the console to check the date and time set on the file server's internal clock. If you want to change the date or time, use the SET TIME command described later in this chapter. The date and time are displayed in the header when you run FCONSOLE.

MONITORING FILE SERVER ACTIVITY

You can use the MONITOR and TRACK ON console commands to monitor certain activities on your file server. These two commands are also helpful when you are trying to diagnose file server problems.

The MONITOR Console Command

MONITOR is by far the most useful console command for diagnostic purposes. This command produces a display showing activity for workstations currently logged into the file server.

File Server Activity. The top of MONITOR's display screen shows the version of NetWare running on the file server, the current file server utilization, and the current number of disk I/Os pending.

The file server utilization is shown as a percentage. This percentage, updated once a second, indicates how much of the CPU's time is spent handling network requests. In actuality, NetWare tracks how much of the time the CPU sits idle and subtracts that percentage from 100 to get the utilization percentage. A consistently high percentage (over 95 percent) indicates that your server's CPU has just about all the work it can handle. The "Current Server Utilization" shown in FCONSOLE's "File Server Statistics Summary" screen shows the same percentage.

The number of disk I/Os pending reflects how many cache buffers in file server memory contain data waiting to be written to disk. This is the same as the number of "Dirty Cache Buffers" in FCONSOLE. Data held in cache buffers is written to the network disk when the buffers are full, or every three seconds, whichever comes first. A consistently high number here may indicate a bottleneck somewhere in the disk channel. (See Chapter 25 for more details.)

Station Activity. The rest of the MONITOR display is divided into six boxes. Each box represents a workstation or some other entity claiming a file server connection. The station (or connection) number is shown in the upper left corner of each box, followed by the most recent request that connection made to the file server. You can watch requests come and go for each workstation. A box with no information displayed indicates an inactive connection.

Possible connection requests as displayed by MONITOR are:

Alloc Resource	Get File Size	Release File
Begin Trans	Lock File	Release File Set
Clear File	Lock Phy Rec Set	Release Record
Clear File Set	Lock Record	Rename File
Clear Record Set	Log Out	Search Next
Close File	Log Pers File	Semaphore
Clr Phy Rec	Log Phy Rec	Set File Atts
Clr Phy Rec Set	Log Record	Start Search
Copy File	Open File	Sys Log
Create File	Pass File	Unlock Record
Dir Search	Read File	Win Format
End of Job	Rel Phy Rec	Win Read
End Trans	Rel Phy Rec Set	Win Write
Erase File	Rel Record Set	Write File
Floppy Config	Rel Resource	

Most of these will make little sense to you unless you understand NetWare function calls. But some are fairly obvious; for example, Dir Search is displayed when a workstation is running the DOS DIR command or some other command that needs to search a network directory. Read File and Write File are basic disk read and write requests.

End of Job indicates that the workstation has completed its work session and all files have been released. If no other requests appear for that workstation, you can assume after a while that the user is not currently running any applications or using any files. You can probably clear that connection if you need to without the workstation losing any data.

In SFT NetWare with TTS, when a workstation is working on a file flagged "Transactional," the message "Begin Trans" appears next to the station number. For the length of time it takes to complete the transaction (usually less than a second), the message "TRANSACTION" will appear on the line directly underneath. If the workstation is waiting for a file or record to be freed for use, the message "WAITING" will appear instead.

The files that the workstation currently has open are listed in the "File" column, along with the DOS task number and file status under the Status column. All files opened by the same application will usually have the same DOS task number assigned. A "P" in the first column after the task number indicates that other workstations are denied read access to that file while it is open. An "R" in the second column indicates that the workstation has the file open only to read it. A "P" in the third column means other workstations are denied write access to the file. A "W" in the fourth column means the workstation has the file open to write to it. If the file is locked, "Lock" will appear in the Status column.

As an example of what all these codes mean, look at the following sample for a workstation running WordPerfect:

```
File                              Stat
─────────────                     ──────
F:PREFACE.DOC                     3 PRPW
F:EAL}.BV2                        3 PRPW
F:EAL}.TV2                        3 PRPW
F:EAL}.BV1                        3 PRPW
Y:WP.EXE                          3 RP
```

Notice that since all the files listed are being used by WordPerfect, they all have the same DOS task number. The first file is the document the user is currently working on. It is open for both reads and writes, and other workstations will not be able to read from or write to the file while this workstation has it open. The next three files are the WordPerfect temporary files. The last file listed is the WordPerfect executable file (WP.EXE) which is not held open exclusively for this station to read and is not open for a write.

FCONSOLE's connection information is much easier to understand because it doesn't use cryptic one-character codes like MONITOR does. FCONSOLE's "Connection Information" option will also show you a good deal more about what a connection is up to and what files it has open. Supervisors can view a connection's logical and physical record locks, open files and their status, semaphore usage, task information, and total disk I/O and packet requests. We recommend that you use FCONSOLE rather than trying to make sense of the MONITOR display.

One last remark about MONITOR: Don't leave the display running if you don't need it. While MONITOR is running, NetWare has the additional overhead of refreshing its display. While the effect of this overhead on performance is probably not noticeable, you should relieve the OS of this unnecessary duty so it can handle more important tasks. Type **OFF** at the colon prompt to turn off the MONITOR display.

The TRACK ON Console Command

This console command is not documented in Novell's *Console Reference,* but it is often useful for diagnosing file server-to-workstation communications. TRACK ON will display information about broadcast packets that the file server receives and sends.

From the colon prompt, type TRACK ON. You will soon see information similar to this:

```
IN   [A:00001B032BE2]    000CAB1E    1/ 2
IN   [A:00001B032BE2]    LPG          1     LPGPRINT      2
OUT  [A:FFFFFFFFFFFF]    SLASHER      1
```

Interpreting the TRACK ON Display. Packets that the server receives are pre-ceded by "IN," while packets the server sends are preceded by "OUT." The address enclos-ed within brackets indicates the physical node address from which the packet is sent or from which it was received; the letter preceding the address indicates whether that node address is LAN A, B, C, or D. Eight-digit numbers represent network addresses being exchanged by the routing mechanism. One-digit numbers represent the number of "hops" between your file server and other servers. A hop is counted for every router the packet must pass through to get from one network address to another. Routers count themselves as one hop, so one is the lowest number of hops you will see. If more than one possible route exists between two networks, both the minimum and the maximum number of hops are displayed, as in the "1/2" designation in the first line of the sample TRACK ON output.

The first few packets in the sample output represent those sent and received by the internet routing function within the OS. The router receives Routing Informa-tion packets containing the network addresses other routers know about and how many hops away they are. Once a minute, the router sends Server Information packets about itself and other file servers out across the internet. Server Information broadcasts are identified by the destination address of [A:FFFFFFFFFFFF], which means the packet is being sent to all nodes on the network serviced by the LAN A network interface board.

Diagnosing Network Problems with TRACK ON. You can use TRACK ON to help you diagnose situations when workstations are unable to establish a file server connection. When a workstation loads the NetWare shell (IPX.COM, followed by NETx.COM), the following packet exchange takes place between the workstation and a file server:

```
IN   [A:00001B0580B6]    Get Nearest Server
OUT  [A:00001B0580B6]    Give Nearest Server SLASHER
```

NETx.COM broadcasts a "Get Nearest Server" packet over the network, looking for the nearest server of a specific type. Because this is a broadcast packet, all servers of the desired type respond with a "Give Nearest Server" reply packet. The first response that the shell receives (in this case, from server SLASHER) is the one it attaches to for the purpose of logging in. The shell runs LOGIN.EXE from the

SYS:LOGIN directory of that file server. A number of factors can influence which server will respond first; you can never predict exactly which file server a workstation will initially attach to. Users should specify a particular file server when they issue the LOGIN command (as in LOGIN SLASHER/JASON instead of just LOGIN) to be sure they log in to the correct server.

To diagnose a problem workstation, type **TRACK ON** at the file server and reboot the workstation. If you don't see a "Get Nearest Server" packet displayed on the console screen, the workstation could have a problem with cabling, network connectors, its network interface board, or its shell. If the problem is isolated to a single workstation, you can reasonably assume that the network board in the file server is working fine.

Sometimes you will see a string of "Get Nearest Server" and "Give Nearest Server" packets when a workstation tries to boot up. This indicates that the workstation shell is receiving no information back from the file server and is continually resending its initial broadcast. Again, if this problem is an isolated instance, check the cabling, network connectors, and the workstation's network interface board. Conflicting interrupt settings in the workstation's hardware can also cause this problem.

In some instances, you may see one or two "Get/Give" packets and then the workstation shell will hang. This situation could indicate that the shell has received a "Give Nearest Server" reply from the file server, but is having trouble routing to that file server. The most common reason for this problem is that two servers or bridges on the same physical cabling system are giving conflicting network addresses for that physical cabling system. To test for this problem, have another workstation try to access that particular server. If the other workstation has trouble accessing that file server, check the bridge board's configurations and connections. Otherwise, check the problem workstation's cabling or network board.

When several workstations cannot boot up, check the cabling system they have in common. If other areas of the network are working, focus on the network connectors or cabling leading directly into or out of the problem area. When none of the workstations on your network is able to boot up and you see no "Get Nearest Server" or "Give Nearest Server" packets, check the common cabling to the file server and the network interface board in the server. If this situation occurs and you do see the "Get/Give" packets, it means that either the cabling has somehow become a "one-way" signal processor, or the network board in the file server is not functioning properly.

Type **TRACK OFF** when you are finished monitoring packet transmissions. The console screen will stop its tracking feature. To clear the tracking information from the screen, type **OFF** at the colon prompt.

Other Routing-Related Console Commands

The DISPLAY NETWORKS, DISPLAY SERVERS, and RESET ROUTER console commands help you in working with internetwork routing problems.

The DISPLAY NETWORKS Command. To view all the network addresses currently contained in the file server's routing information table, type **DISPLAY NETWORKS** at the console. The console screen will display information similar to this:

```
Known networks:
   000001AB   1/ 2      00000BAD   1/ 2      00001AB1   1/ 2
   000CAB1E   1/ 2      BASEBA11   0/ 1
```

The first number following each network address represents the number of other networks (cabling systems) that a packet must cross to reach that network. The second number represents the estimated time, in "ticks," that it takes for a packet to reach that network. (A tick is approximately 1/18 of a second.)

Note that the display above lists network address "BASEBA11" as being zero networks away. "BASEBA11" is the network address assigned to the network interface board in the current file server. If the server had more than one network board installed, more than one network address would be listed as zero networks away.

You can use the DISPLAY NETWORKS command to obtain a list of network addresses currently in use on the internet. This list is helpful when you are adding a new network to the internet and you need to assign a non-conflicting network address for the new cabling system.

The DISPLAY SERVERS Command. To view a list of the server names stored in the file server's server information table, type DISPLAY SERVERS at the file server console. The console screen will display information similar to this:

```
Known servers:
   LABMAN      1    LPG        1    SLASHER     0
   HISTORY     1    BACKUP     2    LPGPRINT    1
```

The servers displayed include file servers, print servers, backup servers, and any other type of server supported by NetWare 286. The number following each server name represents the number of networks (cabling systems) that a packet must cross to reach that server.Note that the display lists the server from which you typed the DISPLAY SERVERS command as being zero networks away.

You can use the DISPLAY SERVERS command to obtain a list of server names currently in use on the internet. This list is helpful when you are adding a new server on the internet and you need to assign a non-conflicting name for the new server.

The RESET ROUTER Command. Normally, NetWare's adaptive routing mechanism updates its routing information and server information tables every two minutes. This periodic refreshing of the tables handles situations when other servers or routers on the internetwork go down. If a bridge or server goes down and you want to avoid losing packets, or if the routing tables in the file server have become corrupted, type **RESET ROUTER** at the console. This command causes the file server to send routing and server information requests immediately so it can rebuild its tables accurately.

The console will display a "Router has been reset" message to indicate that the routing tables are being updated.

FILE SERVER CONTROL FUNCTIONS

The final console commands we'll look at in this chapter let you actually perform some type of action or make some kind of change on the file server. These include DOS, CONSOLE, SET TIME, ENABLE LOGIN, DISABLE LOGIN, CLEAR CONNECTION, and DOWN.

Switching Between Console and DOS Modes

On a nondedicated file server, a user can be running applications on the file server machine itself when it is in DOS mode. When booted, a nondedicated file server comes up in console mode, as evidenced by the colon prompt (:). To switch the machine to local DOS mode so it can be used as a workstation (while the file server still services the network in the background), type DOS at the colon prompt. The prompt will now look like a normal DOS prompt.

To switch the nondedicated file server back to the console mode to enter console commands, you must have the file CONSOLE.EXE someplace where DOS can find it (either in the A drive or in a directory included in the DOS PATH command). Type A:CONSOLE or just CONSOLE (depending on where CONSOLE.EXE is) to switch the file server back into console mode. The colon prompt will reappear.

Setting the File Server Clock

The SET TIME console command allows you to reset the date and time kept by the file server's internal clock. The format is as follows:

```
SET TIME MM/DD/YY  HH:MM:SS
```

NetWare will also accept the date in spelled-out format, as in September 18, 1990. If you leave off the year, the current year is assumed. NetWare accepts time in either standard 12-hour or 24-hour military format. You can add AM or PM to the 12-hour format for clarity. You can also leave off the seconds if you want.

In FCONSOLE, you can reset the date and time through the "Status" option.

Enabling and Disabling Logins

Supervisors often need to prevent users from logging in to the file server during some types of routine maintenance (backing up, loading new software, and so on). You can type **DISABLE LOGIN** from the console to keep users from logging in to the server. Users already logged in will not be affected; however, if you need them to log out, send them a "Log out now" message via the BROADCAST or SEND command. Once they log out, they cannot log back in until you re-enable logins. Users trying to log in will get an error message stating that "The Supervisor has disabled the login function on server *ServerName*."

To make logins possible again, type **ENABLE LOGIN** at the console. If you shut the file server down after using the DISABLE LOGIN command, logins will be automatically re-enabled when you reboot the server.

In FCONSOLE, you can disable and enable logins through the "Status" option.

Clearing a Station's Connection

The CLEAR STATION command can potentially cause a workstation to lose data, so use it with caution. It is intended to be used only after a workstation has already crashed in the middle of an application, leaving files open and drive mappings established on the server.

User CLEAR STATION to remove all file server resources allocated to a particular workstation and completely sever the workstation's logical connection. In addition to clearing that workstation's connection number in the file server's connection tables. NetWare will close all files the workstation had open and clear out any drive mappings that workstation had set up.

The counterpart to this command in FCONSOLE is the "Clear Connection" option in the "Connection Information" submenu. Only the network supervisor can clear a connection in FCONSOLE; a console operator cannot.

Bringing the File Server Down

To ensure the integrity of the data on your file server, always issue the DOWN command to shut down the file server prior to turning it off to perform repairs or maintenance on it. Before you issue the DOWN command, make sure all users have saved their files and logged out. Send a BROADCAST message and use MONITOR to see that all users are indeed logged out before you continue.

Note that all users logged in from remore workstations or through a communications server wil not receive BROADCAST messages. Consider the effect on these remote users before you bring the server down. If you bring the server down before a user logs out, that user will receive a broadcast message saying "SERVER *ServerName* is down (CTRL-ENTER to clear)." When the user pressers Ctrl-Enter, the logical connection will be gone and any files that user still had open on the server may be corrupted or contain only partial updates.

Before it shuts the file server down, the DOWN command writes all data held in cache buffers to disk, closes all open files, and updates the directory entry tables and FATs on the network disks.

Supervisors (and only supervisors) can accomplish the same task by using the "Down File Server" option in FCONSOLE's main menu. A console operator cannot bring the server down in FCONSOLE.

22 Maintaining Network Disks from the Console

This chapter explains the NetWare console commands used for maintaining network hard disks. These include DISK, MOUNT, DISMOUNT, UNMIRROR, and REMIRROR. It also lists error messages associated with mounting and dismounting removable drives, and unmirroring and remirroring from the console. General-purpose console commands are explained in the preceding chapter. Console commands relating to TTS and VAPs are explained in the following chapter, and the console commands related to printing are explained in Chapter 16.

Most of the hard disk-related console commands covered in this chapter have no directly parallel option in FCONSOLE. If there is an easier way to perform a task than by using the console commands, we will indicate what it is.

THE DISK CONSOLE COMMAND

The DISK console command displays slightly different information, depending on whether or not you are running SFT NetWare. Read the explanation appropriate to your version of NetWare.

Checking Hot Fix and Mirroring with DISK (SFT NetWare)

The DISK console command displays the status of each network disk. With SFT NetWare, you can see which drives are mirrored, which drives are set up for Hot Fix, and which drives are no longer functioning properly. You can also see the number of disk I/O errors on the disk, how many blocks in the Hot Fix Redirection Area are used, and how many are still available.

To view this information, type DISK at the colon prompt on the file server console. The disk information will be displayed in the following format (although the information for disk 00 and disk 01 will be all on one line, disk 02 and 03 on the next line, and so on):

```
              PHYSICAL DISKS STATUS AND STATISTICS

          cha  con  drv     stat    IO Err    Free   Used

     00    1    0    0      M-03    00000     0672   0008
     01    1    0    1      OK      00000     0690   0005
     02    2    1    0      D-01    00004     0623   0006
     03    2    1    1      M-00    00003     0672   0008
     04    2    2    0      NO HOT  00039     0621   0148
```

The first column shows the number NetWare uses to identify the physical disk drive. This is the number that appears in error messages involving hard disks. For example, the error message "Hot Fix turned off on drive 04 (volume VOL2)" refers to the disk listed as number 04 in the DISK display. The "cha," "con," and "drv" columns identify the disk's channel number, controller number, and drive number.

The "stat" column indicates the current status of the disk. Possible status messages are listed below:

M-*nn*   The drive is mirrored (or duplexed) with the disk number indicated and the mirroring feature is functioning normally.

D-*nn*   The drive was mirrored (or duplexed) with the indicated disk, but is now "dead" or has ceased to function. You must either repair or replace the disk and remirror the pair as soon as possible to restore the full fault tolerance of the file server.

OK   Hot Fix is functioning properly on the disk. If the drive was part of a mirrored or duplexed pair whose partner is listed as dead, this disk is still operating normally, but as a single drive. You should re-establish the mirrored pair as quickly as possible.

NO HOT   Hot Fix was previously set up on the disk, but has been shut off due to repeated failures. NetWare won't be able to use the disk until you have reinstated Hot Fix on the drive by running NETGEN. You may have to repair the disk first if the failures are serious.

OFF   The drive is no longer functional. Repair or replace it as quickly as possible and reinstall it with Hot Fix.

The "IO Err" column counts the times a block of data being written to the disk had to be redirected by Hot Fix. "Free" tells how many blocks are left in the Hot Fix Redirection Area, while "Used" shows how many have been used up. The total of the "Free" and "Used" columns equals the number of blocks originally set aside for the Hot Fix area on the disk. Note that all disks will show a minimum of five or six blocks used by Hot Fix. These blocks are not bad blocks; they contain control tables used to manage the Hot Fix area, as well as other OS information.

Ignore the rows of zeroes under the DISK display; these extra rows were included for debugging purposes and were never taken out of the final code. You can clear the DISK display by typing **OFF** at the colon prompt.

The same information about Hot Fix is more accessible through FCONSOLE, but for only one disk at a time. Choose "Statistics" from FCONSOLE's main menu, then choose "Disk Statistics" and select the disk whose Hot Fix information you want to see. The "IO Error Count" corresponds to DISK's "IO Err" column. "Hot Fix Remaining" shows how many blocks are still available in the Redirection Area. FCONSOLE doesn't show the number of blocks currently used by Hot Fix, but you can obtain that figure by subtracting the "Hot Fix Remaining" number from the "Hot Fix Table Size" number shown. The status of Hot Fix will be shown as either "Enabled" or "Disabled," corresponding to "OK" and "NO HOT" in the DISK display.

To check on the status of mirrored and duplexed pairs in FCONSOLE, you must use the "Disk Mapping Information" option under "Statistics." If one of the mirrored drives in a pair has failed, the message "Dead" will be displayed next to the disk number.

Checking Hot Fix Status with DISK (Non-SFT)

With Advanced NetWare or ELS NetWare, the DISK console command displays the Hot Fix status of each network disk. You can see which drives are set up for Hot Fix and which drives are no longer functioning properly. You also see the number of disk I/O errors on the disk, how many blocks in the Hot Fix Redirection Area are used, and how many are still available.

To view this information, type DISK at the colon prompt on the file server console. The disk information will be displayed in the following format (although the information for disk 00 and disk 01 will be all on one line, disk 02 and 03 on the next line, and so on):

```
           PHYSICAL DISKS STATUS AND STATISTICS

           cha   con   drv   stat    IO Err    Free    Used

      00    1     0     0    OK      00000     0672    0008
      01    1     0     1    OK      00000     0690    0005
      02    2     1     0    NO HOT  00004     0623    0006
      03    2     1     1    OK      00003     0672    0008
```

The first column shows the number NetWare uses to identify the physical disk drive. This is the number that appears in error messages involving hard disks. For example, the error message "Hot Fix turned off on drive 02 (volume VOL2)" refers to the disk listed as number 02 in the DISK display. The "cha," "con," and "drv" columns identify the disk's channel number, controller number, and drive number.

The "stat" column indicates the current status of the disk. Possible status messages are listed below:

OK   Hot Fix is functioning properly on the disk.

NO HOT Hot Fix was previously set up on the disk, but has been shut off due to repeated failures. NetWare won't be able to use the disk until you have reinstated Hot Fix on the drive by running NETGEN/ELSGEN. You may have to repair the disk first if the failures are serious.

OFF   The drive is no longer functional. Repair or replace it as quickly as possible and reinstall it with Hot Fix.

The "IO Err" column displays how many times a block of data being written to the disk had to be redirected by Hot Fix. "Free" tells how many blocks are left in the Hot Fix Redirection Area, while "Used" shows how many have been used up. The total of the "Free" and "Used" columns equals the number of blocks originally set aside for the Hot Fix area on the disk. Note that all disks will show a minimum of five or six block used by Hot Fix. These blocks are not bad blocks; they contain control tables used to manage the Hot Fix area, as well as other OS information.

Ignore the rows of zeroes under the DISK display; these extra rows were included for debugging purposes and were never taken out of the final code. You can clear the DISK display by typing OFF at the colon prompt.

The same information about Hot Fix is more accessible through FCONSOLE, but for only one disk at a time. Choose "Statistics" from FCONSOLE's main menu, then choose "Disk Statistics" and select the disk whose Hot Fix information you want to see. The "IO Error Count" corresponds to DISK's "IO Err" column. "Hot Fix Remaining" shows how many blocks are still available in the Redirection Area. FCONSOLE doesn't show the number of blocks currently used by Hot Fix, but you can obtain this figure by subtracting the "Hot Fix Remaining" number from the "Hot Fix Table Size" number shown. The status of Hot Fix will be shown as either "Enabled" or "Disabled," corresponding to "OK" and "NO HOT" in the DISK display.

Viewing File Server Volumes with DISK

This variation of the DISK command works with any level of NetWare (SFT, Advanced, or ELS). As a quick check to see which volumes are on which physical disk, type **DISK *** at the console. The volume names will be displayed in the following format (the "Mir Drv" column appears only with SFT NetWare):

```
                        FILE SERVER VOLUMES

Volume Name    Phy Drv    Mir Drv    Volume Name    Phy Drv   Mir Drv
SYS            00           01        VOL1           02
VOL2           03                     VOL3           03
```

In this example, volume SYS is on a mirrored drive (physical drives 00 and 01). VOL2 and VOL3 are on the same physical disk: disk number 03. You can clear the DISK display by typing **OFF** at the colon prompt.

This is the quickest way to obtain this information about your volumes. You can find it in FCONSOLE, but only in a roundabout way. You would have to select FCONSOLE's "Volume Information" option and choose each volume individually, noting the Primary Disk Number and Mirror Disk Number listed for each one.

Viewing Information About a Specific Volume with DISK

This variation of the DISK command works with any level of NetWare (SFT, Advanced, or ELS). To see information about one of the volumes on your file server, type the DISK command as follows:

```
DISK VolumeName
```

The following information will be displayed about the volume you specify:

```
Information For Volume SYS

Physical drive number      : 00
Physical drive type        : IBM PC AT hard disk or equivalent
IO errors on this drive    :    0
Redirection blocks available:  672
Redirection blocks used    :    6

Mirror physical drive number: no mirror drive

Other volumes sharing these physical drive(s):
none
```

If you are running SFT NetWare and the volume is on a mirrored drive, the same information will be displayed for the other physical drive. You can clear the DISK display by typing **OFF** at the colon prompt.

FCONSOLE doesn't have a single option that corresponds to this variation of the DISK command. But you can see the Hot Fix information for an entire disk by choosing the "Statistics" option in FCONSOLE's main menu, then choosing "Disk Statistics" and selecting the disk whose Hot Fix information you want to see.

MOUNTING AND DISMOUNTING REMOVABLE VOLUMES

SFT and Advanced NetWare 286 support disk subsystems with removable media; ELS NetWare does not. These types of storage media most often take the form of removable hard disks, or (in extremely archaic systems) eight-inch floppy diskettes or diskette "packs." NetWare refers to these as *removable volumes.*

If you have a disk subsystem or disk drive that features removable media, those drives should show a status of "Removable" when you run NETGEN. (NETGEN usually displays the status of drives whenever it lists them by channel, controller, and disk number.) The volume initialization procedure for removable drives is slightly different in NETGEN. See Novell's *286 Installation* manual for details.

After the file server is up and running, you must use the MOUNT console command when you insert a removable volume to bring that volume into service. When you want to remove it, you must use the DISMOUNT console command. These commands have no parallel in FCONSOLE.

Using the MOUNT Console Command

To add a removable volume to the file server, insert the medium that contains that volume and type **MOUNT** at the console. If you are mounting a diskette pack (each diskette in the pack usually contains one volume), type **MOUNT PACK** at the console. This will mount all volumes in the diskette pack at once. If you know the volume number of the removable volume, you can optionally add it to the MOUNT command (for example, **MOUNT 4** would mount removable volume number 04).

The NetWare OS checks the newly inserted medium to see if it has been properly configured and contains a valid volume name (or volume names). If the mount is successful, you will see a message indicating which volumes are now in service on the file server. Users can begin to use the data on those volumes.

If the volume mount is not successful, you will get one of the following error messages:

Error Reading Configuration Info from Removable Disk.

Explanation. The OS cannot read the Disk Configuration tables from track 0 of the removable media.

Severity. Not fatal, but the OS will abort the mounting of the removable volume.

Possible Causes. (1) The removable medium has not been formatted for NetWare. (2) The removable media was not configured properly in NETGEN. (3) The disk-related hardware is not functioning properly. (4) A bad spot in track 0 of the removable disk is resulting in a disk error.

Possible Solutions. Run NETGEN to check the installation and configuration of the removable drive. If the drive was correctly formatted and configured, it should be listed with the status "Removable" in the list of drives NETGEN produces.

If the drive has not been formatted properly for NetWare, or if a disk error has occurred, use COMPSURF to reformat the disk. Then reinitialize the removable volume in the "NetWare Installation" part of NETGEN. Once the volume is mounted successfully, you will need to restore its files from a backup.

ERROR: VOLUME ALREADY MOUNTED.
ERROR: VOLUME *VolumeName* ALREADY MOUNTED.

Explanation. The NetWare OS detected that one of the volumes on the removable disk is already in service on the file server.

Severity. These are only warning messages. The existing volume remains mounted, and the new volume mount is aborted.

Possible Causes. (1) You are trying to mount a removable volume with the same name as a volume already mounted on the system. (2) The disk subsystems are interconnected between file servers, and a volume on one disk subsystem has the same name as a volume on another subsystem.

Possible Solutions. Check the volume names currently in use on the file server (use the **DISK** * console command). Make sure every volume that can possibly be mounted on the file server has a unique volume name. Run NETGEN, if necessary, to change the name of a volume.

Illegal Drive Number Specified

Explanation. You specified with the MOUNT command a volume number that is not defined on the file server, or the number corresponds to a nonremovable volume in the server's Volume Information tables.

Severity. This is a warning message only. The operation of the file server will not be affected.

Possible Causes. You accidentally typed the wrong volume number.

Possible Solutions. Use MOUNT only to mount removable volumes that are defined as such with NETGEN. You can check volume numbers and removable status using FCONSOLE's "Volume Information" option (accessed under "Statistics" in the main menu).

!!! MOUNT ERROR — NO FREE DYNAMIC MEMORY !!!

Explanation. When the file server mounts a removable disk, it creates a buffer in memory to complete the process. The file server did not have enough memory to create this buffer.

Severity. Not fatal, but the removable volume will not be mounted.

Possible Causes. (1) The file server is short on memory in Dynamic Memory Pools 1, 2, or 3. (2) A failure in high memory is causing the file server to use less memory than is actually installed.

Possible Solutions. You cannot increase dynamic memory by adding more memory to the file server. You must decrease the demands made on dynamic memory by having users log out while you mount the volume. (See Chapter 34 for other ways to manipulate dynamic memory.) If you suspect high memory problems, run a diagnostics test on the file server memory. Replace any faulty memory components.

Unknown Removable Type

Explanation. The version of NetWare on your file server does not recognize this type of drive.

Severity. Not fatal, but the OS will abort the mounting of the removable volume.

Possible Solutions. Use only removable drives that have been recommended by Novell for use with your version of NetWare.

Using the DISMOUNT Console Command

Use the DISMOUNT command at the console to change or remove a removable volume that is currently mounted on the file server. You must use DISMOUNT to release the volume before you physically remove the removable media from the file server. You must also DISMOUNT an old removable volume before you insert a new removable volume into the same removable drive.

To dismount a removable volume, first make sure that no users are still working on that volume. Never dismount a removable volume while it is being physically accessed by the disk drive; you could severely damage the drive. When you are ready to dismount the volume, type **DISMOUNT** at the colon prompt. To dismount all volumes in a diskette pack, type **DISMOUNT PACK**. You can optionally add the volume number of the volume you want to remove (as in **DISMOUNT 6**). The DISMOUNT command closes all open files on the volume and updates all directories on the removable media.

You may receive the following error messages when you try to dismount a removable volume:

Drive already dismounted.

Explanation. The removable volume you tried to DISMOUNT has already been dismounted.

Severity. This is a warning message only. The operation of the file server will not be affected.

Possible Causes. Either you forgot that you already dismounted the volume, or you specified the wrong removable volume number in the DISMOUNT command.

Possible Solutions. Check the volume numbers and removable status in FCONSOLE's "Volume Information" option (accessed under "Statistics" in the main menu). If you were using DISMOUNT prior to inserting a new removable volume in the drive, go ahead and insert the new medium and type **MOUNT** to mount the new volume.

Illegal Removable Disk Specification.

Explanation. You specified an invalid volume number in the DISMOUNT command, or a number that is assigned to a nonremovable volume on the file server.

Severity. This is a warning message only. The operation of the file server will not be affected.

Possible Causes. You accidentally typed the wrong number.

Possible Solutions. Use DISMOUNT only to dismount volumes designated as removable. Check the volume numbers and removable status in FCONSOLE's "Volume Information" option (accessed under "Statistics" in the main menu).

Removable Drive *nn* locked for use by station *ss*.

Explanation. The station with connection number ss is still using the removable volume number specified.

Severity. This is a warning message only. The station will be able to continue using the volume.

Possible Solutions. Have the user at station ss log out from the file server. (Type **USERLIST** at any workstation to find out which user is using connection number ss.) Then reissue the DISMOUNT command.

VOLUME *VolumeName* MOUNTED. DISMOUNT VOLUME BEFORE REMOVING!

Explanation. You are trying to remove a mounted removable volume from the file server without first dismounting the volume.

Severity. Not fatal.

Possible Solutions. Use DISMOUNT at the file server console before removing the volume.

*** WARNING *** ACTIVE FILES OPEN ON VOLUME. DISMOUNT?

Explanation. Workstations still have files open on the removable volume you are trying to dismount.

Severity. Not fatal. Depending on how you respond to the prompt, however, data could be lost.

Possible Solutions. The safest way is to answer "No" to the "DISMOUNT?" prompt by typing "**N**." Have users close all the files they have open on the removable volume. Then reissue the DISMOUNT command. If a workstation is hung with files left open, use the CLEAR STATION console command to close its files.

If you answer "Yes" to the prompt by typing "**Y**," NetWare will close all files that any workstations have open on the volume and then proceed with the dismount. If a user was in the middle of processing a transaction or updating a file, that file might be updated with incorrect data.

UNMIRRORING AND REMIRRORING DRIVES FROM THE CONSOLE

(*This section applies to SFT NetWare only.*) You can use the UNMIRROR and REMIRROR console commands to work with mirrored or duplexed drives while the file server is up and running. Because mirroring is an important part of SFT NetWare's fault tolerance, you should unmirror drives only when one of the disks in the pair needs to be repaired or replaced. Even though the other disk will continue to function normally under Hot Fix protection, you should remirror the drives as quickly as possible to restore the full SFT protection of your data.

While the UNMIRROR and REMIRROR commands have no counterpart in FCONSOLE, you can observe the status of the unmirroring and remirroring operations by choosing the "Disk Mapping Information" option under "Statistics" in the main menu. Also, the DISK console command shows the progress of volumes being remirrored.

Using the UNMIRROR Console Command

Before you issue the UNMIRROR command, you need to know the disk number that NetWare has assigned to the physical disk you want to unmirror. The physical drive numbers can range from 0 to 31. Type **DISK** at the colon prompt and note the appropriate number (the disk number is in the left-most column of the display). You can unmirror either drive in a mirrored pair. The disk you choose will be shut down, and the other disk in the pair will continue to function under Hot Fix. If you want to make two mirrored drives into two regular drives with their own volumes, don't use the UNMIRROR command. You must run NETGEN to unmirror the drives and establish new volumes on one of them.

Once you know the disk number, type **UNMIRROR *nn*** at the console to begin the unmirroring process. When the process has completed successfully, you will see the following status message on the console screen:

```
Mirroring turned off on volume VolumeName.
```

If something goes wrong, you may see one of these error messages:

Invalid physical drive specified.

Explanation. The physical drive number you typed in the UMMIRROR command is either out of range (00 to 31) or NetWare couldn't find that disk number referenced in its master system disk tables.

Severity. Not fatal, but the unmirroring operation will be aborted.

Possible Solutions. Check the physical drive numbers by typing the **DISK** console command before you unmirror. Make sure you specify a valid physical drive number with the UNMIRROR command.

Physical drive and its mirror do not exist or are totally shut down.

Explanation. NetWare cannot find a physical drive corresponding to the number you specified in the UNMIRROR command.

Severity. Not fatal, but it will abort the unmirroring operation.

Possible Causes. You may have typed an invalid drive number with UN-MIRROR. The drive could have already been shut down due to repeated disk errors, or it may not be cabled properly to the file server.

Possible Solutions. Make sure you have typed the correct physical drive number in the command. Type **DISK** again to check the status of that drive; it may already be unmirrored or shut down. Check the cabling connections of the disk drive; the drive or its mirrored drive may be physically disconnected from the file server.

Physical drive does not have a mirror.

Explanation. You are trying to UNMIRROR a drive that is currently not mirrored to another drive.

Severity. Not fatal.

Possible Solutions. Make sure the drive number you specify corresponds to a drive that is currently mirrored to another drive.

You cannot un-mirror a drive that is currently being used to re-mirror.

Explanation. The drive number you specified in UNMIRROR corresponds to a drive that is currently in the process of being remirrored.

Severity. Not fatal. The current remirroring operation will continue normally.

Possible Solutions. Wait until NetWare finishes remirroring the drive; then re-enter the UNMIRROR command.

Using the REMIRROR Console Command

The REMIRROR console command restores SFT mirroring protection to a pair of drives previously unmirrored with the UNMIRROR console command. As part of the remirroring process, the data on the operating drive in the pair will be copied over to the newly restored drive. Once the data is identical, the two drives are synchronized, and mirroring protection is restored. If you unmirrored the drives temporarily and didn't bring the file server down, only data that changed on the operational drive will be copied back to the second disk when you remirror the drives. Normally, however, you will bring the file server down after unmirroring the drives because you must remove the unmirrored disk for repairs.

To remirror a pair of drives, you must know the physical drive number of the drive that was unmirrored. If you're not certain what the number is, type **DISK** at the colon prompt and look for a label resembling "D-*nn*" in the "stat" column. This is how DISK identifies an unmirrored disk.

Type the remirror command as follows: **REMIRROR *nn***, where *nn* is the physical disk number of the previously unmirrored drive. The file server will display the following message on the console screen:

```
Checking if the drive has been previously mirrored to the active drive.
```

When the remirroring process begins, you will see a message similar to this one:

```
Remirroring Drive nn
Beginning background copy of all allocated disk areas.
```

The remirroring operation happens in the background while the file server continues to function normally. When it finishes successfully, you'll see this message:

```
Re-mirroring successfully completed.
```

When using the REMIRROR command, you may see these error messages on the console screen:

Already re-mirroring a drive...wait until the current re-mirror finishes.

Explanation. NetWare is in the process of remirroring another set of drives. Only one mirrored pair of drives can be remirrored at a time.

Severity. This is a warning message only. The current remirroring operation will continue.

Possible Solutions. Enter the REMIRROR command again when the current remirroring operation is finished. (Some versions of NetWare 286 retain a series of REMIRROR commands in a "remirror queue" and perform the remirroring operations automatically when the current operation is finished. If this is the case for your version, you needn't re-enter the REMIRROR command.)

Background re-mirror aborted due to drive shut down.
Background re-mirror aborted due to ten write errors in a row.

Explanation. NetWare had to abort the background remirroring process because of disk problems.

Severity. Not fatal, but any current remirroring operation will be aborted as well.

Possible Causes. NetWare encountered ten disk write errors in a row on the drive being remirrored, or the drive ceased functioning altogether. The failure could be in the disk drive itself or in the associated disk channel components.

Possible Solutions. Check all the mechanical components of the failed disk channel. Repair or replace any defective drives, controllers, or disk coprocessor boards. Make sure the drive to be remirrored is turned on, then reboot the file server and try the REMIRROR command again.

Both mirror drives are invalid or marked saying that the other is out of sync. Run NETGEN.

Explanation. NetWare does not know which drive to use as the primary drive in the mirrored pair. Somehow, either both drives are marked as primary drives, or neither drive is listed in the server's drive tables.

Severity. Not fatal, but the remirroring process will be aborted.

Possible Causes. The error may result from a buggy disk driver, faulty hardware (DCBs, controller boards, and so on), or invalid information written on the drives.

Possible Solutions. Bring the server down and run NETGEN again to re-establish disk mirroring for the two drives. If the error persists, check for faulty hardware components along the disk channel. You might also try restoring the OS from a backup, or generating a completely new OS.

Drive being re-mirrored does not have any volumes on it.

Explanation. The drive you are trying to remirror does not contain any NetWare volumes.

Severity. Not fatal, but the REMIRROR command will be aborted.

Possible Causes. You may have typed the wrong drive number, or the drive may not have been properly initialized with NetWare volumes.

Possible Solutions. Make sure you type the correct drive number in the RE-MIRROR command. If the error persists, bring down the file server and run NET-GEN to set up NetWare volumes on the drive.

**Drive was shut down due to an unrecoverable failure
and cannot be re-mirrored.**

Explanation. The physical drive you specified in the REMIRROR command has been shut down because of a fatal disk error.

Severity. Not fatal, but the remirroring process will be aborted.

Possible Causes. When an unrecoverable failure occurs on a drive, NetWare automatically shuts the drive down. The OS will not allow the drive to be re-mirrored until it has been repaired.

Possible Solutions. Bring down the file server and repair or replace the faulty drive. Run NETGEN again to initialize the new disk and re-establish disk mirroring on the drive pair. Then reboot the file server.

Dup copies of redirection tables do not match...new tables will be built.

Explanation. During the remirroring process, NetWare detected that the Hot Fix Redirection Tables on the disks did not match.

Severity. This is a warning message only.

Possible Solutions. No action is necessary. NetWare will automatically re-build the Redirection tables as part of the remirroring operation.

Error reading disk redirection tables...new tables will be built.

Explanation. NetWare could not read the Hot Fix Redirection Tables from the disk you are trying to remirror.

Severity. Not fatal. The OS will build new Redirection Tables on the disk.

Possible Causes. (1) Invalid information has been written to the Redirection Tables. (2) One Redirection Table was updated, but the file server went down unexpectedly before the update of the other table was completed.

Possible Solutions. To be safe, you may want to bring the file server down and run NETGEN again to re-establish Hot Fix on the drive.

Dynamic work memory not available.

Explanation. To remirror a drive, NetWare sets aside a portion of the file server's main memory as a temporary workspace. The file server does not presently have enough dynamic memory available to perform the remirroring operation.

Severity. Not fatal, but the remirroring operation will be aborted.

Possible Causes. All of the dynamic memory in the file server is currently being used by other processes.

Possible Solutions. Reissue the REMIRROR command when fewer users are logged in to the file server. Or, bring down the server and use NETGEN to remirror the drives.

Error reading control tables from the active mirror drive.
Error reading [writing] sector 14 of the active [or new] mirror drive.
Error reading [writing] sector 15 of the new mirror drive.
Error reading the bad block table of the new mirror drive.
Error writing control tables to new mirror drive.

Explanation. All of the above errors indicate that NetWare had trouble accurately reading the tables stored in various sectors on track 0 of either the active mirrored drive or the new drive you are trying to remirror.

Severity. Not fatal, but the remirroring operation will be aborted.

Possible Causes. (1) A failure in the active or new mirrored drive, DCB, controller, or connecting cables. (2) Invalid information written to track 0 of the indicated drive. (3) Bad Redirection Tables on the new mirrored drive, making NetWare unable to use the disk's Bad Block table to rebuild the Hot Fix Redirection Tables.

Possible Solutions. Bring down the file server and check all disk channel hardware. Make sure the indicated drive and its controller are properly cabled and have an adequate power supply. Check the DCB to see that it is properly seated in the file server expansion slot and that the cable connector to the disk subsystem is firmly in place.

Run NETGEN to re-establish Hot Fix and disk mirroring on the drives. If the errors persist, back up the data on the disks and reformat them with COMPSURF. Then initialize the volumes on the disks and re-establish disk mirroring in NETGEN. Reboot the file server.

Invalid disk redirection table...duplicate entry. Run NETGEN.

Explanation. The Redirection Table on the drive you are remirroring contains an invalid duplicate entry.

Severity. Not fatal, but the remirroring operation will be aborted.

Possible Causes. This error may result from the disk drive writing invalid data in the Hot Fix Redirection Area.

Possible Solutions. Run NETGEN to re-establish Hot Fix on the disk. Remirror the drives while you are still in NETGEN. The drives will be mirrored when you reboot the file server.

Invalid disk redirection table...entry out of range.
Invalid redirection table size...building new redirection tables.
Invalid redirection tables...duplicate entry...new tables will be built.
Invalid redirection tables...entry out of range...new tables will be built.

Explanation. These errors indicate that the Redirection Tables on the disk you are remirroring are invalid for the reason specified.

Severity. These are informational messages only. The remirroring operation will proceed.

Possible Causes. These errors may occur if the disk drive has written invalid data in the Hot Fix Redirection Area.

Possible Solutions. No action is necessary. NetWare will automatically rebuild the Redirection Tables as part of the remirroring operation.

Invalid physical drive specified.

Explanation. The physical drive number you typed in the REMIRROR command is either out of range (valid range is from 00 to 31), or NetWare couldn't find that disk number referenced in its master system disk tables.

Severity. Not fatal, but the remirroring operation will be aborted.

Possible Solutions. Check the physical drive numbers by typing the **DISK** console command before you remirror. Make sure you specify a valid physical drive number with the REMIRROR command.

Less than 10 free redirection blocks are available...new tables will be built.

Explanation. NetWare found fewer than ten available blocks in the Redirection Tables on the drive you are remirroring.

Severity. This is a warning message only. The remirroring operation will continue.

Possible Causes. (1) Invalid information has been written to the inactive mirrored drive. (2) The drive has an excessive number of disk errors. (3) The Hot Fix Redirection Area is too small.

Possible Solutions. NetWare will automatically rebuild the Redirection Tables as part of the remirroring process. However, you should monitor the number of Hot Fix blocks used by this disk (either through FCONSOLE or the DISK console command). If the Redirection Area continues to fill up rapidly, you should repair or replace the disk. Increasing the size of the Hot Fix Redirection Area is only a temporary, band-aid solution.

Physical drive is not shut off and/or is not mirrored.

Explanation. The drive you are trying to remirror has not been unmirrored (and therefore shut down) with the UNMIRROR command. Or, the drive was never part of a mirrored pair.

Severity. Not fatal, but the remirroring operation will be aborted.

Possible Causes. You typed the wrong physical drive number. You cannot remirror a drive unless the drive was previously mirrored and is now "unmirrored."

Possible Solutions. Check the drive number with the DISK console command and make sure the one you are trying to remirror says "D-nn" in the "stat" column. Reissue the REMIRROR command with the correct drive number.

Ran out of redirection area on the new mirror drive.

Explanation. The Hot Fix Redirection Area on the drive you are remirroring completely filled up during the background copy process.

Severity. Not fatal, but the remirroring operation will be aborted.

Possible Causes. The Hot Fix Redirection Area may not be big enough to accommodate all the bad blocks on the disk. When you format a disk with COMP-SURF, any bad blocks COMPSURF finds are listed in the NetWare Bad Block table on track 0 of the disk. The Hot Fix Redirection Area, which is normally around two percent of the total disk capacity, must be large enough to absorb these pre-existing bad blocks, plus any other data redirected from bad blocks found by Hot Fix during normal operation of the disk. When you mirror the disk, NetWare updates the Redirection Tables to reflect the Bad Block table. If the redirection area is too small, the Redirection table will not have enough room for the bad block entries in the Bad Block table.

Possible Solutions. If the Hot Fix Redirection Area is smaller than two percent of the total disk capacity, bring down the file server and run NETGEN to enlarge it. Remember that mirrored drives must have the same logical size. So if you change the size of the Redirection Area of one drive (by reducing its logical size in NETGEN), you must also do the same for its mirror partner. While you're in NET-GEN, you may as well re-establish the mirrored pair. Then when you reboot the file server, the disks will be automatically mirrored.

If the Redirection Area is adequate in size but is full, it indicates a worn-out disk. Consider having the drive either repaired or replaced. You can still use NET-GEN to enlarge the Hot Fix Redirection Area, but only as a temporary solution.

Re-mirroring successfully completed...original drive shut off.
Explanation. NetWare successfully remirrored a pair of drives, but the original drive was shut down.

Severity. Not fatal. The newly mirrored drive will continue to operate as a single drive, even though its partner is now shut down.

Possible Causes. At some point during the remirroring process, Hot Fix was disabled on the original drive because the drive's Redirection Area became completely filled up.

Possible Solutions. If the size of the Redirection Area on the original disk was at least two percent of the total capacity, the fact that it is full indicates a worn-out disk. Either repair or replace the drive before you remirror it with its partner. You can still use NETGEN to enlarge the Hot Fix Redirection Area, but only as a temporary solution.

The two drive sizes do not match...drive size on the new drive will be changed.
Explanation. The drive you are trying to remirror has a different logical size than the drive you are trying to mirror it with. Remember, you calculate the logical size of a disk by subtracting the number of blocks reserved for the Hot Fix Redirection Area from the total number of blocks on the drive. Mirrored drives must have the same number of *logical* blocks, but not necessarily the same number of *physical* blocks.

Severity. This is an informational message only.

Possible Causes. The error could be caused by invalid information written to either one or both of the mirrored drives. It could also result from physically exchanging one of the drives with another drive that has been previously mirrored.

Possible Solutions. No action is necessary. NetWare will automatically adjust the number of logical blocks on the drive you are remirroring to match the logical size of its mirror partner.

Too many bad blocks defined...redirection table overflow.
Explanation. When remirroring a newly formatted drive with an existing drive, the OS found more bad blocks on the new drive than its Redirection Table could hold.

Severity. Not fatal, but the remirroring operation will be aborted.

Possible Causes. The Hot Fix Redirection Area on the new disk may not be big enough to accommodate all of its bad blocks. When you format a disk with COMPSURF, any bad blocks COMPSURF finds are listed in the NetWare Bad Block table on track 0 of the disk. The Hot Fix Redirection Area, which is normally around two percent of the total disk capacity, must be large enough to absorb these pre-existing bad blocks, plus any other data redirected from bad blocks found by Hot Fix during normal operation of the disk. When you mirror the disk, NetWare updates the Redirection Tables to reflect the Bad Block table. If the number of bad blocks is large, the Redirection table will not have enough room for the bad block entries in the Bad Block table.

Possible Solutions. A disk that has more than two percent of its storage space in bad blocks is probably going to cause you more grief than it's worth. Either repair the drive or replace it. You can still use NETGEN to enlarge the Hot Fix Redirection Area, but only as a temporary solution.

Replacing a Faulty Mirrored Drive

With SFT NetWare, you can use the UNMIRROR and REMIRROR console commands as a means to quickly replace a troublesome drive in a mirrored pair. Suppose you have physical disks 01 and 02 mirrored, with disk 01 serving as the primary drive in the pair. Suppose also that for disk 02, you start to see a growing number of Hot Fix Redirection blocks in the "Used" column of the DISK command. Remember, the "Used" column in the DISK command shows how many redirection blocks Hot Fix is using. Increasing numbers can mean the disk is wearing out or failing. It is a good idea to back up the system at this point.

Since disk 02 is the one that is flaking out, type **UNMIRROR 01** at the file server console to unmirror the mirrored pair. If you have another disk (identical in size to disk 02) already COMPSURFed and Hot Fixed, you can replace disk 02 with the new disk. Turn off the power to the disk subsystem and remove the power and interface cables to the bad drive. Check the disk drive switch setting and make sure the setting on the new drive matches it. Install the new drive, plug in the interface and power cables, and turn on the subsystem. Type **REMIRROR 01** at the server console; NetWare will re-establish mirroring between disk 01 and the new disk 02.

This procedure will work with disks in an external disk subsystem, as long as you have a drive that is already formatted with COMPSURF and set up for Hot Fix. For instance, a disk from another file server might work. You can unmirror either the primary drive or the secondary drive; whichever drive is left becomes the new primary drive.

If you have problems with internal mirrored disks, you must bring down the file server and turn it off to replace a faulty disk drive. Even so, you can replace the disk in about fifteen minutes. Of course, this doesn't include the time required to COMPSURF the new disk and establish Hot Fix.

23 Maintaining TTS and VAPs

Two features that extend the capabilities of the NetWare operating system are the Transaction Tracking System (TTS), available only with SFT NetWare 286, and the ability to run value-added processes (VAPs) with any version of NetWare 286. This chapter explains TTS in detail, focusing on the commands and procedures for installing, configuring, and maintaining Transaction Tracking. This chapter also explains the general procedure for installing VAPs on your file server. It discusses the VAP console command and other procedures connected with using VAPs on your file server.

SFT NETWARE'S TRANSACTION TRACKING SYSTEM

Maintaining internal data consistency is an essential part of any transaction-based system. Mainframe and minicomputer systems have long provided a sophisticated means of protecting databases, inventory systems, accounting programs, and other transaction-oriented software from problems that can arise from interrupted updates to data files. The designers of SFT NetWare recognized that, in order for distributed processing using PC LANs to become a viable alternative to traditional host-based systems, NetWare would need a transaction-protection mechanism to rival that of host-based systems.

The main advantage of distributed processing over host-based processing is that the combined system processing capacity grows as you add more workstations. The disadvantage is that as you add more components, you increase the probability of a failure somewhere in the system. In response to this inherent vulnerability of distributed systems, Novell developed the Transaction Tracking System (TTS) as a critical part of SFT NetWare's overall system fault tolerance. TTS protects transactional file updates against failure in the file server or at a workstation. Due to this broad range of protection, TTS saves databases more often than disk mirroring or any other SFT NetWare feature.

Many PC LAN database programs include a transaction backout capability as part of the application software. However, NetWare's TTS is an integral part of the network operating system itself. Novell sees several performance advantages to implementing transaction tracking at the OS level, rather than at the application software level. First, because the work is done at the OS level, less data is transferred to and from workstations. Second, TTS can work with the disk caching software to optimize transactional reads and writes. Third, NetWare TTS can provide transaction backout capability to multiuser applications not specifically designed for transaction tracking.

Definition of a Transaction

A *transaction* is a series of writes that must be performed in sequence to form a complete update to a database record or accounting data file. Most database changes, including changes to a single record, consist of a series of writes to several data fields in one or more files. In addition to the database files themselves, many relational database programs employ index files or pointer files to maintain the relationships between the stored data. When a user changes a record or field in the database file, the program must also update the index file and other related files to reflect the change. For example, when a user adds a new invoice to an accounts receivable file, the index file is updated so the program can locate the new invoice quickly. In addition, data from the invoice might also be written to the customer data file and the monthly billing file. Though the user doesn't see the change being integrated through several other files, this transparent shuffling of information must occur to keep the database consistent.

In a distributed system, a number of events can interrupt the transaction before all the related files have been updated. The workstation application might hang; a glitch in the storage media could abort the write operation at the file server; a commercial power failure may suddenly halt the operation of the workstation, the server, or both. Errant applications and operator errors can also interrupt a transaction. When such an interruption strikes mid-transaction, some of the files in the database will be updated and others will not. The result is an inconsistent database. At the very least, an incompletely updated database would have to be reindexed. In more extreme cases, records might be inaccessible or contain incorrect data, or the entire database might have to be rebuilt. Once the damage is done, it is extremely difficult, if not impossible, to trace through the entire database and determine what data is valid and what data is not.

How TTS Protects Against Incomplete Transactions

TTS prevents the problem of an inconsistent database by tracking each transactional file update and storing in a separate work file the information necessary to "back out" of any partially completed transactions. This *automatic rollback* feature allows TTS to abort an interrupted transaction and return the database to the way it was before the transaction was started. In this way, TTS ensures that transactional updates to database files are either wholly completed or wholly abandoned. Once the entire transaction is written successfully to disk, the original data is erased from the work file.

SFT NetWare with TTS tracks updates to all data files flagged with the "Transactional" file attribute. SFT NetWare can support multiple, concurrently active transactions from different workstations, or from different tasks within a single workstation. TTS keeps track of each transaction separately, so that automatic rollback of one transaction does not affect any other transactions concurrently in progress on the server.

Figure 23-1 illustrates the procedure TTS follows when tracking an update to a transactional file. Only data written to disk is recoverable in the event of a system failure; data held in cache buffers is lost. Thus, the original data must be written to disk before the changed data in order for TTS to be able to back out of the transaction and return the database to its original state. One of the reasons Novell implemented transaction tracking at the operating system level is so that TTS can interact with the disk caching software and establish write-ordering relationships between the cache buffers where the original and the changed data reside.

Transaction backouts require two writes (one for the original data and one for the new data) for every file update. Since all writes must be done in order and NetWare must wait for their completion, transaction tracking imposes a slight amount of overhead on the system. This is another reason why Novell implemented TTS at the OS level: to counteract the system overhead by using NetWare's sophisticated disk caching features. With disk caching, data does not have to be immediately written to disk. NetWare can collect updates from many transactions in the same cache buffer and write them all to disk in a single write operation.

TTS must be able to handle both workstation failures and file server failures. (A failure in the network cabling is treated the same as a workstation failure). File server failures are backed out when the file server reboots. When a workstation fails, the file server keeps running and performs an on-the-fly backout of the data being changed by the workstation. NetWare TTS monitors workstation backouts carefully to ensure that transactions from other workstations are not affected.

Step 1: When a transaction begins, TTS writes a "Begin Transaction" record to a temporary work file on the transaction backout volume.

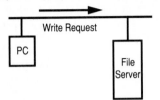

Step 2: The application sends a request to write to record XYZ of "transactional" file ABC.

Step 3: NetWare reads the part of file ABC containing record XYZ into a cache buffer (if it isn't already in cache).

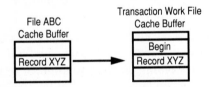

Step 4: TTS copies the original value of record XYZ from file ABC's cache buffer to the transaction work file cache buffer.

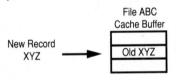

Step 5: As in a normal disk write, NetWare transfers the new value for record XYZ into file ABC's cache buffer first.

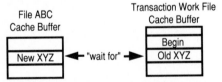

Step 6: TTS establishes a "wait for" relationship between the two cache buffers. The changed record XYZ in file ABC's cache buffer cannot be written to disk until the original record in the work file cache buffer has been written to disk.

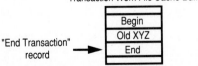

Step 7: Once the changes to record XYZ have been stored in file ABC's cache buffer, NetWare informs the application so that it can move on to something else. However, TTS waits until all changes have been written to disk before writing an "End Transaction" record to the transaction work file.

Figure 23-1: How NetWare TTS keeps track of the information necessary to back out of an interrupted transaction.

Protecting Against Workstation Failure. If the workstation fails part-way through a transaction, but the file server remains operational, TTS aborts the transaction and backs out of it as shown in Figure 23-2.

Step 1: TTS searches backward through the transaction work file to find any orginal data records involved in the aborted transaction.

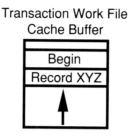

Step 2: TTS copies the original data from the transaction work file to the original file.

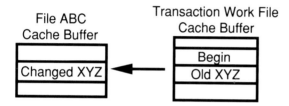

Step 3: Once the original data is written back to disk, TTS writes an "End transaction" record to the transaction work file.

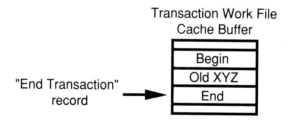

Figure 23-2: How NetWare TTS backs out of a partially completed transaction aborted due to workstation failure.

Protecting Against File Server Failure. If a failure halts the operation of the file server part-way through a transaction, TTS recovers from this failure as shown in Figure 23-3.

INSTALLING TTS WITH SFT NETWARE 286

Unless you have a specific reason *not* to use the Transaction Tracking System, you should install the TTS option with SFT NetWare 286. Installing TTS will benefit transactional applications such as database, accounting, and inventory programs, without affecting non-transactional applications or file server performance.

Step 1: When the file server is rebooted, TTS detects the presence of the transaction work file and scans the transaction work file for incomplete transactions ("Begins" without "Ends").

Step 2: TTS searches backward through the transaction work file to find any original data records involved in the incomplete transaction.

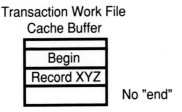

Step 3: TTS copies the original data from the transaction work file to the original file.

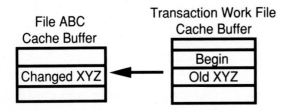

Step 4: Once the original data is written back to disk, TTS writes an "End transaction" record to the transaction work file.

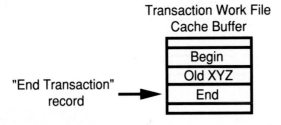

Figure 23-3: How NetWare TTS backs out of a partially completed transaction aborted due to file server failure.

In fact, SFT NetWare automatically uses TTS to track updates to the file server bindery. Without TTS, you have a greater risk of a corrupted bindery if the server fails during a bindery update.

If you have SFT NetWare 286, but the TTS option was not chosen during initial installation, here's how to activate TTS.

Bring down the file server and boot it with DOS. Use your working copies of the NetWare diskettes to rerun NETGEN. Insert the "NETGEN" diskette in drive A and type **NETGEN -C** at the DOS prompt. After loading, NETGEN displays the

"NetWork Generation Options" menu. Choose "Select Network Configuration" from this menu. An "Available Options" submenu will appear. Select "Set Operating System Options" to access this submenu:

Set Operating System Options
SFT NetWare 286 With TTS SFT NetWare 286

(Older versions of NETGEN will display "SFT NetWare Level-II+TTS" and "SFT NetWare Level-II" as the operating system options.) The currently selected operating system will be highlighted. If "SFT NetWare 286" is highlighted, press the Up-arrow key to select the operating system that includes the Transaction Tracking System. Press Enter to return to the "Available Options" submenu.

Now select "Save Selections and Continue" and answer "Yes" to the "Continue Network Generation Using Selection Configurations?" prompt. You will be returned to the "Network Generation Options" menu, with "Link/Configure NetWare Operating System" highlighted. Select this option to regenerate the SFT NetWare operating system to include TTS.

When NETGEN finishes regenerating the OS, the "NetWare Installation" option will be highlighted. Press Enter to go into the Installation half of NETGEN. After the program analyzes the system, verify the hard disk configuration and select "Drive List Is Correct." Then choose "Select Custom Installation Options" from the "Installation Options" menu. Select "Miscellaneous Maintenance" from the "Custom Installation" menu that appears on the screen.

Setting the TTS-Related Options

Two system configuration options come into play with TTS: the transaction backout volume, and the number of transactions. Select "System Configuration" from the "Miscellaneous Maintenance" submenu to set both of these options.

Choosing the Transaction Backout Volume. Until a transaction is completed, NetWare stores the necessary backout information in a temporary work file on the network volume you designate as the "transaction backout volume."

If you don't set it otherwise, the transaction backout volume defaults to the SYS volume. You cannot set aside part of a volume for TTS—you can only designate which volume TTS can use for the transaction backout information. TTS then uses as much disk space on that volume as it needs. The minimum amount of disk space that TTS needs is 1MB; however, depending on the capabilities of your database applications, you may need more than 1MB on the backout volume. The general rule is that the volume used for transaction backout should have enough free space for TTS to keep a copy of the largest transaction (or set of transactions) that your database applications can work with. TTS will disable itself if the server runs out of disk space on the backout volume during a large transaction.

If you are certain that your SYS volume will always have enough free storage space to hold transaction backout information (1MB minimum), the default setting will work fine. To change the default setting, highlight the "Transaction Backout Volume" field and press Enter. Select the volume you want from the list of available volumes that appears.

One way you can increase the efficiency of an SFT NetWare file server running TTS is by having the backout volume on a different hard disk channel than the volume that contains the database files. In other words, set up your hard disks so that the disk containing the backout volume is attached to a different disk coprocessor board than the disk containing the database files. This arrangement allows the database files and the transaction backout files to be updated simultaneously because the operating system can send the disk writes out both channels at once. If the volumes are on the same disk channel, the disk writes must occur one after the other.

Setting the Number of Transactions. The "Number of Transactions" represents the maximum number of user-initiated transactions that TTS can track at the same time. This parameter has nothing to do with the number of files you can have flagged as "Transactional." You can flag as many files "Transactional" as you want; the "Number of Transactions" parameter simply limits the number of transactions TTS can actively track at the same time.

The maximum number of transactions can range from 20 to 200. Each user could potentially have one transaction in progress and another one waiting to be written to disk; therefore, a good general setting for this parameter is twice the number of users on your network. Depending on how big your internetwork is and how large your database files are, you may have to increase the maximum number of transactions. Monitor the peak number of transactions displayed in FCONSOLE to help you fine tune the maximum transactions setting (see Chapter 19).

When adjusting the number of transactions, keep in mind that TTS automatically uses ten transactions to track updates to the bindery. If your server has plenty of memory, set the transaction maximum as high as you need to (up to the maximum of 200). The extra transactions will help the file server during initialization, as well as during bindery updates. If you need to conserve memory for other things, set the transaction maximum to around fifty. TTS works even after it reaches the maximum number of transactions; it just takes longer to process the transactions.

After you have set the TTS parameters, press Escape to return to NETGEN's "Miscellaneous Maintenance" menu.

Completing the TTS Installation

From the "Miscellaneous Maintenance" menu, select "Load Operating System" and set the flag to load the new operating system you have generated. Press Escape until you return to the "Installation Options" menu, choose "Continue Installation," and follow the prompts to load the OS. Exit NETGEN in the usual way. When you reboot the file server, the TTS option will be operational.

Flagging Files "Transactional"

You must flag the data files you want protected by TTS with the "Transactional" file attribute. Never flag .EXE files as "Transactional." Flag the main database file only, not the related key or index files. Once a file is flagged "Transactional," it cannot be deleted or renamed.

You can use either the FLAG command-line utility or the FILER menu utility to set the "Transactional" attribute on a file. Users must have at least Parental, Search, and Modify rights in a directory before they can change the file attributes for files in that directory.

To set the "Transactional" attribute with FLAG, type:

```
FLAG FileName TRANSACTIONAL
```

Replace *FileName* with the directory path and file name of the file you want to make transactional. You can use wildcard characters (* and ?) to flag several files at the same time.

To remove the "Transactional" attribute in order to delete or rename the file, type:

```
FLAG FileName NT
```

See Chapter 7 for information about using FILER to set file attributes.

ENABLING AND DISABLING TRANSACTION TRACKING

Transaction tracking is normally enabled whenever the file server is running. However, if the transaction backout volume runs out of free disk space, TTS will automatically disable itself. To re-enable TTS, type **ENABLE TRANSACTIONS** at the file server console.

If you need to disable TTS temporarily because you are testing a software application, or because you want to speed up the processing of a transactional program, type **DISABLE TRANSACTIONS** at the file server console. NetWare will no longer keep backout files for database transactions until you re-enable TTS.

EXPLICIT AND IMPLICIT TRANSACTIONS

As we have seen, transactions have a distinct beginning and end. TTS can recognize the beginning and end of a transaction in either of two ways: the application can use NetWare function calls to tell TTS when to start and stop tracking the transaction (an *explicit* transaction), or TTS can imply the beginning and end of a transaction based on the application's use of record locks (an *implicit* transaction).

How Explicit Transactions Work

In the NetWare environment, applications can use function calls to control transaction tracking. Applications written using NetWare TTS APIs "explicitly" tell the OS when a transaction is beginning and when the application finishes a transaction. The application programmer must modify the software to define exactly where transactions begin and end.

The advantage of explicit transactions is that the application can clearly identify the beginning and end of all file update sequences, and thus more accurately indicate to TTS when the file updates should be made. Further, users can be assured that the updates contained within the transaction will be written to disk as quickly as possible. Although it is initially time-consuming and costly to rewrite applications, defining explicit transactions ensures an exact definition of transaction boundaries. Applications modified for TTS will also work on a server not running SFT NetWare with TTS, but the transaction tracking functions will not be used.

Novell has made the TTS APIs available to all application developers, but not all developers have chosen to implement TTS. Some of the database programs that use TTS's explicit transaction calls include Novell's Btrieve, DBman from VersaSoft, ZIM from Zanthe, and BBX (Business Basic Extended) or any program written in BBX.

How Implicit Transactions Work

TTS was designed to provide the transaction backout capability to multiuser applications not specifically designed to do backouts. Thus, even database programs that have not been modified to include TTS function calls can use TTS through implicit transactions. Because the application cannot tell TTS when a transaction begins and ends, TTS must "imply" the boundaries of a transaction based on the application's use of logical and physical record locks.

With implicit transactions, TTS implies the start of a transaction whenever the application performs a physical record lock on a file flagged "Transactional," or whenever logical record locks occur while one or more transactional files are open. Likewise, TTS implies the end of a transaction when the record locks are released. Implying the boundaries of a transaction in this way makes sense for most non-TTS applications. When an application locks a group of records in a database, it is essentially asserting control and requesting exclusive access to the records while they are being changed. When the application is finished with the changes, the protection afforded by the record lock is no longer required. The application then releases all locks and relinquishes control of the records.

In the absence of TTS-aware applications, SFT NetWare uses the implicit transaction mode by default. Thus, existing applications do not have to be modified to use TTS with implicit transactions. However, some applications do not conform to the default record-locking model assumed by implicit transactions. To handle these applications, you must use the SETTTS command.

USING SETTTS

Some applications use record locks for purposes other than marking the beginning of a transaction. For example, as a method of copy protection, an application might lock one or more records when you enter the program and leave the records locked until you exit. To allow TTS to work with these types of applications, you can use the NetWare SETTTS command to tell TTS how many logical or physical record locks to ignore before implying the start of a transaction.

The SETTTS command must be issued at the workstation prior to starting the application. Better yet, include the command in the batch file that starts the application. The format for this command is:

```
SETTTS  Logical  Physical
```

Replace *Logical* with the number of logical record locks you want TTS to ignore; replace *Physical* with the number of physical record locks to ignore.

You can set the logical lock threshold, the physical lock threshold, or both. For example, to have TTS ignore two logical record locks and one physical lock before starting a transaction, type **SETTTS 2 1** before entering the application. If you need to specify only a physical lock threshold, set the logical lock threshold to zero. For example, to have TTS ignore one physical record lock before starting a transaction, type **SETTTS 0 1** before entering the application.

In most cases, the logical or physical lock threshold will be 1. If the threshold is set incorrectly, TTS may break file updates into too many transactions, or interpret your entire session in the application as one giant transaction. The desired transaction granularity is lost when one gigantic transaction is created; however, an end transaction is still generated when the application is exited.

One application you must use SETTTS with is dBASE III PLUS v1.0. This version of dBASE III PLUS uses a logical record lock for copy protection, and does not release the lock until you exit the program. You can get around this problem by including the command **SETTTS 1** in the batch file that calls up dBASE III. TTS will then ignore the initial logical lock and start counting a transaction with the next record lock. (Subsequent versions of dBASE III PLUS have rectified the problem and can be used without the SETTTS command.) Other applications that need the lock threshold set to 1 are MicroFocus Cobol and Revelation version G2B. Revelation uses a logical record lock to keep track of how many users are in the program.

Unfortunately, there isn't an extensive list of databases that use a logical or physical record lock for something other than marking the beginning of a transaction. Just about any program that uses logical record locks is a candidate for SETTTS. If you are getting unusually slow response while using TTS, or if your TTS saves occur only when you exit a program, these are signs that the lock threshold isn't set correctly. The best thing to do is call the vendor and ask about the program's record locking sequence. Most vendors will be aware of any problems their applications have running with TTS, and they can probably tell you how many logical or physical record locks to skip over.

Another thing you can do is to start the application from a workstation and open a data file. Log in as supervisor from another workstation, start FCONSOLE, and choose the "Connection Information" options. Select the connection for the workstation on which the application is running. From the "Connection Information" submenu, choose the "Logical Record Locks" option. If the application does perform an initial logical record lock, you will see which task is using the lock and the current status of the lock. Press Escape to leave the logical record lock window. To see if the application uses any physical record locks, choose the "Open Files/

Physical Records" option. Highlight an open file and press Enter. Then, from the "File/Physical Records Information" menu, choose the "Physical Record Locks" option. FCONSOLE will show you if there are any physical record locks on that particular file. Do the same for each open file listed. Add up the number of logical and physical record locks and use those totals as your thresholds in the SETTTS command.

NetWare TTS Quirks

NetWare TTS correctly handles most of the unusual situations that can occur during transaction backouts: file truncations or extensions, multiple changes to the same data area during the same transaction, and errors occurring when the transaction is being backed out. However, some poorly structured programs can end up in a deadlock if they use try to use TTS, particularly with implicit transactions.

Applications normally assume that after each file write, the data has been changed and the user is finished with that data. However, with TTS, data being written to transactional files could possibly be changed several times before the transaction is completed. If an application unlocks the record being updated before the transaction is completed, another user can take over and change the contents of the record. But if the first workstation fails before its transaction is completed, TTS backs out of the transaction and restores the original contents of the record. This backout changes the data out from under the second user and could cause the database to be inconsistent.

To guard against this condition, NetWare holds all locks issued by a workstation until the transaction is completed. Even if the workstation unlocks a record in the middle of a transaction, TTS keeps the lock in force until the transaction is done. This prevents other workstations from accessing the field until it is safe from being changed by a backout. However, holding record locks until the end of transactions creates the potential for deadlocks between workstations. If an application allows records to be unlocked in the middle of transactions to avoid deadlocks, then the fact that TTS retains the lock can cause both workstations to lock up. Fortunately, the deadlock is not serious; when you reboot both workstations, the partial transactions are correctly backed out and database integrity is maintained. This undesirable, but unavoidable, consequence of TTS's transaction backout capability occurs in only a few poorly designed applications.

Many database applications have already been tested and found to work correctly with implicit transactions. With untested applications, you should experiment with implicit transaction backouts before releasing the application into a full-production environment.

TTS-Related Error Messages

The error messages generated by TTS are not documented in the Novell *System Messages* manual. Generally, the error messages are self-explanatory. Some examples include messages like "Backout was requested from station *nn*" or "Backout being aborted due to lack of disk space on volume."

When a transaction is being backed out due to a workstation failure, the following message appears on the server console: "Transaction being backed out for station *nn*." However, with applications that use explicit transaction tracking, this message is not displayed.

INSTALLING VAPs ON THE FILE SERVER

A value-added process (VAP) is a customized, server-based application that runs as an extension to the NetWare operating system in the file server. Typical VAPs associated with NetWare 286 are the Btrieve VAP, the NetWare for Macintosh VAPs, the keyboard-locking VAP, the print server VAP, and the streaming tape backup VAP. These VAPs are provided by Novell. Third-party developers also offer VAPs for print servers, archive servers, database servers, and other types of value-added servers.

To install a VAP, copy the VAP file or files into the SYS:SYSTEM directory of the file server. VAP files usually have the .VAP extension (or some variation, such as .VP0 and .VP1). When you boot the file server, the bootup sequence looks for any VAP files in SYS:SYSTEM and asks you if you want to load them. Loading VAPs is an all-or-nothing proposition in NetWare 286; you either load them all, or you don't load any.

If you want only certain VAPs to load, you must remove or rename all the other VAP files in the SYS:SYSTEM directory. Each VAP will display a sign-on message as it is loaded.

Adjusting the VAP Wait Time

In NetWare v2.15, you can have the file server wait a specific amount of time after it displays the prompt to load VAPs. If no response is received within that time (called the "VAP wait time"), the server will proceed to load the VAPs automatically. This feature allows the server to boot up unattended, if necessary.

The VAP wait time applies only to NetWare v2.15, not v2.12 or previous versions. You set the VAP wait time parameter as a line in the SERVER.CFG file, also located in the SYS:SYSTEM directory. The SERVER.CFG file is a DOS text file that you can edit with a text editor or word processor. The syntax for the VAP wait line is:

```
VAP WAIT nnn
```

where *nnn* is the number of seconds (from 10 to 360) you want the file server to wait for a response to the VAP loading prompt.

THE VAP CONSOLE COMMAND

After the file server is up and running, you can use the VAP console command to find out which VAPs are currently running in the file server. To do this, go to the file server console and type **VAP**. The console screen will display the names and commands associated with all VAPs, in the following format:

```
Value Added Process Names and Commands:

Novell AppleTalk Filing Protocol Gateway — V1.1

Dayna AppleTalk Queue Gateway (AQSVAP) — V1.1
   APPLEQUEUE
   QLIST
   PUBLISH
   UNPUBLISH
```

The Effect of VAPs on File Server Performance

Each VAP requires a certain amount of file server memory and CPU processing time. The number of VAPs that a file server can execute simultaneously is limited by the total amount of memory in the server, the amount of memory used by each VAP, the kinds and sizes of drivers installed, and the version of NetWare being run. Ten VAPs at a time the maximum you can run before server performance becomes unacceptable. If more than ten VAPs are present, the server will attempt to load them all, but it will most likely cause the file server to crash. If they do manage to load successfully, the server will likely ABEND with a General Protection Interrupt (GPI) as soon as you type any console commands.

If the VAP load becomes too much for your file server to handle, you can offload some VAPs—for example, the NetWare for Macintosh VAPs—to external bridges (routers) on the internetwork. You can use the VAP console command at an external bridge console to see what VAPs are loaded on the bridge.

Another thing to remember about VAPs is that they use other file server resources besides just memory: connections, drive mappings, and so on. Since VAPs are not granted special rights or privileges directly from the file server, they must operate (logically) just like any other client on the network. VAPs must log in, map drives, and be granted security rights in the bindery in order to access what they need to on the file server.

The USERLIST command shows you which connections are being used by VAPs, along with those being used by users. It is not uncommon for a VAP to take up four or five connections. But since SFT and Advanced NetWare 286 support up to 100 logical connections at a time, the effect of VAP connections won't manifest itself unless you have close to 100 active workstations on the network. In ELS NetWare, a certain number of "phantom" connections are reserved exclusively for VAPs; therefore, VAPs won't take up any of the four or eight user connections supported by ELS NetWare Level I and Level II, respectively.

Where to Find More Information About Specific VAPs

You can find more information about the VAPs Novell provides in the following NetWare manuals:

Btrieve VAP	*NetWare Btrieve* manual
NetWare for Macintosh VAPs	*NetWare for Macintosh* documentation
Keyboard lock VAP	*Console Reference* manual
Print server VAP	Novell's print server documentation
Streaming tape backup VAP	Novell's streaming tape backup VAP documentation

For other VAPs, refer to the documentation that accompanies the VAP diskettes. The diskettes often contain a README file that gives instructions for loading and using the VAP.

24 UPS and Power Conditioning

Dependable power to the file server and its peripherals is an important component of NetWare's overall fault tolerance. Without dependable power, not even the most sophisticated fault tolerant software provided by SFT NetWare can prevent the loss of valuable data on the LAN. To protect against data loss due to interruptions or fluctuations in commercial power, Novell recommends the use of an Uninterruptible Power Supply (UPS) on all NetWare file servers and attached hard disks. A UPS is a specially-designed power supply, with batteries that can supply power to the file server for short periods. If the commercial power fails, the server runs off the UPS batteries until it can shut itself down gracefully.

To enhance the protection offered by a UPS, all versions of NetWare include a built-in UPS monitoring feature. This feature provides an interface between the UPS unit and the NetWare operating system. Through this interface, the UPS can signal its status to the OS and thereby coordinate the orderly shutdown of the file server.

This chapter first looks at the types of power fluctuations that a UPS must be able to guard against. Then we'll discuss the various types of UPS systems that are available and what their limitations are. Finally, we'll explain how to set up the file server and UPS to use NetWare's UPS monitoring feature.

PROBLEMS WITH COMMERCIAL POWER

Like most other electronic equipment, computers require continuous 120-volt AC power (plus or minus ten percent). Most people assume that, except for occasional outages, this is what the utility company delivers. While this ideal power may be generated at the power plant, much can happen to pollute that power before it gets to your site. Lightning, floods, storms, accidents, or even large loads all coming on-line at once can corrupt commercial power.

Power problems are more common than many people realize. Users often blame hung workstations or lost data on software, when power fluctuations are the real culprit. Many technicians estimate that up to half of the service calls they receive are related to power problems.

A study performed in the early 1970s by IBM and Bell Laboratories concluded that power problems sufficient to interrupt computer operations occur an average of twice a week. Power outages, or blackouts, accounted for less than five percent of these twice-weekly power problems. Other, less serious types of commercial power pollution occur almost every day. Left unchecked, these power imperfections can put undue stress on the file server and its peripherals and can eventually damage both hardware and software.

Types of Power Disturbances

Disturbances to commercial power basically fall into the following categories:

- *Surges*. A power surge is a sudden increase in voltage that can last several seconds.
- *Spikes*. A spike is a burst of high voltage lasting only a fraction of a second. Spikes are also referred to as impulses or transients.
- *Noise*. Noise consists of high-frequency, low-voltage oscillations or "ripples" that originate from such sources as fluorescent lights and heavy equipment motors.
- *Sags*. A sag is a decrease in voltage lasting up to several seconds. Sags make up the majority of power problems.
- *Brownouts*. A brownout is a prolonged sag that usually occurs during periods of peak power usage, when the local utility company's power producing capacity is severely drained. A typical example is a hot summer day when everyone is running air conditioners at full blast.
- *Blackouts*. Also called a power failure or outage, a blackout is the total loss of power. Though dramatic, blackouts are relatively infrequent.

Effects of Power Disturbances

Although blackouts are rare, their effects are potentially the most devastating of all forms of power disturbances. If the blackout occurs during a save to disk, while the file allocation table is being updated, you could lose access to some or all of the files on the disk. All data held in RAM at the time of a power outage is lost as well. The costs of re-entering lost data far exceed the costs of merely replacing a hard disk or power supply.

While the effects of a blackout are immediately obvious, the effects of the other types of power disturbances may be neither immediately obvious nor predictable. Power disturbances can cause glitches in the file server's internal power supply, which in turn can corrupt some of the data held in RAM. If such a disturbance occurs during a discrete operating system routine, the file server may continue to operate normally until that routine is used again. Only then will the server lock up or crash because of the corrupted data in memory.

Power surges are one of the most common causes of hardware problems. Surges put undue stress on certain hardware components, particularly power supplies, and can cause them to fail prematurely. High frequency noise or spikes can lead to read/write errors or parity errors, either of which could cause the computer to hang. Spikes are also a common cause of hardware damage.

Power disturbances can happen in combination, which compounds their potential effects on the system. For example, slight sags in power happen frequently and may not be sufficient to adversely affect computers. If these sags occur during a brownout, though, the power level may be reduced below the acceptable power range that computer equipment needs to operate.

EVALUATING UPS SYSTEMS

A number of power protection devices are currently available for computers. Not all of these devices protect your system against the full range of power problems; some, such as surge suppressors and voltage regulators, are designed only to protect against minor power surges, spikes, and noise. They do not offer protection from the most serious power problems (sags and brownouts), nor do they contain a battery backup—so if the power goes out, so does the network. However, line conditioners, voltage regulators, surge suppressors, and the like do have their place; they are recommended for use with workstations and other less-critical LAN peripherals.

While the UPS is considered the ultimate in power protection for NetWare file servers, not all UPS systems are alike. Early UPS units were designed simply to provide backup power in the event of a blackout, leaving the server completely vulnerable to other types of power irregularities. Newer UPS systems are designed to protect against the full range of power problems.

Types of UPS Systems Available

Generally, UPS systems can be categorized into three types: off-line, on-line, and hybrid. In addition, a new type of power system—the so-called intelligent power supply (IPS) designed specifically for networks—is also available. All UPSes use an internal battery that produces AC power via an inverter. The inverter takes the DC battery charge, changes it to AC, and sends it to the computer's internal power supply. How and when this inverter comes into play largely determines the effectiveness of the UPS.

An *off-line UPS*, or standby power system (SPS), functions by switching from commercial power to battery power when the commercial power drops below a certain voltage level or fails altogether. The inverter is normally off, except during power outages. Because the file server receives power directly from the commercial line as long as it is available, the server remains exposed to such power disturbances as spikes, noise, surges, and brownouts. For this reason, manufacturers of SPS systems often recommend that a line conditioner or voltage regulator be used in addition to the SPS unit itself.

Another drawback of an SPS is that it takes a certain amount of time for the unit's battery to kick in after it senses that the voltage has dropped. Sometimes the file server can't ride through this momentary delay and crashes anyway, especially when voltage on the power line is low. Therefore, the period of time that an offline UPS takes to make the switch is crucial. Generally, an SPS with a switching time of four milliseconds or less is safe to use with a network. The only significant advantage of an off-line UPS is its low cost.

An *on-line UPS* acts like a small solid-state generator. It continuously converts commercial AC power to DC power to keep its battery charged. Its inverter then takes the DC power from the battery and creates new, clean AC power in a steady 120-volt, 60Hz sinewave. The file server runs off the power generated by the UPS at all times. The on-line UPS uses the commercial line voltage to keep its batteries charged, but never to supply power directly to the server. Thus, the on-line UPS completely isolates the file server and its peripherals from the commercial power line (and its inherent power fluctuations) and does not rely on switching between commercial and battery power.

A *hybrid UPS* is typically an off-line SPS enhanced by means of an electronic or ferroresonant conditioner or an interactive design intended to smooth out the load transition from utility-supplied to inverter-supplied power. The output power of a hybrid UPS is only as good as its limited filtering and conditioning capabilities. Descriptions such as "triport," "line interactive," "no break," "load sharing," "bidirectional," and "single conversion" are often applied to hybrids. To add to the confusion, these non-regenerative systems are often labeled as "on-line" products—even though hybrids do not function the same as on-line UPSes. Since neither hybrid nor off-line UPSes regenerate power continuously, users receive raw or partially filtered utility power, giving little or no protection during normal everyday operation. The more sensitive the protected device is, the more severe the potential damage from raw or partially filtered utility power.

A new line of *Intelligent Power Systems* (IPS) is now available. These products are specifically designed to protect the entire network (including workstations and peripherals), not just the file server. They take UPS protection one step farther by adding new software capabilities that work in conjunction with the NetWare operating system itself. This interface to the network operating system goes beyond a simple connection with status indicators of good power or battery charge; using NetWare's built-in UPS monitoring functions to monitor and communicate with sophisticated power supplies, an IPS provides the LAN with several minutes of battery backup. During this time, the IPS transmits messages to any workstations that are still operational and orchestrates an orderly, automatic, and unattended shutdown of the network.

UPS Evaluation Criteria

Since standards for specifications and performance of UPS devices are still in the formulative stages, evaluating their relative merits is rather difficult. With the multitude of power products available, you may wonder what kind of power protection is best for your network. Many systems will do just fine with off-line power backup; others may require the benefits available with on-line backup. In the following pages, we will look at some evaluation criteria for selecting an appropriate power protection system.

What the Experts Recommend. If price is no object, it's best to go with what most power industry experts recommend. The consensus among those in the know seems to be that a true regenerative, on-line, sinewave UPS provides the most complete protection while maintaining a solid output during any power interruption. Of course, these types of systems are the most expensive overall. If your budget is limited, or if you are skeptical of what the experts say, read on. There are other criteria on which you can base your decision.

Range of Protection Offered. At the very least, a UPS must be able to provide continuous 120-volt AC sinewave output at a frequency equal to that of the power line in the event of a power blackout. Since (on the average) oscillations occur daily, and spikes, surges, sags, and brownouts occur weekly, a file server should also be protected from all of these power disturbances.

Many UPS systems offer some protection against spikes, surges, and sags, but overlook brownouts. Off-line and other non-regenerative UPSes typically do not perform well during sustained low voltage conditions. Switching times for these UPSes increase as the commercial voltage decreases. It is not uncommon for a unit with a five-millisecond transfer time at 120 VAC to exceed twenty milliseconds at 100 VAC. Because a brief period of low voltage precedes most blackouts, this occurrence may place a system at even greater risk. Also, off-line and hybrid UPSes can inaccurately sense a brownout as a blackout and prematurely switch to battery. During a sustained brownout, an off-line UPS may completely discharge the battery and potentially "crash" a system, even though the office lights might still be on.

Sinewave Versus Squarewave Output. UPS products are available with either sinewave or squarewave outputs (or some modification thereof). Sinewave is usually considered best because it is the same waveform provided by the utility companies and is the waveform that most electronic equipment is designed to handle. Sinewave is definitely better for LAN hardware because a typical PC contains both linear or RMS-sensitive elements and non-linear or peak-sensitive elements. Squarewave output only approximates the ideal sinusoidal waveform and puts undue stress on RMS-sensitive system elements, while starving the peak-sensitive elements. This can cause overheating and premature hardware failure. The excess energy contained in squarewaves (in the form of harmonics) can get into the logic circuitry and cause sporadic data errors or parity errors.

So-called "computer grade" sinewaves use varying numbers of squarewave increments to approximate a sinewave. These generally provide the required RMS voltage, as well as the peak voltages for which computer equipment is designed. However, these quasi-sinewaves do not provide the precise timing required by many PC monitors. This timing mechanism, known as "zero crossing," regulates how the monitor references its screen scans. Imprecise zero crossings result in "screen swim," a condition in which the screen display appears to breathe or undulate.

It is also important that the waveform output by a UPS be a pure alternating current (AC) type. Even the smallest percentage of direct current (DC) on the output can saturate magnetic loads such as fans and transformers and render them inoperative.

Inrush Capability. This is the capacity required for the UPS's power source to start up all connected loads at a given time. When computers are turned on, the initial power draw is much higher than the normal operating power requirement. If additional equipment attached to the UPS is powered on when the demand for UPS power is already high, a temporary overload can occur. Either the additional device will not receive power, or other equipment attached to the UPS will be shut down. Consequently, on-line UPS devices may require an inrush capacity as high as 1000 percent. On-line UPSes with insufficient inrush capacity cannot be used to power equipment up to the rated output capability of the UPS.

Power Rating. Each UPS unit should have a power rating sufficient to support all hardware that will draw power from the unit. Power ratings are normally specified in terms of volts/amps (VA), as in 150VA or 600VA. You can obtain the VA number by multiplying a product's voltage by its amps (volts x amps also gives the wattage). The more complex the hardware, the more power it uses. A high-end engineering workstation used to run CAD/CAM programs, for example, would have a higher power rating than an IBM XT workstation used for word processing. Certain configurations may have special power requirements, but you're generally in good shape if you simply maintain the power rating specified on the equipment label.

If you aren't sure what power rating you need, consult with the sales engineering staff of the manufacturer of the given unit. Consider not only your current network power needs, but also your long-range expansion plans for the network.

Duration of Backup Power. After a power failure, the UPS's backup power system must be able to maintain power to the server and disk subsystems long enough for the OS to write any data in memory to disk, close all open files, update all tables, and shut the file server down gracefully. Avoid prolonged operation of the file server on UPS batteries in the absence of commercial power, except where there is a critical need. Extended battery-powered operation shortens the life of the UPS battery. Most UPS systems allow you to set a maximum time before the unit either switches back to commercial power or initiates the shutdown of the server.

NetWare Compatibility. A variety of products—ranging in design from simple communication through RS-232 cables to true interactive software that effects a proper shutdown of the file server—claim to communicate with the NetWare operating system. Ask specific questions of vendors regarding what kind of Net-Ware compatibility the product has, how users are notified of power problems, and exactly how the power device interacts with the operating system. Find out whether the UPS hardware supports NetWare's UPS monitoring function that monitors the UPS attached to the file server and informs users of UPS status.

Efficient Operation. To be efficient, the UPS device should not require bringing in a special commercial power line just to run the UPS. It should be able to run from the normal power service available at your site. A UPS should also be as inconspicuous as possible—the smaller, more attractive, and quieter the unit, the better; some models are overly large and rather noisy. Check for simplicity in installation and operation; plug-and-play installation of the power unit and software will make implementation a breeze.

Peculiarities of Your Locale. Your particular location may require special measures for a number of reasons, including nearby radio or television stations, heavy equipment, and industrial sites. Make sure you account for unusual circumstances, such as frequent blackouts or heavy noise.

Since off-line and hybrid UPSes do not continuously regenerate power, they must always transfer the load to battery power when a voltage or frequency problem arises. As a result, output voltage and frequency is typically not well regulated. Off-line or hybrid UPSes are a poor choice for use in industrial parks, rural regions, some foreign countries, and other areas subject to low voltage or frequency instability. These systems are also unacceptable for use in facilities with on-site generators, such as hospitals, oil rigs, remote field sites, and military bases. The slightest irregularities in power can be catastrophic to sensitive process and test equipment, such as blood analyzers, positioning devices, and controlled chemical process equipment.

Cost. As always, cost is an important factor to consider. Low-end SPS and hybrid UPSes with one to three outlets, capable of supplying brief battery backup power, are available for a few hundred dollars. On-line UPS systems can range from $500 to $5,000, depending on network size. Remember to figure in the cost of additional cabling, hardware, and software to go along with the UPS. A bundled UPS package is generally less expensive than buying the components separately.

Power systems, however, are relatively inexpensive when compared to the value of the hardware, software, and data they protect. Most network supervisors find that a UPS more than pays for itself in the long term—and often in the short term.

Protection for Other Network Components

Depending on the types of applications you run on your network, you may want to provide workstations, printers, modems, and other peripherals with some kind of protection. In a small network in which the file server is attached to a UPS, peripherals can also be attached to the same UPS, depending on the power rating and number of receptacles available.

An ideal configuration might include a suitably sized UPS for the file server and a smaller UPS unit at each workstation. Of course, not all network components are adjacent to each other. If you want a workstation to function when the server (which may be located in another department) has survived a blackout, consider a power unit that fits right under the workstation's monitor.

NETWARE'S UPS MONITORING FEATURE

The UPS monitoring function is included in all versions of SFT and Advanced NetWare 286, and in ELS NetWare Level II v2.15. Therefore, most NetWare 286 file servers can be set up to perform UPS monitoring. Through a special interface, the UPS tells the server when the power fails. The file server notifies any users who haven't been affected by the power problem that the server is running on backup power. The users can then save their files quickly and log out. If power is not restored within a few minutes, the server automatically shuts itself down, making sure that all files, directories, and the File Allocation Table (FAT) are internally consistent.

Of course, data that was being processed by workstations, but not yet saved to the file server, is lost if the power fails. If it is important to protect against loss of workstation data, UPSes can be used on them as well.

UPS Monitoring Hardware

To use NetWare UPS monitoring, you need in your file server a board that contains special circuitry, cables, and a socket for connecting to the UPS unit. This UPS circuitry is included on the following boards available from Novell or its OEMs:

- The Novell standalone UPS monitoring board. This is a half-size, 8-bit board whose sole function is to provide UPS monitoring hardware.
- The Novell SS keycard. Although a serialized keycard is no longer required as of NetWare 286 v2.11, some keycards contain the UPS monitoring circuitry. If you have one of these keycards from a previous purchase of NetWare, you can use it to hook up the UPS. (Although NetWare v2.11 and above doesn't check for serialization hardware, the OS software is still serialized.)
- The Novell disk coprocessor board. Most recent versions of the DCB contain UPS monitoring circuitry. Older versions (pre-1987) do not.

An easy way to tell if your old keycard or DCB has UPS monitoring circuitry is to look on the metal mounting bracket on the end of the card. If it has a small, RCA-style jack that looks like you could plug a set of stereo headphones into it, that indicates UPS hardware.

Note that on an IBM PS/2 file server, you connect the UPS through the mouse port of the server; you don't need a separate UPS board.

Setting UPS Jumpers. You must set a few UPS-related jumpers on all of the above types of UPS monitoring boards. These jumpers determine the board's I/O address, the battery low input setting, and the battery on-line input setting. Different UPSes use different methods to signal when the battery is on-line and when it is low. If the jumpers are not set accordingly on the UPS board in the file server, the entire UPS monitoring function will be defeated. You won't get an error message or any other outward manifestation that the jumpers are not correctly set; however, if the UPS monitoring feature fails to function properly during its first power outage, check the jumper settings before you start blaming the UPS unit or the software.

The jumper settings for Novell UPS monitoring hardware are documented in the supplement shipped with the board. Make a note of the I/O address jumper setting, because you'll need it for the SERVER.CFG file.

UPS Parameters in the SERVER.CFG File. The SERVER.CFG file is a DOS text file that you must create in the SYS:SYSTEM directory of the file server. (Prior to v2.15, this file was called CONFIG.UPS.) You can create or edit the SERVER.CFG file with a text editor or word processor. The file contains various parameters relating to the UPS monitoring feature, as well as the VAP and TTS wait time parameters.

The syntax for the four possible UPS parameters in SERVER.CFG is:

```
UPS TYPE = n
UPS IO = nnn
UPS DOWN = nn
UPS WAIT = nnn
```

For UPS TYPE, replace *n* with 1 for the standalone UPS monitor board, 2 for a DCB, 3 for the keycard, or 4 if you are using the mouse port on an IBM PS/2.

For the *nnn* in the UPS IO line, use the I/O address (in hexadecimal notation) corresponding to the jumper settings or factory-preset settings on the UPS monitoring hardware. The following chart summarizes the possible I/O addresses:

Novell keycard	230
Novell Channel 1 DCB	346
Novell Channel 2 DCB	34E
Novell Channel 3 DCB	326
Novell Channel 4 DCB	32E
Novell standalone UPS board	231 or 240 (check the jumpers)
PS/2 Mouse Port	no I/O address parameter needed

The UPS DOWN parameter is the number of *minutes* (from 1 to 30) you want the UPS to sustain power before the NetWare OS shuts down the file server. The number you select should give users time to log out (if they still have power), but not unduly drain the UPS battery. The default UPS down time is three minutes, but you can make it longer or shorter than that. (To accommodate the improved battery capacities of newer UPSes, NetWare v2.15c increases the maximum UPS down time to 64,800 minutes, or roughly 45 days.) If the OS receives the "battery low" signal from the UPS before the specified down time is over, the OS will shut the server down within one minute after receiving the low battery signal.

The UPS WAIT parameter tells the OS how long to wait after UPS power kicks in before informing any operational workstations that the server is on auxiliary power. This accounts for times when the power fluctuates momentarily but is restored within a few seconds. The UPS wait time is specified in *seconds*, and can range from 5 to 300 seconds (five minutes). The UPS wait time must be less than the UPS down time. The default UPS wait time is fifteen seconds.

After you have entered the appropriate parameters in the SERVER.CFG file (only UPS TYPE and UPS IO are required), save the file as a DOS text file in SYS:SYSTEM.

The UPS Console Command

To determine the status of UPS monitoring at any time, type **UPS** at the file server console. A status message will appear, indicating whether UPS monitoring is currently enabled or disabled.

UPS-RELATED ERROR MESSAGES

After you save the SERVER.CFG file in the SYS:SYSTEM directory, the file server will check this directory during the bootup routine. If it encounters any invalid type numbers, misspelled keywords, or extra spaces in the SERVER.CFG file, you will see the following informational message on the console screen:

```
Invalid configuration in SERVER.CFG
```

This message does not abort the bootup, but the UPS monitoring feature will not function properly unless you correct the errors in the SERVER.CFG file and reboot the file server.

If you have correctly installed the UPS monitoring hardware and set up the proper parameters in the SERVER.CFG file, the following message will be displayed when you boot the file server:

```
UPS has been enabled
```

If there is no SERVER.CFG file in the SYS:SYSTEM directory, the file server will boot up normally without displaying any UPS-related message on the console.

Improving File Server Performance

In most networks, just keeping the file server up and running requires a great deal of time and effort. However, the simple fact that a server is working does not necessarily mean that it is operating at its peak performance level. Many do-it-yourself installers fumble their way through a network installation and somehow manage to get the server up, oblivious to the mediocre level of performance they have achieved. Even servers installed by pros may get bogged down in the face of increasing size and demands of the network. As existing LAN hardware and software matures and new technology is introduced, you must not become complacent about your file server's performance.

This section is dedicated to identifying and eliminating potential performance bottlenecks in the file server. In most cases, you can give a sluggish file server a significant performance boost by changing only a few simple aspects of the network.

• Chapter 25 describes how to identify the most common performance bottlenecks in the file server's hard disk channel, LAN communications channel, and CPU. This chapter gives possible remedies for each type of bottleneck, thereby improving overall file server performance.

• Chapter 26 gives tips for upgrading file server hardware and the NetWare operating system to improve file server performance. It also discusses some of the issues involved when adding file servers to the network.

• Chapter 27 explains how to overcome bottlenecks in the LAN communications channel by replacing slow network interface boards, changing an existing board's configuration, or adding a second board to split the network communication load.

• Chapter 28 explains how to overcome bottlenecks in the hard disk channel by adding a new disk channel to split the disk I/O load, adding new hard disk, and replacing old ones.

25 Potential Performance Bottlenecks

In this chapter, we'll look at some of the potential bottlenecks that affect the performance of NetWare 286 file servers. If you suspect that your file server's performance is not up to par, the information in this chapter will help you check the various performance-influencing areas that could be at the root of your server's problems.

THE MOST COMMON NETWORK BOTTLENECKS

Although data exchange across a network seems like a simple process, in reality it is a very complex process involving many hardware and software components. Any one of a number of factors can slow down or clog network performance. Among these factors are:

- The channel from the disk interface board to the host bus
- Disk seek and latency times
- The channel from the LAN interface board to the host bus
- LAN wire bandwidth
- Higher level protocols
- Network schemes used (Ethernet, ARCnet, or Token-Ring)
- The file server microprocessor
- The NetWare operating system (when pushed to its limits)
- The types of applications running on the network

These factors can be grouped into five major areas that interact to determine overall network performance: the network communications channel, the disk channel, the file server machine, the NetWare operating system itself, and the network applications. Most network performance problems can be traced to one of these areas.

Diagnosing Network Bottlenecks

One relatively simple, but not very scientific, way to determine where the performance bottleneck is on your file server is to look at the network utilization statistics. The key statistics that indicate performance are:

• File server CPU utilization percentage (available through FCONSOLE or MONITOR)
• Number of disk I/Os pending (available through FCONSOLE)
• Disk utilization percentage (available by observing the hard disk access light on the server and estimating how much of the time the light stays lit)

The chart in Figure 25-1 will help you pinpoint which area of your file server you should look at as a performance bottleneck, based on these three factors. We'll give more background on each area in the corresponding section in this chapter, along with general suggestions for alleviating the bottleneck condition. We'll discuss specific ways to implement these performance-improvement suggestions in subsequent chapters.

File Server Utilization	Disk I/Os Pending	Hard Disk Utilization	Probable Bottleneck
Low (below 50%)	Consistently large number	Disk light on constantly	Hard disk channel
Low (below 50%)	Zero	Disk light on intermittently	Communications channel
Consistently high (above 80%)	Zero	Disk light on intermittently	File server CPU

Figure 25-1: Chart for diagnosing potential bottleneck areas on your network.

The blame for most performance problems can be pinned on one of these three major bottleneck areas. However, this method of diagnosing bottlenecks is not foolproof; you must take other factors into consideration as well. For example, a slow data transfer speed between the network interface board and the file server CPU can contribute to high file server utilization, even if the file server CPU is fast.

The next three sections of this chapter discuss the issues to consider for each of these major areas, starting with the hard disk channel. At the end of this chapter, we'll look at performance issues that are strictly software-related (the NetWare OS and application programs).

THE HARD DISK CHANNEL

The efficiency of the hard disk channel—how fast it can shuttle data between the disk drive and the OS—is the number-one factor in determining server performance. Figure 25-2 shows the various hardware and software pieces that make up the hard disk channel in a NetWare file server. Poor disk channel performance could be caused by a weak link anywhere along the path from the hard disk to the file server CPU.

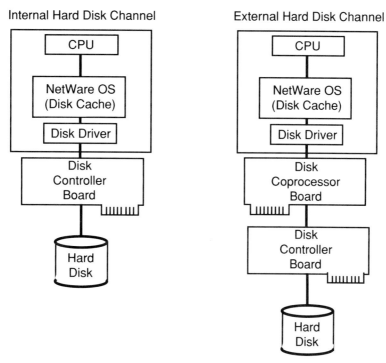

Figure 25-2: The hardware and software components of both internal and external hard disk channels.

As you can see, the disk channel is nearly identical for both internal and external hard disks. The only additional link in the external disk chain is the disk coprocessor board. The DCB usually governs the activity of a number of disk controllers and their attached disks.

Disk Channel Performance Factors

The factors that come into play in determining overall disk channel performance are:

- The disk's seek time
- The disk's interleave factor
- The disk controller type (ST-506, SCSI, or ESDI)
- The type of disk coprocessor board
- The efficiency of the disk driver
- The efficacy of NetWare's disk caching

Seek Time. A hard disk's seek time or access time measures how quickly the disk can locate and retrieve data stored on its surface. This specification is usually given in milliseconds (ms). Typical seek times are in the 30ms to 60ms range. Newer disks using the latest in disk drive technology can achieve 16ms seek times, while the very fastest are claiming seek times of around 10ms. Check the average access time specification for your hard disk. Anything under 30ms is good; if the access time is over 60ms, it may be time to upgrade to newer hard disk technology.

Another important rating related to seek time is the "sustained throughput" of the disk. This rating measures the speed of the entire disk I/O process, from the initial request for data from the CPU to accessing the data on the disk and moving it into memory for use by the requesting application. Sustained throughput is measured in kilobytes per second (KB/s).

Interleave Factor. The interleave factor indicates how many revolutions a hard disk must make to read one full track of data. Interleave helps determine how efficiently data can be transferred between the disk and the file server's memory. To understand interleave, consider the mechanics of how data is read from and written to the disk.

Data is stored in small units called sectors arranged in concentric circles or tracks on the surface of the disk. Most files occupy several sectors on the disk. Imagine a file stored on two sectors—sector A and sector B. When a request comes to read this file, the read/write heads position themselves over the appropriate track and wait for sector A to rotate into position. When sector A is in position, the read/write heads transfer the data to the controller, which passes it on to file server memory via the I/O bus. This transfer takes a certain amount of time, and most systems can't do it fast enough to be ready to grab data from the next physically-adjacent sector before that sector has already spun past the heads. If sectors A and B are placed right next to each other on the disk, the heads have to wait for the disk to make one complete revolution before sector B is once again in position.

Interleave spaces out consecutive sectors of a file so that data transfers can keep up with the rotation of the disk. The interleave factor is specified during the low-level format of the disk (usually done by the COMPSURF utility for NetWare disks). Interleave is usually expressed as a ratio indicating how far apart "consecutive" sectors are spaced. For example, if a disk is formatted with an interleave ratio of 3:1, consecutive sectors are spaced three physical sectors apart on the disk.

The optimal interleave for a disk depends on the efficiency of the data transfer mechanism (the controller and read/write heads). If the data transfer mechanism is fast enough to read every other sector, then a 2:1 interleave ratio (interleave factor of 2) yields the best performance. If you reformatted such a disk with a 1:1 interleave, sectors would be spaced contiguously on the disk, even though the controller isn't able to read contiguous sectors that quickly. The disk would still function with the incorrect interleave, but performance would suffer drastically because the disk has to make extra revolutions to read consecutive sectors of a file.

Hence, an incorrect interleave factor could affect the performance of your network hard disk. For most disks in AT-compatible file servers, the optimal interleave factor is 2. Data transfer on IBM PS/2 machines with the Micro Channel Architecture is fast enough to handle an interleave factor of 1. To make sure your disk is formatted with the correct interleave, contact the disk manufacturer and ask what the optimal interleave should be for your particular hard disks.

Disk Controller. As we have seen, the disk controller plays a big role in the overall performance of a hard disk. The controller is responsible for moving data between the drive and the server's I/O bus. Disk controller boards are generally categorized by the type of interface and data encoding scheme they use. The chart in Figure 25-3 gives the data transfer specifications for various types of disk controller interfaces.

Interface Type	Data Encoding Scheme	Data Transfer Rate
ST-506/412	MFM	5Mbps
SCSI	MFM	5Mbps
ST-506/412	RLL	7.5Mbps
SCSI	RLL	7.5Mbps
ESDI	RLL	10-24Mbps

Figure 25-3: Data transfer rates for common hard disk controller types.

As you can see, disk controllers that use MFM encoding are slower than those that use RLL encoding. Even low-end ESDI controllers provide twice the data transfer rate of MFM.

Before you run out and buy faster controllers, though, remember that the standard AT bus can currently handle data at a rate somewhere between 4Mbps and 8Mbps. IBM's MCA handles data faster, which is why the high-end PS/2 machines come with ESDI controllers. Generally, the disk controller/hard disk combination recommended by the manufacture will give the best possible performance from the hard disk end of the disk channel.

A number of new "caching" disk controllers use on-board RAM to hold large chunks of data prior to transferring it through the I/O bus to file server RAM. The idea behind controller caching is similar to that of NetWare's disk caching: the controller copies more than the requested amount of data into its RAM, anticipating that subsequent requests will be for related data. By servicing requests from RAM instead of accessing the disk each time, a caching controller can make the drive appear to have an access time of less than 1ms.

Disk Coprocessor Board. Using a disk coprocessor board generally increases the performance of the disk channel, because the processing of disk requests is off-loaded from the server CPU to the DCB. A typical DCB contains its own micro-processor and on-board memory so that it can handle disk read and write requests for the host CPU. The DCB also handles read-after-write verification upon completion of all disk write requests. This frees the server CPU to do other things while waiting for disk reads and writes to finish. Use of a DCB yields a significant performance increase over standard AT-type controllers (such as the IBM and Western Digital controllers).

DCBs are available for both the standard AT bus (16-bit board) and IBM's PS/2 Micro Channel Architecture. An Enhanced DCB is also available from Novell reseller channels; this DCB takes advantage of the "SCSI Disconnect" feature to further increase performance.

Disk Driver. The disk driver is a piece of software that provides the communications link between a disk channel and the NetWare OS. Among the disk driver's responsibilities are initializing the disk channel, coordinating channel operations, and handling time-outs and hardware interrupts from the controller.

Novell provides a variety of disk drivers for the most common types of disk channel interfaces. These drivers are included in the NetWare software package. In addition, third-parties can offer their own disk drivers as value-added disk drivers (VADDs). VADDs are difficult to write, and therefore they are not all equally efficient. Many of the earlier VADDs had to be revised due to compatibility problems and bugs. If you suspect that a VADD is hampering the performance of your disk channel, check with the vendor to see if a new version is available.

Disk Caching. As explained in Chapter 3, NetWare uses disk caching (along with a number of other techniques) to improve the disk I/O performance of the file server. The amount of memory you have in the file server largely determines how well disk caching works. You can check the efficacy of disk caching through the "Cache Statistics" and "Summary" options of FCONSOLE. Pay particular attention to the percentage of disk requests serviced from cache and the number of cache misses reported. The percentage of requests serviced from cache should be in the high 90s. If the percentage drops much lower than 95 percent, and you notice a significant rise in the number of cache misses, increase the number of cache buffers by adding more memory to the file server.

Possible Remedies for Disk Channel Bottlenecks

To summarize, then, here are some possible methods for alleviating a bottleneck in the disk channel:

- If the server cache statistics indicate that you don't have enough cache buffers, add more memory to the file server.
- If your disk and controller are slow or outdated, upgrade to faster disk hardware.
- If that doesn't help, add a new disk channel to the existing file server. (NetWare allows up to four external disk channels per server.) This will help distribute a heavy disk I/O load over several channels.
- If your server still can't handle disk I/O traffic, add a new file server to split the network load between two servers.

Chapter 26 explains how to add more memory to the file server. Chapter 29 explains how to perform the rest of these procedures.

THE COMMUNICATIONS CHANNEL

Figure 25-4 shows the various hardware and software components that constitute the LAN communications channel on the file server. If one of these areas is a bottleneck, improving that area will significantly improve performance.

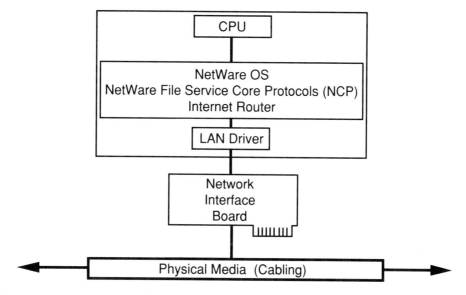

Figure 25-4: Hardware and software components of a NetWare LAN communication channel.

Communications Channel Performance Factors

Four major factors contribute to the overall performance of the network communications channel:

- The raw communications rate of the physical media
- The media access method
- The higher level protocols
- The network hardware/topology

Other related factors include:

- The efficiency of the LAN driver
- The design of the network interface board itself
- The bus bandwidth from the LAN interface board to the host machine

While all of these factors are interrelated in terms of how they affect network performance, we'll explain each one separately.

Raw Communications Rate

The raw communications rate is the speed at which bits of data move along the network cabling. This specification is usually measured in megabits per second (Mbps). Depending on the access method and higher-level protocols used, NetWare can utilize some types of LAN cabling up to 90 percent of their total communications rate capacity. With slower LANs (1Mbps to 2Mbps), a fast file server (such as a 16MHz 386-based machine) can easily outservice the wire's communications capability. In this situation, you can split the network by adding extra network interface boards to the file server; splitting the network in this way can double or triple the effective communications rate.

Media Access Method

The media access method is the way in which network interface boards arbitrate with each other for access to the shared wire. Two methods are currently in widespread use: carrier sense multiple access/collision detection (CSMA/CD) and token passing.

CSMA/CD. On a CSMA/CD (or "carrier contention") network, a network board must wait until no one else is talking on the network before it can talk. Then, as the board sends the packet, it listens to what is being said. If the board doesn't hear itself, another board is talking at the same time. Both boards jam each other, back off for a random amount of time (a different time for each board), then try again.

In theory, CSMA/CD networks are simple to design and move packets more quickly than token-passing systems through light- to medium-load networks. Theoretically, as the network load increases, the probability of collisions increases and performance drops off compared to token-passing systems, whose performance levels out under heavy loads. In actual practice, a 10Mbps Ethernet CSMA/CD network will always outperform a 4Mbps IBM Token-Ring Network. Tests have conclusively shown that in certain situations Ethernet can even outperform 16Mbps Token-Ring. Even though it is statistically possible to generate cases where performance dies because of collisions, in actual practice collisions occur so rarely that their effect is negligible. The higher raw performance of the network becomes the bigger factor.

One disadvantage of carrier contention is that it does not provide a hardware-level acknowledgment that the target node actually received the packet. (Token-Ring networks generally receive this type of acknowledgment from the hardware.) In CSMA/CD networks, any acknowledgment must come from a higher level. Network interface boards that lose a high percentage of packets can cause performance problems. Some of the early Ethernet boards did lose packets, not because the boards didn't see the packets, but because the boards didn't have any memory available to copy them into RAM fast enough. Novell could have added a low-level acknowledgment packet to improve early Ethernet performance, but the improved design of subsequent Ethernet boards has eliminated the problem.

Token Passing. Token passing is more complicated than CSMA/CD. The network interface boards pass a special "token" packet to each other. Possession of the token packet means that the board can send a message if it wants. The trick to token passing is adapting the passing sequence when new boards are added to the ring, and detecting when a board quits operating.

Token passing is more deterministic in guaranteeing access to all workstations. Token-passing networks can be slower in light- and medium-load situations because a workstation must wait its turn before broadcasting. However, in heavy-load situations, token passing ensures that no workstation gets lost in the crunch. IBM chose to use token passing in its Token-Ring LAN products primarily because of the control and predictability it provides.

Higher-Level Protocols

NetWare's low-level LAN communication protocol works best with fairly reliable networks (those in which more than 90 percent of packets sent are actually delivered). However, the communication protocols used at higher levels can also have a significant effect on performance.

NetWare's Internet Packet Exchange (IPX) uses a simple request-response protocol built on top of a datagram or "connectionless" communication protocol. When a workstation sends a request packet to the file server, the file server fulfills the request and sends back a response packet. Thus, there are only two packets sent for each request. The workstation knows that its request was received intact by the server when it receives the response packet.

A "connection-based" protocol involves guaranteed delivery and sequencing of network packets. With this approach, an acknowledgment packet must be relayed to the sending workstation for every packet sent, in effect doubling the number of packets being transmitted over the wire. Acknowledgment packets are typically small, so the amount of data transferred is not doubled, only the number of packets. Any connection-based service requires more processing at both ends of the connection.

Sometimes, a higher level protocol is built on top of a connection-based service. An example of this approach can be seen in certain implementations of NetBIOS. At a higher level, NetBIOS can require an acknowledgment that not only acknowledges the receipt of a packet, but also indicates that the receiving workstation wanted the packet. The lower-level connection service does not know if the work-station wanted the packet or not, so NetBIOS has to send an acknowledgment packet at its level as well. This action doubles the number of packets being sent per file server request. In the worst case, there can be eight packets sent per file server request—one request, one response, and six acknowledgments.

Because of this packet overhead, the use of NetBIOS can degrade network performance. If you are running applications that require NetBIOS, check with the vendor to see if a new version is available that can run without NetBIOS.

Hardware/Topology Performance Comparison

The debate over the performance merits of one networking topology and access scheme over another has been raging since the inception of LANs. Since Net-Ware supports virtually every available type of network hardware and cabling, the question becomes one of which hardware/topology combination yields the fastest throughput on a NetWare 286 network.

Traditionally, the debate revolves around raw transmission speed. The Ethernet camp has claimed that its 10Mbps transmission speed beats Token-Ring's 4Mbps and ARCnet's 2.5Mbps hands down. The IBM Token-Ring camp countered that by coming up with a 16Mbps version. Besides, they claim that Ethernet's CSMA/CD medium access protocol allows collisions on the wire to degrade performance considerably as more workstations are added to the network. The Ethernet proponents respond by pointing out that Token-Ring's token-passing protocol adds a significant amount of overhead, and that when a small number of workstations are passing a large amount of data across the network, time spent passing a token is time that could be better spent transferring actual data. Through it all, the ARCnet community seems quite content with their slower, simpler token-passing alternative.

In theory, their points are all valid. However, when actually implemented on a NetWare 286 network, events don't always adhere to the theoretical norm. One recent set of benchmarks performed jointly by Novell engineers and *PC Week* magazine pitted Ethernet, ARCnet, 4Mbps Token-Ring, and 16Mbps Token-Ring against each other on a NetWare 286 network. As expected, both Ethernet and Token-Ring outperformed ARCnet by a wide margin. Contrary to expectations, however, Ethernet performed significantly better than even 16Mbps Token-Ring, and the data transfer speed of 16Mbps Token-Ring was only slightly faster than the 4Mbps version (although the slowness was attributed more to the LAN driver than to the topology itself). Of course, benchmark results are valid only in the same environment in which they were measured, so you mustn't generalize any particular benchmarks to every network situation. These benchmarks emphasize that you can't look at raw transmission speed alone when determining the overall performance of networking hardware.

Ultimately, the performance claims of any network hardware/topology system must be weighed against a number of other factors: ease of installation, cost per node, quality of manufacturing, efficiency of the associated LAN drivers, availability of supporting hardware (repeaters, hubs, media access units, and so on), flexibility of the topology, cabling types supported, adherence to standards, and compatibility with other systems (Macintosh networks, minicomputers, mainframes, or large-scale network systems such as the TCP/IP-based Internet). With that in mind, here are some guidelines for maximizing network performance by matching the hardware/topology with the usage of the network.

Getting the Best Performance out of Ethernet. Ethernet, with its fast transmission speed and carrier contention access scheme, will yield the best performance on networks where a small number of workstations transmit consistently large files. Software development groups and computer graphics departments are two good examples of this kind of network. Because of its roots in the TCP/IP world, Ethernet is also the logical choice for connectivity to TCP/IP-based networks. IEEE has published the 802.3 Ethernet CSMA/CD standard.

Ethernet Strong Points. On the ease of installation scale, Ethernet ranks about in the middle. Since you typically need to run only a single cable to connect all nodes, cabling costs are low. You can make connections at varying intervals along the cable, which is fairly easy to splice and add on to. Ethernet boards are moderately expensive, but Ethernet LAN drivers are among the most efficient. A wide variety of Ethernet repeaters, transceivers, and terminators are readily available. Originally run only on thick or thin coaxial cable, Ethernet now comes in twisted-pair and fiber optic flavors as well. A number of Ethernet cards are available for Macintosh workstations, and connections to DEC's VAX hosts are usually made over Ethernet.

Ethernet Weak Points. Because an infinite number of collisions could theoretically occur before a packet gets sent, it is impossible to determine the maximum amount of time that may be required to send a packet on a CSMA/CD network. This timing unpredictability is the basis for most arguments against Ethernet's suitability for applications where real-time control of a process is critical. Another drawback of linear-bus Ethernet is that a break in the main trunk cable will bring down the entire network. Ethernet also seems to be more temperamental, demanding more after-installation care and support than ARCnet or Token-Ring networks. Ethernet's fast 10Mbps speed may even be a weak point if you consider that this high speed pushes the electrical limitations of thin copper cable. Without proper shielding, even small amounts of electromagnetic interference can cause significant performance degradation on Ethernet cabling.

Getting the Best Performance out of Token-Ring. Because Token-Ring's deterministic token-passing protocol gives each workstation an equal opportunity to access the network, it performs better in computing environments where a large number of workstations consistently issue many small requests—database and transaction processing environments, for instance. In a token-passing network, you can determine the maximum amount of time that each workstation must wait to access the network. This predictability is important in real-time control applications, such as those commonly found in manufacturing and robotic machinery shops. Because Token-Ring is now the only major LAN supported by IBM (the old IBM PC Network is passe), most IBM minicomputers and mainframes provide for a seamless connection with Token-Ring LANs. This fact makes Token-Ring the choice for IBM-only-no-matter-what operations. IEEE has also published the token-passing method used by Token-Ring as the 802.2 standard.

Token-Ring Strong Points. In networks using a token-passing scheme, performance doesn't degrade as quickly as with carrier contention networks when more workstations are added. Token-Ring throughput stays fairly constant in the face of increasing network traffic, and, of course, you don't have to worry about collisions. Redundant cabling and built-in protocol error handling add greatly to Token-Ring's reliability. If a break occurs in one cable, the network can continue to operate (although at a reduced speed) by switching to the redundant cable. Both versions of Token-Ring are faster than ARCnet, although the actual difference between 16Mbps and 4Mbps Token-Ring is not as pronounced as might be expected. You can bridge a 16Mbps Token-Ring network and a 4Mbps Token-Ring network together in the same NetWare file server (each network will continue to run at its respective transmission speed). The current slowness of Token-Ring has the potential to become a strong point later on. Since Token-Ring does not currently push the limits of either the hardware or cabling, future improvements in both the boards and the drivers could effectively quadruple Token-Ring's performance.

Token-Ring Weak Points. Cost is the most prohibitive factor in Token-Ring networks. The boards, cabling, and other required hardware is expensive. IBM's version requires a multistation access unit (MAU) for every eight users. Other vendors offer more stations per MAU. The ring wiring scheme is more complicated and less flexible than Ethernet's linear bus or ARCnet's combination bus/star scheme. Cabling distances are much more restrictive in Token-Ring; with the IBM cabling system, the maximum distance between nodes is around 700 feet. NetWare 286 Token-Ring drivers are notoriously inefficient, which usually accounts for the relative slowness of Token-Ring networks. As new drivers are written to take advantage of the larger packet sizes that the 16Mbps boards can handle, this bottleneck will be somewhat alleviated. The slow chips used on IBM Token-Ring boards present another performance obstacle. One quirk in Token-Ring's token-passing protocol (as opposed to ARCnet's) is that each station must regenerate the token as it is passed around the ring, slightly reducing its actual throughput.

Getting the Best Performance Out of ARCnet. There is certainly a place for ARCnet, as evidenced by its growing popularity in recent years. Because it also uses a token-passing protocol, ARCnet is well suited to the same types of applications as Token-Ring (as long as high transmission speed is not a requirement).

ARCnet Strong Points. The appeal of ARCnet lies in its being relatively inexpensive, and easy to install, expand, and reconfigure. Its free-form topology adapts itself easily to the most challenging site requirements. If a break occurs in a cable connecting a workstation to a hub, only that workstation will be affected. The rest of the network can continue to operate normally. Even though ARCnet's 2.5Mbps transmissions are significantly slower than Ethernet's or Token-Ring's, this slowness makes the transmissions less susceptible to electromagnetic interference because it doesn't push the limits of the cabling medium. No IEEE standard has been established for the ARCnet token-passing protocol, which is slightly different from the one used by Token-Ring. However, because of the way ARCnet handles the token, its performance is significantly better than Token-Ring's on small networks of ten nodes or less.

ARCnet Weak Points. ARCnet sends out a separate token on the wire for each station on the network (as opposed to Token-Ring, which circulates a single token around the ring). As more ARCnet stations are added, the number of tokens circulating increases, thus slowing down the network's data throughput. Another major drawback of ARCnet is its trouble-prone station addressing mechanism. A single ARCnet network supports up to 255 stations, but each station address must be set manually (usually via a switch block on the boards themselves). If two stations are accidentally set to the same address, the entire network comes to a halt.

LAN Driver

The LAN driver is the piece of software that provides the link between the physical cable/network interface board and the NetWare OS's routing and file service processes. It is the LAN driver's responsibility to build the packets of data that are sent out over the network cabling. The driver also receives packets off the wire and checks them for transmission errors.

Because the LAN driver essentially "runs" its associated network interface board, poor performance by a board is often the fault of a slow or inefficient LAN driver. Regardless of how fast and technologically advanced a network interface board is, it cannot live up to its full performance potential without a LAN driver specifically written to take advantage of the new capabilities of the hardware. For example, IBM's new 16Mbps boards support packet sizes of up to 18KB. However, the NetWare 286 drivers written for these boards transmit data in 1KB packets, thereby limiting the performance of the new boards.

Two Final Hardware Considerations

Two other factors affecting the performance of the LAN communications channel are the design of the network interface board and the amount of bandwidth it provides for transferring data to the file server's I/O bus. The average file server spends upwards of 70-80 percent of its time moving data in and out of the network interface boards. Consequently, if the board is an 8-bit PC-class board, a file server with a fast microprocessor will have to be "wait-stated" down to old 4.77MHz 8088 speeds. Upgrading the network interface boards to zero-wait-state 16- or 32-bit boards can significantly improve file server performance.

Possible Remedies for Communication Channel Bottlenecks

Here is a summary of some of the ways to unclog a bottleneck in the LAN communication channel:

- If you are still using old 8-bit network interface boards in the file server, by all means upgrade to a 16-bit or 32-bit board.
- Upgrade to faster LAN hardware (switching from ARCnet to Ethernet, or from 4Mbps to 16Mbps Token-Ring, for example).
- If wiring problems or expense preclude upgrading, you can often improve network performance by adding a second LAN board to the file server and splitting the LAN into two segments. This approach is like adding an additional lane on the freeway; it allows more data to flow at the same time.
- If your server still can't handle LAN traffic, add a new file server to split the network load between two servers.

Chapter 27 explains how to perform these procedures.

THE FILE SERVER

NetWare 286 was originally written to take advantage of the Intel 80286 16-bit microprocessor. It will run on an 80386- or 80486-based machine, but will not exploit the enhanced features of these newer chips. Nevertheless, the question of what type of file server will yield the better performance is worth considering.

286, 386, or 486

Network performance is influenced by a number of factors, but in most NetWare 286 networks it seems that 80386-based file servers are faster than 286-based servers. Much of the superiority in performance results from the higher CPU clock speeds of 386 machines. In one test using the PERFORM2 utility, a 386-based file server running two networks (Ethernet and Token-Ring) showed a 30-35 percent increase in performance over a 286-based machine running the same network configuration. However, CPU speed is not the only factor to consider; wait states can influence performance just as significantly. For example, it is possible for a 286 file server with fast, zero-wait-state memory to outperform a 16MHz 386 file server with slower memory access.

80486-based file servers were just becoming generally available as this book was written. Given their comparatively high price tag and the fact that NetWare 286 was written for the 80286 chip, using a 486 machine to run NetWare 286 makes little sense.

Another consideration to keep in mind is how soon you plan to upgrade to NetWare 386, which requires a 386- or 486-based file server. If such an upgrade looms in your long-range plans, you can more easily justify a higher investment in hardware that will be used longer.

The Effect of Faster Workstations

Another good question to pose is, what if I keep my slow 286-based file server and just get faster workstations? In 1989, engineers in Novell's NetWare Service and Support Group (NSSG) ran a series of tests to determine the effect of faster workstations on LAN performance. The tests involved running the PERFORM2 network performance analysis program on a switchable-speed workstation. In these tests, doubling the speed of the workstation resulted in a 30-35 percent increase in network throughput. So faster workstations do help overall network performance, as perceived by the workstation users. Of course, most of the performance increase occurs because the applications run faster after being loaded on the workstation, not from any benefit at the file server end.

Another study, published by *LAN TIMES* in 1987, subjected various workstations on an Ethernet network to a battery of tests designed to measure network response time. These tests showed that on a LAN with light to moderate file server utilization (mean percentage below 50 percent), upgrading from a 4.77MHz machine to an 8MHz machine increased that workstation's network response time by approximately 100-125 percent. Going from an 8MHz machine to a 16MHz or 20MHz machine further increased the network response time by approximately 25 percent. The network response times for 16MHz and 20MHz machines were nearly equal. According to the study, this leveling off occurred because the ability of both machines to interact with the network interface boards reaches a threshold at the same point. It is debatable whether this threshold can be attributed to the internal bus architectures, the network interface boards, or the LAN drivers. But under four different application mixes, the network response times on 16MHz and 20MHz workstations were not significantly different.

As the LAN graduates from a medium to heavy load and on to become fully loaded (mean utilization in the 95-100 percent range), the performance benefits of upgrading from a 4.77MHz machine to an 8MHz, 16MHz, or 20MHz machine become insignificant. In other words, under extreme network loads, a 4.77MHz workstation can experience the same network response time as a 20MHz workstation. This situation is most likely caused by a combination of two variables: first, the communications channel may be nearing the threshold at which each client is forced to wait for network access; second, the server may be nearing a threshold where it consistently receives more client requests than it can service. Both of these conditions reduce the benefits of increasing local horsepower, since all workstations experience the same delay in accessing the network.

File Server Memory

Sufficient random access memory is critical to a file server's performance. The server must have enough memory to hold the OS itself, the FATs and directory entry tables for all disks, the number of communication buffers and indexed files specified during installation, and the three dynamic memory pools used by the OS. In addition, the TTS option and any VAPs running in the server take up a certain amount of memory. Whatever is left over is used for disk caching. It is the amount of disk caching memory that makes the most noticeable difference in file server performance.

Options for Upgrading the File Server

If the file server hardware itself appears to be your main performance inhibitor, here are some possible solutions for file server bottleneck:

- Upgrade the file server to a machine with a faster microprocessor.
- Split the network load by adding another server.

Both options involve the purchase of an additional computer, so budgetary constraints will come into play in this decision. If you go the second route and add another server, you will have to consider the issues involved in creating an internetwork (most notably bridging, routing, and backbone cables). Both upgrading the file server and adding another server to the network are explained in the next chapter.

NETWARE OPERATING SYSTEM LIMITATIONS

Your choice of NetWare operating systems can have a major impact on the performance of your network. Whichever one you chose, avoid trying to push the stated maximums to their limits. Typically, these are theoretical maximums that can't all be reached at once in real-life network situations. For example, it's very rare to have 100 users all logged in to an SFT NetWare file server at the same time, with all 100 doing productive work on the LAN. The limits of each NetWare OS are summarized below. (For a more complete comparison between versions, see Appendix A.)

SFT, Advanced, or ELS NetWare

Novell has stratified its operating systems into three classes: System Fault Tolerant (SFT) NetWare, Advanced NetWare, and Entry Level Solution (ELS) NetWare. ELS NetWare is further divided into ELS Level I and ELS Level II. The main idea behind this stratification is to provide varying levels of functionality for networks of varying sizes, purposes, and needs.

SFT NetWare is the top-of-the-line product in the NetWare 286 lineup. Its extra fault tolerant capabilities (disk mirroring and transaction tracking) go beyond the basic fault-tolerance built into the other levels of NetWare. Accordingly, SFT NetWare should be the choice for large workgroups or enterprise-wide networks that need extra protection against data corruption due to disk channel failures, power outages, or other LAN failures.

Here are the stated maximums for SFT NetWare v2.1*x* per file server:

Number of users (connections):	100
File server RAM:	16MB
Total disk storage:	2GB
Number of hard disks:	32
Number of volumes:	32
Volume and file size:	255MB
Number of files open simultaneously:	1,000
Number of LAN drivers:	4
Number of disk drivers:	5

Advanced NetWare is a mid-range product well suited for small- to medium-sized workgroups or departmental LANs with more than eight users. It is virtually identical to SFT NetWare as far as the number of users supported, drivers supported, connectivity options, and basic fault tolerance (redundant FATs and directory entry tables, read-after-write verification, Hot Fix, and UPS monitoring). The only differences are that Advanced NetWare lacks disk mirroring and TTS, and that Advanced NetWare lets you run the OS either dedicated or nondedicated.

ELS NetWare Level II is an eight-user version of NetWare. It supports fewer LAN drivers than Advanced NetWare, and limits you to only internal hard disks. The internetworking and connectivity options are also limited with ELS Level II.

However, ELS Level II provides all the basic fault tolerant features of Advanced NetWare, and is ideal for small businesses and departments with eight users or less. The maximum file size and number of opened files are the same as for Advanced NetWare, although they are typically much smaller because of the internal drive only restriction.

ELS NetWare Level I is a four-user version. Its LAN driver support is even more limited, and there are no provisions at all for internetwork connectivity. ELS Level I is aimed at very small offices of four users or less who simply want to share disk storage and printer resources. Its maximums are the same as for ELS Level II.

Dedicated or Nondedicated OS

With ELS or Advanced NetWare 286, the file server can run NetWare either dedicated (devoted solely to file and printer sharing) or nondedicated (able to run DOS programs at the same time). A dedicated file server offers several performance advantages: performance is higher than in a nondedicated server, and the server is not subject to crashes caused by failure of the workstation software or error on the part of the workstation user. On the other hand, a dedicated server requires the purchase of an additional computer.

In most cases, it's simply more practical for a server to be dedicated, aside from the fact that statistics show that nondedicated servers crash twice as frequently as dedicated servers. Nondedicated servers have three very serious drawbacks. First, a user in a DOS session on the nondedicated server can crash the machine and consequently the whole network. Second, since the nondedicated server has network operations working concurrently with DOS sessions, the operation of the DOS session can slow down the network, and vice versa. And third, since the server has so many network-oriented components, usage of a DOS session can cause interrupt problems.

So what about the extra cost of that additional computer? Because a dedicated server is used only for running the NetWare OS, the display can be the most inexpensive monochrome monitor that money can buy. Weigh the cost of the extra machine against the cost of the potential network downtime you're asking for with nondedicated NetWare.

NETWORK APPLICATION CONSIDERATIONS

One often-overlooked aspect of network performance is the choice of applications to run on the file server. This should actually be the most important factor to consider, as the network's overall performance is intrinsically tied to how fast the users perceive their applications to be running at their workstations.

Types of Network Applications

There are basically three categories of applications typically found on NetWare LANs. The first category includes traditional standalone applications (such as word processors and spreadsheets) that have been modified to run on a network. These revamped applications do not particularly take advantage of the distributed processing capabilities inherent in NetWare. Users run the applications from their workstation, where the entire program is loaded into memory from the copy residing on the file server. Data transfer is heavy between the workstation and file server, because the workstation is essentially using the file server as a large, central hard disk. File locks are generally used to prevent several users from accessing the same file at the same time.

The second category includes distributed-processing applications (such as multiuser database programs) that were developed specifically for network use. In these types of applications, several workstations can access and alter the same data files at the same time. Physical or logical record locks synchronize multiuser access. Still, each workstation loads the application into its own memory and processes all data locally. The file server acts as the source of shared files that the applications (running at the workstations) access through file reads and writes.

The third category encompasses the new generation of server-based applications. In this type of application, the workstations become "clients" of a "server" that performs services other than the usual file services of the traditional file server. The services provided by a server-based application can either be something the workstations cannot do for themselves (usually acting as print server, CD ROM server, or communications gateway involving specialized hardware not locally available to the client) or something the workstations could do for themselves but not as efficiently as the server (as is usually the case with database servers and batch job servers).

The Effect of Applications on Performance

Modified standalone applications and distributed-processing approaches involve a lot of network traffic to and from the server. In the case of a database record search, for example, the workstation would have to tell the file server to lock the file regions it is going to access, then read the database files itself to find the record. Other workstations would be prevented from accessing the locked file regions for the duration of the search, which could necessitate many retries on a heavily-used network.

In a typical server-based approach, the client workstation would simply send a high-level request to the database server to find a record matching the specified criteria. The database server engine takes over from there, interacting directly with the file system to service the request (thus circumventing the file server software entirely). The database server would have to do some synchronization within itself in order to service several client requests simultaneously, but that is easily done. When the server finds the requested record, it sends only that record back to the client workstation.

By concentrating processing at the server and returning to the client only what it needs for its own local processing, many server-based applications significantly reduce packet traffic over the network wire. The amount of actual disk I/O is usually about the same in either approach; however, concentrating processing at the server puts more demands on the file server's CPU. Therefore, if you have a slow file server or LAN topology, server-based applications will perform better because they minimize file server requests. Conversely, the distributed-processing approach performs better with fast file servers and LANs.

Another way to reduce the network traffic generated by an application is to have your most demanding users run applications from a local hard disk instead of from the file server. This setup eliminates the packet traffic involved in copying the application program files from the server to the workstation. The users can still access data files stored on the server, even though they are running the program locally.

26 Upgrading the File Server and OS

Renovating an old house is not an easy task; in fact, it's a major hassle. People usually don't even consider it unless there is a good reason—perhaps the roof leaks, or the walls don't hold heat. Whatever the reason, the renovation will hopefully make the home more livable and prolong its lifespan.

Upgrading a LAN is the same way. While it is a hassle to make changes and learn how to use new features, the decision of whether or not to upgrade must not be based on whatever seems easiest at the moment. It will take some initial effort on your part to do what is required to bring your LAN up to par. You'll have to learn a few new things, maybe even teach the network users some new tricks. But there are justifiable reasons to upgrade:

- To improve the overall performance of the LAN
- To meet the changing needs of the LAN
- To get the latest technology for the best price

This chapter details how to upgrade the file server itself or the NetWare operating system. In some cases, you'll want to upgrade both at the same time.

UPGRADING THE FILE SERVER HARDWARE

Decisions to upgrade network servers are usually based on the assumption that increased server horsepower equals increased performance. In 1988, the *LAN TIMES* performed a set of tests to measure the response times in four different server environments:

- A 4.77MHz IBM XT
- An 8MHz IBM AT
- A 16MHz Novell 386A
- A 20MHz Compaq 386/20

The testbed included 50 AT workstations operating at 8MHz, interconnected with Novell's Ethernet cards and cabling. The tester created a controlled environment by running an identical, automated database application to generate network traffic on each workstation. The network load generated by the database application was intentionally on the high end of network utilization scale (90 percent mean server utilization), in hopes of discovering both the performance ceilings and the effects of incremental load increases.

The tests were run numerous times, first with six workstations, then 12, 20, 30, 40, and finally 50 workstations. In each configuration, the tester measured the network response times in terms of the number of network requests processed per second. Figure 26-1 shows the results for each file server type:

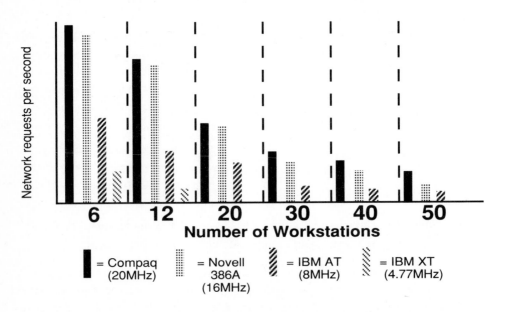

Figure 26-1: Comparative network throughput for different file server types and network sizes.

As expected, the workstations' ability to access the network decreased as the network load increased for all four servers. Most importantly, though, the tests verify the assumption that any increase in server CPU speed makes a difference in the network performance ceiling. The following chart summarizes the performance improvement you can expect when upgrading from one CPU to another.

Server CPU Upgrade	Network Performance Improvement
4.77MHz 8086/8088 to 8MHz 80286)	Four-fold improvement over 4.77MHz performance
8MHz 80286 to 16MHz 80386	Double the 8MHz 286 performance
16MHz 80386 to 20MHz 80386	Marginal improvement under light loads Double the 16MHz performance under heaviest loads

If your current installation is built around an XT file server, you can expect to raise your performance ceiling by 400-800 percent, depending on the CPU speed you choose as part of your upgrade.

Upgrading the File Server CPU

Obviously, the easiest way to upgrade the file server CPU is to purchase an entirely new computer with a faster microprocessor. If you have an XT or 286 AT computer, you can obtain kits to upgrade the motherboard itself. However, this type of retrofitting is not recommended for NetWare file servers. A critical LAN component like the file server should be the highest quality, most reliable computer your budget will allow.

Depending on what type of CPU you are upgrading from, you may also have to upgrade your NetWare operating system at the same time. For example, if you are running the dedicated version of ELS NetWare Level II v2.12 on an 8086-based machine and you want to upgrade to a 286- or 386-based file server, you have two options. One is to use the nondedicated 286 option available in ELS II v2.12. That way you don't have to pay for an OS upgrade; however, you're forced to run nondedicated NetWare. If you want to run dedicated NetWare 286, you must upgrade to ELS II v2.15, Advanced, or SFT NetWare. Check with your NetWare reseller for information on upgrade policies and prices.

Adding Memory to the File Server

Another way to boost the performance of your file server is to add more RAM. As explained in the previous chapter, NetWare needs a certain amount of memory for its basic operations (the OS itself, FATs and directory entry tables, communication buffers, FAT indexes, and dynamic memory pools). The Transaction Tracking System and any VAPs or VADDs require memory as well. Whatever memory is left over is used for disk caching.

An extreme shortage of file server RAM prevents the server from booting up in the first place. You should keep track of the server's memory usage and disk caching statistics in FCONSOLE. An increase in the number of "Cache Misses" indicates that the server needs more memory to create additional cache buffers. The amount of "Unused Server Memory" should be less than 8KB. If it is more than that, it might indicate that memory is not being used efficiently.

What Kind of Memory. In any IBM PC compatible, random access memory can be classified as either conventional, expanded, or extended memory. *Conventional* memory is the memory from 0 to 640KB normally used by DOS. The 8086 CPU was limited to 1MB of addressable memory space, the first 640KB of which was the maximum amount available to DOS. An 80286 CPU running in *real mode* emulates the 8086 and is subject to the same limitations, including the 640KB addressable memory limit. In *protected mode*, the 80286 can address more than 640KB of memory.

Most computers now come with at least 1MB of memory installed. Extra memory can be added to a PC either on the motherboard or through an add-on memory board with RAM chips. To get around the 640KB conventional memory barrier, several companies have come up with ways for DOS to use additional memory beyond 640KB in the form of *expanded* memory. For example, version 4.0 of the Lotus/Intel/Microsoft Expanded Memory Specification (EMS) allows DOS to access up to 8MB of memory by using a "paging" approach. The total amount of RAM set up as expanded memory is divided into 64KB segments, or pages. The PC deals with only one 64KB page at a time, no matter how many megabytes of expanded memory there are. Only applications specifically written to the EMS standard can use expanded memory.

Extended memory is memory above 1MB. Because the 8086 CPU is limited to 1MB of addressable space, extended memory can only be accessed by 80286 or higher CPUs running in protected mode.

While on the surface these three types of PC memory seem quite separate, the distinction can become confusing in real life. For example, many newer PCs use the 360KB of memory between 640KB and 1MB as *shadow RAM*, making it unavailable for use as expanded memory. Worse, extended memory can be remapped to be used as expanded memory.

What does all this memory mishmash mean to NetWare? NetWare requires the file server's memory to be in a continuous block, with no paging. Consequently, NetWare cannot use expanded memory, only conventional and extended memory. Dedicated versions of NetWare 286 use all the extended memory available, up to 16MB. Nondedicated NetWare 286 runs DOS applications in real mode (in the first 640KB of memory), while the OS itself runs in protected mode (using any extended memory above 1MB).

With nondedicated NetWare, it is possible to use both expanded memory and extended memory in the file server. You must set up the expanded memory to be used by DOS applications only, just as you would for a standalone machine. For the nondedicated file server, however, the expanded memory *cannot* be extended memory that has been redefined as expanded. You will most likely have to acquire a separate add-on memory board used exclusively for expanded memory.

How Much Memory. A NetWare 286 file server can have up to 16MB of RAM. So states the marketing literature, anyway. In actual practice, 16MB is an unattainable maximum, for several reasons.

Remember that NetWare uses any memory remaining (after all OS and VAP needs are met) for disk cache buffers. After a certain point, though, you can actually have *too many* cache buffers for NetWare to search through. When this occurs (usually when you have over 800 cache buffers), it can take longer to search through the cache buffers than to physically access the disk. Eight hundred cache buffers represents approximately 3.2MB of memory (800 buffers x 4KB memory per buffer). So if your file server OS and VAPs used up, say, 1.5 to 2MB of RAM (a fairly typical range), you would need at most around 5MB total RAM for effective disk caching. You can check to see how many cache buffers your file server has by using the "File Server Statistics Summary" option in FCONSOLE.

Another memory usage problem occurs (albeit rarely) when you have more than 8MB of extended memory in a server that is running SFT NetWare with TTS. For some reason, NetWare is unable to use all available memory in this case. You can check how much of your server's memory is "unused" via FCONSOLE's "File Server Statistics Summary" option.

So how do you determine how much memory your file server need? Following is a simple method for calculating memory based on either the file server configuration you have already set up or the one you plan to install. As a sample scenario, we'll see how much memory a file server would need to run SFT NetWare 286 with TTS, two 100MB hard disks, the Btrieve VAP, and five indexed files. Assume that we accepted all other NETGEN defaults for number of directory entries, open files, and other parameters.

First, determine the size of the *NetWare operating system file* itself. For most NetWare 286 servers, the NET$OS.EXE file is around 400KB-450KB. With 5.25-inch diskettes, the OS is split into two separate files, NET$OS.EX1 and NET$-OS.EX2, in the SYS:SYSTEM directory. Map a drive to SYS:SYSTEM, then type the following command from any workstation to determine the exact size of the OS:

```
DIR NET$OS.*
```

In our example, let's say the OS totaled 420KB. If you haven't generated the OS yet, use 450KB just to be safe.

Second, determine how much memory it takes to *cache and hash* the FAT and directory entry table of each hard disk attached to the file server. Use the following estimations:

Cache File Allocation Tables	1KB per megabyte of disk capacity
Hash directory entry tables	4 bytes per entry
Cache directory entry tables	32 bytes per entry

NetWare 286 automatically caches all FATs and hashes all directory entry tables. Caching the directory entry tables is an option selectable during installation, but it is highly recommended. If you haven't installed NetWare yet, figure the number of entries for each disk as follows.

Because data is stored on a NetWare disk in logical blocks of 4KB (4,096 bytes), and since each directory entry is 32 bytes long, a block can hold 128 directory entries (32 x 128 = 4,096). The minimum size of a directory entry table is 4 blocks (512 entries). Calculate the default number of directory entries by using the following formula:

512 entries minimum + (128 entries for every 2MB of disk capacity)

This formula assumes an average file size of 64KB; you may need more directory entries if you have many small files, or fewer if you have a small number of large files. A 100MB hard disk containing average-size files would need 6,912 entries in its directory entry table (512 + [128 x 50] = 6,912). The total caching and hashing memory requirements for this disk would be 100KB + 27KB + 216KB = 243KB. Since we have two 100MB disks, the total memory involved here is 486KB.

Third, figure in roughly 500 bytes (0.5KB) of memory for each *communication* or *routing buffer* set aside for the file server. The NETGEN default is 40, so that would make 20KB of memory. (Note that in NetWare v2.15c, the default number of communication buffers was increased to 100.)

Fourth, count 1KB of server memory for each *indexed file*. We specified five indexed files, so that makes 5KB of memory.

Fifth, add in the nonvariables. TTS takes approximately 22KB of memory to run, and the OS needs about 90KB for its dynamic memory pools. The memory used by various VAPs is listed below:

Btrieve VAP	500KB
Keyboard lock VAP	100KB or less
Streaming tape backup VAP	300KB
Macintosh VAPs	3MB or more

Check the VAP or VADD documentation, or contact the third-party vendor, to determine how much memory other VAPs and VADDs require. For our sample server, the total for TTS, dynamic memory, and the Btrieve VAP add up to 612KB altogether.

Now total up the five subtotals to get a grand total of file server memory needed *before* disk caching. In our sample scenario, this grand total would be:

420KB for the NetWare OS
486KB for caching and hashing FATs and directory entry tables
 20KB for communication buffers
  5KB for indexed files
612KB for TTS, Btrieve, and dynamic memory
———
1,543KB total memory before disk caching

The OS will use any memory over and above this roughly 1.5MB for disk cache buffers. Remember, though, we don't want to have more than 800 cache buffers, which translates into about 3.2MB of memory. Installing anywhere from 2MB to 4MB of extended memory, for a total of 3MB to 5MB of RAM, usually yields the best overall performance.

Memory Add-On Boards. Normally, to add extended memory to a personal computer, you must purchase a memory add-on board. Check with the manufacturer of your file server to determine what types of memory add-ons are available. Typically, you get a single board and install banks of RAM chips in 1MB increments, up to a maximum of about 4MB per board.

To avoid potential RAM problems, make sure all of the RAM chips installed on a given memory board are of the same type, or at least have the same speed rating, which is usually given in nanoseconds (ns).

UPGRADING THE NETWARE OS

Upgrading from one version of NetWare to another involves running the NetWare installation programs—NETGEN for SFT and Advanced NetWare, ELS-GEN for ELS NetWare Level II, and INSTALL for ELS NetWare Level I.

A Sample Upgrade Scenario

To better illustrate the process involved in upgrading the LAN, we'll create a sample scenario where an upgrade is needed. While this scenario won't match your situation, you can learn a lot by seeing how someone else handles an upgrade.

Suppose our hypothetical company Stats, Inc. currently has a 286-based file server running nondedicated Advanced NetWare 286. The server has one 40MB internal hard disk, and an external disk subsystem containing two 100MB drives. The disk subsystem is attached to a disk coprocessor board in the file server. A single Ethernet board in the server connects the workstations. The company has a third-party backup system that uses 60MB tape cartridges.

Lately, Stats has grown by leaps and bounds. LAN usage has increased quite a bit, and the old server doesn't seem to be able to handle all the traffic. Stats decides it is time to upgrade to a 386-based file server. They also determine that they need additional fault tolerance and transaction tracking protection for their valuable database information.

Step 1: Obtain the New OS. Stats decides on SFT NetWare 286 with TTS for their new operating system, because of its disk mirroring and transaction tracking capabilities. They call their Novell reseller and find out what they must do to trade in their copy of Advanced NetWare 286 for SFT NetWare 286. When the big red box containing the upgrade software arrives, they're ready to go to work.

Step 2: Determine Hardware Compatibility. Not all NetWare versions support the same network interface boards, internal hard disk types, disk coprocessor boards, or disk subsystems. This is more of a concern when doing a major version upgrade (from NetWare v2.0*x* to v2.1*x*, for example), but you should always check the Novell installation or upgrade documentation just to be sure. In Stats' case, all their existing hardware is compatible. The disk subsystem can be transferred over easily to the new file server. The only trick will be to move the data from the internal hard disk of the current file server to the new one.

Step 3: Back Up All Data. As a precaution, you should *always* back up data before making any changes to the file server configuration. Even though normally no data is lost during an upgrade, having a complete system backup protects you in case something goes haywire. Remember Murphy's Law—if something can go wrong, it will. In a case in which you will be transferring data from an existing hard disk to a new one, you will definitely need a backup on a system that can restore to the new hard disk. Stats perform their system-wide backup using the 60MB tape backup unit.

Step 4: Install the New OS. When you are upgrading to a completely new file server, upgrading is just like installing the OS from scratch. It's helpful to have your configuration documentation handy so you can set the new file server up the same as the old one. If you don't have a record of the network interface board settings, LAN and disk driver configurations, and installation parameters previously chosen, collect that information *before* you start the upgrade. Run NETGEN, ELSGEN, or INSTALL (depending on the NetWare tier) and select the appropriate configuration and installation options.

   If you are upgrading NetWare versions on the *same* file server, the NetWare installation programs will automatically detect and use existing information such as the file server name, the partition table and volume setup, and so on. Here upgrading is a matter of regenerating the new OS and copying it and the accompanying system, public, and login files to the system disk in place of the old ones.

   In our sample scenario, Stats is installing the upgraded OS on a new 386 machine. They run NETGEN, completing the configuration half on one of the network workstations that had a local hard disk. They select NETGEN's hard disk run option. (Avoid running Novell installation programs solely from floppy diskettes unless you want to get your wrists in shape by pulling diskettes in and out of the drive repeatedly.) They specify the same network configuration as in the old file server, except that they chose the "SFT NetWare 286 with TTS" operating system option. Once the new OS is generated and the files downloaded to the floppy diskettes, they bring the old server down, remove the LAN board and DCB, and reinstall them in the new 386 machine. They also reattach the disk subsystem to the DCB. Once they get the 386 machine set up to boot DOS and recognize the new 80MB internal hard disk, they run the installation half on the new file server itself. At this point, they have SFT NetWare 286 running on a new machine. The new SYS volume (on the internal hard disk) contains only the NetWare LOGIN, SYSTEM, PUBLIC, and MAIL directories and utilities—no data yet.

Step 5: Restore the Network Data. If you upgrade within the NetWare v2.1*x* family on the same file server, this step is unnecessary. All data, *including the bindery*, will be intact and existing volumes will be recognized by the new OS. Upgrading from NetWare versions prior to v2.1 requires that you take extra steps to restore the bindery. Refer to the NetWare upgrade documentation for details.

When you install the new version of NetWare on a different server, you must restore network data to the new system. Be careful, when restoring data on the SYS volume, that you do not restore the old LOGIN, SYSTEM, PUBLIC, or MAIL directories over top of the new ones. Doing so will revert your file server back to the previous OS. Other volumes containing strictly data can be restored fully.

Stats creates a new SYS volume on the 80MB internal disk. They restore all directories and files from the old 40MB disk *except* for the LOGIN, SYSTEM, PUBLIC, and MAIL directories. They have DOS directories under SYS:PUBLIC, which they append to the new PUBLIC directory. They don't have to restore any volumes that were on the external disk drives, because those volumes are already recognized by the new OS.

ADDING A FILE SERVER TO THE NETWORK

There was a time when the typical NetWare network consisted of a single file server with a handful of workstations scattered about. Except for the very smallest of network configurations, that time is past. Advances in file server technology and connectivity options have propelled small, single-file-server networks into gigantic internetworks consisting of multiple file servers, bridges, routers, gateways, and other connections to dissimilar systems.

Connectivity through gateways to minicomputers and mainframe systems is not covered in this book. The questions that we will deal with involve the performance issues of setting up a relatively small, self-contained internetwork. These questions are complicated enough in and of themselves: Are two file servers better than one? Should I bridge internally or externally? How do I physically connect multiple servers to achieve the most efficient routing? We'll look at each of these questions separately.

Single or Multiple File Servers

In most normal circumstances, a single file server running NetWare will provide more than adequate performance as long as network usage does not get too close to or exceed the specifications of the OS. As we mentioned before, it is rare to have a full 100 users logged in to an SFT or Advanced NetWare file server and have all 100 doing useful work. A more practical maximum is around 60-75 concurrent connections. When counting the number of connections in use, remember that VAPs take up service connections just as if they were logged in as users.

In the case of ELS NetWare Level I and Level II, you can actually have the maximum of four or eight users logged in at the same time, even if you are running VAPs in the server. This is because in ELS NetWare a certain number of "phantom" connections were provided for the exclusive use of VAPs, apart from the regular user connections.

As the number of workstations on your network grows, you may eventually need to add file servers to your network. Splitting up the network processing load between two or more file servers will help relieve congestion at the file server level. However, before adding another server, you must consider several issues.

One consideration is the practical number of file servers you can possibly have on a NetWare 286 v2.1x internetwork. While no official specification has been issued by Novell, experience has shown that 40-50 file servers is a practical maximum. This is not to say that you cannot have more servers than that on the same internet; before the release of NetWare 386, Novell successfully maintained a NetWare 286-based internet of over 100 servers. However, when the number of file servers exceeds 40 or 50, the routing information tables kept in each file server and bridge become fairly lengthy and unwieldy. Extreme cases can produce such problems as lost server connections and packet traffic jams. These types of problems are more pronounced if a file server running ELS NetWare is placed on the internet. The routing capabilities of ELS NetWare are not as sophisticated as those of Advanced and SFT NetWare; ELS servers can hold (and therefore pass on to other routers) routing information for only 40 servers or fewer.

Keep in mind also that NetWare routers will discard a packet after it has crossed 16 bridges or routing hops. Any nodes separated by more than 16 unique networks won't be able to communicate on the internet.

The whole point here is that you should avoid trying to add too many file servers to the same NetWare internetwork. If you keep the number of servers within reason, having multiple file servers will be beneficial to overall network usefulness. However, when adding servers to an internet, you must consider two other areas: effective use of a backbone cable and the best type of bridging.

Setting Up Backbones for Routing Efficiency

Generally, when you have more than one file server on an internetwork, it is best to use a backbone cable to physically connect the servers. However, before you do this, you must observe a few precautions. To better understand how to set up a backbone for internetworking, let's first briefly review the way in which NetWare's routing and file services interact in the file server.

Each NetWare file server can support up to four internal LAN interface boards with their associated drivers. Attached to each network interface board is a cabling system of some kind. These four "subnetworks" attached to a file server are referred to as LAN A, LAN B, LAN C, and LAN D. It is the internal router's job to sort out all packets that come in through any one of these four LANs and send those not meant for this particular file server back out over the appropriate LAN board. Those packets destined for this file server are passed to the file service processes to be serviced.

Remember that each packet contains the full internet address of its destination: a network address, a node address, and a socket number. Routers, however, are interested only in network addresses. Not until the router sends a packet to the correct network do the node address and socket number come into play. Routers select the quickest path to forward packets to the specified *network*, but they do not discriminate the quickest means of delivering a packet to the designated node and socket. If two routers see the destination network as being the same number of network "hops" away, whichever router responds first will provide the path that the packet will take, even if that path is physically longer.

The file service processes and the router talk to one another through a combination of a file server socket and the LAN A network address. To a router, the file server is just another node on the LAN A network, even though both the router and the file server's file service processes physically reside in the same box. Therefore, the router sends all request packets meant for the file server to LAN A's network address. Packets coming in to the file server over LAN B, LAN C, or LAN D are internally routed to LAN A because, according to the router, the file services logically reside on LAN A.

A NetWare router keeps track of more than just its own host file server. Each router keeps a list (called the routing information table) of all other routers that it knows about, along with their network addresses. Note that these are LAN A network addresses only. If the router receives a request for a different file server, it routes that request to the designated file server's LAN A address. If the packet cannot be sent directly to the LAN A address, the router uses its routing information tables to send the packet to another router that can send it to that file server's LAN A address.

Sample Routing Scenarios. With this in mind, let's look at two configurations often used for internetwork backbones. Figure 26-2 shows the typical setup, where the cable with all the workstations attached to it is designated as LAN A connected to file server PUB. LAN B serves as the backbone, connecting file servers PUB, CORP, ACCTG, and EDUCATION.

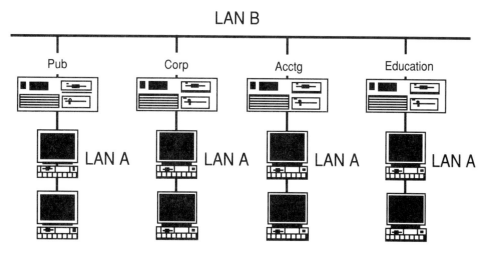

Figure 26-2: A typical internetwork with the backbone configured as LAN B on each file server.

In this scenario, it doesn't matter whether LAN A or LAN B is the backbone, because there is only one path for the workstations to send requests to server PUB. Requests that come in on LAN B are internally routed to the file services.

The second scenario, illustrated in Figure 26-3, offers a means of achieving a redundant connection so that workstations will be able to access either file server if one server connection fails.

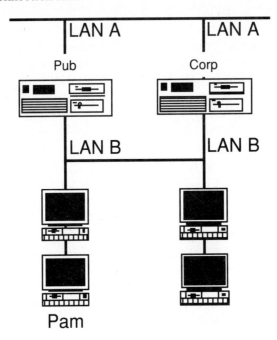

Figure 26-3: An internetwork configuration with redundant cabling.

In this scenario, you essentially have two backbones, with LAN A being used for the internet backbone and LAN B being used to redundantly connect the workstations to the file servers. You should be aware of some inherent problems with such a redundant connection.

Suppose user Pam wants to log in to server PUB on this internetwork. The NetWare shell in Pam's workstation first scans the bindery of whatever file server it was attached to when Pam made the request, looking for server PUB's network address. After the shell finds the address, it issues a "Get Local Target" call to find a route to the network that server PUB claims to be on. The shell uses whatever answer it gets back first. The router sees the file services as logically existing off LAN A; according to the routers in both servers PUB and CORP, LAN A is just one hop away, so either route is available.

Because there are two routes available, server CORP could possibly answer faster than server PUB. In this situation, CORP will answer the "Get Local Target" request and will become the route that Pam will use throughout this session. After such a connection is made, every request that Pam makes goes through server CORP to get to server PUB. Server CORP's router looks at the packet and sees that it is not destined for CORP's file services. CORP then compares the network number to the routing tables and sees that the request is for a node on local LAN A (server PUB).

Because server PUB is known by its LAN A address and CORP has a LAN A connection through the internet, CORP sends the request to the driver on LAN A, which sends the request to server PUB. Since LAN A is the backbone in this scenario, CORP must send the request over the backbone to get to server PUB. That means there is unnecessary traffic running on the backbone. Ideally, a backbone should only be used for file server routing information and for those times when users need the resources on a file server other than their local server.

In this second scenario, all of Pam's requests have an extra hop to get to their destination. Each time she logs in, Pam has a 50 percent chance of going through server CORP instead of server PUB. Since what she needs is a direct connection to PUB, the internet is being unnecessarily cluttered. For most internets, this scenario won't cause much of a problem; when the designated server is only one routing hop away, packets are handled so quickly that users won't notice any performance difference. But as networks grow, the backbone can become a bottleneck if it is used for unnecessary packet transmissions.

The solution for the internet shown in Figure 26-3 is to switch LAN A and LAN B, making sure that local workstations reside on LAN A. Now, when Pam performs a login request, she will have a direct connection to the LAN A address and to PUB's file services. Of course, anyone on a different file server attached to the backbone and trying to use PUB's services has a 50 percent chance of going through the extra routing hop when using PUB's services. But that's acceptable, because those users are requesting the services of a file server to which they are not physically attached.

When there are multiple paths between file servers, you must be careful how you design your network, especially if you want to provide for redundant cabling schemes. Figure 26-4 shows an internet in which the workstation networks are connected to the file servers through LAN A, the internetwork backbone is connected through LAN B, and the redundant cabling scheme uses LAN C. This is the most efficient way as far as routing is concerned.

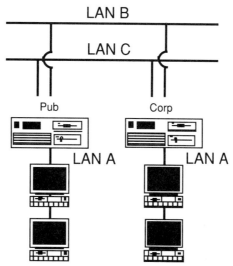

Figure 26-4: This cabling configuration will yield the best results if you want redundant cabling.

If you were to put the backbone on LAN A, you could have all sorts of problems. For instance, if the LAN A server connection were to fail, workstations would no longer be able to route packets over the internet, even though there is another physical connection. This is because the routers will always ask for a path to the LAN A address, where file services are known to reside. The file servers would try to route the connection through LAN A and the packets would only end up in the bit bucket, with workstations getting continuous error messages.

By having the internet on LAN B and the redundant cabling on LAN C, you can ensure that the routing information is sent both ways. This is fine, since the workstation request takes the first routing path that responds to the "Get Local Target" request. If a break stops the routing on LAN B cable, the workstation shell will receive a "Network error on server PUB: Abort or Retry?" error message. It takes about three minutes for the connection to be dropped; the user may have to press "R" (for "Retry") several times before the connection is dissolved. Retrying causes the shell to perform another "Get Local Target" request. The shell will forget about its original route and send the packets over LAN C. When the requested server receives the packet, the packet will be passed internally to its file services.

To summarize, then, configure the local network that attaches directly to your file server as LAN A. Use LAN B or LAN C for your internetwork and redundant cabling networks. Use a backbone only to connect file servers and bridges so they can keep track of each other and so users can access resources on a file server other than their local server. That way, users won't have to go through all the file servers on the internet to get to the resource they seek. It is best to physically attach each user's workstation to the server whose services he or she uses the most. That alone will significantly cut down on internetwork traffic.

Bridge Performance Issues

NetWare provides three options for direct bridging between separate cabling systems in a NetWare internet. You can use *internal bridging*, where you simply install up to four network interface boards in the same file server. Each board supports a separate subnetwork, and the routing mechanism within the file server performs the routing functions.

A second option is to use an existing workstation on the internet as a *non-dedicated external bridge*. In this setup, the workstation runs DOS applications in the foreground; routing operations occur as a background function.

The third option is to add a separate box on the internet to serve as a *dedicated external bridge*. Like a file server, this computer can contain up to four network interface boards. Unlike a file server, the dedicated bridge performs only routing functions. The entire CPU is dedicated to moving packets through the bridge, under the direction of specialized NetWare bridge software.

A study performed by Novell's Systems Engineering Group in 1990 showed that no matter what kind of bridging you use, the network performance (as measured in throughput) will decrease by around 40 percent with one bridge, compared to the throughput achieved when no bridging is used. Each additional bridge added to the internet causes a further degradation of roughly 8 percent, resulting in a cumulative drop in performance of over 80 percent when six bridges are present. This performance degradation is unavoidable if you must bridge, but the effect can be minimized through careful selection of the kind of bridging and the type of computer used for the bridges.

The most inexpensive way to bridge is to use a nondedicated external bridge. All you need is one extra network interface board to install in an existing workstation. However, because a single CPU must split its resources for both running DOS applications and handling bridging operations, performance suffers. Internetwork throughput averages about 40 percent of the no-bridge throughput, and the unfortunate user of the workstation used as the bridge experiences stultifyingly slow response. Reliability suffers as well, because if an application hangs on the workstation side, the bridging side will become inoperative as well.

The main choice, then, is between internal bridging and dedicated external bridging. In terms of cost, internal bridging is cheaper because you don't have to buy a separate computer; you just add network boards to the file server. And internal bridging is fairly reliable; as long as the server is up, the routing operations will continue. However, the performance of an internal bridge is about 10-20 percent lower than that of a dedicated bridge, depending on how busy the file server is. If the server is a fast 80386-based machine, the effect on performance is lessened.

If you're looking for reasonable performance and reliability for the price of a few network boards, and you have a fast file server that is not heavily used on the internet, then internal bridging is the way to go. But if you require maximum performance and reliability, and if you can justify the extra cost of a new machine along with additional network boards, then a dedicated external bridge is the best choice.

27 Unclogging LAN Communication Channels

This chapter covers the procedures you would use to unclog a bottleneck in the LAN communication channel. As outlined in Chapter 25, this communication channel consists of the network interface board and its associated LAN driver, plus the network cabling itself. In this chapter, we'll look at the steps involved in replacing an old network interface board with a new one, reconfiguring an existing network board, and adding a new network board to the file server.

REPLACING A NETWORK INTERFACE BOARD

You may need to replace an existing network interface board in the file server for any of the following reasons:

- You are using an old 8-bit network interface board in the file server and want to upgrade to a 16-bit or 32-bit board of the same type.
- You want to upgrade to a faster LAN hardware/topology (for instance, from ARCnet to Ethernet, or from 4Mbps to 16Mbps Token-Ring).
- An enhanced version of an existing board or LAN driver becomes available.

Whenever you replace a network interface board in the file server, you must regenerate the NetWare OS so it can work with the new board. This involves running NETGEN, ELSGEN, or INSTALL again and selecting the appropriate LAN driver.

As long as the new board works with the type of cabling you already have, you won't have to replace cable, connectors, or any other networking hardware. If you switch hardware/topology schemes, you'll have to rewire the site with new cabling before you can use the new board.

Regenerating and Reinstalling the OS

Let's set up a sample scenario that will demonstrate the steps involved in replacing a network interface board, regenerating the NetWare operating system, and reinstalling it on the server. Suppose you currently have a generic Ethernet board and want to swap it for the high-performance NE1000 Ethernet board. Here's how you would go about making the switch. (These instructions assume that you have the 5.25-inch version of the NetWare diskettes.)

Step 1: Obtain the LAN driver for the board. If the LAN driver for your new board is among those provided with the NetWare OS, you need look no further. However, the list of included LAN drivers changes with every release of NetWare. About the only sure way to tell if the driver is included is to start up NETGEN or ELSGEN, go into the network configuration part of the program, and look at the list of drivers presented when you choose the "Select Loaded Item" option under "Select LAN Drivers" in the "Available Options" menu.

If the driver you need is not listed, check with your NetWare reseller with or Novell itself. Novell offers a Supplemental Drivers Kit containing other OS LAN drivers. Board manufacturers often include a NetWare LAN driver for their board on a separate diskette. These can be loaded directly from the floppy diskette when you run NETGEN or ELSGEN. Note that a supplemental LAN driver diskette must be labeled "LAN_DRV_" plus any three characters other than 001, 002, or ELS.

The LAN driver for the NE1000 is included with most versions of NetWare, so we don't need a supplemental driver diskette for our example.

Step 2: Reconfigure the OS. Your copy of the NetWare OS was custom-generated during the initial installation for your particular combination of LAN and disk drivers. Whenever you change these drivers, you must reconfigure the OS accordingly. You can reconfigure and regenerate the OS without bringing down the file server by running NETGEN or ELSGEN on a workstation that has a local hard disk. After you regenerate the OS at this workstation, the new OS files are saved to floppy diskettes. You must bring down the server to actually install the new OS from these floppies to the file server. (The ELS Level I v2.12 INSTALL program should be run only on the file server itself.)

The exact steps for regenerating NetWare vary slightly between NETGEN and ELSGEN. For our example, we'll show how to regenerate the OS by running NETGEN from a local hard disk. These instructions assume that the files necessary to run NETGEN have been previously loaded onto a workstation's hard disk.

Boot up the workstation and change to the directory on the hard disk that contains the NETGEN.EXE file. (This directory is usually named NETWARE, but it doesn't have to be.) The directory should contain a number of subdirectories with the same names and contents as each of the original NetWare diskettes. Type **NETGEN -C** at the DOS prompt (the "-C" tells NETGEN to run at the custom configuration level). Select the hard disk run option and give NETGEN the drive letter of the hard disk (usually C or D). When the "Network Generation Options" menu appears, choose "Select Network Configuration."

Now choose "Select LAN Drivers." A list of the LAN drivers previously selected should appear in a window, along with a "LAN Driver Options" submenu. Delete the LAN driver for the board you are replacing by choosing "Deselect an Item" and highlighting the driver you want to delete. Pressing Enter completes the deletion. Choose "Select Loaded Item" and highlight the driver for the NE1000 Ethernet board in the list of available LAN drivers. Pressing Enter completes the selection.

You have just selected a new network configuration. Press Escape to save your new selections and return to the "Available Options" menu. Choose "Configure Drivers/Resources" and specify suitable hardware configuration settings for the new board. If the board's IRQ, DMA, I/O address, and memory address jumpers are already set a certain way and that configuration option is available, choose that option. Otherwise, you'll have to set the jumpers on the board to match the option you choose. When you're done, choose "Save Selections and Continue."

Now you need to specify a network address for the new board. To avoid any routing complications, use the same address that was set for the previous board. If you assign a new address, remember that it must be different from the network addresses of the other boards in the server and in any other servers or routers on an internetwork. Type the appropriate address and press Enter. Then press Escape to continue with the program.

The new configuration you just specified will be displayed on the screen. Check it to make sure it is correct, then press Escape twice. Now choose "Save Selections and Continue" again and answer "Yes" to the "Continue Network Generation Using Selected Configuration?" prompt.

Choose "Link/Configure NetWare Operating System" from the "Network Generation Options" menu. This will relink and reconfigure the OS for the new LAN driver. When this is done, choose "Exit NETGEN" and answer "Yes" to the confirmation prompt. Also answer "Yes" to the "Download Needed Files to Floppy Disk?" prompt; insert the diskettes NETGEN asks for. You now have the new OS on the OSEXE-1 (and possibly OSEXE-2) diskette.

Step 3: Install the New Board and OS. Now you must bring down the file server, pull out the old board, and insert the new one. Make sure the jumper settings on the new board match the configuration option you chose in Step 2. The *Guide to Operations* (or similarly titled manual) that came with your file server should contain instructions for installing new boards in the machine. Put the cover back on the server and boot it with DOS 3.3 or above. Make sure the DOS boot diskettes has a CONFIG.SYS file setting FILES = 10.

Insert the NETGEN diskette and type **NETGEN**. (No command line flags are necessary this time.) Select the "Standard Floppy Disk" run option, as you will be running the program from floppies for the installation phase. When the "Network Generation Options" menu appears, choose "NetWare Installation." NETGEN will proceed to analyze the system and present a list of existing disk drives. Since you haven't done anything involving the disk drives, this list should be correct. Highlight "Drive List Is Correct" and press Enter.

Choose "Select Default Installation Options" from the "Installation Options" menu that appears. Using the default option is easier at this stage of the game, because NETGEN will set the "load operating system" flag automatically. Cycle through the screens that appear, pressing Escape to move forward without changing anything. When you get back to the "Installation Options" menu, choose "Continue Installation" and answer "Yes" to the "Install Networking Software on File Server?" prompt. NETGEN will install a new cold boot loader. Press a key when you are prompted to do so. NETGEN will next prompt you to insert the OSEXE-1 and OS-EXE-2 diskettes so it can write the new operating system files to the SYS:SYSTEM directory. Press a key when prompted.

When the "Network Generation Options" menu reappears, exit NETGEN in the usual way. You can now reboot the file server with the new NetWare operating system.

CHANGING AN EXISTING NETWORK INTERFACE BOARD

Although it's not actually a way to increase the performance of the LAN communication channel, you might need to change the jumper settings on an existing network interface board to resolve a hardware conflict in the file server. When you change the settings on the board, you must reconfigure the LAN driver and the NetWare operating system accordingly. The process is similar to the one outlined above for replacing the board, with the following exceptions:

• In Step 2, you need not go into the "Select LAN Drivers" option. The driver is already selected; you just have to choose a new configuration for it via the "Configure Drivers/Resources" option.

• After choosing the new configuration for the LAN driver, select "Configure Operating System" instead of "Link/Configure Operating System." The LAN driver is still linked to the operating system; the OS needs only to be reconfigured to use the new settings.

ADDING A NEW NETWORK INTERFACE BOARD

As explained in Chapter 25, you can often increase the performance of a heavily used LAN communication channel by adding a second network interface board to the file server and connecting half of the workstations to it. This essentially splits the LAN traffic so that all packets don't come in on a single board. Splitting the LAN in this way is a good solution if wiring problems or expense prohibit you from upgrading to a faster hardware/topology combination.

Regenerating and Reinstalling the OS

You must regenerate and reinstall the OS when you add an additional network board. The procedure is slightly different than when you replace an existing network interface board. Usually, when you add a network board, the second board is the same type of board as the first one.

Here's an example of how to add a network interface board, regenerate the NetWare operating system, and reinstall it on the server. In this example, suppose you have an IBM PC Network Adapter II/A in a PS/2 file server and you want to add a second, identical board. Again, we'll assume you're running NETGEN, this time from 3.5-inch diskettes.

Step 1: Obtain the LAN Driver for the Board. The LAN driver for most types of IBM PC Network Adapters is usually included with NetWare. However, check the list of included LAN drivers in NETGEN or ELSGEN to make sure. If the driver is not listed, you can order Novell's Supplemental Drivers Kit or obtain the driver from the board manufacturer.

We chose IBM's PC Network Adapters for this example because the selection of these LAN drivers can be tricky when you put more than one of the same kind of board in the same computer. The original adapter must be configured as a "primary" adapter, and the second one will be an "alternate" adapter. You need a different LAN driver for each type.

Step 2: Reconfigure the OS. It is easier and less disruptive to network users if you reconfigure and regenerate the OS before you bring down the file server. You can do this by running NETGEN on a local hard disk somewhere on the network. The workstation or standalone machine you use should have a 3.5-inch diskette drive (preferably two).

When you run NETGEN from a hard disk, you always start the program from the directory on the hard disk that contains the NETGEN.EXE file. This directory is usually named NETWARE, but it doesn't have to be. This directory should contain a number of subdirectories with the same names and contents as each of the original NetWare diskettes. Type **NETGEN -C** (the "-C" tells NETGEN to run at the custom configuration level). Select the hard disk run option and give NET-GEN the drive letter of the hard disk (usually C or D). When the "Network Generation Options" menu appears, choose "Select Network Configuration."

Now choose "Select LAN Drivers." The "IBM PCN II & Baseband/A (Primary)" driver should appear in the list of previously selected LAN drivers. Choose "Select Loaded Item" and highlight the "IBM PCN II & Baseband/A (Alternate)" driver for the second PCN board. Make sure you choose the driver that says "/A" for Micro Channel Architecture. Choosing the wrong driver will prevent NetWare from booting properly. Press Enter to complete the selection.

With this new network configuration selected, press Escape to save your new selections and return to the "Available Options" menu. Choose "Configure Drivers/Resources" and specify suitable configuration settings for the new board. On boards designed for the Micro Channel Architecture, IRQ, DMA, I/O address, and memory address setting are made through a program on the IBM PS/2 Reference diskette. You may have to run the Reference diskette program later to get the settings on the board to match the option you choose. When you've finished choosing the configuration, choose "Save Selections and Continue."

Specify a network address for the new board. Remember that duplicate network addresses are not allowed within the same server or with any other servers or routers on an internetwork. Type the appropriate address and press Enter. Then press Escape to continue with the program.

The new configuration you just specified will be displayed on the screen. Check it to make sure it is how you want it, then press Escape twice. Now choose "Save Selections and Continue" again and answer "Yes" to the "Continue Network Generation Using Selected Configuration?" prompt.

Choose "Link/Configure NetWare Operating System" from the "Network Generation Options" menu. This will relink and reconfigure the OS to include the new LAN driver. When this is done, choose "Exit NETGEN" and answer "Yes" to the confirmation prompt. Also answer "Yes" to the "Download Needed Files to Floppy Disk?" prompt; insert the diskettes NETGEN asks for. You now have the new OS on the OSEXE-1 diskette.

Step 3: Install the New Board and OS. Now you must bring the file server down and insert the new board. If necessary, run the setup program provided on the IBM PS/2 Reference diskette to make sure the board's settings match the configuration option you chose in Step 2. Put the cover back on the server and boot it with DOS 3.3 or above. Make sure the DOS boot diskettes has a CONFIG.SYS file setting FILES = 10.

Insert the NETGEN diskette and type **NETGEN**. (No command-line flags are necessary this time.) Select the "Standard Floppy Disk" run option, as you will be running from floppies for the installation phase. When the "Network Generation Options" menu comes up, choose "NetWare Installation." NETGEN will proceed to analyze the system and present a list of existing disk drives. Since you haven't done anything involving the disk drives, this list should be correct. Highlight "Drive List Is Correct" and press Enter.

Choose "Select Default Installation Options" from the "Installation Options" menu that appears. Using the default option is easier at this stage of the game, because NETGEN will take over and set the "load operating system" flag automatically. Cycle through the screens that appear, pressing Escape to move forward without changing anything. When you get back to the "Installation Options" menu, choose "Continue Installation" and answer "Yes" to the "Install Networking Software on File Server?" prompt. NETGEN will install a new cold boot loader. NETGEN will next prompt you to insert the OSEXE-1 diskette so it can write the new operating system files to the SYS:SYSTEM directory.

When the "Network Generation Options" menu reappears, exit NETGEN in the usual way. You can now reboot the file server with the new NetWare operating system.

28 Enhancing Hard Disk Channels

This chapter looks at ways to enhance the performance of your file server's hard disk communication channel. As explained in Chapter 25, this communication channel consists of the hard disk and its associated components (power supply, circuit board, and so on), the disk controller board, the disk coprocessor board (for external disk drive channels), the disk driver, and the disk caching mechanism in NetWare itself. In this chapter, we'll look at some of the considerations involved in adding a new disk channel to the file server, reconfiguring an existing channel, and replacing old disk channel components.

ADDING A NEW DISK CHANNEL

If the disk I/O traffic on your file server is too much for one disk channel to handle, you can add another channel to help distribute the load. SFT and Advanced NetWare support up to four external disk channels in addition to the internal disk channel. (ELS NetWare supports only one internal disk channel, so adding a new channel is not an option in ELS networks.)

Besides the performance aspects of having more than one disk channel, you might also want to consider the possibility of disk duplexing. Whereas straight disk mirroring involves pairing two similar disks on the *same* channel, SFT NetWare also allows you to mirror disks on *different* channels to protect against failure anywhere along the disk channel. This is called disk duplexing. (Disk mirroring and duplexing are not supported in Advanced or ELS NetWare.)

A side benefit of having duplexed disks is the disk I/O performance boost associated with *split seeks*. Read requests constitute the majority of requests on most file servers. When the server has duplicate disk channels, SFT NetWare examines each read request and determines which drive—the primary drive or the mirror drive—can service the request the fastest. If the first disk is busy, the OS sends the read request to the second disk. When two or more read requests occur at the same time, NetWare splits the requests between the two channels so they can be answered simultaneously.

Obtaining the Necessary Hardware

Adding a whole disk channel can require some expensive hardware. In most cases, you'll need to purchase at least an additional disk coprocessor board, a new hard disk, a disk subsystem in which to house the disk, and the necessary cabling to hook them all together. Depending on the number and types of disks you buy, you may also need additional disk controller boards and a bigger power supply.

This section will explain in general terms how to reconfigure the OS, program the new DCB, and initialize volumes for a new hard disk channel. Refer to the documentation that comes with your hardware for instructions on actually hooking up the hardware. Figure 28-1 shows a typical disk channel hardware hookup that you can use as a general guide; specific details vary from one manufacturer to another.

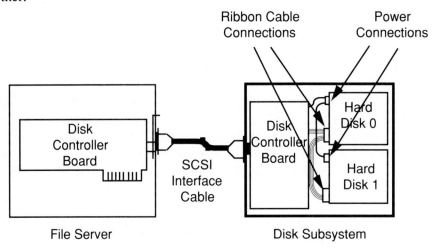

Figure 28-1: Most disk channels consist of a DCB connected to a disk subsystem, which contains one or more controllers and their associated hard disks.

Whatever you do, don't try to wing it, especially when you're dealing with a SCSI bus. Setting the addresses of controllers along the bus and properly terminating both ends of the bus are critical operations.

Regenerating the OS

Whenever you add a DCB to the file server, you must regenerate the NetWare OS so that it recognizes the new DCB. This involves running NETGEN again and selecting the appropriate disk driver.

Novell recently licensed its DCB technology to ADIC Corporation in Redmond, Washington. As a result, DCBs are no longer available directly from Novell. However, the general procedure for adding DCBs is the same for most

NetWare-compatible DCBs currently available. Check the documentation that comes with your DCB to see if it requires any modifications to the normal procedure.

The following instructions explain how to add a typical DCB in an IBM AT-compatible file server and regenerate the NetWare operating system accordingly.

Step 1: Obtain the Disk Driver for the DCB. The NetWare OS includes disk drivers for standard Novell DCBs and 100-percent compatible boards. Your DCB might have come with its own disk driver; as with LAN drivers, these drivers can be loaded directly from the floppy diskette when you run NETGEN. A supplemental disk driver diskette is normally labeled "DSK_DRV_" plus any three characters other than 001.

The disk driver for the Novell DCB is included with NetWare, so we don't need a supplemental driver diskette for our example.

Step 2: Reconfigure the OS. Your copy of the NetWare OS was custom-generated during the initial installation for your particular combination of LAN and disk drivers. Whenever you change these drivers, you must reconfigure the OS accordingly. You can reconfigure and regenerate the OS without bringing down the file server by running NETGEN or ELSGEN on a workstation that has a local hard disk. After you regenerate the OS at this workstation, the new OS files are saved to floppy diskettes. You must bring down the server to actually install the new OS from these floppies to the file server.

The exact steps for regenerating NetWare vary slightly, depending on whether you run NETGEN from floppies or from a hard disk. Here is how to do it for our example, running NETGEN from a workstation's hard disk.

Boot up the workstation and change to the directory on the hard disk that contains the NETGEN.EXE file. (This directory is usually named NETWARE, but it doesn't have to be.) The directory should contain a number of subdirectories with the same names and contents as each of the original NetWare diskettes. Type **NETGEN -D** (the "-D" tells NETGEN to run at the default configuration level). Select the "Hard Disk" run option and give NETGEN the drive letter of the hard disk (usually C or D). When the "Network Generation Options" menu appears, choose "Select Network Configuration."

Now choose "Select Disk Drivers." A list of the disk drivers for all current disk channels should appear in a window, along with a "Disk Driver Options" submenu. Choose "Select Loaded Item" from this submenu. NETGEN will prompt you for a channel number. Enter the next available channel number (2, 3, or 4) and press Enter. Now, in the list of available disk driver types, highlight the driver for the DCB. Press Enter to complete the selection.

You have just selected a new network configuration. Press Escape to save your new selections and return to the "Available Options" menu. Since you selected the default configuration level, NETGEN automatically uses the default hardware configuration settings for the new board.

The new configuration will be displayed on the screen. Check it to make sure it is correct, then press Escape. Answer "Yes" to the "Continue Network Generation Using Selected Configuration?" prompt.

NETGEN will automatically cycle through the relinking and reconfiguring of the OS for the new disk driver. When this is done, choose "Exit NETGEN" and answer "Yes" to the confirmation prompt. Also answer "Yes" to the "Download Needed Files to Floppy Disk?" prompt; insert the diskettes NETGEN asks for. You now have the new OS on the OSEXE-1 and OSEXE-2 diskettes.

Step 3: Install the New DCB and Other Disk Channel Hardware. Now you must bring down the file server and install the new DCB. Make sure the jumper settings match those displayed on the screen in Step 2. After you have installed the DCB, put the cover back on the file server.

Attach the disk subsystem to the DCB according to the documentation that came with the hardware. Set controller addresses and physical disk numbers via the jumper settings on the circuit boards, then connect all hard disks and controllers. Be sure that each end of a SCSI bus is properly terminated with a terminating resistor and that all ribbon cables are properly oriented. (The striped edge usually marks the pin 1 connection.)

You will need to know the disk type (manufacturer and model number, such as Toshiba MK56 or Vertex V185) and the type of controller board each disk is attached to (such as Embedded SCSI or Adaptec 4070). You'll also need to know the controller address setting of each controller.

Step 4: Run the DISKSET Utility. Through the DISKSET option in NETGEN, you must program the DCB so that it knows what disks and controllers it is connected to. Boot the file server with DOS 3.3 or above. Make sure the CONFIG.SYS file includes the line "FILES = 10."

Insert the NETGEN diskette and type **NETGEN**. (No command-line flags are necessary this time.) Select the "Standard Floppy Disk Method" run option, as you will be running from floppies for this phase. When the "Network Generation Options" menu comes up, select "Configuration Utilities." DISKSET will be listed as an option in the resulting menu. (If you are installing a third-party DCB, another configuration utility name may appear as well. Use the utility appropriate for your hardware.)

Go through DISKSET and select the appropriate disk/controller combinations and controller addresses for your new hard disk channel. When you're finished, press Escape and answer "Yes" to the "Save This Information?" prompt. The information you selected will be written to the firmware on the DCB. Press Escape again; select "Return to the Previous Menu" to get back to the "Network Generation Options" menu.

Step 5: COMPSURF the New Disks, If Necessary. COMPSURF is Novell's utility for performing a low-level format on new hard disks never before used with NetWare. In the past, Novell provided hard disks already formatted with COMPSURF. Third-party hard disks all had to be subjected to this new format, even if previously formatted under DOS.

Now many third-party manufacturers sell hard disks preformatted to work with NetWare. You do *not* have to run COMPSURF on these disks. If a disk falls under the "NetWare Ready" category, you *must not run* COMPSURF on that disk. NetWare v2.15c includes a special disk driver option named "NetWare Ready" for disks that have been pretested and prestamped with the appropriate COMPSURF signature. Another case where you do not need to run COMPSURF is with the new Defect-Free Interface (DFI) hard disks. These drives, all thoroughly tested at the factory, have built-in firmware that continuously tests, detects, and replaces defective disk sectors.

If you need to run COMPSURF on a disk, NETGEN will tell you so. Choose "NetWare Installation" from the "Network Generation Options" menu. NETGEN will perform its disk drive analysis. Since you have added new disk drives, make sure the resulting list is correct; then highlight "Drive List Is Correct" and press Enter. If any drives need to be formatted and tested with COMPSURF, NETGEN lists them and tells you to press Escape to continue. Press Escape and then select "Analyze Disk Surface" from the "Network Generation Options" menu.

Run COMPSURF according to the instructions in the Novell *286 Maintenance* manual. Make sure you select the proper interleave and an adequate number of passes for the various tests (the defaults are usually more than sufficient). If a list of known bad blocks came with the disk, entering them before starting speeds up the actual COMPSURF tests. If you don't have such a list, don't worry; COMPSURF will find all bad blocks as part of its testing.

Running COMPSURF can require a substantial amount of time, depending on the size of the disk and the options you choose. To format and test a 20MB hard disk with the default COMPSURF options takes two to three hours. Testing a high-capacity disk (over 200MB) with the default options can take days. When you are finished running COMPSURF for all drives that need it, press Escape until you return to the "Network Generation Options" menu.

Step 6: Reinstall NetWare and Initialize the Volumes. Choose "NetWare Installation" again from the "Network Generation Options" menu. NETGEN will once more analyze all disk drives. The resulting list should be correct at this point. Highlight "Drive List Is Correct" and press Enter.

Choose "Select Default Installation Options" from the "Installation Options" menu. Using the default option is easier at this stage, because it allows NETGEN to do as much as it can automatically. Cycle through the screens that appear, establishing mirrored disk pairs if you need to. For the other screens, press Escape to accept the defaults and move forward in the program.

When you get back to the "Installation Options" menu, choose "Continue Installation" and answer "Yes" to the "Install Networking Software on File Server?" prompt. NETGEN will install a new cold boot loader. Press a key when you are prompted to do so. NETGEN will next prompt you to insert the OSEXE-1 and OSEXE-2 diskettes so it can write the new operating system files to the SYS:SYSTEM directory. Press a key when prompted.

When the "Network Generation Options" menu reappears, exit NETGEN in the usual way. You can now reboot the file server with the new NetWare operating system.

FROM GENERIC DISK TO NETWARE DISK

Before we go further into the other disk channel maintenance tasks in this chapter, it would be helpful to review what is involved in turning a generic hard disk drive into a fully functional network disk on a NetWare file server.

NetWare's Low-Level Format

We already mentioned that each disk drive used with NetWare must be formatted in a particular way. This low-level format, usually performed with the Novell COMPSURF utility, rigorously tests the entire surface of the disk—sector by sector—for any previously undetected disk errors. This extra round of reliability checking is important because it relieves the NetWare OS from having to do any extra error-checking of its own. A disk that cannot pass Novell's rigorous reliability testing is unsuitable for use with NetWare.

After the disk has been low-level formatted and has passed a battery of sequential and random I/O tests, certain key information is written to track 0 on the disk. For example, sector 14 of track 0 is reserved for the NetWare mirror tables, and sector 15 will contain information about the NetWare volumes on the drive. Because track 0 is used for these critical tables, COMPSURF is especially picky about that track and performs a separate reliability check on track 0. A bad sector in track 0 could jeopardize the data on the entire disk.

Partition Tables

After a disk has been formatted for NetWare, you can still create a DOS partition on it if you wish. If you establish both a NetWare and a DOS partition on the disk, the DOS FDISK command will recognize the NetWare partition (FDISK will display its type as "non-DOS"). You would have to use the DOS format command to reformat the DOS partition before you could use it.

Having both a DOS and NetWare partition on the same disk is not recommended, for reasons discussed in more detail in Chapter 7. NETGEN will, by default, set up the entire disk as a NetWare partition. If you use the "Custom Installation Options," you can set up a different partition table via the "Modify Partition Tables" option.

Establishing Hot Fix

After the NetWare partition is set up, a disk must be set up for Hot Fix. A portion of disk space (usually about two percent of the total size) is reserved at the end of the NetWare partition as a Hot Fix Redirection Table. At this point, NetWare also establishes the *logical* size of the drive in 4KB blocks. The logical size of a NetWare drive is equal to the physical size minus the Hot Fix Redirection Area. In other words, the logical size is the amount of disk space actually available for storing data.

Setting Up Mirroring and Duplexing

Once Hot Fix is established and the logical size is known, you can pair two disks that have the same logical size together in the NetWare mirror tables. Mirroring two disks on the same disk channel is called *disk mirroring*; mirroring two disks on separate disk channels is called *disk duplexing*. One disk is designated the primary drive, and the other as the mirror drive. From this point on, NETGEN treats a mirrored pair as a single disk drive. The same volumes will be created on each disk; NetWare will write the same data to both disks. If one disk fails, the OS automatically switches to the other disk in the mirrored pair without losing any data.

Creating NetWare Volumes

Not until you have gone through all the above procedures can you actually set up one or more NetWare volumes on a disk. Volumes represent a physical amount of disk space, as opposed to directories, which can be of variable size. All available space on the disk must be allocated to NetWare volumes before data can actually be written to the disk.

How NetWare Keeps Track of Disks and Volumes

As we mentioned above, NetWare keeps on track 0 various tables that contain information about the file server's disks. The mirror tables contain the logical-to-physical drive mappings necessary for disk mirroring and duplexing to function. The volume tables keep track of which volumes are on which physical disk.

When you move physical disks around in NETGEN, NetWare's tables sometimes get confused and need to be updated. In such an instance, you will see the prompt "Fix the Master System Table?" in the maintenance part of NETGEN. You should always answer "Yes" to the prompt if you have made any changes.

RECONFIGURING A HARD DISK CHANNEL

If you make any changes on an existing external hard disk channel, you must reprogram the DCB for that channel so it knows about the changes. These changes could include:

- Replacing old, slower hard disks with new, faster ones
- Removing a disk from one channel and reattaching it on another channel
- Removing a disk from one file server and "transplanting" it to another file server with data intact
- Replacing old disk controllers boards with either new controller boards or embedded SCSI drives
- Adding new controllers and disks to an existing channel
- Replacing an old DCB with an enhanced DCB

The procedure for reprogramming the DCB for the first five changes is very similar to the one outlined in Step 4 above. As long as you don't add or remove the channels themselves, you need not regenerate the NetWare OS. When you actually remove one DCB and replace it with another that requires a different disk driver, however, you must regenerate the OS to include the disk driver for the new DCB.

Here are some tips for performing each of the tasks listed above. For more details, refer to the instructions in Novell's *286 Maintenance* manual and any specific hardware documentation.

Replacing an Old Hard Disk

Before you do anything to your disk drives, be sure you have a current back-up of all data on all drives attached to the file server. You'll need the backup to restore data from the old hard disk to the new one. Backups of the other disks is strictly a precautionary measure; no data should be lost from them during the process.

You will most likely want the new disk to contain the same volumes as the old disk had. If you're not sure how the volumes are currently set up on the old disk, go into FCONSOLE and select "Statistics" from the main menu. Then choose "Volume Information" and select each volume in turn. For each volume, note the number displayed as the "Logical Drive Number." Then, to find out which physical disk corresponds to what logical drive number, check the "Logical Disk To Physical Disk Mappings" under the "Disk Mapping Information" option in the "File Server Statistics" menu. Make a note of which volumes are on the disk you aim to remove.

Removing a disk involves both deleting the disk from NetWare's master system table (*logical* disk removal) and actually taking the drive off the channel (*physical* disk removal). You should remove the disk logically before you remove it physically.

If the old disk is part of a mirrored pair, you must unmirror the disk pair before you remove the disk. You can unmirror disks while the file server is running by using the UNMIRROR console command. (See Chapter 22 for details.) Or you can unmirror them after the file server is down using the "Modify Mirror Tables" option in NETGEN. The replacement drive should be the same size as the old disk if you intend to reestablish the mirrored pair.

Logically remove the disk by going into NETGEN's "NetWare Installation" option. After the usual drive analysis and confirmation, the "Installation Options" menu appears. Choose "Select Custom Installation Options" from this menu. The following menu appears:

```
┌─────────────────────────────────────────────┐
│            Custom Installation                │
├─────────────────────────────────────────────┤
│   Miscellaneous Maintenance                   │
│   Modify Hot Fix Redirection Tables           │
│   Modify Mirror Tables                        │
│   Modify Partition Table                      │
│   Reinitialize a Disk                         │
│   Remove a Disk                               │
│   Return To Previous Menu                     │
└─────────────────────────────────────────────┘
```

If you need to unmirror a disk pair, do so now with the "Modify Mirror Tables" option. Then select "Remove a Disk." This presents a list of the hard disks that can be removed. (NETGEN won't let you remove the disk containing the SYS volume, because the OS itself is stored in the SYS:SYSTEM directory. If you remove the OS, you don't have a file server anymore.)

NETGEN identifies all disks by channel, controller, and drive number. Make sure you select the correct disk. Answer "Yes" to the "Remove Disk From Master System Table" prompt, then press Escape to return to the "Custom Installation" menu. Choose the "Continue Installation" option to complete the logical disk removal. When that's done, exit NETGEN.

Now you are ready to physically remove the old disk. Bring down the file server and turn off the power to the disk subsystems. Open the disk subsystem containing the old disk and remove the disk carefully. The new disk must be compatible with the connection hardware (ribbon cables and power connectors) in the subsystem. Connect it to the appropriate disk controller (unless it is an embedded SCSI drive, in which case the controller is built in to the drive itself).

When two disk drives are connected to a single disk controller, the jumpers on one of the drives designate that drive as drive 0, while the jumpers on the other drive must be set to indicate drive 1. Check the documentation that came with the drive to make the proper jumper settings. Embedded SCSI drives don't need a drive number jumper setting; they are always drive 0.

Once the replacement disk is physically installed on the channel, turn on the power to the disk subsystems and boot the file server with DOS v3.3 or above. (Make sure the CONFIG.SYS file specifies at least FILES=10.) Start up NETGEN from floppy diskettes and set up the drive just as you would any new hard disk: format it with COMPSURF if necessary, create the NetWare partition, establish Hot Fix, and mirror the drive if appropriate.

When the time comes to create volumes on the new disk, refer to your list of volume names that were on the old drive. Set up the same volumes on the new disk. When you're finished, exit NETGEN and reboot the file server with NetWare. Restore the data from the old disk backup to the same volumes on the new drive.

Moving a Disk from One Channel to Another

When you remove a disk from one channel and reinstall it on another one in the same file server, no data should be lost. However, you should always have a full backup just in case.

All you have to do is run the DISKSET utility to reprogram the DCBs on both channels to reflect the switch. You can run DISKSET without going into NETGEN. The program files necessary to run DISKSET are on the NetWare diskette labeled DSK_DRV_001. Bring down the file server and reboot it with DOS. Then insert this diskette into drive A and type **A:DISKSET**. From this point on, the DISKSET utility runs the same as it does from within NETGEN.

When you reboot the file server with NetWare, users should be able to access data the same as they could before you moved the disk.

Transplanting a Disk to Another File Server

You can remove a NetWare disk and reinstall it, data and all, on a different file server. This procedure is useful when you are upgrading to a faster file server and you want to use the same disks on the new machine. Normally you would transplant the entire disk channel and regenerate the OS with the appropriate disk driver to accept the new channel.

When you transplant a single disk to another file server, you must reprogram the DCB for the channel on which you physically install the disk so it knows there is a new disk on the channel. The "NetWare Installation" portion of NETGEN analyzes the disk drives attached to the file server every time you enter that part of the program. If it finds a disk containing NetWare volumes that weren't there before, NETGEN will add the "Restore a Disk" option to its "Custom Installation Options" menu.

After you select "Restore a Disk," NETGEN displays the transplanted disk's channel, controller, and drive number in a list of "Remove Drives." When you select the disk, NETGEN asks you if you want to "Add Disk to Master System Table." Answer "Yes" to this prompt.

If the transplanted disk contains volumes that have the same names as volumes on the new file server, NETGEN automatically renames the restored volumes according to the default volume naming pattern (VOL1, VOL2, and so on). So, if you transplanted a disk containing a VOL1 to a file server that already had a VOL1 and a VOL2, NETGEN would rename the transplanted disk's VOL1 to VOL3 on the new server.

Replacing Disk Controllers

For performance reasons, you may want to replace an old disk controller board with a controller that uses newer technology. Many new disks, such as embedded SCSI drives, have their controller built in. Because the controller circuitry is more intimately tied to the disk itself, embedded SCSI drives offer quicker data access times than the traditional separate hard disk-controller configuration.

Another new type of controller features on-board RAM (ranging from around 200KB to as much as 4MB) in which the controller caches large chunks of data from the disk. This type of caching at the controller board adds even more speed, on top of that realized from NetWare's disk caching in file server RAM. Typical data access time from the controller's cache memory to file server memory is under one millisecond.

Remember that controllers are designed to work with a specific type of disk interface, such as SCSI, ESDI, or MFM. Before you replace your old disk controller boards, make sure that the new ones will work with the hard disks you already have.

When you replace a disk controller on a channel, you must set the new controller to the same address as the old one and connect it to the disks and the channel bus according to the manufacturer's instructions. After that, you must rerun DISKSET to tell the DCB what type the new controller is.

Adding New Controllers and Disks

You can add new controllers and disks to expand the total storage capacity of a disk channel. The SCSI bus interface supports up to eight controllers (actually seven, because the DCB counts as one controller). Controllers can support either one or two disk drives each. Conceivably, given the right kinds of disks and controllers, you could support up to fourteen hard disks on a single SCSI disk channel.

The power supply is an important consideration when you add controllers and disks in a disk subsystem box. Hard disks draw a substantial amount of wattage from a power supply. Running two disks and a controller off a small power supply may cause extra wear on the components. You are much better off having extra power than too little. Check the disk's documentation or consult with the manufacturer to see what kind of power supply rating a disk requires.

When you add new controllers and disks to an existing disk channel, you must set the controller addresses and disk numbers, then use DISKSET to reprogram the DCB to recognize the new hardware. Run NETGEN to format and initialize the new disks for NetWare.

Replacing a Disk Coprocessor Board

In addition to the traditional DCBs designed for both IBM AT-compatible file servers and IBM PS/2 Micro Channel file servers, Novell has designed an enhanced DCB. The enhanced DCB takes advantage of a feature called SCSI disconnect to improve the overall I/O throughput of the channel.

Whenever you remove one DCB and replace it with another that requires a different disk driver, you must regenerate the OS to include the disk driver for the new DCB. The procedure is similar to that described earlier for adding a whole new disk channel, only you must delete the disk driver for the old DCB and select the new disk driver in its place during the network configuration part of NETGEN.

Once you do that and reboot the file server with the newly regenerated OS, the disks attached to the new DCB should function just as they did under the old DCB.

BACKING UP THE FILE SERVER

Any business or organization that relies on a LAN to store valuable data must protect itself against the possible loss or corruption of that data. Whether due to accidental deletions, hardware failure, sabotage, or some type of disaster (fire, earthquake, and so on), an irretrievable loss of all or part of a company's files can be devastating. A reliable backup and restore system is one of the most critical investments you can make towards protecting data on the network.

With all of NetWare's built-in data protection features, many network supervisors erroneously think of backup systems as an optional peripheral, not as an absolute necessity to the basic operation of the network. Perhaps Novell itself has helped perpetuate this viewpoint because of the company's traditionally weak backup and restore product offerings. If nothing else, Novell's lackluster backup products have spurred the rapid development of an entire industry based on products for backing up NetWare LANs. Any network consultant worth listening to will stress the importance of having not only a good backup system for your LAN, but also an effective plan for using to its fullest advantage whichever backup system you choose.

In this section, we'll look at some of the factors to consider in establishing the best possible backup plan for your network.

• Chapter 29 lists some of the features a good network backup system should have. These criteria will help you evaluate your present backup system and give you ideas for upgrading that system, if necessary. The chapter also looks at some basic principles of an effective backup strategy.

• Chapter 30 gives general information about the backup and restore utilities available from Novell. While these utilities may not represent the best possible solution for backing up and restoring NetWare files, you can use them as part of an overall backup strategy.

29 Establishing a Network Backup Plan

This chapter looks at some of the issues involved in establishing an effective backup plan for your NetWare LAN. While a veritable avalanche of network backup products is currently available on the market, not all of these products are the same. You should carefully evaluate both the network requirements and backup/restore capabilities when deciding on an appropriate backup system for your file server.

We'll look first at the basic requirements needed in a backup program to handle the unique features of NetWare file servers. Then we'll discuss some of the niceties that can make backing up NetWare servers easier. Finally, we'll look at ways of combining these features to create a backup strategy that is as foolproof as possible.

BASIC BACKUP SYSTEM CRITERIA

The overriding requirement for a NetWare file server backup system is that it must able to completely and reliably back up and restore files on a NetWare disk, along with any rights associated with those files. The system should allow you to get the server back up and running quickly, restoring everything exactly as it was before, even after a total server crash. There is little use for a backup system that cannot restore network information completely and accurately.

While backup hardware varies greatly from one manufacturer to another, it is the software accompanying the hardware that marks the biggest difference between systems. Use the following criteria to evaluate the suitability of your present backup system software.

Handling the NetWare File System

Because NetWare has its own file system different from the one used by DOS, you cannot use typical DOS backup programs and procedures to back up NetWare disks. DOS backup programs (such as the BACKUP command) copy only the files, attributes, and directory structures recognized by DOS. NetWare's bindery data, directory rights, trustee assignments, and extended file attributes are not recognized by DOS and therefore cannot be backed up by DOS backup systems. One fundamental feature to look for, then, is whether the backup system is designed to handle the peculiarities of NetWare's file system.

Novell has endorsed a number of third-party backup products for use with NetWare 286, although many good products have not yet received the official stamp of approval. Authorized NetWare resellers receive regularly updated information from Novell about compatible products. NetWire is another good source for backup product recommendations.

Large Files and Directory Structures. With the high-capacity hard disks now available for use in NetWare 286 file servers, files in the multi-megabyte range are becoming more and more common. Directory structures can also grow quite large, with a single volume containing hundreds of directories and subdirectories. Some backup systems cannot handle files over a certain size, or handle more than a specific number of directories. Check the specifications for your backup system to see if you might be running up against these types of limitations.

Macintosh Files. If you are running NetWare for Macintosh and have Macintosh files on the file server, make sure the backup program can handle both the data fork and the resource fork of Macintosh files. Many NetWare-compatible backup programs (including Novell's own MACBACK and v1.0 of NBACKUP) are unable to handle both forks properly. MACBACK does back up Macintosh files, but it creates a resource fork for every file it restores, whether or not the file had one in the first place. NBACKUP v1.0 completely ignores all Macintosh application program files during a backup.

It's a good idea to keep Macintosh files in separate directories, rather than mixing Macintosh files and DOS files in the same directory. Separating the files facilitates using MACBACK to back up the Macintosh directories and other DOS file-oriented utilities to back up directories containing DOS files.

Handling Files That Are Open during Backup

On a typical NetWare file server, many files can be held open for long periods of time. Therefore, another important feature to look at is how the backup system handles files that are open when the backup takes place. Some programs require the file server to be down when you do the backup; in that case, all files are guaranteed to be closed, and open files are not an issue.

Programs that offer on-line backup while the server is up feature a variety of ways to deal with open files. Some systems can back up open files as long as they are flagged Shareable; if a file is open and flagged Nonshareable, the program skips over it and lists it in a log file printed after the backup. The system supervisor can review the log file and try backing up the skipped files later when they are not open.

Other programs will stop and report that a shared file has been encountered, giving the operator the option to abort the backup, retry the file copy, or skip the file. The program maintains a list of skipped files so you can come back to them later. Usually some type of timeout feature is available to allow the system to continue if the backup is running unattended. After so many retries, the system will skip the files and continue its backup.

Support for Various Types of Backup Media

While you shouldn't judge a backup system solely by the type of media it supports, this is an important consideration, especially when you're looking for new software to run with existing hardware. Some of the most common backup media are discussed below.

Magnetic Tape. Offering relatively low cost and widespread availability, magnetic tape cartridges continue to be the main medium used in most backup systems. Quarter-inch cartridge (QIC) tapes come in a variety of capacities ranging from 40MB to over 300MB. Newer systems use 8mm tape and 4mm Digital Audio Tape (DAT) cartridges capable of storing up to 2GB (gigabytes) of data. Normally, these tapes must be formatted before you can use them; buying preformatted tapes therefore saves a considerable amount of time if you need a large number of cartridges.

An important factor to consider is the interchangeability of tape cartridges. We tend to take for granted that media formatted on one machine can be ported to another machine and work just fine (as is usually the case with floppy diskettes and hard disk drives). This is not always the case with magnetic tape cartridges. Some tape cartridges can be used reliably only with the tape drive on which they were formatted. Inserting the cartridge into another tape drive, even one from the same manufacturer, can result in errors in reading the tape. Some manufacturers guarantee that cartridges used for backup on one tape drive can be restored from any other drive in the same hardware series; this capability ensures that, if your regular tape drive fails, you will still be able to restore data by using another tape drive.

Optical Disks. The introduction of optical disk technology several years ago saw almost immediate application in the backup products industry. Back then, the 500MB-800MB storage capacity of a single optical disk was most attractive compared to the under 100MB capacity of QIC tapes. The early optical disks were Write Once/Read Many (WORM) media that could be written to only once, but then read back many times. Rewritable optical disks are now available that allow you to write over data previously written to the disk.

Removable Hard Disks. Removable hard disks can be part of the overall backup system. While removable drives, such as the Bernoulli Box from Iomega, offer limited storage capacity, they are useful for backing up critical data that must be restored quickly if lost. You can access data from a removable hard disk drive much more easily than from a tape or optical disk drive (which both write data sequentially and must perform searches sequentially).

Backup Speed

The speed at which the backup system can copy data is another factor to consider, especially if a great deal of disk storage is attached to your file server. For example, backing up 200MB of data at half a megabyte per minute would take over 6 1/2 hours; at 3MB per minute, it would take slightly over one hour. Average backup speeds range from 2-4MB per minute, although the speed of the network hardware and the performance of the file server itself significantly affect the backup speed.

Although you don't normally think of it, the longer the backup takes, the higher the chances are of a power failure occurring during the backup. The possibility of unauthorized access to the file server is also greater—especially with unattended backup programs that log in to the server with supervisor rights.

Backup Security

Data security is a two-fold concern with NetWare-compatible backup systems. The program must not only protect against unauthorized access during the backup (as mentioned above), but also prevent nefarious users from stealing the backup cartridges and restoring the data they contain to another machine where they have supervisor rights.

To prevent unauthorized users from accessing the server's data through the backup program, some backup systems require a password when starting up the backup or restore program. Other programs offer the ability to assign a password to each data cartridge to prevent unauthorized access to any of the data on the tape. This password is encrypted so that it cannot be read from the tape. Only an authorized operator who knows the password can restore data from the tape.

Another common procedure for enhancing the security of unattended backups is to create a "BACKUP" user account. Set up this account in SYSCON so that user BACKUP can log in only from a specific workstation (network and node address), with only one concurrent connection, and only during the times scheduled for regular backup sessions. (See Chapter 8 for more information about setting up user accounts.) Create a login script for user BACKUP that maps the necessary drives for backing up, calls the backup program, then logs the user out as soon as the backup is finished. (See Chapter 9 for information about login scripts.) Next, set up a batch file to log the user in at a predetermined time.

The final step is to prevent anyone from interrupting the backup session to gain access to the server. Several third-party utilities are available on NetWire to either disable the Ctrl-Break function or lock the workstation's keyboard with a password.

Error Detection and Correction

As with other electronic media, the transfer of data to and from backup media is not an error-free process. Backup systems vary widely in how they handle error detection and correction in backup and restore operations. The two main schemes are read-after-write verification and redundant copies of data on the media. Although both methods have proven reliable, both have drawbacks as well.

With read-after-write verification, after a block of data is written to the backup media, the system compares the backup data to the original hard disk data to verify that the backup copy is an exact duplicate of the original. If a discrepancy is found, the data is read again from the disk and written to a different part of the tape. The verification procedure is repeated to ensure the integrity of the backup copy. Most tape backup systems utilize the read-after-write verification process to detect and correct errors.

The drawback is that, even though data is written to the tape or optical disk without errors, an error can still occur when the system reads back the data during the restore process. Errors caused by dust or micro-debris caught between the drive head and the backup media are called "soft errors" because they are not physical defects, but rather electronic misinterpretations. Read-after-write verification is able to detect and compensate for "hard errors" (physical tape errors), but it does not compensate for soft errors encountered during a restore as effectively as the redundant method.

The redundant method copies each block of data in two different locations on the tape to protect against both media errors and soft errors during restore. If such an error occurs, the system can rebuild the necessary information from the redundant copy of the data. The drawback here is that it takes longer to back up because the system has to make two copies of the data instead of just one.

ADDITIONAL BACKUP SYSTEM FEATURES

It is difficult to draw the line between essential backup features and those that are merely convenient. Depending on the size of your network and other factors, you may consider some of the following features a necessity.

Unattended Backup Capabilities

Babysitting a backup program that requires a lot of operator intervention is, at best, drudgery. Recognizing this fact, vendors of most backup systems include in their products the ability to schedule automatic, unattended backup sessions. You can set up these sessions to run in the middle of the night when network activity is low.

Obviously, you must make sure that the hardware is capable of holding enough information so that changing media is not necessary. Another alternative is a jukebox system that automatically changes cartridges or optical disks when one fills up. Other features that facilitate unattended backup include the ability to run various backup sessions through commands placed in batch files.

Image Backups and File-by-File Backups

Some backup programs (including Novell's streaming tape BACKUP and RESTORE utilities offered with SFT NetWare v2.1) make what is called an "image" backup of a disk. These programs bypass the operating system and talk directly to the disk, copying the sectors one by one in sequence. Image backups are fast because they ignore the directory structure, and they allow you to quickly restore entire disks all at once. On the down side, it's hard to restore a single file or directory with an image backup. Also, the file server must be shut down before the image backup is performed.

The alternative is called "file-by-file" backup. This type of backup copies files separately and allows you to select exactly which files or directories you want to back up. Depending on the sophistication of the program, you can select anything from all files indiscriminately to only files with the .DOC extension that have been modified since the last backup. File-by-file backups offer a great deal more flexibility and make it easier to locate and restore single files or directories. This type of backup can be done while the server is up and running.

Most file-by-file programs allow you to restore files to a different directory than that from which they were backed up. Avoid those that do not; you'll use this feature more often than you might suspect. NetWare-specific programs allow you to select the bindery files only, or files with a certain NetWare file attribute only. Another convenient selection feature is the ability to select only those files modified after a certain date.

Miscellaneous Features

Other convenient backup features include media management functions that help you rotate tape cartridges and keep track of the contents of various backup media. If you have volumes larger than the maximum capacity of a single cartridge, make sure your backup program can span several cartridges without getting confused.

Data compression allows you to cram even more data onto the backup medium. This becomes more and more important as the amount of disk storage on the file server increases. Always keep future expansion in mind when you evaluate the capabilities of a backup system; the backup system must be able to expand right along with the network.

PRINCIPLES OF AN EFFECTIVE BACKUP PLAN

No matter which backup system you have selected, it will do you little good if you don't use it regularly. No excuse is acceptable for missing a scheduled backup session. Problems always seem to attack your network at its most susceptible moment. If you don't have time to do the backups yourself, select a reliable assistant to be responsible for them—but oversee the backup process yourself to make sure it is properly carried out.

As with other aspects of network management, you must plan out your backup strategy carefully. Here are some principles and guidelines for establishing an effective backup plan for your file server.

The Recommended Backup Schedule

You should do a full system backup at least once a week. A full system backup includes all volumes, directories, and files on the file server, including the bindery files, hidden and system files, and the NetWare security associated with the directories and files. Always do a full backup after you install a new backup program. Performing a full backup weekly makes it easier to restore files, because you have only a week's worth of tapes to search through.

In between the full backups, you should back up files that have changed on a daily (or, most likely, nightly) basis. Backing up only modified files conserves room on your backup media because you aren't continually copying the same unchanging files over and over. Back up the trustee rights and bindery files at least once a day as well.

Depending on the applications your users are running and the sensitivity of the data stored on the file server, you may need to back up modified files more often than once a day. The ultimate solution for up-to-the-minute restore capability is an on-line continuous backup system that continually copies file modifications to backup media. This system allows you to restore a file as it was the instant before a problem occurred.

Once a month, go through the files on the server and archive those that are not used regularly and that haven't been changed for a long time. Regular archiving of unused files keeps the server uncluttered and makes disk space available for new files. Transfer archive files to a different type of medium, such as floppy diskettes or optical disks, or to another server. Print out a list of files archived, and store the archive medium in a safe place.

Structuring Directories to Facilitate Backup

Your directory structure can affect the ease or difficulty of backing up the file server. Since static files don't need backup as often as constantly changing files, it's good practice to segregate static files into a volume of their own. For example, application program executable files do not change once you install them on the file server; in fact, you usually flag them Read Only to prevent anyone from altering them in any way. Data files, on the other hand, may change several times every day. If you keep all applications on the SYS volume and put data files on another volume (such as VOL1), you can back up VOL1 daily and back up SYS only monthly.

Rotating Backup Media

To reduce the risk of losing data if a tape cartridge or optical disk goes bad or gets misplaced, you should rotate your backup media. Rotation distributes backed-up data across several cartridges or disks so that the same data isn't always written to the same medium.

Calculate the amount of total backup storage capacity you'll need; buy enough media to handle two or three times that capacity. Divide the media into sets among which you can rotate, and label each cartridge or disk to identify what backup set each belongs in. Keep a written record of which volumes are backed up on which media. Also record the date of each backup, any errors encountered, and the initials of the operator who initiated the backup session.

A number of standard methods exist for rotating backup media. Several are outlined in the *LAN Backup Report* available from Novell's Systems Engineering Department Research Group. (See Appendix C for availability information.)

Storing Backup Media Off-Site

While it may be convenient, it's poor practice to keep your backup media next to the file server. If a fire or other disaster destroys the file server, your backup data will be destroyed with it. You can replace lost hardware, but it is nearly impossible to reconstruct lost data without a sound backup copy. For maximum protection of your valuable data against fires, floods, and other disasters, store the data off-site in a safe place such as a bank deposit vault or a fireproof safe.

30 Using NetWare Backup and Restore Utilities

This chapter looks at the backup and restore utilities that come with NetWare v2.1*x* and suggests possible uses for each utility. Different utilities are shipped with each version of NetWare. We won't go into of detail on how to run these utilities; refer to the Novell documentation for that information. Rather, our intent is to alert you to what is available and what you can do with each utility.

NOVELL'S BACKUP/RESTORE UTILITIES

Over the life of the NetWare 286 product line, Novell has offered a variety of backup and restore utilities. One distinct advantage of using Novell utilities is that you know they can handle NetWare's bindery files, directory rights, trustee rights, and extended file attributes. Here is an overview of the different programs and which versions of NetWare they are available for.

The LARCHIVE and LRESTORE Utilities

These trusty old utilities have been around since the earliest versions of NetWare, and have continued to be offered up through NetWare v2.15c. As of February 1990, they have been replaced by NBACKUP (explained below).

LARCHIVE (Local ARCHIVE) copies NetWare files and directories to a local hard disk, floppy drive, or removable disk. The user interface is a fairly crude command-line prompt interface. When you start the utility, it asks you a series of questions to which you must type in your answers.

In many ways, LARCHIVE is like the DOS BACKUP command. LARCHIVE keeps a log file (ARCHIVE.LOG) that the utility refers to when restoring files. When you back up to floppy diskettes, LARCHIVE stops when the diskette is full and prompts you to insert another diskette. Unlike DOS's BACKUP program, however, LARCHIVE diskettes can be searched and restored from in any order; you need not insert each diskette in sequence to find the files you want.

LRESTORE (Local RESTORE) is the restore counterpart to LARCHIVE. You must run LRESTORE from a network drive on the file server to which you want to restore data. LRESTORE uses the log file (ARCHIVE.LOG) generated by LARCHIVE to restore files to the server.

All network users can use LARCHIVE and LRESTORE to back up and restore files to which they have rights. However, these utilities cannot handle Macintosh files, or files created by a DOS workstation that have since been accessed by a Macintosh workstation.

The NARCHIVE and NRESTORE Utilities

These utilities have been around as long as LARCHIVE and LRESTORE, and have also been replaced by NBACKUP as of February 1990.

NARCHIVE (Network ARCHIVE) copies NetWare files to a different directory on the same file server. It uses the same crude interface as LARCHIVE and generates its own archive log file. NRESTORE (Network RESTORE) is the restore counterpart.

Since these utilities back up files to another area on the file server disks, the data is not protected from file server or disk hardware failures. If you have plenty of extra disk space on the server, you can use NARCHIVE to protect certain files from accidental deletion by users. By using NARCHIVE to copy these files to another network directory, you can restore them more quickly than from local drives or tape backups. To obtain some degree of data protection with NARCHIVE, copy files to a directory on a different disk channel from the channel on which the original data is located.

Any network user can use NARCHIVE and NRESTORE. But, like LARCHIVE and LRESTORE, these utilities cannot handle Macintosh files.

The Streaming Tape BACKUP and RESTORE Utilities

Novell's streaming tape BACKUP and RESTORE utilities are offered only with SFT NetWare v2.1. These utilities were designed to run with the internal Wangtek tape drive found in Novell's old T-286A and T-286B file servers. Installers had to generate a specific version of BACKUP and RESTORE for each file server, using the NETGEN installation program. The .OBJ files for these two utilities were included on the SFT NetWare v2.1 diskettes and accessed in NETGEN via the "Select 'Other' Drivers" option. These utilities require you to bring the file server down before backing up and restoring information.

When Novell discontinued its file server product line, the .OBJ files necessary to generate BACKUP and RESTORE were pulled out of the NetWare operating system software. This is why the "Other" drivers option in NETGEN is no longer used for anything.

The NBACKUP Utility

The NBACKUP utility was originally written as a means of backing up a NetWare 286 file server in preparation for upgrading to NetWare 386 v3.0. As of February 1990, NBACKUP is included with NetWare 286 and allows you to back up and restore files on NetWare 286 servers. It replaces the LARCHIVE, LRESTORE, NARCHIVE, and NRESTORE utilities. You can use NBACKUP while the file server is up and running.

NBACKUP allows you to use any DOS-addressable device or an internal tape drive to back up and restore NetWare files. DOS-addressable devices include floppy diskettes, local hard disks, removable disks, and any other device that can be assigned a drive letter and accessed from DOS. With NBACKUP, you can copy files to other locations on the file server or to other file servers on the internet.

NBACKUP handles Macintosh files as well as DOS files, although NBACKUP v1.0 has a bug, as yet unfixed, that causes the program to ignore Macintosh application program files.

The Streaming Tape Backup VAP

Novell began offering a Streaming Tape Backup VAP in 1989 to replace the functionality of the streaming tape BACKUP and RESTORE utilities. This VAP supports the internal Wangtek tape drives used in Novell's own file servers. As of February 1, 1990, the Streaming Tape Backup VAP comes bundled with all v2.12 and v2.15 NetWare operating systems and works with Wangtek's 60MB and 150MB tape drives.

The VAP, which can be loaded on a file server or external bridge, backs up and restores both DOS and Macintosh files; you can use it to back up multiple servers on an internetwork. It keeps a log of what has been backed up and restored. The VAP requires about 250KB of memory and offers backup speeds of 3MB to 5MB per minute.

The VAP operates in two modes. The first mode closes all files and disables logins so that you can make a complete system backup; the second mode allows users to continue working while the VAP runs in the background, but it does not back up open files.

The MACBACK Utility

The MACBACK utility was offered with the original NetWare for Macintosh software as the only means to back up and restore Macintosh files on the file server. It is still included when you order NetWare for Macintosh, although the NBACKUP utility and the Streaming Tape Backup VAP both handle Macintosh files as well as DOS files.

MACBACK has a few reliability problems that are as yet unresolved. The utility abruptly quits after processing 238 files because it thinks it has run out of disk space. When it restores files, it creates a resource fork whether or not the file had one in the first place. This can cause problems for DOS files and for Macintosh files saved as ASCII files.

Section 3

Troubleshooting

TROUBLESHOOTING THE LAN

Troubleshooting is an inexact science at best; often the source of a problem is not immediately apparent. This is especially true of local area networks where you have a multitude of factors to worry about: file servers, workstations, network interface boards, cabling, hard disks, printers, UPSes, network operating systems, workstation operating systems, shells, protocols, packets, routers, multiuser applications, and so on.

Since this is a file server book, we'll concentrate on problems that involve the file server itself. That narrows the field down to the file server machine, the NetWare OS running on that machine, the applications loaded on the server, the network interface boards in the server, the network hard disks, and other peripherals attached to the server. Of course, we can't completely detach the file server from the cabling systems connected to it. Many file server problems can be identified only by looking at the workstations they affect. As you can see, troubleshooting network problems requires familiarity with a vast range of components.

Depending on your level of LAN expertise, you may or may not be able to accurately pinpoint a problem on the file server by following the suggestions in this book. Knowing what to look for and where the most common problems occur may help you solve some of the simpler problems yourself. If technical support is available, we suggest you use it for the stickier problems. We hope that by reading these troubleshooting chapters, you'll be more informed and prepared to speak with an expert about your network problem.

• Chapter 31 gives general troubleshooting techniques that can be applied to NetWare file servers. It explains the importance of logging network errors and provides a basic troubleshooting chart for isolating common network problems.

• Chapter 32 gives techniques and procedures for resolving the top ten problems that can occur on a NetWare network.

• Chapter 33 gives guidelines for troubleshooting cabling problems, which constitute the overwhelming majority of troubles on any type of network. This chapter also summarizes the cabling rules for the various network topologies.

• Chapter 34 tells how to troubleshoot and remedy a file server that has too few file services processes available for handling network requests. This is one of the trickiest problems to deal with in NetWare 286.

31 Isolating the Problem

Before you can fix a problem with your file server, you need some idea of what is causing the problem in the first place. This chapter gives some tips for identifying and isolating file server problems on a NetWare network. This information will serve mainly as a general guide to troubleshooting; we will present more specific guidelines for actually resolving the problems in subsequent chapters.

GENERAL TROUBLESHOOTING TECHNIQUES

Seasoned troubleshooters and network technicians follow a very precise procedure to isolate and identify the source of a file server problem. By emulating this procedure, you can often eliminate some of the more obvious problems yourself. If you end up calling for help, you can provide more accurate information for the technician to go on.

The rules followed by troubleshooting pros are actually quite simple and are based on nothing more than common sense. They are:

- Try to identify the exact nature of the problem
- Swap components one at a time until you isolate the cause of the problem

Using this two-step "identify/isolate" process will help you diagnose a number of problems on your file server.

Identifying the Source of the Problem

Most file server problems are heralded by something catastrophic: an application hangs, communication with workstations ceases, or the server itself crashes. An error message may or may not appear on the file server monitor. Even if a message does appear, error messages are notoriously vague and hard to decipher. Don't just reboot the server as a knee-jerk reaction. Like a master detective, you've got to gather your clues to solve the case.

The first step in identifying a problem, then, is to analyze the outward symptoms. If you do get an error message, write it down exactly as it appears on the screen in your network error log (more about keeping an error log later in this chapter). The wording of error messages and whether they appear at the server or at a workstation are important clues to where they came from (more on that later, too). The file server may simply hang, or cease operation with no clue as to why. In this case, look for other signs: does the server still have power? Is the monitor dead? Will the server accept any keyboard input at all? Is the disk access light still flashing?

Next, look at the context in which the problem occurred. Try to ascertain what kind of activity was occurring on the network at the time. What VAPs or VADDs were loaded in the server? Were many users logged in, or just a few? What applications were they running? Make a note of which workstations are still operational, if any. If the problem is limited to a single workstation or a group of workstations connected to the same piece of hardware, suspect that piece of hardware first. If the problem affects all workstations running a certain application, that application may be the culprit. If none of the workstations can access the file server, something may be wrong with the LAN communications channel in the file server (NetWare OS, LAN drivers, network boards, cabling, routers, and so on).

Determine whether anything has changed on the network since the file server last functioned properly. If you've just finished running NETGEN or ELS-GEN and you can't get the file server to boot up, there's a pretty good chance that something went wrong during the installation or upgrade. If the file server ran fine until you added that new network interface board or disk drive, chances are the new component could be causing the problem. Even something as minor as deleting a line in a CONFIG.SYS or other configuration file can cause big problems on a network. Keep a detailed record of every hardware and software change in your network logbook.

If the problem occurs while you're trying to boot the file server, note how far the bootup process is able to proceed. Did the server die immediately after reset, or did everything proceed normally until the time came to initialize network interface boards or mount volumes? (See Chapter 39 for a discussion of the normal file server bootup process and possible errors.)

Once you've noted everything you can about the problem, reboot the server and try to make the problem happen again. If the problem reoccurs in exactly the same way over and over, it's easier to identify than a problem that occurs intermittently. If the problem occurs while a certain application is running, try to reproduce the problem with another application or with no applications running.

Isolating the Cause of the Problem

Swapping is the technique used by experts in isolating the cause of a problem. After following the above suggestions for identifying the possible sources of the problem, you should have a fairly good idea of where to start swapping.

If you suspect a hardware problem, remove the questionable component and replace it with an identical component to see if anything changes. One advantage of a network is that you usually have similar network hardware components available in other machines on the LAN. Many network managers keep a small inventory of spare parts on hand just for swapping purposes so they don't have to pilfer them from functional machines.

It is vital that you swap only one component at a time. If you replace a length of cable, the network interface board, and the file server's power supply all at once and the problem is resolved, you'll never know which piece was faulty. If the network functioned well until you added a new piece of hardware, remove the new piece first.

The same principle applies to software problems. If you just added a new piece of software or loaded a new application on the server and now other network applications won't work, remove the new software and see if normal network operation is restored. Whenever you change a software configuration file or batch file, keep a backup copy of the old one to fall back on in case the new one is causing the problems.

KEEPING NETWORK LOGBOOKS

You should keep a *network configuration logbook* describing the exact settings and parameters of each hardware and software component on your network. Chapter 4 describes how to get this logbook started by collecting information about the current configurations of each component of the network. Every subsequent hardware and software change, no matter how minor, should be recorded in the logbook. This configuration logbook will come in handy when you have to call out for support. The first questions support technicians ask is how the file server, workstations, and NetWare operating system are configured.

Also keep a *network error logbook*, either as part of the configuration logbook or separately. The same types of problems tend to reoccur frequently on local area networks. Keep a detailed record that describes every network problem and its solution, no matter who does the repairs: you or a professional service technician. This logbook will be an invaluable resource for future troubleshooting. When future errors occur, check through the logbook to see if that error happened before and if so, what the solution was.

INTERPRETING NETWORK ERROR MESSAGES

Few things are more frustrating than receiving an error message and not being able to determine what the message means or where it came from, let alone how to eliminate the problem that caused the message. One reason error messages are so cryptic is that they are written into the code by engineers who speak an entirely different language than most other people.

Following are some hints for interpreting system and error messages in the NetWare LAN environment. Classifying an error message according its source, its subject, and time of occurence can be very helpful in solving the problem that generated the error.

Determining the Source of Error Messages

Most network supervisors don't realize how many different pieces of software are combined to form a NetWare network. The open architecture of NetWare 286 v2.1*x* opened the door for a myriad of third-party add-ons to the core NetWare operating system. Many error messages that appear on workstations and file servers may not be generated by NetWare at all, but rather by a third-party LAN driver, disk driver (VADD) or VAP, by network application software, or by a workstation operating system (DOS, OS/2, or the Macintosh OS).

Determining the source of the error message can be extremely useful in identifying the problem and eliminating it. The primary key to determining where an error message originates is to observe whether the message is displayed on the file server console or on the workstation.

File Server Console Messages. Error messages that appear on the file server console could be generated by any of these software pieces:

- The core NetWare operating system
- Operating system drivers (LAN drivers, disk drivers, VADDs, or "other" drivers) that have been linked with the OS
- VAPs loaded on the file server
- The file server cold boot loader

Since VAPs, VADDs, and LAN drivers may be written by third-party vendors, these often generate error messages that do not appear in Novell documentation. One way to tell where an error message originated from is to look at how general or specific the wording of the message is.

LAN drivers, disk drivers, VADDs, and VAPs usually generate specific error messages that use the actual name of the component involved. For example, disk drivers often generate disk-specific error messages such as "Unable to reset the PS/2 MFM disk controller." LAN drivers generate LAN hardware-specific errors such as "Error Resetting 3C505 Etherlink Adapter."

Error messages generated by the operating system are typically more general and don't mention disks or boards by name: for example, "Problem with drive 01: Error reading disk redirection data" or "Warning! LAN A DEAD." The cold boot loader generates messages relating to the file server's attempt to boot from a hard disk drive, such as "Checksum error in load file."

Workstation Error Messages. Error messages displayed on a workstation could be generated by the NetWare shell, the workstation operating system, or the specific application running. However, a few error messages generated by the file server operating system appear at workstations instead of at the file server console. Since third-party vendors can supply shell LAN drivers as well as operating system drivers, the error messages these drivers generate may not appear in Novell documentation. But, like file server errors, the generality or specific products named in the message can often help pinpoint the error's source.

For example, a shell LAN driver will generate a specific LAN error message, such as "Error initializing IBM Token-Ring board." Errors that use network terminology, such as "Network Error on Server SLASHER: Error writing to network" are usually generated by the NetWare shell. Workstation operating systems (DOS, OS/2, and the like) produce general file or memory errors, while applications often display messages referring to application-specific details.

Analyzing the Subject of Error Messages

The subject of an error message can be helpful in determining the source of the message and the solution to the problem. Generally, file server console error messages can be classified into one of the following groups:

- The internal operation of the NetWare operating system
- The LAN communication channel
- The disk drives and disk channels
- SFT NetWare disk mirroring and duplexing
- The Transaction Tracking System (TTS)
- The Hot Fix feature
- UPS monitoring
- Printing

The most common error messages occur in the disk drive and System Fault Tolerance areas, such as "Mirroring turned off on volume VOL1 (drive 02 failed)" or "Invalid mirror definition table. Run NETGEN."

Looking at When Error Messages Occur

Generally, NetWare error messages can occur during three distinct stages of network operation. Initialization errors are those that occur when you are booting up the file server. Run time errors are those that occur after the network has been running for a period of time. A third type of error, the consistency check error, can occur either during bootup or during normal operation, whenever the OS checks its data for internal consistency.

Initialization Errors. Initialization errors occur after the file server is reset or turned on, while the operating system software is being loaded. They do not occur after the server has been running for a period of time. Initialization errors are usually fatal errors that halt the system. (Fatal errors are often called "abend" errors because they cause an *ab*normal *end*ing to whatever was running.)

Bootup errors could be caused by improperly configured hardware and software, or by a hardware failure. Examples of these errors include "Invalid Redirection Index Table," "Time out error configuring disk Coprocessor," and "Disk not upgraded to Advanced NetWare" at the file server, and "A File Server could not be found" at the workstation.

Run Time Errors. Run time errors occur after the OS has been properly loaded and initialized, and has been running normally for a time. These error messages are typically caused by hardware failure or power disruptions, though a few are caused by erroneous conditions occurring on the network. Examples of run time errors are: "Abend: NMI Interrupt," "ERROR! Address collision with SLASHER," and "Problem with drive 01: Mirror drive was shut down."

Consistency Check Errors. NetWare's multitasking kernel checks the data stored in memory at various points to ensure that it is consistent with the operation being performed. Most of these consistency checks are performed just before or after critical operations, such as writing data blocks from cache memory to disk. If any of the checks fail, it means that critical data has been corrupted and that continued operation will worsen the situation. Therefore, almost all consistency check errors are fatal and abend the file server.

Examples of consistency check messages are "Dirty cache block has no dirty bits set," "Fatal File System Error: zero First or Current Cluster" and "Stack overflow detected by kernel." Usually the text message generated by a consistency check error is cryptic and difficult to understand unless you know the internal architecture of the NetWare operating system.

Most consistency check errors are caused by memory data corruption. Memory corruption means that data in portions of the system memory are erroneously changed. This condition is commonly attributed to poor power line conditioning on the file server or to hardware memory failure. The latter is particularly true if Non-Maskable Interrupt (NMI) errors frequently occur on the system, since these errors are generated mainly by improperly functioning hardware. Poorly designed applications can also trigger an NMI error.

A Word About Error Message Severity

Not every message you receive from NetWare halts the operation of the network and abends the file server. In addition to these types of messages, which are classified as "fatal," some are considered status messages, while others are considered warning messages.

Status Messages. Status messages simply inform you of current operating system conditions or the successful completion of a process. Most of these messages are not considered errors and typically do not require you to take any specific action, but they can help you in managing the network. Examples of status messages are "Address change detected for SLASHER," "UPS has been enabled," and "Re-mirroring successfully completed."

Warning Messages. Warning messages indicate that, although processing can continue despite the condition mentioned in the message, you should resolve the potential problem condition as soon as possible. If warning messages are not heeded, the problems can reoccur and can quickly become serious. Examples of warning messages are "Hot Fix turned off on drive 02 (volume 03)," "FAT Entry 015A out of bounds in REPORT.OCT," and "Batteries are low. Server will go down in one minute."

Fatal Messages. Abend or fatal error messages are always serious and always halt the system. In errors affecting the file server, the server halts and the error message displays on the console. No further processing takes place until the system is rebooted. Abend errors are usually generated when the software discovers that data being processed is erroneous to the point that automatic recovery is not possible. If the file server continues processing, the result could lead to additional data corruption. Therefore, the system halts operations to prevent further damage.

The majority of abend errors are caused by hardware problems involving memory or disk drives. Examples of fatal error messages are "Abend: Attempt to configure nonexistent drive," "General Protection Interrupt," and "Invalid op code interrupt."

Sources for Error Message Documentation

Many available documents contain specific information on error messages. The NetWare 286 *System Messages* manual describes most NetWare-specific error messages for both file servers and DOS workstations, although many of the file server messages actually apply only to NetWare v2.0a. The manual states that because the v2.1 messages are so similar to those of v2.0a, you should be able to find about 90 percent of the v2.1 messages documented. The other 10 percent were promised in an upgrade supplement, but so far, that supplement has yet to be offered by Novell.

Novell's Electronic Bulletin Board Service, NetWire, and the technical bulletins Novell sends to dealers and distributors are other good sources for advice on NetWare problems and solutions. Many v2.1 error messages not found in the *System Messages* manual are documented on NetWire and in the technical bulletins.

Third-party vendors who supply VAPs or VADDs for NetWare v2.1 may also supply error message documentation with their software. For application-specific error messages, check the manuals that came with the application. Appendix A of the IBM *Disk Operating System Reference* manual contains DOS-specific error messages.

TROUBLESHOOTING CHART

The following pages contain a basic troubleshooting chart that will help you in identifying and isolating common file server problems. Use this as a starting point to lead you to more specific information contained elsewhere in this book. Remember, troubleshooting is not an exact science. About the best you can say is "It could be this," or "It might be that," and "If not, it's probably something else."

Is an error message displayed at the file server console?

YES: Record the exact message in your network error logbook. Follow the suggestions in this chapter to help interpret the message. Check Chapters 39 and 40 to see if the message is covered in this book. If so, follow the guidelines given; if not, check Novell's *System Messages* manual or other sources of error message documentation for instructions relating to the error.

NO: Continue checking other areas listed in this chart.

Does the file server still appear to be operational (powered on, monitor functioning, accepting keyboard input)?

YES: Type the MONITOR console command to see if any workstation activity is taking place (see Chapter 21). Note which connections, if any, are still active. If only one workstation is affected, check for a hardware problem at that workstation. If a group of workstations connected to the same piece of hardware is affected, check the common hardware (hub, wiring concentrator, trunk cable, and so on). See Chapter 33 for help in troubleshooting cabling problems.

Type the TRACK ON console command to see if the server is still sending and receiving packets on the network. If no IN messages appear from other network addresses, check the cabling that connects the file server with other servers or routers (bridges). If there are no OUT messages from the server, check the network interface boards and connections (see Chapter 32). If no IN or OUT messages appear, check for bindery problems (see Chapter 35).

Type the VAP console command to see what VAPs are loaded on the file server. Check the documentation for each VAP for explanations of possible error conditions.

NO: Check the source of power to the file server (UPS or other power protection device). Make sure the unit is still plugged in and functioning properly. Check all power cords and other UPS-to-server connections. Test the wall outlet by plugging something else in, or try plugging the unit into a different outlet. If you don't have a UPS or other device protecting your file server, get one (see Chapter 24).

Check whether the server fan is still running. If not, check the file server's internal power supply. Replace it if faulty or if it does not meet the power specifications required for all internal file server hardware (see Chapter 32).

If the server has power but nothing shows up on the monitor screen, check for monitor problems (see Chapter 32).

If the server has power and the monitor works, but nothing happens when you type at the keyboard, check for keyboard problems (see Chapter 32).

Are any disk access lights flashing on the server or any attached disk subsystems?

YES: Type the DISK console command to check the status of the network hard disks (see Chapter 22). If possible, use FCONSOLE at a workstation to check the status of the server's disk channels (see Chapter 19). See Chapter 32 for other hard disk checks.

NO: Check for hard disk and channel failures (see Chapter 32).

Are any workstations still able to access the file server?

YES: Note which workstations are still operational on the network and what applications they are currently running, if any. Check with the users at any inoperational workstations to see what applications they were running when the problem occurred. If all users of a specific application are down, check that application for problems (see Chapter 32).

Run COMCHECK to test network connections (see Chapter 37). If only one workstation is affected, check for a hardware problem at that workstation. If a group of workstations connected to the same piece of hardware is affected, check the common hardware (hub, wiring concentrator, trunk cable, and so on). See Chapter 33 for help on troubleshooting cabling problems.

NO: Check all aspects of the LAN communications channel in the file server—LAN drivers, network interface boards, cabling, routers, and so on (see Chapter 32).

Have you changed anything recently on the network?

YES: If possible, undo the change and see if network operation is restored. Remove new hardware or software, or restore backup copies of changed configuration and system files.

NO: Continue on down the chart.

Will the file server reboot properly?

YES: Note any unusual messages that might be displayed during the bootup process. Sometimes rebooting the server will solve transient problems, but there is no guarantee that they will not recur. Watch the server closely for a while after rebooting to see if any warning messages appear.

Have users log in and see if the problem happens the same way as before. If so, run through the above checks again. If you still cannot pinpoint the problem, call for professional service.

If everything seems all right for a while, perform the file server checkup in Appendix B to check for possible problems before they can happen again.

NO: Note how far the bootup procedure gets before it dies. See Chapter 39 for more help on errors during file server booting.

Training and experience are the most valuable tools for effective troubleshooting. You probably won't be able to solve every file server problem yourself, but following the guidelines in this chapter will help you gain more insight and competence in tracking down the most common network errors. Don't hesitate to call for service as soon as you feel the problem is out of your league; further tinkering may only make things worse and end up costing you more in the long run.

32 Fixing Common Network Problems

This chapter describes some of the most common problems encountered in a NetWare network and give some possible ways to fix them.

THE TOP TEN NETWORK FAILURES

Here is a list of the top ten causes of problems in NetWare networks, arranged roughly in order of frequency:

- Cabling problems
- Problems arising from incorrect installation
- Hard disk and disk channel failure
- Network interface card failure
- Printer and print queue problems
- Backup and restore difficulties
- Application or other software conflicts
- Corrupt or missing system files
- Commercial power disruptions
- Hardware component or memory failures

CABLING PROBLEMS

Cabling problems, it seems, are ever-present in any kind of network. NetWare LANs are no exception. Since cabling problems constitute the vast majority of network problems, we've devoted an entire chapter to them (see Chapter 33).

COMMON INSTALLATION PROBLEMS

Although most installation-related problems manifest themselves shortly after the network is installed, some may not become apparent until after the LAN has been up and running for some time. Most installation problems can be fixed after the fact, although curing a problem is often more painful than preventing it in the first place. Hiring a professional network installer to install your LAN is probably the best investment you can make towards a smoothly running system.

Yet, despite the complexity of the NetWare 286 installation process, a surprising number of NetWare LANs are installed by non-experts. A survey conducted by Novell's Product Documentation Department in 1988 revealed that nearly 80 percent of the SFT NetWare 286 v2.1 installations had been performed by non-professionals. Typically it's the person who "gets" to be the network supervisor who does the installation. Usually that person's only qualifications were knowing a little bit about PCs or having read the Novell manuals.

For the uninitiated installer, the chance for error lurks behind almost every screen in NETGEN or ELSGEN. This section points out some of the pitfalls that inexperienced installers (and even some of the more experienced ones) encounter when installing NetWare on the file server.

OS Serialization Errors

Copy protection has always been a sore spot in the software industry. Software developers have devised all sorts of ways to prevent piracy and illegal copying of their prime source of revenue. Some of these copy protection schemes worked well; others caused more problems that they were worth. Legitimate software users disliked them all.

Novell's original copy protection scheme involved a piece of hardware called a keycard. A unique serial number was burned into each keycard at the factory, and each set of software diskettes was laboriously serialized to match the number of a particular keycard. After the NetWare operating system was generated, one of the first things it would do upon initialization was check the serial number on the keycard to see if it matched the serial number contained in the OS. If not, the file server refused to boot up.

This hardware-dependent copy protection lasted through SFT NetWare 286 v2.1. With SFT and Advanced NetWare v2.11, Novell experimented with ways for the OS to be serialized in the field rather than at the factory. These early attempts at field serialization proved less than adequate. The whole process hinged around a diskette called GENDATA that contained the serialization data. This GENDATA diskette could not be duplicated, not even to make a legitimate backup copy. NETGEN gave the installer only one chance to enter the correct serial number, after which it was written permanently onto the GENDATA diskette. If the installer entered the number incorrectly (which many did), he or she had to special-order a new GENDATA diskette from Novell.

Beginning with NetWare v2.12 and continuing through all subsequent versions, the whole serialization process was taken out of NETGEN and ELSGEN altogether. Each NetWare OS is still serialized through data on the GENDATA diskette, but you can now make a backup copy of the original GENDATA diskette along with the other NetWare diskettes.

If you see an error message concerning OS serialization, you may have used the wrong GENDATA diskette when generating or regenerating the OS for your file server. Always use your working copy of the GENDATA diskette that came with the NetWare operating system for each particular file server when running NETGEN or ELSGEN for that server. Label the diskettes carefully for each file server if you have more than one on your network. If you run NETGEN or ELSGEN from a hard disk or network drive, delete the GENDATA subdirectory so that the program will ask you for the GENDATA diskette when it needs it.

Conflicting Network Addresses

Another common mistake made in NETGEN or ELSGEN is setting improper network addresses for the network interface boards in the file server. NETGEN/ELSGEN won't let you enter duplicate network addresses for boards within the same file server, but you must also consider network addresses for boards in other file servers or bridges on the internetwork. Duplicate network addresses anywhere on an internetwork cause routing errors to appear on file server and bridge console screens.

The main thing to remember is that, although you set the network address for specific boards in the file server, NetWare uses the network address to identify the *cabling system* that is connected to that board. All nodes physically and directly connected to that cabling system share the same network address, although their node addresses must each be unique. Remember that, although we usually think of nodes as workstations, a node actually represents any network interface board attached to the cable. If you have another file server on the same physical cabling system (such as a backbone cable that connects several file servers), the boards that connect those file servers to the common cabling system must all have the same network address.

If you are getting routing error messages on your internetwork, type the CONFIG console command at each file server to double check the network addresses of each board. Instructions for changing network addresses for file server boards are given in Chapter 20.

Improper Driver Selection or Configuration

The concept of device drivers is vague in the minds of most network users; comprehending their exact purpose and function goes far beyond the limits of what they care to know. So it is not surprising that driver-related problems are as common as they are.

Driver Selection. A few years ago, selecting the right driver for a particular network interface board was fairly easy; for an SMC ARCnet board, you'd choose the SMC ARCnet driver. For the most part, there was a one-to-one correspondence between a particular brand/revision of a network interface board and its associated driver.

Now, the matter is not so clear-cut. As the flavors of network boards become more and more diverse, the differences between them become more and more subtle. Several drivers are now offered for the same type of board, depending on what you want to use it for. The increasing sophistication of Novell workstation and server drivers will only aggravate the driver conflict problem. Successful selection and configuration of the new multiple protocol drivers requires a much higher skill level on the installer's part.

Another frustrating problem is the rapidity with which revisions to a driver are released. By the time the NetWare software goes from Novell's warehouse to a reseller's shelves to the end users, a driver could have been updated several times. Access to Novell's NetWire service on CompuServe is a must to keep up on the latest driver patches and shell fixes.

Driver Configuration. Never assume that a board is set to the factory-default setting—or any other setting, for that matter. Always check the jumpers and switches on the boards themselves to make sure they match with the configuration option you chose for the board in NETGEN/ELSGEN.

For the most commonly used network interface boards, Novell provides installation supplements that show how the switches and jumpers should be set for each configuration option. Other manufacturers of NetWare-compatible boards usually include similar documentation. Keep all hardware documentation on file so you can refer to it readily.

Remember that when you type CONFIG at the file server console, the hardware configuration settings shown are coming from the LAN drivers linked into the OS, not from the boards themselves. About the only sure way to check for driver-board configuration conflicts is to examine the boards firsthand.

Printer Port Foulups

If you are using the file server as your print server (in other words, if your network printers are connected directly to parallel or serial ports on the file server), you must tell NETGEN or ELSGEN which ports you are using for network printers. For printers connected to serial ports, you must also specify the baud rate, word length, number of stop bits, parity, and handshaking protocol set on the printer itself.

Serial ports (or COM ports, as they are also called) are a common source of conflicts in a file server, especially on a network that includes some type of asynchronous communication hardware that uses COM ports to talk to remote workstations or LANs. Check all hardware documentation carefully to determine which COM ports the hardware can be set to use, and make sure only one piece of hardware is trying to use each particular port. Using NETGEN/ELSGEN's Resource Sets for serial port hardware should help avoid these types of conflicts.

HARD DISK AND DISK CHANNEL PROBLEMS

Hard disk technology has improved remarkably over the past several years, resulting in more reliable hard disks and related components. However, the reasonable life expectancy of even the best-cared-for hard disk is only three to five years (five is pushing it). This relatively short lifespan is even more of a concern on a network, where the file server hard disks and their controllers are in almost constant use.

A hard disk malfunction almost always produces an error message on the server, but a failure in the controller or other circuitry may not. Since these are critical parts of the network, you should keep spares in stock or maintain a suitable service agreement for all hard disk channel components.

The following pages list some common problems with hard disks and related disk channel components and give suggestions for solutions.

PROBLEM: A hard disk cannot be accessed by the COMPSURF utility.

Possible Causes. (1) The hard disk is not installed or cabled correctly.
(2) The hard disk controller is not terminated or addressed correctly.
(3) The DCB is not configured properly to recognize the disk.
(4) The communication channel between the DCB, the controller, and the
      hard disk is not functioning.

Possible Solutions. (1) Check the ribbon cables between the hard disk and controller. Be sure Pin 1 of the ribbon cable (usually indicated by a colored stripe) matches up with Pin 1 of the connector. Ensure that the cables from the power supply are seated correctly in the power sockets, both on the hard disk and on the controller. Check the jumper settings on the controller and the hard disk. See the hardware documentation for correct jumper settings.

(2) Check to see that the last controller on the SCSI bus is properly terminated with a terminating resistor. As the first controller on the bus, the DCB should also have a terminating resistor installed. Make sure that each controller connected to the same DCB has its own valid controller address. Follow the hardware manufacturer's documentation carefully to configure the hard disk channel.

(3) Run DISKSET to make sure the hardware configurations stored in the EEPROM chip on the DCB match the actual disk channel configuration in your file server.

(4) Check all components along the disk channel. Make sure the DCB is seated firmly in the file server and that its cable connections are tight. Repair or replace any faulty hardware.

PROBLEM: A hard disk does not pass COMPSURF's track zero test, or COMPSURF encounters an excessive number of bad blocks.

Possible Causes. (1) The hard disk is not installed or cabled correctly.
(2) The hard disk is worn out or damaged.

Possible Solutions. (1) Check the ribbon cables between the hard disk and controller. Be sure Pin 1 of the ribbon cable (usually indicated by a colored stripe) matches up with Pin 1 of the connector. Ensure that the cables from the power supply are seated correctly in the power sockets, both on the hard disk and on the controller. Check the jumper settings on the controller and the hard disk. See the hardware documentation for correct jumper settings.

(2) Replace the hard disk. (See Chapter 28 for details.)

PROBLEM: A hard disk is not listed when you enter the NetWare Installation part of NETGEN/ELSGEN.

Possible Causes. (1) The hard disk is not installed or cabled correctly.

(2) The hard disk controller is not terminated or addressed correctly.

(3) The communication channel between the DCB, the controller, and the hard disk is not functioning.

(4) The DCB is not configured properly to recognize the disk.

(5) The hard disk has not been properly formatted for NetWare.

(6) The INSTOVL.EXE utility was not linked with the correct drivers, or was not configured properly.

Possible Solutions. (1) Check the ribbon cables between the hard disk and controller. Be sure Pin 1 of the ribbon cable (usually indicated by a colored stripe) matches up with Pin 1 of the connector. Ensure that the cables from the power supply are seated correctly in the power sockets, both on the hard disk and on the controller. Check the jumper settings on the controller and the hard disk. See the hardware documentation for correct jumper settings.

(2) Check to see that the last controller on the SCSI bus is properly terminated with a terminating resistor. As the first controller on the bus, the DCB should also have a terminating resistor installed. Make sure that each controller connected to the same DCB has its own valid controller address. Follow the hardware manufacturer's documentation carefully to configure the hard disk channel.

(3) Run FCONSOLE's "Channel Statistics" option (under "Statistics" in the main menu) to determine the status of the hard disk channel. A status line that displays anything other than "Channel is running" indicates a serious disk error.

(4) Run DISKSET to make sure the hardware configurations stored in the EEPROM chip on the DCB match the actual disk channel configuration in your file server.

(5) Run the COMPSURF utility to format and prepare the disk for use by NetWare.

(6) Rerun NETGEN to verify the disk drivers and configurations selected. Make sure your physical disk setup matches the specified configurations.

PROBLEM: The file server will not mount a volume during bootup.

Possible Causes. (1) The hard disk containing the specified volume has failed.

(2) The cable or power to the disk containing the volume has malfunctioned.

Possible Solutions. (1) Replace the hard disk containing the volume. (Be sure to rerun DISKSET if the new disk is different than the old one. Run NETGEN/ELSGEN to initialize the volume. If the SYS volume failed, reinstall the OS.) (2) Check the cabling and power to the hard disk.

PROBLEM: The NetWare OS reports FAT or disk errors when mounting volumes.

Possible Causes. (1) Not enough memory in the file server to mount all volumes. (2) The FAT or directory entry tables have mismatched sectors. This can be due to defective media or the file server being turned off without the DOWN command.

Possible Solutions. (1) Check the file server memory status using FCONSOLE's "Summary" option (under "Statistics" in the main menu). See Chapter 26 for details on adding more memory to the server.
(2) The OS will automatically correct minor directory mismatch errors. For example, if a FAT entry is wrong, the entry will be updated and corrected the next time it is written to. If the errors do not correct themselves, run VREPAIR.

Hot Fix should take care of bad blocks found during normal file server operation. Check the Hot Fix status of the disk by using FCONSOLE's "Disk Statistics" option (under "Statistics" in the main menu). If the number of blocks shown after "Hot Fix Remaining" is under ten, the disk may be worn out and need replacing (see Chapter 28).

NETWORK INTERFACE BOARD PROBLEMS

Problems with network interface boards commonly appear during installation or upgrade. If the problem occurs right after installation, it may indicate that the network board was incorrectly installed. If a problem appears after the board has operated correctly for a time, the board itself may be faulty.

Proper configuration settings are crucial on network interface boards. It is possible for the file server to boot up initially even when you have an incorrect interrupt setting on a network board. The most common conflict (especially on servers with a serial port) is with interrupt line 4 (IRQ 4).

Use the procedures outlined in the following chart to check for network interface board problems in the file server. (The same procedure can be applied to workstations as well.) If the problem persists after you've tried all of the suggested solutions, remove all network boards and see if you can boot the file server with DOS. If not, the fault is probably with another hardware component in the server. If you can boot DOS, replace each network board one at a time and make sure that DOS still boots.

PROBLEM: The file server displays network interface board errors or hangs while trying to initialize a LAN during bootup.

Possible Causes. (1) The network interface board is not installed or seated correctly.
(2) The connector that attaches the board to the network cabling is loose or faulty.
(3) The network interface board is not configured correctly.
(4) The network interface board is defective.
(5) The NetWare OS was not generated with the appropriate drivers and configurations.

Possible Solutions: (1) Make sure that the network boards are seated firmly in the expansion slots and that they have good contact with the expansion bus.
(2) Make sure cable connectors are intact and firmly fastened to all network boards.
(3) Check the board configurations and make sure they match the actual settings on the board.
(4) Swap the board with an identical board that works in another machine, if possible. Don't change anything else. If the server boots with the new board, the old one is probably defective.
(5) Rerun NETGEN/ELSGEN and verify the drivers and configurations selected. Make sure the actual settings on network boards match the configurations chosen in NETGEN/ELSGEN.

PROBLEM: The file server isn't communicating with a group of workstations that are attached to the same cabling system.

Possible Causes. (1) The network interface board controlling that cabling system is not seated or cabled correctly, is not configured correctly, or has failed.
(2) Two boards within the server have the same interrupt setting.
(3) Two different cabling systems have the same network address.
(4) The server does not have enough communication buffers.

Possible Solutions. (1) Check the points listed under the first problem above.
(2) Check which interrupt line is being used by each piece of hardware in the server. If there are conflicts, change the interrupt line settings on the boards. (If you change the configuration of a network interface board in the file server, you must run NETGEN/ELSGEN/INSTALL and regenerate the operating system.)
(3) Check all network boards on the internetwork for conflicting network addresses (see Chapter 20).
(4) Check the status of the communication buffers in FCONSOLE's "Summary" screen (under "Statistics" in the main menu). FCONSOLE calls them "routing buffers." If the peak number used is close or equal to the maximum number, run NETGEN/ELSGEN to increase the maximum number (see Chapter 20).

PROBLEM: FAT errors appear when the file server is first booted after the installation of RX-Net network board.

Possible Causes. The RX-Net board is not connected to an active hub or workstation that is powered on.

Possible Solutions. In order to initialize correctly when the file server is booted, some RX-Net network boards must be connected either to an active hub that is powered on or to another workstation.

PRINTER-RELATED PROBLEMS

Getting NetWare printing set up correctly is an arduous task, due in part to the number of factors involved. Printers must interact with the NetWare OS, parallel or serial ports, the workstation shell, the workstation's operating system, and the application software. In addition, you could have any combination of parallel printers, serial printers, PostScript printers, and LaserWriter printers on the same network.

A few of the most common printer-related problems are described below. For problems specific to certain brands or types of printers, check on CompuServe's NetWire forums, Novell's technical bulletins, or the Technical Information Database (also available from Novell as part of the NetWare Pro package).

PROBLEM: No print queues exist for a network printer.

Possible Causes. (1) Permanent print queue mappings are not set up in the AUTOEXEC.SYS file.
(2) The printer is not properly defined in NetWare's printer tables.

Possible Solutions. (1) If you change the default print queue assignments or queue names, you must include the appropriate console commands in the AUTOEXEC.SYS file (see Chapter 16).
(2) Run the NetWare Installation half of NETGEN/ELSGEN and check the printer tables under the "Miscellaneous Maintenance" option.

PROBLEM: Printing speed is drastically reduced when a nondedicated file server is in DOS mode.

Possible Causes. The switching between protected and real mode on the file server is slow.

Possible Solutions. Make sure the file server is in console mode before you send big print jobs.

PROBLEM: The Print Screen function (accessed by pressing Shift-PrintScreen) does not work on nondedicated file server.

Possible Causes. This function has been disabled to prevent the server from possibly hanging when this particular key sequence is used.

Possible Solutions. Use a third-party program or utility to capture screens if you absolutely need this capability.

PROBLEM: A network printer or plotter works for a while, then generates framing or data transfer errors.

Possible Causes. A glitch has occurred somewhere in the printer interface.

Possible Solutions. Bring down the file server and reboot it. If the printer is connected to a serial port, try switching it to a parallel port (serial-to-parallel converters are available). Remember to redefine the printer port tables in NETGEN/ELSGEN. Check the length of the printer interface cable to make sure it is within the recommended maximum length (around fifteen feet for parallel cables, fifty feet for serial cables).

BACKUP AND RESTORE PROBLEMS

Backing up and restoring network files adequately is another process fraught with potential problems. Here are some general problems often encountered with many backup systems. Again, for problems specific to particular backup/restore systems, check on CompuServe's NetWire forums, Novell's technical bulletins, or the Technical Information Database (also available from Novell as part of the NetWare Pro package).

PROBLEM: Trustee rights are lost when you restore files to the network from a backup.

Possible Causes. The backup program is not NetWare-aware and does not recognize NetWare's extended file information or the bindery files.

Possible Solutions. Switch to a NetWare-compatible backup system that can back up trustee rights and bindery files (see Appendix C for some suggestions).

PROBLEM: Macintosh files are not backed up or restored correctly on the file server.

Possible Causes. (1) The backup program cannot handle both the data fork and the resource fork present in Macintosh files.
(2) You are using Novell's MACBACK utility, which creates resource forks for every file it restores, whether or not the file had one in the first place.

Possible Solutions. (1) Switch to a backup system that can handle both data and resource forks (see Appendix C for some suggestions).
(2) Use Novell's NBACKUP utility, but make sure the version number is later than v1.0 (which completely ignores all Macintosh application program files during a backup).

PROBLEM: The backup program repeatedly skips over certain files because they are always open.

Possible Causes. Backup programs cannot copy files that are open during the backup process.

Possible Solutions. Perform the backups during a period of low network activity when files are more likely to be closed, or have users log out while you perform the backup.

PROBLEM: The DOS BACKUP command does not back up files flagged Shareable on the file server.

Possible Causes. This is a problem with the DOS BACKUP command and some other non-NetWare backup programs.

Possible Solutions. Don't use the DOS BACKUP command to back up net-work files. Use only NetWare-compatible programs (see Appendix C for suggestions).

APPLICATION AND OTHER SOFTWARE CONFLICTS

Network application problems are generally caused by improper installation or configuration of the software. They may or may not affect all users of the application, depending on how the users' workstations are configured.

Listed below are some of the most common problems encountered with network applications in general. NetWire, technical bulletins, and the Technical Information Database are good resources for solutions to application-specific problems.

PROBLEM: An application cannot be installed on a network disk.

Possible Causes. The application may not be designed for network use.

Possible Solutions. Check with the software vendor to see if a network version of the application is available. If not, see Chapter 5 for hints on installing non-network applications.

PROBLEM: A network application cannot find the files it needs to start up.

Possible Causes. (1) NetWare search drive mappings are not properly set up for the applications.
(2) The user does not have appropriate access rights in the application's program directory.
(3) The application was not installed correctly on the network.

Possible Solutions. (1) Make sure the user has search drive mappings to all directories containing the application's program and configuration files. Some applications require two or more search drive mappings. Check the application's documentation for details.
(2) Users need at least Read, Open, and Search rights to run an executable file. Some programs write information back to the executable files, in which case users will need the Write right as well. Check the application's documentation for details.
(3) Reinstall the application in a different directory, taking care to follow the network installation instructions precisely. Remap search drives and reassign trustee rights as necessary.

PROBLEM: A network application cannot find files in a data directory.

Possible Causes. (1) The user does not have sufficient trustee rights in the directory.
(2) The file is currently open for exclusive use by another workstation.

Possible Solutions. (1) Check the user's rights with the RIGHTS utility. A user needs at least Read, Open, and Search rights to see files, and Write and Create rights to write to them. If necessary, grant the user the necessary access rights to the directory (see Chapter 8).
(2) Use FCONSOLE's "File/Lock Activity" option to see if another user has the file open.

PROBLEM: Users cannot write to files even though they have the Open, Write, and Search rights in the directory.

Possible Causes. The files may be flagged Read-Only and thus no one can write to them (not even the supervisor).

Possible Solutions. Shared data files should be flagged Read-Write. Flag them using either FILER or the FLAG command (see Chapter 7).

PROBLEM: An application seems to lock up momentarily at random times, then continues normally.

Possible Causes. (1) The application may be designed to retry a certain number of times when attempting to read a locked record or file, or it may be designed to wait for other users to relinquish the file before it allows others to open it.
(2) NetWare's file caching memory is inadequate.

Possible Solutions. (1) Monitor the file/record locks, using FCONSOLE's "File/Lock Activity" option. If the problem is serious, check with the software vendor to see if there is any solution.
(2) Check the cache buffer status using FCONSOLE's "Cache Statistics" option (under "Statistics" in the main menu). If necessary, add more memory to the file server (see Chapter 26).

PROBLEM: A server-based application (VAP) hangs for no apparent reason.

Possible Causes. The VAP uses one of the same software interrupts that NetWare uses.

Possible Solutions. Unfortunately, there are no industry policies for preventing software interrupt conflicts. Contact either Novell or the VAP vendor for assistance.

PROBLEM: An application is designed to print only to a serial port, so NetWare's CAPTURE command (which captures only parallel ports) cannot redirect the output.

Possible Causes. This usually occurs with CAD applications that are designed to print to serial plotters.

Possible Solutions. Connect a local serial plotter or printer to the workstation running the application. If the application will allow printing to a file, try speci-fying the device name "LPT1:" for the file name. If that doesn't work, save the output to a regular file name and use NPRINT to print the file (see Chapter 17).

PROBLEM: A certain number of users can work just fine in a network application, but additional users are denied access to the program.

Possible Causes. The application has some type of user limit mechanism built in.

Possible Solutions. Check the site license agreement to see if there is a limit on the number of users who can use the program simultaneously. Contact the software vendor for additional licenses if necessary.

CORRUPT OR MISSING SYSTEM FILE PROBLEMS

The NetWare operating system uses a number of configuration files, such as the AUTOEXEC.SYS file, the SERVER.CFG file, and others that are flagged System or Hidden and are for the exclusive use of the OS. (The DIRSTAMP file in each directory is a good example of a NetWare system file.)

These files can be accidentally deleted or become corrupted. Here are some of the problems that can result:

PROBLEM: The file server no longer performs automatic print queue assignments and other console commands right after booting.

Possible Causes. The AUTOEXEC.SYS file is missing or corrupted.

Possible Solutions. Restore the file from a backup, if possible. Otherwise, recreate the file from scratch (see Chapter 16).

PROBLEM: UPS monitoring, TTS wait time, and VAP wait time are not working as expected.

Possible Causes. The SERVER.CFG file is missing or corrupted.

Possible Solutions. Restore the file from a backup, if possible. Otherwise, recreate the file from scratch (see Chapter 24).

COMMERCIAL POWER PROBLEMS

Many network problems can be traced to irregularities on commercial power lines. You should always protect your network equipment with high-quality power protection devices recommended specifically for use in local area networks. See Chapter 24 for more details.

GENERAL HARDWARE AND MEMORY PROBLEMS

Most file servers are regular IBM-compatible personal computers that just happen to be running NetWare instead of DOS. As such, they are subject to the same hardware and memory failures that plague standalone machines. The power supply, motherboard, memory chips, CMOS battery, and other hardware components are all susceptible to failures due to a variety of causes.

One simple way to check for general hardware component problems in the file server is to remove any network boards and see if the file server will boot under DOS. If not, the problem doesn't lie with the networking hardware, but elsewhere in the PC. We recommend taking a class or getting a good book on troubleshooting IBM PCs and compatibles for help in diagnosing hardware problems. Memory problems are best left to a qualified technician to diagnose and correct.

Here are some of the easier hardware problems you can identify and fix yourself:

PROBLEM: The file server doesn't keep track of time correctly, or loses time when the machine is turned off.

Possible Causes. The oscillator on the motherboard is fast or slow, so the system time is similarly fast or slow.

Possible Solutions. When you boot the file server, it reads the date and time from the computer's internal clock that is powered by a CMOS battery. After that, it keeps track of time by counting the machine's clock "ticks." Replace the oscillator.

The CMOS battery may be low or dead. Replace the battery. If neither of these solutions helps, replace the motherboard.

PROBLEM: You get an error reading a diskette in drive A of the file server.

Possible Causes. (1) The floppy diskette is bad or has numerous bad sectors. (2) The hub access hole located in the center of the diskette is not properly aligned with the locking mechanism inside the drive (5.25" drives only). (3) The floppy drive is bad.

Possible Solutions. (1) Try a different floppy diskette. (2) Remove the floppy diskette and shake it. Then, taking care not to touch the magnetic surface of the diskette, spin the diskette a few turns in the jacket by twirling your finger in the hub access hole. (3) If you have an extra floppy disk drive, try swapping them to see if the drive itself is to blame.

MISCELLANEOUS PROBLEMS

Here are a few last problems that don't fall neatly into any one category. Check to see if your file server is experiencing any of these symptoms.

PROBLEM: Console commands do not function correctly or cannot be entered at the file server console.

Possible Causes. The NetWare OS is configured incorrectly or is corrupt.

Possible Solutions. Check all file server board configurations for conflicts in network/node addresses, jumper settings, and so on. Restore the OS from a back-up or regenerate the OS with NETGEN/ELSGEN.

PROBLEM: The file server console screen displays "garbage" characters.

Possible Causes. (1) Two workstations have the same node address on the same cabling system.
(2) Data is corrupted.

Possible Solutions. (1) Check for duplicate station or node addresses on each network address. Check the cabling for bad connections.
(2) Run VREPAIR or restore corrupted data from a backup (see Chapter 36).

PROBLEM: File servers do not recognize each other on the internetwork.

Possible Causes. (1) Incorrect hardware settings in the file server.
(2) Conflicting network addresses on the internetwork.
(3) The bindery is corrupted.

Possible Solutions. (1) Check all file server board configurations for conflicts in network/node addresses, jumper settings, and so on.
(2) Use the CONFIG console command to check network addresses for all servers and routers (bridges) on the internetwork (see Chapter 21).
(3) Run BINDFIX if you suspect a corrupt bindery (see Chapter 35).

PROBLEM: Response from the file server is noticeably slow.

Possible Causes. (1) Faulty network cabling.
(2) Slow or faulty network interface board in the file server.
(3) Slow or faulty hard disk channels.
(4) The file server speed is not set to the highest speed.
(5) The file server is low on memory.
(6) Volumes are large and too full.

Possible Solutions. (1) Test for cabling problems as described in Chapter 33.
(2) Perform the usual network board checks, as described above.
(3) Check the usual hard disk components, as described above.
(4) Check the computer's documentation for how to set switches for the highest CPU speed setting.
(5) Check the file server memory status, using FCONSOLE's "Summary" option (under "Statistics" in the main menu). See Chapter 26 for details on adding more memory to the server.
(6) Archive or delete unnecessary files from the volume. Purge all salvageable files in FCONSOLE.

33 Troubleshooting Cable Problems

Cabling problems account for anywhere from 70 to 90 percent of all LAN problems. Of course, the best way to minimize cable problems is to have your cabling installed by professionals. This is especially true for fiber optic cable, which requires a high level of expertise to handle and splice.

All too often, particularly in smaller LAN installations, the cabling is hurriedly thrown together by either the customer or a dealer ignorant of the finer points of handling cable. The situation is aggravated by the increasing use of un-shielded twisted-pair.

Intermittent problems due to cabling will probably never go away entirely, but here are some suggestions for minimizing downtime due to flaky cabling.

GENERAL CABLING TIPS

The following tips and suggestions apply to all types of cabling used in local area networks.

Test the Cable First

Your cabling system is literally the nerve system of the network. Don't rely on it until it has been fully tested, even if you are using existing wiring. Invest in some basic signal testing equipment, such as ohmmeters and Time Domain Reflectometers. Test new cable while it is still on the spool, before you've routed it through the walls and ceilings.

Adhere to Code

Know and follow your local fire and electric building codes. For example, many codes specify the use of Teflon-jacketed cable in the air handling space between a suspended ceiling and the floor above. If you are not sure what the code requires, obtain professional help.

Avoid Sources of Interference

Coaxial and other types of metal-based cabling are extremely susceptible to electromagnetic and radio frequency (RF) interference. Using shielded cable will help reduce the effects of this interference. You should also consider some less-obvious sources of electromagnetic fields (such as fluorescent lights and power transmission equipment in elevator shafts) when running the cable. Where the cable is routed is as important as what type of cable you use.

Follow the Rules

One of the most common sources of network problems is the disregard, oversight, or outright violation of documented guidelines for installing cable. Improper bus cable termination, inappropriate use of transceivers and hubs, and maximum distances that exceed the limitations are common causes of hardware problems on the network.

Don't push your luck with cabling rules. If the maximum distance for a bus segment is 500 feet, run 475 feet just to be safe. If you are unsure of the exact limitations for a particular type of cabling, consult a professional.

TROUBLESHOOTING NETWORK CABLING PROBLEMS

In general, you should follow a bottom-up approach when trying to isolate a communication problem on the network. Start with the cabling itself, then test the network interface boards, then check other active components (hubs, repeaters, Multistation Access Units, and so on). Novell's COMCHECK utility provides a simple tool for checking the integrity of boards, cable, and other devices all at the same time (see Chapter 37).

Common cabling problems include kinks, breaks, loose connections, improper termination or grounding, and interference. A Time Domain Reflectometer is extremely useful in testing for kinks, breaks, and loose connections. This instrument measures the distance from one end of a trunk segment to the other. If a break or kink occurs somewhere along the line, the distance will read less than the length of the cable. Measure along the cable segment the indicated distance—your break should be close by.

Another common method of testing cable and boards is the loopback test. Many types of boards include this diagnostics capability. Basically, the board sends a signal over the cable and the signal is looped back or returned to the sending device. If the signal does not come back in the same form as it was sent, this change in the signal indicates a problem somewhere along the line.

SPECIFIC CABLING RULES AND TIPS

The NetWare installation supplements spell out most cabling rules for the particular kind of network boards and cable you are using. This book summarizes the basic rules for the three most common types of network cabling: Ethernet (thin and thick), ARCnet, and Token-Ring.

Ethernet Cabling Rules

Ethernet uses a linear bus topology with a CSMA/CD media access scheme that provides a 10Mbps data transfer speed. Ethernet boards are available for use with coaxial, twisted pair, or fiber optic cable. Fiber optic is typically used as a high-speed backbone to which other types of Ethernet-cabled networks are attached. The coaxial cable possibilities include standard (thick) Ethernet and thin Ethernet. Different rules apply to each type of coaxial cable.

When troubleshooting Ethernet cabling, be aware that most Ethernet boards can be set to use either thick or thin Ethernet cable. When set for thick cable, the board expects to be connected to an external transceiver. When set for thin cable, the board will use its built-in internal transceiver.

Rules for Thick Ethernet Cable. The chart in Figure 33-1 summarizes the cabling rules and distance limitations for thick Ethernet cable. This type of cable is also referred to as standard Ethernet, Thicknet, or 10BASE5. (The conversions between U.S. measurements and metrics are approximate.)

Thick Ethernet Cable

Maximum length of a single cable segment	1,500 feet (460m)
Number of transceiver connections per segment	100
Minimum distance between transceiver connections	8 feet (2.5m)
Maximum length of transceiver cable	165 feet (50m)
Maximum total number of devices	1,024 per network
Cable segment termination	Terminate both ends of each segment with a 50-ohm resistor

Figure 33-1: Rules for thick Ethernet cabling.

Testing Thick Ethernet Cabling. You can perform most simple troubleshooting on thick Ethernet cabling with simple tools such as an ohmmeter. Test the integrity of an Ethernet cable segment by removing one of the end terminators and checking for a 50-ohm resistance from the center pin to the shield. A variance of about three percent either way is allowed; any more than this will affect the performance of the cable.

To test a cable-piercing transceiver tap, remove the cover of the tap and locate the center probe (the inner pin) and the braid picks (the two outer pins). Using the ohmmeter, check for a reading of 25 ohms from the center probe to one of the braid picks. A good reading will be between 23 and 27 ohms; any other reading indicates a bad tap. You can remove the tap entirely and wrap the pierced part of the cable with electrician's tape; then try retapping the cable with a new tap a few inches away and test the connection again.

Most Ethernet repeaters and transceivers have LED diagnostic indicators built into the unit. Check the manufacturer's documentation to interpret these diagnostic signals.

Rules for Thin Ethernet Cable. The chart in Figure 33-2 summarizes the cabling rules and distance limitations for thin Ethernet cable. This type of cable (RG-58 coaxial) is also referred to as ThinNet, CheaperNet, or 10BASE2. (The conversions between U.S. measurements and metrics are approximate.)

Thin Ethernet Cable

Maximum length of a single cable segment	600 feet (185m)
Number of device connections per segment	30
Minimum distance between device connections	1.6 feet (0.5m)
Maximum length of transceiver cable (when using BNC transceivers)	165 feet (50m)
Maximum total number of devices per network	1,024
Cable segment termination	Terminate both ends of each segment with a 50-ohm resistor

Figure 33-2: Rules for thin Ethernet cable.

Testing Thin Ethernet Cabling. As with thick Ethernet cabling, you can perform most simple troubleshooting on thin Ethernet cabling with simple tools such as an ohmmeter. Test the integrity of an Ethernet cable segment by removing one of the end terminators and checking for a 50-ohm resistance from the center pin to the shield. A variance of about three percent either way is allowed; any more than this will affect the performance of the cable.

You can quickly locate faulty cable segments with thin Ethernet by moving the terminator along the trunk segment. Start with a workstation at one end of the trunk and insert the terminator into the T-connector that connects to the workstation. Test the resistance as above. If the reading is acceptable, recable that workstation and move to the next one along the trunk. As soon as you get a bad reading, you know which cable segment is faulty.

Rules for Ethernet Twisted Pair. This type of cabling (2-pair, 24-AWG unshielded twisted pair, or 10BASET) has emerged only recently for use with Ethernet. It offers the same 10Mbps speed and CSMA/CD media access method, but allows the nodes to be connected in a star topology. The boards use a transceiver cable and a twisted pair transceiver to connect to a standard telephone-style jack. The twisted-pair cabling then connects to a central splice block.

The maximum length of a twisted-pair segment is 330 feet (100m); only one transceiver device can be attached per segment.

A Note about Fiber Optic Cabling. Due to the complexity involved in splicing and handling fiber optic cabling, its installation and diagnostics are best left to professionals. They have the equipment and expertise necessary to deal with this type of media.

ARCnet Cabling Rules

Traditionally, ARCnet uses a flexible, distributed star topology with a token-passing media access scheme that provides a 2.5Mbps data transfer speed. Newer types of ARCnet boards support a linear bus topology and twisted pair cabling. The coaxial cable used is RG-62 A/U coaxial.

When troubleshooting ARCnet networks, remember that nodes can be removed or turned off without affecting other nodes on the same cabling system. Each node on the same ARCnet cabling system must have a unique node address from 1 to 255. These node addresses are usually set by means of switches on the boards themselves. Duplicate node addresses can cause all kinds of problems.

Rules for ARCnet Coaxial Cable (Star Topology). The chart in Figure 33-3 summarizes the cabling rules and distance limitations for traditional ARCnet coaxial cable. (The conversions between U.S. measurements and metrics are approximate.)

Rules for ARCnet Coaxial Cable (Bus Topology). When using bus-topology ARCnet coaxial cable, the rules are the same as for the star topology, except that the maximum cable length from an active hub is reduced to 1,000 feet (305m). The maximum distance between devices is 400 feet (122m) and you can have up to eight devices per segment. (The conversions between U.S. measurements and metrics are approximate.)

Rules for ARCnet Twisted-Pair Cable. ARCnet also supports the use of 1-pair, 24-AWG unshielded twisted-pair cabling in either a star or bus topology. With either type, the maximum segment length is reduced to 400 feet (122m), but you can have up to ten devices per segment. (The conversions between U.S. measurements and metrics are approximate.)

ARCNET Coaxial Cable (Star)

Maximum cable length from an active hub	2,000 feet (610m)
Maximum cable length from a passive hub	100 feet (30.5m)
Maximum distance between an active hub and a passive hub	100 feet (30.5m)
Maximum total amount of cable (by daisy-chaining active hubs)	20,000 feet (6,096m)
Maximum total number of devices per network	255
Cable termination	Terminate unused passive hub ports with RG-62 terminators. Unused ports on active hubs do not need to be terminated.

Figure 33-3: Rules for ARCnet coaxial cable using the star topology.

Testing ARCnet Cabling. ARCnet cabling is easy to test by swapping cable segments. You can usually isolate a problem by noting which workstations are affected. If all workstations connected to the same active or passive hub go down, replace the cable leading to that hub or, if that doesn't work, replace the hub itself. Most hubs have diagnostic LEDs that indicate whether or not they are functional. Check the manufacturer's documentation for the correct interpretation of these signals.

Token-Ring Cabling Rules

Token-Ring is the LAN technology officially endorsed by IBM. It uses a token-passing scheme over a logical ring topology and provides speeds of 4Mbps or 16Mbps. You can use either IBM Type 1 or Type 3 cabling in Token-Ring networks.

The cabling rules for Token-Ring are more complex, mainly due to the rigidity of the topology and the redundant cabling used to provide built-in fault tolerance. The typical Token-Ring network consists of a series of Multistation Access Units (MAUs) connected in a ring. Each MAU can connect up to eight devices; each ring can support up to 33 MAUs. Therefore, the maximum number of nodes supported by one main ring is around 260. Several main rings can be connected via IBM Token-Ring bridges.

The chart in Figure 33-4 summarizes the major distance limitations in Token-Ring networks. More exact specifications vary, depending on the number of MAUs in the network and the number of wiring closets they are located in. Refer to

Novell's installation supplement for Token-Ring or the IBM *Token-Ring Planning Guide* for more information.

Basic Token-Ring Rules

Maximum total length of the main ring (Type 1 cable)	1,200 feet (366m)
Maximum cable length from a MAU to a workstation (Type 1 cable)	330 feet (100m)
Maximum cable length from a MAU to a workstation (Type 3 cable)	1,000 feet (305m)

Figure 33-4: Rules for Token-Ring cabling.

When calculating total cable length of the ring, assume that each eight-station MAU counts as 16 feet (5m) of cabling. A wide variety of repeaters and hubs are available to extend the distances of a Token-Ring network.

Testing Token-Ring Cabling. Even though Token-Ring cabling is designed to be highly fault tolerant, problems can still occur in the cabling, in the MAUs, or in the network interface boards. If a single workstation fails, check the cable that connects it to the MAU. If all devices on a ring fail, check the outside ring cabling. Remove the Ring-In and Ring-Out cables from each MAU in sequence and see if the devices on that MAU are still communicating. That would indicate a problem in the outside ring cabling. Reattach the Ring-Out cable from a working MAU to the Ring-In connection on the next MAU and repeat the communications test until you have isolated the faulty cable.

MAUs and Token-Ring boards come with a variety of built-in diagnostics capabilities. Check the manufacturer's documentation for details on how to use these diagnostics.

34 Increasing File Service Processes

The NetWare 286 operating system (starting with v2.0*x* and continuing with v2.1*x*) has been around since 1986, when 286-based microcomputers were just catching on in popularity. The OS was designed to make the best possible use of the LAN hardware and software technology available at the time. The fact that NetWare 286 is by far the most widely used network operating system five years later attests to the brilliance and flexibiltiy of the original design.

As with any software product in the face of rapid technological advances, however, some of the original design choices (which were more than adequate when first implemented) can eventually limit how far you can go with the product. Such is the case with NetWare 286 v2.1*x* and its use of the DGroup memory segment. This single 64KB segment was designed to contain, among other things, Dynamic Memory Pool 1, buffers for LAN and disk drivers, disk and volume tables, and stacks for all other internal processes (nearly twenty of them). Whatever is left over is used for file service processes. As LAN and disk driver technology has improved, and as more and more features have been added to NetWare (each taking its toll in DGroup memory requirements), the shortage of memory available for file service processes has become an area of growing concern.

This chapter explains what file service processes are, how they work in NetWare 286 v2.1*x*, and how they are related to the DGroup data segment in file server RAM. By understanding the factors that affect this memory segment allocation, you will be better able to recognize when and why a file server has an insufficient number of file service processes. We'll also summarize some techniques for dealing with this problem.

Much of the information in this chapter is based on a report produced by Novell's Systems Engineering Division in June 1990. The full report is available on NetWire for those who desire more detailed information.

WHAT IS A FILE SERVICE PROCESS?

A file service process (FSP) is a process within a NetWare 286 file server that services packets containing NetWare Core Protocol (NCP) requests for file services. These packets are often referred to as "file service packets." For example, when a workstation wants to read a file from a file server disk, the NetWare shell builds a packet with the appropriate NCP request and sends it to the server. Only FSPs can process NCP requests.

To draw upon the analogy used in Chapter 19, an FSP is like a butler in a large mansion (the file server). Whenever an NCP request arrives at the server, a doorman (the MUX process) passes the request to a butler (FSP). Like a butler, the FSP takes the NCP request to the appropriate room for service, waits for the request to be processed, then escorts the results of the processing back to the door to send them on their way. The FSP then waits for additional NCP requests. At times, more than one NCP request arrives at the same time, or additional NCP requests arrive while an FSP is busy servicing a previous request. To handle these situations, the server usually has several FSP butlers available and waiting by the doorman.

The number of FSPs the file server can make available is limited, however. The maximum number is ten, although a typical server will have from three to seven. If an NCP request packet arrives at the server when all the available FSPs are busy, the doorman places the packet in a "waiting room" (a routing buffer) until an FSP is freed up to handle it.

Problems start occurring when so many NCP requests arrive at once that all available FSPs are busy and all the routing buffers are filled up as well. This condition can occur during periods of heavy NCP request traffic: for example, when large files are being copied, or when certain types of database applications are running. In this situation, the OS has no choice but to discard incoming NCP requests until the FSPs finish with the current NCP requests and those held in the routing buffers. When packets are discarded, workstation application performance slows down because the application must wait while the NetWare shell resends the packets. The performance of the entire network may degrade as well, due to increased traffic on the network cabling. In extreme situations, the NetWare shell will time out, thus losing its connection with the file server.

Diagnosing FSP Shortage Problems

Performance degradations such as the ones described above can be caused by a number of factors, including faulty network interface boards, routing problems, and slow disk channel response. Before you jump to conclusions about what is causing a performance degradation on your network, you should check a few statistics in FCONSOLE to see whether the problem might be due to a lack of FSPs.

First, go into FCONSOLE and select "Statistics" from the main menu. Choose "Summary" from the resulting "File Server Statistics" submenu and note the "Number Of File Service Processes" listed. For most small networks, two or three file service processes is enough; larger networks may need three or more. If the number shown is less than two, you definitely have a shortage of FSPs. Press Escape to leave the "Summary" screen.

Now choose "LAN I/O Statistics" and look at the "File Service Used Route" entry. This entry represents the number of times an NCP request had to wait in a routing buffer because no FSPs were available to service it. (Note that the "File Service Used Route" counter will reset to zero after it reaches 65,536. If the counter has rolled over between two measurements, you must add 65,536 to the second measurement to get an accurate reading.) Look also at the number of "File Service Packets" shown on this screen. This number represents the total number of file service packets (mostly NCP requests) serviced by the file server. Divide the "File Service Used Route" number by the total number of "File Service Packets." A result of more than .10 (more than ten percent of all file service packets having to wait in routing buffers) is another indication that your server is short on FSPs.

To be doubly sure that your diagnosis is correct, observe these statistics at various times during the day over a period of several days. Compare the readings to see if there are any radical differences in the numbers during periods of heavy server utilization. Evidence of an FSP shortage may not appear until a certain application is running or a particular activity is being performed.

You cannot associate a particular network interface board or file server peripheral with using a certain number of FSPs. To get an accurate picture of why your server is running short on FSPs, you need to look at how the various options and peripherals configured on your file server use the DGroup data segment in the file server RAM.

COMPONENTS OF THE DGROUP DATA SEGMENT

The DGroup data segment consists of a number of components vital to the NetWare operating system, including file service processes. The size of DGroup memory is fixed at 64KB because the Intel 286 microprocessor segments RAM into 64KB blocks. You cannot increase the size of DGroup memory by adding more memory to the file server. The only way to affect how much of DGroup memory is allocated to FSPs is to reduce the amount of the 64KB used by the other DGroup components. Here is a list of components contained in DGroup memory and the minimum-maximum amount of memory taken up by each component:

• The Global Static Data area contains all global variables defined for the NetWare OS and its linked LAN and disk drivers. This area can take anywhere from 28.0 to 39.3KB of memory.

• The Process Stack area provides stack space for all NetWare processes. This area takes about 7.0-10.5KB of memory.

• The Volume and Monitor Table area holds information used by the MONITOR console command, as well as the volume tables for all disk volumes mounted on the server. Depending on the number of volumes, this area can take from 0.2KB to 11.5KB of memory.

• Dynamic Memory Pool 1 is a workspace used by virtually all NetWare processes and routines for such procedures as maintaining disk drive mappings and servicing file server requests. The size of this workspace can range from 16.0KB to 20.9KB, although most of the time it is between 16KB and 17KB in size.

• The File Service Process Buffer area is where incoming NCP requests are queued prior to either being serviced by an FSP or sent to wait in a routing buffer. The number of file service process *buffers* directly determines how many FSPs are available. This area in DGroup memory ranges from 1.5KB to 12.8KB in size.

Each of these DGroup memory components is explained in more detail below.

Global Static Data Area

This area is typically the largest single segment allocated in DGroup memory because it contains all of the global variables defined by the NetWare operating system. The amount of memory allocated to this area has increased with each successive version and revision of the OS, as shown in Figure 34-1:

Operating System	DGroup Allocation
Advanced NetWare v2.15	28,454 bytes
Advanced NetWare v2.15 (Nondedicated)	28,518 bytes
SFT NetWare v2.15	28,444 bytes
SFT NetWare with TTS v2.15	28,596 bytes
Advanced NetWare v2.15c	28,466 bytes
Advanced NetWare v2.15c (Nondedicated)	28,530 bytes
SFT NetWare v2.15c	28,466 bytes
SFT NetWare with TTS v2.15c	28,608 bytes

Figure 34-1: NetWare operating system DGroup allocation table.

The Global Static Data area also contains global variables defined by whatever LAN drivers and disk drivers (including VADDs) are linked in with the OS. In this respect, you can affect the size of this area by changing the number and types of LAN and disk drivers you configure in NETGEN. Figure 34-2 shows the amount of memory allocated for each driver:

LAN Driver	DGroup Allocation
Novell Ethernet NE1000	301 bytes
Novell Ethernet NE2000	406 bytes
Novell Ethernet NE/2	356 bytes
Novell Ethernet NE2000 W/AppleTalk	881 bytes
Novell Ethernet NE/2 W/AppleTalk	837 bytes
Micom-Interlan NP600	243 bytes
3Com 3C501 EtherLink	403 bytes
3Com 3C505 EtherLink Plus (2012)	405 bytes
3Com 3C505 EtherLink Plus (1194)	573 bytes
3Com 3C505 Etherlink Plus W/AppleTalk	798 bytes
3Com 3C503 EtherLink II	388 bytes
3Com 3C523 EtherLink/MC	258 bytes

IBM Token-Ring	644 bytes
IBM Token-Ring Source Routing	3,920 bytes
Novell RX-Net	256 bytes
Novell RX-Net/2 — SMC PS110	259 bytes
SMC Arcnet/Pure Data	256 bytes
Novell NL1000 & NL/2 (AppleTalk)	108 bytes
Novell Star Intelligent NIC	160 bytes
AT&T StarLAN	103 bytes
Corvus Omninet	162 bytes
IBM PC Cluster	1,044 bytes
IBM PCN (Original Adapter)	606 bytes
IBM PCN II & Baseband	696 bytes
Gateway Communications Inc. G/NET	241 bytes
Proteon ProNET-10 P1300/P1800	356 bytes
Generic NetBIOS	1,526 bytes
IBM Async (Com1/Com2)	3,203 bytes
Async WNIM	9,942 bytes
Telebit P.E.P. Modem/WNIM	9,952 bytes

Disk Driver	**DGroup Allocation**
IBM AT hard disk controller	170 bytes
Novell Disk CoProcessor - AT	783 bytes
IBM PS/2 Model 30 286 MFM	138 bytes
IBM PS/2 MFM disk controller	152 bytes
IBM PS/2 ESDI disk controller	180 bytes
Industry Standard ISA or AT Controller	292 bytes

Figure 34-2: LAN and disk driver DGroup allocation table.

When you link in more than one LAN driver in NETGEN, the amount of memory for global variables shown above is allocated in DGroup for each driver. If the same LAN driver is loaded twice, the memory is allocated twice. For example, if you configure the OS for a Novell Ethernet NE2000 board and a Novell RX-Net board, the total DGroup allocation is 662 bytes (406 + 256 bytes). If you configure the OS for two NE2000 boards, the DGroup allocation is 812 bytes (406 bytes x 2).

If the same disk driver is loaded more than once, the amount of memory for its global variables is allocated only once. For example, if you configure the OS for an ISA disk driver and the Novell DCB driver, the total DGroup allocation is 1,075 bytes (292 + 783 bytes). However, if you configure the OS for two Novell DCBs, the total DGroup allocation is only 783 bytes.

Process Stacks Area

NetWare allocates stack space in DGroup memory for each of the following OS processes:

Standard OS processes	7,136 bytes
TTS Stack	250 bytes
Print Spooler Stack	668 bytes

A separate stack of 668 bytes is allocated for each spooled printer port defined for the file server in NETGEN. You can influence how much total space is allocated to the Process Stacks area by removing TTS from the file server (if you don't need it) and by reducing the number of ports spooled for printers in NETGEN. Using external print server software to handle network printers eliminates the need for print spooler stacks in DGroup memory.

Volume and Monitor Tables

The Monitor Table stores information used by the MONITOR console command to display its file server monitor screen. This table requires a fixed amount of 84 bytes of DGroup memory. The amount of memory required for the volume tables varies according to the number of volumes mounted on the server, how big they are, and the maximum number of directory entries defined for each volume in NETGEN/ELSGEN. (Volumes on mirrored disks are not counted twice.)

Each volume mounted on the server takes 84 bytes. In addition, each megabyte of disk space in the volumes requires 1.75 bytes. Every 18 directory entries allocated for all volumes takes up 1 additional byte. Fractional values are rounded up to the next highest whole number.

For example, if your server has only one volume mounted, and that volume (SYS) is 145MB in size with a maximum of 9,600 directory entries, you could figure the amount of memory taken up by the Volume and Monitor Tables as follows:

Monitor Table (fixed at 84 bytes)	84
Volume Table (1 volume at 84 bytes)	84
145MB at 1.75 bytes (rounded up)	254
9,600 directory entries at 1 byte per 18 entries (rounded up)	534
Total DGroup memory used	956 bytes

Dynamic Memory Pool 1

Dynamic Memory Pool 1 is used as a temporary workspace by virtually all NetWare processes and routines. As needed, NetWare can allocate anywhere from 2 to 1,024 bytes or more (128 bytes is the average amount) to a process for short periods of time. When the process is finished, it returns the memory to the pool so other processes can use it.

NetWare processes and routines that run more or less continuously in the file server hold memory allocated out of Dynamic Memory Pool 1 on a semi-permanent basis. These processes and the amount of memory they require are shown in Figure 34-3. Those marked with an asterisk (*) are, for all practical purposes, permanent allocations, because you must bring down the file server and reconfigure the NetWare OS to change these allocations.

Process or Routine	Dynamic Memory Pool 1 Allocation
Drive Mappings	16 bytes per map assignment, per workstation
*Additional drive information	614 bytes per physical drive
*Process Control Blocks	30 bytes each (30 allocated initially)
*Semaphores	8 bytes each (40 allocated initially)
Auto Remirror Queue	6 bytes per drive to be remirrored
Apple Macintosh file support	6 bytes per open Macintosh file
Workstation support	10 bytes per logged in workstation
*Disk Storage Tracking Process	962 bytes (if Accounting is enabled)
Spool Queue entries	46 bytes per spooled print job
Queue Management System	30 bytes per queue
QMS Queue servers	8 bytes per queue server, up to a maximum of 25 queue servers
*Volume Names	Up to 18 bytes per mounted volume
*VAPs	130 bytes per VAP (for stack space)

Figure 34-3: Semi-permanent allocations from Dynamic Memory Pool 1.

Running out of available workspace in Dynamic Memory Pool 1 may or may not generate an "ABEND" error message. In some versions of NetWare, print jobs either disappear until some memory in Dynamic Memory Pool 1 becomes available, or they are lost altogether. Any reference to "dynamic workspace" in an error message can refer to Dynamic Memory Pool 1, 2, or 3. Check the "File Server Statistics Summary" screen in FCONSOLE to see which memory pool is out of workspace.

Because of the way in which NetWare allocates the memory in Dynamic Memory Pool 1, you cannot manipulate its size to gain additional FSPs. You should, however, manage the semi-permanent Dynamic Memory Pool 1 allocations to avoid a shortage of RAM in this memory pool.

File Service Process Buffers

These are the buffers allocated in DGroup for incoming file service packets containing NCP requests. Technically, file service processes are not actually part of DGroup memory, but the number of FSP buffers available directly determines how many FSPs your server will have. If the server has four file service process *buffers* available, it will have four FSPs.

A file service process buffer requires the following amount of DGroup memory:

106 bytes	for workspace
768 bytes	for stack space
94 bytes	for a packet reply buffer
512-4,096 bytes	for a packet receive buffer

The size of the packet receive buffer is variable to accommodate the varying packet sizes handled by different network interface boards. The total size of an FSP buffer, then, depends on the largest packet size used by any of the LAN drivers linked in to the OS.

For example, suppose you have configured the OS for an Ethernet driver with a packet size of 1,024 bytes and an ARCnet driver with 4,096 byte packets. The size of all FSP buffers for this server would be 5,064 bytes (106 + 768 + 94 + 4,096 bytes). The bigger packet size used by the ARCnet driver causes all of the FSP buffers to be larger, even though the Ethernet driver uses smaller 1,024-byte packets. For this reason, you should avoid having LAN drivers that use widely varying packet sizes on the same file server. One possible solution is to move offending large-packet LAN drivers and their associated network interface boards to an external bridge instead of using them on the file server.

A few other factors come into play with FSP buffers and DGroup memory. Regardless of the number of FSP buffers, the OS allocates one additional 94-byte reply buffer in DGroup memory. If any of the LAN drivers linked into the OS support direct memory access (DMA), the OS may have to set aside a portion of DGroup memory as unusable. The reason for this is that some DMA chips cannot handle addresses correctly across physical 64KB boundaries in RAM. If the receive buffer within an FSP buffer happens to straddle a physical 64KB boundary, the OS will skip to the next boundary and not use the remaining memory in that 64KB segment. Depending on the size of the receive buffer and the location of the boundary overlap, the amount of memory skipped over could be as much as 4,095 bytes. Of course, you can avoid this problem by not using LAN drivers that require DMA.

Figure 34-4 illustrates how the OS compensates for drivers that use DMA:

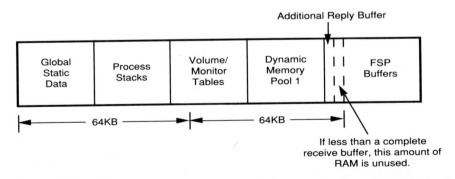

Figure 34-4: If the receive buffer for a LAN driver using DMA does not coincide with a physical 64KB boundary in file server memory, the OS must skip over some memory to accommodate this shortcoming.

LAN Driver Packet Sizes. The table in Figure 34-5 shows various LAN drivers, their packet and FSP buffer sizes, and whether or not they use DMA.

LAN Driver	Max.Packet Size	DGroup Buffer	H/W DMA
Novell Ethernet NE1000	1,024	1,992	No
Novell Ethernet NE2000	1,024	1,992	No
Novell Ethernet NE/2	1,024	1,992	No
Novell Ethernet NE2000 W/AppleTalk	1,024	1,992	No
Novell Ethernet NE/2 W/AppleTalk	1,024	1,992	No
Micom-Interlan NP600	1,024	1,992	Yes
3Com 3C501 EtherLink	1,024	1,992	No
3Com 3C505 EtherLink Plus (2012)	1,024	1,992	Yes
3Com 3C505 EtherLink Plus (1194)	1,024	1,992	Yes
3Com 3C505 ELink Plus W/AppleTalk	1,024	1,992	Yes
3Com 3C503 EtherLink II	1,024	1,992	Yes
3Com 3C523 EtherLink/MC	1,024	1,992	No
IBM Token-Ring	1,024	1,992	No
IBM Token-Ring Source Routing	1,024	1,992	No
Novell RX-Net	512	1,480	No
Novell RX-Net/2 — SMC PS110	512	1,480	No
SMC Arcnet/Pure Data	512	1,480	No
Novell NL1000 & NL/2 (AppleTalk)	1,024	1,992	No
Novell Star Intelligent NIC	512	1,480	No
AT&T StarLAN	512	1,480	No
Corvus Omninet	512	1,480	No
IBM PC Cluster	512	1,480	No
IBM PCN (Original Adapter)	1,024	1,992	Yes
IBM PCN II & Baseband	1,024	1,992	No
Gateway Communications Inc. G/NET	1,024	1,992	No
Proteon ProNET-10 P1300/P1800	1,024	1,992	No
Generic NetBIOS	2,048	3,016	No
IBM Async (Com1/Com2)	512	1,480	No
Async WNIM	512	1,480	No
Telebit P.E.P. Modem/WNIM	512	1,480	No

Figure 34-5: Packet sizes, FSP buffer sizes, and DMA usage of various LAN drivers (in bytes).

How the OS Allocates DGroup Memory

NetWare allocates DGroup memory in roughly the same order as we have presented the DGroup components. First, the OS allocates enough space for its own global variables and those needed by LAN and disk drivers. Then space is allocated to process stacks and the volume and monitor tables. Next, the OS sets aside 16KB as a minimum amount for Dynamic Memory Pool 1. The space reserved for FSP buffers is determined as follows:

- The OS sets aside 94 bytes as a one-time allocation for the additional reply buffer.
- The OS determines how big the receive buffer needs to be (based on the largest LAN driver packet size). If any LAN driver supports DMA, the OS might have to set aside up to 4,095 bytes as unused memory, depending on whether the receive buffers straddle 64KB boundaries.
- The remaining RAM is divided by the total FSP buffer size, up to a maximum of ten FSP buffers.
- Any leftover DGroup memory is added to the 16KB initially allocated to Dynamic Memory Pool 1 to make this pool as large as possible.

Once you understand this process, you can use it to determine how close your file server is to gaining another FSP. Follow these steps:

1. Calculate the FSP buffer size.
2. From the maximum memory in reported for Dynamic Memory Pool 1 in FCON-SOLE, subtract 16,384 bytes (the minimum size of Dynamic Memory Pool 1).
3. Subtract that difference from the FSP buffer size. The result tells you how many more bytes must be freed up in DGroup to gain an additional FSP.

For example, suppose you determined that the FSP buffer size was 1,992 bytes and the size of Dynamic Memory Pool 1 was 16,804 bytes. Subtracting 16,384 from 16,804 leaves 420 bytes. When you subtract 420 from 1,992, you find that you need 1,572 more bytes available in DGroup memory in order to gain an additional FSP.

To free up 1,572 bytes in DGroup memory, you might remove three spooled printer ports (freeing up 668 bytes each), or you might reduce the maximum number of directory entries configured for volumes by 28,296 (freeing up 1 byte for every 18 entries). Either of these possibilities would free up the necessary memory in DGroup RAM; however, if the current RAM usage in Dynamic Memory Pool 1 is close to the maximum, your best choice would be to use the option that leaves you with additional RAM remaining for Dynamic Memory Pool 1. In this instance, that choice would be removing the three spooled printer ports (which leaves 432 bytes for Dynamic Memory Pool 1).

These suggested solutions may not be possible on your file server if you don't have an external print server, or if your volumes need all the directory entries they can get. The next section discusses other possible ways to free up DGroup memory.

FREEING UP MEMORY IN THE DGROUP SEGMENT

The following discussion lists ways of freeing up DGroup memory, roughly in order of their impact on a typical file server's operation. As mentioned above, you won't be able to use some of these methods for your particular server configuration.

Increasing the Number of Communication Buffers

While increasing communication buffers does not involve the DGroup memory segment, doing so may improve performance if a significant number of packets are waiting in communication buffers for FSPs to become available.

Removing Spooled Printer Ports in NETGEN

Another possibility for freeing up this memory is to reduce the number of spooled printer ports configured for the file server in NETGEN. Each spooled printer requires a stack of 668 bytes in DGroup memory. If you currently have five network printers attached to the file server, getting rid of three of those printers would free up 2,004 bytes (2KB) of memory. If you need all five printers, consider purchasing external print server software to eliminate all spooled printers from the file server. Removing all five spooled printers would free up 3,340 bytes of DGroup memory. You may have to dedicate a separate machine on the network for use as the print server.

Decreasing the Maximum Number of Directory Entries

If you have plenty of headroom in the directory entry tables configured for your file server volumes, you may be able to free up a little DGroup memory by decreasing the number of directory entries. However, do not go into the program NETGEN/ELSGEN to decrease the number of directory entries without checking first to see how many you can safely reduce without losing data.

As new directories and files are created on the server, NetWare adds entries to the directory entry tables sequentially. NetWare keeps track of the highest directory entry used in the table as the "peak" directory entry reported in FCONSOLE. However, deleting directories and files leaves holes in the directory entry table. These holes are included in the number of "free" directory entries reported in FCONSOLE. NetWare eventually fills these holes with subsequent new directory entries.

When you bring down the file server and run NETGEN/ELSGEN to reduce the number of directory entries, NETGEN/ELSGEN doesn't check first to see if the directory entries about to be deleted are in use or not; the program simply reduces the size of the table by the number of entries you specify. If your directory entry table is fragmented, it is possible for you to delete part of the table that is in use.

To determine the safe number of entries you can eliminate in the directory entry table, go into FCONSOLE and select "Statistics" from the main menu; then select "Volume Information" and choose the volume for which you need to adjust the number of directory entries. Subtract the "Peak Directory Entries Used" from the number of "Maximum Directory Entries" shown. The result is the number of free directory entries that you can safely manipulate without losing access to files.

Changing LAN Drivers

There are two ways to affect DGroup memory by changing the LAN drivers in your file server configuration. The packet size used by LAN drivers has the biggest impact on FSP allocations, since the packet size determines the divisor NetWare uses when dividing up leftover DGroup memory for FSP buffers. The larger the packet size, the bigger the FSP buffer must be, resulting in a smaller number of available FSPs. Check first with the manufacturer of your network interface boards for any new LAN drivers that use a smaller packet size. If you have multiple LAN drivers in the same file server and one uses a significantly larger packet size than the others, move that LAN driver and its associated network interface board to an external bridge.

Second, remember that it is possible to lose up to 4,095 bytes of DGroup memory with LAN drivers that require DMA. If any of your LAN drivers use DMA, change to drivers that don't use DMA to prevent the OS from creating unusable holes in DGroup memory.

Removing TTS from SFT NetWare

If you are running SFT NetWare 286 with TTS, but you are not running any applications that use TTS, you can remove TTS from the file server. (You remove TTS by rerunning NETGEN and selecting the non-TTS operating system option. See Chapter 20 for details.) The process stack for TTS requires 250 bytes of DGroup memory, while global variables for TTS can use 142 to 152 additional bytes. Thus, removing TTS could free up around 400 bytes of memory in the DGroup segment.

Remember that, even if you don't use applications that require TTS, SFT NetWare uses TTS when performing updates to the bindery files. If you remove TTS, these bindery updates will no longer be protected against corruption due to interruptions that may occur before the update is completed.

Decreasing Total File Server Disk Space

Supporting a large amount of disk storage can have a considerable impact on DGroup RAM allocation, mainly due to the number of directory entries that must be configured to accommodate the disk space. For example, a total of 10,000 directory entries for all network volumes would use up 13,584 bytes of DGroup memory. Consider splitting up the disk storage between two file servers, if possible.

Using Novell's Dynamic Memory Pool 1 Patch

As a last resort, Novell offers a patch fix that might help "qualified" NetWare 286 servers gain one or two additional FSPs. This patch works by reducing some of the memory available to Dynamic Memory Pool 1. Other sources have started offering similar patches, but these are not officially sanctioned by Novell; don't use them unless you really know what you're doing.

Because these patches decreases the amount of memory in Dynamic Memory Pool 1, using a patch may have some potentially negative side effects. Most notably, you will have less memory space to dedicate to network drive mappings.

If you have a large number of regular network users who each set up many drive mappings, you may not be able to use the patch.

The Novell-approved patch is available through LANSWER technical support, who will make sure your server will really benefit from the patch. Call LANSWER for additional information and exact instructions.

USING NETWARE'S DIAGNOSTIC
AND REPAIR UTILITIES

Every copy of NetWare 286 comes with a set of diagnostic and repair utilities. The BINDFIX, VREPAIR, and COMCHECK utilities are helpful in fixing problems with the file server bindery, repairing minor hard disk problems, and checking the LAN communications channel. Another utility, PERFORM2, is available through NetWire. PERFORM2 is a network performance test that you can use to run benchmark tests on your file server.

     • Chapter 35 explains how to run the BINDFIX utility to correct errors that can creep into the file server's bindery database.

     • Chapter 36 explains how to use the NetWare VREPAIR utility to repair minor directory entry table and File Allocation Table errors. It also lists error messages that indicate the need to run VREPAIR.

     • Chapter 37 discusses how to use the COMCHECK utility to check the soundness of the connections between the network workstations and the file server.

     • Chapter 38 tells how to do your own benchmark tests using the PERFORM2 utility provided by Novell. These benchmarks provide a point of reference for gauging file server performance in your own network configuration.

35 Fixing the Bindery with BINDFIX

The bindery is a small database of named "objects" stored in the file server. An object can be a user, a resource, a file server, a user group—anything that has been given a name. Each bindery object has a set of properties associated with it that contains information about the objects. These properties include passwords, groups, security information, and so on. The bindery is contained in two files located in the SYS:SYSTEM directory: NET$BIND.SYS and NET$BVAL.SYS. The NET$-BIND.SYS file contains the object names and properties; NET$BVAL.SYS contains the property values.

WHEN TO RUN BINDFIX

If a file server crashes when the bindery database is in the middle of updating some information, the bindery pointers could end up pointing where they shouldn't. This can cause all kinds of problems in the system security. Some of the problems that can occur are:

- User names cannot be deleted or modified.
- A user's rights cannot be modified.
- Users cannot change their own passwords.
- Errors referring to the bindery are being displayed at the file server console.
- Users get an "unknown server" error message when they run CAPTURE, even though they are capturing on the default server.

BINDFIX is a useful utility for fixing these types of errors that may exist in the bindery after a file server crash. There is a certain amount of redundancy within the bindery that BINDFIX takes advantage of to reconstruct bindery information.

RUNNING BINDFIX

BINDFIX will work on all NetWare 286 file servers running NetWare v2.1x. It is a good idea to run VREPAIR before you run BINDFIX, as it is helpful to have the volumes intact before working on the bindery.

The file server must be up and running in order for you to run BINDFIX. So if the server is down, reboot it and log in as SUPERVISOR (or a user with supervisor equivalence) from any available workstation.

Important: BINDFIX closes the bindery files when it starts running. No users should be logged in or attempt to log in while you are running this utility. To be safe, log out any users currently logged in, then disable file server logins through FCONSOLE until you are finished fixing the bindery.

Because BINDFIX should be run only by the network supervisor, the BINDFIX.EXE file is located in the SYS:SYSTEM directory. Normally only the supervisor has rights in this directory. If you have a drive mapped to SYS:SYSTEM, change to that drive. If you don't have a drive mapped to SYS:SYSTEM, set your default drive there by typing **CD SYS:SYSTEM**.

To start the program, type **BINDFIX** and press Enter. You will see this message:

```
Rebuilding Bindery. Please Wait.
```

The first thing BINDFIX does is close the NET$BIND.SYS and NET$BVAL.SYS bindery files and make backup copies of them. These backup copies are renamed with an .OLD extension. If BINDFIX is for some reason unsuccessful in reconstructing the bindery, these .OLD files contain all the information necessary to restore the bindery back to its original state through the BINDREST program.

BINDFIX will next scan the current bindery files for inconsistencies and attempt to correct any problems it finds. You can follow its progress by watching the screen output:

```
Checking for invalid nodes.
Checking object's property lists.
Checking properties to see that they are in an object property
        list.
Checking objects for back-link property.
Checking set consistency and compacting sets.
Building available lists and new hash tables.
There are XX Object Nodes and XX Property Nodes free.
Checking user objects for standard properties.
Checking group objects for standard properties.
Checking links between users and groups for consistency.
```

The term "node" in these messages refers to the types of records that are kept within the bindery database, not workstation nodes on the network.

You will next see this prompt:

```
Delete mail directories of users that no longer exist? (y/n):
```

Respond "Yes" to this prompt, as mail subdirectories are of no use whatsoever for users that have been deleted (unless you are planning to restore those users from a backup at a later time). You will then see the following messages and another prompt:

```
Checking for mail directories of users that no longer exist.
Checking for users that do not have mail directories.
Delete trustee rights to users that no longer exist? (y/n):
```

Answer "Yes" again. BINDFIX will scan the directories on all mounted volumes and remove any trustee assignments to users that have been deleted, displaying its progress on the screen like this:

```
Checking Volume SYS. Please wait.
Checking Volume VOL1. Please wait.
```

Now comes the moment of truth: BINDFIX will say whether it has successfully completed the bindery check or not. Either way, you will be returned to the DOS prompt.

If BINDFIX did *not* successfully complete the bindery check, type **BINDREST** at the DOS prompt and press Enter. BINDREST will restore the information from the .OLD bindery files, returning the system to its previous state. In this case, you're no better off than you were when you started, but at least the bindery problems are not fatal—mostly just nuisances.

If BINDFIX says it was successful, you now have a bindery that's internally consistent once again. Go get yourself a candy bar and celebrate.

36 Using the VREPAIR Utility

This chapter explains when and how to run the NetWare VREPAIR (Volume REPAIR) utility. This utility corrects minor hard disk problems resulting from corrupted or mismatched File Allocation Table (FAT) and Directory Entry Table entries. VREPAIR is a nondestructive utility; no data is written over or deleted in the volume VREPAIR tries to fix.

WHEN TO RUN VREPAIR

As explained in Chapter 7, NetWare's FATs and Directory Entry Tables contain critical information that the file server must have in order to locate directories and files on its hard disk volumes. (If necessary, review the section on FATs and Directory Entry Tables in Chapter 7.) VREPAIR attempts to recover data from a volume after incorrect information has been written to the volume's FAT or Directory Entry Table. Bad information in these tables can result from:

- Defective or worn-out hard disks
- Unexpected power loss to the file server, or severe power fluctuations
- Shutting off the file server before bringing it down properly

Proper installation, use, and maintenance of the file server will save you from having to run VREPAIR in most cases. More specifically, you can avoid the above three causes of data loss by installing NetWare's Hot Fix feature, using an Uninterruptible Power Supply (UPS), and following the correct procedure for bringing down the file server.

Normally, Hot Fix takes care of minor defects on hard disk storage media. Hot Fix must be installed on every disk used by NetWare. If the defects become so rampant that NetWare shuts off Hot Fix, or if other disk hardware components fail, VREPAIR may be able to help you recover some of the data from the disk.

Novell recommends that all file servers and their attached disk subsystems be protected from unexpected power loss through the use of a UPS. In the event of a long-term commercial power line failure, the UPS provides battery backup power to the server long enough for it to shut itself down gracefully, thus preserving the integrity of the FATs and Directory Entry Tables. However, some UPS systems do not protect adequately against power fluctuations that often cause just as much damage as full-fledged outages. VREPAIR may be able to help in these situations as well.

The proper way to bring down a file server is to have all users close their files and log out, then use either the DOWN console command or the "Down File Server" option in FCONSOLE. However, when your file server mysteriously hangs, you usually have no choice but to turn it off without issuing the DOWN command. When the file server is downed with a file still open, file allocation pointers used in the FAT become misaligned and no longer point to the next block of information in that file. This misalignment also affects the Directory Entry Tables because they rely on the FAT tables for data retrieval. Of course, any data still held in the cache buffers in file server memory that has not been updated on the hard disk will be irretrievably lost.

VREPAIR can fix the directory and FAT entries, but it can do nothing for data lost from file server memory. VREPAIR's primary purpose is to restore the integrity of the FATs and Directory Entry Tables; its secondary purpose is to recover data, if possible. VREPAIR may not be able to recover lost data at all; therefore, you cannot rely on VREPAIR to take the place of regular system backups.

Error Messages that Necessitate VREPAIR

Here are some of the most common error messages that indicate the need to run VREPAIR on the file server. These messages are displayed on the file server screen, usually when you are rebooting the server after it has gone down unexpectedly. We have included a brief explanation of each message and its possible causes. The solution is the same for all of these errors: run VREPAIR.

nnnn FAT blocks are marked used, but included in no file.
Explanation. The OS is having trouble using the disk's FAT to piece files together. Certain blocks in the FAT are marked as being used by files on the disk, but they do not actually correspond to any specific file.

FAT Write Error: copy = n FAT sector = nnnn volume = VolumeName
Explanation. The read-after-write verification of a sector written to one of the two copies of a disk's FAT failed, and Hot Fix was unable to redirect the bad sector to a good sector in the Redirection Area. "Copy = 0" indicates the primary copy of the FAT is affected; "Copy = 1" indicates the secondary or duplicate FAT copy is affected.

This is a serious error because it indicates that Hot Fix is probably no longer functioning on the disk. If running VREPAIR doesn't solve the problem, check for faulty components along the disk channel (disk drive, controller, DCB, and cabling). Repair or replace any defective channel hardware. You may have to run COMPSURF to reformat the drive.

*** WARNING *** Directory sector *nnnn* data mirror mismatch.
*** WARNING *** FAT Table sector *nnnn* data mirror mismatch.

Explanation. In SFT NetWare, duplicate copies of the FATs and Directory Entry Tables are kept on both drives in a mirrored pair. When a directory entry changes, the OS updates the Directory Entry Tables and FATs on both drives. This error indicates that, due to a power failure or improper downing of the file server, the primary and secondary (mirror) copies of the specified directory or FAT sector do not match.

When this error occurs during bootup, the prompt "Cancel mount?" follows the message. If you answer "No" and allow the volume to continue mounting, NetWare will *not* automatically update the secondary drive copy to match the primary drive copy. The OS will use the copy on the primary drive and treat the directory or FAT sector on the mirrored drive as if it contained no active file entries. Eventually, a request to write to the sector will cause the OS to update the mirror copy to match the primary copy.

If you answer "Yes" to cancel mounting of the volume, the file server will continue to boot, but that volume will not be available to users.

This error indicates significant problems in the FATs and Directory Entry Tables and will probably be accompanied by other error messages. It is best to bring the file server down and run VREPAIR on the volume, rather than trying to mount the volume with damaged tables.

*** WARNING *** DISK READ ERROR. CANCEL MOUNT?

Explanation. While trying to mount a volume, the OS encountered a disk read error while reading *both* copies of the volume's Directory Entry Table. (All 2.1x versions of NetWare keep two copies of the FAT and the Directory Entry Table for each disk volume.)

You can choose either to continue mounting the volume or to cancel the volume mount. If you answer "No" to the prompt, the OS will mount the volume, but some data may be inaccessible due to the read error. If you answer "Yes" to cancel mounting of the volume, the file server will continue to boot, but that volume will not be available to users.

This error indicates significant problems in the Directory Entry Tables and will probably be accompanied by other error messages. It is best to bring the file server down and run VREPAIR on the volume, rather than trying to mount the volume with a damaged Directory Entry Table.

*** WARNING *** FAT Entry *nnnn* marked bad in *FileName*.

Explanation. While scanning the FAT for the links to the specified file, the OS server detected that one of the FAT entries is linked to a physical sector on the disk that has been marked as bad. NetWare will automatically truncate the file in its internal tables at the point where it encountered the bad entry. This change is made in memory, but is not immediately written to the disk. The volume will continue to mount.

If you have a good backup copy of the file, you can delete the file and then restore it from the backup media. Otherwise, run VREPAIR to fix the problem.

*** WARNING *** FAT Entry *nnnn* multiple allocation in *FileName*.

Explanation. While scanning the FAT for a volume, the OS detected that the indicated FAT entry shows two different files claiming to be using the same physical disk area. The file named in this message is the second file that claims the disk space. This error indicates data corruption in at least one, but possibly both, files involved. NetWare will automatically truncate the second file so that it no longer claims the disputed block on the disk. This change is made in memory, but is not immediately written to disk. The volume will continue to mount.

If you have a good backup copy of the file, you can delete the file and then restore it from the backup media. Otherwise, use VREPAIR to find the names of the files that claim the same physical area. Restore any files that VREPAIR can't recover from the most current backup.

*** WARNING *** FAT Entry *nnnn* out of bounds in *FileName*.

Explanation. The FAT link points to a data block beyond the end of the physical disk. A file's FAT link points to the next physical area the file occupies. The OS reports this error and treats it as a file link error by truncating the file. This error is not fatal; the volume will continue mounting.

Since the file indicated in the error message has already been truncated automatically by the OS, the best solution is to erase the file and restore it from a backup.

*** WARNING *** FAT Entry *nnnn* out of order in *FileName*.

Explanation. The physical disk entries in a file's FAT map are out of consecutive order. The OS logically keeps track of where each physical disk block belongs, both by linkage order and by allocation number. This information is kept in a file so that operating systems such as CP/M, which allow files to be created with large holes in them, will work correctly on the file server. If NetWare discovers a FAT order error, it truncates the file and reports the problem. The OS assumes that a FAT order error is a symptom of a FAT link error. FAT link errors occur when one file has been accidentally linked into the disk allocation list of a different file. This error is not fatal; the volume will continue mounting.

If running VREPAIR fails to correct the problem, erase the file and restore it from a backup copy.

WARNING: FATAL DIR ERROR ON VOL *VolumeName*
   DIR SECTOR nnnn.
WARNING: FATAL DIR ERROR ON VOL *VolumeName*
   FAT SECTOR *nnnn.*

The file server detected a disk read error while reading a volume directory or FAT. Two copies of all directory entry tables and FATs are kept on each system volume. If a read failure occurs on one copy, the file server will automatically retry the read using the secondary directory/FAT copy. This error message will be displayed only if a directory/FAT sector read failed on both directory copies.

These errors are not fatal; the server will continue to operate as if the directory/FAT sector had contained no active file entries. However, this error indicates significant problems in the directory area and will probably be accompanied by many other error messages. You should run VREPAIR on the volume to repair the bad sectors before allowing users to access the volume.

** WARNING ** Sector *nnnn* **DIR Table** *n* **Read Error on** *VolumeName.*
** WARNING ** Sector *nnnn* **FAT Table** *n* **Read Error on** *VolumeName.*

Explanation. The OS could not read a sector from a volume's directory entry table or FAT. In the message, n indicates which directory is faulty (0=primary, 1=back-up or mirror directory).

These errors are not fatal. If a directory/FAT sector is bad, the file server will automatically switch to the mirrored backup copy of the faulty sector. The file server will continue to function correctly using the backup directory sector unless that sector is also bad. However, the directory mirror will no longer function for this sector until the read error is corrected. You should run VREPAIR on the volume to repair the bad sectors before allowing users to access the volume.

One FAT Error that Doesn't Require VREPAIR

The file server will automatically fix errors like "FAT allocated with no file" error messages in the course of running. In due time, the file server overwrites these erroneous entries with a proper FAT entry.

*** WARNING *** FAT Entry nnn marked used with no File.

Explanation. The file server detected that FAT entry *nnn* has a disk block allocated to a file but that no file is linked to the disk block. The OS automatically deallocates the block in its internal memory tables. The change will be updated on the disk when the block is reallocated for another file. Since the OS automatically deallocates the block and repairs itself, you can safely ignore this error message.

THE VREPAIR PROCEDURE

With NetWare 286 v2.1x, a custom version of VREPAIR is generated along with the OS during installation. Be sure you use the version of VREPAIR that matches your file server's disk configuration. If you run NETGEN/ELSGEN from a hard disk, the finished VREPAIR.EXE file is placed in the UTILEXE-2 directory. It is a good idea to download this file to a floppy diskette, because that's the most practical way to run it.

Here is a list of what you'll need to successfully run VREPAIR:

• Your working copy of the UTILEXE-2 diskette (5.25" format) or UTILEXE diskette (3.5" format) containing the VREPAIR.EXE file generated specifically for your file server
• The name(s) of the volume(s) to be repaired (usually specified in the error messages)
• If you want a printed copy of VREPAIR's error report, attach a parallel printer to the LPT1 port on the file server. Define it as network printer 0. (Due to a bug in VREPAIR, no other printers can be defined for the file server.)

Even though VREPAIR is nondestructive, you should *always* make a full backup of your disks before running VREPAIR, just to be safe. The VREPAIR utility may take up to two hours to run, depending on the number of errors it encounters.

To run VREPAIR, have all users log out, then bring down the file server using the DOWN console command. Boot the server with DOS and start VREPAIR by inserting the appropriate diskette and typing **VREPAIR**.

The Drive List Screen

You will first see a screen that shows the version of VREPAIR you are running, the number of cache buffers, and a list of network disk drives similar to this one:

```
Drive:  1. Maxtor V185
Drive:  2. Vertex V170

 Select drive number?
```

Select the drive that contains the volume(s) you wish to fix. The system volume (SYS) is always on the hard drive listed as number 1.

The Volume List Screen

Next, you will be presented with a list of volumes on that drive, similar to this one:

```
Drive 1 contains the volumes:

  1. SYS
  2. VOL1

 Select the volume?
```

Type the number of the volume you wish to test first and press the Enter key.

VREPAIR Options

VREPAIR has three different options, which you select by answering questions as you run the utility.

The Printer Option. VREPAIR first asks you if you want to print out the error report that will be generated:

```
Do you want a printed report of any errors or corrections made
    [Yes or No]?
```

When VREPAIR discovers an error, it presents information about the error along with the suggested solution. It also pauses after each error and solution, so you will have to be present to press the Enter key for each error. This information will be sent either directly to network printer 0 or it will be displayed on the screen.

If you want a printout of this information, attach a printer to LPT1, type "**Y**", and press the Enter key. Type "**N**" if you do not want a printout.

Be sure you have only one parallel printer attached to the file server when using the printer option; otherwise, VREPAIR will hang trying to locate the printer. The printer option prints the errors and solutions without pauses. Be sure you have enough paper if you think you are having a lot of problems.

The Bad Block Test Option. You will next see the following question:

```
Do you want to test for Bad Blocks [Yes or No]?
```

VREPAIR will check all the data blocks on the disk surface to determine if any data blocks are bad. If it encounters a bad data block, it will attempt to write the information in that block to another block on the disk and add the bad block to the bad block table.

Testing for bad blocks adds considerable time to VREPAIR. Unless you are having read or write errors to disk, you probably won't need to use this option. Type "**N**" or "**Y**" and press the Enter key.

The Recover Lost Blocks Option. You will then be prompted:

```
Do you want to recover lost blocks as files [Yes or No]?
```

In the process of checking files on the file server, VREPAIR may encounter blocks that are not connected to any valid file name, and that are not marked as "free" either. To save these data blocks as files, type "**Y**" and press the Enter key. The files will be saved in the root directory of the volume that is being checked.

To identify these files, you will see an eight-digit file name, followed by a three-digit extension. For example, in the case of a file block, you would see VF392890.F38. In the case of a directory block, you would see VF738764.D29.

There is no guarantee that the blocks will be large enough to be helpful. Generally, these blocks are only fragments of files, and you would need expertise and a good text editor to piece this information together into a file again. So unless you hope to rescue a file you desperately need, type "**N**" and press the Enter key. VREPAIR will free up these blocks for future use.

Confirming the VREPAIR Options. You will next see a screen that allows you to confirm your choices for VREPAIR's three options:

```
Printer Option: Enabled
Bad Block Test Option: Enabled
Recover Lost Blocks Option: Disabled

Is this correct [Yes, No, Abort]?
```

To confirm your choices, type "**Y**" and press the Enter key. To change any of these, type "**N**" and you will be returned to the "printer" option. To abort the VREPAIR utility, type "**A**" and press Enter and you will return to the drive selection screen.

The VREPAIR Test Cycle

Once you verify the options, VREPAIR will begin checking the volume. Depending on the options you chose, you will see a display similar to this one:

```
Checking Volume: SYS

Checking For Bad FAT Blocks>..................................<
Checking For Bad Dir. Blocks>.................................<
Checking For Bad Data Blocks>.................................<
Checking For Mirror Mismatches>...............................<
Checking Directory>...........................................<
Checking Trustees>............................................<
Checking Files>...............................................<
Purging Salvage Files>........................................<
Checking Reserved FAT>........................................<
Checking FAT>..................                              <
```

During this time, the screen will display VREPAIR's progress by a series of dots filling in the space on each line. In the sample display above, the dots indicate that VREPAIR has finished up to about halfway through the "Checking FAT" stage.

Responding to VREPAIR's Error Messages. When VREPAIR finds an error, it displays a message indicating the nature of the error detected and VREPAIR's proposed solution. Note that these solutions will not actually be written to the disk until you tell it to do so at the end of the testing sequence.

For example, if VREPAIR finds a lost file block, you will see a message similar to this one:

```
<— Lost file at Slot 79 —>

Corrected Entry follows:

File Entry
Name: VF392890.F38
Path: SYS:
Attribute: 20     1st FAT: 13A
File Size: 4096


<—————————— end —————————>
```

If you enabled the printer option and attached a printer, VREPAIR will print all of these messages. If you disabled the printer option, you will see the following question:

```
Abandon Error Report [Yes or No]?
```

If you want to see the rest of the error messages in the current sequence, answer "No". If you want to abandon the current sequence and proceed with the VREPAIR tests, answer "Yes". You will again see the VREPAIR test progress screen shown above.

The Final Question. After the tests are all over, you will see the following prompt:

```
Make corrections permanent [Yes or No]?
```

To actually write VREPAIR's proposed solutions to the hard disk, type "**Y**" and press Enter. You'll see something like the following on the screen:

```
Updating vol: SYS
Saving Directory>                                                  <
Saving FATs>                                                       <

Press Enter to continue.
```

If no errors were found, you will see the following:

```
No errors in Volume: SYS

Press Enter to continue.
```

To run VREPAIR on another volume on the same drive, press the Enter key once. To return to the drive list screen, press the Enter key twice. To leave the VREPAIR utility, press the Enter key three times. After you're finished with VREPAIR, you will have to reboot the file server; the program does not return you to DOS. Be sure to remove the diskette from drive A before you reboot.

WHEN VREPAIR DOESN'T HELP

VREPAIR is a useful tool for fixing file and directory problems caused by power failure or by downing the server improperly. But if the problems are consistent and are getting worse to the point where you need to COMPSURF the hard drive, consider replacing the hard drive altogether. If your site has a history of power problems, either purchase an Uninterruptible Power Supply (UPS) or have the UPS you are using upgraded or repaired.

37 Checking Connections with COMCHECK

NetWare comes with a diagnostic utility named COMCHECK (for COMmunication CHECK). This utility provides a quick check to see if two or more stations are able to communicate properly across the network cable. Novell installation manuals suggest that COMCHECK be used after all networking hardware is initially installed to test for proper connections. You can also use COMCHECK any time while the network is running to isolate faulty cable segments or network interface boards. This chapter explains how COMCHECK works and gives pointers on running COMCHECK either while the network is up and running or when the file server is down.

HOW COMCHECK WORKS

COMCHECK uses NetWare's Internet Packet Exchange (IPX) protocol to perform point-to-point communication checks. IPX.COM is the part of the NetWare workstation shell that handles communications with the file server and with other workstations on the network. IPX is a lower level "connectionless" protocol, meaning that it doesn't have to establish a logical connection between sender and receiver; IPX simply transmits a packet to an intended destination. If that destination sends back a response packet, IPX knows that the packet was received safe and sound.

Of course, in order for a packet to be successfully transmitted between two stations on the network, the *physical* connection must be intact. A faulty component anywhere along the channel from the LAN driver, through the network interface board, and out onto the cable itself can prevent a network station from communicating properly.

Because COMCHECK uses only IPX, the network doesn't necessarily have to be up and running for you to check connections. If you want check workstations' connections to the file server with COMCHECK, you will have to bring the file server down first. You normally don't have to generate an IPX.COM file for the network interface boards in the file server like you do for workstations; rather, you select the appropriate LAN drivers and link them into the NetWare operating system itself. To include the file server in your COMCHECK testing, however, you must run the NetWare SHGEN (SHell GENeration) program to generate a valid IPX.COM file for the server's primary network board (the one designated as LAN A in NETGEN).

Limitations of COMCHECK

COMCHECK can check connections across only one physical cabling system at a time. If you have more than one network interface board in your file server (for example, an Ethernet board and a Token-Ring board), you can only check communications between stations physically connected to the same cabling system. You can check all the Ethernet workstations to see if they are all talking to each other, and you can run COMCHECK again (after generating a new shell for the server) to check the Token-Ring workstations to see if they are all talking to each other. But you can't use COMCHECK to see if an Ethernet workstation can talk to a Token-Ring workstation. For that, you need a more sophisticated point-to-point communication testing program.

What COMCHECK Will Tell You

In the course of running COMCHECK, you may discover the following types of LAN communication problems:

- Mismatched settings between those configured in a workstation's IPX.COM file and the actual switch or jumper settings on the network interface board
- Defective or improperly seated network interface boards
- Loose or faulty connectors between boards and cabling
- Faulty or broken cable segments between two workstations
- Duplicate or illegal station (node) address settings on network interface boards having the same network address

While COMCHECK is not sophisticated enough to pinpoint exactly where the communication fault lies, it does provide enough information to help you deduce by the process of elimination where the problem lies.

RUNNING COMCHECK WHEN THE FILE SERVER IS UP

If only one or two workstations on your network are having trouble communicating, you can run COMCHECK to test the physical connections without bringing down the file server. You will need two things to run COMCHECK:

- The DIAGNOSTIC diskette that came with your NetWare software package. This diskette contains the COMCHECK.EXE program.

• A valid IPX.COM file generated specifically for each workstation you are going to test. This file should already exist on the workstation's network boot diskette or boot directory on a local hard drive.

The "Loading IPX" Test

If the affected workstations are hung or have lost their network connection (some type of error message will usually appear to indicate that a file server cannot be found or that the shell is no longer attached to any file server), reboot each workstation using the normal network boot procedure.

Most workstations have commands in the AUTOEXEC.BAT file that automatically load IPX and NET3 or NET4 before logging in to the file server. If this is the case, watch the screen during the bootup. If IPX loads successfully, the screen will display the correct LAN driver type and hardware configuration settings for the workstation.

If IPX does not load successfully, the failure to load could indicate one of the following two problems:

• The boot diskette contains the wrong IPX.COM file for the workstation's network board and its hardware settings. Type **IPX I** from the boot drive (either A: if the workstation boots from a floppy diskette or C:\ if it boots from a local hard disk). This command will display the LAN driver and hardware settings for which the IPX.COM file was configured. If these don't match the actual board and settings in the workstation, rerun SHGEN to generate the correct IPX.COM file.
• IPX will not load properly if the network interface board is defective. Most network boards come with their own diagnostics programs; run the appropriate diagnostics to determine if the board is good. If the board passes but IPX still won't load, try swapping the workstation's board for an identical board that you know is good. If IPX loads properly, then you know that something is wrong with the old board (even though it passed its own diagnostics).

As long as the board is good and IPX.COM is configured properly, IPX should load successfully. A faulty cable segment or bad connector shouldn't make any difference at this point, since no packets are actually sent out through the board until you load NET3 or NET4.

For COMCHECK, you don't need to load NET3 or NET4. If the AUTO-EXEC.BAT file already did that successfully and has established a connection to the file server, then you know the physical connection between that workstation and the file server is good. Usually, though, if a workstation is having communication problems, NET3 or NET4 will not be successful. In any event, you should now have at least IPX.COM loaded on the workstation.

The COMCHECK Test

Insert the NetWare DIAGNOSTIC diskette and change to drive A. Then type **COMCHECK**. A prompt will appear, asking you to supply "Unique User Information." Enter something that will uniquely identify this workstation for the COMCHECK test: "Lisa's Workstation" or "Station #1," for example. You will then see this screen:

NetWare Communication Check	v2.00		Friday	July 13, 1990	10:44 am

Network	Node	Unique User Information	Yr Mo Dy Hr Mn Sc *
BA5EBA11	00001B035F59	Jason	90/07/13 10:44:16 *

In addition to the unique user information you just typed, the display also shows the network address of the cabling system being tested under the "Network" column. The "Node" column shows the station or node address set on the network interface board itself. Notice the asterisk (*) to the right of the current date and time. The asterisk indicates the station on which you are currently running COMCHECK. Leave the display running while you start COMCHECK at additional workstations.

Move to the next workstation along the cable and repeat the above procedure. Reboot the workstation if necessary and at least load IPX.COM. Then insert the DIAGNOSTIC diskette and type **COMCHECK** at that workstation. Within fifteen seconds, a screen similar to this one should appear, showing information about both workstations currently running COMCHECK:

NetWare Communication Check	v2.00		Friday	July 13, 1990	10:44 am

Network	Node	Unique User Information	Yr Mo Dy Hr Mn Sc *
BA5EBA11	00001B035F59	Jason	90/07/13 10:44:16 *
BA5EBA11	00001B035F88	Freddy	90/07/13 10:44:32 *

If the second workstation information doesn't appear after fifteen seconds, you probably have a faulty or broken cable connection somewhere between the first and second workstation.

First, make sure that the network interface board in the second workstation is seated properly. A number of intermittent network problems are caused by a board that isn't quite inserted all the way into the expansion bus. Turn off the power to the workstation and remove the network board. If the contacts on the bottom of the board look dirty, clean them, using a pencil eraser. (Be careful not to get eraser crumbs inside the computer and to clean them all off the board before reinserting it.) Examine the slot on the PC's expansion bus to see if any of its contacts are bent or broken off. If so, use a different slot when you reinsert the board. Push the board firmly down into the connection slot and screw it in place. If you don't attach the board firmly with the screw, it's possible to knock the board out of alignment when you reattach the connector to the cabling system.

Next, check all the physical connections between the two machines: T-connectors, transceivers, drop cables, hubs, and so on. Some types of cable (such as thin Ethernet) are extremely temperamental and can break or come loose with even the slightest jostling. Swap any faulty components you find with new ones.

Last, if the stations are on ARCnet cabling, double-check the node addresses of both boards. Duplicate node addresses are a concern only with ARCnet networks where you set the station address manually on each board. (Ethernet and Token-Ring boards use other means to ensure that their node addresses are all unique.) Two ARCnet workstations with the same station address on the same network address will always prevent at least those two workstations from communicating on the network. In some cases, it prevents *all* workstations from being able to communicate.

Now try COMCHECK again at the second workstation. Information for both workstations should appear after fifteen seconds. If so, you now have a sound physical connection between the two. If not, you'll need to resort to more sophisticated cable troubleshooting tools (see Chapter 33).

You can run COMCHECK on as many workstations as you need to. COMCHECK lets you adjust two parameters: the broadcast delay period and the dead timeout period. The broadcast delay period (number of seconds between updates) is set to fifteen seconds by default. If you set it for less, the file server response time to workstation requests will decrease dramatically due to the flood of COMCHECK broadcasts out on the wire. Keep this in mind if users are currently working on the network while you run COMCHECK.

The dead timeout period defines how long COMCHECK will wait, once a workstation fails to send an update packet, before it pronounces that workstation "dead." This timeout period applies only to workstations already running COM-CHECK and listed on the screen. COMCHECK indicates a dead workstation by bolding the information for that workstation on all the other COMCHECK screen displays. The default dead timeout period is sixty seconds. It must always be at least ten seconds more than the broadcast delay period.

Once you have COMCHECK running in all of the workstations you want to test, observe the COMCHECK screen display for a few minutes. The time column should be updated every fifteen seconds for workstations that are communicating properly through IPX. If any line turns bold, it indicates that particular workstation has stopped sending update transmissions for some reason. As long as that doesn't happen, you can be assured of two things:

• The physical connections between all listed workstations are okay. That doesn't necessarily imply that all physical connections everywhere are okay.
• IPX packets are getting through on these physical connections. That doesn't preclude the possibility of conflicts or problems involving some higher level protocol that is using the cabling.

RUNNING COMCHECK WITH THE FILE SERVER DOWN

If you want to include the file server in the COMCHECK test, you must bring the file server down. The only other software you'll need (besides the DIAG-NOSTIC diskette and the workstations' IPX.COM files) is an IPX.COM file for each network interface board in your file server that you want to test.

To generate this IPX.COM file, first find out what type of boards you have and what hardware settings have been made on them. The easiest way to do this is to type **CONFIG** at the file server console while the server is up and running. The resulting display will show you the type of board and the IRQ, DMA, I/O address, and memory address settings for each board in the file server. Write down the information shown to use when generating the shell files.

Next, follow the instructions given in your Novell installation manual for running the SHGEN program. Generating an IPX.COM for the file server's board works exactly the same as for a workstation board. Be sure to download the newly generated IPX.COM file to a floppy diskette so you can load IPX at the server.

When you run COMCHECK, treat the file server just like any other workstation. Be sure to load the correct version of IPX.COM for the particular file server network board you are testing. For example, if you have an NE1000 board and an IBM Token-Ring board in the server, load the IPX.COM file you generated for Novell Ethernet NE1000 to test the connections to the NE1000. Then reboot and load the IPX.COM file for IBM Token-Ring to test the Token-Ring network connections.

38 Using the PERFORM2 Utility

This chapter explains how to run your own benchmark tests using the PERFORM2 utility available on NetWire. The PERFORM2 utility is an improved version of the older PERFORM utility. PERFORM did not slave the testing workstations together so that starting one workstation synchronizes the start of all workstations in the test; the newer PERFORM2 slaves all testing workstations together.

PERFORM2 measures data throughput on the network in kilobytes per second (KB/sec). Four aspects of the network affect data throughput: the type of file server, the networking hardware/topology used, the type of operating system, and the LAN driver used in the file server to transfer information to the network board.

PUBLISHED BENCHMARKS

Novell has published benchmarks using PERFORM2 in the *LAN Evaluation Report 1986*. The report shows the throughput for 286A, PC AT, PC XT, and 68B file servers running on eleven different network topologies, using PC ATs as workstations. Figure 38-1 reproduces the report's statistics, including the "Actual Maximum Single Station Throughput" and "Available Maximum Working Bandwidth" for the 286A and PC AT servers on the most common network types.

Actual Maximum Single Station Throughput (KB/sec)

NETWORK TYPE	SERVER TYPE	
	286A	PC AT
SMC ARCnet	70.67	64.41
3Com EtherLink	174.93	144.40
3Com EtherLink Plus	140.06	116.85
IBM PC Network	24.68	23.64
IBM Token-Ring	85.65	80.97

Available Maximum Working Bandwidth (KB/sec)

NETWORK TYPE	SERVER TYPE	
	286A	PC AT
SMC ARCnet	115.31	104.54
3Com EtherLink	235.15	167.40
3Com EtherLink Plus	410.11	278.30
IBM PC Network	34.83	33.62
IBM Token-Ring	241.33	226.17

Figure 38-1: Benchmarks for network throughput and bandwidth using PERFORM2.

This data was generated on a network with six IBM PC AT workstations running PERFORM2.EXE. The parameters were Read, Overlaid, 4,096 bytes, and 100 times. For testing IBM Token-Ring, the 286A server required a wait state to function correctly.

These published benchmarks do not include listings for PCs or XTs as workstations, and therefore may not accurately reflect your network situation. The benchmarks do, however, reflect a fairly typical topology/server relationship that can be useful for anyone in the market for a new server or cabling topology.

RUNNING PERFORM2

You can run PERFORM2 on one or more workstations on a network. To test the full bandwidth of most network board and cable combinations, you must run PERFORM2 on at least six AT-type workstations.

PERFORM2 uses standard DOS functions to create, open, read from, and write to the simple DOS files that it creates. PERFORM2 writes to and reads from these files during the testing process. These files are created and opened in the directory that you are in when you start PERFORM2.

The network must be up and running before you execute PERFORM2. To run a PERFORM2 practice test, make a test directory (by typing **MD TEST** at the DOS prompt). Be sure the TEST directory is either in a place that all workstations have rights to access, or create a user that has rights to the TEST directory and have each workstation running PERFORM2 log in as that user.

Now change to the TEST directory (by typing **CD TEST**) and copy the PERFORM2.EXE and PERF$RUN.OVL files into the TEST directory from wherever you have those files stored. (When you run the ARC program on the PERFORM.ARC file you download from NetWire, you end up with two files: PERFORM2.EXE and PERF$RUN.OVL. If you haven't yet un-arced these files, put the PERFORM.ARC and the ARC program into the TEST directory and run the ARC program.)

Type **PERFORM2** and press the Enter key. You will see a screen with three sections—Parameters, Results, and Status:

```
                    Novell Network Performance Test
─────────────────────────────────────────────────────────────────────────
                 │ Read record / Write record      (R/W)      WRITE
  Parameters     │ Overlayed or Sequential I/O      (O/S)      OVERLAYED
                 │ Record Size                   (1 - 4096)    4096
                 │ Iterations to perform         (1 - 1000)    1
─────────────────────────────────────────────────────────────────────────

                 │ Type   Size   I/Os  Bytes I/O    Time    ┌─────────┐
  Results        │                                          │ KB / Sec│(K = 1024)
                 │ W O    4096     0            0    0.00    │  0.00   │
                 │                                           └─────────┘
─────────────────────────────────────────────────────────────────────────

  Status         │
                 │ Select Options and press <F1> to start test, ^C to exit
                 │
─────────────────────────────────────────────────────────────────────────
```

Setting PERFORM2's Parameters

The parameter section displays five parameters; only the first four are user-definable. You toggle the settings for these parameters by typing the letters or numbers shown in parentheses to the right of the parameter. The fifth parameter displays the number of stations in the test.

The "Read record/Write record" parameter determines whether you will execute reads or writes. You must perform the write test first to create a file for the read test to access.

The "Overlayed or Sequential I/O" parameter determines how the test file in the TEST directory will be read or written. With *overlaid* I/O, the read or write operation occurs over the same record within the file. This is the way to test non-disk performance factors, since all writes and reads (after the first one) are made to the disk cache buffers in file server RAM. With *sequential* I/O, the reads and writes are performed on consecutive records in the file. Sequential writes can take up a lot of disk space; they may use up more memory than is available for disk caching, causing writes/reads to occur to the disk rather than to the cache buffers. Since you are testing network throughput rather than disk access, use the overlaid setting (which is the default).

You can set the "Record Size" parameter anywhere from 1 byte to 4,096 bytes (4KB). To achieve the most accurate results, use the entire 4,096 record size for both read and write tests. Be sure to use the same size for the read tests that you used with the write tests.

"Iterations to Perform" indicates the number of records you want to read or write. In the read test, the more iterations are performed, the more accurate the final results will be. For the write test, however, set this parameter to 1.

Performing a Practice Test

As a practice test, set the parameters to WRITE, OVERLAYED, 4,096 for the record size, and 1 for the number of iterations. As instructed on the screen, press the F1 key to begin the test. PERFORM2 will execute the write test, displaying the results in the "Results" section of the screen:

```
                      Novell Network Performance Test
═══════════════════════════════════════════════════════════════════════
               │ Read record / Write record      (R/W)      WRITE
 Parameters    │ Overlayed or Sequential I/O      (O/S)      OVERLAYED
               │ Record Size                  (1 - 4096)     4096
               │ Iterations to perform        (1 - 1000)     100
               │ Stations in Test                            1
═══════════════════════════════════════════════════════════════════════
               │
               │ Type  Size  I/Os  Bytes I/O    Time  ┌KB / Sec┐(K = 1024)
 Results       │                                      │        │
               │ W S   4096    1        4096    0.05  │  80.00 │
               │                                      └────────┘
───────────────────────────────────────────────────────────────────────
               │              Test completed successfully
 Status        │
               │ Select Options and press <F1> to start test, ^C to exit
               │
═══════════════════════════════════════════════════════════════════════
```

The "Status" section of the screen shows the current status of the test. While the test is running, you will see "Test in progress." When a test is completed successfully, the message "Test completed successfully" appears.

After the write test is completed, set the "Read record/Write record" parameter to "READ" by using the Up arrow key to highlight that field and then typing "R" to toggle the setting to "READ." Next, move down to the "Iterations to perform" parameter and type "1000." Press the F1 key to begin the read test. When the read test is finished, record the test results displayed in the "KB/Sec" box. This number indicates the network throughput for that particular workstation. Repeat the write/read test on another workstation; you will notice that the results are most likely different for each type of workstation (PCs, ATs, 386 machines, and so on).

If you are curious about the server utilization percentage during the tests, type **MONITOR** at the file server console before starting PERFORM2 and watch the "Utilization (%)" display in the center of the screen while you run the PERFORM2 tests. Because updating the MONITOR display requires a certain amount of processing overhead, using the MONITOR command affects network throughput results. All benchmarks in the *LAN Evaluation Report 1986* were performed with the MONITOR command active. Be consistent when you run your tests: either leave the MONITOR command on while you run PERFORM2 or turn it off with the OFF console command.

RUNNING PERFORM2 ON MULTIPLE WORKSTATIONS

To run PERFORM2 on multiple workstations, have all workstations log in and change to the TEST directory. PERFORM2 will automatically create a file with a unique name for each workstation, so any number of workstations can run PERFORM2 in that directory. Be sure each workstation has sufficient rights to perform read/writes within the TEST directory.

Type **PERFORM2** on all workstations you want to include in the test. The "Stations in test" parameter will increase with each added workstation. PERFORM2 synchronizes the input on all participating workstations, so the parameters you enter on one keyboard are set on all other workstations in the test. Set the parameters to WRITE, OVERLAYED, 4,096 for the record size, and 1 for the number of iterations. Start the write test by pressing F1 on only one workstation; all other workstations will begin the write test at the same time.

After the write test finishes, set the parameters on one workstation to READ, OVERLAYED, 4,096 for the record size, and 1,000 for the number of iterations; then press the F1 key. The other workstations will change to the read parameters and begin testing as well. It is important to specify at least 1,000 iterations, as some workstations will enter the read test later than others.

Record the read test results displayed in the "KB/Sec" box. After you have performed the write/read tests and recorded the results for all participating workstations, press Alt-F10 on one workstation to cause every workstation in the test to exit to DOS.

After you have run the write test on all workstations, you can drop a workstation from the read test and still get accurate results. However, you cannot add workstations in the read test that were not included in the initial write test. If you want to include other workstations in the read test, you must run the write test again. The write test creates an extension file specific to the each workstation in the test. If you try to run a read test on a workstation that has not run the write test, you will receive the message "Test aborted due to I/O failure," along with instructions to run the write test first. PERFORM2 will complete the testing without the "writeless" workstation, but it will give the KB/sec average as though that workstation were tested. This situation won't provide accurate benchmarks, so be sure to run the write test for each added workstation.

To perform benchmarks for your network, first run PERFORM2 as described above on all workstations attached to your file server; record the "KB/Sec" results. Then press the Escape key on one workstation, run the read test, and record the "KB/Sec" information again. (Remember, you can drop a workstation from the read test, but you cannot add a workstation without rerunning the write test.)

Repeat this procedure, dropping one workstation at a time, until all workstations are out of the PERFORM2 program. These results are your network benchmarks; save them in your network logbook for future use.

HOW TO USE YOUR BENCHMARK RESULTS

The benchmark results you gather with the PERFORM2 utility can help you in several ways. First, you can compare your results to the benchmarks published in the *LAN Evaluation Report 1986*. Your results probably won't match these benchmarks exactly, but they can give you a general feel for the kind of performance you can expect from various network topologies. This performance information is useful when you are considering adding on to your network. Also, Appendix A of the *LAN Evaluation Report 1986* contains information that can help you determine network traffic and decide whether it will help to split your network load by adding another network board to your file server.

Whatever you use them for, be sure to record your benchmark results for future reference. If you later suspect that your network is starting to bog down, run PERFORM2 again and compare the results to the earlier benchmarks. If performance degradation is obvious, you have two choices—live with it, or do something about it. Chapter 25 explains how to identify performance bottlenecks and gives methods for improving file server performance.

HANDLING FILE SERVER
ERROR MESSAGES

The final chapters of this book list the various error messages that you might see displayed on the file server console. For each error message, we give a short explanation of the error, the severity of the error (if known), possible causes for the error, and possible solutions for fixing the error. Refer to these chapters first when you encounter an error message at the file server. If the message is not listed in Chapter 39 or 40, check Chapter 16 for printing-related error messages, Chapter 22 for hard disk-related error messages, and Chapter 36 for FAT- and directory entry-related error messages.

• Chapter 39 discusses the procedures that take place when you start up a NetWare 286 file server. It explains the possible errors you might encounter when booting the file server, and tells you what to do about them.

• Chapter 40 list and explains what to do about some of the more common error messages that occur after the file server has been up and running for a while.

39 Errors During Bootup

Many of the error messages you receive at the file server display during the bootup process when you first turn on the server. This chapter follows the normal file server bootup procedure and indicates which errors could occur and what to do about them.

REBOOTING THE FILE SERVER

The exact procedure for rebooting a file server is different for dedicated and nondedicated file servers. The instructions are summarized below. (Check the Novell installation manuals for more precise instructions. Some machines (such as the IBM PS/2 Model 50Z) require a slightly different procedure.)

Rebooting a Dedicated File Server

You can boot a dedicated file server either from floppy diskettes or from the system disk. Most PCs used as file servers have a bootable hard disk; however, some non-Novell file servers cannot be booted from the system disk if they contain a Novell disk coprocessor board (DCB).

Once the OS has been generated and copied to the SYS:SYSTEM directory along with the cold boot loader, simply make sure there is no floppy diskette in drive A of the server and perform a cold boot. You can do this by using a reset key or switch, or by turning the machine off and back on again. Be sure to wait at least ten seconds to give the machine a chance to completely stop before you start it up again. (The Ctrl-Alt-Del method doesn't always work for rebooting a file server.)

To boot the server from floppy diskettes, you need your working copy of the OSEXE-1 diskette (and OSEXE-2 with 5.25" format). Boot the server with DOS v3.*x* or higher. Then insert OSEXE-1 in drive A. Type **NET$OS**, and follow the prompt to insert OSEXE-2 if necessary.

Rebooting a Nondedicated File Server

Generally (unless you have a DOS partition on the system disk), you must boot a nondedicated file server from floppies. To do this, you must create a boot diskette for the server. Format a new diskette, using the DOS FORMAT command with the /S parameter so the diskette will be able to boot DOS. Copy the NET$OS.EXE file from OSEXE-1 to the new boot diskette. Then copy NET3.COM or NET4.COM (depending on your version of DOS) from SHGEN-1. Finally, copy CONSOLE.EXE from the GENDATA or BRUTILS diskette.

Now create an AUTOEXEC.BAT file on the new diskette. This batch file will contain a single line: **NET$OS**. This command will prompt you to insert OS-EXE-1 and OSEXE-2 to load the nondedicated OS. Do not include any other lines in this AUTOEXEC.BAT file, especially a "PROMPT=" command. Doing so will cause "invalid COMMAND.COM" problems for the workstation side of the server.

Insert the new boot diskette into drive A of the file server and reboot the machine. After DOS loads and runs the AUTOEXEC.BAT file, insert the OSEXE-1 and OSEXE-2 diskettes as prompted. After the date and time appear, you will see a prompt to "insert disk with batch file." This refers to the boot diskette. Once you reinsert it, the DOS prompt (A>) will appear and the server will be up and running in DOS mode. Type **CONSOLE** to switch to console mode.

Normal Bootup Screen Messages

This section describes the normal messages you see as the file server reboots. Some of these may not appear on your file server, depending on which version of NetWare you are using.

Cold Boot Loader Message. The first message you see when you reboot a dedicated file server from the system disk is the cold boot loader message:

```
Novell SFT NetWare  File Server Cold Boot Loader
(C) Copyright 1983, 1988 Novell, Inc.  All Rights Reserved
```

The cold boot loader is copied to track 0 of the system disk at the end of the NetWare Installation part of NETGEN/ELSGEN. It searches for NET$OS.EXE in the SYS:SYSTEM directory and loads the NetWare OS into the file server memory.

Some versions of NetWare v2.12 and higher have difficulty with the cold boot loader and require you to boot DOS first. If you find this annoying, a corrected cold boot loader file is available from Novell's NetWire forum on CompuServe. The file is called LOAD21.ARC. After downloading this file, rerun the NetWare Installation part of NETGEN/ELSGEN and set the "Load Operating System" flag to copy the new cold boot loader onto the system disk.

NetWare OS Initialization. The file server next initializes the NetWare operating system and gives it as much memory as is available. No message appears during this phase unless memory is severely limited or defective.

Volume Mounting Messages. The newly initialized OS proceeds to mount each volume defined in the NetWare volume tables, starting with the SYS volume. The message

```
Mounting Volume SYS
```

appears during this process. A similar message is displayed for each additional volume. If any disk errors or directory mismatch errors are encountered while mounting a volume, an error message will appear. Serious errors may include a prompt asking you if you want to abandon the volume mount.

TTS Initialization Message. If the server is running SFT NetWare with TTS, the following message will be displayed on the screen:

```
Initializing Transaction Tracking System
```

Bindery and Queue Check Messages. The following messages are displayed while the OS checks the bindery and the queues defined on the file server:

```
Checking Bindery
Checking Queues
```

The OS will indicate any problems it finds during these checks as well.

Network Interface Board Initialization. The OS next initializes each network board installed in the file server, as indicated by messages similar to the following:

```
Initializing LAN A
```

If the a network board is faulty or improperly installed, error messages may be generated at this point.

NetWare Version Information. After network boards are initialized, the file server displays information about the version of NetWare that just loaded, similar to this one:

```
Novell SFT NetWare 286 v2.15C
(C) Copyright 1983, 1989 Novell Inc.
All Rights Reserved.
```

The Error Log Message. Any significant errors encountered during the bootup process are recorded in a text file named SYS$LOG.ERR file in the SYS:SYSTEM directory. This procedure is indicated by the following message:

```
SYSTEM ERRORS RECORDED IN SUPERVISOR FILE SYS$LOG.ERR
```

Supervisors can read this file through SYSCON's "View File Server Error Log" option under "Supervisor Options" in the main menu. Since it is a DOS text file, it can also be printed for a permanent record of file server errors. After resolving the errors, you can clear the error log file to keep it from becoming too large.

File Server Date and Time. NetWare initially reads the date and time from the file server's internal clock. You can change the date and time by using the SET TIME console command or the FCONSOLE utility.

Console Prompt. The file server console prompt is a colon (:) to distinguish it from a DOS prompt (usually A> or C>). This prompt is where you enter console commands.

OS INITIALIZATION ERROR MESSAGES

The following error messages may appear during the initialization of the NetWare OS:

Invalid number of FCBs requested from configuration information.

Explanation. The OS is setting up the File Control Block (FCB) storage area in file server memory, but the number of FCBs requested is invalid. The number of FCBs allocated is determined by the maximum number of open files configured in NETGEN/ELSGEN (must range between 20 and 1,000).

Severity. Fatal—abends the bootup of the file server.

Possible Causes. (1) The OS file is corrupt.
(2) A hardware failure occurred in a disk drive, controller, DCB, or memory.

Possible Solutions. (1) Run NETGEN to check the setting for the maximum number of open files (it should be between 20 and 1,000). Then reboot the server. If the error persists, restore the OS from a backup.
(2) Check the memory and the disk-related hardware in the file server. Repair or replace any faulty components.

NetWare/286 requires running on an IBM PC/AT or equivalent.

Explanation. The OS checks the file server's ROM BIOS during bootup to determine whether the file server is suitable for running NetWare.

Severity. Fatal—abends the bootup of the file server.

Possible Causes. (1) You tried to boot NetWare 286 on a computer that is not an IBM PC AT or compatible, or an IBM PS/2 Model 50 and above.
(2) You have changed the ROM BIOS, or the ROM BIOS is defective.

Possible Solutions. (1) Use a Novell-approved IBM PC AT or PS/2 compatible file server.
(2) Check the ROM BIOS chip to make sure that it is seated properly, that is does not have any bent pins, and that it is not corrupted. Also make sure that the ROM BIOS is IBM PC AT compatible.

Network Operating System software is not serialized for this network.

Explanation. The SFT NetWare 286 v2.1 serialization check discovered that the serial number on the key device does not match the serial number of the OS. (This error does not apply to NetWare versions 2.11 and above that do not require a key device.)

Severity. Fatal—abends the bootup of the file server.

Possible Causes. The OS serial number and the hardware serial number on the Novell keycard or DCB are not the same.

Possible Solutions. Check the keycard or DCB to make sure the serial number matches the serial number of the OS you are loading on the file server. If the error occurs after the first time you bring the server up, check for faulty components on the key device.

NO FREE SPACE TO VERIFY DIRECTORIES
NO FREE SPACE TO VERIFY FAT TABLES

Explanation. During bootup, the OS creates a buffer in memory to check for discrepancies between the duplicate copies of the volume directory entry tables and FATs. NetWare maintains two copies of these tables as part of its Level I fault tole-ance.

Severity. Warning (not fatal). The file server will continue to boot as usual. However, the OS will not be able to check for discrepancies between the two copies of the directory entry tables and FATs. This compromises some of the built-in fault tolerance of NetWare.

Possible Causes. (1) The file server does not have enough dynamic memory available to create a buffer big enough to compare the duplicate tables.
(2) A failure in high memory is causing the file server to use less memory than is actually installed.

Possible Solutions. (1) This process uses memory in Dynamic Memory Pool 1. You cannot increase dynamic memory by adding memory boards. Therefore, you will have to decrease the demands made on dynamic memory by manipulating the allocations made in this area of memory. See Chapter 34 for details.
(2) Run diagnostics test on the file server memory, or have it checked by other means. Replace any defective memory hardware.

Non-dedicated Server not running on top of DOS.

Explanation. When a nondedicated OS initializes the file server, it checks to make sure that DOS has been loaded first. The nondedicated file server "task swit-ches" between the DOS workstation functions (running in 286 real mode) and the file server functions (running in 286 protected mode), but DOS must be loaded first.

Possible Causes. You tried to boot the file server with a nondedicated NetWare OS before loading DOS in the file server.

Possible Solutions. Boot the system with DOS before typing the NET$OS command. Do not use nondedicated NetWare with any operating system other than DOS.

Not enough memory above 640K to run the server (requires 384K).

Explanation. The nondedicated NetWare OS requires at least 1MB of RAM in the file server (1.5MB for v2.15c). The first 640KB of RAM is used by the DOS workstation function; all memory above 640KB is used for the NetWare file server operations. The OS requires at least 384KB (800KB in v2.15c) in order to run, but typically needs much more than that to run well.

Possible Causes. (1) The file server does not have enough RAM to run non-dedicated NetWare.

(2) A failure in high memory is causing the file server to use less memory than is actually installed.

Possible Solutions. (1) Add more extended memory to the file server. Make sure the file server has at least 1MB of memory installed.

(2) Run a diagnostics test on the file server memory, or have it checked by other means. Replace any defective memory hardware.

Operating System / Server Mismatch.

Explanation. The OS found that the file server hardware does not conform to the version of NetWare trying to load.

Severity. Fatal—abends the bootup of the file server.

Possible Causes. Your file server hardware does not conform to the NetWare OS.

Possible Solutions. Install the version of the OS specific to the file server.

DISK ERRORS DURING BOOTUP

The following error messages may appear prior to or during the mounting of volumes when you are booting the file server:

Error marking mirror bad...Run NETGEN.

Explanation. The OS detected problems with a mirrored pair of disk drives, then encountered a write error while trying to write this data to the mirrored drive.

Severity. Fatal—abends the bootup of the file server.

Possible Causes. (1) A failure has occurred in the disk drive, controller board, DCB, or cables for either of the mirrored drives.

(2) The power supply to the disk drives has failed.

Possible Solutions. (1) Repair or replace the bad disk drives, controllers, DCBs, or cables that are causing the problem. Use NETGEN to remirror the drives before rebooting the server. If the error persists, restore the OS from a backup, or generate a new OS.

(2) Repair or replace the power supply.

Error reading disk redirection data.
Error reading disk redirection information on sector 14. Run NETGEN.

Explanation. The OS could not correctly read the Hot Fix Redirection data on a disk drive.

Severity. Warning—the server will not be able to use the drive until the problem is resolved.

Possible Causes. (1) A failure has occurred in the disk drive, controller board, DCB, or connecting cables.

(2) The file server has written invalid information to the disk.

Possible Solutions. (1) If you suspect hardware problems, check the disk drive to see that it is properly cabled and has power. Check the controller board and DCB to make sure they are properly seated and cabled. Repair or replace any bad disk drives, controllers, DCBs, or cables.

(2) If the drive is mirrored, you can fix the error using REMIRROR after the server is booted. REMIRROR will rebuild the redirection tables automatically. If the drive is not mirrored, use NETGEN to re-establish Hot Fix.

If the error persists, back up all data on the disk and run COMPSURF to reformat the drive. Then run NETGEN to re-establish Hot Fix, mirroring, and volumes. Restore the data from the backup to the disk.

Invalid Redirection Index table.
Invalid redirection table. Run NETGEN.

Explanation. The OS found inconsistencies in a disk's Hot Fix Redirection Table during bootup.

Severity. Warning—the file server will proceed to boot up, but will not be able to use the drive until the problem is resolved.

Possible Causes. The disk drive has written invalid data over the Hot Fix Redirection Area.

Possible Solutions. Run NETGEN to re-establish Hot Fix on the drive.

Mirror copies of disk redirection information do not match. Run NETGEN.

Explanation. During bootup, the OS detected that the two copies of the Hot Fix Redirection table stored on a disk do not match. Two copies of the Hot Fix Redirection table are stored on each physical disk to ensure disk integrity.

Severity. Warning—the file server will proceed to boot up, but will not be able to use the drive until the problem is resolved.

Possible Causes. (1) The file server has written invalid data over the Hot Fix Redirection Area.

(2) One redirection table was updated on the disk, but the file server lost power before the other table could be updated.

Possible Solutions. Run NETGEN to re-establish Hot Fix.

Mirror drive was shut down.

Explanation. During bootup, the OS shut down one of the drives in a mirrored pair.

Severity. Warning—the file server will continue to boot, but will not be able to use the drive until the problem is resolved. (You should resolve the problem as soon as possible to restore SFT mirroring protection for your data.)

Possible Causes. (1) A failure occurred in the disk drive, controller, DCB, or connecting cables.

(2) The file server has written invalid information to the disk.

Possible Solutions. (1) Check the disk drive to see that it is properly cabled and has power. Check the controller board and DCB to make sure they are properly seated and cabled. Repair or replace any bad disk drives, controllers, DCBs, or cables.

(2) Run NETGEN to re-establish Hot Fix and mirroring on the disk.

If the error persists, back up all data on the disk and run COMPSURF to reformat the drive. Then run NETGEN to re-establish Hot Fix, mirroring, and volumes.

Mirror drives are not the same size...Run NETGEN.

Explanation. During bootup, the OS detected that two disks in a mirrored pair have a different number of logical blocks.

Severity. Warning—the file server will continue to boot, but will not be able to mirror the drives until the problem is resolved. (You should resolve the problem as soon as possible to restore SFT mirroring protection for your data.)

Possible Causes. (1) Either drive of a mirrored pair has written invalid data over the Redirection table.

(2) One of the drives was exchanged with a drive that was previously mirrored in a different mirrored pair.

Possible Solutions. (1) Run NETGEN and specify identical logical block sizes for both mirrored disk drives.

(2) Run NETGEN and specify identical logical block sizes for both mirror-ed disk drives.

Mirroring not supported under NetWare SFT Level I.

Explanation. A file server previously set up for SFT NetWare Level II was booted with SFT NetWare Level I. Disk mirroring is supported only under SFT NetWare Level II.

Severity. Warning—the file server will continue to boot, but no disk mirroring will take place.

Possible Causes. You restored an old version of the NetWare operating system to a recently upgraded file server.

Possible Solutions. If you want to run the OS that does not support mirroring, use NETGEN to turn off disk mirroring, then reboot the file server. If you want to run SFT NetWare Level II, run NETGEN to generate and copy an SFT NetWare Level II OS to the server, then reboot.

Only *nn* redirection blocks available on drive *dd*.

Explanation. While initializing a drive, the OS finds that it has fewer than ten redirection blocks available in the Hot Fix Redirection Area. The *nn* represents the number of redirection blocks left, and *dd* represents the drive number.

Severity. Warning—the file server will continue to boot, but you should fix the problem as soon as possible to avoid losing data.

Possible Causes. (1) The Hot Fix Redirection Area is smaller than the recommended default size (approximately 2 percent of the total disk capacity).

(2) The Hot Fix Redirection Area is adequate in size but it is full.

Possible Solutions. (1) Run NETGEN to enlarge the size of the Hot Fix Redirection Area. Remember that if you enlarge the Hot Fix Redirection Area on one drive in a mirrored pair, you will also have to enlarge the redirection area on the corresponding mirrored drive to match.

(2) A full disk redirection area usually means the disk drive has serious problems. Consider having the drive either repaired or replaced. You can still use NETGEN to enlarge the redirection area, but you should consider this as only a temporary solution.

Problem with drive *nn*: Error reading disk redirection information on sector 14.

Explanation. During bootup, the OS could not correctly read the disk redirection information on sector 14 of the drive currently being mounted.

Severity. Warning—the file server will continue to boot, but will not be able to use the drive until the problem is resolved.

Possible Causes. (1) A failure occurred in the disk drive, controller, DCB, or connecting cables.

(2) The file server has written invalid information to the disk.

Possible Solutions. (1) If you suspect hardware problems, check the disk drive to see that it is properly cabled and has power. Check the controller board and DCB to make sure they are properly seated and cabled. Repair or replace any bad disk drives, controllers, DCBs, or cables.

(2) If the drive is mirrored, you can fix the error using REMIRROR after the server is booted. REMIRROR will rebuild the redirection tables automatically. If the drive is not mirrored, use NETGEN to re-establish Hot Fix.

If the error persists, back up all data on the disk and run COMPSURF to reformat the drive. Then run NETGEN to re-establish Hot Fix, mirroring, and volumes.

Problem with drive *nn*: Drive not set up for Hot Fix.

Explanation. During bootup, the OS detected that a physical drive was not set up for Hot Fix.

Severity. Fatal—you must set up Hot Fix on all drives before the OS can be booted on the server.

Possible Causes. Hot Fix was not properly installed on the indicated disk drive.

Possible Solutions. Run NETGEN and set up Hot Fix on all drives attached to or installed in the file server.

Problem with drive *nn*: Duplicate copies of disk redirection data do not match.
Problem with drive *nn*: Error reading disk redirection data.
Problem with drive *nn*: Invalid disk redirection table...duplicate entry.
Problem with drive *nn*: Invalid disk redirection table...entry out of range.

Explanation. During bootup, the OS detected errors relating to the Hot Fix Redirection Area of the disk.

Severity. Warning—the file server will continue to boot, but will not be able to use the drive until the problem is resolved.

Possible Causes. (1) A failure occurred in the disk drive, controller, DCB, or connecting cables.

(2) The file server has written invalid information to the disk.

Possible Solutions. (1) If you suspect hardware problems, check the disk drive to see that it is properly cabled and has power. Check the controller board and DCB to make sure they are properly seated and cabled. Repair or replace any bad disk drives, controllers, DCBs, or cables.

(2) If the drive is mirrored, you can fix the error using REMIRROR after the server is booted. REMIRROR will rebuild the redirection tables automatically. If the drive is not mirrored, use NETGEN to re-establish Hot Fix.

If the error persists, back up all data on the disk and run COMPSURF to reformat the drive. Then run NETGEN to re-establish Hot Fix, mirroring, and volumes.

Problem with drive *nn*: Mirror drive was shut down.

Explanation. During bootup, the OS detected that one drive in a mirrored pair of drives was shut down.

Severity. Warning—the file server will continue to boot, but will not be able to use the drive until the problem is resolved. (You should resolve the problem as soon as possible to restore SFT mirroring protection for your data.)

Possible Causes. (1) A failure occurred in the disk drive, controller, DCB, or connecting cables.

(2) The file server has written invalid information to the disk.

Possible Solutions. (1) If you suspect hardware problems, check the disk drive to see that it is properly cabled and has power. Check the controller board and DCB to make sure they are properly seated and cabled. Repair or replace any bad disk drives, controllers, DCBs, or cables.

(2) Run NETGEN to re-establish Hot Fix and mirroring on the disk.

If the error persists, back up all data on the disk and run COMPSURF to reformat the drive. Then run NETGEN to re-establish Hot Fix, mirroring, and volumes.

VOLUME MOUNTING ERROR MESSAGES

The following error messages may occur when volumes are being mounted during file server bootup:

Abandon Volume Mount?

Explanation. While trying to mount a volume, the OS detected potentially serious errors. This prompt actually appears at the end of several error messages.

When to Answer Yes. Type "**Y**" if the error preceding the prompt indicates a potentially serious problem. This will stop the volume from being mounted and accessed by file server users until you can take appropriate steps to correct the errors and recover valuable data on the volume. All other volumes on the file server will be mounted, and the file server will be initialized. When the file server comes up, users will not be able to access data residing on the damaged volume. Run VREPAIR to repair FAT and directory entry table errors. If necessary, restore damaged files from a backup.

When to Answer No. Type "**N**" if the preceding error indicates a "data mirror mismatch" or similar wording. This will continue the volume mounting process. The OS will perform as many corrective actions as it can to try to resolve the problems encountered. As files that contain errors are used and rewritten, the OS will automatically repair all data mirror or directory mismatches.

Abandon Error Report?

Explanation. While trying to mount a volume, the OS detected a string of inconsistencies in the directory entry table or FAT. This prompt actually appears after several other operating system messages. You can choose whether or not to display all the inconsistencies found by typing "**Y**" or "**N**" after the prompt. Either way, the file server will mount the volume and attempt to fix the problem. As the files that have the errors are used and rewritten, the file server will automatically repair all "data mirror mismatch" errors.

Not enough memory to cache volume *nn*.

Explanation. The file server does not have enough memory to cache the directory entry tables of the indicated volume. The OS requires 4KB of memory to cache a directory (32 bytes per directory entry) on a volume.

Severity. Warning—the file server will proceed to boot up, but because the volume's directory is not cached, the file server's performance may be sluggish.

Possible Causes. (1) The file server does not have enough memory available for the amount of disk space (volumes) it must support.
(2) A failure in high memory is causing the file server to use less memory than is actually installed.

Possible Solutions. (1) Add more extended memory to the file server and reboot.
(2) Run diagnostics tests on the file server memory or have it checked by other means. Replace any defective memory hardware.

TOO MANY VOLUMES ON SYSTEM

Explanation. The file server tried to mount more than the maximum of 32 volumes supported in NetWare 286.

Severity. Warning—the file server will proceed to boot up, but no more volumes will be mounted. (A file server can support up to 32 volumes, but it also needs sufficient memory to cache the directories and FATs for each volume.)

Possible Causes. Too many volumes have been defined in the NetWare volume tables.

Possible Solutions. Run NETGEN to reduce the number of volumes to less than 32. If necessary, decrease the number of volumes by increasing the amount of disk space assigned to each volume. We recommend assigning only one volume to each physical disk drive. This allows the maximum number of physical disks possible to be used on the file server.

If the disk is larger than 255MB, you must create multiple volumes on the disk. (Drives over 255MB are supported only in NetWare v2.15c).

!!! VOLUME MOUNT ERROR — NO FREE ALLOCATION SPACE !!!

Explanation. When the file server boots, the OS keeps track of volumes as they are mounted. To update the Volume Name table, the OS must create a buffer in dynamic memory. This error indicates that there was not enough dynamic memory space available to create this buffer.

Severity. Warning—the file server will continue to boot, but the current volume will not be mounted. If NetWare cannot mount the first volume (SYS), the server will come up, but no volumes will be mounted.

Possible Causes. (1) The file server does not have enough dynamic memory available to add the volume name to the Volume Name table.

(2) A failure in high memory is causing the file server to use less memory than is actually installed.

Possible Solutions. (1) This process uses memory in Dynamic Memory Pool 1. You cannot increase dynamic memory by adding memory boards. Therefore, you will have to decrease the demands made on dynamic memory by manipulating the allocations made in this area of memory. See Chapter 34 for details.

(2) Run diagnostics test on the file server memory, or have it checked by other means. Replace any defective memory hardware.

BINDERY AND QUEUE ERROR MESSAGES

The following error messages may appear when the OS checks the bindery and queues during bootup:

ERROR—CANNOT OPEN BINDERY FILES.

Explanation. The file server bindery is a small database containing the names of users, their rights, the file servers to which they are attached, and so on. The bindery files, named NET$BIND.SYS and NET$BVAL.SYS, are located in SYS:SYSTEM.

Severity. Warning—the file server will proceed to boot up, but bindery errors must be fixed before users can log in.

Possible Causes. (1) The bindery files do not exist in the SYS:SYSTEM directory.

(2) The OS is unable to create new bindery files after it has failed to locate any existing ones.

(3) Existing bindery files are damaged or corrupted.

(4) The directory entry table on the SYS volume is full, or the volume itself is full.

(5) The file server does not have enough RAM to support all the hard disks attached to it.

Possible Solutions. (1) The OS automatically tries to rebuild the bindery if it cannot find the bindery files during bootup. However, the OS initializes the rebuilt bindery to its default state; the only users defined will be SUPERVISOR and GUEST. Restore the bindery files, if possible. Otherwise, you must re-create all users and groups and re-assign the NetWare security rights.

(2) Restore the bindery files from the most recent backup. Then reboot the server.

(3) Run BINDFIX to repair damaged bindery files, or restore good bindery files from a backup.

(4) Run NETGEN to increase the maximum number of directory entries for the SYS volume, or follow the instructions for regaining volume space in Chap. 7.

(5) Add more memory to the file server.

LAN INITIALIZATION ERROR MESSAGE

The following error message may occur during the initialization of network interface boards when the file server is booted:

No LAN Processor Boards are responding.

Explanation. The OS could not establish communication with any network interface boards during bootup.

Severity. Fatal—abends the file server bootup.

Possible Causes. (1) No network boards are installed in the file server.

(2) The network interface boards in the file server are not installed correctly.

(3) The network interface boards in the file server are defective.

Possible Solutions. (1) Make sure the file server has at least one properly connected network interface board installed.

(2) Check for configuration conflicts between boards in the file server. Make sure boards are firmly seated in the expansion bus and are properly connected to the network cabling system.

(3) Swap a suspected board with one that you know is good to see if the problem lies with the board. Replace any defective hardware.

40 Errors During Operation

This chapter lists some of the error messages that can appear on the file server console while the server is running. These error messages are grouped into general console messages, messages that appear when you are bringing down the server, error messages dealing with physical disk drives or disk channel components, and error messages caused by memory failure in the server. Where two or more error messages are similar, the messages are listed together.

Most of these messages will be preceded by "Abend:" to indicate that NetWare has encountered a fatal problem that prevents further operation of the server. ("Abend" is short for *ab*normal *end*ing.) The OS regularly performs internal consistency checks before critical operations to ensure the integrity of the data involved; an abend error usually results from a failed consistency check.

GENERAL FILE SERVER CONSOLE MESSAGES

The following general messages can appear on the file server console screen:

??? UNKNOWN COMMAND ???

Explanation. You have entered a console command that the file server does not recognize.

Possible Causes. The syntax of the console command you entered is invalid, or the spelling of the command is incorrect.

Possible Solutions. Re-enter the console command with the correct spelling and format.

Bindery Object List Warning
Bindery Property List Warning

Explanation. The OS detected a problem with the objects listed in the file server's bindery (the names of users, groups, other file servers, and so on) or their properties. Properties can be such things as passwords, trustee rights, and internetwork addresses.

Severity. A warning message. The file server will continue to operate, but users may experience difficulties changing their passwords or logging in.

Possible Causes. The bindery files may be damaged, which can result from the file server being turned off or halted by a power failure before it is properly shut down with the DOWN command.

Possible Solutions. Run the BINDFIX utility to repair the bindery files (see Chapter 35), or restore the bindery files from a backup copy.

ERROR—CANNOT OPEN BINDERY FILES.

Explanation. The OS could not open the bindery files.

Severity. Warning—the file server will continue to operate, but users will not be able to log in.

Possible Causes. (1) The SYS volume was mounted improperly.
(2) The file server has run out of memory space for directory handles.

Possible Solutions. (1) Reboot the file server; watch the console screen to see if the SYS volume mounts properly. If not, the OS may be corrupt. Restore the OS from a backup copy, or regenerate a new OS with NETGEN/ELSGEN.
(2) Add more memory to the file server. If the server has adequate memory, run a memory diagnostics test and replace any faulty memory chips.

FATAL ERROR—NOT ENOUGH MEMORY TO SUPPORT DISK DRIVES.
NOT ENOUGH MEMORY TO SUPPORT DISK DRIVES.

Explanation. The file server does not have enough memory installed to cache the FATs and directory entry tables of all volumes found on the network disk drives.

Severity. Fatal—the operation of the file server will be terminated.

Possible Causes. The file server could be attempting to mount more disk volumes than it has memory to support. Or, a memory failure could be affecting the normal amount of memory the file server can use.

Possible Solutions. Run a diagnostics test to make sure the file server memory is good. Replace any faulty memory chips. If memory checks out all right, decrease the amount of disk storage to be mounted by eliminating a volume or two from the server (if possible). Or, add extended memory to the file server. Each megabyte of disk storage requires about 1KB of file server memory.

Fatal File System Error: zero First or Current Cluster.
File System internal error: zero First or Current Cluster.

Explanation. The OS performed a consistency check before attempting to extend an existing file and the consistency check failed.

Severity. Fatal—the operation of the file server will be terminated.

Possible Causes. The file is corrupted due to disk errors or memory failure.

Possible Solutions. Reboot the file server. If the error persists, run VREPAIR to fix minor disk errors. Check disk channel components and repair or replace any defective hardware. Run a diagnostics test to make sure the file server memory is good. Replace any faulty memory chips.

General protection interrupt.

Explanation. The 80286 CPU received an interrupt on line 13, which sig-nals a memory protection violation. On the 80286 chip, interrupts 9 through 12 usually handle memory protection interrupts. A serious problem, such as an attempt to write to a memory segment defined as read-only, will trigger interrupt 13.

Severity. Fatal—the operation of the file server will be terminated.

Possible Causes. Data stored in the CPU's registers or in file server memory has been seriously altered due to a hardware conflict or memory failure of some kind. Insufficient RAM in the file server (below the minimum recommended amount) can also cause a GPI.

Possible Solutions. If the GPI occurs during bootup, check to make sure you have at least the minimum recommended amount of memory installed in the file server. Check for hardware conflicts among boards in the file server. If you have recently added a VAP or VADD to the server, remove the VAP or VADD and reboot the server to see if that could be causing the GPI. Run a diagnostics check on the file server's memory and replace any defective RAM chips. Make sure the UPS is functioning properly to protect the file server from power glitches. If the error persists after you have removed any third-party VADDs or VAPs, contact Novell.

NMI interrupt

Explanation. The 80286 CPU received a signal on its Non-Maskable Interrupt (NMI) line but was unable to identify the source of the interrupt.

Severity. Fatal—the operation of the file server will be terminated.

Possible Causes. (1) A board in your file server is trying to use the same I/O or memory addresses as another piece of hardware in the file server. For example, since the Channel 1 DCB uses the I/O base address 340h, no other board can use this I/O address.

(2) Faulty or insufficient memory can generate this error.

(3) Defective hardware can also cause NMI interrupt errors.

Possible Solutions. (1) Reconfigure the boards in your file server to eliminate I/O and memory address conflicts. Rerun NETGEN/ELSGEN to generate a new OS and reinstall it on the file server.

(2) If the error persists, run a diagnostics check on the file server's memory. Replace any defective RAM chips and add more memory, if necessary.

(3) Check all hardware in the file server; repair or replace any defective hardware.

No cache blocks available for allocation.

Explanation. The OS could not allocate any disk cache blocks due to an insufficient amount of file server memory.

Severity. Fatal—the operation of the file server will be terminated.

Possible Causes. The file server does not have enough memory to support the amount of disk storage connected to it. Or, a failure in high memory is causing the file server to use less memory than is actually installed.

Possible Solutions. Run a diagnostics test on the file server memory. If the memory checks out, add more memory to the file server to make more cache buffers available.

!!! No Dynamic Work Space Available !!!
Out of dynamic memory.

Explanation. The OS ran out of free dynamic memory space.

Severity. Warning—the file server will continue to operate, but users may not be able to access file server resources.

Possible Causes. (1) All available memory space in Dynamic Memory Pool 1, 2, or 3 is used up.

(2) A failure in high memory is causing the file server to use less memory than is actually installed.

Possible Solutions. (1) You cannot increase the amount of *dynamic* memory by adding memory to the file server; you must reduce the demands made on dynamic memory by manipulating the allocations to this area of memory. See Chapter 34 for more information on dynamic memory usage.

(2) Run a memory diagnostics test; replace any defective memory hardware.

Not enough memory available for cache blocks.

Explanation. The file server has run out of memory for additional disk cache buffers.

Severity. Warning—disk I/O performance will be degraded.

Possible Causes. All available memory in the file server is used up by other processes.

Possible Solutions. Add more memory to the file server. The OS needs 4KB of cache memory for each volume directory block cached, plus a minimum of eight additional blocks of cache memory for file caching.

Not enough memory available for locks work space.

Explanation. The file server does not have enough memory for file locking workspace.

Severity. Warning—the file server will continue to operate, but users may not be able to access file server resources.

Possible Causes. (1) The file server does not have enough memory.

(2) All available memory space in Dynamic Memory Pool 1, 2, or 3 is used up.

(3) A failure in high memory is causing the file server to use less memory that is actually installed.

Possible Solutions. (1) Add memory to the file server. The OS needs at least 2KB of memory for file locking, plus 100 bytes for each file that can be opened on the file server. The maximum amount of memory that can be consumed by the NetWare file locking system is 64KB.

(2) Reduce the demands made on dynamic memory by manipulating the allocations to this are of memory. See Chapter 34 for more information on dynamic memory usage.

(3) Make sure the file server's memory is good and that all of it is being used by the file server.

NOT ENOUGH MEMORY FOR DISK FAT TABLES.

Explanation. The file server does not have enough memory to store the File Allocation Tables (FAT) for all mounted volumes.

Severity. Warning—the file server will continue to operate, but users may not be able to access file server resources.

Possible Causes. (1) The file server does not have enough memory.

(2) All available memory space in Dynamic Memory Pool 1, 2, or 3 is used up.

(3) A failure in high memory is causing the file server to use less memory that is actually installed.

Possible Solutions. (1) Add memory to the file server. The OS needs 1KB of memory for each megabyte of mounted disk space to store the FATs.

(2) Reduce the demands made on dynamic memory by manipulating the allocations made to this area of memory. See Chapter 34 for more information on dynamic memory usage.

(3) Make sure the file server's memory is good and that all of it is being used by the file server. The OS requires 1KB of memory for each megabyte of mounted disk space for storing the FAT.

Out of non-dedicated work stacks.

SwitchToReal ran out of non-dedicated work stacks.

Explanation. All four of the stacks that nondedicated NetWare allocates in memory for handling real-mode interrupts were in use when another real-mode interrupt occurred.

Severity. Fatal—the operation of the file server will be terminated.

Possible Causes. Software running in the nondedicated server contains poorly written interrupt routines that take a long time to service. Some of the boards installed in the server use interrupts and are interrupting too often.

Possible Solutions. Do not install boards that use interrupts in a nondedicated file server. Do not use interrupt-driven hardware or software with nondedicated NetWare. Especially avoid real-time applications.

Out of memory...too many FCBs requested.

Explanation. The file server does not have enough memory to handle the maximum number of open files configured in NETGEN/ELSGEN. A File Control Block (FCB) is created for each open file. The OS requires 40 bytes of memory space for each file that is open simultaneously in the network. The maximum possible number of FCBs is 1,000.

Severity. Fatal—the operation of the file server will be terminated.

Possible Causes. (1) The number of open files configured for the file server is too high for the amount of memory the server has.
(2) The file server has run out of memory in Dynamic Memory Pool 1, 2, or 3.
(3) A failure in high memory is causing the file server to use less memory than is actually installed.

Possible Solutions. (1) Run NETGEN/ELSGEN to reduce the maximum number of files that can be open simultaneously. Allow for at least five files per workstation attached to the server. If necessary, add more memory to the file server.
(2) Reduce the demands made on dynamic memory by manipulating the allocations made to this area of memory. See Chapter 34 for more information on dynamic memory usage.
(3) Make sure the file server's memory is good and that all of it is being used by the file server.

Stack overflow detected by kernel.

Explanation. The OS performed a consistency check on the memory stack used by a completed process or a task-switched process, and found that the process used too much stack memory.

Severity. Fatal—the operation of the file server will be terminated.

Possible Causes. An invalid device driver, modified type table, or memory overflow error in the file server.

Possible Solutions. Check all device drivers or type tables on the file server. To free up additional memory for use by stacks, rerun NETGEN/ELSGEN and reduce the maximum number of open files. If the error persists, reinstall the OS.

WARNING — CANNOT CREATE MESSAGE FILE!!!

Explanation. The temporary file used to store broadcast messages cannot be created in the SYS:SYSTEM directory of the file server.

Severity. Warning—the file server will continue to operate, but you won't be able to send broadcast messages until the problem is fixed.

Possible Causes. The file cannot be created due to a lack of workspace or an insufficient number of directory entries on the SYS volume.

Possible Solutions. The SYS volume must have at least 2MB-3MB of free disk space and 20-40 free directory entries. Use CHKVOL or VOLINFO to check the free space and number of directory entries available on the SYS volume. Run NETGEN/ELSGEN to allocate more disk space or (preferably) more directory entries on the SYS volume. Or, have users delete all unnecessary files from the SYS volume.

WARNING: INSUFFICIENT MEMORY TO HASH DIRECTORIES.

Explanation. The file server does not have enough memory available to hash all the directories of the mounted volumes.

Severity. Warning—the file server will continue to operate, but its performance will be considerably degraded.

Possible Causes. (1) The file server needs more memory.
(2) A failure in high memory is causing the file server to use less memory than is actually installed.

Possible Solutions. (1) Make sure the file server has sufficient memory available for directory hashing. To hash directories, the OS requires eight bytes of memory for each configured directory entry on a volume.
(2) If the file server has adequate memory, run a memory diagnostics test; replace any faulty memory chips.

WARNING! LAN *n* DEAD.

Explanation. The OS can no longer communicate with the network interface board configured as LAN *n* in the file server (where *n* could be A, B, C, or D).

Possible Causes. (1) A bad connection between the network board and the file server.
(2) Faulty cabling on the network.
(3) A defective network interface board.

Possible Solutions. (1) Check the seating of the network interface board in the file server.

(2) Check the connections to the network cabling and the cabling itself.

(3) If neither of these checks fixes the problem, replace the network interface board.

MESSAGES WHEN BRINGING DOWN THE SERVER

The following messages may appear when you use the DOWN console command to shut down the file server:

*** WARNING *** ACTIVE FILES OPEN. HALT NETWORK?

Explanation. At least one workstation still had files open when you issued the DOWN command. If the workstation is in the middle of a transaction or file update, data may be lost if you continue with the shutdown of the server.

To abort the shutdown procedure, answer "No" by typing "**N**" at the prompt. Wait until the workstation is finished and has logged out; then type DOWN again. If the workstation is hung with files open, use the CLEAR STATION console command to break the connection.

If you answer "Yes" to the "HALT NETWORK?" prompt, the OS will close all open files (whether the workstations are through with them or not) and shut down the server.

The Server has been Shut Down. Please Re-Boot to Restart.

This status message indicates that the file server has been successfully brought down with the DOWN command. All open files have been closed, cache buffers have been written to disk, directory entry tables and FATs have been up-dated, and the OS has been shut down. Note that even though the disk operations are nonfunctional, the server still acts as a router on the internetwork while it is shut down.

As the message indicates, you must perform a cold boot to restart the file server. Either reset the server or turn the server off and back on again.

ERROR MESSAGES DEALING WITH PHYSICAL DISK DRIVES

The following error messages result from problems with network disk drives or other disk channel hardware:

Attempt to configure a non-existent disk.
Attempt to configure a non-existent drive.

Explanation. The OS tried to configure a disk drive that is not attached to the file server.

Severity. Fatal—the operation of the file server will be terminated.

Possible Causes. (1) A drive was physically removed from the file server, but the OS has not been reconfigured with NETGEN.

(2) The disk channel configuration programmed into the EEPROM of a disk coprocessor board with DISKSET does not correspond to the actual channel configuration.

Possible Solutions. (1) Run NETGEN and remove the disk in the NetWare Installation part of the program. Reload the OS and reboot the file server.

(2) Rerun DISKSET and make sure the DCB configuration agrees with both the configuration set in NETGEN and the actual disk channel configuration.

Channel *n* was shut down due to unrecoverable failure.

Explanation. The OS detected a serious error, such as a timeout or invalid interrupt from a DCB, that forced a shutdown of the indicated disk channel (1, 2, 3, or 4).

Severity. Not fatal unless the channel containing the SYS volume is shut down. Any remaining disk channels will continue to operate.

Possible Causes. Bad connections somewhere along the disk channel, or faulty channel hardware (disk drive, controller, cabling, or DCB).

Possible Solutions. Check the seating of the DCB in the file server. Make sure the cabling between the controller boards and disk drives is intact and firmly connected. Repair or replace any faulty components.

Disk CoProcessor got a premature interrupt.

Explanation. When a DCB finishes processing a disk request for the OS, the DCB sets a flag in its internal, dual-ported RAM and sends an interrupt request to the file server CPU. When the CPU receives the interrupt request, it checks the DCB flag as an internal consistency check. The DCB interrupt flag was not valid.

Severity. Fatal—the disk channel will be shut down. If the channel contains the SYS volume, the operation of the file server will be terminated.

Possible Causes. (1) The on-board memory of the DCB has been overwritten or has failed.

(2) Other boards in the file server use the same interrupt (IRQ) line as the DCB.

(3) Power or hardware failures.

Possible Solutions. Reboot the file server. If the error persists, check for other cards in the file server that might be using the same IRQ line that the DCB is using. Also check the file server's memory and power line conditioning.

Disk CoProcessor had a ROM checksum error.
Disk CoProcessor returned invalid error code from diagnostics.
Disk CoProcessor timed out performing diagnostics.

Explanation. The OS instructs the DCB to perform a diagnostics test at various times. The DCB did not pass its own internal self-diagnostic tests, for the reason indicated.

Severity. Fatal—the disk channel will be shut down. If the channel contains the SYS volume, the operation of the file server will be terminated.

Possible Causes. (1) Bad connection between the DCB and the file server system board.

(2) Improper SCSI bus termination.

(3) Poor power supply regulation.

(4) Memory or other hardware failure on the DCB.

(5) On older revision DCBs, the timeout error might appear if no controllers or drives are connected to the DCB.

Possible Solutions. (1) Check the EEPROM on the DCB for bent pins. Clean the connector on the DCB and reseat the board.

(2) Make sure a terminating resistor has been properly installed on only the last controller physically connected to the SCSI bus.

(3) Check the power supply to ensure that the proper DC power is reaching the DCB.

(4) Replace the DCB, if defective.

(5) On older DCBs, make sure that at least one disk drive/controller is connected to the disk channel.

Disk Error on drive 0, sector 14.

Explanation. The OS could not read from sector 14 of a drive. This sector contains information about the Hot Fix Redirection table.

Severity. Fatal—the OS will shut off Hot Fix on the disk and render it un-usable.

Possible Causes. A defective or worn-out disk drive.

Possible Solutions. Run NETGEN to re-establish Hot Fix on the disk. If the problem persists, repair or replace the disk.

DISK NOT FORMATTED FOR NETWARE NETWORK

Explanation. The OS tried to initialize a disk and found that it has not been formatted for NetWare.

Severity. Not fatal unless the OS is trying to mount the primary disk in a mirrored pair of drives.

Possible Causes. The disk has not been formatted with COMPSURF. Track 0 of the disk may have been overwritten or damaged.

Possible Solutions. If the disk has not been formatted, run COMPSURF on the disk, then run NETGEN to initialize the disk with NetWare volumes. If the drive does not pass the COMPSURF test, you must replace the drive. If track 0 of the disk drive is bad, restore the disk's files from a backup (after running COMPSURF and NETGEN).

DISK NOT UPGRADED TO ADVANCED NETWARE

Explanation. The OS tried to mount a disk, but discovered that the disk was formatted with a version of NetWare below Advanced NetWare v1.0.

Severity. Fatal—the disk cannot be used.

Possible Causes. Incomplete upgrade of the file server disks. Track 0 of the disk may have been overwritten or damaged.

Possible Solutions. Run NETGEN to upgrade the disk to NetWare 286 v2.1*x*. If track 0 of the disk drive is bad, restore the disk's files from a backup (after running COMPSURF and NETGEN).

Drive not set up for Hot Fix.

Explanation. The OS tried to set up a drive for SFT NetWare mirroring or duplexing, but the drive has not previously had Hot Fix established on it.

Severity. The file server will not be able to use the disk until Hot Fix is established. Run NETGEN to set up Hot Fix on the drive.

Error configuring Disk CoProcessor.

Explanation. The DCB has passed the self-diagnostics test, but has returned an error condition to the disk driver after attempting to configure itself. A DCB configures itself by trying to access each of the disks programmed into its EEPROM. If the DCB is unsuccessful in accessing these disks, the DCB returns an error condition to the driver, which in turn generates this error message.

Severity. Fatal—the disk channel cannot be accessed.

Possible Causes. A hardware problem with a disk drive, controller, or interface cables. Since the DCB passed its self-diagnostics test, the DCB itself should be okay.

Possible Solutions. Check all disk drives, controllers, and interface cables connected to the DCB. Repair or replace any faulty components.

ERROR READING NETWARE CONFIGURATION INFORMATION

Explanation. The OS could not read the disk configuration tables from track 0 of the system disk (the disk containing the SYS volume).

Severity. Warning—the file server will continue to operate, but will not be able to access all disk drives.

Possible Causes. Incorrect disk configuration, faulty disk-related hardware, or a bad disk sector on track 0.

Possible Solutions. Use NETGEN to check the disk drive configuration. If you find a disk error, make a backup of the disk's files and run COMPSURF to reformat the disk. If the disk fails the COMPSURF test, replace the disk. Repair or replace any other defective hardware you might find. If necessary, reinstall the OS and restore the files from a backup.

Error resetting external disk controller.
Error resetting the PC/AT hard disk controller board.

Explanation. The OS tried to reset an external or internal disk controller board three times without success.

Severity. Fatal—the disks connected to the controller cannot be accessed.

Possible Causes. A defective disk controller board, or loose or faulty cabling.

Possible Solutions. Make sure the disk interface cables are intact and properly connected. Reseat the disk controller board. If the error persists, repair or replace the controller board.

Invalid Disk ReDirection Index table.

Explanation. The Hot Fix Redirection table has become corrupted. (The Redirection table contains the information used by Hot Fix to redirect data from bad blocks on the disk.)

Severity. Fatal—the disk cannot be used until Hot Fix has been re-established.

Possible Causes. (1) The Hot Fix Redirection table has been overwritten with invalid data.
(2) You attempted to mirror drives larger than 255MB with a version of SFT NetWare prior to v2.15 Revision C.

Possible Solutions. (1) Run NETGEN to re-establish Hot Fix on the disk.
(2) Upgrade to SFT NetWare 286 v2.15c.

Invalid Mirror abend.

Explanation. The OS detected a serious problem in the SFT NetWare disk mirroring process.

Severity. Fatal—the operation of the file server will be terminated.

Possible Causes. (1) A hardware failure in the mirrored disk drives, controller, DCBs, or associated cables.
(2) A failure in file server memory.

Possible Solutions. Reboot the file server. If the error persists, run NETGEN to re-establish mirroring. If that doesn't work, check all disk channel components and replace any defective hardware. Run a memory diagnostics test and replace any faulty memory chips.

Invalid mirror definition table...refers to unknown or duplicate drive. Run NETGEN.
Invalid mirror definition table. Run NETGEN.

Explanation. The Mirror Definition table, which contains the SFT NetWare mirroring information, has become corrupted. (Although non-SFT versions of NetWare do not support disk mirroring, they still use the information in the Mirror Definition table.)

Severity. Fatal—the operation of the file server will be terminated.

Possible Causes. The disk drive has written invalid data over the Mirror Definition table.

Possible Solutions. Use NETGEN to re-establish the disk mirroring assignments. If the error persists, restore the OS from a backup, or generate a new OS and reboot the file server.

Map To Logical request made with invalid physical drive.

Explanation. An OS routine called "Map to Logical," which keeps track of physical and logical drive numbers, was called with an invalid physical drive number.

Possible Causes. A disk-related hardware failure, poor power line conditioning, memory failure, or a corrupted OS.

Possible Solutions. Reboot the file server. If the error persists, reinstall the OS, then check the UPS power line conditioning and memory.

Mirroring turned off on volume *VolumeName* (drive *nn* failed).

Explanation. The OS shut off mirroring of the disk containing the specified volume.

Severity. Not fatal, but it will prevent at least one volume from having a mirrored backup. (You should resolve the problem as soon as possible to avoid losing valuable data.)

Possible Causes. A failure in the disk drive, controller, DCB, power supply, or interface cabling of a mirrored drive.

Possible Solutions. Check all disk channel components and repair or replace any faulty hardware. Run NETGEN to re-establish the mirrored pair, or run REMIRROR after rebooting the file server.

Time out error configuring Disk CoProcessor.
Time out on the first Disk CoProcessor.
Time out on the second Disk CoProcessor.

Explanation. The disk driver attempted to configure or program a DCB, but the DCB did not return a completion code within a specified amount of time.

Possible Causes. (1) Improper disk channel configuration.

(2) Faulty disk drive, controller, DCB, or interface cables.

(3) Hardware conflicts with other boards in the file server.

Possible Solutions. (1) Rerun DISKSET to check the disk channel configuration. Make sure the configuration programmed on the DCB matches the actual disks attached to the channel.

(2) Check all disk channel components and repair or replace any faulty hardware.

(3) Make sure that the DCB's IRQ settings do not conflict with other boards in the file server. If two DCBs are installed in the file server, they must be configured for different channels.

Volume *VolumeNames* have been completely shut down due to channel failure.

Explanation. The OS detected a fatal error, such as a timeout or invalid interrupt from the DCB, on the disk channel containing the volumes mentioned.

Severity. Not fatal, unless the channel containing the SYS volume is affected. Any remaining channels containing volumes will continue to operate.

Possible Causes. Faulty hardware along the disk channel, including the DCB, the disk controller board, the disk drive, and the cable connections between these components.

Possible Solutions. (1) Make sure the DCB is properly seated and that the connections between the DCB, the disk controller boards, and the disk drives are tight and properly cabled. (The colored edge of the flat ribbon cable always goes to pin number 1.) Check for defective cables or broken components. If you suspect faulty disk channel components, call your Novell authorized reseller for assistance.

Warning. disk write error in file *FileName*.

Explanation. Read-after-write verification failed when the OS tried to write the specified file to disk. This message is one of the few OS messages that is displayed at a workstation instead of at the file server console.

Severity. Warning—the specified file is corrupted, and Hot Fix has probably been turned off on the disk.

Possible Causes. The OS turned off the Hot Fix redirection feature on the disk, due to an unrecoverable disk channel error.

Possible Solutions. If the user is still in the application when this error occurs on the workstation, have the user try to save the file again, using a different file name. Do not delete the original file; rather, rename it with a .BAD extension (if possible) so that another disk write won't try to use the same bad area on the disk. Run VREPAIR to diagnose and repair minor disk problems. Re-establish Hot Fix on the drive by rerunning NETGEN/ELSGEN, if necessary.

!!! WARNING !!! ERROR MOUNTING DRIVE *nn* OF CONTROLLER *nn*.

Explanation. The OS could not mount the specified drive attached to the specified controller due to a disk read error.

Severity. Warning—the disk cannot be accessed by the file server.

Possible Causes. (1) The hard disk has not been formatted for NetWare. (2) A hardware failure occurred in the disk channel hardware.

Possible Solutions. (1) Use COMPSURF to format the drive. Then initialize volumes on the disk with NETGEN/ELSGEN and reboot the file server. (2) Check the disk channel components and repair or replace any faulty hardware.

Write Error: dir = *nnn* file = FileName vol = *VolumeName*.

Explanation. The read-after-write verification failed when the OS tried to write the indicated file on the specified volume.

Severity. Warning—the specified file is corrupted, and Hot Fix has probably been turned off on the disk.

Possible Causes. The OS turned off the Hot Fix redirection feature on the disk due to an unrecoverable disk channel error.

Possible Solutions. Run VREPAIR to diagnose and repair minor disk problems. Re-establish Hot Fix on the drive by rerunning NETGEN/ELSGEN, if necessary.

ROUTING MESSAGES

The following messages may appear because of routing problems or internetwork address conflicts:

Address change detected for ServerName.

Explanation. The OS has detected a change in the internetwork address of the specified file server. The message is displayed on the console of each file server and bridge that detects the change.

Severity. Only a warning—the internet will continue to function.

Possible Causes. The network address or node address for LAN A was changed on another file server, or an OS with a different LAN A network address is installed on the server. An internetwork address change in LAN B, C, or D of another file server will not produce this message.

Possible Solutions. No action is necessary. The routing information tables will be automatically updated in each server or bridge.

BAD PACKET ENCOUNTERED

Explanation. The message will be displayed on the file server console if the console is in TRACK ON mode and a bad router packet is received.

Severity. Only a warning.

Possible Causes. The error may be caused by transmission problems with the cables or the network interface boards. Improper cable type, improper cable termination, or extended cable lengths can cause packets to be lost or distorted.

Possible Solutions. Check cable types, cable termination, and cable lengths. If none of these seem to be the cause, check the network boards. If several file servers are cabled through a large internetwork, you will have to inspect the entire network.

ERROR! Address collision with *ServerName*.
!!!ROUTER CONFIGURATION ERROR!!! ROUTER *Address* claims LAN A is *Address*.
WARNING!!! MULTIPLE ROUTERS WITH SAME INTERNET ADDRESS!

Explanation. The routing process within the OS discovered that it has the same network address for LAN A as another router on the internetwork. If two or more file servers are not directly connected to the same cabling system, the network address of each file server must be unique.

Severity. Warning—users won't be able to access the specified file server.

Possible Causes. (1) The LAN A board in your file server is using the same network address as a LAN A board in another file server on the internetwork.

(2) A break exists in the backbone cable between two file servers. The two file servers, which have the same network address because they used to be connected to the same backbone cable, are still connected to the internetwork through alternate cabling routes.

Possible Solutions. (1) Use the CONFIG console command to find duplicate network addresses. Rerun NETGEN to change one of the duplicate network addresses for a LAN A board. Make sure the new network address is unique.

(2) If the two conflicting network addresses correspond with the backbone cable address, check for a break in the cabling between the two file servers.

ERRORS CAUSED BY MEMORY FAILURE

The following Abend errors may be caused by a memory failure in the file server. Memory failures can be caused by poor power line conditioning, static electricity, faulty RAM chips, or a corrupted operating system file. If electronic components such as RAM chips are defective, they usually fail within the first ten days of use.

The meaning of these error messages is significant only to someone who understands the inner workings of NetWare. Brief explanations of each message are included in the NetWare *System Messages* manual, but generally all you need to know is that the error is caused by a memory failure. Use the following diagnostic procedure for all of these memory errors:

Memory Diagnostics Procedure

First, try rebooting the file server. If the error occurs again, try restoring the OS from a backup or regenerating the OS from scratch. If that doesn't work, check the UPS power line conditioning. Run a diagnostics test on the file server memory. Check to see that RAM chips are properly installed and that all chips on the same memory expansion board have the same speed rating. Repair or replace any faulty memory components. If these errors persist after you have checked all of these possibilities, contact Novell.

Here is the list of errors most likely to be caused by memory failure in the file server:

Allocated cache block not found in Sector Index.
An invalid message number was returned to the background cache
        write process.
Bad block returned via Free.
Bound interrupt.
Breakpoint interrupt.
Cache Block Not Released During FlushCache.
CacheRelease on non-used cache buffer.
Check specific message no such message in kernel.
ClearFileStation with files open.
DeAllocate semaphore attempted on active semaphore in kernel.
DeAttachFile invalid file handle.
DetachFile invalid file handle.
Destroy Process not processed in kernel.
DIRECTORY ACCESS BY UNAUTHORIZED PROCESS.
Dirty cache block has no dirty bits set
Disk release call to illegal cache block.
Divide overflow interrupt.
Double exception interrupt.
FlushBuffer with a non-zero use count.
Global Descriptor Table overflow...too many segments defined.
Illegal Sector Number to Cache.
INT0 Detected interrupt.
Invalid drive passed to disk process.
Invalid op code interrupt.
Invalid process id passed by interrupt procedure to kernel.
Invalid semaphore number passed to kernel.
Invalid task state interrupt.

LinkTree invalid file handle.
Message sent to invalid process in kernel.
NDetachFile invalid file handle.
NextRemoveFile invalid file handle.
No Dirty Bits Set On Dirty Block.
No PCBs available in kernel.
NO PRE-FETCH FOR DIRECTORY WRITE REQUEST.
No semaphores available in kernel.
NReAttachFile invalid file handle.
NRemoveStationFile invalid file handle.
Out of message packets in the Kernel
Over 64K segment requested by AllocSeg.
Processor extension not supported.
Processor extension overrun interrupt.
RemoveFromSectorIndex called with invalid cache buffer.
Reply requested to non-existent message in kernel.
ResetBeingUsed called on unused cache buffer.
ResetBeingUsed call to cache block not being used.
Segment not present interrupt.
Semaphore created with negative initial value in kernel.
SetBeingUsed already being used in cache.
SetBeingUsed call to cache block already set.
SetBeingUsed out of semaphores.
Single step interrupt.
Stack segment overrun interrupt.
StationRemoveFile invalid file handle.
Timer Process out of Control Blocks.
Too large a message request sent to kernel.

Appendices

A Differences between NetWare 286 Versions

Since the original SFT NetWare 286 v2.1, each new version of NetWare 286 has included various changes—new features, new utilities, support for new hardware, different installation procedures. This appendix will help you sort out what's what so you can identify the unique concerns of your particular version of NetWare 286.

We'll take a chronological approach in order to highlight the changes from one release to another. At the end, we'll summarize the major differences in a chart for comparison purposes.

Note that Novell strongly encourages customers to upgrade to the latest versions of NetWare within the stratum appropriate for their network—ELS I, ELS II, Advanced, or SFT. One major advantage of upgrading is to avoid the annoyances of Novell's outdated copy-protection schemes. Versions of NetWare 286 that incorporated copy protection through a keycard (v2.1) or a non-copyable GEN-DATA diskette (v2.11) are no longer available from Novell.

SFT NETWARE 286 VERSION 2.1

This flagship release heralded the new era of NetWare v2.1 functionality. Released in December of 1987, SFT NetWare v2.1 offered over 100 enhancements and new features to improve on v2.0a versions of NetWare. We don't have room here to list every one, but we will cover the highlights for those holdouts (and you know who you are) who have just made the switch from v2.0a to v2.1x.

A New Operating System

The SFT NetWare v2.1 operating system consolidated the system fault tolerant features available in various v2.0a versions into one OS. What was previously known as SFT Level I (directory and FAT duplication, read-after-write verification, and Hot Fix) and Level II (disk mirroring and disk duplexing) were bundled together in SFT v2.1. The Transaction Tracking System (TTS) was included as an option in the basic OS. UPS Monitoring was also included, with the necessary jacks built in on Novell's keycards and disk coprocessor boards.

Because Novell considers the SFT NetWare product line to be their most reliable operating system, SFT v2.1 was available only as a dedicated operating system. Nondedicated versions were available only in the Advanced and ELS (Entry Level Solution) product lines.

Starting with SFT v2.1, the NetWare operating system was opened up to third-party developers. New APIs and other interfaces allowed specialized value-added processes (VAPs) and value-added disk drivers (VADDs) to run in the file server and have more direct access to the server's CPU and RAM. The VAP capability paved the way for various multitasking, server-based applications (such as print servers, backup servers, and others) to run in the file server as extensions to NetWare. The VADD capability freed NetWare from its v2.0a restriction of using only hard disks formatted, tested, and sold by Novell.

A New Installation Procedure

The flip side of allowing VADDs turned out to be a much more complex installation procedure. Not only did the OS have to be specially configured for the network interface boards that would be installed in the file server, it also had to be configured for whatever kind of disk and tape drives would be installed. The installation program had to allow installers to select the correct LAN drivers, disk drivers, and "other" drivers (for tape drives), configure them so there were no hardware conflicts, and then link the selected drivers with the NetWare OS. File server utilities that needed to talk to the hard disks (like COMPSURF, VREPAIR, and DISKED) had to be custom-linked as well.

The program Novell came up with was called NETGEN. In addition to all this configuring and linking, NETGEN absorbed all the functionality of v2.0a's PREPARE and INSTALL utilities. The DISKSET and COMPSURF utilities were made available as well as options within NETGEN. With NETGEN, then, you can configure the OS and its associated drivers, link them all together, assign network addresses, program the disk coprocessor boards, format the hard disks, install partition tables, establish Hot Fix, set up drive mirroring, name the file server, set the configurable OS parameters, create NetWare volumes, and ready the network printer ports—all from one mega-utility.

In addition to NETGEN, SFT v2.1 included a new workstation shell-generation program (SHGEN) and an external bridge-generation program (BRGEN). The new SHGEN allowed network boards in workstations to be set to hardware configurations other than the default. BRGEN handles the configuration and generation of the external bridge routing software.

New Supervisor Utilities

SFT v2.1 brought new utilities to help the network supervisor manage users, security, and the file server itself. Foremost among these new supervisor utilities were MAKEUSER (which allowed multiple users to be created all at once), SECURITY (which analyzed the server for possible security holes), and FCONSOLE (which allowed remote control of certain file server console functions and access to server utilization and performance statistics).

The user options in SYSCON were expanded to include enhanced password and login security. The supervisor could require users to change their passwords (now encrypted so no one—even the supervisor—can see them) and set restrictions on password length and reusability. The supervisor also had greater control over when users can log in and from what workstations. An intruder detection feature helped track down unauthorized access to the server. The new OS also performed security checks every 30 minutes and could force users to log out if they were not authorized to be using the network. Accounting features were also added to SYSCON so that supervisors could charge users for network services such as connection time and disk usage.

New command line utilities such as GRANT, REVOKE, and TLIST offered quick ways of managing trustee rights assignments from the DOS prompt. Repair utilities such as BINDFIX and VREPAIR were bundled with the OS. Other new utilities such as ARCONFIG and LCONSOLE were included to improve communications with remote networks.

To set up network printers and print queues, v2.1 offered three new printing utilities: PRINTDEF, PRINTCON, and PCONSOLE. CAPTURE and ENDCAP replaced their v2.0a SPOOL and ENDSPOOL counterparts.

New User Utilities

SFT v2.1 saw the inclusion of several new utilities for users, as well as the enhancement of previous v2.0a utilities. These included NDIR, USERLIST, VOLINFO, and VERSION, among others.

Updated Hardware and Software Support

In keeping with Novell's commitment to work with new industry-standard hardware and software as it comes along, SFT v2.1 supported the then-new IBM PS/2 machines as both workstations and file servers, and workstation operating systems such as DOS 3.3, PC-MOS 386, and Windows/386.

Serialization

SFT v2.1 retained v2.0a's keycard method of copy protection. A specially serialized keycard, or DCB, was shipped with each NetWare OS. The OS software was also serialized to run only if the matching key device was installed in the file server. Novell has since eliminated this hardware-dependent copy protection scheme.

SFT AND ADVANCED NETWARE VERSION 2.11

Novell next planned to release a 2.1 version of Advanced NetWare that included all of the features of SFT v2.1 except disk mirroring and TTS. As before, Advanced NetWare was to run as either a dedicated or nondedicated operating system. However, in between the release of SFT v2.1 and the planned release of Advanced v2.1, Novell decided to go with a new serialization procedure that could be performed in the field. Not only would this relieve Novell of the burden of having to individually serialize each OS in-house, it would also eliminate the frustrations of network downtime when the server's key device failed. In addition, a few minor fixes to the v2.1 OS were needed.

Field Serialization

Consequently, Advanced NetWare was released as v2.11, along with a new SFT v2.11, in May of 1988. Both used the new field serialization process that relied on the GENDATA diskette. Because this diskette contained the OS serialization information, it was made so that it could not be copied. While the whole procedure sounded good in theory, in practice it was problematic. Installers had only one chance to input the correct serial number for the OS. Once it was written to the GENDATA diskette, there was no way to change the serial number. If installers accidentally entered the wrong serial number, they had to request a new GENDATA diskette from Novell and start all over.

Improvements to NETGEN

Another major complaint addressed in v2.11 involved the NETGEN program. SFT v2.1's NETGEN program required an inordinate amount of shuffling diskettes in and out of the floppy drive. While installers could relieve some of this by copying the files onto a hard disk, NETGEN provided no automatic procedure to do this. For v2.11, NETGEN was revised to include four installation methods: the standard floppy disk method, a RAM disk method (which used extended memory to cut down on the number of disk swaps), a local hard disk method (which provided an automatic procedure for uploading the files to a hard disk), and a network drive method (same thing, only to a network hard disk).

SFT, ADVANCED, AND ELS NETWARE LEVEL II VERSION 2.12

Later in 1988, Novell released an update to SFT and Advanced NetWare v2.11 and introduced ELS NetWare Level II v2.12. For all of these v2.12 products, the GENDATA diskette was made fully copyable to eliminate the serialization bugaboos inherent to v2.11. All other functionality for SFT and Advanced NetWare remained the same. A revised on-line HELP facility was also included with all v2.12 products.

ELS NetWare Level II Features

ELS NetWare Level II is an eight-user version of NetWare. While similar in functionality to Advanced NetWare, ELS supports a smaller number of network interface boards and works only with internal disk drives on IBM XT or AT compatibles or PS/2 Models 50 and above (including the Model 50Z and Model 70). The 286 version can run either dedicated or nondedicated, but the 86 option (for IBM XTs) runs only dedicated. A core set of the twelve most popular LAN drivers is shipped with ELS, but a supplemental driver kit is also available.

The only internetworking option that comes with ELS NetWare Level II is a remote asynchronous connection through a COM1/COM2 board. An ELS Level II file server can be connected via an external bridge to other servers on an internet, but the bridge software does not come with the ELS package.

ELS NetWare comes with a scaled-down version of NETGEN called ELS-GEN. Some of the options have been rearranged, and the ones that don't apply to ELS Level II have been taken out, but ELSGEN is basically the same as NETGEN.

ELS Level II v2.12 introduced a new user creation utility called USERDEF. USERDEF acts as a front end to the more complicated MAKEUSER utility and consolidates the important steps in creating users into a single utility. With USER-DEF, you can create groups of new users, give them a basic login script, and define their security restrictions and group membership.

ELS Level II v2.12 was also the first release in which Novell included pre-defined print device definition files for the most popular network printers. These files can be copied directly into a file server's PRINTDEF database, making network printer setup much easier.

SFT, ADVANCED, AND ELS NETWARE LEVEL II VERSION 2.15

In order to integrate Macintosh workstations into the NetWare 286 world, the OS had to undergo many changes—some major, some more subtle. SFT and Advanced NetWare v2.15 were originally introduced to accommodate NetWare for Macintosh. Later, Macintosh support was ported to ELS NetWare Level II.

Changes in the Rights

The most significant Macintosh-related change involved NetWare's rights, specifically the Parental right. Whereas before the Parental right was needed to create, delete, or rename subdirectories, those capabilities were reassigned to the Create, Delete, and Modify rights respectively.

Changes in the Utilities

FILER and NCOPY were modified to be able to copy both the data fork and the resource fork of Macintosh files. Also, a new FLAGDIR command was introduced to allow users to designate a directory as Normal, System, Hidden, and Private (matching the possible Macintosh folder attributes).

Other subtle changes were not Macintosh-related. For example, password synchronization over all attached file servers was incorporated into the SETPASS command, and the USERLIST and SLIST commands gained the ability to do wild-card searches.

SFT AND ADVANCED NETWARE VERSION 2.15 REV C

In September 1989, Novell released a maintenance update for SFT and Advanced NetWare v2.15. The update is identified as "Rev C" (revision C).

Rev B was never released, but Rev C contained everything Rev B had and more. Rev C fixed many problems that surfaced after the initial release of v2.15 and provided some enhancements to existing features.

Fixes

Rev C corrects the following problems, some of which had been around since before the first v2.15:

• When a server broadcasted its list of known servers, it omitted every eighth server in its bindery.

• A server with a partitioned hard disk could ABEND if someone tried to copy from the DOS partition to the NetWare partition.

• The external bridge software would not support the WNIM card.

• The serial port on the server did not support even parity for printers.

• Large drives with multiple volumes could be set to the default size only.

• Unmirrored hard drives larger than 255MB containing multiple volumes could ABEND the server when a remirror was attempted.

New or Enhanced Features

In addition to these problem fixes, Rev C added some new features and enhanced some existing features. Here's a quick rundown:

• Support for Macintosh in general was improved, paving the way for Net-Ware for Macintosh v1.1.

• Support for large drives (over 256MB) was enhanced, and DISKSET was modified to provide direct support for NetWare-ready drives previously supported only under the generic SCSI option.

• The "AT Fixed Disk Controller" choice in NETGEN was renamed to "Industry Standard (ISA or AT Comp.) Disk Controller" to be more in step with industry terminology as EISA bus file servers became available.

• To accommodate improved UPS systems, the maximum time for the UPS DOWN parameter was extended from 30 minutes to 64,800 minutes (45 days).

• All utilities that send passwords to the server were modified to encrypt passwords before sending them out over the wire.

New Utilities and Shells

The USERDEF utility, originally included only with ELS NetWare, was added to SFT and Advanced NetWare to give all NetWare users access to USER-DEF's simplified way of creating users in bulk. The DOS workstation shell was enhanced to allow users to change the hardware configuration settings (IRQ, DMA, base I/O address, and memory address) via the SHELL.CFG file, without regenerating the whole shell. Other shell enhancements provide more flexibility when working with NetBIOS.

ELS NETWARE LEVEL I VERSION 2.12

In 1990, Novell released a 2.1x version of ELS NetWare Level I (previously available only as a v2.0a product). ELS Level I v2.12 is a four-user version of NetWare tailored for small network needs. It can run either dedicated or nondedicated. ELS Level I provides a simple installation procedure that lets you link in one of the three most popular LAN drivers. Unlike ELS Level II, ELS Level I restricts you to the three drivers included with ELS Level I—no option is available to load and select supplemental drivers.

ELS Level I does not allow for internetworking, and it supports only PC-compatible workstations running DOS 3.*x*. It offers UPS monitoring and includes Novell's new NBACKUP tape backup software.

THE VERY LATEST FOR NETWARE 286

Some new enhancements were just being made as this book was being written. As of February 1990, Novell bundles two products with NetWare 286 that were previously available separately: the Print Server software and the Streaming Tape Backup VAP. A Name Service and new DOS workstation shells have also been announced for NetWare 286.

The Print Server uses the standard NetWare printing utilities and print queues, but allows for up to sixteen network printers instead of five. The network printers can be attached to the file server, a dedicated workstation, or any user workstation.

The Backup VAP is a server-based implementation that replaces the traditional NetWare BACKUP and RESTORE software. Files can be backed up to a wider range of devices while the file server is up and running. A companion program called NBACKUP is run from workstations and can back up local data as well as network files.

NetWare 286's Name Service will be regulated via a new NETCON utility that will replace SYSCON. By using NETCON and other replacement utilities, network managers will be able to define groups of servers as a "domain" and manage all of the users and groups within that domain, rather than on a server-by-server basis.

NETWARE 286 FEATURE COMPARISON CHART

The following chart summarizes the features supported in all current versions of NetWare 286 v2.1x:

Feature	ELS I v2.12	ELS II v2.15	Advanced v2.15	SFT v2.15
Mode of operation	286 nonded 386 nonded	86 ded 286 non 386 non	286 ded/non 386 ded/non	286 ded 386 ded
Bus support	AT, MCA	AT, MCA	AT, MCA	AT, MCA
Max. number of users	4	8	100	100
Installation process	INSTALL	ELSGEN	NETGEN	NETGEN
Network boards supported	1	1 (2 for Mac support)	4	4
Topologies supported	3	12*	12*	12*
Third-party LAN driver support	No	Yes	Yes	Yes
Macintosh support	No	Yes	Yes	Yes
Internetworking support	None	Async remote connection	Yes	Yes
SFT level	I	I	I	II
TTS option	No	No	No	Yes
UPS monitoring	No	Yes	Yes	Yes
Btrieve VAP	No	Yes	Yes	Yes
MHS VAP	No	Yes	Yes	Yes
External bridge software	No	No	Yes	Yes

*Approximately twelve drivers are bundled with the OS; additional drivers are available in a Supplemental Driver Kit.

B Routine File Server Checkup

You can save yourself a good deal of trouble by anticipating file server problems before they happen and taking steps to minimize their impact on the network. This appendix outlines a routine file server maintenance checkup that you should perform on a regular basis (at least once a week).

FILE SERVER CHECKS

Check the following statistics dealing with the file server itself. (Most of these numbers are available in FCONSOLE's "File Server Statistics Summary" screen, accessed by selecting "Statistics" from the main menu, then "Summary" from the resulting submenu. Exceptions are noted below.)

- *File server utilization.* If the utilization consistently exceeds 60 percent, add more memory or reconfigure the network applications to reduce the load on the file server's CPU.
- Number of *file service processes* available after booting the server. Fewer than two FSPs could indicate trouble. See Chapter 34 for details.
- *Total server memory, unused memory,* and memory in *Dynamic Memory Pools 1, 2,* and *3.* If the total memory listed does not match what you have installed, run a diagnostics check on file server memory. Monitor the other memory statistics for other possible memory problems.
- *Peak number of connections* versus the *maximum number of connections* supported by the file server. If these two numbers are getting closer, you may need add another file server to split your network in half.
- *Peak number of open files* versus the *maximum number of open files.* If the peak number is approaching 70 percent of the maximum, raise the maximum number in NETGEN/ELSGEN.

• *Peak number of indexed files* versus the *maximum number of indexed files*. If these two numbers are getting closer, reconfigure the OS with NETGEN to support more indexed files.

• Check to see that *login is enabled* (select the "Status" option from FCONSOLE's main menu).

• Check the *file server date* and *time* (use "Status" option of FCONSOLE or TIME console command)

• Check the file server error log, SYS$LOG.ERR (select "Supervisor Options" from SYSCON's main menu, then "View File Server Error Log.")

HARD DISK CHECKS

Make the following checks to ascertain the status of the network hard disks, disk channels, and disk caching:

• Check SFT *disk mirroring* and *duplexing* status (select "Statistics" from FCONSOLE's main menu, then "Disk Mapping Information").

• Check to see that *Hot Fix* is still enabled on all disks (use the DISK console command, or select "Statistics" from FCONSOLE's main menu, then "Disk Statistics").

• Monitor the count of *Hot Fix blocks used* on each disk (use DISK console command, or select "Statistics" from FCONSOLE's main menu, then "Disk Statistics"). If this number increases suddenly and continues to ncrement rapidly, the disk surface may be worn out and need to be replaced.

• Monitor the count of *disk I/O errors* (use DISK console command, or select "Statistics" from FCONSOLE's main menu, then "Disk Statistics").

• Check the *disk caching statistics* by selecting "Statistics" from FCONSOLE's main menu, then "Cache Statistics." If the number of disk requests serviced from cache is less than 90 percent, either add more memory to create more disk cache buffers, move applications or data to local hard disks, or add another file server to accommodate high-volume applications. If the thrashing count is greater than 0, add more memory to create additional cache buffers.

• Check the status of each *disk channel* by selecting "Statistics" from FCONSOLE's main menu, then "Channel Statistics." The status should be "Running" for each channel.

VOLUME CHECKS

Check the following information for each volume mounted on the file server:

• Make certain that all volumes are mounted and that they are hashed and cached as configured (select "Statistics" from FCONSOLE's main menu, then "Volume Information").

• Run VOLINFO to check for volumes that are running out of free disk space or free directory entries. 1MB is the lowest amount of disk space you should allow a volume to have. If necessary, remove unneeded files from the volume and run NETGEN/ELSGEN to configure more directory entries.

TTS CHECKS

Check the following aspects of SFT NetWare's Transaction Tracking System (TTS) if your file server uses it:

• Run VOLINFO to check the remaining disk space on the transaction backout volume. You should always have at least twice as much free disk space as the largest possible transaction size (1MB minimum).
• Check the "Status" option in FCONSOLE's main menu to see that TTS is still enabled.
• Check the peak number of transactions versus the maximum (select "Statistics" from FCONSOLE's main menu, then "Summary"). If these two numbers are getting closer, run NETGEN to increase the configured maximum number of transactions.

BENCHMARK CHECKS

Run the PERFORM2 utility while the file server is operating normally so that you have some benchmark results to compare with when diagnosing a file server performance problem. (See Chapter 38 for details.)

C Useful Troubleshooting/ Maintenance Tools

This appendix outlines some of the network management services available from Novell. It also contains a list of selected tools and utilities for troubleshooting and maintaining NetWare 286-based file servers. This list is by no means exhaustive; it does, however, contain a few representative products in each category that should give you an idea of what's available.

SERVICES AVAILABLE FROM NOVELL

Novell offers a number of services to NetWare users. This section briefly explains some of the more useful helps Novell provides. For more information, contact Novell at (800) 526-5463.

Novell's NetWire Forums

A number of useful tools and maintenance helps are available from Novell's NetWire forums on CompuServe. NetWire offers a wide range of information about Novell products and services, including press releases, financial information, and technical bulletins. Of most interest to network supervisors are the hardware and software compatibility lists, NetWare workstation shells, other program files, updates and patches, and the technical bulletin boards.

If you have a modem and a CompuServe account, subscribe to NetWire; then you can access these forums and download data from NetWire any time of the day or night.

On-Site and Consulting Services

Novell offers on-site service agreements to help you keep your network running smoothly. You can get a standard service agreement that covers you during normal working hours (8 a.m. to 5 p.m. Monday through Friday), or you can get an extended maintenance agreement to cover weekends as well.

Novell's NetWare Services and Support Group (NSSG) houses several consulting groups that can help you with the initial design, installation, and maintenance of your LAN. In addition, the Systems Research Department publishes a series of application notes pertaining to critical NetWare design and management issues.

NetWare Pro

Novell's NetWare Pro package offers a number of valuable aids for the network manager. These aids can help in providing network management, technical support, and user training. The package includes access to the Novell Technical Support Hot-Line, the NetWare Care diagnostics software, and the Computer Based Training for both users and system supervisors. You can also obtain the Technical Information Database, an on-line text retrieval system cataloging a wealth of information about Novell product compatibility, error messages, and technical bulletins.

ANTI-VIRUS UTILITIES

The following third-party utilities are useful in controlling computer viruses on local area networks:

Clean-up
Viruscan
McAfee Associates
4423 Cheeney Street
Santa Clara, CA 95054
(408) 988-3832

Flu Shot +
Software Concepts Design
594 Third Avenue
New York, NY 10016
(212) 889-6438

Disinfectant
GateKeeper
Vaccine
(Available from on-line services or through users groups)

BACKUP PROGRAMS (NETWARE-INTEGRATED)
These backup programs are NetWare-aware, meaning they can handle Net-Ware's bindery files and security rights:

Data Library
Advanced Digital Information Corp.
P.O. Box 2996
Redmond, WA 98073
(800) 336-1233
(206) 881-8004

NOV-XX000 Series
Emerald Systems
12230 World Trade Drive
San Diego, CA 92128
(800) 767-7267

FileSECURE
Tallgrass Technologies, Inc.
11100 West 82nd Street
Lenexa, KS 66214
(913) 492-6002
(800) 825-4727

MaynStream
Maynard Electronics
460 East Semoran Blvd.
Casselberry, FL 32707
(800) 237-4929
(407) 331-6402

BIOS
The BIOS available from Award Software is a good, general-purpose BIOS that will work with file servers running nondedicated NetWare.

Award Software, Inc.
130 Knowles Drive
Los Gatos, CA 95030
(408) 370-7979

BOOT ROMS CERTIFIED FOR NETWARE V2.1x

BOOT ROMS CERTIFIED FOR NETWARE V2.1x

BOOT ROMS CERTIFIED FOR NETWARE V2.1x

The following companies manufacture boot ROMs certified to run with the Remote Reset feature of NetWare 286:

Acer 5279 (for the Acer 5270 board)
Acer Technologies
401 Charcot Ave.
San Jose, CA 95131
(408) 922-0333

Ethernet (for the AST Ethernet board)
Ethernode (for the AST Ethernode board)
AST Research
2121 Alton Pkwy.
Irvine, CA 92714
(714) 863-1333

ARCnet (for the SMC PC, PC-100, and PC 110 boards)
(also for Novell RX-Net boards)
3C501 (for 3Com 3C501 boards assembly 345, 780 and 1221)
3Station (for 3Com 3Station boards)
NE1000 (for Novell NE1000 boards)
NE/2 (for Novell NE/2 boards)
NE2000 (for Novell NE2000 boards)
NI5010 (for MICOM NI5010 boards)
PCN II (for IBM PC Network II boards)
Token-Ring (for IBM Token-Ring boards)
PC-Terminal (for PC-Terminal boards)
Novell, Inc.
122 East 1700 South
Provo, UT 84601
(801) 379-5900

Pronet-4 (for Pronet-4 boards)
Proteon Inc.
Two Technology Drive
Westborough, MA 01581
(617) 898-2800

WD8003E (for WD8003E boards)
Western Digital
2445 McCabe Way
Irvine, CA 92714
(800) 638-5323
(714) 474-2033

NE1000/RPL (for use with Wyse WY212M terminal)
Wyse
3571 North First Street
San Jose, CA 95134
(408) 433-1000

CABLE TESTING AND TROUBLESHOOTING

The following products can help you test for and troubleshoot problems with the network cabling system:

Emonitor
ARCmonitor
Brightwork Development Inc.
766 Shrewsbury Avenue
Jerral Center West
Tinton Falls, NJ
(800) 552-9876
(201) 530-0440

LAN Specialist
Cabletron
Cabletron Industrial Park
10 Main St., Box 6257
E. Rochester, NH 03867
(603) 332-9400

DATA COMPRESSION UTILITIES

Apart from their data compression capabilities, these utilities can generate check sums to help you compare two files when checking for viruses:

ARC
System Enhancement Associates
21 New Street
Wayne, NJ 07470

PKZIP
PKWare
7545 North Port Washington Road, Suite 205
Glendale, WI 53217-3422

FILE/DISK MANAGEMENT UTILITIES

These utilities help you manage directories and files on NetWare volumes:

Navigate
Performance Technology
800 Lincoln Center
San Antonio, TX 78230
(512) 349-2000

XTreeNet
Executive Systems, Inc.
4300 Santa Fe Rd.
San Luis Obispo, CA 93401
(800) 634-5545
(805) 541-0604

MEMORY-RESIDENT TEXT EDITOR

You can use the following utility to develop customized help screens for your network menu system:

Sidekick
Borland International
1700 Green Hills Rd.
Scotts Valley, CA 95066-0001
(800) 543-7543
(408) 438-8400

MENU SYSTEMS

The following menu systems are fully compatible with NetWare:

Saber Menu
Saber Software Corp.
P.O. Box 9088
Dallas, TX 75209
(800) 338-8754

LANShell
LAN Systems Inc.
300 Park Ave. South
New York, NY 10010
(800) 458-5267
(212) 473-6800

Windows Workstation
Automated Design Systems, Inc.
375 Northridge Rd., Suite 270
Atlanta, GA 30350
(800) 366-2552
(404) 394-2552

MHS-COMPATIBLE E-MAIL PROGRAMS
These e-mail packages are compatible with Novell's Message Handling Services (MHS):

The Coordinator
Action Technologies
2200 Powell Street, 11th Floor
Emeryville, CA 94608
(415) 654-4444

Da Vinci eMAIL
Da Vinci Systems
PO Box 5427
Raleigh, NC 27650
(800) 326-3556
(919) 781-5924

NETWORK MANAGEMENT UTILITIES
The following are general-purpose network management utilities specially designed for use on Novell networks:

Frye Utilities for Networks
Frye Computer Systems, Inc.
200 Clarendon St.
Boston, MA 02116
(617) 247-2300

LANshadow
LAN Systems Inc.
300 Park Ave. South
New York, NY 10010
(800) 458-5267
(212) 473-6800

Monitrix
Cheyenne Software, Inc.
55 Bryant Avenue
Roslyn, NY 11576
(800) 243-9462
(516) 484-5110

NETmanager
Brightwork Development Inc.
766 Shrewsbury Avenue
Jerral Center West
Tinton Falls, NJ
(800) 552-9876
(201) 530-0440

NetWare Care
Novell, Inc.
122 E. 1700 S.
Provo, UT 84606
(800) 453-1267

PRINT SERVER PRODUCTS

The following print server programs allow you to offload network printing from the file server to another personal computer on the network:

LANspool
LAN Systems Inc.
300 Park Ave. South
New York, NY 10010
(800) 458-5267
(212) 473-6800

PS-Print
Brightwork Development, Inc.
766 Shrewsbury Avenue
Jerral Center West
Tinton Falls, NJ
(800) 552-9876
(201) 530-0440

PROTOCOL ANALYZERS

Protocol analyzers can help in diagnosing and troubleshooting problems with network cabling and packet transmissions:

LANalyzer
Novell, Inc.
LANalyzer Products Division
2180 Fortune Dr.
San Jose, CA 95131
(800) 392-3526
(408) 434-2300

The Sniffer
Network General
4200 Bohannon Drive
Menlo Park, CA 94025
(800) 952-6300

REMOTE WORKSTATION ACCESS UTILITIES

These utilities allow you to take over and control any workstation on the network from your own workstation:

Close-Up/LAN
Norton-Lambert
PO Box 4085
Santa Barbara, CA 93140
(805) 964-6767

LAN Assist Plus
Fresh Technology
1478 North Tech Blvd., Suite 101
Gilbert, AZ 85234
(602) 497-4200

NETmanager
Brightwork Development Inc.
766 Shrewsbury Avenue
Jerral Center West
Tinton Falls, NJ
(800) 552-9876
(201) 530-0440

REPORT AND AUDIT TRAIL UTILITIES

These utilities produce network usage reports and provide an audit trail of logins, logouts, and other important events:

Lomax Network Management Report Utilities
J.A. Lomax Associates
695 DeLong Ave., Suite 130
Novato, CA 94947
(415) 892-9606

LT Auditor
Blue Lance
PO Box 430546
Houston, TX 77243
(713) 680-1187

NETreports
Brightwork Development, Inc.
766 Shrewsbury Avenue
Jerral Center West
Tinton Falls, NJ
(800) 552-9876
(201) 530-0440

SOFTWARE METERING PRODUCTS

These products allow you to keep track of the number of users currently using network applications:

SiteLock
Brightwork Development Inc.
766 Shrewsbury Avenue
Jerral Center West
Tinton Falls, NJ
(800) 552-9876
(201) 530-0440

Turnstyle
Connect Computer
9855 West 78th St. #270
Eden Prairie, MN 55344
(612) 944-0181

UNINTERRUPTIBLE POWER SUPPLY SYSTEMS

The following UPS systems are designed particularly for use with Novell file servers:

Benchmark Series
Viteq Corp.
10000 Aerospace Road
Lanham, MD 20706
(301) 731-0400

ONGUARD
Clary Corp.
320 West Clary Ave.
San Gabriel, CA 91776
(818) 287-6111

UPS 800 RT
American Power Conversion
PO Box 3723
Peace Dale, RI 02883
(401) 789-5735

FailSafe IPS
Elgar Electronics
9250 Brown Deer Road
San Diego, CA 92121
(619) 450-0085

MISCELLANEOUS UTILITIES

Net-Aware (a utility that can help turn
single-user applications into networkable programs)
LANSMITH
406 Lincolnwood Place
Santa Barbara, CA 93110
(800) 522-4567

INDEX

C

D

G

H

V

W